THE LEAST OF MY BROTHERS
Matthew 25: 31-46
A History of Interpretation

SOCIETY OF BIBLICAL LITERATURE

DISSERTATION SERIES
J. J. M. Roberts, Old Testament Editor
Charles Talbert, New Testament Editor

Number 114

THE LEAST OF MY BROTHERS
Matthew 25: 31-46
A History of Interpretation
by
Sherman W. Gray

Sherman W. Gray

THE LEAST OF MY BROTHERS
Matthew 25: 31-46
A History of Interpretation

Scholars Press
Atlanta, Georgia

THE LEAST OF MY BROTHERS
Sherman W. Gray

Ph.D., 1987
Catholic University of America
(Washington D.C.)

Advisor:
Rev. Joseph A. Fitzmyer, S.J.

© 1989
The Society of Biblical Literature

Nihil Obstat:
July 5, 1989
John J. Toomey, J.C.D., P.A.
Censor Librorum

Imprimatur:
July 10, 1989
Edward Michael Egan, J.C.D, D.D.
Bishop of Bridgeport, CT

The *nihil obstat* and *imprimatur* are official declarations that a book or pamphlet is free of doctrinal and moral error. No implication is contained therein that those who have granted the *nihil obstat* and *imprimatur* agree with the contents, opinions, or statements expressed.

Grateful acknowledgment for permission to use copyrighted material is made to the following publishers: Oxford University Press (*The Coptic Version of the New Testament in the Southern Dialect.* Vol. 1: The Gospels of S. Matthew and S. Mark. ed. G.W. Horner, 1911-1924; *The Coptic Version of the New Testament in the Northern Dialect (Bohairic).* Vol. 1: The Gospels of S. Matthew and S. Mark. ed. G.W. Horner, 1898) and The British and Foreign Bible Society (*The New Testament in Syriac*, 1966).

Library of Congress Cataloging in Publication Data

Gray, Sherman W.
  The least of my brothers : Matthew 25: 31-46 : a history of interpretation / Sherman W. Gray.
  p. cm. -- (Dissertation series / Society of Biblical Literature : no. 114)
  ISBN 1-55540-344-1 (alk. paper). -- ISBN 1-55540-345-X (pbk. : alk. paper)
  1. Bible. N.T. Matthew XXV, 31-46--Criticism, interpretation, etc.--History. I. Title. II. Series: Dissertation series (Society of Biblical Literature) ; no. 114
BS2575.2.G73 1989
226'.206'09--dc19   89-6088
                                                                  CIP

Printed in the United States of America
on acid-free paper

"... kto szanuję swoją matkę będzie nagrodzony przez Pana."

z Księgi Syracydesa 3:4

Dla moich dwóch Matek

TABLE OF CONTENTS

Acknowledgments	xv
Abbreviations	xvii

Chapter I

Preliminaries

The Greek Text of Matt 25:31-46	1
The "Identity Dialogue" in the Vulgate and the VL	2
The Syriac Text of Matthew 25:31-46	3
The "Identity Dialogue" in Sahidic Coptic	4
The "Identity Dialogue" in Bohairic Coptic	4
Textual Criticism	5
References to the OT	6
The Context	7
The Interpretation of Matt 25:31-46	8
Notes to Chapter I	10

Chapter II

The Patristic Period

The Apostolic Fathers	11
Fathers of the Later Second Century	
Justin Martyr	12
Irenaeus of Lyons	12
Anonymous Writings of the Second Century	14
Fathers of the Third Century	
Eastern writers	
Clement of Alexandria	16
Origen	17
Firmilian of Caesarea in Cappadocia	22
Gregory Thaumaturgus	22
Archelaus of Cascar	23
Methodius of Olympus	23

Table of Contents

Peter of Alexandria	24
Western writers	
Tertullian	25
Hippolytus of Rome	26
Pontianus of Rome	27
Cyprian of Carthage	27
Commodianus	29
Anonymous Writings of the Third Century	29
The Great Patristic Century (AD 325 - 431)	
Eastern writers	
Eusebius of Caesarea	31
Aphraates	33
Pachomius	34
Eusebius of Emesa	35
Basil of Ancyra	36
Athanasius of Alexandria	37
Ephraem of Nisibis	39
Basil the Great	42
Horsiesi	44
Cyril of Jerusalem	45
Gregory Nazianzus	46
Macarius of Egypt	46
Gregory of Nyssa	47
Didymus the Blind	48
Asterius of Amasea	49
Epiphanius	49
John Chrysostom	50
John the Dwarf	53
Palladius	54
Nilus of Ancyra	54
Western writers	
Gaudentius of Brescia	55
Firmicus Maternus	56
Hilary of Poitiers	56
Ambrose of Milan	57
Ambrosiaster	59
Chromatius of Aquilea	60

Table of Contents

Maximus of Turin	60
Rufinus of Aquilea	61
Aponius	62
Paulus Orosius	62
Pelagius	63
Sulpicius Severus	65
Jerome	65
Augustine of Hippo	69
Paulinus of Nola	72
The Clementines	73

From the Council of Ephesus to the Second Council of Constantinople (AD 431-553)

Eastern writers

Cyril of Alexandria	75
Isidore of Pelusium.	77
Callinicus	78
Hesychius of Jerusalem	78
Basil of Seleucia	79
Theodoret of Cyr	80
Gennadius of Constantinople	82
Ps-Eusebius of Alexandria	82
Procopius of Gaza	83
John of Gaza	84
Jobius	85

Western writers

Laurentius of Novae	86
John Cassian	86
Peter Chrysologus	87
Quodvultdeus of Carthage	89
Arnobius the Younger	90
Patrick of Ireland	91
Valerian of Cemele	91
Leo the Great	92
Epiphanius Latinus	94
Prosper of Aquitane	95
Salvianus of Marseilles	96
Faustus of Riez	97

Table of Contents

      Avitus of Vienne   98
      Fulgentius of Ruspe   99
      Remigius of Rheims   100
      Eugippius   100
      Caesarius of Arles   101
      Benedict of Nursia   104
   Anonymous Writings   105
From the Second Council of Constantinople to the End of the Patristic Era (AD 554 - 750)
   Eastern writers
      Nicephoras of Antioch   106
      John Climacus   107
      Anastasius Apocrisiarius   108
      Maximus the Confessor   108
      Antiochus the Monk   109
      Anastasius of Sinai   110
      Germanus of Constantinople   111
      Andrew of Crete   112
      John Damascene   113
   Western writers
      Cassiodorus   114
      Council of Mâcon   115
      Gregory of Agrigentum   115
      Gregory of Tours   116
      Leander of Seville   116
      Gregory the Great   117
      Isidore of Seville   119
      Donatus of Besançon   120
      Valerius of Bancona   120
      Eligius of Noyon   121
      Fructuosus of Braga   121
      Waldebertus of Luxeuil   121
      Audoenus of Rouen   122
      Julian of Toledo   122
      Bede the Venerable   123
   Anonymous writings   125
Notes to Chapter II   126

Table of Contents

Chapter III

The Middle Ages (AD 850 - 1399)

Eastern Writers
    Isho'dad of Merv   149
    Symeon the New Theologian.   149
    Theophylact of Bulgaria   152
    Euthymius Zigabenus   153
    Theophane Cerameus   154
    Dionysius Bar Salibi   155
    Anonymous writers.   156

Western Writers
    Paul the Deacon   157
    Christian Druthmar   160
    Haymo of Halberstadt   161
    Rabanus Maurus of Mainz   162
    Paschasius Radbertus   163
    Remigius of Auxerre   166
    Anselm of Laon   167
    Bruno of Asti   168
    Rupert of Deutz   169
    Ralph of Laon   170
    Zachary of Besançon   170
    Peter Comestor   171
    Hugh of Saint Cher   172
    Bonaventure   174
    Albert the Great   176
    Thomas Aquinas   178
    Nicholas of Lyra   180
    Ludolph of Saxony   182

Notes to Chapter III   183

Table of Contents

Chapter IV

The Renaissance and Reformation (AD 1400 - 1699)

The Fifteenth Century
    Bernardine of Siena   191
    Alphonsus Tostatus   192
    Denys van Leeuwen   194
The Sixteenth Century
    Catholic Writers
        Desiderius Erasmus   195
        Antonius Broickwy   196
        John Wild   197
        Cornelius Jansen the Elder   198
        The Douai-Rheims New Testament   200
        Juan Maldonado   200
        Manoel De Sa   202
    Protestant Writers
        Ulrich Zwingli   202
        Martin Luther   203
        John Calvin   206
        Augustine Marloratus   208
The Seventeenth Century
    Catholic Writers
        Wilhem Hessels van Est   209
        Sebastian Barradas   211
        Francis Luca of Bruges   212
        Robert Bellarmine   215
        James Tirinus   216
        Cornelis Cornelissen van den Steen   217
        Cornelius Otto Jansen   218
        John Bourgesius   219
        Giovanni Stefano Menochio   220
        Daniel van Breen   220
        Filippo Picinelli   221
        Antoine Furetiere   221
        Charles Marie de Veil   222
        Anonymous Priest of the French Oratory   222

Table of Contents

Jacques Bénigne Bossuet	223
Pasquier Quesnel	224
Protestant Writers	
David Pareus	224
John Piscator	226
Huig de Groot	227
Giovanni Diodati	228
Joseph Hall	228
Henry Hammond	228
Matthew Poole	229
Richard Ward	230
Samuel Clarke	231
Notes to Chapter IV	231

Chapter V

The Modern Era (AD 1700-1986)

Authors of the eighteenth century	241
Authors of the nineteenth century	244
Authors of the twentieth century	255
Notes to Chapter V	272

Chapter VI

Conclusions

Results of the historical study	331
Observations	351
Notes to Chapter VI	360
Bibliography	365
Author Index	437

ACKNOWLEDGMENTS

A doctoral dissertation is never the work of one person alone. To Father Joseph A. Fitzmyer, S.J., my director, and to Father Francis Gignac, S.J. and Father Thomas Halton, my readers, go my sincere thanks for their guidance and helpful critique. To my Ordinary, Bishop Walter W. Curtis, and to Bishop William J. McCormack, Msgr. Andrew Cusack, Doctor Robert Wickenheiser, Msgr. Ernest Gatta, Msgr. Thomas Dade, and all the priests and parishioners of St. Bernard's, Riverdale, MD, I owe a special debt of gratitude. My sincere appreciation is also extended to Fathers Francis Martin, Joseph Zalotay, Alexei Michalenko, Roman Obrycki, Thomas Byrd, Willfried Brieven and Mr. Ragnar Sissener; as well as to my colleagues, classmates and former students who prodded me on and brought me so much joy in the process of my research and writing: Gary Gunville, Joseph McCue, William Thompson, James Caldarella, Robert Kippley, Remy Schoone, Jack Evans, Michael Kavanaugh, Richard Canty, Jack Healy, David Buescher, Jack Roach, Michael Bransfield, Robert Antonelli, Paul Moglia, Samuel and Kay Maceri, Michael and Marilyn Zingarelli, David Givey, James McVey, Charles Talar, Paul Wirhun, and Samuel Giese. I could not have finished this work without them. A special word of thanks to John Bollier, Assistant Librarian at Yale Divinity School, New Haven, CT.

ABBREVIATIONS

With very few exceptions, only those works that are abbreviated in the style sheet of *The Catholic Biblical Quarterly* 46 (1984) 401-408 are abbreviated in this study. Those abbreviations are as follows:

AB	Anchor Bible. Garden City, NY: Doubleday, 1964—
ACW	Ancient Christian Writers. Westminster, MD: Newman, 1946–
AnBib	Analecta biblica. Rome: Biblical Institute, 1952–
ANF	A. Roberts and J. Donaldson (eds.). The Ante-Nicene Fathers. 11 vols. New York: Scribner, 1886-99. Reprinted, Grand Rapids: Eerdmans, 1979-82.
AsSeign	*Assemblées du Seigneur*. Paris: Cerf, 1962–
ATANT	Abhandlungen zur Theologie des Alten und Neuen Testaments. Zurich: Zwingli, 1944–
AusBR	*Australian Biblical Review*. Melbourne: Fellowship for Biblical Studies, 1951–
BAC	Biblioteca de autores cristianos. Madrid: Editorial católica, 1947–
BeO	*Bibbia e oriente*. Milan: Gruppo biblico Milanese, 1959–
BETL	Bibliotheca ephemeridum theologicarum lovaniensium. Louvain: Publications universitaires de Louvain, 1948–
BEvT	Beiträge zur evangelischen Theologie. Munich: Kaiser, 1940–
BFCT	Beiträge zur Förderung christlicher Theologie. Gütersloh: Bertelsmann, 1897–
BGBE	Beiträge zur Geschichte der biblischen Exegese. Tübingen: Mohr, 1955–
BJRL	*Bulletin of the John Rylands University Library of Manchester*. Manchester: The John Rylands Library, 1903–

Abbreviations

BK	*Bibel und Kirche.* Stuttgart: KBW, 1946–
Bib	*Biblica.* Rome: Biblical Institute, 1920–
BibLeb	*Bibel und Leben.* Düsseldorf: Patmos, 1960–
BSac	*Bibliotheca Sacra.* Dallas, TX: Dallas Theological Seminary, 1844–
BTB	*Biblical Theology Bulletin.* Rome: Collegio internazionale di Gesù, 1971–
BZ	*Biblische Zeitschrift.* Paderborn: Schöningh, 1903–
CB	*Cultura bíblica.* Madrid: AFEBE, 1944–
CBQ	*The Catholic Biblical Quarterly.* Washington, DC: CBA, 1939–
CBQMS	Catholic Biblical Quarterly—Monograph Series. Washington, DC: CBA, 1971–
CCG	Corpus christianorum. Greek Series. Turnhout: Brépols, 1977–
CCL	Corpus christianorum. Latin Series. Turnhout: Brépols, 1953–
CCM	Corpus christianorum. Medieval Series. Turnhout: Brépols, 1971–
CNT	Commentaire du Nouveau Testament. Paris: Delachaux & Niestlé, 1949–
CSCO	Corpus scriptorum christianorum orientalium. Louvain: Imprimerie orientaliste, 1903–
CSEL	Corpus scriptorum ecclesiasticorum latinorum. Vienna: Gerald, 1866–
DBSup	L. Pirot and A. Robert (eds.). *Dictionnaire de la Bible, Supplément.* Paris: Letouzey & Ané, 1928–
DTC	*Dictionnaire de théologie catholique.* 15 vols. Paris: Letouzey & Ané, 1930-50.
EBib	Etudes bibliques. Paris: Gabalda, 1903–
EncJud	Cecil Roth et al. (eds.). *Encyclopaedia Judaica.* 16 vols. Jerusalem: Keter, 1971-72.
ETR	*Etudes théologiques et religieuses.* Montpellier: Faculté de théologie protestante de Montpellier, 1926–
EvK	*Evangelische Kommentare.* Stuttgart: Kreuz, 1968–

Abbreviations

EWNT	H. Balz and G. Schneider (eds.). *Exegetisches Wörterbuch zum Neuen Testament.* 3 vols. Stuttgart: Kohlhammer, 1980.
ExpTim	*Expository Times.* Edinburgh: Clark, 1889–
FRLANT	Forschungen zur Religion und Literatur des Alten und Neuen Testaments. Göttingen: Vandenhoeck & Ruprecht, 1903–
GCS	Die griechischen christlichen Schriftsteller der ersten drei Jahrhunderte. Leipzig/ Berlin: Hinrichs/Akademie, 1897–
HNT	Handbuch zum Neuen Testament. Tübingen: Mohr, 1907–
HTR	*Harvard Theological Review.* Cambridge, MA: Harvard University, 1908–
IB	G. A. Buttrick (ed.). *The Interpreter's Bible.* 12 vols. Nashville: Abingdon, 1952-57.
ICC	International Critical Commentary. Edinburgh: Clark, 1895–
Int	*Interpretation.* Richmond, VA: Union Theological Seminary, 1947–
JBC	R. E. Brown et al. (eds.). *The Jerome Biblical Commentary.* 2 vols. Englewood Cliffs, NJ: Prentice-Hall, 1968.
JBL	*Journal of Biblical Literature.* Middletown, CT: Pelton & King, 1881–
JSNT	*Journal for the Study of the New Testament.* Sheffield: Sheffield University, 1978–
JTS	*Journal of Theological Studies.* Oxford: Clarendon, 1899–
Judaica	*Judaica: Beiträge zum Verständnis des jüdischen Schicksals in Vergangenheit und Gegenwart.* Zürich: Zwingli, 1945–
LB	*Linguistica biblica.* Bonn/Röttgen: Linguistica biblica, 1970–
LCL	T. E. Page and W. H. D. Rouse (eds.). The Loeb Classical Library. Cambridge, MA: Harvard University; London: Heinemann, 1913–

Abbreviations

LSJ	H. G. Liddell and R. Scott. *A Greek-English Lexicon*. 2 vols. Revised, H. S. Jones and R. McKenzie. Oxford: Clarendon, 1951.
LumVie	*Lumière et vie*. Bruges: Abbaye de S. André, 1951–
MeyerK	H. A. W. Meyer. *Kritisch-exegetischer Kommentar über das Neue Testament*. Göttingen: Vandenhoeck & Ruprecht, 1832–
MNTC	Moffatt New Testament Commentary. London: Hodder & Stoughton; New York: Harper, 1928–
NCB	New Century Bible. New York: Frowde; Oxford: University Press, 1904–
NCCHS	R. C. Fuller et al. (eds.), *New Catholic Commentary on Holy Scripture*. London: Nelson, 1969.
NCE	M. R. P. McGuire et al. (eds.). *New Catholic Encyclopedia*. 17 vols. New York: McGraw-Hill, 1967-79.
NLTC	H. Hurter. *Nomenclator literarius theologiae catholicae*. 5 vols. New York: Franklin, 1903.
NovT	*Novum Testamentum*. Leiden: Brill, 1956–
NovTSup	Novum Testamentum, Supplements. Leiden: Brill, 1958–
NRT	*La nouvelle revue théologique*. Tournai: Casterman, 1869–
NTAbh	Neutestamentliche Abhandlungen. Münster: Aschendorff, 1909–
NTD	Das Neue Testament Deutsch. Göttingen: Vandenhoeck & Ruprecht, 1932–
NTS	*New Testament Studies*. Cambridge: University Press, 1954–
OBO	Orbis biblicus et orientalis. Freiburg, Schweiz: Universitätsverlag; Göttingen: Vandenhoeck & Ruprecht, 1973–
ODCC	F. L. Cross and E. A. Livingstone (eds.). *The Oxford Dictionary of the Christian Church*. 2d ed. London: Oxford University, 1974.

Abbreviations

PCB	M. Black and H. H. Rowley (eds.). *Peake's Commentary on the Bible.* London/New York: Nelson, 1962.
PG	J. P. Migne. Patrologia graeca. Paris: Garnier, 1857-87.
PL	J. P. Migne. Patrologia latina. Paris: Garnier, 1844-82.
PLSup	A. Hamman. Patrologia latina. Supplementum. 5 vols. Paris: Garnier, 1958-74.
PO	F. Nau and R. Graffin. Patrologia Orientalis. Paris: Firmin-Didot, 1904–
RB	*Revue biblique.* Paris: Gabalda, 1892–
RevExp	*Review and Expositor.* Louisville, KY: Southern Baptist Theological Seminary, 1904–
RevistB	*Revista bíblica.* Buenos Aires: Editorial Guadalupe, 1939–
RevScRel	*Revue des sciences religieuses.* Strasbourg: Faculté catholique de théologie, 1921–
RHPR	*Revue d'histoire et de philosophie religieuses.* Strasbourg: Bureau de la Revue, 1921–
RNT	A. Wikenhauser and O. Kuss (eds.). Regensburger Neues Testament. Regensburg: Pustet, 1956–
SBJ	*La sainte bible de Jerusalem.* Paris: Cerf, 1948–
SBM	Stuttgarter biblische Monographien. Stuttgart: KBW, 1967–
SBS	Stuttgarter Bibelstudien. Stuttgart: KBW, 1965–
SC	Sources chrétiennes. Paris: Cerf, 1943–
ScEccl	*Sciences écclesiastiques.* Montréal: Les éditions de l'immaculée conception, 1948–
SJT	*Scottish Journal of Theology.* Edinburgh: Oliver & Boyd, 1948–
SNTSMS	Society for New Testament Studies Monograph Series. Cambridge: University Press, 1965–
ST	*Studia theologica.* Lund: Gleerup, 1947–
STANT	Studien zum Alten und Neuen Testament. Munich: Kösel, 1960–

Abbreviations

TBT	*The Bible Today*. Collegeville, MN: Liturgical Press, 1962–
TDNT	G. Kittel and G. Friedrich (eds.). *Theological Dictionary of the New Testament*. 10 vols. Grand Rapids: Eerdmans, 1964-76.
THKNT	Theologischer Handkommentar zum Neuen Testament. Berlin: Evangelische Verlagsanstalt, 1928–
TLZ	*Theologische Literaturzeitung*. Leipzig: Hinrichs, 1876–
TQ	*Theologische Quartalschrift*. Tübingen: Ravensburg, 1819–
TRE	G. Krause and G. Müller (eds.). *Theologische Realenzyklopädie*. 14 vols. Berlin/New York: de Gruyter, 1977–
TS	*Theological Studies*. Woodstock, MD: Woodstock College, 1940–
TSK	*Theologische Studien und Kritiken*. Berlin: Evangelisches Verlagsanstalt, 1828–
TToday	*Theology Today*. Princeton, NJ: Princeton Theological Seminary, 1944–
TU	Texte und Untersuchungen zur Geschichte der altchristlichen Literatur. Leipzig: Hinrichs; Berlin: Akademie, 1882–
VC	*Vigiliae christianae*. Amsterdam: Brill, 1947–
VS	Verbum salutis. Paris: Beauchesne, 1931–
WA	J. C. F. Knaake et al. (eds.). *D. Martin Luthers Werke. Kritische Gesamtausgabe*. 79 vols. Weimar: Böhlau, 1883-1941.
WMANT	Wissenschaftliche Monographien zum Alten und Neuen Testament. Neukirchen-Vluyn: Neukirchener Verlag, 1960–
WUNT	Wissenschaftliche Untersuchungen zum Neuen Testament. Tübingen: Mohr, 1950–

CHAPTER I

PRELIMINARIES

A. *The Greek Text of Matthew 25:31-46*

³¹Ὅταν δὲ ἔλθῃ ὁ υἱὸς τοῦ ἀνθρώπου ἐν τῇ δόξῃ αὐτοῦ καὶ πάντες οἱ ἄγγελοι μετ' αὐτοῦ, τότε καθίσει ἐπὶ θρόνου δόξης αὐτοῦ·
³²καὶ συναχθήσονται ἔμπροσθεν αὐτοῦ πάντα τὰ ἔθνη, καὶ ἀφορίσει αὐτοὺς ἀπ' ἀλλήλων, ὥσπερ ὁ ποιμὴν ἀφορίζει τὰ πρόβατα ἀπὸ τῶν ἐρίφων,
³³καὶ στήσει τὰ μὲν πρόβατα ἐκ δεξιῶν αὐτοῦ, τὰ δὲ ἐρίφια ἐξ εὐωνύμων.
³⁴τότε ἐρεῖ ὁ βασιλεὺς τοῖς ἐκ δεξιῶν αὐτοῦ· δεῦτε οἱ εὐλογημένοι τοῦ πατρός μου, κληρονομήσατε τὴν ἡτοιμασμένην ὑμῖν βασιλείαν ἀπὸ καταβολῆς κόσμου.
³⁵ἐπείνασα γὰρ καὶ ἐδώκατέ μοι φαγεῖν, ἐδίψησα καὶ ἐποτίσατέ με, ξένος ἤμην καὶ συνηγάγετέ με,
³⁶γυμνὸς καὶ περιεβάλετέ με, ἠσθένησα καὶ ἐπεσκέψασθέ με, ἐν φυλακῇ ἤμην καὶ ἤλθατε πρός με.
³⁷τότε ἀποκριθήσονται αὐτῷ οἱ δίκαιοι λέγοντες· κύριε, πότε σε εἴδομεν πεινῶντα καὶ ἐθρέψαμεν, ἢ διψῶντα καὶ ἐποτίσαμεν;
³⁸πότε δέ σε εἴδομεν ξένον καὶ συνηγάγομεν, ἢ γυμνὸν καὶ περιεβάλομεν;
³⁹πότε δέ σε εἴδομεν ἀσθενοῦντα ἢ ἐν φυλακῇ καὶ ἤλθομεν πρός σε;
⁴⁰καὶ ἀποκριθεὶς ὁ βασιλεὺς ἐρεῖ αὐτοῖς· ἀμὴν λέγω ὑμῖν, ἐφ' ὅσον ἐποιήσατε ἑνὶ τούτων τῶν ἀδελφῶν μου τῶν ἐλαχίστων, ἐμοὶ ἐποιήσατε.
⁴¹τότε ἐρεῖ καὶ τοῖς ἐξ εὐωνύμων· πορεύεσθε ἀπ' ἐμοῦ [οἱ] κατηραμένοι εἰς τὸ πῦρ τὸ αἰώνιον τὸ ἡτοιμασμένον τῷ διαβόλῳ καὶ τοῖς ἀγγέλοις αὐτοῦ.
⁴²ἐπείνασα γὰρ καὶ οὐκ ἐδώκατέ μοι φαγεῖν, ἐδίψησα καὶ οὐκ ἐποτίσατέ με,

⁴³ξένος ἤμην καὶ οὐ συνηγάγετέ με, γυμνὸς καὶ οὐ περιεβάλετέ με, ἀσθενὴς καὶ ἐν φυλακῇ καὶ οὐκ ἐπεσκέψασθέ με.
⁴⁴τότε ἀποκριθήσονται καὶ αὐτοὶ λέγοντες· κύριε, πότε σε εἴδομεν πεινῶντα ἢ διψῶντα ἢ ξένον ἢ γυμνὸν ἢ ἀσθενῆ ἢ ἐν φυλακῇ καὶ οὐ διηκονήσαμέν σοι;
⁴⁵τότε ἀποκριθήσεται αὐτοῖς λέγων· ἀμὴν λέγω ὑμῖν, ἐφ' ὅσον οὐκ ἐποιήσατε ἑνὶ τούτων τῶν ἐλαχίστων, οὐδὲ ἐμοὶ ἐποιήσατε.
⁴⁶καὶ ἀπελεύσονται οὗτοι εἰς κόλασιν αἰώνιον, οἱ δὲ δίκαιοι εἰς ζωὴν αἰώνιον.

B. The "Identity Dialogue" in the Vulgate and the VL[1]

35 Esurivi enim et dedistis mihi manducare; sitivi et dedistis mihi bibere [et potastis me]; hospes eram [peregrinus fui] et collexistis (collegistis) [suscepistis, tollegistis] me;

36 nudus et operuistis (cooperuistis) [vestistis, texistis] me; infirmus et visitastis me; in carcere eram et venistis ad me.

37 Tunc respondebunt ei iusti dicentes: Domine, quando te vidimus esurientem et pavimus (te); sitientem et dedimus tibi potum [potavimus te]?

38 Quando autem te vidimus hospitem [peregrinum] et colleximus (collegimus) [suscepimus] te, aut nudum et cooperuimus [vestivimus, teximus] (te)?

39 Aut quando te vidimus infirmum aut in carcere et venimus ad te?

40 Et respondens rex dicet [dixit] illis: Amen dico vobis quamdiu [in quantum] fecistis uni de his fratribus meis minimis [uni horum fratrum meorum minimorum] mihi fecistis.

....

42 Esurivi enim et non dedistis mihi manducare; sitivi et non dedistis mihi potum [potastis me];

43 hospes eram [peregrinus fui] et non collexistis (collegistis) [recipistis, suscepistis] me; nudus et non operuistis (cooperuistis) [vestistis] me; infirmus et in carcere et non visitastis me.

Preliminaries 3

⁴⁴ Tunc respondebunt (ei) et ipsi dicentes: Domine, quando te vidimus esurientem aut sitientem aut hospitem [peregrinum] aut nudum aut infirmum vel in carcere et non ministravimus tibi?

⁴⁵ Tunc respondebit illis dicens: Amen dico vobis quamdiu [in quantum] non fecistis uni de minoribus his [uni ex minimis istis] nec mihi fecistis.

C. *The Syriac Text of Matthew 25:31-46*

ܟܕ ܕܝܢ ܢܐܬܐ ܒܪܗ ܕܐܢܫܐ ܒܫܘܒܚܗ: ܘܟܠܗܘܢ ܡܠܐܟܘܗܝ ܩܕܝܫܐ ܥܡܗ. ܗܝܕܝܢ ܢܬܒ ܥܠ ܟܘܪܣܝܐ ܕܫܘܒܚܗ. ܘܢܬܟܢܫܘܢ ܩܕܡܘܗܝ ܟܠܗܘܢ ܥܡܡܐ ܘܢܦܪܫ ܐܢܘܢ ܚܕ ܡܢ ܚܕ ܐܝܟ ܪܥܝܐ ܕܡܦܪܫ ܥܪܒܐ ܡܢ ܓܕܝܐ. ܘܢܩܝܡ ܥܪܒܐ ܡܢ ܝܡܝܢܗ ܘܓܕܝܐ ܡܢ ܣܡܠܗ. ܗܝܕܝܢ ܢܐܡܪ ܡܠܟܐ ܠܗܢܘܢ ܕܡܢ ܝܡܝܢܗ ܬܘ ܝܪܘܬܘ ܡܠܟܘܬܐ ܕܡܛܝܒܐ ܗܘܬ ܠܟܘܢ ܡܢ ܬܘܪܡܝܗ ܕܥܠܡܐ. ܟܦܢܬ ܓܝܪ ܘܝܗܒܬܘܢ ܠܝ ܠܡܐܟܠ. ܘܨܗܝܬ ܘܐܫܩܝܬܘܢܢܝ. ܐܟܣܢܝܐ ܗܘܝܬ ܘܟܢܫܬܘܢܢܝ. ܥܪܛܠ ܗܘܝܬ ܘܟܣܝܬܘܢܢܝ. ܟܪܝܗ ܗܘܝܬ ܘܣܥܪܬܘܢܢܝ. ܒܝܬ ܐܣܝܪܐ ܗܘܝܬ ܘܐܬܝܬܘܢ ܠܘܬܝ. ܗܝܕܝܢ ܢܐܡܪܘܢ ܠܗ ܙܕܝܩܐ ܐܪܝ ܐܡܬܝ. ܚܙܝܢܟ ܟܦܢܐ ܘܬܪܣܝܢܟ ܐܘ ܨܗܝܐ ܘܐܫܩܝܢܟ. ܘܐܡܬܝ ܚܙܝܢܟ ܕܐܟܣܢܝܐ ܐܢܬ ܘܟܢܫܢܟ ܐܘ ܕܥܪܛܠܝ ܐܢܬ ܘܟܣܝܢܟ. ܘܐܡܬܝ ܚܙܝܢܟ ܟܪܝܗܐ ܐܘ ܒܝܬ ܐܣܝܪܐ ܘܐܬܝܢ ܠܘܬܟ. ܘܥܢܐ ܡܠܟܐ ܘܐܡܪ ܠܗܘܢ ܐܡܝܢ ܐܡܪ ܐܢܐ ܠܟܘܢ ܕܟܡܐ ܕܥܒܕܬܘܢ ܠܚܕ ܡܢ ܗܠܝܢ ܐܚܝ ܙܥܘܪܐ ܠܝ ܗܘ ܥܒܕܬܘܢ. ܗܝܕܝܢ ܢܐܡܪ ܐܦ ܠܗܢܘܢ ܕܡܢ ܣܡܠܗ ܙܠܘ ܠܟܘܢ ܡܢܝ ܠܝܛܐ ܠܢܘܪܐ ܕܠܥܠܡ. ܗܝ ܕܡܛܝܒܐ ܠܐܟܠܩܪܨܐ ܘܠܡܠܐܟܘܗܝ. ܟܦܢܬ ܓܝܪ ܘܠܐ ܝܗܒܬܘܢ ܠܝ ܠܡܐܟܠ. ܘܨܗܝܬ ܘܠܐ ܐܫܩܝܬܘܢܢܝ. ܘܐܟܣܢܝܐ ܗܘܝܬ ܘܠܐ ܟܢܫܬܘܢܢܝ. ܘܥܪܛܠܝ ܘܠܐ ܟܣܝܬܘܢܢܝ. ܘܟܪܝܗ ܘܒܝܬ ܐܣܝܪܐ ܘܠܐ ܣܥܪܬܘܢܢܝ. ܗܝܕܝܢ ܢܥܢܘܢ ܐܦ ܗܢܘܢ ܘܢܐܡܪܘܢ. ܡܪܢ ܐܡܬܝ ܚܙܝܢܟ ܟܦܢܐ ܐܘ ܨܗܝܐ ܐܘ ܐܟܣܢܝܐ ܐܘ ܥܪܛܠܝܐ ܐܘ ܟܪܝܗܐ ܐܘ ܒܝܬ ܐܣܝܪܐ ܘܠܐ ܫܡܫܢܟ. ܗܝܕܝܢ ܢܥܢܐ ܘܢܐܡܪ ܠܗܘܢ. ܐܡܝܢ ܐܡܪ ܐܢܐ ܠܟܘܢ ܕܟܡܐ ܕܠܐ ܥܒܕܬܘܢ ܠܚܕ ܡܢ ܗܠܝܢ ܙܥܘܪܐ ܐܦ ܠܐ ܠܝ ܥܒܕܬܘܢ. ܘܢܐܙܠܘܢ ܗܠܝܢ ܠܬܫܢܝܩܐ ܕܠܥܠܡ. ܘܙܕܝܩܐ ܠܚܝܐ ܕܠܥܠܡ.

D. The "Identity Dialogue" in Sahidic Coptic

³⁵ ⲁⲓϩⲕⲟ ⲅⲁⲣ ⲁⲧⲉⲧⲛ̄ⲧⲙ̄ⲙⲟⲓ. ⲁⲓⲉⲓⲃⲉ ⲁⲧⲉⲧⲛ̄ⲧⲥⲟⲓ. ⲛⲉⲓⲟ ⲛ̄ϣⲙ̄ⲙⲟ ⲡⲉ. ⲁⲧⲉⲧⲛ̄ϣⲟⲡⲧ̄ ⲉⲣⲱⲧⲛ̄. ³⁶ ⲛⲉⲓⲕⲏ ⲕⲁϩⲏⲧ ⲡⲉ. ⲁⲧⲉⲧⲛ̄ϯ ϩⲓⲱⲱⲧ. ⲛⲉⲓϣⲱⲛⲉ ⲡⲉ ⲁⲧⲉⲧⲛ̄ϭⲙ̄ⲡⲁϣⲓⲛⲉ. ⲛⲉⲓϩⲙ̄ ⲡⲉϣⲧⲉⲕⲟ ⲡⲉ ⲁⲧⲉⲧⲛ̄ⲉⲓ ϣⲁⲣⲟⲓ. ³⁷ ⲧⲟⲧⲉ ⲥⲉⲛⲁⲟⲩⲱϣⲃ̄ ⲛⲁϥ ⲛ̄ϭⲓⲛ̄ⲇⲓⲕⲁⲓⲟⲥ ⲉⲩϫⲱ ⲙ̄ⲙⲟⲥ. ϫⲉ ⲡϫⲟⲉⲓⲥ ⲛ̄ⲧⲁⲛⲛⲁⲩ ⲉⲣⲟⲕ ⲧⲛⲁⲩ ⲉⲕϩⲕⲁⲉⲓⲧ ⲁⲛⲧⲙ̄ⲙⲟⲕ ⲏ ⲉⲕⲟⲃⲉ ⲁⲛⲧⲥⲟⲕ. ³⁸ ⲛ̄ⲧⲁⲛⲛⲁⲩ ⲇⲉ ⲉⲣⲟⲕ ⲧⲛⲁⲩ ⲉⲕⲟ ⲛ̄ϣⲙ̄ⲙⲟ ⲁⲛϣⲟⲡⲕ̄ ⲉⲣⲟⲛ. ⲏ ⲉⲕⲕⲏ ⲕⲁϩⲏⲧ ⲁⲛϯ ϩⲓⲱⲱⲕ. ³⁹ ⲛ̄ⲧⲁⲛⲛⲁⲩ ⲇⲉ ⲉⲣⲟⲕ ⲧⲛⲁⲩ ⲉⲕϣⲱⲛⲉ ⲏ ⲉⲕϩⲙ̄ ⲡⲉϣⲧⲉⲕⲟ ⲁⲛⲉⲓ ϣⲁⲣⲟⲕ. ⁴⁰ ϥⲛⲁⲟⲩⲱϣⲃ̄ ⲇⲉ ⲛ̄ϭⲓⲡⲣ̄ⲣⲟ ⲛϥ̄ϫⲟⲟⲥ ⲛⲁⲩ. ϫⲉ ϩⲁⲙⲏⲛ ϯϫⲱ ⲙ̄ⲙⲟⲥ ⲛⲏⲧⲛ̄. ϫⲉ ⲉⲫⲟⲥⲟⲛ ⲁⲧⲉⲧⲛ̄ⲁⲁⲥ ⲛ̄ⲟⲩⲁ ⲛ̄ⲛⲉⲓⲥⲛⲏⲩ ⲉⲧⲥⲟⲃⲕ̄ ⲁⲛⲟⲕ ⲡⲉⲛⲧⲁⲧⲉⲧⲛ̄ⲁⲁⲥ ⲛⲁⲓ. ...

⁴² ⲁⲓϩⲕⲟ ⲅⲁⲣ ⲙ̄ⲡⲉⲧⲛ̄ⲧⲙ̄ⲙⲟⲓ. ⲁⲓⲉⲓⲃⲉ ⲙ̄ⲡⲉⲧⲛ̄ⲧⲥⲟⲓ. ⁴³ ⲛⲉⲓⲟ ⲛ̄ϣⲙ̄ⲙⲟ ⲡⲉ. ⲙ̄ⲡⲉⲧⲛ̄ϣⲟⲡⲧ̄ ⲉⲣⲱⲧⲛ̄. ⲛⲉⲓⲕⲏ ⲕⲁϩⲏⲧ ⲡⲉ. ⲙ̄ⲡⲉⲧⲛ̄ϯ ϩⲓⲱⲱⲧ. ⲛⲉⲓϣⲱⲛⲉ ⲡⲉ. ⲁⲩⲱ ⲉⲓϩⲙ̄ ⲡⲉϣⲧⲉⲕⲟ. ⲙ̄ⲡⲉⲧⲛ̄ϭⲙ̄ⲡⲁϣⲓⲛⲉ. ⁴⁴ ⲧⲟⲧⲉ ⲥⲉⲛⲁⲟⲩⲱϣⲃ̄ ϩⲱⲟⲩ ⲟⲛ ⲉⲩϫⲱ ⲙ̄ⲙⲟⲥ. ϫⲉ ⲡϫⲟⲉⲓⲥ ⲛ̄ⲧⲁⲛⲛⲁⲩ ⲉⲣⲟⲕ ⲧⲛⲁⲩ ⲉⲕϩⲕⲁⲉⲓⲧ ⲏ ⲉⲕⲟⲃⲉ ⲏ ⲉⲕⲟ ⲛ̄ϣⲙ̄ⲙⲟ ⲏ ⲉⲕⲕⲏ ⲕⲁϩⲏⲧ ⲏ ⲉⲕϣⲱⲛⲉ ⲏ ⲉⲕϩⲙ̄ ⲡⲉϣⲧⲉⲕⲟ ⲙ̄ⲡⲛ̄ⲇⲓⲁⲕⲟⲛⲉⲓ ⲛⲁⲕ. ⁴⁵ ⲧⲟⲧⲉ ϥⲛⲁⲟⲩⲱϣⲃ̄ ⲛⲁⲩ ⲉϥϫⲱ ⲙ̄ⲙⲟⲥ. ϫⲉ ϩⲁⲙⲏⲛ ϯϫⲱ ⲙ̄ⲙⲟⲥ ⲛⲏⲧⲛ̄. ϫⲉ ⲉⲫⲟⲥⲟⲛ ⲙ̄ⲡⲉⲧⲛ̄ⲁⲁⲥ ⲛ̄ⲟⲩⲁ ⲛ̄ⲛⲉⲓⲕⲟⲩⲓ. ⲁⲛⲟⲕ ⲡⲉ ⲙ̄ⲡⲉⲧⲛ̄ⲁⲁⲥ ⲛⲁⲓ.

E. The "Identity Dialogue" in Bohairic Coptic

³⁵ Ⲁⲓϩⲕⲟ ⲅⲁⲣ ⲟⲩⲟϩ ⲁⲧⲉⲧⲉⲛⲧⲉⲙⲙⲟⲓ. ⲁⲛⲃⲓ ⲟⲩⲟϩ ⲁⲧⲉⲧⲉⲛⲧⲟⲓ. ⲁⲓⲟⲓ ⲛ̄ϣⲉⲙⲙⲟ ⲟⲩⲟϩ ⲁⲧⲉⲧⲉⲛϣⲟⲡⲧ ⲉⲣⲱⲧⲉⲛ.

³⁶ Ⲛⲁⲓⲃⲏϣ ⲟⲩⲟϩ ⲁⲧⲉⲧⲉⲛϩⲟⲃⲥⲧ. ⲛⲁⲓϣⲱⲛⲓ ⲟⲩⲟϩ ⲁⲧⲉⲧⲉⲛϫⲉⲙⲡⲁϣⲓⲛⲓ. ⲛⲁⲓⲭⲏ ϧⲉⲛ ⲡⲓϣⲧⲉⲕⲟ ⲟⲩⲟϩ ⲁⲧⲉⲧⲉⲛⲓ ϣⲁⲣⲟⲓ.

³⁷ Ⲧⲟⲧⲉ ⲉⲩⲉⲉⲣⲟⲩⲱ ⲛⲁϥ ⲛ̄ϫⲉⲛⲓ|ⲑⲙⲏⲓ ⲉⲩϫⲱ ⲙ̄ⲙⲟⲥ. ϫⲉ ⲡⲉⲛⲟ̄ⲥ̄ ⲉⲧⲁⲛⲛⲁⲩ ⲉⲣⲟⲕ ⲛ̄ⲑⲛⲁⲩ ⲉⲕ-ϩⲟⲕⲉⲣ ⲟⲩⲟϩ ⲁⲛⲧⲉⲙⲙⲟⲕ. ⲓⲉ ⲉⲕⲟⲃⲓ ⲟⲩⲟϩ

ⲁⲛⲧⲥⲟⲕ. ³⁶ ⲓⲉ ⲉⲧⲁⲛⲛⲁⲩ ⲉⲣⲟⲕ ⲛ̄ⲑⲛⲁⲩ ⲉⲕⲟⲓ
ⲛ̄ϣⲉⲙⲙⲟ ⲟⲩⲟϩ, ⲁⲛϣⲟⲡⲕ ⲉⲣⲟⲛ. ⲓⲉ ⲉⲕⲃⲏϣ
ⲟⲩⲟϩ, ⲁⲛϩⲟⲃⲥⲕ. ³⁹ ⲓⲉ ⲉⲧⲁⲛⲛⲁⲩ ⲉⲣⲟⲕ ⲛ̄ⲑⲛⲁⲩ
ⲉⲕϣⲱⲛⲓ. ⲓⲉ ⲉⲕⲭⲏ ϧⲉⲛ ⲡⲓϣⲧⲉⲕⲟ ⲟⲩⲟϩ, ⲁⲛⲓ
ϣⲁⲣⲟⲕ.
⁴⁰ Ⲟⲩⲟϩ, ⲉϥⲉⲉⲣⲟⲩⲱ ⲛ̄ϫⲉⲡⲓⲟⲩⲣⲟ ⲉϥⲉϫⲟⲥ ⲛⲱⲟⲩ. ϫⲉ
ⲁⲙⲏⲛ ϯϫⲱ ⲙ̄ⲙⲟⲥ ⲛⲱⲧⲉⲛ. ϫⲉ ⲉⲫⲟⲥⲟⲛ ⲁⲧⲉ-
ⲧⲉⲛⲁⲓⲧⲟⲩ ⲛ̄ⲟⲩⲁⲓ ⲛ̄ⲛⲁⲓⲕⲟⲩϫⲓ ⲛ̄ⲥⲛⲏⲟⲩ ⲛ̄ⲧⲏⲓ.
ⲁⲛⲟⲕ ⲡⲉⲧⲁⲣⲉⲧⲉⲛⲁⲓⲧⲟⲩ ⲛⲏⲓ. ...
⁴² Ⲁⲓϩⲕⲟ ⲅⲁⲣ ⲟⲩⲟϩ, ⲙ̄ⲡⲉⲧⲉⲛⲧⲉⲙⲙⲟⲓ. ⲁⲓⲓⲃⲓ
ⲟⲩⲟϩ, ⲙ̄ⲡⲉⲧⲉⲛⲧⲥⲟⲓ. ⁴³ ⲛⲁⲓⲟⲓ ⲛ̄ϣⲉⲙⲙⲟ ⲟⲩⲟϩ,
ⲙ̄ⲡⲉⲧⲉⲛϣⲟⲡⲧ ⲉⲣⲱⲧⲉⲛ. ⲛⲁⲓⲃⲏϣ ⲟⲩⲟϩ, ⲙ̄ⲡⲉ-
ⲧⲉⲛϩⲟⲃⲥⲧ. ⲛⲁⲓϣⲱⲛⲓ ⲟⲩⲟϩ, ⲙ̄ⲡⲉⲧⲉⲛϫⲉⲙ-
ⲡⲁϣⲓⲛⲓ. ⲛⲁⲓⲭⲏ ϧⲉⲛ ⲡⲓϣⲧⲉⲕⲟ ⲙ̄ⲡⲉⲧⲉⲛⲓ
ϣⲁⲣⲟⲓ.
⁴⁴ Ⲧⲟⲧⲉ ⲉⲩⲉⲉⲣⲟⲩⲱ ϩⲱⲟⲩ ⲉⲩϫⲱ ⲙ̄ⲙⲟⲥ. ϫⲉ ⲡⲉⲛⲟ̅ⲥ̅
ⲉⲧⲁⲛⲛⲁⲩ ⲉⲣⲟⲕ ⲛ̄ⲑⲛⲁⲩ ⲉⲕϩⲟⲕⲉⲣ ⲓⲉ ⲉⲕⲟⲃⲓ ⲓⲉ
ⲉⲕⲟⲓ ⲛ̄ϣⲉⲙⲙⲟ ⲓⲉ ⲉⲕⲃⲏϣ ⲓⲉ ⲉⲕϣⲱⲛⲓ ⲓⲉ ⲉⲕⲭⲏ
ϧⲉⲛ ⲡⲓϣⲧⲉⲕⲟ. ⲟⲩⲟϩ, ⲙ̄ⲡⲉⲛϣⲉⲙϣⲏⲧⲕ.
⁴⁵ Ⲧⲟⲧⲉ ⲉϥⲉⲉⲣⲟⲩⲱ ⲛⲱⲟⲩ ⲉϥϫⲱ ⲙ̄ⲙⲟⲥ. ϫⲉ ⲁⲙⲏⲛ
ϯϫⲱ ⲙ̄ⲙⲟⲥ ⲛⲱⲧⲉⲛ. ϫⲉ ⲉⲫⲟⲥⲟⲛ ⲙ̄ⲡⲉⲧⲉⲛ|-
ⲁⲓⲧⲟⲩ ⲛ̄ⲟⲩⲁⲓ ⲛ̄ⲛⲁⲓⲕⲟⲩϫⲓ. ⲟⲩⲇⲉ ⲁⲛⲟⲕ ⲙ̄ⲡⲉ-
ⲧⲉⲛⲁⲓⲧⲟⲩ ⲛⲏⲓ.

F. *Textual Criticism*

There are three textual variants of significance in vv 40 and 41 that should be considered.

<u>25:40</u> The words τῶν ἀδελφῶν μου are omitted in B* 1424 ff¹ ff² and in Clement of Alexandria, Eusebius of Caesarea and Gregory of Nyssa. This omission is most likely the result of the influence of the absence of these words in v 45.

<u>25:41</u> The article οἱ is omitted in ℵ B L 0128. 0135. 33 *pc*. Witnesses for its presence are A D W Θ 067^{vid}. 074 $f^{1.13}$ 𝔐. The

word is enclosed in brackets in the Nestle-Aland text, indicating that the editors consider its authenticity doubtful.[2]

τὸ ἡτοιμασμένον is found in $\mathfrak{P}^{45}$ ℵ A B K L W Δ Θ Π 067. 074. 0128. 0135. 0136. f^{13} 𝔐 lat sy sa bo goth arm eth geo Diatessaron Tertullian[1/2] Hippolytus Origen[gr,lat] Eusebius Hilary Basil Apostolic Constitutions Didymus Augustine Cyril. ὃ ἡτοίμασεν ὁ πατήρ μου is found in D f^1 it mae Justin Irenaeus[lat] Hippolytus Origen[lat3/5] Cyprian Ps-Clement Hilary Petilianus Augustine. τῷ ἡτοιμασμένῳ is found in F 1009 1344 1[1663] and ὃ ἡτοίμασεν ὁ κύριος is witnessed in Clement Tertullian[1/2] (Origen[lat]). It is possible that ὃ ἡτοίμασεν ὁ πατήρ μου was the original reading and was shortened to the passive participle τὸ ἡτοιμασμένον to agree with ἡτοιμασμένην in v 34; or that τὸ ἡτοιμασμένον was original and ὁ πατήρ μου was introduced into v 41 in order to provide a parallel to τοῦ πατρός μου of v 34. Because of the weight of the external evidence, the UBS committee chose τὸ ἡτοιμασμένον, the shorter reading, and assigned this passage a B rating, indicating some degree of doubt. τῷ ἡτοιμασμένῳ and ὃ ἡτοίμασεν ὁ κύριος were seen to be developments of the other two readings.[3]

G. *References to the OT*

There are no exact quotations from the OT in Matt 25:31-46, but there are allusions with some correspondence in wording with the LXX. In three cases, marked with an asterisk (*), there is similarity of idea but no verbal correspondence.

v 31	Dan 7:13; Deut 32:43; 33:2 LXX; Zech 14:5; *1 Enoch* 61:8; 62:2-3; 69:27,29.
32	Dan 7:14; Joel 4:12; Ezek 34:17, 20.
33	Ezek 34:17, 20.
34	Ps 109;1; Isa 65:23.
35a	Isa 58:7; Ezek 18:7,16; Tob 4:16.
35c	Isa 58:7; Job 31:32.
36a	Ezek 18:7,16; Tob 4:16.

36b	Sir 7:35.*
40	Prov 19:17.*
41	Ps 6:9.*
42	Job 22:7.
46	Dan 12:2.

H. *The Context*

It is widely agreed among commentators that Matt 25:31-46 concludes the major discourse of the last of the so-called formal teaching discourses in Matthew. What is debated among scholars is exactly where this final discourse begins and whether Matt 25:31-46 is to be regarded as an independent unit or not.

I am most convinced by the arguments of B. W. Bacon that, exclusive of a preamble (chaps. 1-2) and an epilogue (26:3--28:20), Matthew can be divided into five parts, each beginning with narrative material and ending with a discourse. Each of the five parts of Matthew is terminated with the formula καὶ ἐγένετο ὅτε ἐτέλεσεν ὁ Ἰησοῦς . . . which occurs at 7:28; 11:1; 13:53; 19:1; and 26:1.[4]

I disagree with Bacon in his making the debate with the Pharisees (23:1-39) part of the fifth discourse. I would include it with the preceding narrative material and, along with J. Lambrecht[5] and L. Cope,[6] see chaps. 24-25 as a unit. Matt 24-25, sometimes called the parousia discourse, can be divided into three large sections: (a) 24:1-35 (in which, following Mark closely, he gives information about events leading to the parousia); (b) 24:36-25:30 (in which, using parables mainly from Q and his own Parable of the Ten Virgins, he exhorts his readers to vigilance); and (c) 25:31-46 (a description from his *Sondergut* of the universal judgment at the parousia).[7] The center of attention throughout this final Matthean discourse is the return of Christ at the end of the age. He is represented as looking beyond his imminent passion and offering encouragement to his disciples about the time before his return. L. Cope[8] has observed that each of the first four formal discourses in Matthew contains some reference to judgment in its concluding section: 7:23b; 10:42; 13:49; 18:35. The fifth discourse is concluded, not by a simple reference to future judgment, but by an extended description of the final event. Thus Matt 25:31-46 can be viewed as an intriguing technique to conclude not only the fifth discourse but all the preceding discourses of Jesus as well

To appreciate fully the position that the scene of the last judgment has in Matthew, it is not sufficient to see it merely as a conclusion. Looking at the larger context, it would seem that 25:31-46, in a proleptic fashion, is integrally related to the Great Commission that occurs a few chapters later (28:16-20) where the disciples are sent to the very same people (πάντα τὰ ἔθνη) that are to be gathered before Christ at the end of time. The two scenes have to be taken together; in any attempt at exegesis, the judgment that takes place in 25:31-46 cannot be viewed apart from the events described in 28:16-20.

I. *The Interpretation of Matt 25:31-46*

The Matthean scene of the final judgment belongs to that select category of biblical passages that have exerted tremendous influence on Christian preaching, praxis, literature, and art. Verses 31-34,41,46 have been used by untold writers, ancient and modern, to remind their readers of the certainty of eternal reward and punishment. Verses 35-40, 42-45, which constitute what I shall term in this dissertation "the dialogue of the needy Christ" or simply the "identity dialogue," have been employed to exhort to greater Christian almsgiving. Throughout the centuries exegetes have found in this passage grounds for charity without bounds, interpreting it as a command to Christian and non-Christian alike to care for every needy human being. In recent years, however, voices have been raised that seriously challenge that interpretation and claim that Matt 25:35-40,42-45 does not provide a legitimate basis for Christian concern for the poor and needy of the world. The two problem areas in the interpretation of the pericope continue to be the identity of πάντα τὰ ἔθνη in v 32 and ἑνὶ τούτων (τῶν ἀδελφῶν μου) τῶν ἐλαχίστων in vv 40, 45. What is the make-up of "all the nations?" Is it to be understood in its Jewish sense of all who are not Jewish, or in its Christian sense of all who are not Christian, or in its widest possible sense of all human beings? Who are the "least of my brothers?" Are they the disciples, or all Christians, or Jews, or any human being who is in need?

Rudolf Brändle has observed that "a comprehensive treatment of the history of interpretation and influence of this pericope is lacking."[9] Several monographs and numerous articles deal with the exegesis of Matt 25:31-46, but no work exists that attempts to give as complete a survey as possible of the history of its interpretation. This study is intended to fill that lacuna. In the following pages I shall examine what ancient, medieval, and modern authors have had to say about the Matthean judgment scene, placing special emphasis on the make-up of πάντα τὰ ἔθνη in v 32, or on the verses pertaining to the identification of Christ with "the least" (vv 35-40,42-45). In order that there may be some control in this study, I shall consider a passage to be an allusion to or interpretation of the Matthean pericope only if the same Greek words (or in the case of the Vg, the same Latin words) are present that are found in the biblical text.

Literature is replete with casual references to vv 31-34,41,46 to prove the divinity of Christ, his equality with the Father, his superiority over Satan, or simply to remind the reader that there will be final accountability for human actions, that the bliss of heaven or the fires of hell are eternal, or that it was not part of God's original plan that human beings be punished. A discussion of these aspects of the passage would produce a volume in itself and therefore have to be left beyond the consideration of this study, unless they shed light on an author's interpretation of "all the nations" or "the least of my brothers." In the chapters that follow I shall from time to time describe an author as having a "restrictive," "narrow," or "particularist" viewpoint regarding the identity of "the least." By this I mean that he considers the needy in the passage to be Christ's apostles or members of the Christian community in general. The terms "expansive," "all-encompassing," or "universalist" indicate that an author sees the beneficiaries of vv 35-40,42-45 as all men and women.

In the pages that follow I shall investigate the interpretation of Matt 25:31-46 in the following historical periods: A. *The Early Church*. This section will deal with eastern and western writers of the patristic period. B. *The Middle Ages*. This chapter will cover the period of time from the beginning of the ninth century to the Renaissance. C. *The Reformation and Counter-Reformation*. This period will include the Renaissance and will deal with both Catholic and Protestant exegesis primarily in the sixteenth and seventeenth centuries. D. *The Modern Era*. This section will begin with the eighteenth century and conclude with the present. In the final chapter I shall classify and offer a critical assessment of the various interpretations of Matt 25:31-46, especially in regards to the understanding of "the least" in vv 40,45.

NOTES TO CHAPTER I

[1] Significant textual variants found in the Clementine edition (*Bibliorum sacrorum juxta Vulgatam Clementinam* [Vatican: Typis polyglottis, 1951] will be included in parentheses. Variants found in the VL (*Itala: Das Neue Testament in altlateinischer Überlieferung* [4 vols.; ed. A. Jülicher; Berlin: de Gruyter, 1938] 1.187-89) are included within brackets.

[2] E. Nestle, E. Nestle, K. Aland, M. Black, C. Martini, B. Metzger, A. Wikgren (eds.), *Novum Testamentum Graece* (26th ed.; Stuttgart: Deutsche Bibelstiftung, 1981) 74.

[3] B. M. Metzger, *A Textual Commentary on the Greek New Testament* (London/New York: United Bible Societies, 1971) 63-64.

[4] B. W. Bacon, *Studies in Matthew* (New York: Holt, 1930) 80-82.

[5] J. Lambrecht, "The Parousia Discourse: Composition and Content in *Mt.*, XXIV-XXV," *L'Evangile selon Matthieu* (BETL 29; ed. M. Didier; Gembloux: Duculot, 1972) 309.

[6] L. Cope, "Matthew 25:31-46: The Sheep and the Goats Reinterpreted," *NovT* 11 (1969) 32-44, esp. p. 33.

[7] Lambrecht, 311-313. Not all, however, agree. J. S. Sibinga ("The Structure of the Apocalyptic Discourse, Matthew 24 and 25," *ST* 29 [1975] 72) argues, from a numerical arrangement, that the Parable of the Talents (25:14-30) forms an unbreakable unit with 25:31-46.

[8] "Matthew 25:31-46," *NovT* 11 (1969) 33-34.

[9] R. Brändle, *Matt 25:31-46 im Werk des Johannes Chrysostomos* (BGBE 22; Tübingen: Mohr, 1979) 1.

CHAPTER II

THE PATRISTIC PERIOD

The Apostolic Fathers

A careful study of the Apostolic Fathers,[1] the earliest Christian writings after the NT, reveals that we can nowhere with any certitude find a direct quotation or even a definite allusion to Matt 25:31-46. *1 Clem.* 59.4 ("... heal the sick [ἀσθενεῖς] ... feed the hungry [πεινῶντας] ... raise up the weak [ἀσθενοῦντας]");[2] Ign. *Smyrn.* 6.2 ("... they have no concern for ... the hungry or the thirsty [πεινῶντος ἢ διψῶντος]");[3] and Pol. *Phil.* 6.1 ("... the presbyters must comfort all the sick [ἐπισκεπτόμενοι πάντας ἀσθενεῖς]")[4] reflect similar social concerns as Matt 25:35-36, but the points of verbal contact are so slight that an allusion to the Matthean pericope might not be clearly intended. This may be an indication that the Matthean gospel was not yet widely known by the end of the first century.[5] Otherwise, how account for the fact that in passages dealing with fraternal charity and the necessity of almsgiving, where one would expect the words of the Matthean Christ to be quoted, they are not? The very strong probability exists that any references in these early writings to the six acts of charity mentioned in Matt 25:35-36 come from the same sources that Matthew might have used: Isa 58:7; Ezek 18:7,16; Job 22:7; 31:32; and Tob 4:16.

What we do see in the writings of the Apostolic Fathers are various Christian communities concerned with putting acts of charity into practice among their own people. The second-century Christian would not have the same kind of global concern as ours in this century. In the Apostolic Fathers there is nothing to indicate that the charitable concern of the Christian extended beyond the faith community. On the contrary, in almost every passage concerned with the same issues as Matt 25: 35-36 there is some restricting element, a word or a phrase, that makes it clear that the good works being discussed are envisaged in terms of other Christians.

Fathers of the Later Second Century

Justin Martyr (ca. AD 100 - 166)

Justin, writing from Rome at about the middle of the second century, is the first church Father to quote from Matt 25:31-46. In his *Dialogue with Trypho* 76.5 he quotes v 41 to prove that Christ has his own power and majesty, distinct from that of the Father. In the remainder of his extant writings he alludes three times (*Apol.* 1.28; 1.51; and 2.8)[6] to those verses of the Matthean passage that show Christ as equal to the Father and the Messiah foretold by the Hebrew prophets.

Justin is caught up with the christological controversies of the early church, and so it is not surprising that in his treatment of Matt 25:31-46 he is concerned only with those six verses (31-34,41,46) demonstrating Christ's power and judgment. No passage in his works refers to those verses (35-40,42-45) stating Christ's identity with the poor and suffering. In *Apol.* 1. 61-67 he describes elements of the contemporary structure of the Christian liturgy and tells us that it was customary at every Eucharist for the Christians to take up a collection to be used to aid five classes of people: orphans and widows, the sick, those imprisoned, strangers, and those in any kind of need.[7] It would have been appropriate at this point to buttress his argument by quoting Matt 25:35-36, but he does not do so.

Irenaeus of Lyons (ca. AD 130-203)

Irenaeus, the first great anti-gnostic theologian, is the first church Father to quote from the verses in the Matthean pericope that have to do with Christ's identification of himself with the needy. His most important work, *Adversus Haereses*, is not extant in the Greek original but in a very literal Latin translation.[8] Out of eighteen references to Matt 25:31-46 in *Adversus Haereses* only two are quotations from the "identity dialogue." In *Adv. Haer.* 4.18, 6 he argues that we give to God when we give to our fellow human beings:

> ... even though God does not need what comes from us, we need to offer something to God. As Solomon says: 'He who has compassion on the poor lends to the Lord.' God, who has no need of anything, accepts our good works in order to give us in return his own goods. As the Lord says: '... I was hungry and you fed me; I thirsted and you gave me to drink. I was a stranger and you took me in, naked and you covered me, ill and you took care of me. I was in prison and you visited me.'[9]

Irenaeus quotes Prov 19:17 along with Matt 25:35-36 to substantiate his argument. This could be an indication that the object of his concern is any poor and needy person.

In *Adv. Haer.* 4.30, 3, opposing Marcion's contention that the Israelites sinned by despoiling the Egyptians before their departure from Egypt (Exod 12:35-36), Irenaeus quotes Matt 25:35a,36a in the context of insisting that Christians of his own day benefit from the security and prosperity of the pagan Roman world.[10] Hence, because Christians receive from others, they are to share what they have with others. Irenaeus is silent here about the exact identity of the needy that Christians must help, but the fact that he mentions that Christians receive benefits from the pagan Romans might indicate that non-Christians are likewise to be included as benefactors of Christian charity.

Irenaeus is also important in the history of exegesis of Matt 25:31-46 because, as far as I could discover, he is the sole witness to the heretical, gnostic use of the passage. In *Adv. Haer.* 1.5,1 he gives the impression that Ptolemy, the mid-second-century disciple of Valentinus, understood Matt 25:33 (the separation of the sheep and goats) to refer to the demiurge's creation. From psychic substance he created those beings comparable to God that the Valentinian gnostics called "the right"

14   Matthew 25:31-46

(δεξιά/dextras); while those beings that sprang from passion, or matter, were called "the left" (d ριστερά/sinistras).[11] Irenaeus gives his own understanding of Matt 25:33 in *Adv. Haer.* 5.28, 1: on the last day true Christians will be separated from heretics. [12]

Anonymous Writings of the Second Century

There are nine extant anonymous writings from the second century that might possibly refer to Matt 25:31-46: the Greek *Apocalypse of Peter, The Martyrdom of Polycarp, the Letter of the Churches of Lyons and Vienne, The Acts of the Martyrs Andochius, Thyrsus and Felix, 2 Clement, The Acts of Thomas, The Epistle of the Apostles, The Sibylline Oracles,* and *The Sentences of Sextus.* In none of these writings is there an exact quotation. Most of them allude to vv 41, 46 to prove that Christians, especially martyrs, will enter eternal life, while nonbelievers and heretics will perish.

The only texts important for our investigation are the apocryphal *Acts of Thomas* and the anonymous homily known as *2 Clement.* They are the only ones that allude to Matt 25:35-36.

In the *Acts of Thomas* 145, just before his death "Thomas" describes his own life as an apostle in terms that bring to mind vv 35-36 from the Matthean judgment scene:

> . . . Behold, therefore, I have fulfilled your work and accomplished your command; and I have become poor and needy and a stranger (wĕʾaksĕnāyāʾ/ξένος) and a slave, despised and a prisoner (wĕʾasîrāʾ/δέσμιος) and hungry (wĕkapnāʾ/πειναλέος) and thirsty (waṣhiyāʾ/διψαλέος) and naked (wĕʿarṭelāyāʾ/ἐξουδενωμένος) and weary for your sake.[13]

I agree with J. B. Lightfoot[14] and the Committee of the Oxford Society of Historical Theology[15] that there is an allusion to v 46 in *2 Clem.* 6.7: ". . . if we disregard his commandments, nothing will deliver us from eternal punishment (ἐκ τῆς αἰωνίου κολάσεως) . . . ."[16] Since Matt 25:46 is the only passage in the NT and the LXX where κόλασις is used in conjunction with αἰώνιος, it is "hard to escape the impression that (2 Clement) is using (Matthew's) gospel directly or indirectly."[17]

In 2 Clem.17:4-5 the author presents an exhortation illustrated by a judgment scene reminiscent of Matt 25:

> For the Lord said, "I am coming to gather all nations, peoples and tongues." This refers to the day of his appearing, when he will come to redeem us, each according to his deeds. And the unbelievers shall see his glory and might, and they will be astonished to see that sovereignty over the world belongs to Jesus, and they will say, "Woe is us, for you really did exist, *and we did not know it* nor did we believe and obey the elders who preached to us of our salvation." (Οὔαι ἡμῖν ὅτι σὺ ἦς, καὶ οὐκ ᾔδειμεν καὶ οὐκ ἐπιστεύομεν, καὶ οὐκ ἐπειθόμεθα τοῖς πρεσβυτέροις τοῖς ἀναγγέλλουσιν ἡμῖν περὶ τῆς σωτηρίας ἡμῶν.)[18]

I agree with J. R. Michaels who sees in the italicized words an allusion to the puzzled questions of the damned in Matt 25:44 and an implicit connection between their fate and their obedience to or treatment of the elders. Thus, "the least" in the Matthean setting, according to "Clement," would be the πρεσβύτεροι of the church.[19]

While there is no certainty that the anonymous authors of the *Acts of Thomas*[20] and *2 Clement* had the Matthean judgment scene in mind, there remains a possibility that they did. If that be the case, these two writings could be the earliest indication that the needy described in Matt 25:35-40, 42-45 were seen to be the apostles and other messengers of the gospel.

Fathers of the Third Century

Eastern Writers

Clement of Alexandria (ca. AD 150 - 216)

Titus Flavius Clemens is the first to identify the beneficiaries of the good works described in Matt 25:31-46 as Christians. Of the eight references to the Matthean pericope that I was able to find in his works, five are actual quotations of verses from the "identity dialogue."

In his *Quis dives salvetur* 30:1-5, Clement quotes vv 34-40 in full, in conjunction with the restrictive Matt 10:40, to make the point that ". . . whatever is done to a disciple the Lord accepts as done to himself . . . ." [21]

The other four quotations are found in *Paedagogus* and *Stromata*, but the recipients of charity are never explicitly identified as believers. In *Paed*. 3.4.30,3 Clement, as a moralist and close observer of the customs of his times, quotes Matt 25:40 (without τῶν ἀδελφῶν μου) to excoriate the wealthy who take more delight in accumulating and caring for their pet animals than they do in caring for orphans, widows, and the aged.[22] The fact that in this same context he also quotes Prov 19:17, which applies to all the poor, may be an indication that he has even non-Christian needy in mind.

In *Paed*. 3.12.93,4-5 Clement quotes a near semblance of v 40 ("whatever you have done to these little ones [τοῖς μικροῖς τούτοις], you have done to me") in conjunction with vv 34-36,46b to encourage stingy Christians to be more free with their possessions when it comes to sharing with the needy.[23] There is nothing here either to indicate that Clement has a restrictive view of the needy, unless an argument can be made that in the above quotation μικροῖς was used because he had in mind the μικρῶν of Matt 10:42, a verse that is concerned with charity to the disciples.

In his *Stromata* Clement likewise quotes twice from the dialogue of the needy Christ. He is not concerned here with moral issues, but rather with heretical views regarding marriage and the nature of God. In *Strom.* 3.6.54,3 he cites vv 35-36a and v 40 (without τῶν ἀδελφῶν μου) as part of his argument in favor of marriage against a certain Carpocrates and his followers who rejected it. The gnostics sought an "immoral communion" with God by means of their strict continence. The communion with himself that God is interested in, says Clement, is best illustrated by the charitable works described in the "identity dialogue." The fact that he then quotes Prov 3:27 and 19:17 could be a strong indication that he includes all needy people in his concept of "the least." [24]

In *Strom.* 2.16.73,1-2 Clement cites v 35ab and a slight variation of v 40 ("ὃ γὰρ ἑνὶ τούτων τῶν ἐλαχίστων πεποιήκατε, ἐμοὶ πεποιήκατε") to prove that God can be said to have human affections: "As then [God] is nourished [τρέφεται], though not personally, by the nourishing of one whom he wishes nourished; so he rejoices, without suffering change, by reason of him who has repented."[25]

It is noteworthy that with Clement of Alexandria we see the first moral and pastoral use of the Matthean pericope. In three of the five uses of the "identity dialogue" he is concerned with caring for the needy. And yet Clement is generally silent regarding the exact identity of "the least." In light of the fact that, of the five quotations having to do with the needy, only *Quis dives salvetur* 30.1-5 can be interpreted with certainty as espousing the restrictive viewpoint, it would be difficult to place him firmly in the camp of those who see "the least of my brethren" as Christians only. There is really not enough evidence to decide one way or the other.

Origen (ca. AD 185 - 255)

The successor of Clement as head of the catechetical school in Alexandria was Origen, the most prolific writer of the early church. He was by far the most influential, and yet controversial, exegete of the third century. Even though his scriptural exegesis is at times heavily colored by his neoplatonic worldview,[26] Origen's importance as an expositor of the sacred texts should not be undervalued. He is the first commentator to recognize the problem of "the nations" in v 32, a problem that has plagued modern scholarship. He asks whether all peoples who ever existed are meant, or only those who will be alive at the time of the parousia. Will they be only those who believe in Christ or even nonbelievers? His conclusion is that it is not clear from the text exactly what is meant by τὰ ἔθνη. (Cf. *Comm. ser.* 70: ". . . non satis est manifestum").[27] He is exceptionally important for this study because he is the first to give us a commentary as such on Matthew's Gospel, even though his comments on Matt 25:31-46 are preserved in a work entitled *Commentariorum series*, a Latin translation by Rufinus. Origen did not limit his comments on Matt 25:31-46 to his *Commentary on Matthew*. His extant works are sprinkled with quotations and allusions to the Matthean judgment scene. Out of a total of forty-six references to Matt 25:31-46, twenty-five are concerned with those verses that comprise the "dialogue of the needy Christ." All but one of these references (*De oratione* 11.2) are found in his so-called exegetical works.[28] Out of these twenty-five references (fifteen actual quotations and ten allusions) twenty-one can be used to show that Origen held the restrictive view with regard to the identity of those who were in need. For him the "least of my brothers" were undoubtedly Christians.

Only one text can be interpreted in a nonrestrictive sense. In *Hom. in psalm.* 2.1, in a discussion of the close interrelation between Christ and his members, Origen alludes to vv 35-36, 40:

> . . . [Christ] says he is the one who is hungry [esuriat] among us, he is the one who is thirsty [sitiat] among us, and naked [nudus] and sick [aeger] and the stranger [hospes] and the one hidden in prison [retrusus in carcerem], and he states that whatever will have been done to one of his least ones [uni ex minimis suis] was done to him . . . .[29]

A few lines later he speaks of the body of Christ as comprising "the entire human race, even more, perhaps the totality of all creation [Christus ergo cuius omne hominum genus, imo fortassis totius creaturae universitas corpus est . . .]."[30]

As to be expected, the largest number of references to the identity of the needy are to be found in what is extant of Origen's own *Commentary on Matthew* and in *Commentariorum series*, Rufinus' translation of his remarks on the last six chapters of Matthew. His commentary on Matt 25:42-43 in *Comm. Ser.* 73 best sums up his views regarding the identity of those with whom Christ so closely associates himself:

> When the saints are in need of food, he [Christ] also is hungry [esurit]. When others of his members need medicine, he too, weak [infirmus] as it were, also needs it. And when others are in need of being taken in, he himself, as if a traveler, seeks in them "where he can lay his head."... Wherefore he says: 'I was ill and in prison and you did not visit me.' If a member of Christ is in prison [in carcere], then he himself [Christ] is not free of prison....[31]

In other passages where he cites or alludes to the "identity dialogue," Origen refers to the recipients of the charity or injustice inflicted by others as "those who are the flesh of Christ by the acquisition of the Spirit" (*Strom.* 10),[32] "those who are in the church" (fragment on Ps 68:24),[33] "those who believe in him" (*De orat.* 11.2; *Comm. in Rom.* 7.5),[34] "the martyrs" (*Hom. in Jer.* 14.7),[35] "Christians, who are the feet of Christ" (*Comm. ser.* 77),[36] "the poor faithful" (*Comm. ser.* 68),[37] and "those who preach the gospel" (*Comm. ser.* 61).[38] In his *Comm. in Matt.* 13.2, commenting on Matt 17:12-13, Origen says that the torments the Jews inflicted on John the Baptist were inflicted on Christ, who said, "... because of the weak [ἀσθενοῦντας], I was weak [ἠσθένουν]; because of the hungry [πεινῶντας], I was hungry [ἐπείνων], and because of the thirsty [διψῶντας], I was thirsty [ἐδίψων]."[39] If Origen intended to allude here to Matt 25:35-36, it could be an indication that his conception of "the least" was wider than Christians, unless, because of the close association between the Baptist and Christ, he considered John to be a disciple.[40]

Origen is perhaps most well known for his tendency to spiritualize the scriptures, to reach beyond the literal and try to grasp a deeper meaning. His observations on Matt 25:31-46 do not escape this allegorical or spiritualizing tendency. His understanding of Matt 25:35-36 was in no way restricted to the six physical works of mercy mentioned by Christ. He claimed that everything done to the disciple, whether physically, mentally, or spiritually, was done to Christ. In *Comm. ser.* 1.1, commenting on the Pharisee who tempted Christ (Matt 22:34), he says that anyone who questions a learned person with the purpose of tempting him is doing to Christ precisely what the Pharisee did. And then, after quoting Matt 25:35-36,40, he comes to his main point:

> Everything that happens to the holy ones of Christ, whether caused by those loving them or tempting them, he [Christ] takes unto himself.... When a just man, either blasphemed or something else, suffers an injury, put Christ there saying to those who did it: By the fact that you did it to one of these least ones [uni ex minimis istis] you injured me, you blasphemed me.[41]

In *Comm. ser.* 72 Origen ponders whether v 35 refers to simple, bodily benefactions or rather spiritual works, and comes to the conclusion that "whoever does a good work [opus bonum] in one way or another [sive hoc sive illo modo] . . . is giving food [cibum] and drink [potum] to the hungry and thirsty Christ [Christo esurienti et sitienti]"[42] In *Hom. in Gen.* 10.3 he links Jesus' request to the Samaritan woman for a drink of water (Jn 4:7) with his statement of thirst in the Matthean judgment scene (Matt 25:35) and claims that Christ, in reality, is thirsting for our faith; [43] and in *Comm. ser.* 137 he depicts Christ thirsting for the drink of our virtuous lives, free of all bitterness.[44] In *Comm. ser.* 72, commenting on v 35c, he claims that we receive Christ as a traveler when we take him into our hearts by receiving the words of his missionaries and feed him with the abundance of our virtues:

> When we prepare our hearts with various virtues to receive him or those who belong to him, we receive him as a pilgrim

into the home of our heart, fashioning a large, ornate and elegant banquet hall for the reception of Christ, a pilgrim in the world, and the rest of his disciples. For when we receive their words, we seem to have received their very selves into us, and, through them, Christ, whose word they carry.[45]

The garments with which we clothe the naked are the virtues of "mercy, chastity, meekness and humility" (*Comm. in ser.* 72)[46] which are fostered in those who accept Christian teaching; while in *Comm. in Matt.* 12.23, Origen quotes v 42a to insist that the one who fails to feed Christ is the one who is a scandal to the brethren: "Even more so such as these would be called by Jesus a scandal to him; and by being a scandal to him, they would certainly be a scandal to his brothers among whom, as he says, there 'is the one who is hungry and you did not give me to eat . . . .' "[47] In *Hom. in Ps.* 2.1 he paraphrases vv 35-36,40 to make his point that the sick to be visited are the members of Christ's body who are ill with serious sin.[48] And in *Comm. ser.* 72 Origen claims that since this world was a prison for Christ, it is likewise a prison for those who believe in him; consequently, when we visit the faithful, for any reason whatsoever, we are visiting those in prison.[49]

For Origen, as for most of the Fathers, those who are commanded to perform these good deeds are Christians. In *De orat.* 11.2 he states that even the saints in heaven, who pray for Christians on earth, continue to minister to Christ who attributes to himself the sufferings of those who believe in him.[50] Those who fail to do the six works of Matt 25:35-36, however, are a mixture of Christians and non-Christians. Among the Christians to fall under Christ's indictment are those who are stumbling blocks to their fellow believers (*Comm. in Matt.* 12.23),[51] those who speak evilly or falsely regarding their brother Christians (*Hom. in Ps.* 3.12),[52] and those who betray (to the unbelievers?) the disciples (*Comm. ser.* 83).[53] Among the non-Christians to be singled out for indictment by Origen are the persecutors of the martyrs (*Hom. in Jer.* 14.7),[54] heretics who mislead the faithful with their false doctrines (*Comm. in*

Matt. 12.23),[55] and especially the Jews. In a fragment on Ps 36:22, with a possible allusion to Matt 25:37, he says rather scathingly:

> As he [Christ] says: You fed him [τοῦτον ἔθρεψας], you fed me [ἐμὲ ἔθρεψας]. So as a consequence he might say: You reviled him, you reviled me. In truth, they curse God who do not know him . . . .The Gentiles bless God, wherefore they inherit the kingdom; but the Jews, blaspheming him, are lost forever.[56]

The question could be asked whether "Gentiles" in the above quotation refers solely to Gentile Christians or pagan Gentiles as well. From my reading of Origen, it would be quite unthinkable for him to include pagans among those to be saved.

Firmilian of Caesarea in Cappadocia (d. AD 268)

In the only extant work we have of Firmilian, *Letter 75*, written to Cyprian against Pope Stephen I, and dealing with the rebaptizing of heretics, there is an allusion to v 35b. In par. 23 Firmilian spiritualizes the second Matthean work of mercy, seeing "the drink" as baptism. He says to those who refuse baptism to converts from heretical sects, "you denied the drink of the church to those who are thirsty [. . . sitientibus ecclesiae potum negasti . . . .]"[57] One could conclude that Firmilian had a universal view of the recipients in this passage since he would hardly have considered heretics to be Christians.

Gregory Thaumaturgus (ca. AD 213 - 270)

One fragment from the writings of Gregory contains a reference to the Matthean judgment scene. In *De simulatione* 5.8, a fragment commenting on Jer 9:8-26, he quotes v 40 in full and says that we will hear from Christ those very words: ". . . if we do anything to our neighbor [εἰς τὸν πλησίον] not formed in charity. By the same token, if we do anything evil to a brother [εἰς τὸν ἀδελφόν], falsified by fraudulent hypocrisy or any other sin, we likewise offend God."[58] The sense seems to be universal. The word "brother" seems to refer to a Christian, but the contrasting way "neighbor" is used leads me to think it is not meant to be another way of saying brother, but to signify another category of people. As does Origen, Gregory takes Matt 25:40, which is originally an encomium, and turns it into an indictment.

Archelaus of Cascar (ca. AD 277-78)

In his *Disputation with Manes* 38, Archelaus, a bishop of Mesopotamia, quotes Matt 25:41, 44 to prove that Christ will not be indulgent on the last day even though those on the left hand beseech him for mercy.[59] Apparently in his evangelizing attempts the heretic Manes would use a form of interrogation. Archelaus reminds his readers that at the judgment those to be condemned will use the same interrogative style to justify themselves, and that Manes and his followers will be in their midst. Apparently it did not occur to Archelaus that the saved also use the same interrogative format (vv 37-39).

Methodius of Olympus (d. ca. AD 311)

This stalwart opponent of Tertullian and Origenist allegorism has left us only three possible allusions to the Matthean pericope. In a moving passage in his *De vita* 8.3-4 Methodius says emphatically that the one who will be numbered among those on the Judge's right hand is the one who shares his clothing with the poor and naked [dem Nackten], gives food to the hungry [die Speise Fordernden], drink to the thirsty [dem Durstenden], invites the homeless under his roof, is concerned with the plight of prisoners [Gefangenen] and helps to alleviate the suffering of the sick [dem durch Krankheit Leidenden].[60] Nothing in this passage seems to indicate a restrictiveness in his viewpoint regarding the identity of "the least."

In *De lepra* 12.4 in the context of an exhortation on humility, Methodius alludes to vv 35a,36a and possibly v 40 when he states:

> ... it is fitting to be lowly before men who are in the same condition just as it is fitting to give food and clothing to the hungry [τῷ πεινῶντι] and the naked [τῷ γυμνῷ].... For God takes pleasure in these things and ascribes that haste to himself [ἥδεται γὰρ τούτοις ὁ θεὸς καὶ εἰς ἑαυτὸν ταύτην ἐπαναφέρει τὴν σπουδήν].[61]

There is the same open-endedness here regarding the identity of the needy as in *De vita* 8.3-4.

It is only when we read further that we get the inkling that Methodius might be concerned primarily with charity to Christians. In *De lepra* 16.8-10 he alludes to v 35c, but this time it is unmistakenly in the context of Christians aiding Christians. He states that "we must honor strangers [die Fremden] and the poor, for in them Christ is known,"[62] and he complains that his hearers "are not compassionate, shutting up pity in the face of our *brotherhood* [gegen unsere Bruderschaft]."[63] He sees selfishness as the culprit and accuses both bishops and laity of looking out for their own profits.

Because the available evidence is so sparse, it is difficult to come to a conclusion regarding Methodius' understanding of the recipients of his fellow Christians' charity. If he were to have understood Matthew's "least" to be Christians, he would certainly have been in step with other eastern theologians of his century.

Peter of Alexandria (d. ca. AD 311)

In *Homily 8*, a Maundy Thursday sermon attributed[64] to this Patriarch of Alexandria, another forceful foe of Origen, there is an allusion to Matt 25:35-36:

> ... for he [Christ] said: By this everyone shall know that you are my disciples if you love one another. Let us visit those who are sick [marenjempšini ᵉnni etšoni], and let us go to those who are imprisoned; let us clothe those who are naked [marentihiōou ᵉnnē etchēkahēou], let us give him to drink who is

thirsty [ᵉntenetseoua efobi], let us feed him who is hungry [marentemmeoua efhkait] with our bread, so that Jesus Christ our God may call us to his supper with his saints.⁶⁵

The juxtaposition of the restrictive verse John 13:35 and the allusions to the Matthean "identity dialogue" are an indication, I believe, that in this particular passage Peter has Christian sick, imprisoned, naked, thirsty and hungry in mind.

Western Writers

Tertullian (ca. AD 160 - 225)

Of the ten references in the works of Tertullian to Matt 25:31-46 there is only one quotation. It is of v 41 in *Adversus Hermogenum* 11.3.⁶⁶ Tertullian is very attracted to the descriptions of blessedness and hell fire in the Matthean judgment scene. Eight of the ten references are to vv 34,41 and 46, and Tertullian uses them to his own advantage to prove that heretics will be condemned (*De praescriptione haereticorum* 24.1),⁶⁷ that the reward and punishment described in these verses is eternal (*Ad nationes* 1.19,6),⁶⁸ or to explain why Christ did not redeem the fallen angels (*De carne Christi* 14.2).⁶⁹

In the two instances that Tertullian does allude to the characteristics of the "needy Christ," he seems to be speaking of Christians. In *Scorpiace* 11.3, alluding to v 36c, he says: ". . . when he [Christ] wishes a brother to be visited in prison [cum in carcere fratrem vult visitari], he is commanding that those about to confess [i.e., suffer martyrdom] be the object of solicitude."⁷⁰ And in *De oratione* 26.1, speaking of not dismissing a brother who has entered our homes without prayer, he makes the statement: "You have seen the brother, he [Christ] says; you have seen your Lord [Vidisti, inquit, fratrem; vidisti dominum tuum]." ⁷¹ The statement is a possible allusion to vv 37-40,44-45 and makes the most sense if the visiting brother is a Christian.

Hippolytus (ca. AD 170 - 235)

In the authentic works of this early Roman exegete there are only two quotations from the Matthean pericope, both of them from vv 32-34 and 41. In a fragmentary comment on Gen 49:16-20, *The Blessings of Moses* 2,[72] and in *Demonstratio de Christo et Antichristo* 65,[73] Hippolytus sees the apostles as the "blessed" of v 34 and all those who have refused to believe in Christ as the condemned of v 41. But in *De consummatione mundi* 40-48,[74] a discourse that may be falsely attributed to Hippolytus,[75] the entire Matthean judgment scene is reenacted and the author provides an insight into the identity of the saved, the condemned, and the recipients of the charity from those on the right. The "least" of v 40 are Christians, for those who are called to the kingdom are saved because of their concern for the poor who are called Christ's "limbs" [μέλη], the same terminology used in the Pauline epistles [76] to describe the union between Christ and the baptized:

> Then again the King of Kings will answer, saying to them: Whatever you have done to one of these least ones, my brothers, you have done to me. As often as you have shown hospitality to, clothed, fed or given drink to my members, the poor, whom I publicly proclaimed to you, you have done it to me. [ἐφ' ὅσον οὓς προεῖπον ὑμῖν ἐξενοδοχήσατε, ἐνεδύσατε καὶ ἐθρέψατε καὶ ἐποτίσατε τὰ μέλη μου, τοὺς πτωχούς, ἐμοὶ ἐποιήσατε.] [77]

The saved are a vast potpourri from the Old and New Testaments, including the prophets, the patriarchs, the apostles who suffered with Christ, the martyrs, hierarchs who said Mass daily and maidens who remained chaste. The condemned include nonbelievers, especially the Jews who will "have to look upon him whom they pierced,"[78] but also the baptized who, even though they were chaste and mortified their flesh and gave up their property, "did not observe mercy or cast hatred of their brother from their souls."[79]

Pontianus of Rome (d. AD 235)

In *Letter 2*, a letter "On Brotherly Love" to all bishops, Pontianus, pope from ca. 230-235, quotes Matt 25:40 (without τῶν ἀδελφῶν μου) to explain that a Christian who relieves an afflicted brother, delivers a captive, or consoles a mourner will be rewarded by Christ to whom the action was really done:

> Beloved, strive to raise the oppressed and always help those having need; for whoever relieves his afflicted brother, lifts the spirits of the apprehensive and consoles the dying will be rewarded by him, to whom the whole matter was done, who said: Whatever you did to one of these least ones, you did to me.[80]

It could be argued, I suppose, that Pontianus had all human beings in mind as the object of Christian concern; but when one takes into consideration the fact that he uses the term "brother," that the letter elsewhere concerns itself with internal affairs of the church, and that in this letter Christians who "unceasingly help the brethren" are termed children of God in contradistinction to the children of the devil, then it seems plausible that Pontianus' horizon is narrow. He is concerned with Christians helping Christians.

Cyprian of Carthage (ca. AD 210 - 258)

Jerome tells us that Cyprian was very fond of reading Tertullian.[81] Yet in his use of the Matthean judgment scene Cyprian seems far less concerned than Tertullian with doctrinal matters and much more interested in the practical matters of tending the needy. That would account for his concern with those verses that deal with almsgiving. Out of a total of eleven references to the Matthean pericope, nine have to do with the words of the needy Christ. In one of his earliest works, *Testimonia ad Quirinum*, he twice quotes in full the entire pericope (*Test. ad Quir.* 2.30; 3.1),[82] and then a little later on (3.109)[83] he quotes v 36 in his concern that the sick be visited. In this work Cyprian gives no indication as to whether the recipients of Christian solicitude are to be fellow Christians only or everyone. In fact, from the catena of Old and New Testament texts used to bolster the message of the Matthean Christ, it could be argued that Cyprian's horizon of social concerns was universal.

Such is not the case, however, when one moves to his later works. In *De dominica oratione* 33, in a strong allusion to v 40, he says:

> ... those who give alms among the members of God's household according to his commands, because they fear what God commands to be done, do themselves also deserve to be heard by God.... When one has pity on the poor, he lends to God; and he who gives to the least gives to God [qui dat minimis Deo donat]....[84]

In *De opere et eleemosynis* 16, 23-24 he gives us the clearest indication of his understanding of Matt 25:40. In paragraph 16 he says: "... by almsgiving to the poor we are lending to God ... and when it is given to the least, it is given to Christ [cum datur minimis Christo datur]...."[85]

In paragraphs 23-24 he quotes the Matthean pericope in its entirety to make his point. That Cyprian is here urging Christians to take care of other Christians is obvious because, immediately after quoting Matt 25:31-46, he launches into a lengthy description of the love exhibited by the early church and quotes Gal 6:10 to urge his listeners to do good, especially to those of the "household of the faith" [maxime autem ad domesticos fidei].[86]

This same concern for fellow believers is further manifested by Cyprian in *Letter 60.* 3, a letter he sent in AD 253 to the Numidian bishops. He quotes v 36bc as the rationale for his sending 100,000 sesterces for the redemption of Christians who were captured and sold into slavery.[87]

Commodianus (fl. ca. AD 248-258)

This poet and "beggar of Christ," as he calls himself, gives us only one possible allusion to Matt 25:35-36 in his extant works. In the *Instructiones* 2.18 he says: "In your riches make yourself a sharer to the weak. Give of your labor, clothe the naked [nudum vesti]. Thus do you conquer."[88] Commodianus gives no indication here of any exclusivity of outlook. Though the evidence is scanty, and we are not even certain that he has Matt 25:35-36 in mind, there is the sense in this work that his charitable concerns extend beyond the Christian community.

Anonymous Writings of the Third Century

There are five anonymous writings of the third century that make reference to the "identity dialogue": [1] *Didascalia Apostolorum*, [2] *Ecclesiastical Canons of the Holy Apostles*, [3] the first Pseudo-Clementine epistle *De virginitate*, [4] an ancient unnamed hymn from the Fayûm, and [5] *De decem virginibus*.

According to *Didascalia Apostolorum* 11 and 15, in an obvious allusion to v 33, the pagans are those who stand on the left hand of the judge.[89] *Didascalia Apostolorum* 19 quotes Matt 25:34-40 (with variant readings in vv 34 and 40) to urge that bishops do everything they can for their Christian brethren condemned to martyrdom by the unbelievers for the sake of Christ:

> And you shall not be ashamed to go to them when they are in prison. And when you do these things, you shall inherit everlasting life for you become sharers in their martyrdom. Indeed, let us learn how our Lord said in the Gospel: 'Come unto me [dtw lwty], all you blessed of my Father, inherit the kingdom which was prepared for you from before [qdm] the foundations of the world .... All that you did to one of these little and inferior ones [z'wr' wbṣyr'], you did to me.'[90]

The same narrow interpretation of "the least" could also be argued in the apocryphal *Ecclesiastical Canons of the Holy Apostles* 22 where Andrew says:

> Let the deacons perform good works, looking around everywhere night and day, not despising the poor [πένητα] or being partial to the rich. Let them be understanding of the one who suffers and not omit [him] from the collection. They shall persuade those able to do so to lay up treasures by their good works, having before [them] the words of our teacher: You saw me hungry and you did not feed me [εἴδετέ με πεινῶντα καὶ οὐκ ἐθρέψατέ με].[91]

Although there is nothing in the above to prove definitively that only Christian poor are to be the concern of the deacons, from other early sources[92] we know that the collection taken up at the Christian liturgy was used primarily for the poor among the believers.

In three remaining works, *De virginitate, De decem virginibus,* and an ancient hymn from the Fayûm, there are references to Matthew's "identity dialogue," but the interpretation is not so narrow.

In the first of two epistles traditionally ascribed to Clement of Rome,[93] *De virginitate* 1.12.4-6, Matt 25:36b is quoted (although in a slightly variant form) to show that we should visit the sick: "Let us approach the brother or sister who is sick [aegrotantes] . . . for it is a beautiful and profitable matter to the servants of God who act according to the commands of the Lord who said: 'I was ill [aegrotus] and you took care of me' and things similar to this."[94] The apparent narrow interpretation could be deceiving, since in the same epistle a few verses later (1.12.8) there is the command to love the "brethren and strangers" as we have been taught by the Lord [. . . fratres atque peregrinos diligamus propter Deum et propter eos qui credunt in Deum].[95] Is the author contrasting Christian members of the local community (brethren) with Christians passing through (strangers), or Christians in general (brethren) with non-Christians (strangers)? Unfortunately, the text sheds no light on his precise meaning.

In *De decem virginibus*, once ascribed to Victorinus of Pettau but now judged to be anonymous, there are definite allusions to vv 35-36, 45. The treatise, a commentary on the parable of the ten virgins (Matt 25:1-13), makes the point, so often made in patristic literature, that the wise virgins are those who, among other virtues, give freely to the widow and orphan, visit the sick [infirmos visitat] and imprisoned [carceres penetrat], give bread and drink to the hungry and thirsty [esurientes pane satiat, sitientes potu recreat] and welcome the stranger,[96] because "negligence of God is negligence of one's brothers" [neglegentia in Deum, neglegentia in fratres suos].[97] The point is forcefully made in this little work that the virgins who extend this charity are neither Jews nor heretics; yet nowhere is there any indication regarding the exact identity of the recipients.

The same seemingly universal appeal to charity is present in an anonymous ancient hymn from the Fayûm. In what appears to be an allusion to Matt 25:35,46 we read: "Now work out your inheritance. Now is the time, now, to give richly to those who hunger [τοῖς πεινῶσι]. God said to feed strangers [ξένους . . . διατρέφειν]. Receive as guests [ξένιζε] the strangers [ξένους] and the helpless so that you may escape the fire."[98]

Fathers of the Great Patristic Century

(AD 325 - 431)

Eastern Writers

Eusebius of Caesarea (ca. AD 260 - 340)

Eusebius was concerned with proving that the coming and the growth of the Christian faith were prophesied in the OT. This apologetic interest permeates many of his works and is even present in his use of the Matthean pericope. In his extant works I was able to find sixteen references to Matt 25:31-46. Most of these quote or allude to vv 31-34 to prove that Christians are the ones that will be on the right hand of the judge and invited to enter the kingdom. Only six references pertain to those verses dealing with the needy Christ.

In *Comm. in Ps.* 49.13, commenting on the verse "Do I eat the flesh of strong bulls or is the blood of goats my drink?" Eusebius, reflecting Origen's influence upon him, tends to spiritualize the acts of mercy, hinting that acts of thanksgiving or theological works can be substituted:

> God's food is that of which he spoke: I was hungry and you fed me; I thirsted and you gave me to drink. Nourished by this, I [sic] shall say: Whatever you did to one of these least ones, you did to me. He can be sacrificed to by means of words, through acts of thanksgiving [διὰ εὐχαριστίας] and speaking about him [διὰ θεολογίας]. If anyone has promised anything to God, let him fulfill it by means of deeds.[99]

In *Comm. in Ps* 68:22-25, quoting Matt 25:35ab, he explains that Christ is fed by the orthodox faith, pious life and upright living of the true believer. The one who adds gall to his food [εἰς τὸ βρῶμα αὐτοῦ χολὴν ἐμβάλλει] and offers him sour wine [οἶνον ἐκτροπίαν] is the one who blasphemes and dabbles with atheistic and false doctrines.[100]

In his *Demonstratio Evangelica* 1.6 Eusebius quotes v 35c in the context of his apologetics. Commenting on Job 31:32 (". . . I opened my door to wayfarers"), Eusebius sees the statement of this hospitable patriarch ("who existed even before Abraham") as a prefigurement of the teaching of the Christian faith that would open its arms to the Gentiles.[101]

There is only one instance where Eusebius gives a hint that he might have a restrictive view regarding the identity of "the least." In a lengthy discourse in his *Comm. in Ps.* 40.2-4 he quotes Matt 25:34-36,40 (without τῶν ἀδελφῶν μου) and then quotes Matt 5:3 (μακάριοι οἱ πτωχοὶ τῷ πνεύματι) to elucidate, saying: "By these words the Savior proclaimed blessed those who are philosophers according to God and because of the divine command take care of the poor who were his disciples and apostles."[102]

Aphraates (ca. AD 280 - 345)

The first of the Syriac Church Fathers, sometimes called "the wise man of Persia" has left us a work containing 23 documents called *Demonstrations*. In *Dem.* 6.1 he alludes to vv 33 and 36b: "Let us visit [nes'ûr] the Lord in the sick [bakrîhê'] so that he may invite us to stand at his right . . . ."[103] In *Dem.* 20. 5 he quotes vv 35ab,36a,35c,36bc,40-41,45 and paraphrases vv 37-39, 42-44 to encourage Christians to help the Lord in the persons of the poor, sick and needy. In his quotation of v 40 he uses the word "small" [daqdĕqe'], the Syriac equivalent of the Greek μικροί, and in his quotation of v 45 he uses the term "needy" [sĕnîqe'] instead of "least" [zĕ'ûre²].[104]

At first glance it seems Aphraates is silent about the exact identity of the "small" and "needy," but when one closely reads *Demonstrations* 20, one realizes that he marshalls a catena of OT and NT texts on the poor to prove his point that the "small" and "needy" are the Christians and the rich are the Jews. He sees the poor and unfortunate of Amos 5:11 and Isa 41:17-19 as the Christians who have been called forth from the Jewish people.[105] In *Dem.* 20.16 he quotes Matt 25:40 (without τῶν ἀδελφῶν μου and ἐλαχίστων) in the context of interpreting Luke 16:9 (. . . ἑαυτοῖς ποιήσατε φίλους ἐκ τοῦ μαμωνᾶ τῆς ἀδικίας, ἵνα ὅταν ἐκλίπῃ δέξωνται ὑμᾶς εἰς τὰς αἰωνίους σκηνάς). And a few lines later, quoting John 15:15, he makes the point that the ones called "friends" by Christ are the apostles.[106] Thus it seems clear that in the understanding of Aphraates "the least" of Matt 25:40, 45 are the apostles and possibly all Christians. He quotes lavishly from the "identity dialogue" and other scriptural texts pertaining to the rich and poor in the context of an anti-Jewish apologetic; therefore, one is never quite sure whether he is primarily concerned with the moral and pastoral issue of caring for the needy or the doctrinal issue of proving that the Jews are no longer God's chosen.

Pachomius (ca. AD 290 - 346)

In the biographies of Pachomius, sometimes referred to as the father of the coenobitic life, one gets the impression that this monk's view of "the least" was narrow. To exemplify the spiritual foundation for the hospitality that Pachomius always showed to visiting monks from other monasteries, the anonymous author of his life (*Bohairic Life* 40;[107] *First Greek Life* 40;[108]) quotes v 40 with the addition of the very restrictive element τῶν πιστευόντων εἰς ἐμέ [109] from Matt 18:6. And in another episode (*First Greek Life* 125), relating how the brothers would sit around after the evening meal searching the Scriptures "for their salvation," his biographer gives us a rather spiritual interpretation of v 40. It is again quoted with the restrictive interpolation from Matt 18:6. In this case, the recipients of the charity are the uneducated monks: "Those who were able and appointed to have care did it [i.e., expound the Scriptures] as servants of God, for 'Insofar as you did this,' says the Lord, 'to one of those who believe in me, you did it to me.'"[110]

In Pachomius' own works, probably because he is writing for his brother monks, we see for the most part the same restrictive interpretation of the "identity dialogue." In *Instructions* 37 he paraphrases vv 45-46 to show the danger the monk is in when he fails to love his brother monk: "He will say to you: Inasmuch as you hate your brother, I am he whom you hate [jeephoson kmoste ᵉmpekson anok petekmoste ᵉmmoï], and you will go off to eternal torment [ᵉntok de eknabōk eukolasis ᵉnšaeneh] because you are inimical to your brother."[111]

In two different passages in *Letter* 3 Pachomius alludes to v 43c in order to upbraid those monks who failed to visit the sick of the community. In par. 3 he states: "Because of that, the same was done to him because he forgot the law of his God and did not visit the sick [καὶ οὐκ ἐπεσκέψατο τοὺς ἀσθενεῖς]."[112] And in par. 9 he says: "O man, how long will you not hear the voice of him who tells you: Pause and know that I am God. But they did not pause; instead each one followed his own soul.

They did not visit the sick [οὐκ ἐπεσκέψαντο τοὺς ἀσθενεῖς]."[113]

The one instance in Pachomius' own works where a verse from the "identity dialogue" might be used in a universal sense is found in *Paralipomena* 41. There Pachomius quotes v 40 (without τῶν ἀδελφῶν μου) to emphasize the unbreakable relationship between the first commandment to love God and the second command to love one's neighbor: "For in every evil that a man does, especially when he rejects the second commandment, he will also reject the first one, as it is said: Inasmuch as you have done it to one of the least of these, you did it to me."[114] A strong indication that "the least" in the above quote could be any human being is the fact that, immediately following this passage, Pachomius utters what is probably the most all-encompassing prayer in his works. He prays that all Jews, pagans, Christians, and even the barbarians be saved for the Lord.[115]

Eusebius of Emesa (d. ca. AD 359)

This lesser-known Eusebius was a disciple of his namesake Eusebius of Caesarea to whom some of his works were attributed. In *De Fide adversus Sabellium* 2 he quotes Matt 25:40 (without τῶν ἀδελφῶν μου but with the very restrictive clause τῶν πιστευόντων εἰς ἐμέ from Matt 18:6) and interprets it in a very narrow sense to mean Christians. In a moving diatribe against heretics, he states that the true Christian is the real brother, and that whatever is done for or against a true Christian is done for or against Christ: "For, he said, whatever you did to one of these least ones who believe in me [uni ex minimis istis qui credunt in me] you did to me, whether good or evil.... For let the brother be the true Christian; the true Christian, for Christ is true."[116]

In another possibly authentic work, *De Avaritia* 16, Eusebius quotes vv 42,43b, and 44a to explain that Christ puts aside his glory and clothes himself with the nakedness of the poor:

> How shall we dare go to Jesus who said and will say: I was hungry and you did not feed me; I thirsted and you did not give me to drink; I was naked and you did not cover me. We will say to him what was written that we would say: When did we see you hungry? You do not see Jesus, you see someone in need of clothing [nudum vides a vestimento]. Does not that visible naked one [nudus] show forth Jesus?[117]

I could find nothing in the work to support the narrow view that the needy are Christians only.

In *Homily* 45. 5,7, a work found in the Pseudo-Eusebian collection of Gallican Sermons that were long attributed[118] to this author, we find Matt 25:40, 42ab used in what seems to be a universal sense:

> . . . we heard the Lord in the gospel speaking with unspeakable dignity and love: Whoever has done [something] to one of these least ones, has done [it] to me [Qui fecit uni ex minimis istis, mihi fecit]. These words commend to us, by heavenly authority, the works of almsgiving.[119]
> . . . for he will carry none of those possessions he believed he owned - just as the prophet said: For when he dies he shall take none of it; his wealth shall not follow him down [Ps 49:18]. Among the indefensible pleas will be heard: I was hungry and you did not feed me; I thirsted and you did not give me to drink.[120]

There is no evidence in the homily that the author thought of the recipients of this charity as Christians only.

Basil of Ancyra (d. ca. AD 366)

This famous *homoiousian* published little, but in his *De Virginitate* he twice quotes from the dialogue of the needy Christ to encourage his listeners to love their neighbors as themselves.

In *De Virginitate* 11, Basil quotes vv 36a,35a and 36b to encourage Christians to be of assistance to Christ by helping the neighbor: "But if you love your neighbor [τὸν πλησίον σου] as yourself, because of this commandment we are eager to be of assistance to the one who said: I was naked [γυμνὸς] and you covered me, hungry [πεινῶντα] and you fed me, ill [ἀσθενοῦντα] and you took care of me."[121]

In chap. 37 he again takes up the theme of loving the neighbor and buttresses his argument by quoting v 40 (without τῶν ἀδελφῶν μου and ἐλαχίστων, but with the addition of τῷ σῷ νυμφίῳ, probably attracted here from the Parable of the Ten Virgins [Matt 25:1,5,6,10]):

> But there must be love of one's neighbor, because 'You shall love your neighbor as yourself;' and the groom handed over this precept to the bride. He said: You shall certainly love and whatever you do to one of these, you do to me your bridegroom [καὶ ἐφ' ὅσον ἑνὶ τούτων ποιεῖς, ἐμοὶ τῷ σῷ νυμφίῳ ποιεῖς].[122]

Basil gives us no indication, one way or the other, whether he conceives of "the neighbor" to be Christians or all men and women in general.

Athanasius of Alexandria (ca. AD 296 - 373)

Among the authentic works of this implacable foe of Arianism there are eight references to Matt 25:31-46. Five are quotations of v 34 to remind orthodox Christians of the joy they will inherit on judgment day. The remaining three references are to the dialogue of the needy Christ. In his *Expositio in Psalmos* 40.2 Athanasius quotes Matt 25:40 together with Prov 19:17 to remind Christians of their duties to the needy: "The Lord, who is light, will free those who love the poor . . . for through Solomon he said: He who has compassion on the poor lends to the Lord; and especially through his own mouth: Whatever you did to one of these least ones, you did to me."[123] The sense here seems to be universal; I could find no element in the discourse that would limit Christian charity to fellow Christians.

There is a slightly more restrictive sense, however, in his *History of the Arians*. In 2.13,3, paraphrasing v 45 to show that the Arian bishop Gregory will suffer because he withheld church monies from widows and social outcasts, Athanasius has Christ say: "Insofar as you have dishonored [ἠτίμασας] them, you have dishonored me."[124] In the same vein, in his attempt to show that the Arians were not true followers of Christ, in 7.61,1 he quotes vv 35ab and 40 (without τῶν ἀδελφῶν μου and with μικρῶν instead of ἐλαχίστων), in conjunction with Luke 12:33, to upbraid the Arian clergy after they had received the churches of Alexandria from the civil authorities for not using church funds for the care of the widows that had long been supported by the orthodox clergy: "For the Lord commanded that the poor be remembered, saying: Sell your possessions and give alms; and: I was hungry and you fed me, I thirsted and you gave me to drink. For whatever you have done to one of these little ones [τῶν μικρῶν τούτων], you have done to me."[125] Since widows held a special office in the early church, I think a true interpretation of the above two passages would see Athanasius concerned not with widows in general, but with Christian widows. This restrictive concern of his could be accountable for the attraction of τῶν μικρῶν τούτων into v 40 from Matt 10:42, a verse concerned with charity to the disciple.

Among the works that have been attributed to Athanasius on insufficient grounds,[126] there are two that have quotations from Matt 25:31-46. In *Passionem et Crucem Domini* 34, there is the use of v 40 (without τῶν ἀδελφῶν μου and with μικρῶν instead of ἐλαχιστῶν) to make the point that those who neglect the needy (the sense seems to be universal) are similar to the Jews who rejected Christ:

> He who does nothing for the poor man [τὸν πένητα] slanders the Lord as the Jews did . . . he who neglects the hungry, thirsty and naked poor man [πένητα πεινῶντα καὶ διψῶντα καὶ γυμνόν] is similar to the Jews who rejected the Lord and gave him wine with vinegar . . . as the Lord himself says in the gospels: Whatever you have done to one of these little ones [τῶν μικρῶν τούτων], you have done to me.[127]

Ps-Athanasius uses v 40 here as an indictment, rather than an encomium, and therefore has it addressed to those on the left rather than on the right. The attraction of τῶν μικρῶν τούτων from Matt 10:42 could be an indication that his concept of the needy is restricted.

In the *Quaestiones ad Antiochum Ducem*, v 35 is quoted twice to support almsgiving. In *Question* 89 in response to the query whether the merciful are more blessed than the miracleworkers, Athanasius states that when Christ invites those on his right into his Father's kingdom, it will not be because they worked signs and wonders or did any other good thing, but because "I was hungry and you fed me, and so forth."[128] There is no indication as to the identity of the beneficiaries.

In *Question* 86, however, he quotes v 35ab and interprets it in the narrow sense. When asked whether it is better to worship God in churches or to distribute alms to the needy, Ps-Athanasius makes the point that the poor, especially those subjected to torments *for the faith of Christ*, are the true temples of God.[129]

Ephraem of Nisibis (ca. AD 306 - 373)

This great Syrian poet left us his *Commentary on the Gospel* in accordance with Tatian's *Diatessaron*,[130] but surprisingly he does not include a discussion of Matt 25:31-46,[131] even though he quotes vv 34 and 41 four times in his discussion of other pericopes (*Commentary* 6.26; 7.25; 8.13; 18.16).[132] But in three sermons to his brother monks, attributed to him without dispute, Ephraem quotes from the dialogue of the needy Christ to encourage the monks to support their weaker brethren, to offer true and sincere love to one another and not to neglect the visitation of the sick in the monastery. In *Ad Imitationem Proverbiorum*, he alludes to v 43c and quotes v 40 (adapting it to the second person singular):

> If your brother labors under some weakness, support and help him that you would merit to hear from the Lord on that day: What you did [ἐποίησας] to one of these least, my brothers, you did [ἐποίησας] to me. The one who neglects the sick [ἀσθενοῦς] provokes the law giver and the one who rejoices in the fall of his brother, will go to serious ruin.[133]

Ephraem's view of "the least" here is the narrower one that one would expect of someone speaking to his brother religious. But in the other two sermons there is not the same certainty that Ephraim is speaking only of Christian needy when he exhorts his brothers to charity. In *Epistola ad Joannem* he quotes both v 40 and v 45 (inserting τῶν ἀδελφῶν μου from v 40 into v 45 as well) to make his point:

> In all things and to all (εἰς πάντας) offer true and sincere love to one another . . . for he is not a liar who said: Whatever you did to one of the least of my brothers, you did to me. To those, however, who closed the bowels of mercy he said: Whatever you did not do to one of the least of my brothers, you did not do to me [ὃ ἑνὶ τῶν ἀδελφῶν μου τῶν ἐλαχίστων οὐκ ἐποιήσατε, οὐδὲ ἐμοὶ ἐποιήσατε].[134]

In the third sermon, *In Secundum Domini Adventum*, alluding to vv 35c, 36ac, he says that those who will stand on the Lord's right are

> . . . the ones who . . . were merciful, loving orphans and widows, receiving the guest [οἱ ξενοδοχοῦντες], clothing the naked [οἱ τοὺς γυμνοὺς περιβάλλοντες], visiting those detained in prison [οἱ τοὺς ἐν φυλακῇ ἐπισκεπτόμενοι], receiving laborers, visiting the sick and those now grieving . . . forgiving the sins of their brothers and keeping the deposit of faith pure and unbroken by any heresy. These stand at the right [ἐκ δεξιῶν] . . . .[135]

And then paraphrasing vv 42-44 with a staccato-like succession of present participles, he says that those on the left did not listen to Christ's voice:

> You did not serve me nor feed me when I was hungry, nor give drink to me when I was thirsty, nor accept me when I was a stranger, nor clothe me when I was naked nor visit me when I was sick, nor come to me when I was in prison . . . ἐμοὶ γὰρ οὐ διηκονήσατε οὐδὲ πεινῶντα ἐθρέψατε οὐδὲ διψῶντα ἐποτίσατε οὐδὲ ξενοδοκήσατε οὐδὲ ἐνδύσατε γυμνητεύοντα

οὐδὲ ἀσθενοῦντά με ἐπεσκέψασθε οὐδὲ ἐν φυλακῇ ὄντος μου ἤλθετε πρός με ....[136]

Ephraim does not specifically say here that those to be helped are only Christians. What can be said with certainty from this passage is that in his mind heretics would not be among the saved.

In four other works, attributed to Ephraem with some doubt, there is the same ambivalence regarding the identity of "the least." In *De Poentitentia*, he quotes v 40 (without τῶν ἀδελφῶν μου), to prove that "... he also feeds [τρέφει] God by various almsgivings ...."[137] There is the possibility that the recipients of the monks' charity are meant to be only other Christians, for in the same context Ps-Ephraem speaks of "all of us being in the one bread of Christ" [οἱ γὰρ πάντες ἐν τῷ ἑνὶ ἄρτῳ τοῦ Χριστοῦ] and says "we are one body" [ἓν σῶμα ἐσμέν].[138] One could infer that beneficiaries as well as benefactors are included in the term "all of us."

In *Institutio ad Monachos* v 40 is paraphrased in a very short form (ἑνὶ τούτων ἐποιήσατε, ἐμοὶ ἐποιήσατε) in conjunction with Matt 10:42 and John 13:14, two verses that clearly refer to charity done to a disciple. This could be an indication that v 40 is to be interpreted in the same narrow light, except that Ps-Ephraem makes a point of taking the restrictive edge off the phrase μόνον εἰς ὄνομα μαθητοῦ in Matt 10:42 by explaining that it means offering charity "out of the love of Christ."[139]

In *De Amore Pauperum* 26 there seems to be the same nonrestrictive use of v 40 (without τῶν ἀδελφῶν μου) used in conjunction with the nonrestrictive Prov 19:17: "The one who is merciful to the poor is merciful--with interest--to God himself who said: Whatever you have done to one of these least you have done to me. The one who receives a stranger [τὸν ξένον] under his roof receives Christ himself."[140] Then alluding to v 35c and finally quoting v 36c, Ephraem states:

> The boast of Christians is to wash the feet of the brethren ... the boast of Christians is compassion and the reception of strangers [ξενοδοχεία] .... The boast of Christians is to re-

ceive always at their table the poor, orphans and strangers [ξένους].... The boast of Christians is to visit those in prison [τοὺς ἐν φυλακῇ ἐπισκέπτεσθαι] ... as is fitting a true disciple of the one who said: I was in prison and you came to me.[141]

In the above quotation, if the phrase "to wash the feet of the brethren" were taken as his main thought and everything that followed it were seen as its exemplification, much like a catena of phrases following a colon in modern English, then it might possibly be argued that in Ephraem's mind the various categories of the needy were all disciples. I do not find the evidence strong enough, however, to build a valid case for the restrictive viewpoint here.

The universal horizon also seems to permeate *In Christo Obdormientes* where Ephraem quotes v 40 in full and alludes to vv 35-36 throughout a lengthy passage describing the day of judgment when the "brothers of Christ," among them the poor [πένητες], strangers [ξένοι], those imprisoned [οἱ ἐν φυλακαῖς] and the sick [οἱ ἐν ἀσθενείαις], will show Christ "what you did for them, how you fed [δέδωκας] them, gave them drink [ἐδίψας], gave them rest and served them .... Christ will turn to you who stand on his right and say: Whatever you did to one of these least, my brothers, you did to me."[142] The "least" would certainly be Christians, but they might very well be non-Christians as well.

Basil the Great (ca. AD 330 - 379)

Of the ten references in the authentic works of Basil to the "dialogue of the needy Christ," seven can be interpreted as having to do with needy Christians. As to be expected, the majority of the references to Matt 25:31-46 are found in Basil's ascetical works: the *Moralia*,[143] the *Longer Rule*,[144] and the *Shorter Rule*.[145] Because Basil is primarily concerned with monastic life in these three works, he quotes from the "dialogue of the needy Christ" to encourage his religious to have greater concern for their brother monks.

In *Reg. Fus. Tract.* 34.2 the objects of the monks' charity are those "consecrated to Christ." He quotes v 40 to remind those who hold the office of distributing necessary articles to the community: "... you minister not to men but to the Lord himself who ... regards as offered to himself the honor and esteem shown to those who are consecrated to him...."[146] As if to emphasize this narrow interpretation, Basil will often quote from the "identity dialogue" in conjunction with other scriptural quotations that specifically refer to *intra-Christian* charity and community living or explicitly identify the disciples by the term "brother": Matt 12:50 in *Reg. Fus. Tract.* 34.2;[147] 2 Thess 3:11-12 in *Reg. Fus. Tract.* 4.1;[148] John 13:35 in *Reg. Fus. Tract.* 3.1;[149] 1 Cor 16:1-2 in *Mor.* 48.6;[150] and Heb 13:1 in *Mor.* 69.2.[151]

This same narrow concept of "the least" is also found in other works that are doubtfully attributed to Basil. In *Letter 8.* 8, written to Caesareans who were experiencing some form of persecution,[152] v 36a is quoted in conjunction with Acts 9:4:

> ... he [Christ] once spoke of himself as persecuted: 'Saul, Saul, why do you persecute me,' he says on the occasion when Saul was hurrying to Damascus with a desire to imprison the disciples. Again, he calls himself naked when any one of his brethren is naked: I was naked and you covered me.... So all those things which happen to hurt us he makes his own, taking upon himself our sufferings in his fellowship with us. [153]

In *Constitutiones Asceticae*[154] v 40 is quoted twice, in 1.1 and 23. In chap. 1.1 it is quoted in full to remind those who live in monastic community that whether they receive guests (ξένους) or wait on the sick (ἀσθενοῦντες) they serve Christ himself.[155] In chap. 23, v 40 is quoted to impress upon the monks the exalted state of their calling:

> ... the zeal and benevolence shown them [the monks] is transferred to the Lord who said: Whatever you did to these least, my brothers, you did to me. If he claims as his own what is done to the least, how much more will he claim what is

done to the chosen [εἰ δὲ τὰ τῶν ἐλαχίστων οἰκειοῦται, πολλῷ μᾶλλον τὰ τῶν ἐκλεκτῶν οἰκειώσεται].[156]

It might be argued that Basil is making a distinction between non-Christians and Christians; however, in the context it makes more sense if the distinction is seen between the ordinary Christian ("the least") and the monk ("the chosen").

In the sermon *De Renuntiatione Saeculi* 9 this same restrictive use of the "identity dialogue" is evident. In the context of encouraging the brothers to minister to one another, Ps-Basil quotes vv 35-36 to exhort the monks to serve one another as if it were Christ himself they were serving.[157]

It is possible that Basil's narrow interpretation of "the least" is influenced by the narrow audience for whom these monastic works were intended; therefore, to get a more accurate reading of his true position, it would be necessary to consult works that were meant for an audience beyond the walls of the monastery. Unfortunately, such evidence does not abound. Quotations from the "identity dialogue" are found in two authentic works that seem to have a wider intent, *Homiliae in Psalmos* 14.6[158] and *Homilia in illud: Destruam* 8;[159] but there is nothing in these two works to indicate that only the Christian needy are to be helped.

In *De Misericordia et Judicio*, a work that seems to be intended for the general public yet may very well be apocryphal,[160] vv 34-40 are quoted extensively in a narrow sense to prove that "kindness shown to the saints [ἁγίους] is piety toward Christ" and "the neediness of the *disciples* [τῶν μαθητῶν ἔνδεια] ... is a source of true riches [to the wealthy man] who "nourishes the soldiers of Christ [στρατιώτας τρέφεις Χριστοῦ] and becomes thereby a co-worker with Christ."[161]

Horsiesi (d. ca. AD 380)

As the successor of Pachomius, Horsiesi, sometimes referred to as Orsisius, wrote a treatise of 56 chapters entitled *Doctrina de Institutione Monachorum* or more simply *The Testament*, in which he twice refers to the dialogue of the needy Christ. In par. 47, a section extolling the well known hospitality and charity of his mentor Pachomius, Horsiesi alludes to vv 35a, 36a: " . . . Pachomius gave a hospice to wayfarers [peregrinis hospitium tribuens] . . . he provided bread in hunger [panem in fame] . . . and clothing in nakedness [vestimentum in nuditate] . . . ."[162] There is nothing in the above text to suggest that Pachomius was charitable only to Christians.

In par. 15, however, Horsiesi quotes v 45 with a more restrictive meaning. He finds it necessary to deal with intramonastic problems and reminds the housemasters of the individual religious communities to be more solicitous of their religious brethren, warning them that what they fail to do for their brother monks they fail to do for Christ.[163]

Cyril of Jerusalem (ca. AD 313 - 386)

In his work *Catecheses* Cyril has 7 references to Matt 25:31-46. Only two of them refer to the "identity dialogue." In *Cat.* 8.6 he argues against the heretics who say that money is evil and quotes vv 35a and 36a to show the tremendous good a person can do with his money.[164] In *Cat.* 15.26, Cyril quotes vv 35-36 in their entirety to show the necessity of good works. As do so many of the other eastern fathers, he uses the Parable of the Ten Virgins (Matt 25:1-13) in conjunction with Matt 25:31-46 to clarify his point: we must not be confident merely because we have the lamp (of faith), but must see to it that we keep it burning with the oil (of good works).[165]

Cyril gives us no clue as to the identity of the poor and needy to be helped. It could be an indication that he has a universal horizon in this regard. He is very much a universalist when it comes to the interpretation of v 32. In *Cat.* 15.24 he understands τὰ ἔθνη to mean that "every race of mankind will be present" [πᾶν γένος ἀνθρώπων τότε παρέσται] at the final judgment.[166] In *Cat.* 15.25, commenting on v 33, he explains that the righteous are called sheep because the whiteness of their wool symbolizes the newly baptized or newly confessed, while goats, like Esau who lost his birthright, are known for their hair.[167]

Gregory Nazianzus (AD 329 - 389)

There are only two references to the "identity dialogue" in the works of this close friend and collaborator of Basil. In *Oration* 3. 2 Gregory makes a strong allusion to v 43a when he complains to the people because they did not turn out to hear him preach at Easter. He says: " . . . and we were as strangers whom you did not welcome [καὶ οὐδὲ ὡς ξένους ἡμᾶς συνηγάγετε]."[168] The possibility exists that Gregory had a restrictive view of the "identity dialogue" and understood the "strangers" of Matt 25:35c and 43a to be the apostles; and that the awareness of himself as the apostle rejected by his own flock influenced his choice of an allusion. This, however, cannot be substantiated.

In *Oration* 26. 6 there is a possible allusion to v 40. After a long exhortation to communal charity in which he cites 1 Tim 5:10, Gregory adds: " . . . we have said this that you might learn to do good to Christ by doing good to one of the little ones [. . . ἀλλ' ἵν' ὑμεῖς μάθητε Χριστὸν εὖ ποιεῖν διὰ τοῦ καὶ τῶν μικρῶν τινα εὖ ποιεῖν]."[169] The fact that this verse follows closely after the citation of 1 Tim 5:10, in which widows are encouraged to "wash the feet of the saints," could be an indication that Gregory's perspective of Matt 25:40 is narrow. In fact, such an understanding of v 40 could account for the use of the positive τῶν μικρῶν, which is used to refer to Christians in Matt 10:42, rather than the more usual superlative τῶν ἐλαχίστων.

Macarius of Egypt (ca. AD 300 - 390)

Macarius of Egypt, also called the Great, quotes from the Matthean pericope in his *Spiritual Homilies* 30.9.[170] Citing vv 43a,42ab, he interprets them in the very spiritual sense of feeding and clothing Christ in our souls:

> . . . He endured to suffer many things . . . that he might come to our soul and make his abode with it. For this cause the Lord says to those on the left hand in the day of judgment . . .

I was a stranger and you did not take me in; I was hungry and you did not feed me; I thirsted and you gave me no drink. His food and his drink, his clothing and shelter and rest is in our souls. Therefore he is always knocking, desiring to enter into us . . . every soul that has not now received him within and given him rest, or rather found rest in him, has no inheritance in the kingdom of heaven . . . .[171]

In a spurious work,[172] *De Oratione* 8, in the context of fraternal charity or ministry to one's fellow monks, Ps-Macarius paraphrases v 40 (ἐφ' ὅσον ἐποιήσατε ἑνὶ τούτων, ἐμοὶ ἐποιήσατε) in conjunction with the more restrictive Matt 10:42 to remind the monks that they should not observe fraternal charity for human rewards and recognition, but for love of God. Since he is speaking on the topic of intramonastic charity, one would surmise that his interpretation of "the least" would be narrow. But in his exegesis of Matt 10:42, he understands the qualifying phrase μόνον εἰς ὄνομα μαθητοῦ to mean "from reverence and love of Christ," thus giving us a slight hint that he might have a more universal outlook.[173]

Gregory of Nyssa (ca. AD 330 - 395)

This youngest brother of Basil the Great seems to have had a more universal understanding of "the least" in Matt 25:40 than his brother. Gregory quotes from the Matthean dialogue in five of his works: *Comm. on the Song of Songs* 10;[174] *De Beatitudinibus* 5;[175] *De Pauperibus Amandis* 2;[176] *Oratio Funebris de Flacilla*;[177] and *De Instituto Christiano*.[178] In four out of the five cases the meaning seems to be non-restrictive. He gives us no indication that only Christian needy are to be helped. This broader horizon could be reflected by the fact that three times (in *De Pauperibus Amandis* 2;[179] in *Oratio Funebris de Flacilla* [180] and in *De Instituto Christiano*[181]) Gregory quotes v 40 without the restrictive τῶν ἀδελφῶν μου.

The one work in which a case for the restrictive horizon might be argued was written for monks and could possibly be spurious.[182] In *De Instituto Christiano* a paraphrase of v 40 (without ἐλαχίστων and τῶν ἀδελφῶν μου) is used in conjunction with Matt 10:42 where the beneficiary is clearly a disciple:

> God demands nothing that cannot be accomplished. He says: Whoever gives a cup of cold water to one of these little ones because he is a disciple will not go without his reward. What could be easier than this command? The reward of such a light and easy work is a heavenly one. Again he says: Insofar as you did it to one of these, you did it to me.[183]

The fact that v 40 is used with Matt 10:42 could be an indication that Gregory identifies the τούτων of v 40 with the μικρῶν of 10:42.

Didymus the Blind (ca. AD 313 - 398)

There are only two references to the "identity dialogue" in Didymus' *De Trinitate*. In *De Trin.* 3.3, arguing that "the creator and savior of all speaks, assuming the identity of creatures," Didymus juxtaposes Acts 9:4 (in which there is the unmistakable identification of Christ and his persecuted disciples) with Matt 25:35ab.[184] This juxtaposition could very well indicate that his understanding of Matt 25:35 was similar: that he understood the hungry and the thirsty, with whom Christ identified, to be Christians.

In *De Trin.* 3.15 Didymus paraphrases v 40 (ὃς ἐὰν ποιήσῃ ἑνὶ τούτων τῶν ἐλαχίστων, ἐμοὶ ἐποίησεν). He uses it in conjunction with Acts 1:1 (. . . ὧν ἤρξατο ὁ Ἰησοῦς ποιεῖν τε καὶ διδάσκειν . . .) to show that Christ is more interested in deeds than in words, arguing his point from the fact that ποιεῖν appears in the inspired text (Acts 1:1) before διδάσκειν. The text sheds no further light on Didymus' understanding of "the least."[185]

The Patristic Period

Asterius of Amasea (ca. AD 400)

This famous preacher of Asia Minor, in the course of two extant homilies that take up the theme of God's dispossession of the Jews, makes a number of references to Matt 25:31-46. He quotes v 34 to prove that "the Gentiles" (*Homily 15*)[186] or "the church" (*Homily 16* 5.1)[187] will be the ones to inherit the kingdom, in contrast to the Jews who have lost it. In *Hom. 16* 5.1 he quotes vv 34-36 and v 40 (with neither ἐλαχίστων nor τῶν ἀδελφῶν μου) but gives no indication of a restrictive viewpoint.[188] Likewise in *Hom. 16* 5.12, in the context of proving that the Jews are no longer the chosen, he cites vv 34-36 and 40 (without τῶν ἀδελφῶν μου) to show that the Christians are the heirs of the kingdom because of their charity to the poor: "Who is the one who will inherit? The one who has fed the poor and, by means of the poor, the Christ."[189]

A few pages later, however, he quotes v 43b in the context of a prayer that Satan would not denude the church "the spouse of Christ" and look upon her with ridicule in her nakedness as Ham ridiculed the nakedness of his father Noah: "Therefore, even now he [Satan] wishes to strip naked your spouse that, seeing you naked in suffering like Noah, she may mock you. Wherefore you would disinherit her and say: Depart from me, cursed. I was naked and you did not cover me."[190] The evidence is far too sparse to come to any conclusion regarding Asterius' viewpoint on the identity of "the least."

Epiphanius (ca. AD 315 - 403)

This great foe of Origenist theology refers to Matt 25:31-46 only once. In his chief work, *Panarion* 61.4,1, he understands vv 35ab, 36a in a narrow sense, for he quotes them as justification for the presence of the women who ministered to Christ and his disciples:

> Our Savior . . . did not reject those women around him who ministered to him and his apostles. For it is written: Joanna, the wife of Herod's steward Chuza, Susanna and many others

assisted them out of their means [Luke 8:3]. For this was so that the Scripture might be fulfilled which said: I was hungry and you fed me, I thirsted and you gave me to drink, I was naked and you covered me.[191]

The implication is that just as Christ and his disciples had no earthly possessions but had to rely on the generosity of others to sustain them, so the clergy of Epiphanius' day are to rely on the charity of their fellow Christians.

John Chrysostom (ca. AD 347 - 407)

Without a doubt John Chrysostom refers to Matt 25:31-46 more than any other church father. The Matthean Gospel is the most quoted biblical book in his works,[192] and the final judgment scene, together with the Sermon on the Mount, are by far the most quoted pericopes from that gospel. I agree with Rudolf Brändle that Matt 25:31-46 is primarily responsible for the formation of Chrysostom's ideas on social justice and is the major impetus behind his priestly and pastoral activity.[193] In forty-nine extant works (twenty-nine authentic and twenty doubtful or spurious) there are 170 quotes and 220 allusions. And yet Chrysostom is very free with the texts of Scripture, quoting most often from memory. In the nearly four hundred references in his works there are only four full, verbatim quotations and twenty-three partial verbatim quotations.[194] The majority of the references are to vv 34,41 which are technically beyond the scope of this study. Among the references to the actual dialogue of the needy Christ (vv 35-40; 42-45) the verses that are most quoted are v 35 and its negative counterpart v 42.

The best place to begin the study of Chrysostom's interpretation of Matt 25:31-46 is the one work where he specifically comments on the pericope, his *Homilies on Matthew* 79-80.1.[195] Here we see Chrysostom's literal approach, so characteristic of the Antiochene school. He tells us that the meaning of πάντα τὰ ἔθνη in v 32 is all mankind [πᾶσα ἡ τῶν ἀνθρώπων φύσις][196] and makes many distinctions between the saved and the condemned. The condemned are not cursed by the Father but by their own works (hence the omission of τοῦ πατρός μου in v 41); they are called "kids" (ἔριφοι) and not "goats" (τράγοι) because, unlike the sheep, they are unproductive,[197] and their punishment, unlike the "kingdom" in v 34, was not prepared for them (hence the omission of ὑμῖν in v 41) but for Satan. That ambivalence regarding the identity of "the least" that we have seen in most of the Fathers so far and that is present also in the writings of Chrysostom, is present as well in this passage. In his comments on v 40 the impression is given that "the least" are the poor in general, but when he explains the meaning of v 45, he becomes restrictive. Quoting v 45 (with the strange addition of τῶν ἀδελφῶν μου from v 40)[198] he states that the objects of our charity must be the lowly, poor, outcast, the unknown and the contemptible:

> ... not meaning by these the monks only ... but every believer [ἕκαστον πιστόν]. Even though he be a secular person [βιωτικός], if he is hungry [πεινῶν] and famished, naked [γυμνός] and a stranger [ξένος], [Christ's] will is that he should have the benefit of all this care. For baptism and the partaking of the divine mysteries render a man a brother [ἀδελφὸν γὰρ ὁ βάπτισμα ἐργάζεται καὶ ἡ τῶν θείων μυστηρίων κοινωνία].[199]

From the remaining works of Chrysostom, however, there emerges a clearer picture of his concept of the identity of the beneficiaries of Christian charity. In the genuine works of Chrysostom there are sixty references to one verse or another of the actual "dialogue of the needy Christ." In forty-one of these references, Chrysostom gives us no indication whatsoever whether the needy are Christians only or everyone. In eight instances it is certain that he has Christians only in mind: *Adversus Judaeos* 3.1;[200] 67 *Hom. in Gen.* 65.4;[201] *Hom. in Matt.* 79.1;[202] 88.1-89.3;[203] *Hom in Joh.* 59.4;[204] *Hom. in Acta Apost.* 45.3;[205] *Hom. in Rom.* 30.4;[206] and *Hom. in 1 Cor.* 21.7.[207] In three instances there is high probability that Chrysostom has only Christian needy in mind: 67 *Hom. in Gen.* 55.3;[208] *Hom. in 2 Cor.* 30.4;[209] and *Hom. in 1 Tm.* 14.2.[210] In five instances, however, (*Hom. in Phil.* 1.5;[211] *Hom. in 1 Cor.* 10.4;[212] *Hom. in Matt.* 35.5; [213] *Hom. in Joh.* 60.4 [214] and possibly *De Lazaro* 2.5[215]) in what may very well be his true position on the matter, he makes a distinction between Christians and non-Christians and claims that our charity must go out to all. Perhaps the clearest expression of this viewpoint is found in his *Homilies on Philippians* 1.5. Using a participial form frequently, Chrysostom quotes v 35a (πεινῶντά με γὰρ . . . εἴδετε καὶ ἐθρέψατε) and states that a hungry person has a right to be fed because he is hungry and because he is Christian: "Twofold is the claim. If he that is simply hungry ought to be fed, much more is it the case when he that is hungry is also a believer [Διπλοῦν τὸ δικαίωμα. εἰ δὲ τὸν ἁπλῶς πεινῶντα δεῖ τρέφειν, πολλῷ μᾶλλον ὅταν καὶ ἅγιος ὁ πεινῶν ᾖ]."[216]

From this evidence Chrysostom is the first to make a clear distinction between Christian poor and nonChristian poor and to state specifically that even the nonbeliever must be the object of Christian charity. The overall observation of R. Brändle is correct that Chrysostom "in no way understands 'the least' of Matt 25:40,45 exclusively as brothers of the faith."[217] With Chrysostom we have a true universalism with regards to the identity of "the least"; he has every needy human being in mind. However, like Paul (cf. Gal 6:10), Chrysostom has that specifically Christian perspective that sees a believer as a brother in a narrower sense than the nonbeliever. He can be said to "see two concentric circles. The wider circle includes all men as brothers; the other only brothers of the faith. Solidarity with the Christian brother is for John an additional, an entirely distinct motive for charitable concerns."[218]

In the works of Ps-Chrysostom this "interaction" between the two circles, which is certainly found in the authentic works, is not as evident. Out of twenty-one references to those verses which constitute the basis of our study, there is only one instance where there is specific mention of Christian poor. In *De Poenitentia* 2.2-3, v 40 is quoted followed by a list of those Ps-Chrysostom considered to be the least:

Amen, amen I say to you whatever you did to one of these least, the poor, the abject, strangers, the lowly, the despised, the mutilated, those involved in tragedy, those in need, the hungry, thirsty, those wounded, afflicted, infirm and in trouble; whatever you did to one of these, you did to me; you took care of my members, you served me, you gave rest to my soul.[219]

Then v 34 is quoted followed by an invitation to various categories of people to enter heaven, among them "those who were hungry and thirsty because of Christ" [δεῦτε οἱ δι' ἐμὲ πεινάσαντες καὶ διψήσαντες].[220] The subjects of the participles are obviously Christian, but it is not clear whether they are in the same category as those in the above list who are definitely to be identified with "the least" in v 40.

Also included in the litany of those invited to enter the kingdom are "those who fed those who were hungry and thirsty because of my name" [δεῦτε οἱ τὰς ψυχὰς τῶν πεινώντων καὶ διψώντων διὰ τὸ ὄνομά μου ἐμπλήσαντες].[221] The statement is ambiguous. If διὰ τὸ ὄνομά μου is intended to modify ἐμπλήσαντες, as it modifies the corresponding main participles in the statements preceding this one, then we are told nothing specific about the identity of the needy. If it is taken to modify πεινώντων and διψώντων, however, the needy are obviously Christian.

John the Dwarf (d. after AD 407)

As recorded in *Apophthegmata Patrum* 10. 27, Abba John quotes Matt 25:36c to encourage his monks to remain in their cells: "Watching means to sit in the cell and to be always mindful of God. This is what is meant by: I was in prison and you came to me [. . . φυλακή ἐστι τὸ καθίσαι ἐν τῷ κελλίῳ καὶ μνημονεύειν τοῦ θεοῦ πάντοτε. Καὶ τοῦτό ἐστι τὸ, Ἐν φυλακῇ ἤμην καὶ ἤλθετε πρὸς μέ]."[222] John not only spiritualizes the sixth Matthean work, but he also drastically changes the meaning of the verse. In Matthew the imprisoned is Christ in the person of "the least," while in the above text the imprisoned is the monk and the visitor is Christ. John seems to give φυλακή its etymological meaning of "a watching" or "a guarding" rather than "a prison." If that be the case, a better translation of v 36c in the above quotation would be: "I was on watch and you [Christ] came to me."

Palladius (ca. AD 365 - 425)

This historian of early monasticism paraphrases Matt 25:35a in his *Dialogue on the Life of St. John Chrysostom* 12 in the context of contrasting Chrysostom's custom of eating alone with the lavish banquets given by his predecessors in the see of Constantinople:

> Just as the champion horse no longer able to race about the stadium is relegated to the mill where he trudges round and round in an endless circle, so it is with the teacher when too weary to impart lessons of virtue. He then casts out the net of the dining table; would that it were among the hungry and the needy from whom he might win the blessing of the Lord: For I was hungry and you fed me [. . . Ἐπείνων καὶ ἐχορτάσατέ με].[223]

There is no indication here that "the hungry" and "the needy" are exclusively Christian. Palladius seems to have the same universal outlook as his friend and mentor John Chrysostom.

Nilus of Ancyra (d. ca. AD 430)

In *Tractatus ad Eulogium* 26, this faithful disciple of John Chrysostom, who is also erroneously called Nilus of Sinai, quotes v 40 to encourage the monk Eulogius to be hospitable to monks from other monasteries, even inviting them to table. If Abraham entertained guests who turned out to be angels, then the monks should exhibit such hospitality, not to receive mere angels, but God himself who said what was done to the least was done to him.[224]

In two other works that might not be authentic, *Peristeria*[225] and *De Malignis Cogitationibus*,[226] Ps-Nilus' view seems to be a bit more universal. In *Peristeria* 12.12, in an oratorical style reminiscent of John Chrysostom, he quotes v 40 in a very truncated manner (ὃ τούτοις ἐποιήσατε, ἐμοὶ ἐποιήσατε) to encourage his listeners to reflect on that moment at the last judgment when they will be publicly thanked by Christ for their generosity to him in the person of the poor.[227] The same truncated form of v 40 in used in the same treatise in 4.13[228] and 9.5.[229] The sense in all three citations is universal.

In *De Malignis Cogitationibus* 12 Ps-Nilus quotes v 36bc, with the same non-restrictive outlook, to remind his brother monks that visiting the sick [ἀσθενοῦντας] and looking after those in prison [τοὺς ἐν φυλακῇ ἐπισκέπτεσθαι] is not only following the command of Christ, but is also one of the best ways to dispel evil thoughts and put the demons to flight.[230]

Western Writers

Gaudentius of Brescia (4th to 5th century AD)

This friend of Ambrose refers to Matt 25:31-46 eight times in his extant sermons. Five of these references are to the "identity dialogue," but only twice does he give an exact quotation. In *Tractatus* 18.6-7 he quotes vv 34-36, 40 from one of the OL versions and alludes to vv 37-39:

> For he says: 'Come blessed of my Father, possess the kingdom which was prepared for you from the beginning of the world [ab origine mundi]; for I was hungry and you fed me, I thirsted and you gave me to drink, I was a stranger [peregrinus] and you took me in, naked and you covered me, ill and you took care of me; I was in prison and you visited me. To those bashfully and reverently making the excuse: Lord, when did we see you with these needs and minister to you? he will reply: 'Amen I say to you, when you did [it] to one of these

least, you did [it] to me [. . . cum fecistis uni ex minimis istis, mihi fecistis]. Therefore it does not seem absurd to anyone that they, whose cause we undertake, are said to receive us since the receiver himself, our Lord Jesus, . . . asserts that in them he was hungry [esurisse] and thirsty [sitisse] and a stranger [peregrinum] and naked [nudum] and ill [infirmum] and imprisoned [carceratum].[231]

In *Tractatus* 13. 29 he quotes v 45 in the context of a description of those Christians who do not show love for God: "Nor does that person love God who has no compassion for the poor in whom Christ asserts that he is either nourished or neglected. For whenever you have not done [it], he says, to one of these least ones, you have not done to me."[232] There is no indication in the above quotations or in the three places where Gaudentius alludes to vv 40, 45 (*Tractatus* 13. 24, 31; 18. 7)[233] that he has only Christian needy in mind. The texts are neutral in the sense that there is no indication whatsoever as to the exact identity of the beneficiaries.

Firmicus Maternus (d. after AD 360)

As an incentive to greater concern for the neighbor, this famous Sicilian rhetorician cites Matt 25:40 (without the restrictive τῶν ἀδελφῶν μου) in his treatise *Consultationes Zacchaei et Apollonii* 3.1: "The Lord in the gospel taught that he was supported in the persons of the lowly when he said: Amen I say to you, what you have done to one of these least, you have done to me." [234] The quotation comes in the midst of a catena of OT and NT verses (Matt 22:37, 39; Sir 29:15; Prov 19:17; Ps 37:25-26; Job 29:12 [LXX]; 2 Cor 9:6-7; Isa 58:6, 9) that have the poor in general in mind. There is no indication here of a narrow interpretation of "the least."

Hilary of Poitiers (ca. AD 315 - 367)

In his *De Trinitate*, a work less concerned with an exposition of Trinitarian doctrine than with the proof of the divinity of

Christ, Hilary has three quotations from Matt 25:31-46. None of them is from the so-called dialogue of the needy Christ, but in *De Trin.* 9. 25 he quotes v 34 as an indication of the reward for those who put love of neighbor on the same level as love of self. He goes on to say that the one who gives a neighbor as much as he gives himself will be saved.[235] The sense seems to be universal; there is nothing to indicate that Christians only or Christians primarily are to be the objects of charity.

In his *Commentarius in Evangelium Matthaei* 28.1, however, Hilary's viewpoint is restrictive. He sees the separation between the sheep and the goats in v 33 to be that between believers and nonbelievers. Alluding to vv 35-36 and 40, Hilary claims that the least with whom Christ identifies himself are believers:

> [Christ] indicates that he is in his least, that is, in those servants of his in a low position, and that he is fed with those who are hungry, quenched with those who are thirsty, comforted with those who are strangers, clothed with those who are naked, visited with those who are sick and consoled with those who are troubled. For he is poured into the bodies and minds of all the faithful to such an extent that the accomplishment of these works of humanity merits his grace, while their refusal causes him offense.[236]

Ambrose of Milan (ca. AD 339 - 397)

Ambrose had a great admiration for Origen. Perhaps this explains the fact that, like the famous Alexandrian allegorist, he often interprets Matt 25:31-46 in a far from literal way and in a manner that pertains to Christians only. Out of eight references in his works to those verses that comprise the dialogue of the needy Christ, four can be taken to refer to Christians. In *De Officiis Ministrorum* 2. 28 Ambrose exhorts his clergy to raise money for the ransom of Christian captives, even to the point of melting down their sacred vessels. Worrying that captured Christians will succumb to pagan religious practices, he states: " . . . it is far better to preserve souls for the Lord than gold . . . .

The chalice redeems from the enemy those whom [Christ's] blood has redeemed from sin."[237] Quoting v 35 and paraphrasing v 40 ("Quod enim uni horum fecistis, mihi fecistis"), he recounts the story of how Lawrence of Rome, when asked to produce the treasures of the church for the civil authorities, appeared in company with all the Christian poor.[238]

This same restrictive viewpoint is found in *Letter* 41.23 to his sister. Commenting on the woman in the gospels who anointed Christ's feet with oil, Ambrose says that the feet of Christ must continually be anointed. Quoting v 40 (without the restrictive τῶν ἀδελφῶν μου) he explains that the feet of Christ are those with whom Christ identified himself in the Matthean judgment scene, and that "whoever loves even the lowest of the holy people (qui etiam infimos plebis sacrae diligit) kisses these feet."[239] Then, in a rather allegorical interpretation of the "identity dialogue," he implies that every time the church administers the sacraments of penance or baptism she ministers to the needy feet of Christ.[240]

The same allegorical interpretation of these verses is found in two other works. In *De Mysteriis* 9. 57 he alludes to v 36c in a rather strange way. In the context of a discourse on the eucharist he suggests that when Christians eat and drink at the sacred mysteries, it is actually Christ who is being fed and nourished since "he says that in our persons he is in prison (sicut in nobis . . . in carcere esse se dicit)."[241] In his *De Poenitentia* 1. 7, 32 he quotes v 36b ("Et aeger eram et visitastis me") to accuse the Novatian schismatics, who will not absolve certain Christians, of being guilty of not visiting Christ who is sick in his followers who are in the state of sin and wishes to be visited in the sacrament of penance.[242]

Certainly, even though Ambrose was influenced by Origen, he does not interpret Matt 25:40,45 as narrowly as Origen did. There are passages in his works where he speaks of "the least" in terms of the needy in general, or at least puts no restriction on the beneficiaries of the charity of his congregation. In *De Viduis* 9. 54 he paraphrases v 40 to encourage lazy widows to perform charitable acts: "For no idle person ministers to Christ.

Minister to the poor and you have ministered to Christ. For what you did to one of these, he said, you did to me."[243]

The same nonrestrictive sense of the poor is also found in two citations in *Expositio Evangelii secundum Lucam*. In 4. 6, in the context of a discussion of Christ becoming man for our benefit, he alludes to v 36c when he states, " . . . he [Christ] is in prison with the poor man (in carcere cum paupere est) . . . ."[244] In 6. 27, in the same commentary on Luke, Ambrose notes that Christ's seeming indifference to the poor in Mark 14:7 and Matt 26:11 ("The poor you will always have with you . . . ") is offset by the identification of himself with "the least" in Matt 25:40 (quoted without τῶν ἀδελφῶν μου).[245] He goes on to encourage his readers to imitate the woman who anointed Christ: "If you desire grace, increase charity. Place upon the body of Jesus the faith of the resurrection, the odor of the church, the ointment of communal charity. And thus, going out, you will give to the poor."[246] One is not quite sure here whether Ambrose means all poor or Christian poor. His use of the terms "body of Jesus" and "communal charity" might indicate that in this passage he has in mind Christian needy. Perhaps, like Chrysostom, Ambrose had a universal outlook regarding the identity of "the least," but at the same time recognized the priority of the claim that the Christian poor had on the generosity of their fellow believers.

Ambrosiaster

This anonymous author[247] refers to Matt 25:31-46 twice. In his commentary on 1 Tim 4:8 he sums up the entire pericope in one sentence, but gives no indication of the exact identity of the beneficiaries: "Finally the evangelical word testifies that those who were generous to the brothers, serving [them] under various titles, would enter eternal life, while those disagreeing with this work, [would enter] eternal fire."[248]

In his commentary on 2 Cor 8:14, however, Ambrosiaster quotes v 40 in what seems to be a narrow sense:

Those who believe and who are engaged in business or the arts or have inherited material resources are to minister to the needs of the saints (sanctorum inopiis), that in turn, in the beyond, the saints, when they are rich and these are needy, might share with them, as if paying them back for their service, just as the Lord says: As often as you did [it] to one of these least ones, you did [it] to me [quamdiu fecistis uni ex minimis istis, mihi fecistis].[249]

Chromatius of Aquilea (d. AD 407)

In one of his few extant treatises, Chromatius deals with a biblical text in the same allegorical way that was encountered in the works of Ambrose. In *Tractatus* 29.3,1, commenting on Christ's command to the Christian to keep his hair groomed whenever he fasts (Matt 6:17), Chromatius argues that the anointing of the head in this text really refers to almsgiving: "Hence to anoint the head is to perform charity to one's neighbor. This charity is done to the Lord who, according to the apostle, is understood as the head of man. The same Lord said: As often as you did [it] to one of these least, you did [it] to me."[250] There is nothing in the passage to indicate that only Christian poor are to be the concern of the almsgiver.

Maximus of Turin (d. after AD 408)

In *Sermon* 27.1, a sermon to his priests, Maximus alludes to Matt 25: 35a, 36ac to stress that the priest must be involved in what he calls "spiritual banking" [spiritale mercimonium]:

> Of what value to us is the feeding of the poor [pauperum . . . refectio], the covering of the naked [nudorum protectio] and the visitation of the imprisoned [carceratorum visitatio], except that what is spent on them is not deducted from our account but is increased, and, in a sense, for the giver business is conducted with a certain profitable interest. The hungry poor man [pauper esuriens] is the rich man's treasure . . . .[251]

The fact that Maximus frequently asks his hearers to look ahead to the day of judgment, when the poor to whom they have given alms will speak up for them, is an indication that he did indeed have the Matthean "identity dialogue" in mind in the above quotation. There is nothing in the sermon to indicate that only Christians are to be the beneficiaries of the priests' charity.

Rufinus of Aquileia (ca. AD 345 - 410)

In his *Commentary on the Apostles' Creed* 34, Rufinus quotes Matt 25:32 in his discussion of the return of Christ to judge the living and the dead. He understands πάντα τὰ ἔθνη in the universal sense of all peoples.[252]

In *Interpretatio novem orationum Gregorii*, a translation of nine treatises of Gregory Nazianzus, Rufinus sharpens two possible allusions to the "identity dialogue" that are not seen as clearly in Gregory's original sermons. In *De grandinis vastatione* 18, Rufinus alludes to vv 40 and 42a: "Another was unmerciful to the widow and the orphan and did not share his bread with the hungry; rather he did not feed the hungry Christ who is fed in each of these least ones . . . [immo potius esurientem Christum non refecit, qui in singulis quibusque minimis pascitur . . . ."[253] There is nothing here to indicate that "the least" are only Christians. In *De Pentecoste* 5, however, Rufinus adds an allusion to v 40 that would seem to refer to Christians who either suffer for the sake of Christ or are well-treated:

> Even now he [Christ] suffers many of these things. Indeed he suffers and endures at the hands of those who hate, and at the hands of those who love he experiences nothing less than what they themselves experience. For he who does [it] to one of his least, does [it] to him . . . [Horum multa etiam nunc patitur: ab his quidem qui oderunt patitur et fert, ab his vero qui diligunt fert nihilo minus quae ipsi patiuntur. Qui enim facit uni ex minimis eius ipsi facit . . .].[254]

The evidence is far too scant to come to any firm conclusion regarding Rufinus' understanding of "the least." The fact that he would interpolate a clear reference to v 40 into the context of a discussion of Christ's identity with ill-treated and well-treated Christians, could be an indication that his understanding of "the least" was narrow.

Aponius (fl. ca. AD 405 - 415)

In his *Explanatio in Canticum Canticorum* 7, Aponius, commenting on Cant 4:9, paraphrases vv 34-36 as an incentive for Christians to adorn the Church with their charity: "In this way do his people shine with such splendor before the judgment seat of Christ when it is spoken by that blessed mouth: Come blessed of my Father. For I was hungry and thirsty, I was naked, I was a stranger; I was sick. I was in prison and you ministered to me."[255]

A few chapters later, *Exp. in Cant. Cant.* 10, Aponius paraphrases vv 37-39, 44, in order to impress upon his readers the necessity of doing good works in secret: "These works are hidden away in so many secret places (to be made public on the day of judgment) that even those who performed them are hardly aware of them, saying to Christ the judge who praises them: Lord, when did we see you or when did we minister to you?"[256] The above quotations are in the context of what seems to be an exhortation to intracommunity charity. Aponius speaks at length of feeding and nourishing those who become members of the church, not only with the Eucharist and daily sustenance, but also with the church's doctrines. In that sense it can be said that he uses these quotations from the "identity dialogue" in a narrow way.

Paulus Orosius (d. after AD 417)

This companion of Augustine refers to the Matthean judgment scene only once in his works. In *Liber Apologeticus* 18. 9, written against Pelagianism, Paulus paraphrases v 37 ("Lord, when did we see you and do these things to you?") in the context of his argument that, *pace* Pelagius, no one can attain ultimate perfection in this life and that even the just, on judgment day, will be ignorant of certain matters and will have to rely on the goodness of the judge for their salvation.[257] The text is used strictly in a doctrinal sense and is an indication that Paulus, like every other writer of the early church, interpreted the Matthean pericope in a very realistic sense as an exact description of the parousia. The text gives no indication of his view of "the least."

Pelagius (d. after AD 418)

This British monk, who is most remembered for his disputes with Augustine, was a firm champion of the necessity of good works for salvation, and he often quoted from Matt 25:31-46 to underscore this point. Three of the seven references to the Matthean pericope in his authentic works are quotations from the "identity dialogue." In addition, a doubtful work contains a reference to the pericope.

In *Epistola de malis doctoribus* 14. 5 Pelagius quotes vv 41 (with the Western variant) and 42ab to prove his point that the good who do nothing are just as deserving of punishment as those who do evil:

> ... the Lord testified that not only those doing evil, but also the good doing nothing, would be deserving of eternal fire, when he said: Depart from me, cursed, into eternal fire which my Father prepared for the devil and his angels. For I was hungry and you did not feed me, I thirsted and you did not give me to drink, and so forth. He did not say these things to those not believing, but to sinners....[258]

This same emphasis on the necessity of good works is found in *Fragmenta Vindobonensia* 10. Pelagius cites vv 34-36 to prove that fasting and abstinence without works of mercy is of no avail:

> I beg that you fast less than what you are able to do and make up for it by giving food to the hungry and drink to the thirsty.

> Clothe the naked; receive strangers and the poor; assist those in trouble so that with the others you might be worthy to hear: Come, blessed of my Father, partake of [percipite] the kingdom which was prepared for you from the beginning [ab origine] of the world. For I was hungry and you fed me, I thirsted and you gave me drink [potastis me]. I was naked and you covered me; I was ill and you took care of me; I was in prison and you visited me. He who wished to earn this by fasting or abstinence alone will in no way be able to hear these words.[259]

In light of Pelagius' insistence on the necessity of good works for salvation, it is surprising to read his advice to the Roman woman Demetrias upon learning that she is to consecrate her virginity to Christ. In *Ad Demetriadem* 22, Pelagius alludes to vv 35ac and 36ab and quotes v 40 as part of his encouragement to Demetrias to become more contemplative:

> But, I pray you, let your grandmother and mother undertake this responsibility [i.e., almsgiving] in your stead.... Let it be their duty to nourish the hungry with food [esurientes alere cibo], to clothe the naked [vestire nudos], to visit the sick [visitare infirmos], to give shelter to strangers [peregrinos tecto suscipere], and in hope of eternal reward to make a loan to Christ in his poor, who said: Whatever you did to one of these, the least of my brothers, you did to me.[260]

There is no indication whatsoever in the above works that Pelagius had a narrow interpretation of "the least." He gives us no clue as to their identity. His interest in the passage seems to spring more from the dogmatic and apologetic concern that faith alone is useless to save, than from the pastoral and moral concern that the poor be attended to.

The same universal outlook regarding the recipients of Christian charity is found in a work that is doubtfully attributed to Pelagius. In *Admonitio Augiensis* Ps-Pelagius quotes v 43a in the context of encouraging greater hospitality:

Behold Jesus walks about in front of the door looking for a place to stay. Let us receive him into the bedroom of our heart, that he might receive us into the blessedness of his kingdom. Let us beware lest he, knocking at the door for a long time in any poor whatsoever, not suffer injury and say to us: I was a stranger and you did not take me in.[261]

Sulpicius Severus (ca. AD 360 - ca. 420)

The same absence of a restrictive point of view is found in two works of Sulpicius Severus. In his famous *Life of St. Martin* 3. 4 he quotes v 40 (without the restrictive τῶν ἀδελφῶν μου) in the context of relating how the sainted catechumen of Tours shared half his cloak with a beggar, and then that night in his dreams saw Christ wearing the tattered cloak.[262] And in a doubtful work, *Letter* 2. 7, written to his sister Claudia on the subject of virginity, he quotes vv 41-42 to show that righteousness consists in more than simply not doing evil.[263] There is nothing in either text to indicate a narrow point of view; the poor and needy are presented in a seemingly universal way.

Jerome (ca. AD 342 - 420)

With regard to the πάντα τὰ ἔθνη of v 32, Jerome was a universalist. In his *Commentary on Jeremiah* 6. 25, 3 he tells us that the meaning of the verse is that all mankind will be subject to judgment.[264] With regard to his views on the identity of the sheep and the goats in vv 32-33, we are fortunate for the existence of his letter to Marcella. Evidently, Marcella had specifically asked Jerome whether the sheep could be identified as Christians and the goats as heathens. In *Letter* 59. 2[265] he refers her to his own work *Contra Jovinianum* 2. 18 wherein he explains that the sheep are all the righteous and the goats are all the unrighteous, Christian sinners included.[266] In his *Commentary on Jonah* 3. 6-9[267] and the *Treatise on Psalm 15* 8[268] he also includes Christian sinners among the goats. From the *Commentary on Isaiah* 8. 25, 1-5[269] and 14. 50, 11,[270] however, we know that Jerome included the Jews among the condemned. In *Comm. in Is.* 2. 5, 17 he places the Gentiles on the right saying that they shall graze on what the Jews deserted.[271] The implication is that the Jews are on the left.

With regard to the identity of "the least" Jerome is by far the most restrictive among the western authors. This could reflect his strong dependence on Origen's commentaries. Of the nine passages in his works where he refers to the dialogue of the needy Christ, six (*Comm. in Matt.* 25. 33;[272] *Letters* 4.1;[273] 58. 6-7;[274] *Comm. in Is.* 16. 58, 6-7;[275] and *Comm. in Ezek.* 6.18,11;[276] 14. 46,16-18[277]) give the reader the impression that Jerome opted for the narrow interpretation; and two passages (*Letter* 54.12[278] and *Apologia contra Rufinum* 3.17[279]), while identifying the needy as anyone (with the exception of heretics), give Christian poor a very strong preference.

In *Comm. in Matt.* 25. 33, Jerome is the first to address explicitly the problem regarding the exact identity of "the least." He states that the view that Christ is present in all the poor is too free an interpretation:

> To us the understanding was liberal that in every poor man Christ hungering was fed, thirsting was quenched, a stranger was led to shelter, naked was clothed, sick was visited, and shut up in prison had the solace of a comforter. But from that which follows: 'When you did [something] to one of these least, my brothers, you did [it] to me,' it seems to me that it was not said about all the poor in general, but about those who are poor in spirit, towards whom he extended his hand and said: 'My brothers and my mother are those who do the will of my father.'[280]

In *Letter* 58. 7 written to Paulinus of Nola, Jerome says that Christ is to be fed, clothed and welcomed in the Christian: "The true temple of Christ is the believer's soul. Adorn it, clothe it, offer gifts to it, welcome Christ in it. What use are walls blazing with jewels when Christ in his poor is in danger of perishing from hunger?"[281]

In *Letter* 4.1 he thanks Florentius for having "supported, fed, clothed and visited Christ"[282] in the person of Heliodorus, a needy priest living with Jerome.

In his *Commentary on Ezekiel* 14.46,16-18 he quotes v 40 (without τῶν ἀδελφῶν μου and ἐλαχίστων) and alludes to vv 35-36ac to make his point that wealthy men, upon entering the priesthood, should not give their money to their children but to the Christian poor:

> Therefore, the priest who is wealthier, when he enters the priesthood, should not give his excess possessions to his children but to the poor and holy brethren and to the household members of the faith . . . that they may return to the Lord what belongs to the Lord, who says in the gospel: 'Whatever you did to one of these, you did to me.' He is the one who is received in hospitality in the poor, he is visited in prison, he is the naked one covered, the thirsty one who drinks, the hungry one who is filled.[283]

In two of his letters Jerome makes it clear that, even though Christians are to have preference, non-Christians should also be attended to, as long as they are not members of a heretical Christian sect. He is the most clear about this in *Apologia contra Rufinum* 3.17 where, quoting v 43a, he explains: "We receive all who come to us at the monastery. For we are apprehensive about the fact that Mary and Joseph did not find a place at the inn, and we fear that Jesus would exclude us, saying: I was a stranger and you did not take me in. Only heretics we do not receive . . . ."[284] The same sentiments seem to be expressed in *Letter* 54.12, a letter of guidance to a widow named Furia. Jerome alludes to vv 35a, 36ab to recommend Paul's advice in Gal 6:10: "Give to everyone that asks of you, but especially to those who are of the household of the faith: clothe the naked, feed the hungry, visit the sick. As often as you extend your hand, think of Christ."[285] Jerome then seems to indicate that Furia should be on her guard against aiding anyone who is not of the Lord, by stating: "See to it that, when the Lord your God asks an alms of you, you do not increase riches which are not his."[286] If this last statement were taken to refer to all who are not Christian, it would be a flagrant contradiction of the universal sentiment expressed in the first part of the quotation. The most plausible reading would interpret it to mean those belonging to heretical Christian sects.

Origen's strong influence on Jerome is further seen in the fact that Jerome sometimes spiritualizes the meaning of the six works in Matt 25:31-46. In *Comm. in Ezek.* 6.18,11, in a strange mixture of realism and allegorism, he quotes v 36a and sees as the naked not only those without clothing but also the heathen in need of baptism: " . . . since the Savior said: 'I was naked and you covered me,' we are to give covering to the naked; and to those naked of faith and virtue we are to give the clothing of Christ, about which it was written: 'For all of you who have been baptized in Christ have put on Christ.' "[287]

In his *Commentary on Isaiah* 16. 58, 6-7, Jerome quotes vv 34-36, 40 and understands the corporal works mentioned in Matthew and Isaiah to be spiritual works. Sheltering the homeless means leading those freezing outside of the faith into the warmth of the church;[288] clothing the naked means covering them with baptism, the "tunic of Christ;"[289] feeding the hungry signifies instructing souls in the doctrine of the church;[290] and loosening the Isaian shackles means delivering those bound by heresy.[291] The passage is brought to a close with a reminder that all are to be the recipients of the Christian's charity, with special attention given to those who are believers: "And when, he says, you have done these things and your generosity to all will have been seen, [take care] especially not to look down on the household members of the faith."[292]

Perhaps, like Chrysostom, Jerome envisions two concentric circles: the wider circle of all the poor and the inner circle of Christian poor. But he is more insistent than Chrysostom on the fact that the preferential beneficiaries of Christian charity are to be members of the believing community. In that sense he is more narrow than Chrysostom, especially in his outspokeness about heretics not sharing at all in Christian almsgiving. It seems that whenever Jerome treats the works of mercy in a more literal, corporal sense, he tends to be restrictive in his outlook;

while he becomes much more universal in horizon when he allegorizes the works, seeing them as spiritual deeds.

Augustine of Hippo (AD 354 - 430)

Augustine is second only to Chrysostom in the number of times he refers to Matt 25:31-46. There are 114 references to the Matthean pericope scattered throughout twenty-nine of his undisputed works. Of the total number of references, forty-four refer to the dialogue of the needy Christ. Nowhere does Augustine specifically state that "the least" are the poor in general; in slightly more than a third of these forty-four references, however, it is obvious that the Christian poor are meant. Seventeen citations are definitely restrictive in their viewpoint, and four others could possibly be interpreted in the same light.

On a number of occasions (*Sermons* 56.6;[293] 57.5;[294] 58.3;[295] and *Enarr. in Ps.* 9.9[296]) Augustine states that the scene of the last judgment, which he always interprets in a literal way, is the answer to Matt 6:10, the second petition of the Lord's Prayer. In *Enarr. in Ps.* 9. 9 he tells us that the πάντα τὰ ἔθνη of v 32 is to be understood in the widest possible sense of all humanity.[297] Like so many spiritual writers of his age, Augustine frequently makes reference to those verses of the pericope (31-32,34,41,46) that he feels prove the power and divinity of Christ and the certainty and interminability of reward and punishment. He has much to say about the identity of the sheep and goats. For Augustine the sheep are Christians. He identifies them by various names: the body of Christ (*De Agone Christiano* 28),[298] good Christians (*Contra Litt. Petiliani* 3. 2, 3),[299] orthodox Christians (*Sermon* 146. 2),[300] those who convert to Christianity to please God and not men (*De Catech. Rudibus* 17. 27),[301] Gentiles who have become Christian (*De Consensu Evang.* 3. 25, 86),[302] martyrs (*Tract. on John* 21.14),[303] saints of Christ (*Tract. on John* 25. 2),[304] believers in eternal life (*Sermon* 127.1, 9),[305] the baptized (*De Symbolo ad Catech.* 4.12),[306] the just and the righteous (*De*

Trin. 1.13, 31),³⁰⁷ those redeemed by Christ's blood (*Tract. on John* 68. 2);³⁰⁸ - but the common denominator of all is their belief in Christ. In *Enarr. in Ps.* 72. 7 he includes the prophets of Israel among the saved,³⁰⁹ but it is obvious that he considers them "Christian" in the sense that they believed in and foretold the coming of the Messiah.

The goats, however, include a wide mixture of Christians, heretics, Jews and pagans. Among the Christians who are condemned are those who do not do the will of God (*Contra Faust.* 5.3; *De Bapt. contra Don.* 4.19, 26; *Contra Litt. Petiliani* 2. 23, 54),³¹⁰ those who convert to Christianity merely to please men (*De Catech. Rudibus* 17. 27),³¹¹ those who do not keep God's commandments (*Enarr. in Ps.* 9.9; 58.12; 62.9; 64.17),³¹² and especially the wealthy who do not share their resources with the poor (*Enarr. in Ps.* 4.2; 49. 3).³¹³

Among the non-Christians, Jews and heretics receive the most scathing rebukes from Augustine. A favorite theme with Augustine is that the Jews, who will be forced on judgment day to look on Christ "whom they have pierced" (Zech 12:10) (*Tract. on 1 John* 4. 5; *Tract. on John* 21.13),³¹⁴ will be condemned because they continue to be the enemies of Christ in Augustine's own day (*Enarr. in Ps.* 44.13; 78. 3; *De Consensu Evang.* 3. 25, 86).³¹⁵ Pelagius and his followers (*De Pecc. Meritis et Rem.* 3.6),³¹⁶ as well as all other heretics who persecute the orthodox Christians and mock true Christian belief (*Enarr. in Ps.* 99. 6; 146. 8),³¹⁷ will meet the same fate as pagan civil tyrants (*Enarr. in Ps.* 91.11; 125. 8)³¹⁸ and all other unbelievers (*Enarr. in Ps.* 89.15; *Tract. on John* 44. 6; 95.1).³¹⁹

Unlike Chrysostom and Jerome, Augustine nowhere in the forty-four references to the "identity dialogue" specifically mentions that non-Christians are to be within the scope of the believer's charity. The majority of his references dealing with "the least" are neutral; that is, they give us no indication whatsoever as to the identity of the beneficiaries. In 17 instances, however, (*De Trin.* 15.19, 34;³²⁰ *De Civ. Dei* 17.18; 21. 27;³²¹ *De Bapt. contra Don.* 5. 21, 29³²² *De Consensu Evang.* 3. 25, 86; 4. 5, 6;³²³ *Tract. on John* 21. 7;³²⁴ *Enarr. in Ps.* 37. 2,10; 38.

2, 6; 40. 5;[325] *Sermon* 103.1; 113.1; 123. 4-5; 133. 8; 137. 2;[326] *Sermo Morin Guelfer.* 13.1;[327] *Sermo Morin* 11. 6[328]) Augustine comes down clearly on the side of those who hold a restrictive viewpoint; and this same interpretation could be plausibly argued in four other passages (*Tract. on John* 50. 6; 51.12; *Enarr. in Ps.* 50.11; *Sermo Lambot* 4).[329] For Augustine baptism produces "not only Christians but Christ" (*Tract. on John* 21. 7),[330] and to emphasize his strong belief in what seems to be almost a physical unity between Christ and the believer, he frequently quotes vv 35-40 in conjunction with Acts 9:4-5 and other scriptural passages where Christ clearly identifies himself with the suffering Christian (*Tract. on John* 21. 7; *Sermon* 123. 4-5; 133. 8; *Enarr. in Ps.* 38. 5; 40. 5; *De Consensu Evang.* 4. 5, 6; *Sermo Morin Guelfer.* 13).[331] This strong sense of an almost physical identity between "the head in heaven" and his "members on earth" pervades many of the passages in which Augustine addresses himself to the issue of almsgiving. The "least" of v 40 are the very members of Christ's body (*De Trin.* 15.19, 34; *De Civ. Dei* 17.18; *Enarr. in Ps.* 37.10; 38. 2);[332] In *Sermon* 137. 2 he quotes vv 34-40 and concludes that "the least" are the feet here on earth of the head who dwells in heaven:

> He is now in heaven, yet he suffers here as long as his church suffers here. Here Christ is hungry [esurit], here he is thirsty [sitit], is naked [nudus], is a stranger [hospes], is sick [infirmatur], is in prison [in carcere]. For whatever his body suffers here he said that he himself suffers . . . . For he said to them: 'Whatever you did to one of these least, you did to me.' It is the same in our own body. The head is above, the feet are on earth; yet in any crowd or throng of men, when anyone treads on your foot, does not the head say: 'You are treading upon me?' No one has trodden on your head or on your tongue; it is above in safety. No harm has happened to it. And yet, because by the bond of charity there is unity from the head even to the feet, the tongue does not separate itself from the feet, but says: 'You are treading on me,' when no one has touched it. As the tongue which no one has touched says, 'You are treading on me,' so Christ the head, whom no one stepped on, said, 'I was hungry and you gave me to eat.'[333]

In other passages those with whom Christ identifies himself in vv 40, 45 are variously described as "those who left all and followed him" (*Sermon* 113.1),[334] and "other Christians" (*Tract. on John* 21. 7; *De Civ. Dei* 21. 27; *De Bapt. contra Don.* 5. 21, 29).[335] In *De Consensu Evang.* 4. 5, 6, one of the classic passages in Augustine to show the strict unity he envisioned between Christ and the disciple, he quotes vv 40, 45, along with such texts as Matt 10:40; Luke 10:16 and Acts 9:4, to argue that one cannot be for Christ and against his disciples, nor conversely against Christ and in favor of his disciples.[336] In *Enarr. in Ps.* 50.11 Augustine states that "the least" of vv 40, 45, whom he calls "saints," will actually be included with the angels who will come with Christ at the end of time; and he gives the impression that they will somehow or other have a part to play in the actual process of judging their benefactors as well as those who neglected them.[337]

It would be tempting to place Augustine in the same category with Chrysostom and Jerome and call him a universalist with a special propensity for the Christian needy. But, as I have already mentioned, nowhere does he explicitly state that the Christian has a duty to be charitable to all; yet, in many places he is very clear and uncompromising about the duty Christians have to take care of their own. So it might be much closer to the mark to say that he has a narrow viewpoint regarding the identity of "the least," a kind of narrowness, in fact, not attested to since Origen. Probably undergirding this rather restrictive viewpoint is Augustine's familiarity with the teaching of the apostle Paul, especially the concept of the so-called mystical body and such community-centered sentiments as those expressed in Rom12:13a ("Look on the needs of the saints as your own . . . ") and Gal 6:10 (. . . "let us do good to all men, but especially those of the household of the faith).

Paulinus of Nola (AD 353 - 431)

This contemporary and friend of Augustine, Ambrose and Jerome cites Matt 25: 31-46 nine times in his extant works. Five of these references are allusions to the "identity dialogue." Three of these allusions (*Letters* 1.1;[338] 13. 22[339] and 32. 20[340]) give no indication that the objects of charity are meant to be Christians, but the remaining two references indicate that Paulinus might have had a narrow understanding of "the least."

In *Letter* 5. 3, written to thank Sulpicius Severus for some act of generosity to him, Paulinus alludes to v 40 in conjunction with Matt 10:41a:

> ... recompense shall be made you at the resurrection of the just by him who bears witness that he is loved and welcomed in his least (ab eo qui et in minimis suis se diligi testatur et recipi). By his own words he makes himself a debtor on behalf of even a false or useless servant who belongs to his name, saying: He who receives a prophet in the name of a prophet shall receive the reward of a prophet.[341]

In a second letter to Sulpicius Severus, *Letter* 23. 43, Paulinus again alludes to v 40 and makes a clearer connection between "the least" and Christians:

> For he [Christ] deigns to be to us whatever we his poor servants have been to him. He mingles with us and implants us in him, so that what he has received from us is put to our own profit. He regards all that is given to us, that is, his least, as having been given to him [Ita enim se immiscet nobis, ac nos sibi conserit, ut quod ipse accepit, nobis proficere faciat; qui quod nobis, id est, minimis eius tribuitur, sibi acceptum ferat].[342]

Anonymous Writings

The anonymous group of writings which purports to relate the history of Clement of Rome, and hence termed the "Clementines,"[343] has seven references to the Matthean verses that pertain to this study. In the introductory *Epistle to James* and in the following 20 *Homilies* there are five references to the dialogue of the needy Christ, two of them definitely reflective of the restrictive viewpoint.

In the *Epistle to James* 9. 3-4, alluding to vv 35-36, Pseudo-Clement exhorts the Christians to share their food with "all who are brothers according to God" (πᾶσιν τοῖς κατὰ θεὸν ἀδελφοῖς) and to take care to

> ... feed the hungry (πεινῶντας τρέφετε) and give drink to the thirsty (διψῶσι παρέχετε ποτόν); clothe the naked (γυμνοῖς ἔνδυμα), visit the sick (τοὺς νοσοῦντας ἐπισκέπτεσθε) and help as much as possible those in prison (τοῖς ἐν φυλακαῖς . . . βοηθεῖτε); receive strangers (τοὺς ξένους . . . λαμβάνετε) into your own homes with all eagerness....[344]

In *Homilies* 3. 69 the same sentiments are repeated in an allusion to vv 35-36. Christians are asked to love the brothers and to share their own possessions with them:

> If you love your brothers (τοὺς ἀδελφοὺς ὑμῶν), you will steal nothing of theirs but will rather give [them] what is yours. You will feed the hungry (πεινῶντας γὰρ θρέψετε), give drink to the thirsty (διψῶσιν ποτὸν παρέξετε), clothe the naked (γυμνοὺς ἐνδύσετε), visit the sick (νοσοῦντας ἐπισκέψεσθε), help as much as possible those in prison (τοῖς ἐν εἱρκταῖς . . . βοηθήσετε), and gladly receive strangers into your homes (ξένους . . . ἀποδέξεσθε), treating no one with hatred.[345]

That a narrow, intracommunity charity is meant is made clearer by the fact that this passage is included in a discussion of internal community problems. The author goes on to discuss those who stay away from the community assembly because of their grievances against fellow Christians.

In *Homilies* 11. 4; 12. 32; 17. 7[346] and in *Recognitions* 5. 23, 2-3,[347] however, we get the sense that the author is a true universalist. In *Recognitions* 5. 23, 2-3, alluding to vv 35-36, Ps-Clement refutes the argument that Christians worship images of the invisible God and claims that, on the contrary, they worship God in his only image, man, by giving

... food to the hungry (esurienti cibum), a goblet to the thirsty (sitienti poculum), a garment to the naked (nudo indumentum), service to the sick (aegro ministerium), hospitality to the traveler (peregrino hospitium) and the necessities to those in prison (in carcere posito necessaria) . . .[348]

In the same context of the above passage he identifies this object of Christian charity as every one: "If you should truly wish to honor the image of God, you will do good to man . . . for in every man is the image of God . . . ."[349] The same sentiment is found in *Homilies* 17. 7 in a possible allusion to v 40: "The one wishing to honor God should honor his visible image, that is, man. Whatever anyone does to man (whether good or bad) is done to him [i.e., God]."[350] Thus the evidence would indicate that, even though Ps-Clement used the Matthean "identity dialogue" on occasion to encourage intracommunity almsgiving, he also realized that the concerns of Christian charity went beyond the boundaries of the believing community. He makes explicit the fact that every human being is the proper object of a Christian's concern. In that sense he is similar to Chrysostom and even a bit wider in his scope than Jerome.

From the Council of Ephesus to the Second Council of Constantinople

(AD 431 - 553)

Eastern Writers

Cyril of Alexandria (d. AD 444)

This celebrated foe of Nestorius refers to Matt 25:31-46 43 times in twenty-two of his works. Only nine citations (eight quotations and one allusion) have to do with the "identity dialogue." The remainder of the references are to vv 31-34, 41 and 46 and, in the majority of cases, are used to prove Christ's divinity and his equality with the Father.

For Cyril the phrase πάντα τὰ ἔθνη of v 32 seems to mean all human beings. In *De recta fide* 59 he interpets it to mean "the world" (τὴν οἰκουμένην)³⁵¹ and in *Quod beata Maria sit deipara* he says it means "all flesh" (πᾶσα σάρξ) as in Ps 65:3.³⁵² In *Explanatio in psalmos* 36. 22, however, he leaves his reader with the impression that he might understand πάντα τὰ ἔθνη in terms of Gentile Christians. In the context of describing those who bless and curse God, Cyril alludes to Matt 25:35a (". . . you fed this one, you fed me [τοῦτον ἔθρεψας, ἐμὲ ἔθρεψας] . . . ") and then states: "The Gentiles [τὰ ἔθνη], however, bless Christ and so they inherit the kingdom. The Jews, on the contrary, who blaspheme him are, at the end, obliterated and utterly destroyed."³⁵³ The allusion to v 34 in the above quotation, and the fact that it is found in conjunction with an allusion to v 35a, may be an indication that when Cyril uses the term τὰ ἔθνη he may also have πάντα τὰ ἔθνη of v 32 in mind.

Five of the nine references to the "identity dialogue" (*Quod unus sit Christus*;³⁵⁴ *Exp. in ps.* 36. 22;³⁵⁵ *Thesaurus*;³⁵⁶ *Scholia de incarnatione* 37;³⁵⁷ *In epist. ad Heb.* 13.16³⁵⁸) are in the context of controversy with the Nestorians and others who, in Cyril's estimation, made too great a distinction between the human and divine natures of Christ. Cyril quotes v 40 (always without τῶν ἀδελφῶν μου) as part of his argument that the hypostatic union that exists in the person of Christ is even more intimate than the moral union that exists between Christ and the poor. In these instances Cyril gives us no indication that he has a narrow viewpoint regarding the identity of "the least."

Four references to the dialogue between the judged and the judge are found in works that are more pastoral in nature rather than purely theological. It is in these pastoral works that we are given the slight impression that Cyril might have been primarily concerned with helping Christian needy. In *Homilia paschalis* 19. 3 he quotes vv 34-36, 40 (without τῶν ἀδελφῶν μου) to encourage charity to the "poor and wretched."³⁵⁹ It would seem that Cyril had all the poor in mind, except that a few paragraphs before the quotation from Matthew he quotes Deut 15:11, a verse that has to do with the Hebrews taking care of their own Hebrew poor.

In his *Commentary on Amos* 2. 7, Cyril again quotes v 40 (without τῶν ἀδελφῶν μου) to encourage almsgiving to those "weakened by painful troubles and the burden of poverty."[360] There is no indication here that the poor are Christians only.

In his *Commentary on Luke* 21. 3-4, he quotes v 40 (without τῶν ἀδελφῶν μου) in what seems to be an appeal to intracommunity charity:

> He [Christ] counts as offerings and takes unto himself what we do for the brethren who are grieved by poverty. For he said: Truly I tell you that whatever you have done to one of these little ones, you have done to me .... As I said, therefore, our deeds are indeed done to those who are our fellows and brethren, but God takes it unto himself ....[361]

The sense that Cyril has a narrow view of "the least" here is heightened by his additional quotation of Deut 15:7-10, a text that encourages the Hebrews to look after their Hebrew brethren in need.

This seemingly narrow interpretation, however, might not be a true reflection of Cyril's position. Earlier in the same commentary, *Comm. in Luc.*14.12, he cites vv 35ab, 36 and 40 (with neither τῶν ἀδελφῶν μου nor τῶν ἐλαχίστων) in a much more universal context, to encourage Christians to deliver themselves from eternal punishment: "The way in which to deliver ourselves is to live in virtue--to comfort the brethren who are grieved with poverty, and open our hand wide to all who are in need, and to sympathize with the sick."[362] From the above text it becomes clearer that Cyril had a universal outlook regarding the identity of "the least." His concern was certainly for the Christian needy, but, perhaps as did Chrysostom and Jerome before him, he exhibited a care that went beyond the boundaries of his faith community.

Isidore of Pelusium (d. ca. AD 450)

Isidore considered himself a disciple of John Chrysostom, and the latter's strong literal and universalistic approach to the

Matthean pericope seems to have influenced his own moral concern for social service.[363] In one of his extant letters, *Letter 88*, in answer to Bishop Asclepius' consternation that Christ would have been so unconcerned with the poor when he allowed the woman to anoint his feet with the precious ointment (Mark 14:3-9 par), Isidore quotes v 40, along with Matt 5:7; 9:13 and 12:7, to emphasize Christ's over-riding concern for the needy: "The one who said, 'Blessed are the merciful' and 'I want mercy, not sacrifice' and 'Whatever you did to the least of my brothers, you did to me' would in no way go back on his concern for the poor . . . .If anyone says: I want to consecrate something [to God], order him to give it to the poor."[364] There is nothing that hints of restrictiveness here. Even though the evidence is so scant, because of Isidore's close association with Chrysostom he could have held the same universal horizon regarding the beneficiaries of Christian charity as Chrysostom did. Oddly, Chrysostom's prolific use of the Matthean pericope is not duplicated in the works of Isidore. Out of his numerous extant letters, there is one reference to the Matthean dialogue of the needy Christ, even though his works are replete with themes of liberality and magnanimity.[365]

Callinicus (d. ca. AD 450)

In his *Vita sancti Hypatii* 4. 4, Callinicus quotes Matt 25:34-36,40 and alludes to vv 37-39 with what appears to be a universal application. He describes how the monk Hypatius was entirely at the service of those afflicted with illness, both within and without the monastery; and how he travelled far and wide to find the sick and those wounded and bring them into the monastery so he could care for them.[366] There is no indication of any restrictive understanding of "the least."

Hesychius of Jerusalem (d. after AD 451)

There are six references to Matt 25:31-46 in the extant works of this monk who enjoyed great doctrinal authority in Palestine because of his scriptural commentaries. Only two of the references to the Matthean pericope refer to the "identity dialogue," and in both cases there is no indication that Hesychius held a restrictive viewpoint with regard to "the least."

In his *Commentary on Leviticus* 7. 26, Hesychius quotes v 40 (without τῶν ἀδελφῶν μου) in his exegesis of Lev 26:9: "[God] indeed increases us when he makes the small good things we have done appear great. For he multiplies small things, causing them to grow into many. Increasing and magnifying our virtues, did he not say: As often as you did it to one of these least ones, you did it to me?"[367]

Commenting on Ps 103:4b in his *In psalmos* 102. 4, he cites vv 34-35ab:

> If you were compassionate to your neighbor (πρὸς τὸν πλησίον), he will grant you for your crown the kingdom of heaven, saying: Come, blessed of my Father, and inherit the kingdom prepared for you from the beginning of the world. For I was hungry and you fed me, I thirsted and you gave me to drink, and what follows.[368]

Basil of Seleucia (d. ca. AD 459)

In the 41 extant sermons bearing the name of Basil there are three citations of Matt 25:31-46. The only reference to the words of the "needy Christ" is found in Oratio 26 where, in a lengthy peroration, Basil quotes vv 35, 42-43a to urge his listeners to greater almsgiving:

> I was hungry and you fed me, I thirsted and you gave me to drink; I was a stranger and you took me in. For what you give to my own, you reap from me. For their sake I am naked and a stranger and a wanderer and poor. The gift is theirs; the gratitude is mine. I am tormented by their pleas. Before the judgment win over the judge by your gifts. Give him the occasion of exercising benevolence; supply him with a reason for forgiveness . . . . What deeds, therefore, condemn us with the devil? I was hungry and you did not feed me, I thirsted and you did not give me to drink. I was a stranger and you did not

take me in, naked and you did not cover me . . . . Let us put out the fire by mercy; by charity to one another [τῇ πρὸς ἀλλήλους φιλανθρωπίᾳ] let us turn aside the threats against one another [καθ' ἡμῶν]; let us be compassionate to each other [πρὸς ἀλλήλους] . . . .[369]

"To my own" in the above quotation indicates that the needy to be assisted are Christians. This narrow understanding of "the least" is further evidenced by the fact that the above quotation was given in the context of a discussion of John 10:11b (" . . . the good shepherd lays down his life for the sheep") and was obviously meant to bolster intracommunity charity.

Theodoret of Cyrus (ca. AD 393 - 466)

This last great representative of the School of Antioch has 13 references to Matt 25:31-46 scattered throughout seven of his extant works. Only four of these references are to the "identity dialogue," and in each of them it seems Theodoret has a narrow interpretation of "the least."

In *Graecorum affectionum curatio* 11. 63-64, Theodoret quotes vv 31-36, alludes to vv 37-39; and then, possibly influenced by his fellow Syrian, Eusebius of Emesa, he quotes v 40 with the restrictive addition taken from Matt 18:6: "Whatever you have done to one of the least of my brothers who believe in me [ἑνὶ τούτων τῶν ἀδελφῶν μου τῶν ἐλαχίστων τῶν πιστευόντων εἰς ἐμέ], you have done to me."[370]

This influence of Matt 18:6 is seen again in *Letter* 131, sent to Longinus to thank him for his assistance when Theodoret was imprisoned. He quotes v 36c and then v 40 (without τῶν ἀδελφῶν μου but with the restrictive τῶν πιστευόντων εἰς ἐμέ and the superfluous μικρῶν from Matt 18:6):

> You have shared in our suffering not only by a consoling letter but also by sending the very revered and religious deacons Matthew and Isaac. I know very well you will hear from the just judge: I was in prison and you came to me. Even though we are wicked and weak and weighed down with a large burden of sins, the Lord is rich and generous. Therefore, he

speaks not of great people but of little people when he says: What you have done to one of the least little ones who believe in me [ἐνὶ τῶν σμικρῶν[371] τῶν ἐλαχίστων τῶν πιστευόντων εἰς ἐμέ], you have done to me.[372]

This same narrow interpretation of "the least" may be present in Theodoret's *Commentary on the Song of Songs*. In 4. 6, 11, commenting on Cant 6:11 [LXX], he again combines the positive μικρῶν with the superlative ἐλαχίστων in what seems to be an allegorizing of the Matthean passage: "I shall give you my breasts, that is, the springs of my teaching. For whatever is given to them you consider conferred upon yourself, saying: Whatever you did to one of the least of these little ones [ἐνὶ τῶν μικρῶν τούτων τῶν ἐλαχίστων], you did to me."[373] The Christian instruction that is given to "the least" here is ambiguous. If Theodoret is talking about instructing already baptized Christians, then obviously he has a narrow interpretation of "the least" in mind. If he means the evangelization of non-Christians, however, then he could have a much broader understanding of the recipients in v 40.

We are given some further elucidation in this matter a few chapters later in the same commentary. In *Comm. on the Sg of Sgs* 4. 7,11-13, interpreting Cant 7:13 [LXX], Theodoret quotes v 40 (with the same peculiar combination of μικρῶν and ἐλαχίστων): "Wherefore, she says, there I shall give you my breasts. For you make your own whatever is done to them, and you say: Whatever you have done to one of the least little ones [ἐνὶ τῶν μικρῶν τῶν ἐλαχίστων], you have done to me."[374] In this second quotation the breasts are meant to be the works of charity to be performed for the "lowly and the small" [ταπεινὰς καὶ μικράς]. Theodoret leaves the reader with the impression that he is speaking here about those in the church, for in this same passage he says, "Let us investigate . . . those who by now have accepted the preaching, as to whether a sprout has blossomed."[375] If his use of τῶν μικρῶν in the above two passages was influenced by the restrictive Matt 18:6, then it is further indication that Theodoret has a narrow interpretation of "the least."

Gennadius of Constantinople (d. AD 471)

One reference to Matt 25:31-46 exists in the extant works of this exegete and orator. In his *Commentary on Genesis* 1. 26, expounding on the word "image" in Gen 1:26, Gennadius quotes vv 40, 45 (without τῶν ἀδελφῶν μου and with τῶν μικρῶν in place of τῶν ἐλαχίστων):

> If I should consider what "image" means in our usage, I would discover that an image is to be venerated because of what it portrays. My thinking about the image is clearly referred to what it represents. Therefore, the Lord himself in the Gospels says: Whatever you have done to one of these little ones, you have done to me; and whatever you have not done to one of these, you have not done to me.[376]

There is no indication here that Gennadius has a restrictive viewpoint with regard to the identity of "the least."

Ps-Eusebius of Alexandria (fifth to sixth century AD)[377]

There are two references to the Matthean pericope in the sermons of Ps-Eusebius. In *Sermon* 21.1-5, a lengthy discourse on almsgiving and Lazarus and the rich man, almost the entire pericope is quoted as the author reenacts the judgment scene and includes his listeners in the scenario.[378] Throughout the sermon there is no hint that those to be helped are Christians only, until near the end, in chap. 5, Ps-Eusebius paraphrases v 44 (omitting the fifth work, the visitation of the sick) and adds a comment that could indicate a narrow interpretation:

> What will they say on behalf of themselves in the presence of the incorrupt judge? Lord, when did we see you hungry, or thirsty, or a stranger, or naked or in prison and not minister to you? The virtue-loving Lord will answer them: Yes, as you say, you did not see me. Nevertheless, every hour you saw brothers, my members [τὰ ἐμὰ μέλη], who were distressed by hunger, thirst and cold....[379]

The phrase τὰ ἐμὰ μέλη calls to mind 1 Cor 12:12 and Paul's teaching on the union of Christ and Christians in one body. It would be inconceivable that Ps-Eusebius would have non-Christians in mind when he used this phrase.

There might also be a narrow use of v 40 in *Sermon 8*, a homily on the proper commemoration of the feasts of martyrs. Ps-Eusebius encourages his listeners to invite anyone they meet to their banquets on the feasts of martyrs and to consider the invited as the martyrs themselves:

> ... do not doubt that, in truth, the martyrs themselves come to the banquet of those who zealously and properly celebrate the com- memorations of the saints. Just as the Savior says: Whoever will have done [something] for one of these least, has done [it] for me [ὃς ἂν ποιήσει ἑνὶ τούτων τῶν ἐλαχίστων, ἐμοὶ ἐποίησεν]. And elsewhere: The one who receives you receives me. If, therefore, the one who receives the poor shows that he receives Christ, then the one who receives them in the name of the martyrs receives the martyrs themselves and has the reward and the advantage with the saints, just as the Lord said: The one who receives a prophet in the name of a prophet shall receive a prophet's reward.[380]

Whom does Ps-Eusebius have in mind when he speaks of "the least" in the above paraphrase of v 40? Any poor person invited to the banquet or the martyrs who come in the disguise of the poor? Since v 40 is used in conjunction with the restrictive Matt 10:40 (which refers to the apostles), there is the strong possibility that "the least" in the above quotation refers to the martyrs who secretly attend the banquets given in their own honor.

Procopius of Gaza (ca. AD 475 - 538)

In the extant works of Procopius, the first Greek author known to have used the literary form known as ἐκλογαί or *catenae*, there are eleven references to Matt 25:31-46, but only one reference to the "identity dialogue" as such. In his *Commentary on the Song of Songs* 5.1, Procopius rambles on in a disjointed series of associated ideas as he attempts to elucidate the meaning of Cant 5:1 [LXX]:

> ... the live plants of the garden produce bread for God according to what is written: I was hungry and you fed me. The bread of happiness, however, is good works sweetened with the honey of the commandments. Again, in a way, the flowering plants of the garden pour out wine. To these he says: I thirsted and you gave me to drink, mixing wine with milk, the food of human nature that is pure and simple and childlike and without sorrow, cleansed of every cause of evil.[381]

Procopius allegorizes the Matthean works, seeing the food and drink of a pure, upright life, good works and the observance of the commandments being given to Christ himself rather than to the poor. For this reason the text is neutral; we are given no insight into his view of "the least."

In his *Commentary on Isaiah* 65, Procopius seems to interpret πάντα τὰ ἔθνη in the universal sense. Stating that Isa 66:18 [LXX] is fully understood only in the light of the Gospel, he quotes Matt 25:31-32 and adds: "For the old law gathered one nation [ἐν ἔθνος] and one tongue. Christ, however, [gathered] all nations together with those saved from Israel [πάντα μετὰ τῶν σωθέντων ἐξ Ἰσραήλ], saying: Hear this, all nations."[382] It could be argued from the above quotation that Procopius understood that not everyone from Israel was to be saved. Hence there is the possibility that he would not include those Jews who did not become Christians among πάντα τὰ ἔθνη of v 32.

John of Gaza (d. ca. AD 550)

This disciple of the more famous Varsanuphius was also referred to as John the Prophet. He left several letters of spiritual direction that contain three references to Matt 25:31-46, but only one citation of a verse from the words of the "needy Christ." In *Questions and Answers* 124, in response to the inquiry of a certain monk Andrew as to whether he should care for his sick religious superior even though the superior refused to command him to do so, John paraphrases v 36b importing the verb διακονεῖν from v 44:

> Do anything you can to refresh the old man for it pleases God more than divine services . . . The old man should not protest when he is ministered to by you, but ought to give thanks to God and pray for you . . . . Every man ought to live according to his measure and condition in the fear of God, thanking Him always that by means of him others get their reward. Then let him not bear a grudge towards him who wants to hear Him who says: I was sick and you ministered to me [ἠσθένησα καὶ διηκονήσατέ μοι].[383]

Obviously, since it is a question here of a monk serving his brother monk, John's use of this verse from the "identity dialogue" is narrow.

Jobius (mid-sixth century AD)

Little is known of this Byzantine monk except that he wrote against Severus, the Monophysite Patriarch of Antioch. In his *De incarnatione* 3, in the context of a discussion of God's great love for mankind, Jobius quotes v 40 (without τῶν ἀδελφῶν μου) as an elucidation of the parable of the merciless official (Matt 18:21-35):

> . . . the one to whom ten thousand talents was remitted, thinking little of the charity of the remittor, became angry with his fellow servant; he therefore outraged the Lord who for love of mankind [τῆς αὐτοῦ φιλανθρωπίας] takes to himself the [injuries] of his servants [τὰ τῶν δούλων]. For he says: What you have done to one of these least, you have done to me.[384]

There is nothing in the passage to indicate that Jobius held a restrictive interpretation of "the least." The phrase "his servants" seems to be universal, a further illustration, as it were, of "mankind."

Western Writers

Laurentius of Novae (fifth century AD)[385]

In *Homily* 2, a sermon on almsgiving, Laurentius makes frequent use of Matt 25:35-36, 40 (without τῶν ἀδελφῶν μου) to encourage his listeners to silence the cry of the poor with their alms so that on the day of judgment they would be publicly acclaimed by the poor they had assisted.[386] His quotation of v 36a (Nudus fui et dedistis mihi indumentum)[387] is unattested by any of the versions. This could indicate that Laurentius is quoting from memory and has cast the verse into the same grammatical format as v 35ab. There is no indication anywhere in the sermon of a restrictive viewpoint. He frequently identifies those to be helped as "the hungry," "the poor," "the blind, the deaf, the lame, the crippled, widows and orphans, strangers, travellers, foreigners and men of this type needing any help,"[388] but nowhere does he give the slightest indication that he has primarily Christians in mind.

John Cassian (ca. AD 360 - 435)

As did so many other Christian authors before him, Cassian, in his struggle with Nestorian heretics, resorted primarily to those verses in the Matthean pericope that he felt could be used to prove Christ's divinity. In two of his conferences with the famed Abbot Moses of Scete in the Egyptian desert, there are references to verses that comprise the identity dialogue. In the *First Conference of Abba Moses* 9, v 35ab is quoted in the inquiry of the monk Germanus as to why the doing of good deeds will cease at death:

> ... why ... will works of mercy ... be taken from us and not remain with their authors? Especially since the Lord himself promises the reward of the kingdom of heaven in exchange for these works, saying: For I was hungry and you fed me; I thirsted and you gave me to drink, and so forth. How, there-

fore, can those things which lead their performers into the kingdom of heaven be taken away?[389]

In the *Second Conference of Abba Moses* 2, v 35ab is likewise quoted in the context of a discussion as to whether, of all the virtues, almsgiving will bring a monk to God the quickest: " . . . some argue for the following of charity, that is, humanitarian deeds, because the Lord in the gospel promises very specially that for these he will give the kingdom of heaven, saying: For I was hungry and you fed me; I thirsted and you gave me to drink, and so forth."[390] The idea of limiting one's charity to brother monks or fellow Christians, as found in the works of other Egyptian ascetics such as Pachomius and Macarius, is not present in Cassian's account of Moses' conference. Whether this universalizing tendency is authentic or whether it reflects the filter of Cassian's own western "horizon," is unknown.

Peter Chrysologus (ca. AD 400 - 450)

This bishop of Ravenna, renowned for his oratory, refers to Matt 25:31-46 thirteen times in thirteen of his 176 extant sermons. Eight of these references are to the "identity dialogue." The majority of the quotations are of v 35 (*Sermons* 9. 4;[391] 14. 4;[392] 39. 4;[393] 41. 4;[394] 42. 6;[395] and 121. 4[396]). Characteristic of Peter's use of this verse is *Sermon* 41. 4, a Lenten homily, which portrays his vivid style, his famous *antitheses*, and clever turn of phrase:

> Man, give God what he wants if you want what you want from God given to you. I want mercy: it is the voice of God. God seeks mercy from us, and if we give [it], what will he say? What was read today: I was hungry and you fed me; I thirsted and you gave me to drink . . . . He who gives bread to the hungry will give himself a kingdom; he who denies a cup of water to the thirsty, will deny himself the fountain of life.[397]

Only once does Peter quote v 40 and, characteristic of what seems to be a universal outlook, it is without the restrictive τῶν ἀδελφῶν μου. It is found in the same *Sermon* 42. 6: "God in heaven eats the bread which the poor on earth have received. Whatever you did to one of these least, you did to me. Therefore, give bread, give drink, give clothing, give shelter, if you want to have God as a debtor and not as a judge."[398] There seems to be a universalism regarding the needy in these sermons of Peter. He never explicitly states that the Christian must be concerned with all, but one is left with the impression that his concern for the poor reaches beyond the boundaries of the church.

Only in one sermon are we left with the distinct impression that "the least" to be cared for are the preachers of the gospel, and that those who will be condemned for their neglect are the Jews. In *Sermon* 95. 5-6, commenting on the anointing of Jesus' feet just before his passion (Mark 14:3-9 par.; John 12:1-8), Peter alludes to vv 31-32, 40 and quotes vv 42, 43a in the context of a comparison between the synagogue and the church:

> Brothers, the church today hears Christ in the home of the Pharisee, that is, the synagogue, beset with every sorrow and total deception, suffering, crucified and buried. Nevertheless by such injury she is not held back from the fervor of the faith, but she carries the oil of Christian chrism. Because she did not deserve to see the physical face of Christ, she stands behind, not with regard to place, but time. She clings to his footsteps in order to follow [him], and she pours forth now tears of desire rather than conscience. The one she did not deserve to see leave, she deserves to see return. She, therefore, pours out tears on his feet which she drenches with overflowing love, when she holds in the hands of good works the feet of those who preach the good news of his kingdom. She washes with the tears of charity, she kisses with the lips of [her] testimony, and she pours out all the ointment of mercy, until, having turned to her--what does "having turned" mean? It means, having returned--he says to Simon, he says to the Pharisees, he says to those denying [him], he says to the people of the Jews: I entered your home and you did not give me water for my feet. When does he say this? When he will have come in the majesty of his Father and will have separated the just from the unjust, as a shepherd who separates sheep from

goats, he will say: I was hungry and you did not feed me; I thirsted and you did not give me to drink; I was a stranger and you did not take me in. Which is to say: You did not give water for my feet. She, however, when she washed my feet, anointed my feet, kissed my feet, did to slaves what you did not do to the Lord. She did to the feet what you denied to the head; she imparted to the least [minimis] what you refused to your author.[399]

Quodvultdeus of Carthage (d. AD 453)

In three of his works Quodvultdeus refers to the Matthean pericope six times, but only two references are to the "identity dialogue."

In *Dimidium temporis in signis Antichristi* 30, he quotes vv 31-34, 35a, 41 (according to the western variant: "Depart into the everlasting fire which my Father has prepared for the devil and his angels"), 42a, 45 and a variant of v 46 ("The unrighteous [impii] will go into eternal burning [ambustionem]; the just, however, into eternal life") to underscore his main point that there will be a day of judgment and we will be judged by our deeds of mercy.[400] He is not even concerned here with the identity of those to be aided.

In *Liber promissionum* 2.13, in the context of making his point that the almsgiving recommended by Christ is more effective than the sacrifices commanded in Leviticus, Quodvultdeus alludes to vv 33, 35ac, 36:

> This [i.e., almsgiving] is what extinguishes the eternal fires, this is what is opposed to sins, this is what feeds the hungry Christ in the poor [Christum pascit esurientem in paupere], this clothes the naked [vestit nudum], this visits the sick [visitat infirmum], this receives the stranger in hospitality [peregrinum hospitio recipit], this is what takes away every distress of prison [omnem angustiam carceris tollit] . . . this is what distinguishes the lambs from the goats . . . .[401]

Again, Quodvultdeus gives us no indication as to the identity of the needy. His main concern in the passage is the superiority of NT almsgiving over OT sacrifices.

In his *De symbolo* 1. 8, 5, discussing Christ's return to judge the living and the dead, he quotes v 41 and interprets it as applying to the Jews:

> He will come so that he who stood under judgment might judge. He will come in that form in which he was judged, so that the Jews might look upon the one they pierced, might recognize the one they denied ... so as to convince them the Truth might say: Behold the man whom you crucified, behold God and man in whom you were unwilling to believe .... You who were not redeemed by the price of my blood, you are not mine; depart from me into the eternal fire which was prepared for the devil and his angels.[402]

It is difficult to assess whether or not this use of v 41 reflects an understanding of the entire pericope in which the Jews are pitted against Christians and, in a reversal of the judgment they expect, are condemned, while the Christian Gentiles are saved. Most probably it does not. Quodvultdeus cites v 41 elsewhere (*Dimidium temporis* 30;[403] *Liber promissionum* 1.1; 2. 41[404]) with regard to Christian sinners and those who do not perform the mandated acts of charity.

Arnobius the Younger (d. after AD 455)

This semi-pelagian writer has one reference to the Matthean pericope in his extant works. In *Comm. in Ps.* 40, commenting on Ps 41:2, Arnobius quotes vv 42-43ac from what appears to be the VL:

> It is known to all that there are five senses in man: sight, hearing, smell, taste and touch. As well as all of these there is the intention, which becomes strong by the nourishment of wisdom and grows fat on the food of memory. This is what is treated, therefore, at the beginning of this psalm, so that it

might have regard for the needy and the poor. For everyone is able to see him [i.e., the needy and the poor], but, it says, unless he shall have had regard for the needy and the poor, he will not be blessed and on an evil day the Lord will not deliver him. For the real needy and poor one says: I was hungry and you did not feed me; I thirsted and you did not give me to drink [sitivi, et non potastis me]. I was a stranger and you did not take me in [hospes fui, et non suscepistis me]; I was ill and you did not take care of me. Blessed is the one who recognizes that the needy and the lowly is Christ . . . .[405]

There is nothing in the passage that betrays a restrictive outlook regarding the needy.

Patrick of Ireland (ca. AD 390 - 460)

In his *Confessions* 56, Patrick seems to allude to Matt 25:40: "Behold I now commend my life to my most faithful God for whom I am carrying out this mission, in spite of my lowliness. Because he is not a respecter of persons, he has chosen me for this office so that I might be [his] servant, one of his least [ut unus essem de suis minimis minister]."[406] Patrick's use of v 40 here is narrow, as he seems to equate himself in his missionary role to the Irish with the Matthean "least."

Valerian of Cemele (d. ca. AD 460)

Valerian has eight quotations from the "identity dialogue" in six of his 20 extant sermons. In every case, he is concerned with pastoral and moral issues, rather than doctrinal, and his outlook is universal. In *Homily* 7. 3-4, in the context of exhorting his listeners to increased almsgiving, he quotes vv 34-35ab, 36a:

> Without a doubt, however, the one who sends his treasures ahead of him to heaven, will be free of the punishments of the deep. Hear what God offers: Come, blessed of my Father, possess with me [mecum] the kingdom promised you from the beginning of the world. I was hungry and you fed me; I

thirsted and you gave me to drink; I was naked and you covered me [nudus eram et vestistis me].[407]

A few lines later he leaves no doubt as to the universality of his outlook. Asking who are to be the recipients of Christian charity, he states:

> ... all those related to us through the fact that they were born. Why should no person be excepted from our charity? Why is no selection to be made? Because something which is meeting a necessity does not require an order in the disbursement. Why do you need to ask whether the one who makes the request is Christian or Jew, heretic or pagan, Roman or foreigner, free man or slave? When necessity is pressing, you do not need to discuss the person. Otherwise, in separating out those unworthy of your charity, you may likewise lose the Son of God.[408]

This definite universalism of Valerian could also be manifest in his use of v 40. Both times that he quotes the verse (*Hom.* 4. 7 and 9. 4)[409] he does so without the restrictive τῶν ἀδελφῶν μου. The omission could be deliberate. An indication of this might be the fact that in *Hom.* 9. 4 he quotes v 40 in conjunction with Matt 10:42, and omits even the restrictive phrase εἰς ὄνομα μαθητοῦ from the latter.[410]

Leo the Great (d. AD 461)

The same pastoral use of Matt 25:31-46 that is found in the writings of Valerian is found in those of Leo the Great. Nine of his ninety-six extant sermons contain ten references to the Matthean pericope. In *Serm.* 9. 2, paraphrasing v 32, Leo interprets πάντα τὰ ἔθνη in the widest possible sense: "Peoples of all nations will be gathered before the throne of his power, and every human being whatsoever, born in all ages in the entire earth [quidquid hominum universis saeculis toto terrarum orbe progenitum est], will stand in the sight of the judge."[411]

There are six quotations of verses from the "identity dialogue." He quotes vv 35-36 (*Serm.* 45. 3);[412] v 42 (*Serm.* 18. 3);[413] and four times uses v 40. *Serm.* 45. 3[414] is the only instance where he quotes v 40 in its entirety. In *Serm.* 87. 4[415] and 94. 4[416] he uses a shortened version, omitting τῶν ἀδελφῶν μου as well as τῶν ἐλαχίστων: *Quod uni horum fecistis, mihi fecistis.* In *Serm.* 91. 3, in the context of a discussion of the necessity of being aware of Christ in the poor in the same way that we must be aware of his presence in the sacrament, Leo, in a use of the verse that is not often attested, quotes v 40 with τῶν ἀδελφῶν μου but without τῶν ἐλαχίστων:

> ... you should partake of the sacred table so that you might in no way waver concerning the truth of the body and blood of Christ. For what is believed by faith is consumed by mouth, and in vain do those who dispute what is received respond 'Amen.' As the prophet says: Blessed is he who has regard for the lowly and the poor. The one who is the praiseworthy distributor of clothing and food with regard to the needy is the one who knows that he is feeding and clothing Christ in the poor, for he himself says: As long as you did [it] to one of my brothers, you did [it] to me.[417]

In all of the above quotations there is no indication of any limitations to Leo's concept of Christian charity. It seems to be universal. That his compassion was in fact universal is proven in his own writings. In two sermons Leo clarifies his thinking with regard to the recipients of Christian almsgiving. In *Serm.* 89. 5 he states:

> Your benevolence should come to the aid of all the needy, whoever they might be; but be especially mindful of those who are members of the Body of Christ and who are united to us in the unity of the Catholic faith. For we owe more to those who are our own, by their participation in the same grace, than to others who have in common with us only the community of nature.[418]

The same sentiments of universal charity, with preference for Christians, are found in *Serm.* 41. 3:

> Although the poverty of the faithful is especially to be helped, those who have not yet received the Gospel are also to be pitied in their trouble: for the common bond of nature in all men must be loved. It obliges us to act kindly to those who, in any condition whatsoever, are subject to us, especially if they are already reborn by the same grace and redeemed by the same price of Christ's blood.[419]

Thus, as did Chrysostom, Leo saw the world in two concentric circles: Christians were to be given special care, but no one was to be excluded from Christian charity. As A. K. Squire states, "Nothing is more striking in Leo's penitential preaching, and indeed in his preaching as a whole, than his insistence upon the claim of all men to our compassion, simply on the ground of their being men."[420]

Epiphanius Latinus (fl. ca. AD 441 - 461)

In the work *Interpretatio evangeliorum* there are four references to Matt 25:31-46. The only references to the "identity dialogue" are found in chap 38, a long commentary on the Matthean judgment scene, in which almost every verse of the pericope is quoted or alluded to. Following the quotation of vv 31-32, we are told that πάντα τὰ ἔθνη is interpreted in its widest sense: "He who they said was a man will himself raise up and judge all peoples [omnes gentes], every person according to his works. Every race of mankind [omne genus hominum] will see him . . . ."[421]

Epiphanius' understanding of "the least" seems to be narrow. He quotes vv 35ab, 37 and 38b and then adds:

> The Lord is hungry not in himself but in his holy ones [sanctos suos]. The Lord is thirsty not in himself but in his poor [pauperes suos]. The Lord, who clothes all, is naked not in himself but in his servants [servos suos]. The Lord, who can heal all the sick and take away death itself, is sick not in him-

self but in his servants [servos suos]. The Lord, to whom belong the heavens and the earth, is a stranger not in himself but in his servants [servis suis]. Our Lord, who can free every man from tribulation, is in prison not in himself but in his holy ones [sanctos suos]. You see, therefore, beloved, that the holy ones [sancti] are not alone, but that the saints [sancti] suffer all these things because of the Lord, just as the Lord, on account of them, suffers all these things with them.[422]

A few lines later he quotes vv 40-42, 44 and 45 (with the addition of τῶν ἀδελφῶν μου!) and then states: "The Lord did not say to them: Depart from me, you cursed, because you perpetrated murder or committed adultery or robbery. No. But: I was hungry and thirsty in my servants and you did not minister to me."[423] In the above quotations it seems that Christians are meant to be the objects of charity. Surely, "holy ones" or "saints" would only be used of baptized Christians. It is highly probable that "servants" refers to the same group of people.

Prosper of Aquitaine (ca. AD 390 - 463)

This layman, who was a close friend of Leo the Great, produced many works in defense of the teaching of Augustine. He refers to Matt 25:31-46 12 times in three of his works, but only once refers to the "identity dialogue." His interpretation of "the least" in that one reference, possibly due to the influence of Augustine, is narrow. In *Expositio psalmorum* 140. 3, commenting on Ps 141:3 ("O Lord, set a watch before my mouth, a guard at the door of my lips."), Prosper links v 40 (surprisingly without τῶν ἀδελφῶν μου τῶν ἐλαχίστων) to Acts 9:4, which refers to the members of the church, and interprets it in the same restrictive sense:

> The head does not need this guard and this fortification, does he? Instead he pleads the cause of his body, and he asks for himself what will be useful for his members. For he is the one who said: Since you did [it] to one of these, you did [it] to me [Cum enim uni eorum fecistis, mihi fecistis], and to the one persecuting the church he says: Why do you persecute me?

He is the one who, in their persons, asks, saying: O Lord, set a watch before my mouth, a guard at the door of my lips.[424]

In *De vocatione omnium gentium* 2. 8, Prosper seems to give the impression that not only is πάντα τὰ ἔθνη of v 32 to be interpreted in the universal sense, but that by the day of judgment all those gathered for judgment will be Christian. Alluding to vv 31-33 he states:

> ... we read that when the Son of Man shall sit upon the seat of his majesty, before which all the nations [omnium gentium] will be gathered, he will place some on his right and others on his left. Those on his right will be praised for their works of charity, while to those on his left no other reproach will be made than their neglect of mercy and kindness. They also had received the faith but they did not practice charity; they will be condemned not for not having preserved, but for not having increased, the gift they received.[425]

Salvianus of Marseilles (ca. AD 400 - 480)

The three extant writings of this priest and orator contain only one reference to the "identity dialogue." In *Adversus avaritiam* 4. 20, an epistle written under the pseudonym of Timothy and addressed to the universal church, Salvianus quotes vv 35ab and 42 to encourage the wealthy to give their possesions to the church for the relief of the poor, and then says:

> None of his servants [nullus servorum suorum] is exiled, none is tormented by cold and want of clothing, with whom he is not suffering. Christ alone feels hunger with the hungry, and he alone feels thirst with the thirsty. Therefore, insofar as it pertains to his compassion, he is in need more than others. For every needy person is in need only for himself and in himself, but Christ alone begs in the universality of all the poor [in omnium pauperum universitate].[426]

In the same passage Salvianus writes: "[Christ] does not seek generosity for himself; he seeks it for his own [in suis] . . . ."[427] The above quotations are evidence of a universal interpretation of "the least." Salvianus certainly realizes that Christians are to be helped by the church (as evidenced by the expressions "his servants" and "his own"), but as did Leo and Chrysostom before him, he also sees every poor and needy person as the proper object of Christian charity when he writes "the universality of all the poor."

Faustus of Riez (ca. AD 408 - 490)

This theologian from the School of Lerins refers to Matt 25:31-46 13 times in ten different works. Eight of these references are quotations from the "identity dialogue," four of which (*De revelatione corporis beati Stephani* 7;[428] *Homily* 45. 5;[429] *Sermon* 15;[430] and *De spiritu sancto* 2. 4[431]) contain v 40 (always without τῶν ἀδελφῶν μου). These four passages contain nothing that would indicate that Faustus had a narrow concept of "the least." In fact, one of them could be interpreted to mean that he had a truly universal interpretation of the verse. In the sermon *De revelatione corporis beati Stephani* 7, alluding to vv 35a, 36a and quoting v 40, he says:

> Since our God testifies that he is clothed in the one who is cold [algente vestiri], fed in the hungry [esuriente refici] and honored in the poor - saying as much: Whoever has done [it] to one of these least, has done [it] to me [Qui fecit uni ex minimis istis, mihi fecit]--it follows that it must be believed that he would say and feel thus about his own chosen ones [de electis suis]: The reverence which anyone strives to give to my holy ones [sanctis meis], he renders to me. It is just that the one who honored me with his blood should be honored in my name.[432]

A contrast is evident in the above passage between "the least" [minimis], who are all human beings, and the "chosen ones" [electis], who obviously are the Christians.

In one passage, however, there is an indication that when Faustus quotes from the "identity dialogue," he might have only Christians in mind as the beneficiaries. In the treatise *De spiritu sancto* 2. 4, commenting on the unity that exists in the person of Christ, he gives v 35ab as an example:

> ... how can he [John the Evangelist] assert that before the passion, resurrection or day of ascension the Son of Man had descended from heaven and yet remain in the heavens, unless by the reasoning of truth this is solved through the unity of the person? Just as in another place the person of the head and the body is united, when it is said: I was hungry and you fed me, I thirsted and you gave me to drink. What does the unity of the person accomplish here? Man is fed and God is refreshed; the foot is comforted and the head testifies that it feels alleviation. [433]

It would be hard to imagine that Faustus would conceive of all mankind as the body of Christ. Most likely, in the above quotation he has Christians in mind. This single narrow use of a verse from the "identity dialogue," however, cannot justify the conclusion that Faustus held a narrow interpretation of "the least," especially in view of the universal use of v 40 already discussed, and the fact that out of eight references to the words of the "needy Christ" only one might lend itself to a narrow interpretation.

Avitus of Vienne (d. ca. AD 519)

In *Homily* 19, a sermon on the meeting of Zacchaeus and Jesus (Luke 19:1-10) given on the occasion of the dedication of the cathedral in Geneva, Avitus quotes vv 35c and 40 (without τῶν ἀδελφῶν μου):

> Because today the builder has recognized well his worth: I was a stranger and you received me and whatever you did to one of these least, you did to me--may Christ advance in hospitality, may he enter what he is drawn to, receive what is offered, bless what he instituted, restore what he promised.[434]

Avitus makes the distinction between the building and the land. Most likely he refers to the cathedral itself as opposed to the lands surrounding the cathedral that are to be used for the upkeep of the poor. Nowhere in the homily does he give an indication that his concern is only for the Christian poor.

Fulgentius of Ruspe (AD 468 - 533)

This thoroughgoing follower of Augustine referred to Matt 25:31-46 12 times in eight different works, but only two of his references are to the "identity dialogue."

In *De veritate praedestinationis* 2. 44, Fulgentius alludes to vv 35-36, 40 in the context of defending monks and others who, though held in low esteem by the world, will be on Christ's right hand:

> Who will dare call vessels of dishonor those stationed on the right to whom the Lord will give the kingdom because of this, that they fed him hungry and thirsty in his least, they clothed the naked, they received the stranger in hospitality, they visited the sick and the one put in prison [eum in suis minimis esurientem sitientemque paverunt, vestierunt nudum, susceperunt hospitio peregrinum, visitaverunt infirmum et in carcere constitutum]? Who dares to call vessels made for dishonor all those whom the potter himself says will go into eternal life?[435]

There is nothing here to indicate a narrowness of perspective regarding "the least."

In *Epistle* 19. 4, however, written to Faustinus, in a moving series of antitheses, Fulgentius gives the impression that by "the least" he might mean those who are Christian. After quoting vv 42-43, he states:

> If the one who does not visit the sick and imprisoned servants of Christ [famulos Christi] is relegated to eternal fire, what do we say is to be done to those who, either by the squalor of prisons or the banishment of exiles, violently afflict the ser-

vants of God [Dei famulos] who follow the sole truth of the faith?[436]

It would be difficult to comprehend the term "servants of Christ" as a description of those not Christian. In the above quotation Fulgentius is not contrasting "servants of Christ" with "servants of God who follow the sole truth of the faith," as one might too quickly conclude. The two terms are meant to describe one and the same reality: Christians. He is contrasting, rather, the idea of "not visiting," a sin of omission, with "afflicting," a sin of commission.

Remigius of Rheims (ca. AD 438 - 533)

In his *Testament* 1245-46, the bishop of Rheims, quotes vv 40 (omitting τῶν ἀδελφῶν, but keeping μου) and 45 in the context of a discussion of someone who undergoes excommunication:

> Let everything that the church is accustomed to repeat about the person of Judas, Christ's traitor, and about evil bishops be repeated about him through each and every church, because the Lord says: As often as you did [it] to one of my least, you did [it] to me; and as often as you did not do [it] to these, you did not do [it] to me. Therefore, let it not be doubted that what is approved in the head is to be understood in the members. . . .[437]

It seems that Remigius understands vv 40, 45 in a narrow sense and is using them here to bolster the unity between his metropolitan see and the suffragan sees dependent on him. Thus his argument would run: what is approved in the head (i.e., the see of Rheims) should be approved in the members (i.e., the suffragan sees) since Christ declares in Matt 25:40,45 that there is an identification between himself and his members.

Eugippius (ca. AD 455 - 535)

In the *Thesaurus Augustinianus*, a work of 352 chapters composed entirely from the writings of Augustine, Eugippius includes twelve references to Matt 25:31-46, but only three of them pertain to the "identity dialogue." Verse 40 is quoted in *Thes.* 180[438] and 242,[439] and v 45 is quoted in *Thes.* 142.[440] All three citations are used in a narrow sense, but, unfortunately, since they are taken from Augustine's works, they cannot strictly be used as evidence of Eugippius' understanding of "the least."

In the *Life of St. Severin*, which is his own composition, Eugippius has what may be an allusion to v 42a. When Severin learns that in a famine-stricken town a widow has been hoarding huge quantities of grain for her own use, he says to her sarcastically: "Help yourself, then, rather than the poor, with the goods which so far you have decided to hold back while Christ goes hungry [Quamobrem subveni tibi potius quam pauperibus, ex his quae adhuc te aestimas Christo esuriente servare]."[441] In this passage there is no indication of a narrow outlook regarding the poor.

Caesarius of Arles (ca. AD 470 - 542)

This great moral preacher refers to Matt 25:31-46 forty-two times in thirty of his original works,[442] most of them sermons. Twenty-one of the references are quotations from the "identity dialogue," and ten of these contain v 40. Everytime Caesarius quotes v 40 in his original sermons, he does so without τῶν ἀδελφῶν μου. This could be a deliberate reflection of his universal outlook.

There is only one passage in which Caesarius seems to use a verse from the "identity dialogue" in an exclusively narrow way. In *Sermon* 26. 3 he quotes vv 35bc, 36bc in the context of discussing Christ's union with persecuted and suffering Christians:

> See the Lord's goodness, brothers: now he is seated at the right hand of the Father in heaven, and still he deigns to work with us on earth. He does not shy away from being hungry with us, being thirsty with us, being cold with us, being a stranger with us, even dying or being cast into prison with us. Or is what I am suggesting perhaps not true, brothers? Let us

ask the Lord himself, and in his goodness he will deign to explain this more fully. I was thirsty, he says; I was a stranger, I was sick, I was in prison and you came to me.[443]

Yet, a few paragraphs later, in *Serm.* 26. 5, Caesarius quotes v 40 in a more neutral context in which one has the sense that any needy person may be in his mind: "For as often as a poor man approaches your home, without a doubt it is Christ who comes, the one who said: As often as you did [it] to one of these least, you did [it] to me."[444] This same neutral use of v 40 is found in six other passages: *Sermons* 46. 4;[445] 156.3;[446] 158.6;[447] 158A;[448] 228.6,[449] and *Epistle* 2.[450] No specific indication is given with regard to the identity of "the least," but there is the sense that Caesarius has all the needy in mind.

In two of his works v 40 is used in a specifically universal context. In *Serm.* 25.1 he states: "For God is cold and hungry in all the poor in this world [in hoc mundo in omnibus pauperibus], as he himself said: As often as you did [it] to one of these least, you did [it] to me."[451] In *Serm.* 199. 3, upbraiding those who never take a stranger into their spacious homes, he says: "What excuse shall we be able to give . . . unaware, rather not believing, that Christ is welcomed in every stranger [in omnibus peregrinis], as he himself said: As often as you did [it] to one of these least, you did [it] to me."[452] This same universal compassion is articulated in *Serm.* 29. 3-4, where Caesarius quotes vv 34-35a to make his point:

> What is true charity? That which loves all men [omnes homines] as itself. It is true charity which reaches out to enemies as well as to friends . . . if a man does not possess this charity, he will not be able to see God or deserve to hear: Come, you blessed, take possession of the kingdom; for I was hungry and you fed me . . . . Let us possess such great charity, brothers that we can love all men [omnes homines] with our whole hearts. If you love all mankind [totum genus humanum] as yourself, there will not remain a door through which sin can enter into you.[453]

In *Serm.* 27. 3, an appeal to the faithful to support monks and others who must give all of their time to spiritual pursuits, Caesarius quotes v 40 in a narrow sense in conjunction with Gal 6:10, and yet makes the point clearly that those beyond "the household of the faith" are also the proper beneficiaries of Christian charity. Speaking of the monks and the clergy as Christ's poor, he states:

> Therefore no one should hesitate to give to the poor, for the hand of the poor is Christ's treasury; what he receives on earth he stores up in heaven. Thus the Lord himself has also said: When you did [it] for one of these least, you did [it] for me. Let us listen to the apostle when he says: . . . do good to all men, but especially to those who are of the household of the faith. Who are of the household of the faith, brothers, if not good clerics, monks and all other servants of God who flee the hindrances of this life, are devoted to God, and engaged in reading and prayer? According to our means we must give to all who ask, but to God's servants who are ashamed to ask we must give even if they have not asked [Omnibus quidem petentibus, secundum quod possumus, dandum est: servis autem dei, qui petere a nobis erubescunt, etiamsi non petierunt, ingerendum est].[454]

Caesarius is not making a distinction here between monks who ask and monks who are ashamed to ask, but rather between all who might ask for assistance [omnibus quidem petentibus] and monks and clergy [servis autem dei], who are ashamed to ask. Thus it seems that even though Caesarius followed Augustine closely in many doctrinal matters, he was not all that influenced by him with regard to the use of the "identity dialogue." Caesarius held a much broader outlook concerning the scope of Christian charity than did Augustine.

In two of his sermons Caesarius gives us an insight into his understanding of those who will be gathered for judgment. Evidently it was his belief that only Christians were to be among the πάντα τὰ ἔθνη of v 32. In *Serm.* 157. 4, quoting v 42a, he asks his listeners to contemplate the reason why the goats will be condemned:

It is not going to be said: Because you committed murder, because you committed adultery, because you seized the property of another, but only this are they going to hear: For I was hungry and you did not feed me .... Believe most firmly that Christians and Catholics are going to hear it, if they will to persevere in evil deeds. Neither pagans nor heretics nor Jews are coming to judgment, because it is written of them: He who does not believe is already judged.[455]

Benedict of Nursia (ca. AD 480 - 550)

In his *Rule of the Monastic Life* Benedict has three references to Matt 25:31-46. The only narrow use of the "identity dialogue" is found in *Regula* 36. 2-3. Benedict quotes vv 36b and 40 (without τῶν ἀδελφῶν μου) to encourage his monks in their care of the sick members of the monastery: "Before all and above all it is necessary to care for the sick, serving them as though they were truly Christ, since he said: I was ill and you took care of me, and: What you did to one of these least, you did to me."[456]

In *Regula* 4.15-16, which contains an allusion to v 36ab,[457] and 53.1, which contains a quotation of v 35c, Benedict's understanding of those to be assisted is much more universal. In fact, in *Regula* 53.1 he gives concrete indication that even non-Christians are to be assisted by the monks:

All strangers who suddenly show up are to be welcomed as if they were Christ, since he will say: I was a stranger and you welcomed me; due honor is to be shown to all, especially to members of the household of the faith and strangers [et omnibus congruus honor exhibeatur, maxime domesticis fidei et peregrinis].[458]

In the above quotation, especially, Benedict shows the same approach to Christian charity that was first evidenced in the writings of Chrysostom: in the monks' exercise of charity Christian beneficiaries are to have priority, but their concern must also extend beyond the boundaries of the faith.

Anonymous Writings

Four anonymous works from the middle of the sixth-century, probably written by an Arian bishop of an unknown see,[459] contain quotations from the "identity dialogue." Three of them (*Homily* 20; *Sermons* 19 and 31) are found under the name Chrysostomus Latinus, and one (*Homily* 4) is attributed to Origenes Latinus.

In *Hom.* 4, commenting on Matt 6:17, Ps-Origen quotes v 40 (without τῶν ἀδελφῶν μου and with *pusillis* rather than *minimis*) to make his point that anointing the head is caring for the poor and needy:

> Anoint and arrange [your hair] by means of compassion for the poor [and] almsgiving for the needy. By means of those things, therefore, anoint your head, your Lord Christ, so that he might say to you: When you did [it] to one of these tiny ones, you did [it] to me [Quando fecisti uni ex pusillis istis, mihi fecisti.[460]

There is no indication in the passage of a restrictive horizon regarding those who benefit from the Christian's charity. If the term *pusillis* was attracted to Matt 25:40 from Matt 18:6 where it is used in a narrow way (. . . unum de pusillis istis qui in me credunt . . .), it could be an indication that the author had the same narrow outlook here; but the evidence is too scanty to come to any conclusion in that direction.

The same nonrestrictive attitude is present in the works of Chrysostomus Latinus. In *Sermon* 31 he quotes vv 42-43 (with his own interpolation) in the context of describing pharisaical Christians:

> . . . they look down on strangers, they despise the naked, they do not reach out to the poor. What do these look forward to in the future, if not that sentence about which the Lord spoke: I was hungry and you did not feed me; I thirsted and you did not give me to drink; I was naked and you did not cover me; in sorrow and you did not comfort me [in tribulatione, et non es-

tis me consolati]; ill and you did not visit; in prison and you did not come?[461]

Verses 42-43, with the same interpolation found in the above passage, are likewise used in *Serm.* 19 in the context of the author's commentary on Ps 91:7 ("Though a thousand fall at your side, ten thousand at your right side . . . ") where he states that those who fall fall from the right side and end up on the Lord's left side to hear the words of condemnation.

In *Hom.* 20, commenting on the hungry Jesus who came looking for figs and found none (Matt 21:18-22), Ps-Chrysostom uses v 35a in a different sense than Matthew. The concrete identification between Christ and "the least" has disappeared as the author interprets the verse in a strictly spiritual sense:

> There is in the tree, however, a likeness of man to whom the Lord comes, hungry. What does the Lord who hungers for man desire be given him, if not what he himself gave to God the Father? My food, he said, and my drink is that I should do the will of him who sent me . . . . The duties of the servant are the rich food of the Lord. You work hard [at them] and the Lord is nourished; you are obedient and the Son of God is richly fed. I was hungry, he said, and you gave me to eat.[462]

From the Second Council of Constantinople to the End of the Patristic Era
(AD 554 - 750)

Eastern Writers

Nicephorus of Antioch (sixth century AD)

In his *Life of Simeon Stylites the Younger* 4. 32, Nicephorus quotes v 40 (without τῶν ἀδελφῶν μου) in the context of a talk given by Simeon to his followers:

> Indeed almsgiving is accustomed to obtain mercy for those who are merciful towards the needy and to free them from

serious difficulties. Christ himself testifies and says that mercy shown to a poor man is to be considered shown to himself. For he says: As often as you did [it] to one of these least, you did [it] to me. This is true to such an extent that the one who does not have mercy on his brother is to be considered as having publicly denied the Son of God . . . .[463]

There is nothing in the talk to indicate a narrow interpretation of "the least." The term "brother" in the above quotation could be used in a universal sense, for a few lines later Simeon speaks of "regarding everyone as one and seeing Christ in everyone."[464]

John Climacus (ca. AD 570 - 649)

In his *Ladder of Paradise*, inveighing against an activism that he considered to be destructive of the contemplative life, John Climacus twice quotes from the "identity dialogue." In chap. 13 he quotes v 36b as an example of the type of incentive that listlessness would employ to get a monk to leave his cell: "The entertaining of guests is the suggestion of listlessness and it encourages that alms be given by the work of one's own hands. It eagerly recommends that the sick be visited, calling to mind the one who said: I was ill and you took care of me."[465] This same polemic against activism is present in chap. 26, scholion 25, where v 35a is quoted as the basis of those who would not recognize the value of contemplative activity: "[The activist] says that activity devoid of manual labor is without reward and is easily undone. Excuses are contrived as the reason for his works. That saying of Christ: You gave me to eat, and what follows, are the works and kinds of works [to be done]."[466] There is no indication in the above passages as to the identity of those to be cared for.

Anastasius Apocrisiarius (ca. AD 655)

This friend of Maximus the Confessor refers once to Matt 25:31-46 in his few extant works. In his *Letter to Theodosius* 8, evidently written from exile, he recounts his sufferings and quotes vv 34, 35c in the context of describing hospitality received from a fellow Christian and his family:

> May [Christ] make them worthy of that place which in the future is to be on the right and capable of hearing that divine and meek voice which will say: Come, blessed of my Father, inherit the kingdom prepared for you from the beginning of the world: because I was a stranger and you welcomed me, and so forth.[467]

Anastasius can be said to use v 35c here in a narrow way, since he is applying the verse to his own experience of having received hospitality.

Maximus the Confessor (ca. AD 580 - 662)

This staunch adversary of Monotheletism has eight references to the Matthean pericope in six of his extant works, but only three of these are references to the words of the needy Christ. The only rather complete quotation from the "identity dialogue" is of v 40 (without τῶν ἀδελφῶν μου) and is found in *Mystagogia* 24: "Indeed Scripture has shown that the one who is in need of help . . . is God. For whatever you have done, it says, to one of these least, you have done to me. God is the one speaking . . . ."[468] There is nothing in the passage to indicate that Maximus is speaking only of Christian poor.

The same seemingly universal outlook is found in two other works in a partial quotation of and an allusion to the "identity dialogue." In *Epistle* 1 he alludes to vv 35-36:

> You were the eye of the blind and the foot of the lame and the father of the invalid. You shattered the millstones of the wicked and from the midst of their teeth you plucked the booty. The main thing, I might say, is that you feed the hun-

gry, you give drink to the thirsty, you welcome strangers, you cover the naked, you visit the sick and you minister to those who are in prison [πεινῶντας διατρέφεις, καὶ διψῶντας ποτίζεις, καὶ ξένους περιστέλλεις, καὶ γυμνοὺς περιβάλλεις, καὶ ἀσθενοῦντας ἐπισκέπτῃ, καὶ τοῖς ἐν φυλακαῖς διακονεῖς].[469]

In *Capita de caritate*, scholion 17, he gives a partial quotation of vv 40, 45: "In truth the Lord shows in the gospels that to be ill-disposed towards one's neighbor is against the will of God, when he says: Whatsoever you have done or whatsoever you have not done, listing the different kinds of love and hatred."[470]

Antiochus the Monk (seventh century AD)

This monk of the famed St. Sabas Monastery in Palestine has eight references to Matt 25:31-46 in his moral work *Pandecta Scripturae Sacrae*, six of them to the "identity dialogue."

Four of the quotations are in contexts which lead one to believe that Antiochus has his fellow monks or fellow Christians in mind. In *Pan.* 60, speaking of the care needed not to bring sorrow upon anyone, he quotes vv 40, 45 in conjunction with the more restrictive Johannine and Pauline concepts of community:

> The one who loves his brother, loves God; whoever does not love his brother does not love God, according to the Apostle John. It is then clear that the one who grieves his brother, grieves God. For it says: Do not grieve the Holy Spirit with whom you were sealed [Eph 4:30] . . . . Again: Whatever you have done to one of these least, my brothers, you have done to me. And: Whatever you have not done to one of these, you have not done to me.[471]

The same sense that Antiochus is speaking of intracommunity harmony, either in his monastery or in the wider Christian community, is found in *Pan.* 88 (where he quotes vv 40, 45 in the context of service to those in the monastery);[472] *Pan.* 97 (where he links vv 35, 36a with Heb 13:1-2, Titus 3:13 and Rom 16:23

which are expressions of Christian hospitality);[473] and *Pan.* 99 (where he quotes v 36bc together with Gal 6:10 and Phil 4:15-16,18b, Paul's expression of gratitude for assistance received from fellow Christians).[474]

In *Pan.* 91 Antiochus rearranges v 40 and uses it in a neutral sense. In a discourse about the necessity to empathize with someone in trouble, he comments on the meaning of Qoh 9:8 (. . . spare not the perfume for your head): " . . . by means of the poor pour out the perfume of your almsgiving upon your head, Christ. For he is our head who says: To me have you done whatever you did to the least, my brothers ['Εμοὶ ἐποιήσατε ὅσα τοῖς ἐλαχίστοις τοῖς ἀδελφοῖς μου ἐποιήσατε]."[475] There is no indication here of a narrow interpretation of "the least."

In *Pan.* 99 Antiochus quotes vv 35ac, 36b and alludes to v 36c and tells us implicitly that his viewpoint his universal:

> I was a stranger, he says, and you welcomed me. I was hungry and you fed me; I was ill and you took care of me. The one, therefore, who visits those in sickness or in prisons [ἐν φυλακαῖς] or in difficulties, visits God the Word who became poor for our sakes, as he himself testifies. It is clear and incontestable to everyone that it is a beautiful thing to visit orphans and widows in their distress and those with many children, above all those of the household of the faith [μάλιστα δὲ πρῶτον καὶ τοὺς οἰκείους τῆς πίστεως].[476]

By his explicit mention of charity to fellow Christians in the above passage, in contrast to charity to everyone, Antiochus gives evidence of his universal interpretation of "the least," even though he would give preference to Christian needs.

Anastasius of Sinai (ca. AD 630 - 700)

In his *Questions and Answers* 14, responding to whether it is more useful to give money to the church or to the poor, Anastasius quotes the beginning of v 34 and alludes to vv 35c, 36ac to explain that the poor are always in need, while many churches are already too wealthy: "The Lord, praising those who were on his right by saying: Come, blessed of my Father, was mindful of nothing else except almsgiving to the poor and strangers [ξένους] and the naked [γυμνοὺς] and those in prison [ἐν φυλακῇ]."[477] There is nothing in Anastasius' own words that would indicate a narrow viewpoint. In the catena of opinions from the Fathers that follows this answer, however, he quotes Chrysostom[478] and Basil the Great,[479] both of whom use verses from the "identity dialogue" in a narrow way. It is uncertain whether this inclusion of a narrow use of the "identity dialogue" found in the works of previous Fathers in any way reflects Anastasius' own understanding of "the least."

Germanus of Constantinople (ca. AD 634 - 733)

This first bishop to denounce publicly the Iconoclasts has two references to Matt 25:31-46 in a Good Friday sermon, *In dominici corporis sepulturam*. Germanus quotes vv 34, 35c, 36ab, interpolating his own additions by which he interprets the Matthean acts in the most literal sense, and applies them to Christ in the circumstances of his death and burial:

> Let us imitate Joseph and Nicodemus, those beautiful hosts of Christ who were more illustrious than Abraham himself. For they did not unknowingly receive in hospitality angels, but the very Lord of angels. Rewarding them for their kindness, he will say: Come, blessed of my Father. Inherit the kingdom prepared for you, for I was naked and you covered me, clothing [me] with burial shrouds. Sick due to the voluntary crucifixion and the agony of death, and you visited me. A stranger and dead, and you welcomed me, concealing [me] in a new tomb.[480]

A few paragraphs further, however, he restores the Matthean identity between Christ and the poor. He quotes v 40 in the context of arguing that the Christian can participate in the deeds of Joseph of Arimathea and Nicodemus by their concern for the needy they meet every day:

For the beggar who stands outside your door, that one full of sores, sick and with torn clothing, bears the person of Christ: whatever consideration you extend to him is transferred to the one who sits at the right hand of the Father. For that promise of his is true: Whatever you did to one of these least, my brothers, you did to me.[481]

Germanus gives no indication in this work that his understanding of "the least" is restrictive.

Andrew of Crete (ca. AD 660 - 740)

In *Oratio 7*, a sermon about the Lord's Transfiguration, Andrew quotes vv 35-36 to prove his point that, just as Christ, the Wisdom of God, created everything in six days, so he enumerated six different types of human kindness that he accepts as done to himself.[482] He then alludes to the six Matthean acts in vv 35-36 and quotes v 40 (without τῶν ἀδελφῶν μου) to underscore his point that every disciple must come down from the Mount of Transfiguration and serve the transfigured Christ in those who are in need:

> ... thus shall he give food and drink to the hungry and thirsty Christ [θρέψει μὲν καὶ ποτίσει Χριστὸν πεινῶντα καὶ διψῶντα], the salvation of all ... thus by means of the needy he shall possess him who lives in *all who receive him in faith*. He will welcome him, a stranger; he will clothe him, naked; he will heal him, sick, and he will not overlook him, detained in prison [διὰ τῶν δεομένων τὸν πᾶσιν εἰσοικισθέντα τοῖς λαβοῦσιν αὐτὸν διὰ τῆς πίστεως· συναγάγοι δὲ ξενιτεύοντα, ἐνδύσει δὲ γυμνητεύοντα, θεραπεύσει δὲ ἀσθενοῦντα, καὶ ἐν φυλακῇ καθειργμένον οὐ παρόψεται] ... by an affection for what is external he shall not place boundaries on the kindness of the loving Lord—for this is what is meant, I dare to say, with regard to what is written: As often as you did [it] to one of these least, you did [it] to me—but he will penetrate to the interior of what is seen and give attention to spiritual sufferings and be concerned about a proper cure.[483]

If the italics in the above quotation are taken to refer to Christ living in the faithful who are needy, then Andrew is using these verses from the "identity dialogue" in a narrow sense. If they are interpreted to refer to Christ living in the Christian benefactor, then the above use of vv 35-36, 40 gives no indication on Andrew's part of a restrictive understanding of "the least."

John Damascene (ca. AD 675 - 749)

John of Damascus, traditionally considered the last of the Eastern Fathers, refers to Matt 25:31-46 fifteen times in five of his works. Only two of these references are to verses from the "identity dialogue." In the *Life of Barlaam and Joasaph* 9.71, in the context of proving that there will be reward and punishment for the deeds done in one's lifetime, he quotes vv 31-36, in conjunction with Matt 10:42, and then adds: "Why does he say this? Because he considers the kind acts we do to the needy [εἰς τοὺς δεομένους] as done to himself."[484] Even though John quotes vv 35-36 in conjunction with the more restrictive Matt 10:42, there is no other indication that he considers the needy here in a restrictive sense.

This same neutral viewpoint is found six chapters later, in *Barlaam and Joasaph* 15.126, where he alludes to v 40:

> In various places the Master mentions almsgiving and generosity to the poor [τῶν πενήτων], as we learn in the Gospel. Thus you should most assuredly send your entire treasure ahead of you by the hands of the needy [ταῖς τῶν δεομένων χερσίν], for whatever you shall do to these the Master considers done to himself [ὅσα γὰρ εἰς τούτους ποιήσεις, ἑαυτῷ ὁ Δεσπότης οἰκειούμενος] and will reward you many times over.[485]

As in the previous passage, there is no indication here of a restrictive viewpoint with regard to the identity of "the least."

Western Writers

Cassiodorus (ca. AD 485 - 580)

This statesman-turned-monk has 46 references to Matt 25:31-46 in his *Expositio psalmorum,* but only four of these references pertain to the "identity dialogue." The remainder of the references are to vv 34, 41 and 46 and are inserted whenever there is any mention of future reward or punishment.

In *Expositio* 49. 7[486] and 80. 9-10,[487] Cassiodorus quotes v 35ab in a neutral sense as an example of the kind of testimony that God will give about his faithful at the judgment. In these quotations we are given no information about the identity of those who were helped by Christian generosity.

In *Expositio* 58.17, however, he quotes v 40 (without τῶν ἀδελφῶν μου) in what appears to be a restrictive sense. Commenting on the meaning of the words "you have become my support" in Ps 59:17, he states:

> He [the psalmist] has exposed how humanity has rejoiced in Christ the Lord, for he [Christ] has become my [humanity's] support. For he [Christ] is acknowledged when the entire church is saved. That is the meaning of the statement: If anyone has done [it] to one of these least, he has done [it] to me.[488]

Even though Cassiodorus' exegesis is sometimes hard to follow, it is evident in the above quotation that he is linking Christ and his church and that here he understands "the least" of v 40 as members of Christ, i.e. of the church.

The same narrow interpretation of "the least" is found in *Expositio* 40. 2. Speaking of almsgiving in general, Cassiodorus quotes Luke 6:30a ("Give to all who beg from you") to underline his point that in almsgiving the giver is not to be concerned with the receiver's merits or lack thereof, but is to give to all. But then he states that greater care must be taken to be generous to holy men (presumably monks), and he quotes v 40 (without τῶν ἀδελφῶν μου) to buttress his argumentation: "But greater care is to be given that we should come to the relief of holy men in any need because of Christ our Lord, who in his own judgment will say about his own poor: Who has done [it] to one of these least, has done [it] to me."[489]

Council of Mâcon (AD 585)

Decree 11 of the Council of Mâcon alludes to v 35c to encourage bishops and laity alike to be practitioners of hospitality:

> Not only does the Lord Jesus admonish us to be practicers of hospitality when he says he was received in the guest [cum se dicit in hospidem (sic) receptum fuisse], but also his apostle in almost all his commands. Therefore, most blessed brothers, each one of us should exhort to this work not only himself, but also the minds of all the faithful, so that by works of mercy they might be able to intercede with God for our sins and reconcile us to him by means of true hospitality.[490]

There is no indication in this conciliar decree that only Christians or especially Christians are to be received as guests.

Gregory of Agrigentum (d. ca. 594)

In his *Explanatio super Ecclesiasten* 2.12, commenting on Qoh 2:24, Gregory quotes v 40 to show the evil involved in building up assets for oneself while neglecting the needs of the poor:

> Growing rich, however, in any way one can and using the produce of wealth for oneself and one's own needs without allowing the needy and the poor to be partakers of it is evil and the bearer of evil rewards. For it was concerning them that the Lord said: As often as you did [it] to one of these least, my brothers, you did [it] to me.[491]

There is no indication here of a restrictive understanding of "the least."

Gregory of Tours (ca. AD 540 - 594)

Gregory has two references to Matt 25:31-46 in *Lives of the Fathers*, a hagiographical work of twenty biographies. In *Vitae patrum* 4. 4, describing the charity of Bishop Quintianus, he alludes to v 40:

> [Quintianus] was magnificent in almsgiving. Whenever he saw any poor man whatsoever crying out, he would say: Hurry, I pray, hurry and minister to the poor man the necessary means of livelihood ... perhaps it is he who in the gospel commanded that he be fed in the least of the poor [forsitan ipse est qui se per evangelicae lectionis seriem reficiendum in pauperibus minimis esse mandavit].[492]

In *Vitae patrum* 11, writing of Abbot Aridius, Gregory quotes vv 36c and 40 (without τῶν ἀδελφῶν but maintaining μου):

> When Aridius heard that many were imprisoned under sentence of death in a certain city, he was mindful of the word of the Lord which said: I was in prison and you came to me, and: As often as you did [it] to one of my least ones, you did [it] to me, and he wondered if there were any way he might be able to free them.[493]

Gregory manifests no indication of a narrow understanding of "the least."

Leander of Seville (ca. AD 550 - 600)

In *De institutione virginum et contemptu mundi* 4, a rule for women religious written for his sister Florentina, the Archbishop of Seville quotes v 36b in order to encourage the nuns to care for their sick sisters in the monastery: "If a sister is ill, help her with zealous and kind attendance ... consider that the illnesses of the sisters and their weakness are your own suffering, so that you may well hear the words of the Lord, who felt in his own body the wounds and cures of his people: I was ill and you took care of me."[494] Obviously, since Leander is concerned here with the care of religious women, his use of v 36b can be considered narrow.

Gregory the Great (ca. AD 540 - 604)

Scattered throughout eight different works of Gregory the Great are 26 references to Matt 25:31-46. Twelve of these references are to the "identity dialogue:" eight quotations can be classified as neutral, three narrow and one, possibly, universal.

The majority of the references to the words of the needy Christ are found in Gregory's *Moralia*, a moral exposition of the Book of Job. In *Moralia* 6. 7, 9;[495] 6. 30, 48;[496] 15. 31, 37;[497] 26. 27, 51;[498] and *Epistle* 12. 2[499] he quotes vv 35-36 in a neutral manner. He gives no indication as to the identity of those to be helped. The same open-endedness is found in *Moralia* 15.19, 23[500] and 26. 27, 50,[501] where Gregory quotes vv 42-43 to make his point that those who steal from the poor will be punished more severely than those who fail to give to the poor.

Gregory quotes v 40 five times. In *Homilia in evangelia* 40.12[502] and *Epistle* 12. 2,[503] his use is neutral, that is, he gives no indication whether the poor are everybody or Christians only. In three instances, however, he uses v 40 in a narrow context. In *Moralia* 16. 2. 2, commenting on Job 22:3, he states:

> ... [God] has no need of the wealth of a servant. On the contrary he confers, rather than receives, goodness, so that the goodness that has been offered is not of use to him, but rather to those who receive it and then to those who give it. Without a doubt, when he comes to judge, the Lord says: As often as you have done [it] to one of these least, my brothers, you have done [it] to me. It is with extraordinary tenderness, out of compassion for his own, that Christ says this. And because of this he who is our head, he who is helped in his own members by our good deeds, helps us.[504]

The same restrictive use of v 40 is found in *Epistle* 9.226. Writing in AD 599 to a certain Asclepiodotus in Gaul, Gregory quotes v 40 (without τῶν ἀδελφῶν μου) to encourage him to give aid, sustenance and support to Hilary, a fellow Christian: "For whoever relieves an afflicted brother frees the captive [brother] or consoles the sorrowing [brother], is repaid by the very one to whom, without a doubt, the entire thing is done. For he says: What you did to one of these least, you did to me."[505] In *Homilia in evangelia* 23. 2, his use of v 40, in conjunction with v 35c, likewise seems narrow. He quotes v 35c in conjunction with Heb 13:1-2 and 1 Pet 4:9, quotations that have to do with intracommunal charity. Then he tells the tale of the head of a family who was accustomed to showing hospitality. One day an unfamiliar guest appeared and was led to the table. When the host turned around to get the pitcher of water to wash his hands, the guest disappeared. That same night the Lord appeared to the host in his dreams and said:

> On other days you received me in my members; yesterday, however, you received me myself. Behold, coming for judgment he will say: Whatever you did to one of these least, you did to me. Behold, before the judgment when he is welcomed in his members, he looks for his hosts himself; yet, nonetheless, we are lazy when it comes to the grace of hospitality.[506]

There is an indication, however, that Gregory might have a truly universal understanding of the "identity dialogue." In his *Book of Pastoral Rule* 3. 20 he quotes vv 42-43 to make the same point he makes in his *Moralia* 15.19, 23:[507] if those who do not give to the poor will be punished severely, then how much more culpable will be those who defraud and steal from the poor. The quotation is found in the context of a discussion as to whether the poor who are wicked should be the object of a Christian's charity. Gregory quotes Luke 6:30a ("Give to all who beg from you . . . "), but then qualifies his apparent universality by appealing to Sir 12:4a ("Give to the good man, refuse the sinner . . . ") and Tob 4:17b (. . . "do not share them [i.e., your bread and wine] with sinners"). He must have had second thoughts about this restrictiveness, however, since he further qualifies his position, stating that a Christian can give to the wicked if he looks, not upon their sin, but upon their human nature: "For he distributes his bread to the needy sinner, not because he is a sinner, but because he is a man; he certainly does not support a sinner, but a poor just man, for he loves in him not the sin but [his] nature."[508] Even though Gregory never explicitly tackles the question of whether non-Christians should receive Christian charity, it stands to reason that his argument of the superiority of human nature in the above quotation would be reflective of a totally universal outlook.

In *Homilia in evangelia* 19. 5[509] and *Moralia* 26. 27, 50-51,[510] Gregory indicates that, as did Caesarius of Arles, he believes only Christians will be judged. Gregory understands πάντα τὰ ἔθνη of v 32 as all humanity, but he divides the two main classes of people, the elect and the reprobate, into two further classes in each category: the judged and the unjudged. Only believers are to be included among the goats. Unbelievers have already been judged by their unbelief. They will rise, says Gregory, not for judgment but for torment. Those who will hear the words of condemnation from the judge are those Christians without sufficient good works.[511]

By the same token, among the elect are the sheep who will be judged and those who, having no need of judgment, will be co-judges with the Lord. Gregory says that these elect who have no need of judgment are those who have surpassed the precepts of the law by the perfection of virtue. They are the ones (presumably the monks) who have given up everything to follow Christ.[512]

Isidore of Seville (ca. AD 560 - 636)

There are nine references to Matt 25:31-46 in the works of Isidore, three of them to the "identity dialogue."

In *Quaestiones in Vetus Testamentum* 4.1, commenting on Gen 2:24, Isidore says it refers to Christ who left his Father in heaven and his mother, Judaism, in order to cling to his wife, the church. Then, quoting v 40 (without τῶν ἀδελφῶν μου), he indicates that he understands "the least" to be Christians: "From then on we have accepted in Christ the precept that Adam accepted figuratively, because every single Christian uniformly bears the person of Christ, for the Lord himself said: What you have done to one of these least, you have done to me."[513]

In *Liber Sententiarum* 3.60,10 he quotes vv 35-36a, 41-42 to underscore his point that almsgiving removes sin and that the absence of charity in one's life will result in condemnation.[514] There is no indication here of a restrictive viewpoint.

In *De ecclesiasticis officiis* 5.19, expounding on the duty a bishop has to be hospitable, Isidore quotes v 35c in a context that might indicate he has a universal outlook with regard to those received as guests:

> His hospitality should be outstanding, so that he might welcome everyone [omnes] with kindness and charity. For if all the faithful desire to hear what is in the gospel: I was a stranger and you took me in, how much more the bishop, whose home ought to be the shelter of all [cunctorum]. A layman has fulfilled the duty of hospitality by receiving one or two [guests]; a bishop, however, unless he shall have received everyone [omnes], is inhuman.[515]

Donatus of Besançon (ca. AD 592 - 651)

In his *Regula ad virgines*, a rule for women religious, Donatus quotes vv 36b, 40 in a narrow sense, encouraging care of the sick nuns: "As we already said above, care for the sick sisters should be displayed above and before all else. Let them be served as if it were Christ, for he himself said: I was ill and you took care of me; and: What you have done to one of these least, my brothers, you have done to me."[516]

Valerius of Bancona (ca. AD 655)

In *Opuscula* 12, a discussion of false and hypocritical monks, Abbot Valerius quotes v 40 (without τῶν ἀδελφῶν but maintaining μου) in a narrow context as he equates "the least" with the faithful monks: ". . . despising God, they [the false monks] obey the devil . . . but to the Lord, whose most faithful servants they persecute and hate, who said: What you did to one of my least, you did to me, to him they are enemies, runaways, hateful and strangers."[517]

Eligius of Noyon (fl. AD 640 - 658)

Eligius has two references to the "identity dialogue" in his extant sermons. In *Homily* 9, a sermon on the Good Samaritan, he quotes v 40 in the context of encouraging Christians to give of their own food and drink to the poor so that they might hear those words from Christ at the judgment.[518] In *Homily* 11, a sermon on almsgiving, Eligius includes vv 35ab, 36a and 40 in a catena of scriptural quotations lauding the benefits of charity.[519] In neither sermon is there any indication of a restrictive outlook on his part. Eligius appears to have all the needy in mind.

Fructuosus of Braga (ca. AD 600 - 665)

In his *Regula monastica communis* 10, laying down regulations for abbots of monasteries, Bishop Fructuosus quotes v 35c in a narrow sense since he understands it to refer to monks: "[Abbots] are to live at one common table with their brothers who are guests and travellers, because it was of them that the Lord said: I was a stranger and you took me in."[520]

Waldebertus of Luxeuil (ca. AD 629 - 670)

In his *Regula ad virgines* 3, a rule for the women religious of his diocese, Waldebertus quotes v 40 (without τῶν ἀδελφῶν μου) in the context of discussing the duties of the monastic porter or gatekeeper: "Among other duties they are to have care for the poor, strangers and guests: for in these Christ is received, as he himself says: Whatever you did to these least, you did to me."[521] There is no restrictiveness of outlook here.

Audoenus of Rouen (ca. AD 609 - 683)

In his *Life of St. Eligius* 15, Audoenus three times refers to the "identity dialogue." He first quotes vv 35c, 40 in the context of describing the necessity of the Christian to love everyone, even the enemy, and of being receptive to all.[522] A few pages later in the same chapter, he again quotes v 40 in the midst of a discussion on tithing. In this instance Audoenus is a little clearer with regard to his universalism:

> ... do not be selective when it comes to showing mercy, lest by chance you pass over someone who is worthy to receive, for you do not know into whom Christ deigns to come. Know that whatever you offer to the poor or stranger on earth, you give to the one sitting in heaven who said: Whoever receives you, receives me; and, As often as you did [it] to one of my least ones, you did [it] to me.[523]

Even though v 40 is quoted here in conjunction with Matt 10:40a, which refers to Christ's disciples, the tenor of the whole work calls for a wide understanding of "the least."

The third quotation from the "identity dialogue" is found a few pages later and occurs in the midst of a realistic description of the judgment. Audoenus quotes vv 31-40, but he is not concerned here with almsgiving. His main focus is the certainty and universality of judgment. He tells us that his understanding of πάντα τὰ ἔθνη in v 32 is the widest possible: "all nations under heaven will be summoned ... every person, both male and female ... the good and the evil, saints and sinners, everyone born from the beginning of the world ...."[524]

Julian of Toledo (d. AD 690)

In his *Prognosticon futuri saeculi* 3. 33 Julian quotes vv 35a, 42a. Influenced by the commentaries of Gregory the Great and Isidore of Seville, he divides all those present on the day of judgment into four categories: the Christian perfect who have left everything to follow Christ and will not be judged but will be co-judges with him; the Christian elect who will be judged and saved, to whom Matt 25:34-36 will be addressed;[525] those outside the church who will not be judged and will perish; and Christians who will be judged and perish and will hear Matt 25:41-43.[526] Julian gives no consideration at all to the identity of those who are helped or neglected by Christians.

Bede the Venerable (ca. AD 673 - 735)

The last of the Western Fathers has thirty-four references to Matt 25:31-46 scattered throughout seventeen of his works. Fifteen of these references are to the "identity dialogue," seven of which are quotations of v 40.

Bede is important because he is one of the few Fathers to have written a commentary on the Gospel of Matthew as such.[527] In that commentary, *In Matthaei evangelium expositio* 4. 25, Bede states that πάντα τὰ ἔθνη of v 32 is to be understood in its widest sense. As did Gregory the Great, Isidore of Seville and Julian of Toledo before him, Bede believes that only Christians will be subject to the judgment. All those who are outside the church will perish without being judged; while those who left everything to follow Christ will be co-judges with him.[528]

Commenting on vv 35-36, Bede interprets the six Matthean works allegorically and says they can be understood to refer also to spiritual works of mercy:

> In truth according to a higher understanding they show the perfection of charity, by which the one hungering and thirsting for justice is refreshed with the bread of the word and the drink of divine wisdom; and by which the one straying from the way of the truth is led by penitence into the hospitality of Mother Church; and by which the one who is sick in faith is tended to, and by which the one placed in the prison of difficulties, tribulations and sorrow is uplifted by the help of consolation.[529]

Commenting on v 40, Bede quotes from Jerome's *Commentary on Matthew* 25. 33[530] to indicate that he understands "the least" in the same restrictive manner: "As often as you did [it] to one of these brothers of mine, and so forth. It seems that this is spoken about the poor in spirit to whom, stretching forth his hand, he had said: My brothers and my mother are the ones who do the will of my Father who is in heaven."[531]

This same narrow understanding of "the least" is found in four other passages where Bede quotes v 40. In his *Commentary on the Song of Songs* 5. 6, expounding on the meaning of Cant 6.1, he states:

> He [Christ] feeds in gardens because they are his members to whom the fruits of justice are done; and not only should physical almsgiving be understood here, but spiritual as well, since he predicted he would say at the judgment: As often as you did [it] to one of these least, my brothers, you did [it] to me.[532]

In his *Commentary on Luke* 3.10,16, Bede alludes to v 40, linking it to Luke 10:16 which refers to the disciples: " 'He who rejects you, rejects me' can be understood in this way: the one who does not show mercy to one of my least brothers [uni de fratribus meis minimis] does not show it to me, since it was for these that I received the form of a slave and the condition of a pauper . . . ."[533] In *Expositio Actuum Apostolorum* 9. 4, as did so many writers before him, Bede creates a linkage between Acts 9:4 and Matt 25:40:

> [Christ] did not say: Why are you persecuting my members? but: Why are you persecuting me? because in his body, which is the church, he still suffers from enemies. He even proclaims that the benefits conferred on his members are done to himself, when he says: I was hungry and you fed me; and by way of explanation he added: As often as you did [it] to one of these least, you did [it] to me.[534]

In *Homily* 2. 4, a Holy Week sermon on Mary's anointing Jesus' feet, he understands "the least" of v 40 to be members of the church:

'The head of the Lord' can be rightly interpreted as the Mediator himself between God and men who is the head of the church; 'the feet,' however, can be easily understood as his lowest members whatsoever [ultima quaelibet membra eius] about whom, at the end, he will say: As often as you did [it] to one of these least, my brothers, you did [it] to me.[535]

In two passages, however, *In epistolam Jacobi* 1. 27[536] and *De muliere forti* 4 (where he uses *minoribus* in place of *minimis*),[537] Bede quotes v 40 in a neutral sense, giving no indication of a restrictive viewpoint.

Anonymous Writings

There are two anonymous writings from the seventh century that make reference to the Matthean "identity dialogue." In *Sermo de symbolo* 2, discussing the seven means by which sin is forgiven, the author quotes vv 35-36 in a nonrestrictive sense to elucidate the fifth way:

The fifth remission is by means of true charity, that is, by works of mercy, just as the Lord himself said: I was hungry and you fed me; I thirsted and you gave me to drink; I was a stranger and you took me in; naked and you covered me; ill and you took care of me; I was in prison and you came to me. These are the six works of mercy.[538]

The same non-restrictive attitude is apparent in *De decem virginibus*, a sermon on Matt 25:1-13, in which v 40 (without τῶν ἀδελφῶν μου) is quoted. The anonymous author states that Matt 25:9 (Go to the dealers and buy yourselves some . . .) is to be understood with regard to the poor. The poor, he says, are the merchants who sell us the oil necessary for the lamps of our souls:

For Christ was accustomed to carry on this business by means of [the poor]: for in them he accepts earthly things in order to return heavenly; he accepts perishable things and will give in return the eternal. Thus he himself finally said: As often as you did [it] to one of these least, you did [it] to me.[539]

NOTES TO CHAPTER II

[1] See B. Altaner and A. Stuiber (*Patrologie* [Freiburg: Herder, 1978] 43-44) who use the term "Apostolic Fathers" to refer to only ten works: *1 Clement*, the seven epistles of Ignatius, Polycarp's *Epistle to the Philippians* and the fragment of Quadratus.

[2] J. B. Lightfoot, *The Apostolic Fathers* (2 vols.; Hildesheim: Olms, 1973), 1/2. 175.

[3] Ibid., 2/2. 305.

[4] Ibid., 2/3. 332.

[5] The influence of Matthew upon *1 Clement* and the Ignatian epistles is debated. D. A. Hagner (*The Use of the Old and New Testaments in Clement of Rome*. [NovTSup 34; Leiden: Brill, 1973] 171) concludes that we cannot "affirm with complete confidence that Clement was dependent upon the written synoptic gospels as we know them today." He claims that any similarities between Clement and the New Testament can be explained by the common fund of Jewish-Christian terminology. The Committee of the Oxford Society of Historical Theology (*The New Testament in the Apostolic Fathers* [Oxford: Clarendon, 1905] 61) concludes that we have in *1 Clement* "references to some written or unwritten form of 'catechesis' . . . current in the Roman church . . . which may go back to a time before our gospels existed." As regards the Ignatian epistles, the Committee of the Oxford Society (*The New Testament in the Apostolic Fathers*, 79), R. Grant (*The Formation of the New Testament* [New York: Harper & Row, 1965] 102), and V. Corwin (*Saint Ignatius and Christianity in Antioch* [New Haven: Yale University, 1960] 67) would be willing to concede that Ignatius knew and used Matthew's gospel. E. Massaux (*Influence de l'Evangile de saint Matthieu sur la littérature chrétienne avant saint Irénée* [BETL 75; Leuven: University Press, 1986] 132) argues forcefully that Matthew was known by Ignatius, whereas H. Koester (*Synoptische Überlieferungen bei den apostolischen Vätern* [TU 65; Berlin: Akademie, 1957] 61) is less convinced:"Daraus ist zu schließen, daß Ignatius Mt-Evangelium nicht benutzt haben wird." W.

R. Schoedel (*Ignatius of Antioch* [Hermeneia; Philadelphia: Fortress, 1985] 9) maintains the same opinion.

[6] PG 6. 372, 404, 457.

[7] Ibid., 420-432.

[8] A number of fragments from the lost Greek original are preserved in the works of Hippolytus, Eusebius, and Epiphanius, so that much of the Greek text can be reconstructed. The date of the Latin translation still poses a problem for scholars and is given anywhere from AD 200 to 420. See J. Quasten, *Patrology* (3 vols.; Westminster, MD: Newman, 1950-60), 1. 291, and Altaner-Stuiber, *Patrologie*, 111.

[9] SC 100. 613, 615.

[10] Ibid., 783.

[11] SC 264. 76.

[12] SC 153. 349.

[13] Cf. W. Wright, *Apocryphal Acts of the Apostles* (2 vols.; London: Williams & Norgate, 1871; reprinted, Amsterdam: Philo, 1968) 1. 314, for the Syriac text. The Greek is found in R. A. Lipsius and M. Bonnet, *Acta Apostolorum Apocrypha* (2 vols.; Leipzig: Mendelssohn, 1891-1903) 2/2. 252. The Syriac version is much closer to the biblical text than the Greek version is. There is a discrepancy concerning the original language of *The Acts*. Wright (*Apocryphal Acts*, xiv) states that the Syriac was translated from the Greek text, while the anonymous author of the article "Acts of Thomas," *ODCC*, 1370, holds for a Syriac original.

[14] Lightfoot, *The Apostolic Fathers*, 1/2. 222.

[15] Committee of the Oxford Society, *The New Testament in the Apostolic Fathers*, 130.

[16] Lightfoot, *The Apostolic Fathers*, 1/2. 222.

[17] Committee of the Oxford Society, *The New Testament in the Apostolic Fathers*, 130.

[18] Lightfoot, *The Apostolic Fathers*, 1/2. 254.

[19] J. R. Michaels, "Apostolic Hardships and Righteous Gentiles: A Study of Matt 25:31-46," *JBL* 84 (1965) 27-37, esp. p. 32.

[20] The author of *The Acts of Thomas* could have been influenced rather by Paul's account of his own apostolic hardships in 2 Cor 11:23-27. See J. R. Michaels, *JBL* 84 (1965) 32-35, for a detailed comparison of 2 Cor 11:23-27 and *The Acts of Thomas* 145 with Matt 25:35-36. He concludes that the author of the *Acts* has apparently preserved a traditon that merges the Pauline and Matthean passages.

[21] GCS 17/2.179-180.
[22] GCS 12. 98.
[23] Ibid., 287.
[24] GCS 15. 221.
[25] Ibid., 151.
[26] Influenced by a form of Platonism, Origen argues that all creatures preexisted this life and descended from a higher to a lower realm. He uses the Greek καταβολή of Matt 25:34 to bolster his position, interpreting it to mean not a "beginning" but a "throwing down," a "descent" (*De Princip.* 3. 5, 4 [SC 268. 224]). Other indications of his unique theology are found in his discussion of the punishment in Matt 25:41,46. He reasons that God punishes only for the eventual conversion of the punished (*Hom. in Jer.* 12. 5 [SC 238. 28]) and even hints at the possibility that the punishment of Satan and his angels might not be eternal (*De Princip.* 1. 6, 3 [SC 252. 202]).
[27] GCS 38.164-165. Origen acknowledges that some of his contemporaries hold the opinion that the division would involve only believers, but it is not clear whether he includes himself in their category or not. He seems to hold the universalist position with regard to πάντα τὰ ἔθνη since he states that Christ will be manifest to "everyone, the good as well as the evil, the believers as well as the unbelievers."
[28] Origen's exegetical works are of three kinds: the *scholia* (philological and historical notes on obscure verses or passages), the *commentaries* (a well-developed interpretation of the scriptural text), and the *homilies* (dogmatic, moral and mystical instructions drawn from the scriptures). The scholia and the commentaries have not fared as well with the passage of time as have the homilies.
[29] PG 12.1329.
[30] Ibid., 1330.
[31] GCS 38.172.
[32] PL 26. 406. It is quoted by Jerome: "Licet enim infirmi sint et caro comparatione spiritus appellentur; caro tamen Christi sunt."
[33] PG 12.1516.
[34] GCS 3. 322; PG 14.1115.
[35] SC 238. 80.
[36] GCS 38.185.
[37] Ibid., 160.
[38] Ibid., 141.
[39] GCS 40.183.

⁴⁰Origen's reference to "spiritual and holy beings" (*Comm. in Joh.* 1. 73 [SC 120. 94]) and "the just" (*Hom. in Ps.* 3.12 [PG 12.1348]) as representatives of "the least" of vv 40, 45 could be used to bolster the argument that he considered the saints of the OT in his perspective. These two references, however, are in a context where he specifically mentions Christians, so the greater probability is that he means these terms to be synonymous with Christians.

⁴¹GCS 38. 2.

⁴²Ibid., 168.

⁴³GCS 29. 96.

⁴⁴GCS 38. 282.

⁴⁵Ibid., 169.

⁴⁶Ibid.

⁴⁷GCS 40.121.

⁴⁸PG 12.1329. " . . . si aliquis ex nobis qui membra eius dicimur aegrotat, et aliquo peccati morbo laborat, id est, si alicuius peccati macula inuritur, et non subjectus Deo, recte ille nondum dicitur esse subjectus, cuius sint membra illi qui non sunt subjecti Deo."

⁴⁹GCS 38.170. "Deinde omne quod hic est, carcer est Christi et eorum qui sunt ipsius. Propterea eamus ad eos, qui in domo vinculorum istorum habentur quasi in carcere, et sunt in hoc mundo degentes quasi carcere naturae necessitate constricti. Cum ergo abierimus ad tales et omne opus bonum fecerimus in eis, visitavimus eos in carcere et Christum in eis."

⁵⁰GCS 3. 322. καὶ ταῦτα τοῦ Χριστοῦ ὁμολογοῦντος καθ' ἕκαστον τῶν ἀσθενούντων ἁγίων ἀσθενεῖν ὁμοίως καὶ ἐν φυλακῇ εἶναι καὶ γυμνιτεύειν ξενιτεύειν τε καὶ πεινᾶν καὶ διψᾶν.

⁵¹GCS 40.121.

⁵²PG 12.1348.

⁵³GCS 38.195.

⁵⁴SC 238. 80.

⁵⁵GCS 40.121.

⁵⁶PG 17.132.

⁵⁷CSEL 3/2. 826. It is numbered among the letters of Cyprian.

⁵⁸*Analecta Sacra* (4 vols.; ed. J. B. Pitra; Paris: Jouby & Roger, 1876-84) 3. 592.

⁵⁹ANF 6. 212. Cyril of Jerusalem also quotes from this disputation in his *Catecheses* 6. 27 (PG 33. 585).

[60] GCS 27. 216. The text is preserved for us only in a Slavonic version, but its authenticity should not be doubted. See H. Musurillo, *Saint Methodius* (ACW 27; Westminster, MD: Newman, 1958) 7. As the Slavonic text was not available to me, I had to rely on the German translation of G. N. Bonwetsch in GCS 27. 209-216.

[61] Ibid., 466-467.

[62] Ibid., 472. The Greek of the text is not available, so I had to rely on the German translation of G. N. Bonwetsch.

[63] Ibid.

[64] M. Geerard (*Clavis Patrum Graecorum* [4 vols.; Turnhout: Brépols, 1983] 1. 209) considers the work spurious.

[65] See O. H. Burmester, "The Homilies of the Holy Week Lectionary," *Le Muséon* 45 (1932) 50, 69.

[66] CCL 1. 406.

[67] Ibid., 205.

[68] Ibid., 39.

[69] CCL 2. 899.

[70] Ibid., 1090.

[71] CCL 1. 273.

[72] PO 27. 124-125.

[73] GCS 1. 45

[74] Ibid., 305-309.

[75] H. Achelis (*Hippolytstudien* [TU 16/4; Leipzig: Hinrichs, 1897] 79) says it is a compilation from the *De Christo et Antichristo* and the homilies of Ephraem and was not "concocted" before the ninth century.

[76] 1 Cor 6:15; 12:12, 27; Rom 12:5.

[77] *De Consum. Mundi* 44. GCS 1. 307.

[78] Ibid., 40. GCS 1. 305.

[79] Ibid., 48. GCS 1. 309.

[80] PG 10.166.

[81] *De Vir. Illust.* 53. PL 23. 663.

[82] CCL 3. 72, 85-86.

[83] Ibid., 174.

[84] CCL 3A.111.

[85] Ibid., 65.

[86] CCL 3A. 71.

[87]PL 4. 361. This is Letter 62 in G. W. Clarke, *The Letters of Cyprian of Carthage* (3 vols.; ACW 46; New York: Newman, 1986) 96, 284 n. 10.

[88]CCL 128. 57.

[89]CSCO 407. 128, 165. There is a discrepancy about the dating. B. Altaner and A. Stuiber (*Patrologie*, 84) state that the *Didascalia* was written "most probably in the first half of the third century," while J. R. Michaels (*JBL* 84 [1965] 35) dates the work in the late fourth century. The original Greek has been lost. The work has been preserved, however, in Syriac.

[90]CSCO 407.186-87.

[91]Adolf Harnack, *Die Lehre der zwölf Apostel* (TU 2/1-2; Leipzig: Hinrichs, 1884) 235.

[92]E.g., Justin Martyr, *Apol.* 1. 61-67. PG 6. 420-432.

[93]Recent critics do not uphold the authenticity of Clementine authorship. Most scholars judge these two epistles to have been composed in the third century. See B. Altaner and A. Stuiber, *Patrologie*, 47.

[94]F. X. Funk, *Patres Apostolici* (2 vols.; Tübingen: Laupp, 1881) 2.12.

[95]Ibid., 12-13.

[96]PLSup 1.173-174.

[97]Ibid., 174.

[98]Lines 13-14. See B. P. Grenfell and A. S. Hunt, *The Amherst Papyri* (2 vols.; London: Frowde, 1900) 1. 25. See also C. Wessely, PO 4 (1908) 207.

[99]PG 23. 436-437.

[100]Ibid., 749.

[101]GCS 23. 26.

[102]PG 23. 361, 364.

[103]R. Graffin, *Patrologia Syriaca* (2 vols.; Paris: Firmin-Didot, 1894-1907)1. 241. See also G. Bert (ed.), "Die Unterweisung von den Bundesbrüdern," TU 3 (Leipzig: Hinrichs, 1887) 89-113, esp. p. 90.

[104]*Patrologia Syriaca* 1. 901; See also G. Bert (ed.), "Die Unterweisung von der Unterstützung der Armen," TU 3. 315-328, esp. pp. 317-318.

[105]G. Bert, "Die Unterweisung von der Unterstützung der Armen," TU 3. 322.

[106]*Patrologia Syriaca* 1. 920; See also G. Bert, "Die Unterweisung von der Unterstützung der Armen," TU 3. 324.

[107] A. Veilleux (ed.), "The Bohairic Life of Pachomius," *Pachomian Koinonia* (3 vols.; Cistercian Studies Series 45-47; Kalamazoo, MI: Cistercian Publications, 1980-82) 1. 23-266, esp. p. 64.

[108] A. Veilleux (ed.),"The First Greek Life of Pachomius," *Pachomian Koinonia* 1. 297-407, esp. p. 325.

[109] This restrictive addition from Matt 18:6 is omitted from the *Vita Altera*, the Latin translation of Pachomius' life (See H. van Cranenburgh, *La vie latine de Saint Pachome* [Subsidia hagiographica 46; Bruxelles: Société des Bollandistes, 1969] 164).

[110] A. Veilleux, *Pachomian Koinonia* 1. 386.

[111] CSCO 159.15; See also A. Veilleux (ed.), "The Instructions of St. Pachomius," *Pachomian Koinonia* 3. 13-48, esp. p. 30.

[112] H. Quecke, *Die Briefe Pachoms* (Textus patristici et liturgici 11; Regensburg: Pustet, 1975) 101. See also A. Veilleux (ed.), "The Letters of St. Pachomius," *Pachomian Koinonia* 3. 51-78, esp. p. 53.

[113] H. Quecke, *Die Briefe Pachoms*,104. See also *Pachomian Koinonia* 3. 56.

[114] A. Veilleux (ed.), "Paralipomena from the Life of Holy Pachomius," *Pachomian Koinonia* 2.19-66, esp. p. 66.

[115] Ibid.

[116] PG 24.1070.

[117] E. M. Buytaert, *Eusèbe d'Émèse: Discours conservés en latin* (2 vols.; Louvain: Bureaux de la Revue,1953-57) 1. 354.

[118] J. Quasten (*Patrology*, 3.351) seems to agree with those who find no positive reason to ascribe these works to Eusebius. I include the works here for lack of a better place to treat them.

[119] CCL 101A. 539.

[120] Ibid., 541.

[121] PG 30. 689.

[122] Ibid., 744.

[123] PG 27.196.

[124] H. G. Opitz (ed.), *Athanasius Werke* (Berlin/Leipzig: de Gruyter, 1935) 189.

[125] Ibid., 217.

[126] M. Geerard (*Clavis Patrum Graecorum*, 2.45,48) lists *In Passionem et Crucem Domini* and *Quaestiones ad Antiochum Ducem* as spurious works of Athanasius.

[127] PG 28. 248.

[128] Ibid., 652.

[129] Ibid., 649.

[130] The Syriac text of the *Diatessaron* is no longer extant. The Latin text, attributed to Ammonius of Alexandria, can be found in PL 68. 251-358.

[131] After a discussion of Luke 12:35 (*Diat.* 43. 39-42) he immediately begins comment on John 13:1-15 (*Diat.* 44.10-33).

[132] SC 121.136-137, 153, 165, 326.

[133] J. and E. Assemani (eds.), *S. Ephraemi Opera Omnia, Graece, Syriace Latine* (6 vols.; Rome: Salvioni, 1732-46) Gr. 1. 81.

[134] Ibid., Gr. 2. 189.

[135] Ibid., 197.

[136] Ibid., 198.

[137] Ibid., Gr. 3.169.

[138] Ibid.

[139] Ibid., 350, 354.

[140] Ibid., 21.

[141] Ibid., 22.

[142] Ibid., 270-271.

[143] It is a work composed of 80 rules applicable not only to monks but to all Christians.

[144] The *Regulae Fusius Tractatae* is a synopsis of 55 lectures that treat of the most important aspects of monastic life.

[145] The *Regulae Brevius Tractatae* is a series of 313 answers to specific questions on the religious life.

[146] PG 31.1001.

[147] Ibid.

[148] Ibid., 1025.

[149] Ibid., 917.

[150] Ibid., 772.

[151] Ibid., 812.

[152] J. Quasten (*Patrology* 3. 224) claims this letter must be assigned to Evagrius Ponticus.

[153] PG 32. 261.

[154] J. Quasten (*Patrology* 3. 213) maintains that the origin of the *Constitutiones Asceticae* is uncertain.

[155] PG 31.1328.

[156] Ibid., 1412.

[157] Ibid., 645. J. Quasten (*Patrology* 3. 219) does not include this work among Basil's authentic sermons.

[158] PG 29. 264.

[159] PG 31. 261-277. It is a homily on Luke 12:18.

[160] M. Geerard (*Clavis Patrum Graecorum* 2.170) considers it a spurious work, and J. Quasten (*Patrology* 3. 219) does not include it among Basil's authentic works.

[161] PG 31.1712.

[162] A. Boon, *Pachomiana latina* (Louvain: Bureaux de la Revue, 1932) 140. The text is preserved in the Latin translation of Jerome. See also A. Veilleux (ed.), "The Testament of Horsiesos," *Pachomian Koinonia* 3.171-215, esp. p. 206.

[163] A. Veilleux, *Pachomian Koinonia* 3.181.

[164] PG 33. 632.

[165] Ibid., 908.

[166] Ibid., 904.

[167] Ibid., 905.

[168] SC 270.180.

[169] PG 35.1236. Rufinus' translation of this passage brings out the allusion to v 40 much more clearly. See CSEL 46.173-174: " . . . sed haec diximus ut vos discatis Christo facere per ea quae uni ex minimis eius facitis . . . ."

[170] J. Quasten (*Patrology* 3.163-165) says that the authorship of these homilies is still a mystery, but that they were not written by Macarius of Egypt. He suggests that they arose from Messalian circles in Syria.

[171] *Fifty Spiritual Homilies* (Willits, CA: Eastern Orthodox Books, 1974) 228.

[172] J. Quasten (*Patrology* 3.168) denies its authenticity. He suspects that the *De oratione* attributed to Macarius is in reality a paraphrase of the second section of Gregory of Nyssa's *De instituto christiano*. R. Staats, however, in *Makarios-Symeon: Epistola Magna. Eine messalianische Mönchsregel und ihre Umschrift in Gregors von Nyssa "De instituto christiano"* (Göttingen: AAW, 1984) argues that *De instituto christiano* is a redaction of Macarius' *De oratione*.

[173] PG 34. 860.

[174] PG 44. 989.

[175] Ibid., 1261.
[176] PG 46. 473.
[177] Ibid., 889.
[178] Ibid., 305.
[179] Ibid., 473.
[180] Ibid., 889.
[181] PG 46. 305.
[182] W. Jaeger (*Two Rediscovered Works of Ancient Christian Literature: Gregory of Nyssa and Macarius* [Leiden: Brill, 1954] 119) holds that it is genuine. J. Quasten (*Patrology* 3. 274) agrees with him. However, M. Canévet ("Le 'De Instituto Christiano': est-il de Grégoire de Nysse? Problèmes de critique interne," *Revue des études grecques* 82 [1969] 404-423) continues to question its authenticity.
[183] PG 46. 305.
[184] PG 39. 816.
[185] Ibid., 864.
[186] PG 40. 397.
[187] Ibid., 405.
[188] Ibid.
[189] Ibid., 408.
[190] Ibid., 412.
[191] PG 41.1044. This work of Epiphanius is also referred to as *Adversus Haereses*.
[192] Cf. C. Baur, "Der Kanon des heiligen Johannes Chrysostomos," *TQ* 105 (1924) 258-271, esp. p. 260.
[193] R. Brändle, *Matt 25:31-46 im Werk des Johannes Chrysostomos*, (BGBE 22; Tübingen: Mohr, 1979) 3. " . . . Matt 25:31-46 das soziale Handeln des Chrysostomos geformt hat und zum Movens seiner priesterlichen und seelsorgerlichen Tätigkeit und schließlich zur integrativen Kraft seiner theologischen Leitideen geworden ist."
[194] Ibid., 38.
[195] PG 58. 717-724. These are part of 90 homilies on Matthew's Gospel delivered by Chrysostom at Antioch in AD 390.
[196] PG 58. 717.
[197] In his *De Diabolo Tentatore* 3.3 (PG 49. 267) Chrysostom elucidates further, stating that a "kid is unfruitful and is not able to con-

tribute services either by its milk or by progeny, or by its hair, to those who possess it on account of the immaturity of its age."

[198] Brändle (*Matt 25:31-46 im Werk des Johannes Chysostomos*, 36) makes the observation that this addition in v 45 is all the more conspicuous because Chrysostom includes τῶν ἀδελφῶν μου in his quotations of v 40 only twice.

[199] PG 58. 718.
[200] PG 48. 862.
[201] PG 54. 564.
[202] PG 58. 718.
[203] Ibid., 779.
[204] PG 59. 328.
[205] PG 60. 318.
[206] Ibid., 666.
[207] PG 61.179.
[208] PG 54. 483.
[209] PG 61. 610.
[210] PG 62. 574.
[211] Ibid., 188.
[212] PG 61. 87.
[213] PG 57. 409.
[214] PG 59. 332.
[215] PG 48. 989.
[216] PG 62.188.

[217] R. Brändle, *Matt 25:31-46 im Werk des Johannes Chrysostomos*, 249. He bases his conclusion on three arguments: (1) Chrysostom in a number of places in his works calls for all the needy, even pagans and Jews, to be helped, and in his entire corpus he refers to the restrictive Gal 6:10 only three times; (2)With only two exceptions (*Hom. 67 in Gen.* 41. 7 [PG 53. 384] and 55. 3 [PG 54. 483]) he omits τῶν ἀδελφῶν μου when quoting v 40; and (3) in his discussion of Matt 18:10 he sees the μικρῶν as everyone (PG 54. 249-250). I am not completely convinced by his second argument. In four partial quotations of v 40 in which Chrysostom deals specifically with Christian needy (*67 Hom. in Gen.* 65. 4 [PG 54. 564]; *Hom. in Acta Apost.* 45. 3 [PG 60. 318]; *Hom. in Rom.* 30. 4 [PG 60. 666]; *Hom. in 1 Tm.* 14. 2 [PG 62. 574]) he omits τῶν ἀδελφῶν μου, so its absence or presence may not be indicative of his viewpoint of the identity of the needy.

[218] Ibid., 250.
[219] PG 60. 702.
[220] Ibid.
[221] Ibid.
[222] PG 65. 213
[223] PG 47. 40.
[224] PG 79.1128. J. Quasten (*Patrology* 3. 503) suggests that the work really belongs to Evagrius Ponticus.
[225] J. Quasten (*Patrology* 3. 503) claims *Peristeria* was composed at Alexandria in the middle of the fifth century AD, and that Nilus of Ancyra cannot be its author.
[226] *De malignis cogitationibus* is included among Nilus' works by Migne (PG 79.1199-1234) but not even mentioned by M. Geerard (*Clavis Patrum Graecorum* 3.174-182) nor by J. Quasten (*Patrology* 3.497-504) in their discussions of the works of Nilus.
[227] PG 79. 964.
[228] Ibid., 841.
[229] Ibid., 872.
[230] Ibid., 1213.
[231] CSEL 68.154.
[232] Ibid., 122.
[233] Ibid., 121, 123, 157-158.
[234] PL 20. 1148-1149.
[235] PL 10. 301.
[236] SC 258. 216, 218.
[237] *De off. min.* 2. 28, 137-138. PL 16. 140-141.
[238] Ibid., 2. 28, 140. PL 16. 141.
[239] PL 16. 1119.
[240] Ibid.
[241] SC 25. 190.
[242] SC 179. 80.
[243] PL 16. 251.
[244] CCL 14.107.
[245] Ibid., 183-184.
[246] Ibid., 184.

[247]Nothing certain about the identity of Ambrosiaster is known. He is called by that name since his commentaries on the Pauline epistles were long thought to be the work of Ambrose. Erasmus was the first to question that assumption. See "Ambrosiaster," *ODCC*, 44, as well as A. Stuiber, "Ambrosiaster," *TRE* 2. 356-362, esp. pp. 356-357.

[248]CSEL 81/3. 274.

[249]CSEL 81/2. 260.

[250]CCL 9A. 339.

[251]CCL 23.105.

[252]CCL 20.168.

[253]CSEL 46. 257. Cf. Gregory's original: Ὁ δὲ χήραν καὶ ὀρφανὸν οὐκ ἠλέησεν, οὐδὲ μετέδωκεν ἄρτου καὶ τροφῆς ὀλίγης τῷ δεομένῳ, μᾶλλον δὲ Χριστῷ τῷ τρεφομένῳ διὰ τῶν καὶ μικρῶς τρεφομένων. PG 35. 960. It is less clearly an allusion to verses 40, 42a.

[254]CSEL 46.147. The allusion to v 40 is not found in the original Greek of Gregory Nazianzus. Cf. PG 36. 436.

[255]PLSup 1. 913.

[256]Ibid., 975.

[257]CSEL 5. 632.

[258]PLSup 1.1441.

[259]Ibid., 1566.

[260]PL 33.1114.

[261]PLSup 1.1699.

[262]SC 133. 258.

[263]PL 20. 231.

[264]CCL 74. 317.

[265]PL 22. 587.

[266]PL 23. 312-313.

[267]CCL 76. 407.

[268]CCL 78. 379.

[269]CCL 73. 325.

[270]CCL 73A. 557.

[271]CCL 73. 75.

[272]CCL 77. 243-244.

[273]PL 22. 335.

[274]Ibid., 583-584.

[275]CCL 73A. 666-667.

[276] CCL 75. 239.
[277] Ibid., 702.
[278] PL 22. 556.
[279] CCL 79. 89.
[280] CCL 77. 244.
[281] PL 22. 583. "Verum Christi templum anima credentis est; illam exorna, illam vesti, illi offer donaria, in illa Christum suscipe."
[282] PL 22. 335. "... Christum sustenasti, pavisti, vestisti, visitasti...."
[283] CCL 75. 702.
[284] CCL 79. 89.
[285] PL 22. 556.
[286] Ibid.
[287] CCL 75. 239.
[288] CCL 73A. 667. "... non habentes calorem fidei, sed extra Ecclesiam frigoribus infidelitatis algentes, et inopes atque peregrinos, induc, ait, in domum Ecclesiae...."
[289] Ibid. "... ut vestiti Christi tunica, nequaquam maneant in sepulcris...."
[290] Ibid. "... frangat doctrinae ecclesiasticae esurientibus panem suum...."
[291] Ibid. "... ut solvat omne vinculum iniquitatis, quo simplices quique credentium haereticorum fraudibus colligati sunt."
[292] Ibid.
[293] PL 38. 381.
[294] PL 38. 388.
[295] Ibid., 393-394.
[296] CCL 38. 63.
[297] Ibid., 63.
[298] CSEL 41.129.
[299] CSEL 52.164.
[300] PL 38. 797.
[301] CCL 46.152
[302] CSEL 43. 393.
[303] CCL 36. 221.
[304] Ibid., 249.
[305] PL 38. 706.
[306] CCL 46.196.

[307] CCL 50. 78.
[308] CCL 36. 498.
[309] CCL 39. 976.
[310] CSEL 25. 273; 51. 253; 52. 54.
[311] PL 40. 331.
[312] CCL 38. 63; 39. 719, 779, 819.
[313] Ibid., 14, 553.
[314] PL 35. 2008; CCL 36. 220.
[315] CCL 38. 486; 39.1068; CSEL 43. 391-393.
[316] CSEL 60.132-133.
[317] CCL 39.1383; 40. 2110.
[318] Ibid., 1264; 1842.
[319] Ibid., 1229; 36. 384, 565.
[320] CCL 50A. 510.
[321] CSEL 40/2. 255, 575.
[322] CSEL 51. 287.
[323] CSEL 43. 391-393, 399
[324] CCL 36. 216.
[325] CCL 38. 339, 345, 383, 387, 428.
[326] PL 38. 613, 648, 685-686, 742, 755.
[327] PLSup 2. 573.
[328] Ibid., 681.
[329] CCL 36. 435, 444; 38. 585; PLSup 2. 766.
[330] CCL 36. 216.
[331] CCL 36. 216; PL 38. 685-686, 742; CCL 38. 386, 428; CSEL 43. 399; PLSup 2. 572.
[332] CCL 50A. 510; CSEL 40/2. 255; CCL 38. 345, 383.
[333] PL 38. 755.
[334] Ibid., 648.
[335] CCL 36. 216; CSEL 40/2. 575; 51. 287.
[336] CSEL 43. 399.
[337] CCL 38. 585.
[338] PL 61.154.
[339] Ibid., 220.
[340] Ibid., 340.

341 Ibid., 169.

342 Ibid., 284.

343 J. Quasten (*Patrology* 1. 61-62) claims that the question of the dating and authorship of the Clementines has thus far defied every attempt at solution. He suggests that they were written by a Jewish Christian belonging to a heretical sect, possibly in Syria, and that the original document from which the *Homilies* and *Recognitions* were taken was written in the third century but is now lost. B. Altaner and A. Stuiber (*Patrologie*, 135) claim that the version of the *Homilies* and *Recognitions* that is known to us today was written somewhere in the course of the fourth century, before AD 381. G. Strecker (*Das Judenchristentum in den Ps-Klementinen* [TU 70; Berlin: Akademie, 1958] 267-270) is a bit more specific about the dating. He claims that the *Grundschrift* that lies at the base of the *Homilies* and *Recognitions* was written in the middle of the third century, while the *Homilies* were written in the first decade of the fourth century and the *Recognitions* were not written much before AD 350.

344 GCS 42.13.

345 Ibid., 81.

346 Ibid., 155, 190-191, 232-233.

347 GCS 51.178.

348 Ibid.

349 Ibid.

350 GCS 42. 232-233.

351 P. E. Pusey (ed.), *Sancti Cyrilli archiepiscopi alexandrini opera* (7 vols.; Brussels: Culture et Civilisation, 1965), 7. 176.

352 PG 76. 277.

353 PG 69. 940.

354 SC 97. 360.

355 PG 69. 940.

356 PG 75. 497.

357 Pusey, *S. Cyrilli opera*, 6. 576.

358 Ibid., 5. 419, 425.

359 PG 77. 832.

360 Pusey, *S. Cyrilli opera*, 1. 403.

361 Cyril of Alexandria, *Commentary on the Gospel of Luke* (reprinted and translated, R. Payne Smith; Astoria, NY: Studion, 1983) 551.

[362]Ibid., 414-415.

[363]Even though Isidore lived so close to Alexandria, he stood out firmly against Alexandrian allegorism in his exegesis of scripture and aligned himself with the Antiochene school.

[364]PG 78. 532.

[365]J. Quasten (*Patrology* 3.181) states that, on the basis of a literary analysis of his letters, we should not put much credence in the traditional view that Isidore was a pupil of John Chrysostom.

[366]SC 177. 84, 86.

[367]PG 93.1143.

[368]Ibid., 1280.

[369]PG 85. 308.

[370]SC 57. 413.

[371]σμικρῶν is the Ionian and the Old Attic form for μικρῶν. The form is often found in the Koine. See LSJ 2.1133, as well as F. T. Gignac, *A Grammar of the Greek Papyri of the Roman and Byzantine Periods* (2 vols.; Milan: Cisalpino, 1976, 1981) I. 122.

[372]PG 83.1348-1349.

[373]PG 81.181.

[374]Ibid., 197.

[375]Ibid.

[376]PG 85.1632.

[377]The name "Eusebius of Alexandria" designates a legendary biography and a collection of 22 sermons, purportedly written by the man Cyril of Alexandria chose to be his successor. The identity of the author of this collection remains a mystery. Since these works were cited as early as the seventh century, they must have been written sometime during the fifth and sixth centuries. See F. Nau, "Eusèbe d'Alexandrie," *DTC* 5/2.1526-1527.

[378]PG 86. 424-429.

[379]Ibid., 429.

[380]Ibid., 357.

[381]PG 87/2.1672.

[382]Ibid., 2712.

[383]D. J. Chitty, "Varsanuphius and John: Questions and Answers," *PO* 31 (1966) 449-616, esp. p. 608.

[384]PG 86/2. 3317.

[385] Very little is known about this writer. B. Altaner and A. Stuiber (*Patrologie*, 391) simply state that he was bishop of Novae at the beginning of the fifth century.
[386] PL 66.107-109.
[387] Ibid., 108.
[388] Ibid., 109.
[389] PL 49. 493.
[390] Ibid., 526.
[391] CCL 24. 66.
[392] Ibid., 89.
[393] Ibid., 222.
[394] Ibid., 235.
[395] Ibid., 240.
[396] CCL 24A. 729.
[397] CCL 24. 235.
[398] Ibid., 240.
[399] CCL 24A. 589-590.
[400] CCL 60. 212-213.
[401] Ibid., 83-84.
[402] Ibid., 325.
[403] Ibid., 212.
[404] Ibid., 12, 111.
[405] PL 53.382.
[406] SC 249.128.
[407] PL 52. 714.
[408] Ibid., 715.
[409] Ibid., 705, 721.
[410] Ibid., 721.
[411] CCL 138. 34.
[412] CCL 138A. 266.
[413] CCL 138. 75.
[414] CCL 138A. 266.
[415] Ibid., 545.
[416] Ibid., 580.
[417] Ibid., 566.

[418] Ibid., 554.

[419] Ibid., 235-236.

[420] A. K. Squire, "Universal Compassion in Leo the Great," *Studia patristica* 13 (TU 116; Berlin: Akademie, 1975) 280-285, esp. p. 282.

[421] PLSup 3. 899. Very little information is available about the author. A. Erikson (*Sancti Epiphanii episcopi interpretatio evangeliorum* [Lund: Gleerup, 1939], vi) admits that he is not yet positively identified. He claims that his native language was Latin and that he could not have written before the fifth century. He conjectures that he might have been the Epiphanius who usurped the See of Seville in Spain between AD 441-61 or the Bishop of Benevento sometime in the fifth or sixth centuries. See "Epiphanius (3)," *A Dictionary of Christian Biography* (ed. W. Smith and H. Wace; 4 vols.; New York: AMS, 1967) 2.156.

[422] PLSup 3. 900.

[423] Ibid., 902.

[424] CCL 68A. 178.

[425] PL 51. 693.

[426] CSEL 8. 307-308.

[427] Ibid., 307.

[428] CCL 101B. 824.

[429] CCL 101A. 539.

[430] CSEL 21. 283.

[431] Ibid., 140.

[432] CCL 101B. 824. This homily is found among the works of Eusebius Gallicanus where it is given the title *Sermon 1*.

[433] CSEL 21.140.

[434] PLSup 3. 810.

[435] CCL 91A. 520.

[436] Ibid., 629.

[437] CCL 117. 486.

[438] CSEL 9. 605.

[439] Ibid., 786-787.

[440] Ibid., 509.

[441] PL 62.1172.

[442] Eight sermons included in the works of Caesarius (CCL 103-104) contain references to the "identity dialogue," but they will not be considered in this discussion since they are sermons of his predecessors

which he freely borrowed and just as freely acknowledged. *Sermons* 17, 19, 24, 131, 132, and 183 are from Augustine, *Sermon* 31 is from Salvianus, and *Sermon* 197 belongs to Faustus of Riez.

[443] CCL 103.116.
[444] Ibid., 117.
[445] Ibid., 207.
[446] CCL 104. 637.
[447] Ibid., 648.
[448] Ibid., 649.
[449] Ibid., 904.
[450] PL 67.1133.
[451] CCL 103. 112.
[452] CCL 104. 805.
[453] CCL 103. 127-128.
[454] Ibid., 121.
[455] CCL 104. 642. The same sentiments are expressed in *Serm.* 209.3. Quoting vv 41-42a, Caesarius compares the final judgment to the activity of winnowing and threshing described in Matt 3:12 and then states: "That threshing floor which the Lord in the Gospel promised that he would fan is known to contain neither heretics nor pagans but only Catholic Christians" (CCL 104. 836).
[456] SC 182. 570.
[457] SC 181. 456.
[458] SC 182. 610, 612.
[459] See E. Dekkers, *Clavis Patrum Latinorum* (Sacris erudiri 3; 2d ed.; Steenbrugge: Abbatia S. Petri, 1961), 155, 162.
[460] PLSup 4. 869.
[461] PLSup 4.832. The author could have had 2 Cor 1:4a in mind (" . . . qui consolatur nos in omni tribulatione ut possimus et ipsi consolari eos qui in omni pressura sunt . . . ") when he composed the additional verse.
[462] Ibid., 714.
[463] PG 86/2. 3016.
[464] Ibid.
[465] PG 88. 860.
[466] Ibid., 1041.
[467] PG 90.175.

[468] PG 91.713.
[469] Ibid., 373.
[470] PG 90.1076.
[471] PG 89.1613.
[472] Ibid., 1704.
[473] Ibid., 1729.
[474] Ibid., 1736.
[475] Ibid., 1713.
[476] Ibid., 1732-1733.
[477] Ibid., 464.
[478] Ibid. He quotes an allusion to vv 35ac, 36a from Chrysostom's τοῦ κατὰ Ματθαῖον: "Whatever you shall have done to a brother who is hungry [πεινῶντα] and a stranger [ξένον] and naked [γυμνόν] . . . ."
[479] Ibid., 465. He quotes from Basil's τῶν Ἀσκητικῶν in which v 40 is used in a narrow way.
[480] PG 98. 288.
[481] Ibid., 289.
[482] PG 97. 941.
[483] Ibid.
[484] St. John Damascene, *Barlaam and Joasaph* (LCL; London: Heinemann, 1914) 120.
[485] Ibid., 214.
[486] CCL 97. 444.
[487] CCL 98. 753.
[488] CCL 97. 528.
[489] Ibid., 373.
[490] CCL 148A. 244.
[491] PG 98. 836.
[492] PL 71.1025.
[493] Ibid., 1125.
[494] A. C. Vega (ed.), *S. Leandri Hispalensis de institutione virginum et contemptu mundi*. (Scriptores ecclesiastici hispano-latini veteris et medii aevi 16-17; Escorial: Monasterio Augustiniano, 1948) 103.
[495] CCL 143. 290.
[496] Ibid., 318-319.
[497] SC 221. 68.

[498] PL 76. 379.
[499] CCL 140A. 969.
[500] SC 221. 46.
[501] PL 76. 378.
[502] Ibid., 1312.
[503] CCL 140A. 969.
[504] SC 221.140.
[505] CCL 140A. 800.
[506] PL 76.1183.
[507] SC 221. 46.
[508] PL 77. 85.
[509] PL 76.1157.
[510] Ibid., 378-379.
[511] Ibid., 378.
[512] Ibid., 379.
[513] PL 83. 218.
[514] Ibid., 733-734.
[515] Ibid., 786.
[516] PL 87. 279.
[517] Ibid., 438.
[518] Ibid., 628.
[519] Ibid., 635.
[520] Ibid., 1119.
[521] PL 88.1056.
[522] PL 87. 526.
[523] Ibid., 534.
[524] Ibid., 545.
[525] CCL 115.107.
[526] Ibid., 108.

[527] In addition to Bede, only Origen, John Chrysostom, Hilary of Poitiers, Jerome, and Cyril of Alexandria comment on Matt 25:31-46 as part of a larger commentary on the Gospel of Matthew. Cyril restricts his comments to Matt 25:31.

[528] PL 91.109. The same fourfold division is found in *Homily* 1.13 (CCL 122. 90).

[529] Ibid., 109.

[530] CCL 77. 244.
[531] PL 91.110.
[532] Ibid., 1175.
[533] CCL 120. 218.
[534] CCL 121. 44.
[535] CCL 122. 210.
[536] CCL 121.193.
[537] PL 91.1042.
[538] PLSup 4. 2162.
[539] PL 88.1076.

CHAPTER III

THE MIDDLE AGES

Eastern Authors

Isho'dad of Merv (d. ca. AD 850)

In his *Commentary on Matthew* 19, the Nestorian bishop of Merv gives no insight into his understanding of the "identity dialogue" or πάντα τὰ ἔθνη of v 32. He comments only on Matt 25:31,41,46. In a discussion as to which angels will accompany Christ at the judgment, Isho'dad cites the opinion of Theodore of Mopsuestia, whom he refers to as the Interpreter, that only the guardian angels below the firmament are referred to in v 31 and not the angels who serve at God's throne.[1] Commenting on v 41, he stresses that hell was not created for man but for Satan and his minions, a point that is found in almost every commentary on this verse.[2] There is a trace of anti-Jewish rhetoric in Isho'dad's discussion of v 46 that leaves the reader with the impression that, in his perspective, at the judgment the Jews would find themselves at the left of Christ: " . . . life is common to both parties, but on account of the torment it is not counted as life to these [the condemned]; as it is said in the prophet about the Jews, that there is no life in their life."[3]

Symeon the New Theologian (AD 949 - 1022)

The most famous of Byzantine mystical writers left no commentary as such on Matthew 25:31-46, but in three of his works he has fourteen references to the "identity dialogue," and devotes an entire chapter in his *Catecheses* to an exposition of his understanding of the six Matthean acts of mercy.

In his *Gnostic and Practical Theological Chapters* 3. 91-96, Symeon includes four quotations and one allusion to the words of the needy Christ[4] and leaves the reader with the impression that he understands the six works to be corporal and "the least" to be everyone:

> If [Christ] has condescended to assume the features of every poor man and make himself like all the poor, it is so that none of his faithful should ever raise himself above his brother, but that each one should look on his brother and his neighbor as his very God and consider himself the least of all . . . .[5]

This same universal and literal approach to the pericope is found in his *Book of Ethics* 7[6] and in *Catecheses* 7.10; [7] 21. 3; [8] and 30.11.[9]

In *Catecheses* 9, however, which is entitled "Works of Mercy," Symeon understands the six Matthean works to be spiritual, as well as corporal, and interprets "the least" in a much narrower perspective. In 9. 2, quoting vv 40, 42, he states:

> As for the junior monks, they should be subject to the seniors for the Lord's sake; as for the seniors, they should behave toward the juniors as toward their true children because of the Lord's commandment: Whatever you did to any one of these least, you did to me [Ἐφ' ὅσον ἐποιήσατε ἑνὶ ἑκάστῳ τούτων τῶν ἐλαχίστων, ἐμοὶ ἐποιήσατε]. The Lord did not . . . say this merely of those stricken with poverty and destitute of bodily food. He said this no less of all our other brethren who are wasting away, not through any famine of bread and water, but from the famine of the neglect of God's commands and failure to obey them. As the soul is more valuable than the body, so spiritual food is more necessary than bodily food. It is of this that I think the Lord spoke when he said: I was hungry and you did not feed me, I thirsted and you gave me no drink, rather than of bodily food which is subject to corruption; for he truly suffers thirst and hunger for the salvation of each one of us.[10]

In his attempt to show that the mere corporal understanding of the Matthean acts is not enough to procure salvation, Symeon, in *Catecheses* 9. 3, gives the example of Mary of Egypt who went off to the desert and won heaven without ever performing any of the six corporal works of mercy.[11] Like Mary, says Symeon, the Christian is to have a spiritual understanding of these works and see them as means of ministering to the Christ who dwells within the baptized. In *Catecheses* 9. 5, paraphrasing v 40 and alluding to vv 35-36, 42a, 43c, he says:

> When you are hungry and thirsty for his sake it is reckoned as food and drink for him. How? Because by these and similar actions you cleanse your soul and rid yourself of the famine and squalor of passions.... Whatever you do to yourself he counts as though he undergoes it himself and says: Whatever you did to the least one, your soul, you did to me [Ἐφ' ὅσον ἐποίησας τῇ ἐλαχίστῃ ψυχῇ σου, ἐμοὶ ἐποίησας] ... if you ignore yourself and ... leave your soul in the famine of laziness or the thirst of indifference or imprisoned in the dungeon of this filthy body through gluttony or love of pleasure, lying in filth, squalor, and deepest gloom as though it were dead, have you not treated Christ's brother with contempt? Have you not abandoned him to hunger and thirst? Have you not failed to visit him when he was in prison?[12]

This same spiritual understanding of the Matthean acts is expressed again in *Catecheses* 15. 5 where Symeon, quoting v 34 and alluding to vv 35-36ab, insists that they refer to a ministry to Christ within the Christian soul:

> Come, O blessed of my Father, inherit the kingdom prepared for you, because you fed me when I was hungry for your salvation by practicing my commandments, you gave me to drink, you clothed me, you welcomed me, you visited me by cleansing your hearts from every spot and defilement of sin.[13]

Theophylact of Bulgaria (d. AD 1070)

In his *Enarratio in Evangelium Matthaei* 25: 31-46, Theophylact does not even discuss the question of those who are to be gathered before the throne. Most of his commentary on vv 31-33 is taken up with an explanation as to why the saints are called sheep (they are meek, productive, and useful) and the condemned goats (they are confused, wander out onto precipices and are sterile).[14] Elaborating on v 34, he makes the point that Christ does not say "receive [λάβετε] the kingdom" but "inherit [κληρονομήσατε] the kingdom," since it belongs to the just as their patrimony. Theophylact seems to be aware of the problem of the identity of "the least." Commenting on v 40, he states: "He calls the least brothers, either his own disciples or simply all the poor. For every poor man is a brother of Christ insofar as he is poor, inasmuch as Christ lived in poverty."[15] From the above quotation it is clear that Theophylact's understanding of "the least" is universal, but a few paragraphs later in his commentary, possibly influenced by Symeon the New Theologian, he understands the six Matthean works in a decidedly spiritual way and sees the Christian as the beneficiary:

> Feed Christ who is hungry for our salvation. For you have fed and given drink to Christ, if you have fed and given drink to the one hungry for teaching. For Christ is in the Christian and faith is nourished and increased by teaching. Whenever you see anyone who is estranged from his heavenly homeland, receive him, that is, when you enter heaven bring him with you lest, after preaching to others, you yourself are rejected. If anyone has thrown off the garment of incorruption with which he was clothed at baptism and is naked, clothe him. Take care of the weak in faith (as Paul says), and visit the one shut up in prison, that is, in this dark body, giving him admonition as if it were splendor. Fulfill all six forms of charity in a corporal manner, but also in a spiritual manner. Since our nature is twofold, corporal and spiritual, so these works are to be accomplished in a twofold manner.[16]

In his remarks on v 41, Theophylact emphasizes that the punishing fire was not created for the condemned, but for the devil and his minions. This is an indication, he says, that the condemned are liable to punishment because of their own free will.[17] Commenting on v 46, he states that the words κόλασιν αἰώνιον are a clear argument against Origen's position that ultimately the condemned will be released from their punishments and join the just in heaven.[18]

Euthymius Zigabenus (d. ca. AD 1122)

The exegetical works of this Byzantine theologian are remarkable for the account they take of the literal sense of the Scriptures, an achievement that is unusual among the later Greek exegetes.[19] This less spiritual approach to the Matthean "identity dialogue" is evident in Euthymius' *Commentarium in Matthaeum* 61, where he treats the six works solely in a corporal sense. According to Euthymius vv 35-36 are addressed to the Christians only. He sees the six works as a sort of compendium of the entire Gospel: "It is clear that he addresses these words to Christians alone to whom the precepts of his Gospel were directed."[20] Euthymius insists that every word, work and thought of man will be examined by the judge, but in this scene, he says, Christ uses the sole criterion of concern or lack of concern for one's fellow man to indicate the primacy and necessity of the virtue of love: "For love is the trademark by which every Christian is able to be recognized. By this, he says, will all know that you are my disciples, if you have mutual love among yourselves."[21] The above quotation of John 13:35 in the context of a discussion of Matt 25:35-36 would seem to indicate that Euthymius understood "the least" to be fellow Christians, but a few paragraphs later, commenting on v 40, he indicates a broader horizon, leaving the reader the impression that anyone poor and needy could be the proper beneficiary of the Christian's charity: "The poor he called brothers, since he undertook a nature and abasement similar to theirs and also because they shared in his poverty."[22]

Euthymius does not even discuss the components of πάντα τὰ ἔθνη in v 32, but in his remarks on that verse states that only Christians will undergo the separation to the right and the left.[23] Quoting Ps 1:5, he insists that the unbelievers are not the concern of Christ in this scene: "He will have no word for the unbelievers; all of them will be condemned by him together. For he says: The wicked will not arise at the judgment [οὐκ ἀναστήσονται ἀσεβεῖς ἐν κρίσει], that is, they will not rise to be judged but to be punished."[24] Euthymius' vision of the judgment scene is a bit unclear. Are the unbelievers present with the believers before the throne and thus included in πάντα τὰ ἔθνη? His observations that Christ's words are addressed to believers alone would seem to preclude this. Yet his comment in the above quotation that the wicked will rise to be punished might indicate his belief that they would be present as onlookers. What is certain from Euthymius' commentary is that he considers Matt 25:31-46 to be a description of the judgment of Christians alone.

Theophane Cerameus (d. AD 1140)

This archbishop of Taormina, Sicily, left no commentary on Matthew as such, but in his lengthy Greek *Homiliae de tempore* 18 he presents his exegesis of Matt 25:31-46. He is a universalist in regard to the meaning of πάντα τὰ ἔθνη: all of humanity, from the beginning of creation, will be gathered in the same place.[25] Commenting on vv 35-36, he states that the six Matthean works are to be understood as a compendium of all the virtues.[26] Arguing that six is the perfect number because of its various numerical components, Theophane says that the fact six works are mentioned is an indication that they represent the "perfection of virtue" in the same way that God's perfection is symbolized by the six days of creation in Genesis 1.[27] The works of mercy are to be understood in a spiritual as well as a corporal manner: "Since man is twofold, exterior and interior, the observation of the precepts will be twofold."[28] In addition to the literal meaning of vv 35-36, the Christian is to refresh the one "hungry for the Divine Word," take in the "stranger deprived of his heavenly home by perverse deeds," teaching and exhorting him so as "to cover him with the garment of virtue." Those incarcerated in the "dark prisons of ignorance" are to be visited with the "light of knowledge," while the sick to be tended to are those who are "weak in faith."[29]

Theophane does not comment on v 40, but is taken up with the fact that "the least" in v 45 are not addressed as "brothers" as they are in v 40. In his attempt to explain the difference, he is ambiguous. He leaves the reader with the impression that either "the least" of v 40 ("the least" of the saved) is an entirely different category than "the least" in v 45 ("the least" of the damned) or else "the least" in vv 40, 45 is the same category, namely, those on the right; but Christ refuses to call them "brothers" when speaking to the damned because the damned are no longer his brothers:

> Perhaps [Christ] accommodates his speech to his opinion of each of them. The just were concerned in this life about the poor as if they were the brothers of Christ; the wicked, however, rejected them as the lowest and most wretched of people.... Those who with a strong and patient spirit bore the inconveniences of poverty, as did the ulcerated Lazarus, and did not raise their voices in blasphemy because of the evils they suffered, are placed at the right and named the brothers of Christ. Those, however, who, in addition to material poverty, lacked the riches of virtue were banished to the left and also removed from the family of Christ. To all on both sides receiving the reward of their merits he speaks in a demonstrative way and, as if with his finger, points out the one of whom he is speaking; he calls the poor located on the right brothers, while those who occupied the left he does not dignify with this name.[30]

Dionysius Bar Salibi (d. AD 1171)

As did Isho'dad of Merv, Dionysius, in his *Commentarii in Evangelia* Matt 25:31, speculates as to how many and what type of angels will accompany Christ. He disagrees with

Theodore of Mopsuestia and Isho'dad in this matter and concludes that πάντες οἱ ἄγγελοι must be taken at its face value to mean all angels.[31] His interpretation of πάντα τὰ ἔθνη in v 32 is just as universal; he states that it means "all men."[32]

As expected of a Syrian exegete, Dionysius has a spiritual understanding of the six Matthean works, but not to the extent that that was discernible in the works of Symeon the New Theologian and Theophylact. He approaches the text more in the literal manner of the Antiochene School. Commenting on v 35, he states:

> *For I was hungry*: by means of the poor I ate and was filled. And notice that he seeks only bread from us, not a multitude of necessities. Again, *I was hungry*: that I might save you. *And you fed me*: you became obedient from the heart and abandoned sin. The hunger of our Lord, therefore, is our salvation. *I thirsted*: he asks only a drink of water from us. *I was a stranger*: where are those who reject strangers? Let them know that in their hatred they reject Christ. *I was ill*: he did not say: You healed me, but: *You took care of me*, teaching that he demands from man nothing beyond his power. *I was in prison*: he did not say: You led me out of prison, but: *You came to me*, showing that he demands nothing from man except what is in his power.[33]

Dionysius' understanding of "the least" might well be universal. In his brief remarks on v 40, he gives no indication that he has only Christians in mind: "He calls the unknown, strangers, and the worthless 'his brothers;' we, however, who are formed from the same clay, are ashamed to call them our brothers. He called them 'little ones' [ze ure] because they are humble and lack the things of this world."[34]

Anonymous Writings

The anonymous *Scholia vetera in Matthaeum*, which might have been compiled by Leo Patricius in the ninth or tenth centuries AD,[35] do not address the problems of the identity of "the least" or the composition of πάντα τὰ ἔθνη. Its only comments are brief and concern Matt 25:33, 34, and 42. The just are compared to sheep, it is stated, because sheep are useful: they produce wool, offspring, milk, and cheese. Goats, however, are nonproductive and wicked by nature, as are the condemned who are wicked of their own free will.[36] The comment on v 34 stresses the use of the word κληρονομήσατε rather than λάβετε,[37] and the scholion on v 42 simply rehashes the biblical text, adding nothing new.[38]

Western Authors

Paul the Deacon (ca. AD 720 - 800)

This famous chronicler, who is sometimes referred to as the "Father of Italian History," left no commentary on the Gospel of Matthew, but in his *Homiliae de tempore* 73, written for the first Monday in Lent, the only day in the medieval western ecclesiastical calendar when Matt 25:31-46 was read liturgically, he gives his interpretation of the pericope. In his remarks on vv 31-33, Paul insists that Christ will return to judge "all men, from the first man, Adam, until the one who will be born at the end of the world, those from the beginning of the world who are now dead, and those who will be found alive in their bodies."[39] Christ will return in human form to point out the heresy of those who say that after his resurrection and ascension he no longer had a human nature. Paul acknowledges that the majority of exegetes understand the throne of judgment to be a cloud, but he says a more suitable understanding of the throne would be the church, since Christ, when he appears, will sit in the midst of his church to glorify her.[40] As were Chrysostom and Jerome, Paul is at pains, in his discussion of the sheep and the goats, to point out that the wicked are called "young goats" (*haedos*) because they are useless and incapable of producing offspring, and are not to be associated with the useful "she-goat" (*capra*). Reflecting the tradition that first surfaced in the writings of Gregory the Great, Paul divides all those gathered before the throne into four classes: the just who will co-judge with Christ (the apostles and those who left all to follow Christ), the just to be judged (Christians who are to be saved), the wicked to be judged (Christians to be condemned), and those already judged (all who are not Christian). He understands the judgment described in this pericope to pertain only to Christians, the two categories that are to be judged.[41]

Paul has a literal understanding of the six merciful acts described in vv 35-36, but he insists that a spiritual understanding of the works produces a charity more pleasing to God:

> ... charity is to be shown not only to a brother's flesh, which will die, but much more to his soul, which will always survive .... Therefore, whoever nourishes the hungry and thirsty with the bread of the word and the water of wisdom performs works of perfect charity. Whoever by sacred admonition recalls one wandering from the way of truth and by penance receives him into the house of the holy Church, truly performs works of piety. Whoever, according to the Apostle, receives the weak in faith and imparts the solace of compassion and a word of consolation to the one shut up in the prison of tribulations ... indeed fulfills the duties of true love and will therefore be remunerated with piety's reward.[42]

In his commentary on v 40, Paul indicates that, even though a universal understanding of "the least" could be supported by the evidence, a more valid interpretation would see "the least" as Christians, especially the monks who live in voluntary poverty:

> Certainly what he says: Whatever you did to one of my least, you did to me, can be understood generally of every poor man, since alms given to any needy person whatsoever because of Christ is received by [Christ] himself. But when the Lord notably and as if pointing says: to one of these least, he shows that he is not speaking in general about any poor whatsoever, but only about those who are poor in spirit, who because of God endure voluntary poverty. These the faithful should particularly support from their own resources, and

should become friends with them, so that they might be received by them into the eternal dwellings of the kingdom of heaven.[43]

The same narrow outlook is evident in his remarks on v 45. As if to underscore this restrictive viewpoint, Paul interpolates into the verse τῶν ἀδελφῶν μου from v 40 and adds the further restrictive commentary that Christ is benefited only when the benefactor is Christian as well and does not operate out of human respect:

> . . . as often as you did not do [it] to one of these least, my brothers, you did not do [it] to me. Whoever neglects to give benefit to the humble and despised members of Christ proves that he is in no way devoted to Christ, and therefore can never feel pleased that he gave him anything. Take note of the fact that here, as above [in v 40], mention is made of unity, when it states: As often as you did not do [it] to one of my least, you did not do [it] to me. By this it is proven that the generosity of one who strives to give with a simple intention of the heart in the unity of the Catholic faith is acceptable to God. The charity of the person, however, who is separated from the unity of the faith by heretical depravity, or who by his good work seeks human praise, is judged sinful and unworthy by Christ.[44]

Paul seems to place a heavy emphasis on predestination in his commentary. In his remarks on v 34 he does not make the familiar distinction between κληρονομήσατε and λάβετε, but dwells instead on the fact that the just were "predestined and preordained" for the kingdom.[45] Commenting on v 41, he nowhere mentions the all too common observation that eternal punishment was not created for man, but instead makes the point that the wicked were "preordained" for this eternal punishment together with Satan and his cohorts.[46]

Christian Druthmar (d. ca. AD 850)

This monk of the celebrated monastery of Corbie, in his *Expositio in Matthaeum Evangelistam* 56, clearly indicates that he considered "the least" to be Christians and that, as did so many commentators before him, he interpreted the Matthean works in a corporal and spiritual manner:

> I was hungry in my members. Which is my Church. And you fed me. Either material or spiritual food. I thirsted and you gave me to drink. Just as the food is spiritual, so is the drink . . . . . I was naked and you covered me. It is corporal and spiritual nudity . . . . Ill and you took care of me. Those who call upon God the Father, whether in sickness of body or sickness of soul, must be visited . . . . I was in prison and you visited me. The prison can be understood as anguish and cowardice of the spirit. The exercise of all these works of piety can be understood in a corporal and spiritual manner.[47]

Commenting on v 40, Druthmar emphasizes his restrictive outlook further by predicating of "the least" qualities not found in the biblical text, but perhaps included in the marginal *glossae* of the manuscripts at his disposal: "What he said about these least, his brothers, is to be emphasized: that is, they believe in God the Father, they call upon him, and they are not puffed up, but humble in spirit."[48]

In his remarks on vv 31-34 Druthmar states that "all men, good and bad" will be present at the judgment; and in a possible reference to the controversy over the angels found in the works of the eastern commentators, he claims that all nine ranks of the angelic creation would be present as well.[49] The judgment will not take place, as some think, in the "Valley of Josaphat, a place in Judea," but in the air as indicated by Paul in 1 Thess 4:17.[50] Contrasting ἐκ δεξιῶν αὐτοῦ in v 34 with ἐξ εὐωνύμων in v 41, Druthmar makes the point that the possessive pronoun is missing in v 41 because God does not have a left, that is an evil, side.[51] He ends his commentary with a lengthy discourse on Origen's error and how κόλασιν αἰώνιον in v 46 is a refutation of that error.⁵²

Haymo of Halberstadt (d. ca. AD 853)

In his *Homiliae de tempore* 29, given on the first Monday of Lent, Haymo says nothing specifically about his understanding of the six works, but he does interpret "the least" of v 40 in a narrow way. At the same time he indicates that charity performed for anyone is done to Christ:

> Granted that Christ is received in all the poor and that almsgiving to all is given to him, nevertheless in this world he especially designates those who are poor not in body, but in spirit: those who left their possessions for God, as did the apostles and their imitators, over whom the Lord, extending his hands, said: Behold my mother and my brothers.⁵³

Haymo is influenced here by Jerome's observations on Matt 25:40,⁵⁴ but he clarifies the concept of the "poor in spirit" by indicating that they are to be understood as the apostles and their imitators, namely the religious who took a voluntary vow of poverty.⁵⁵

Haymo understands v 32 in a universal sense: Christ will come to judge the "human race" [genus humanum].⁵⁶ Commenting on v 33, he states that the just are compared to sheep because they imitate the innocent Christ who was led as a sheep to his slaughter; while the wicked are called goats, not only because they imitate the petulance and wildness of a goat, but also (and here he again shows his dependence on Jerome) because in the OT a goat was always sacrificed for the people's sins.⁵⁷ He understands v 34 as proof that the elect were saved by the "foreknowledge and predestination of God,"⁵⁸ and concludes his homily with the usual refutation of Origen's error provided by v 46.⁵⁹

Rabanus Maurus of Mainz (ca. AD 776 - 856)

This abbot of the famed monastery at Fulda, in his *Commentarium in Matthaeum* 7. 25, follows Paul the Deacon's observations on Matt 25: 31-46 so closely that he must have had a copy of Paul's commentary in front of him as he wrote. In his comments on vv 40, 45, however, Rabanus deviates significantly from Paul's commentary. This could be an indication that he held a wider understanding of "the least" than Paul did.

In his commentary on v 40, Rabanus simply quotes Jerome. He would thus understand the "poor in spirit" to be Christians, but, unlike Paul the Deacon, he does not more narrowly identify them as monks: "To me it does not seem to be spoken about the poor in general, but about those who are poor in spirit, to whom [Christ], stretching out his hand, had said: These are my brothers and my mother; they perform the will of my Father in heaven."[60]

In his remarks on v 45 Rabanus continues to follow the commentary of Paul almost verbatim, but, in a further manifestation that he might have a wider view than Paul regarding "the least," he omits the restrictive words "members of Christ" that follow "humble and despised": "As often as you did not do [it] to one of these lesser ones [minoribus], you did not do [it] to me. Whoever disdains to help the least [minimis], that is, the humble and despised, cannot feel glad that he ministered to the king of the humble, that is, the judge of all."[61] Continuing to quote from Paul the Deacon, Rabanus indicates that the donor must be a believer if the gift is to be regarded as offered to Christ: " . . . whatever is given to God should be offered through the unity of faith and peace and with a simple intention . . . ."[62]

Rabanus has another revealing omission in his commentary. In his remarks on v 41, he follows the thought of Paul the Deacon that the fire was preordained by God for the devil and his angels, but he omits the words "and for the condemned" that are found in his *Vorlage*.[63] This is most assuredly a reflection of Rabanus' controversy with the heterodox monk Gottschalk who, restricting the universal saving will of God, taught that some are predestined to eternal fire.

Rabanus' commentary on Matt 25:32-36 is no longer extant due to "the savagery of soldiers" in some past war,[64] so we are at a loss as to his views on πάντα τὰ ἔθνη in v 32 and the six works described in vv 35-36. Since he follows Paul the Deacon so closely in the rest of his commentary, however, it would seem plausible that he would likewise have followed him in the pages that are missing. Hence, Rabanus possibly was a universalist in regard to πάντα τὰ ἔθνη and viewed the six works from a spiritual as well as a corporal perspective.

Paschasius Radbertus (ca. AD 790 - 865)

This important Benedictine theologian of the monastery of Corbie produced such a thorough and important commentary on Matthew that it was to become one of the main sources of the *Glossa ordinaria*, the standard medieval commentary on the Bible.[65] In his *Expositio in Matthaeum* 11. 25, 31-46, Paschasius not only treats Matt 25:31-46 as the last of the parables, but, as did Chrysostom, he insists that it can be properly understood only if taken together with the two parables that precede it: the Parable of the Ten Virgins (Matt 25:1-13) and the Parable of the Silver Pieces (Matt 25:14-30). Each parable, he claims, can be divided into the saved (the wise virgins, the two industrious servants, and the sheep) and the condemned (the foolish virgins, the one lazy servant, and the goats).[66] Matthew places the last judgment scene immediately before the account of Jesus' passion to show that the judgment he endured at the hands of men would have a bearing on his judgment of the world.[67]

Paschasius directly addresses the problem of v 32 and, following Origen's commentary closely, asks whether πάντα τὰ ἔθνη refers to "all peoples that existed in all generations of the world; or only those who at the end of the world will still be alive; or only those who believed in the Gospel of Christ . . . ."[68] He insists that all people who ever existed, "the good as well as the bad, the believers and the unbelievers,"[69] will be gathered before Christ who will appear in bodily form and sit on his throne, the church.[70] To counter those who object that no spot on earth is large enough for such a convocation, Paschasius explains that all will appear in their resurrected state, free from the limitations of space;[71] and that since Christ in his resurrected state is everywhere and is absent from no place on earth, he will be present simultaneously to all, wherever they may be, in the eyes of their minds.[72]

In his remarks on v 33, Paschasius pretty much copies the commentary of Jerome. Commenting on v 34 he emphasizes the predestination of the just, but warns the reader to beware of heretics who, following a suggestion made in Origen's commentary that there are "other blessed who are inferior,"[73] use v 34 to claim that there will be some not blessed by the Father, but nevertheless saved since they will be blessed by Christ. All who undergo judgment and are saved, says Paschasius, are included in the εὐλογημένοι of v 34, just as all the condemned are referred to by κατηραμένοι in v 41.[74]

Paschasius understands the six Matthean works in a corporal as well as a spiritual manner: ". . . whether corporally or spiritually, anyone who . . . refreshes the body with material food or the soul with spiritual food feeds and refreshes God in his members."[75] He continually makes the point that the the six acts of love include all the other virtues, since wherever love is present "all the virtues are preserved."[76] Consequently, as did Origen, he claims that no one can argue that the sole criterion of judgment is humaneness or inhumaneness.[77] There is no doubt that in Paschasius' view "the least" are Christians. Commenting on vv 35-36, he states:

> For I was hungry and you fed me. Here is commended the great unity between Christ and the great sacrament of the Church, regarding which the Apostle says that the two will be in one flesh, that is, Christ and the Church; so that he is the head and all the elect are members in one body of the one head . . . . Wherefore, only those moved by the spirit of God are the sons of God, the brothers of Christ, and they live in the body of Christ. As I mentioned, the great unity between them is in this place [vv 35-36] commended by the Lord, so that he

testifies that whatever you do to one of them is, in a strange way, done entirely to himself.[78]

Not only are "the least" Christians; Paschasius makes it very clear that they are the apostles and others who preach the gospel and leave everything for Christ. He quotes 2 Cor 8:14 to elucidate his narrow understanding of vv 35-36.[79]

In his observations on vv 42-43, Paschasius gives more evidence of his narrow interpretation of the beneficiaries:

> Just as Christ is hungry and suffers in his body which is the Church, so is he fed and refreshed [in the Church] ... in each one of his saints he is fed with food and refreshed by drink; naked, he is clothed; a stranger, he is welcomed; in prison, he is consoled; and sick; he is visited .... If Paul is truly sick with the sick and suffers with all the brothers, how much more does Christ, the head of the entire Church ....[80]

Commenting on v 40, Paschasius indicates that "the least" will be present at the judgment, not among those to be saved or condemned, but, as a third category, as co-judges with Christ. They are the ones referred to in Matt 19:27-29 who gave up all to follow Christ; hence, they will judge with Christ:

> Christ says in a demonstrative manner: Whatever you did or did not do to one of these least, my brothers. Hence, the sense is clear that those about whom he speaks, to whom he seems to extend a finger as if pointing, will be present. They will therefore be with the Lord at the same judgment; not that they might be judged, as I said, but that they might judge, for they left behind all their possessions and even themselves for the sake of Christ. Because of Christ they were judged in the world, and therefore ... they will judge others.[81]

In a lengthy description Paschasius compares "the least" to Paul and the other apostles and says that the sufferings of "the least" are the same as those mentioned by Paul in 2 Cor 11:23-27.[82] He proceeds to quote Jerome's comments on v 40, and then states that the co-judges with Christ are called "the least" either in comparison to Christ, or because their number will be exceedingly small,[83] or, as Origen claims, because they were considered least by the world, or else because they, due to their humility, considered themselves to be the lowest.[84] Paschasius ends his discussion of v 40 with what seems to be a plea for special consideration for preachers and professed religious:

> Wherefore as household members in the faith are always more chosen, so let those who labor at the word of God and display in themselves the discipline of Christ be more honored with every indulgence of humanity. It is for such as these that a great reward is acquired and the religion of Christ venerated.[85]

In his remarks on v 45, he makes an issue of the absence of τῶν ἀδελφῶν μου. By not referring to "the least" as "my brothers" when he addresses the condemned, says Paschasius in a weak argument taken from Origen, Christ shows the grandeur and the excellence of the deeds of the just and refuses to give undue attention to the condemned.[86]

Commenting on v 41, he again quotes Origen and says that the condemned are not addressed as "condemned by my Father" because the Father is the author of blessing and not malediction. Each one of the condemned, claims Paschasius, is the author of his own condemnation. That is also the reason for the absence of the possessive pronoun αὐτοῦ that one would expect to follow ἐξ εὐωνύμων in v 41; since God is not the source of condemnation, he has no left side.[87]

In his commentary on Matthew Paschasius follows Origen and Jerome closely. The only concept that he seems to develop a bit more in depth is the idea that "the least" are the apostles and others who left everything to follow Christ.

Remigius of Auxerre (ca. AD 841-908)

The medieval philosopher Remigius of Auxerre wrote a *Commentarius vastus in Matthaeum,* but as yet this commentary remains unpublished.[88] J. P. Migne states that there are manuscripts of it in the library of the elector of Bavaria as well as in libraries in Venice and Vienna.[89] Remigius is an important commentator because he is quoted often in the works of those who came after him. It is difficult to know Remigius' viewpoints because so many may have quoted him without giving him proper credit. Those who did acknowledge their dependence on him, however, were Zachary of Besançon, Thomas Aquinas, and Ludolph of Saxony. It is from their commentaries that a partial reconstruction of his interpretation of Matt 25:31-46 is made possible.

Remigius' views on the identity of "the least" remain unknown, but he seems to be a universalist in regard to πάντα τὰ ἔθνη of v 32, stating that "these words prove that the resurrection of men shall be real."[90] Agreeing with Paul the Deacon, he states that Christ will return at the judgment in human form to refute the error of those who say that after his resurrection he no longer possessed a human nature,[91] and that the throne upon which he will sit is "the Church in which he will appear in his omnipotence."[92] Remigius emphasizes the predestination of the just in his comment on v 34 and notes, as he also does when he comments on vv 37-39, that the conversation between Christ and the elect is not a verbal transmission but takes place in their consciences.[93]

Anselm of Laon (d. AD 1117)

In his *Enarrationes in Evangelium Matthaei* 25,[94] Anselm follows closely the commentaries of his predecessors in which are contained the ideas of the Fathers, especially Origen and Jerome. He does not consider Matt 25:31-46 to be a parable, as did Paschasius Radbertus, but rather an actual description of the final judgment. He sees the Church as the throne of Christ's majesty before which will appear all peoples "of every time, every condition and every sex."[95] He repeats the opinion begun with Gregory the Great that those present at the final judgment will fall into one of the four traditional categories.[96] In wording that betrays his reliance on the commentary of Paul the Deacon, Anselm interprets the six Matthean works in a corporal as well as a spiritual manner and, quoting Jerome, states that "the least" are not the poor in general, "but only those who are poor in spirit who, having put aside their own will, do the will of the heavenly Father."[97] His observations on v 41 seem to contain a rebuke to Gottschalk and his followers who held for the predestination of the condemned: " . . . the wicked are finally taken away so that they might not see the glory of God and are sent into the eternal fire which was prepared for the devil and his angels, not for men, from the beginning of the world . . . ."[98]

Bruno of Asti (d. AD 1123)

This abbot of Monte Cassino and later bishop of Segni simply reiterates the thoughts of the Fathers and his more immediate predecessors in his *Commentaria in Matthaeum* 4. 25. He interprets πάντα τὰ ἔθνη in a universal way: "it will not be difficult to gather all nations if it was not difficult to create and resuscitate them;"[99] and understands "the least" in a restrictive manner. Commenting on v 40 he states: "Christ is received in his own members: for all Christians are his own members. They are therefore called Christians because they are members of Christ."[100] Bruno does not indicate in his commentary whether he holds a spiritual interpretation of the six works or not. In his remarks on vv 34-36, he gets sidetracked by a discussion of predestination from which he does not recover.[101] This excursus on predestination is likewise found, and more fully developed, in his *Homiliae de tempore* 29, a sermon on Matt 25:31-46, in which he seems to be speaking of what would later be called "consequent predestination" which takes into account the good or evil deeds of men: "If you do these things, be certain and believe without doubt that you are destined for eternal life. But if with an obdurate heart you refuse to do these things and persevere in this evil, know for sure that you are predestined to death."[102]

Rupert of Deutz (ca. AD 1075 - 1130)

This monastic theologian gives his interpretation of Matt 25:31-46 in his work *De Trinitate et operibus eius* 42. 9, 8-24, in a discussion of the final gift of the Spirit, "fear of the Lord." Rupert understands πάντα τὰ ἔθνη in a universal way: all mankind in their resurrected state will be gathered for judgment and will fall into one of the four categories first mentioned by Gregory the Great and repeated in almost every medieval commentary.[103]

In his discussion of vv 35-36 Rupert makes a causal link between the six Matthean acts and the reward of the kingdom: "There are, therefore, six works of mercy *after which and because of which* is said: Come, blessed of my Father, possess the kingdom."[104] The six works are a reflection of the six days of divine activity at the creation, since the kingdom was prepared, not "before the beginning of the world," but "at the beginning of the world."[105] As God rested on the seventh day, so the kingdom promised to the blessed in v 34 is that sabbath rest that is the subject of Heb 4:3-6.[106] Rupert treats the six works of mercy in a purely corporal manner, stating that they belong by nature to Christians involved, as was Martha, in the active life, and hence will be the criteria used for their judgment.[107] Christian contemplatives who follow the example of Mary, says Rupert, are not able to fulfill the six Matthean works since they have already relinquished everything for Christ. They will not be judged, but will be included in the category of those who will be co-judges with Christ, who, Rupert states, are the ones Christ refers to as "the least":

> Who are the least to whom, as if with a finger, he points: As often as you did [it] to one of my least ones, he says, you did [it] to me? Who are they, or where are they, since he says this to all who are stationed on the right? They are of another order, namely the order of those who, as we said above, are not judged but judge, according to the promise of the one who said: Because you left everything and followed me, in the

resurrection when the Son of Man will sit on the throne of his majesty, and so forth.[108]

Rupert makes the point strongly that Christ did not say "what [quod] you did to my least" but rather "as long as [quandiu] you did [it] to my least." Hence, at the judgment the criterion of time or duration will be taken into consideration so that "the one who ministered longer will have more of the reward."[109]

In his remarks on v 41 Rupert gives evidence that he had at hand a Bible containing the variant reading "qui praeparatus est diabolo et angelis eius,"[110] for he argues from the prefix *prae* that the eternal fire was created before the kingdom, and hence before the world.[111]

Ralph of Laon   (d. AD 1133)

The commentary on Matthew 25:31-46 in the *Glossa ordinaria* or *Glossa communis*, the standard medieval commentary on the Scriptures, was long thought to be the work of Walafrid Strabo (ca. AD 808-849). In fact, it was compiled by Ralph, the brother of Anselm of Laon,[112] who comments only on vv 31-34, 37, 40, 42, 44, and 46. He did not consider Matt 25:31-46 to be one of the parables, but a realistic description of the parousia.[113] The comments on v 32 have to do with the division of those gathered into the four traditional categories; there is no discussion of πάντα τὰ ἔθνη as such. The *Glossa* reflects the influence of Jerome throughout, especially in its discussion of why the wicked are called goats and the fact that those on the right are predestined for the kingdom. Jerome's narrow understanding of "the least" is also seen in the brief commentary on v 40: "Of these brothers: My brothers and mother are those who do the will of my Father."[114]

Zachary of Besançon   (d. ca. AD 1152)

In his *De concordia evangelistarum* 3.151, a commentary on a harmony of the Gospels modeled on that of Ammonius of

Alexandria,[115] Zachary merely compiles the opinions of commentators who preceded him, especially Chrysostom, Jerome, Augustine, Paul the Deacon and Rabanus Maurus. He does not give a clear opinion regarding πάντα τὰ ἔθνη, but it might be presumed that he is a universalist since he states that all those gathered for the final judgment will fall into one of the four Gregorian categories.[116] He agrees with earlier commentators who see "the throne" as the church[117] and understand the six works of mercy in a spiritual as well as a corporal manner.[118] For Zachary "the least" are Christians. In his remarks on v 40, he reiterates the narrow interpretation of Jerome,[119] and in his comments on vv 42-43, repeats the well known observation found in Augustine's *Sermon* 137. 2:

> Christ is the head of the Church; the Church is his body. In our body the head is on top, while the feet are on the ground. In a crowd of men should someone trample on your foot, would not your head say: Why do you trample on me? As the tongue, therefore, which no one touches, says: Why do you trample on me? so Christ the head, on whom no one tramples, will say: I was hungry and you did not feed me, and so forth.[120]

Reflecting the concerns of his own age, Zachary dedicates the greater part of his commentary on Matt 25:31-46 to a discussion of the location and nature of the "eternal punishment" mentioned in v 46.[121]

Peter Comestor (d. ca. AD 1179)

This author of the *Historia scholastica*, a biblical commentary which ranked with the *Glossa ordinaria* as a standard textbook in the Middle Ages, was called "Comestor" or "Manducator" because he was regarded to have "eaten and digested the scriptures."[122] His comments on the Matthean "identity dialogue," found in *In evangelia* 145, comprise three sentences:

Then the judge will mention the works of mercy which are, namely, to feed the hungry, give drink to the thirsty, receive the stranger, clothe the naked, visit the sick, console the imprisoned. The seventh, to bury the dead, is written in Tobit. There will be mention of nothing else, since all will know their own merits for which they will be saved or condemned.[123]

Peter seems to understand only the literal sense of vv 35-36. For the first time, possibly, the burial of the dead (Tob 1:17-18; 2:4; 12:12-13) is linked to the six Matthean works to form what will come to be called the "seven corporal works of mercy." Peter sheds no light on the composition of πάντα τὰ ἔθνη or the identity of τῶν ἀδελφῶν μου τῶν ἐλαχίστων. As was Zachary, he is much more taken up with a lengthy discussion of the location, intensity and nature of the fire in vv 41, 46.[124]

Hugh of Saint Cher (d. ca. AD 1263)

This Dominican prior from Paris, with the assistance of his friars, compiled a new apparatus to the entire Bible, supplementing the *Glossa ordinaria* with additional excerpts from the scriptures and the Fathers and drawing on commentators of the twelfth and early thirteenth centuries.[125] In his remarks on Matt 25:31-46 in *In Evangelia secundum Matthaeum, Lucam, Marcum et Joannem*,[126] Hugh readily manifests this penchant to explain a passage of Scripture by the use of another passage.

With regard to v 32 Hugh seems to be a universalist: he says that Christ, seated on "his throne, that is, the Church in which his omnipotence will appear," will gather all peoples before him by. Hugh does not explicitly address the issue of the make-up of πάντα τὰ ἔθνη, but the fact that he quotes Joel 4:2, Rom 14:12, 1 Cor 15:22, and 2 Cor 5:10 as commentary on v 32 is an indication that he has all humanity in mind.

His interpretation of the six Matthean works is spiritual as well as corporal, but in his commentary on vv 35-36 the spiritual understanding is more predominant than the corporal:

> I hungered in myself for the salvation of men . . . . And you gave me as food your very selves by believing and working . . . . I thirsted in my own for justice . . . you fed me by helping, inviting and congratulating them . . . . I hungered in my own for the bread of doctrine . . . . I hungered in my own for material bread . . . . I thirsted in my own for the drink of wisdom . . .[127]

In his listing of the corporal works, Hugh, possibly influenced by Isa 58:6 and the capture of Christians in the Crusades, changes "visitation" of the captive to "redemption" of the captive, and, reflecting the influence of Peter Comestor, adds the Tobian seventh work to form a sort of mnemonic jingle that was to become popular in the Middle Ages: "The works of mercy touched on here are six, namely, to visit the sick, give drink to the thirsty, visit the hungry, redeem captives, clothe the naked, welcome strangers. The seventh is (Tobit 2) to bury the dead. Whence: Visito, poto, cibo, redimo, tego, colligo, condo."[128]

To elucidate the meaning of v 40, Hugh quotes Sir 19:23 [Vg] and Matt 12:50, which figured prominently in Jerome's interpretation: "He says this because not all the least are his brothers. Eccl 19: There is one who humbles himself wickedly. Matt 12: Whoever does the will of my Father who is in heaven is my brother and sister and mother."[129] Commenting on v 45, he reiterates the beginning of John Chrysostom's comment on the same verse in *Homilies on Matthew* 79.1: "What are you saying? They are your brothers and you call them least? For this very reason they are brothers, because they are lowly, because they are outcast."[130]

In the above quotations Hugh is obviously referring to the interpretations of Jerome and Chrysostom, but he omits from their comments phrases that more clearly identify "the least" as Christians. Is this an indication that Hugh holds for a wider interpretation? I think not. Most likely Hugh's understanding of "the least" is that they are Christians. He is aware that his readers would be familiar with the comments of Chrysostom and Jerome; so even a partial quotation of their thoughts would indicate to his readers that he held the same narrow viewpoint.

Bonaventure (ca. AD 1217 - 1274)

The Franciscan Giovanni di Fidanza, who came to be called Bonaventure, left no commentary on the Gospel of Matthew, but in his extant works there are so many quotations and allusions from Matt 25:31-46 that they form an unofficial commentary on the Matthean pericope. As an exegete and a spiritual writer Bonaventure was to have a great and lasting influence, especially in the Franciscan schools, so it was no surprise that in AD 1685 the Italian Capuchin Bartholomew de Barberiis published a *Glossa in Sacram Scripturam* that was based solely on the writings of the Seraphic Doctor.[131]

With regard to πάντα τὰ ἔθνη in v 32, Bonaventure is a universalist. Not only will all human beings in their resurrected bodies be gathered, but the angels as well. The just will see the divinity, as well as the humanity, of Christ; the wicked will see only his humanity. The throne upon which Christ will sit for judgment will be the cross, with all the instruments of the passion, in the midst of a shining cloud. The just are to be stationed at his right, not only because the right signifies the spiritual realities in which they were interested, but also because at the crucifixion the good thief hung on Jesus' right.[132]

Christ, in v 34, addresses the elect first and enumerates their good works in order to inflict further punishment on the damned by letting them see what they lost. As did so many commentators before him, Bonaventure stresses that the just were predestined for the kingdom, which he says is nothing other than God himself.[133]

Only the six works of mercy in vv 35-36 are used as the criteria for judgment, says Bonaventure, because they contain the fullness of mercy, and because Christ wishes to show that the indispensable trademark of the Christian must be love; hence these works are of precept and not supererogatory.[134] Bonaventure interprets the works in a corporal and spiritual manner, with a decided emphasis on the spiritual, and sees them refer not only to the needy members of Christ but to the human Jesus as well:

> ... he himself in his most blessed Passion hungered greatly for our justice, and had a spiritual thirst on the cross, together with a corporal hunger and thirst ... feed him in yourself and in your heart or at least in the poor. He was a stranger since when his death was imminent he said: My kingdom is not of this world ... let us welcome this stranger inside ourselves or in his members .... He was naked on the cross and showed himself that way to us so that we might clothe him with the garment of charity, especially in his members .... He was sick with sorrows and full of tribulation for us; let us visit him ... especially in his members. He was a captive for us ... let us go to his captive members. Note also that he showed himself a captive of love in the Eucharist so that we might ascend to him, a captive, and receive from him the remission of sins.[135]

Jesus himself performed these six works in his passion as an example for his followers: he quenched the thirsty with his blood poured out on the cross; he fed the hungry by means of his body, consumed on the cross with the fire of love and present in the Eucharist; he welcomed the stranger, namely the good thief; he denuded himself in order to cover the fears of men; he left heaven to visit sick mankind and carried their infirmities to the cross; and for three days he visited those captive in hell.[136]

There are eight quotations of v 40 (only three include the phrase τῶν ἀδελφῶν μου) and three quotations of v 45 in the works of Bonaventure. In three of his works, *Epistola de 25 memorialibus* 19,[137] *Comm. in Lucam* 9. 88,[138] and *Sermo in Epiphaniam* 3. 2,[139] Bonaventure states, with no further specification, that "the least" are the little ones, the poor or the humble. In the remaining eight quotations, however, he clearly identifies "the least" as Christians. In *Comm. in Lucam* 19. 9 they are called "members of Christ."[140] In *Comm. in Joannem* 13. 24[141] and *Comm. in Lucam* 10. 26[142] they are the apostles and disciples sent out to preach by Christ, including the preachers of Bonaventure's own day. In *Comm. in Lucam*

16.16[143] and *Apologia pauperum* 12. 35,[144] Bonaventure says they are the monks and others who voluntarily gave up everything to follow Christ and hence will be co-judges with him at the parousia. In *Comm. in Lucam* 14. 30, he quotes Chrysostom's views[145] on the subject and says that Christ was speaking, not only of his disciples and those who embraced the monastic life, but of every believer.[146] In his *Legenda Sancti Francisci* 7. 8[147] and *Expositio super regulam* 1. 2,[148] he explains that the "the least" are the Franciscans. They are called "Fratres Minores" because they are to regard themselves as the ones Christ was referring to in vv 40 and 45.[149]

In his remarks on vv 41 and 46, Bonaventure stresses that the wicked are not condemned by the Father, but by their own evil works.[150] He devotes an inordinate amount of space discussing the locale and nature of the punishing fire. It is located, he says, beneath the earth; after the wicked have been absorbed into a huge hole in the ground made by God they will fall into hell.[151]

Bonaventure's understanding of Matt 25:31-46 is highlighted by the sevenfold aspect he sees to everything. He delineates seven elements in the blessing of v 34[152] as well as in the curse of v 41.[153] The elect are saved because of the seven works of mercy (he says that "the burial of the dead," though not explicitly mentioned, must be taken into consideration)[154] and the wicked are condemned because of the seven capital sins.[155]

Albert the Great (ca. AD 1206 - 1280)

This Dominican theologian, philosopher and scientist believed that in scriptural exegesis the literal sense was to be considered first without necessarily neglecting the allegorical.[156] This approach is evident in his *Enarrationes in Matthaeum* 25. 31-46 where, for the most part, he abandons the spiritual approach of the Fathers and previous commentators. One is immediately struck by the fact that in his exegesis of Matt 25:31-46, Albert uses Scripture to prove Scripture; he uses a plethora of scriptural quotations, sometimes from Matthew, but most often not, to comment on the verse in question.

He does not consider Matt 25:31-46 to be a parable, but treats it as a bona fide description of the parousia.[157] Nor does he recognize the problem of πάντα τὰ ἔθνη in v 32, but simply quotes Joel 4:2 and 2 Cor 5:10, leaving the reader with the impression that he is a universalist.[158] Neither does Albert recognize a problem with the identity of "the least." Quoting only the beginning of v 40, he offers a brief explanation that gives no indication that he has a restrictive viewpoint: "These matters are clear . . . . For as a pauper, having experienced the needs of the poor, shining now in the glory of his judicial power he says that everything done to the poor is done to himself. Woe, therefore, to those who persecute the poor and needy . . . ."[159]

Albert's treatment of vv 35-36 shows his originality in scriptural exegesis as well as his expertise as a scholastic philosopher well versed in Aristotelian categories. He states that the six Matthean works are used as the sole criteria of judgment because "it is the nature of the human being to overflow in acts of responsibility towards the neighbor."[160] The six Matthean acts, he claims, are works, not of justice but of obligation, that counteract the natural and accidental defects, both internal and external, that destroy the substance of man. The natural internal defects of hunger and thirst are attacked by feeding the hungry and giving drink to the thirsty (vv 35ab). The natural external defect of tempestuous winds and rain is offset by hospitality (v 35c), while the natural external defect of the weather in regards to its quality, that is, hot or cold, is counterattacked by clothing the naked (v 36a). The accidental interior defect of sickness is offset, he claims, by visitation of the sick (v 36b) and the accidental exterior defect of violence is attacked by consolation of the imprisoned (v 36c).[161] He includes the burial of the dead as one of the necessary works of mercy, but not mentioned in vv 35-36 because " . . . granted Christ is said to be hungry in the poor, it cannot be said correspondingly that he dies in the dying, since a dead person is truly not called a member of a living head."[162]

In his brief comments on vv 42-43, Albert mentions the "perfect who will judge with Christ" and says that the exposure or opening (propalatio) of their hearts is their judgment.[163] Nowhere does he complete the traditional Gregorian tetrad by mentioning that unbelievers will also not be judged. This could be an indication that Albert's view of the categories present for the parousia is threefold rather than fourfold.

Thomas Aquinas (ca. AD 1225 - 1274)

We possess Thomas' commentaries on Matthew in two forms: *expositions*, written entirely by him, and *lectures*, transcriptions of Thomas' oral teaching made by a listener chosen by him. The *Catena aurea super Matthaeum* was written by Thomas but is technically considered to be a *Gloss*, not a commentary, since it is nothing other than an elucidation of the biblical text by "chains" of passages derived from the Fathers and early medieval commentators. In his treatment of Matt 25:31-46,[164] Thomas lists the opinions of Origen, Chrysostom, Jerome, Augustine, Gregory the Great, Remigius of Auxerre, and Rabanus Maurus, without any comment of his own.

It is only in his *Reportationes super Matthaeum* 25. 31-46, lectures transcribed by one of his students, that we encounter Thomas' own views on the Matthean pericope. He considers the pericope, not as a parable, but an actual account of the judgment. As did previous commentators, he links the pericope closely to the passion narrative. Christ will come to judge in human form, not only to be seen by the wicked who cannot see his divinity, but also because it was in human form that he was judged.[165] The throne of judgment is not to be interpreted in a material sense; it is the angels and the holy ones referred to in Matt 19:28.[166] Thomas understands πάντα τὰ ἔθνη in its widest sense as "all men who are born, from Adam until the end of the world," even infants who, "although they possess nothing of their own merit, nevertheless have something [to be judged], either guilt from the sin of the first man or grace from the sacrament of Christ."[167]

All will be gathered, says Thomas, but not all will be gathered for the same purpose. Two classes of people, those who left behind their possessions to follow Christ and those who do not believe in Christ, will be gathered merely to receive their sentence. The remaining two categories, "the sheep," i.e., Christians involved in secular affairs who made good use of their possessions, and "the goats," i.e., secular Christians who were selfish with their possessions, will undergo the discussion of merits described in vv 35-40 and 42-45. Thomas ascribes to the opinion of Origen that "the sheep" will be gathered into the air while "the goats" will be left on the earth. A physical gathering in one spot is not to be envisioned, he says, but rather a spiritual gathering. At the moment of the parousia, wherever men happen to be on earth they will be present to Christ immediately and spiritually undergo a judgment which will not occur vocally and over a period of time, but inwardly and instantaneously in their intellects.[168]

Thomas insists that the six Matthean works are mentioned by Christ to show that salvation is the result, not only of God's blessing, but of man's free will. The six works, or lack thereof, are not to be regarded in a literal way as the sole criteria for salvation, he claims, or interpreted merely in terms of others or in a physical manner:

> [The six works] signify that charity is to be shown not only to the neighbor, but to one's self as well. If one is obliged to feed the hungry, much more is he obliged to feed his hungering self, and the same with the other works. They are likewise not only corporal works of charity but spiritual as well; therefore, whatever man does for his own good or that of his neighbor is contained totally in a work of mercy. Hence, everything is contained in these works or in their opposites.[169]

As did Albert, Bonaventure and Hugh of Saint Cher before him, Thomas includes the burial of the dead among the works of mercy and quotes the popular mnemonic device to that effect;[170] but, manifesting his scholastic penchant for the categories of Aristotle and his dependence on the views of his teacher Albert, he says that only six works are mentioned because they are the works that offset the defects to which man is liable: the general internal defects of hunger and thirst; the general external defects of nakedness and loneliness; the particular intrinsic or natural defect of sickness, and the particular extrinsic defect of any tribulation.[171]

In his remarks on v 40, Aquinas indicates a narrow understanding of "the least":

> As often as you did [it] to one of these least, my brothers, you did [it] to me. Matt 10:40: Who receives you, receives me: because the head and the members are one body. And he says "brothers" because they are brothers who do the will of God: hence Matt 12:48 where it says that, extending his hands toward his disciples, he said: These are my brothers.[172]

They are called "the least," says Thomas, for three reasons: because they are "the least" in the eyes of the world, because of their own humility (Matt 11:25), and because thereby Christ wishes to teach that those who have no ability to repay should be the special objects of charity.[173] Continuing his discussion, Thomas asks, in effect, whether the non-Christian can be included in the category of "the least of my brothers." He admits that "all, good and evil, are brothers of God according to nature," but "only the good are [God's brothers] according to grace." It is the latter to whom Christ refers in vv 40, 45. Charity can be shown to the sinner, claims Thomas, but only in the case of extreme necessity for the alleviation of nature. It should be shown first and foremost [magis et prius] to the just.[174]

In his brief remarks on v 45, Aquinas reinforces his restrictive understanding of τῶν ἐλαχίστων by quoting Luke 10:16 ("He who rejects you, rejects me") which was addressed to the disciples.[175]

Nicholas of Lyra (ca. AD 1270 - 1340)

This Franciscan theologian, because of his wide knowledge of the biblical languages and the history of Christian exegesis, has been called the "best-equipped biblical scholar of the Middle Ages."[176] Commenting on Matt 25:31-46 in his *Postilla super totam Bibliam*,[177] the first scriptural commentary to be printed, he links the pericope with the two parables that precede it, calling it "the third parable that has to do with the active, to whom it pertains to exercise themselves in the acts of mercy."[178] Nicholas does not seem to be aware of the problem of πάντα τὰ ἔθνη in v 32. It is possible that he interprets it in the widest sense since his only comment on the verse is: "Because no one will be able to hide."[179]

In his remarks on vv 35-36, Nicholas speaks of seven works of mercy and calls the precept to bury the dead "the fifth work of mercy" as if it were included among the Matthean works. Borrowing concepts from Aristotle's *De anima*, he divides the needs of man into three essential categories: food and drink, provisions that are necessary for him to exist (sine quo non potest esse); clothing and shelter, provisions that are necessary for him to exist well (sine quo non potest bene esse); and burial, which is needed after this life. These needs are common to all, he says, and are taken care of by the first five works of mercy. The two remaining works, visitation of the sick and the imprisoned, respond to accidental needs that are not common to all, but found in some.[180] There is no hint in Nicholas' commentary of treating the Matthean works in a spiritual manner; this could be an indication of his distaste for allegoristic interpretations. In fact, at the close of his commentary he states:

> It must also be considered that there is no mention here of the spiritual works of mercy, since they pertain, for the most part, to prelates whose concern it is to instruct others and lead them to salvation. Here, however, as was seen, it is a question of the judgment about the status of those who are active.[181]

From the above quotation it is clear that Nicholas makes a distinction between the adherents of the contemplative life and those of the active life, and would agree with those commentators who would not include the contemplative monks or religious among those to be judged. In his eyes Matt 25:31-46 describes the judgment of those with possessions who are fully involved in the active life.

Nicholas has a restrictive view of "the least." After quoting the seven-word mnemonic device first used by Hugh of Saint Cher, he states: "[Christ] considers these seven works, however, done to Christ's faithful because of Christ, done entirely to himself, since the faithful are his members. On the contrary, whatever is denied to the faithful, he considers to be denied to himself."[182]

Ludolph of Saxony (d. AD 1378)

This Carthusian spiritual writer devotes a considerable amount of attention to Matt 25:31-46 in his celebrated *Vita Christi*, a meditation on the gospels that is interwoven with prayers and extensive Patristic citations,[183] but he breaks no new ground in the exegesis of the pericope. His comments are a compilation of quotations from John Chrysostom, Gregory Nazianzus, Jerome, and Augustine, as well as Remigius of Auxerre, Rabanus Maurus and his immediate predecessor Nicholas of Lyra.

Ludolph is a universalist with regard to v 32: he says that, seated on the throne of his Church, Christ will gather "all peoples of every time, every condition and every age, for no one will be able to escape notice or lie hidden."[184]

"The least," in his understanding, are Christians. Commenting on v 40, he seems to have Jerome's commentary in mind as he says: "*Amen I say to you as often as,* that is, every time, *you have done [it],* that is, exhibited the works of mercy, *to one of these least, my brothers, you have done [it] to me.* They are brothers because they did the will of the Father; they are least because they were humble and lowly."[185] Quoting Augustine, he clarifies further that "the least" are monks and religious: "The least are those who belong to Christ; they are those who have given up everything and followed him, and whatever they had they distributed to the poor so that, disentangled, they might serve God without worldly shackles . . . ."[186] He reiterates this narrow view that "the least" are believers in his remarks on v 45. He quotes the famous passage from Augustine's *Serm.* 137. 2 in which Christ, the head, complains when his members, the feet, are trampled on,[187] and paraphrases as well the comment of Nicholas of Lyra:

> Christ considers these seven [works] done to the faithful because of Christ, done to himself; and on the contrary, whatever is denied to the faithful, he considers denied to himself. The faithful are his members; because of this he grants eternal life to those performing the works of mercy, and to those neglecting them he renders punishment.[188]

Ludolph includes the Tobian work of burying the dead along with the six Matthean works and interprets them in a corporal and spiritual way, with a decided emphasis on the spiritual. He includes in his commentary, almost verbatim, Nicholas of Lyra's strictly corporal approach to the seven works that is based on Aristotelian concepts, but he omits Nicholas' comments that these works are not to be interpreted spiritually.[189] Instead, quoting at length from Chrysostom and Gregory Nazianzus about the primacy of the soul over the body, he insists that the spiritual ministration to souls is the higher meaning of the seven works of mercy.[190]

NOTES TO CHAPTER III

[1] "Commentary on Matthew," *The Commentaries of Isho'dad of Merv* (5 vols.; ed., M. D. Gibson; Cambridge: University Press, 1911) 2.169.
[2] Ibid.
[3] Ibid.
[4] SC 51.110-111.
[5] Ibid., 111.
[6] SC 129.176.

[7] SC 104. 76.
[8] Ibid., 358.
[9] SC 113. 216.
[10] SC 104.104, 106.
[11] Ibid., 110.
[12] Ibid., 114, 116, 118.
[13] Ibid., 234.
[14] PG 123. 429.
[15] Ibid., 432.
[16] Ibid., 433.
[17] Ibid., 432.
[18] Ibid., 433.
[19] "Euthymius Zigabenus," *ODCC*, 484. See also G. Podskalsky, "Euthymios Zigabenos," *TRE* 10. 557-558.
[20] PG 129. 640.
[21] Ibid.
[22] Ibid., 641.
[23] Ibid., 640.
[24] Ibid.
[25] PG 132. 398.
[26] Ibid., 402.
[27] Ibid., 406.
[28] Ibid., 407.
[29] Ibid.
[30] Ibid., 410.
[31] "Commentarii in Evangelia," *CSCO* 95 (1931) 58-61, esp. p. 58.
[32] Ibid., 59.
[33] Ibid., 59-60.
[34] Ibid., 60.
[35] This is the opinion of M. Geerard (*Clavis patrum graecorum* [4 vols.; Turnhout: Brépols, 1980] 4. 229).
[36] PG 106.1157, 1160.
[37] Ibid., 1160.
[38] Ibid.
[39] PL 95.1215.

[40] Ibid.
[41] Ibid., 1215-1216.
[42] Ibid., 1216-1217.
[43] Ibid., 1217.
[44] Ibid., 1218.
[45] Ibid., 1216.
[46] Ibid., 1218.
[47] PL 106.1470.
[48] Ibid.
[49] Ibid., 1469.
[50] Ibid.
[51] Ibid., 1470.
[52] Ibid., 1471.
[53] PL 118. 204.
[54] *Comm. in Matt.* 4. 25, 40. CCL 77. 244.
[55] PL 118. 204.
[56] Ibid., 203.
[57] Ibid.
[58] Ibid., 204.
[59] Ibid.
[60] PL 107.1097. Cf. Jerome's remarks on Matt 25:40 in CCL 77. 244.
[61] Ibid., 1098.
[62] Ibid.
[63] Ibid., 1097.
[64] See J. P. Migne, PL 107.1095, note.
[65] "Paschasius Radbertus," *ODCC*, 1039.
[66] CCM 56B.1257.
[67] Ibid., 1241.
[68] Ibid., 1241-1242.
[69] Ibid., 1245.
[70] Ibid., 1243.
[71] Ibid., 1244.
[72] Ibid.
[73] GCS 38.167.
[74] Ibid., 1248.

[75] Ibid., 1250.
[76] Ibid., 1243.
[77] Ibid., 1250.
[78] Ibid., 1249.
[79] Ibid., 1250.
[80] Ibid., 1256.
[81] Ibid., 1252.
[82] Ibid.
[83] Ibid.
[84] Ibid., 1257.
[85] Ibid., 1253.
[86] Ibid., 1257.
[87] Ibid., 1253.
[88] See "Remigius of Auxerre," *ODCC*, 1173.
[89] PL 131.49.
[90] *Sancti Thomae Aquinatis opera omnia* (7 vols.; ed. R. Busa; Stuttgart/Bad Cannstatt: Frommann-Holzboog, 1980) 5. 230.
[91] Ibid.
[92] He is quoted in the commentary of Zachary of Besançon. PL 186. 488.
[93] He is quoted in the commentary of Ludolph of Saxony, *Vita Domini nostri Jesu Christi e sacris quatuor evangeliis* (Lyons: Coffin & Plaignard,1644) 537.
[94] The authorship of this commentary is disputed. The anonymous author of the article "Anselm of Laon" in *ODCC*, 61-62, claims that it is to be dated in the middle of the twelfth century, possibly the work of a certain Geoffrey Babion.
[95] PL 162.1463.
[96] Ibid., 1464.
[97] Ibid.
[98] Ibid.
[99] PL 165. 284.
[100] Ibid., 285.
[101] Ibid., 284-285.
[102] PL 165. 784. It is a sermon for the first Monday in Lent.
[103] CCM 24. 2112-2113.

104Ibid., 2115.

105Ibid., 2114.

106Ibid. Rupert makes the same connection between Genesis 1 and Matt 25:35-36 in his *De Gloria et honore Filii Hominis super Matthaeum* 5. See CCM 29.150-151.

107Ibid., 2116. These same sentiments are expressed by Rupert in *De Trinitate et operibus eius* 7. 7, 31. See CCM 21. 466-467.

108Ibid., 2117.

109Ibid., 2118-2119.

110This variant is found in AFDΦν. Cf. *Biblia sacra iuxta vulgatam versionem* (3d ed.; ed. R. Weber; 2 vols.; Stuttgart: Deutsche Bibelgesellschaft, 1983) 2.1567.

111CCM 24. 2122.

112See "Glossa ordinaria," *ODCC*, 572.

113PL 114.166.

114Ibid.

115J. Leclercq, "The Exposition and Exegesis of Scripture from Gregory the Great to St. Bernard," *The Cambridge History of the Bible* (3 vols.; ed. G. W. Lampe; Cambridge, University Press, 1969) 2.183-197, esp. p. 191.

116PL 186. 490.

117Ibid., 488.

118Ibid., 489.

119Ibid.

120Ibid. 490. Cf. PL 38. 742.

121Ibid., 490-492.

122B. Smalley, "The Bible in the Medieval Schools," *The Cambridge History of the Bible*, 2.197-220, esp. p. 206.

123PL 198.1613.

124Ibid., 1613-1614.

125B. Smalley, *Cambridge History of the Bible*, 2. 206-207.

126In *Hugonis de Sancto Charo opera omnia* (8 vols.; Lyons: Huguetan & Barbier, 1668-69) 6. 79.

127Ibid.

128Ibid.

129Ibid.

130Ibid. Cf. PG 58. 718.

[131] B. de Barberiis, *Glossa in Sacram Scripturam* 4 vols.; Lyons: Anissonios, Posuel & Rigaud, 1685.

[132] Ibid., 4. 276-277.

[133] Ibid., 277-278.

[134] Ibid., 278. See the sermon "De Trinitate" 1. 2 in *Sancti Bonaventurae opera omnia* (10 vols.; ed. A. A. Parma; Quaracchi: College of St. Bonaventure, 1882-1901) 9. 348.

[135] B. de Barberiis, *Glossa in Sacram Scripturam*, 4. 279.

[136] Ibid.

[137] *S. Bonaventurae omnia opera*, 8. 495.

[138] Ibid., 7. 244.

[139] Ibid., 9.158.

[140] Ibid., 7. 475. See B. de Barberiis, *Glossa in Sacram Scripturam*, 4. 279-280.

[141] *S. Bonaventurae omnia opera*, 6. 428.

[142] Ibid., 7. 260-261.

[143] Ibid., 7. 408.

[144] Ibid., 8. 328.

[145] *Hom. in Matt.* 79.1. PG 58. 718.

[146] *S. Bonaventurae omnia opera*, 7. 368.

[147] Ibid., 8. 525.

[148] Ibid., 8. 393.

[149] B. de Barberiis, *Glossa in Sacram Scripturam*, 4. 280.

[150] Ibid., 282.

[151] Ibid., 283.

[152] Ibid., 277.

[153] Ibid., 281.

[154] Ibid., 278.

[155] Ibid., 282.

[156] "Albertus Magnus," *The Oxford Dictionary of the Christian Church*, 30. See also P. Simon, "Albert der Grosse," *TRE* 2.177-184, esp. pp. 181-182.

[157] *Alberti Magni opera omnia* (38 vols.; ed. S. C. A. Borgnet; Paris: Vivès, 1890-99) 21.137.

[158] Ibid., 138.

[159] Ibid., 142.

[160]Ibid., 140.
[161]Ibid., 140-141.
[162]Ibid., 140.
[163]Ibid., 143.
[164]*Sancti Thomae Aquinatis opera omnia* 5. 230-232.
[165]Ibid., 6. 211.
[166]Ibid., 212.
[167]Ibid.
[168]Ibid.
[169]Ibid.
[170]Ibid. "Visito, poto, cibo, redimo, tego, colligo, condo."
[171]Ibid.
[172]Ibid., 213.
[173]Ibid.
[174]Ibid.
[175]Ibid.
[176]"Nicholas of Lyra," *ODCC*, 972.
[177](Strassburg: Mentelin, 1469; Reprinted, 4 vols.; Frankfurt/Main: Minerva, 1971).
[178]Ibid., 4. *ad loc*. There is no pagination in the 1971 reprint, hence *ad loc*. references will be given.
[179]Ibid., *ad loc*.
[180]Ibid., *ad loc*.
[181]Ibid., *ad loc*.
[182]Ibid., *ad loc*.
[183]*Vita Domini nostri Jesu Christi e sacris quatuor evangeliis* (Lyons: Coffin & Plaignard,1644) 537-539.
[184]Ibid., 537.
[185]Ibid.
[186]Ibid., 538.
[187]Ibid. See PL 38. 742.
[188]Ibid., 539. Cf. Nicholas of Lyra, *Postilla*, 4. *ad loc*.
[189]Ibid.
[190]Ibid., 538.

CHAPTER IV

THE RENAISSANCE AND REFORMATION

The Fifteenth Century

Bernardine of Siena (AD 1380 - 1444)

This famous Franciscan reformer did not produce a commentary on Matthew, but in two sermons, *De ultimo judicio*[1] and *De judicio generali*,[2] which are more like theological treatises, he gives a rather thorough exegesis of Matt 25:31-46.

According to Bernardine, πάντα τὰ ἔθνη of v 32 is interpreted in the widest sense to include all humanity of "every sex and age."[3] The angels who accompany Christ in judgment are, he says, "the evangelically perfect . . . the Virgin, . . . John the Baptist, . . . the apostles and their perfect imitators, who will sit on thrones to judge their inferiors" as indicated in Matt 19:28.[4] Unlike Paschasius Radbertus and many of the medieval commentators, however, Bernardine does not identify those who accompany Christ in judgment as "the least" of v 40. In *De judicio generali* 2.3, he addresses the question pointedly: "But who are the least of whom Christ speaks here? And why are they not placed among those to be judged, or seen to be placed among the co-judges? To which we answer: Those least are men perfected in humility who for three reasons were not expressly named at the coming of the Judge."[5] Bernardine then continues at length to give the three reasons why "the least" were not mentioned prior to v 40: (1) to show more clearly their identity with Christ; (2) because of their greatness they were included among the angels in v 31; and (3) it is the nature of the scriptures to omit something at first, but then to mention it later.[6]

Bernardine does not state directly that "the least" are Christians, but that that is his understanding is indirectly evident from his discussion of the nature of the Matthean works and the response of the just. He states that the burial of the dead is not included among the works in vv 35-36 because "works of mercy are done to neighbors insofar as they are members of Christ. The dead person, however, insofar as he is dead, is not a member of Christ, for Christ is always alive as Heb 7:25 states."[7] In his discussion of vv 37-39, Bernardine argues that the just are not really ignorant of their good works but respond as they do because of their overwhelming "admiration over such great unity of Christ the head and his members . . . ."[8]

In *De judicio generali* 2.3 he treats the Matthean works solely in a literal manner, and sees them, in much the same way as Albert and Nicholas of Lyra saw them, as the all-inclusive antidote to the natural and accidental, external and internal, miseries that afflict human nature.[9] In *De ultimo judicio* 3. 2, however, he states, " . . . mention is made only of the corporal works of mercy because by means of these the works of spiritual mercy are designated."[10] Food and drink, he says, represent the strong doctrine by which the weak faithful are protected from interior temptations; sheltering the homeless and clothing the naked represent the spiritual works of mercy that protect from external temptations; while visitation of the sick and imprisoned refer to the obligation to counteract a debilitation of spirit caused internally by grief or externally by sin.[11]

Alphonsus Tostatus (AD 1400 - 1455)

In his *Commentaria in septem partes Matthaei*[12] Tostatus directly addresses the religious identity of "the least" and is adamantly universal in his outlook. Only twice in his observations, in Questions 392-393,[13] does he claim that Christ refers to "the least" as brothers because "all those who believe in Christ are especially called brothers"[14] and "are members of the one body whose head is Christ."[15] In all other instances his view is universal. In Question 393, "Why does Christ call the poor 'brothers'?" he states:

> ... all men are called brothers insofar as they are of the same nature and take their origin from one first [man] ; in view of this they are brothers. Christ, however, is true man and descended from Adam insofar as the substance of his body is concerned ... the poor, however, are men; therefore, Christ is their brother.[16]

In Question 397, Tostatus asks whether "the least" of Matt 25:40 refers to all the poor, both good and evil, or only to monks, or apostles and disciples. He bases his universal understanding of v 40 on his universal understanding of πάντα τὰ ἔθνη in v 32:

> ... it is clear that God will say this [v 40] to all men, that is, good and evil, who existed in every time, but it is clear that in many times there were no monks ... and there were not prophets and disciples in every time, and they will not always be, for now we see neither prophets nor disciples. Therefore, it is necessarily understood of the poor who exist in every time .... No one should be damned except for something he is able to do and does not do, and a great difficulty should not be placed in the path to salvation. To befriend prophets and disciples is not in our power because now there are no prophets and disciples ... therefore, salvation should not depend on doing good to them alone, but on doing good to all, even to those who are not disciples of Christ, or prophets, but lowly [parvuli] ....[17]

Countering those who would cite τῶν μικρῶν τούτων in the more restrictive Matt 10:42 to prove the narrowness of Matt 25:40, Tostatus states right from the start that they cannot be compared. Matt 25:40 is concerned with all the poor, he says, while Matt 10:40-42 has to do solely with the disciples of Christ who are sent out to preach. Christ adds the qualitative εἰς ὄνομα μαθητοῦ in 10:42 to protect the reward of the donor. Even should a false prophet or false disciple come along seeking alms, as long as the donor is under the impression that the beggar is *bona fide*, he will be rewarded for his charity.[18]

Tostatus objects to the position of Jerome and others who say that while "the least" do not have to be apostles and disciples of Christ, they must nonetheless be just men who do the will of God:

> ... 'brother' is used in an equivocal sense, as Jerome himself asserts, and so all are called brothers who descend from one father. Because we and the man Christ descend from one father ... that is, Adam, we are called brothers. The Apostle calls him our brother because he shares with us flesh and blood (Hebrews 2) ... for this reason, therefore, not only the good but also the evil are called his brothers. That alms be given not only to the good but also to the evil is therefore consonant with this passage.[19]

Tostatus clearly states that even the unbeliever is included in "the least." In Question 397, as part of his fifth reason why Matt 25:40 refers to all the needy, he quotes Gal 6:10 and adds: "... the Apostle admonishes that good is to be done to all men, not only to the good, and not only to the evil about whom there is a doubt whether they are good or evil, but also to the evil who are clearly evil, namely the unbelievers, who are not able to be good as long as they are unbelievers...."[20]

Denys van Leeuwen (AD 1402 - 1471)

This theologian and mystic of the Charterhouse of Roermund, better known as Dionysius the Carthusian, compiled a series of very extensive commentaries on the Scriptures. In his *Enarratio in Matthaeum* 40, he treats of the Matthean judgment scene.[21] Commenting on Matt 25:40, Dionysius is just as much a universalist as Tostatus, but he does insist that those who befriend the poor do so out of love for Christ:

> ... as long as you did [it] to one of these least brothers of mine, that is to any needy person insofar as he is lowly and

despised in this world, you did [it] to me. For these are my mystical body and my flesh, and I am grateful for the good done to them as if it were done to my own person, as long as it was done to them out of love and because of me.[22]

Dionysius ponders Jerome's position that by "the least" are meant "the poor in spirit . . . belonging to his flock,"[23] but decides to opt for the universal understanding of the phrase, insisting that "it is meritorious to do good to any poor whatsoever because of God . . . ."[24]

His understanding of πάντα τὰ ἔθνη is likewise universal. Commenting on v 32, he says that "peoples of all times, ranks, conditions, ages and states will be gathered before him by angels."[25]

Dionysius argues that burial of the dead should be added to the six Matthean works,[26] and to those who may be troubled by the fact that the corporal works of mercy cannot be performed by "many poor and religious, especially cloistered religious and hermits,"[27] he says that the Matthean works really stand for the spiritual works of mercy, which are superior to, and more meritorious than, the corporal works and can be performed by everyone.[28]

The Sixteenth Century

Catholic Authors

Desiderius Erasmus (ca. AD 1469 - 1536)

In his celebrated translation of the Greek NT into classical Latin, first published in 1516,[29] this renowned scholar dealt only with matters of textual criticism with regard to Matt 25:31-46. In his *Tomus primus paraphraseon in Novum Testamentum*,[30] however, published eight years later, Erasmus gives us his views on the meaning of vv 32 and 40.

He interprets πάντα τὰ ἔθνη universally, stating that "all the nations of the whole world shall be called before him, for no man, high or low, can escape that judgment."[31] In his comments on v 40, however, Erasmus is ambiguous as to whether he interprets "the least" in a universal or restrictive manner. At first glance it seems that his understanding is universal:

> Then the king shall say openly that he would account done to him whatever is given to any one of them whom the world despises for their poverty and lowliness. Yet he despised them not, inasmuch as he honored them with the name of brothers. He shall say: Truly I say to you, although I who am lord of all have no need of anyone's help, inasmuch as you did these things for my sake to any of these my poor little brothers, you did them to me.[32]

As the comment stands, it could be interpreted to mean anybody who is poor and lowly. At the beginning of the paragraph, however, in his comments on vv 34-36, Erasmus says that those who are saved are to inherit the kingdom "because of the ills and displeasures which you have suffered for my sake."[33] They are the ones "whom the world considers vile and accursed, but whom my Father considers honorable and praiseworthy."[34] Commenting on v 45, he states that those "whom the world flattered and praised, but are vile and accursed by my Father and me"[35] will be condemned because they did not minister to those held "in little regard by the world."[36] In light of the close similarity between the terms used to identify οἱ εὐλογημένοι in v 34 and τῶν ἐλαχίστων in vv 40, 45, it may be truer to Erasmus' intentions to see "the least" as the neediest or lowliest in the category of the saved, and hence Christians, because he states that those who are offered the kingdom suffered for the sake of Christ.

Anthony Broickwy (d. ca. AD 1541)

In his *Enarrationes in quatuor evangelia* 115,[37] this Capuchin scholar interprets Matt 25:31-46 by a catena of scriptural quotations that are interspersed, ever so infrequently, with his own comments. He is a universalist with regard to those who will be judged: " . . . the entire race of mortals will be divided into two categories . . . . No man, however, no matter how high or low, will be able to flee from that judgment . . . since it will have to do with the accurate judgment of God, to whose eyes everything is visible."[38]

His interpretation of "the least," however, seems to be restrictive. In his sparse comment on v 40, he says that "the least" are those disciples who did the will of God in Matt 12:50,[39] and in his brief remarks on v 45 states that " . . . the needy Christ is refreshed or neglected in his members."[40]

John Wild (AD 1495 - 1554)

This Franciscan scholar seems to be taken up with rebutting the views of the Reformers in his commentary on Matt 25:31-46. His remarks on the Matthean judgment scene are found in his *In sacrosanctum Jesu Christi domini nostri evangelium secundum Matthaeum commentariorum libri quatuor*[41] and are primarily concerned with stressing the need of good works for salvation:

> Are we not going to be judged by works, therefore, since, as it is clear from the above, even the foolish virgins who had lamps were rejected? . . . he will surely judge according to faith, but because works, especially works of charity, are indicative of faith, he says that the judgment will be according to works. Wherefore, because faith and an external work are an integral work, he will therefore judge according to the integral work and not according to its parts. Here, however, you see which works are to be required at the judgment, especially works of charity.[42]

Wild states at the very beginning of his commentary on the pericope that Matt 25:31-46 is not a parable but a clear presentation of what will actually happen at the judgment.[43] This literal approach is evident in his discussion of the nature of the works. He says that only external works of charity are listed and only those demands are made that can be performed by all in order to emphasize (*pace* the Calvinistic idea of predestination) the universality of salvation.[44]

He is a universalist. Commenting on v 32, he states that "all men will be gathered in an instant"[45] and that "the entire human race will be divided into two parts . . . ."[46] In his remarks on v 40 he identifies "the least" as "not only the great apostles, but any lowly one [minimum quemque]" and reminds us that on the day of judgment "any poor man whatsoever [pauper quispiam]" that we have assisted will be more valuable to us than our friends and even the saints.[47]

Cornelius Jansen the Elder (AD 1510 - 1576)

This bishop of Ghent, not to be confused with his more famous nephew Cornelius Jansen, the bishop of Ypres, has a rather lengthy commentary on Matt 25:31-46 in his *Commentarius in concordiam evangelicam*.[48] He does not specifically address the problem of the identity of πάντα τὰ ἔθνη in v 32, but since he refers to Christ here as "the judge of everyone" and quotes 2 Cor 5:10a to elucidate the meaning of the Matthean verse, it can be surmised that he interprets it in the universalist sense.[49]

Jansen is very clear in his commentary that vv 35-36 are addressed only to Christians. The unbelievers, who have already been judged and about whom there will be no discussion of works, "will not be condemned because of the absence of works of mercy, but because of the absence of faith."[50] He claims that the preceding Parable of the Talents was addressed to the apostles and leaders in the Church, while this pericope, which he does not include among the parables,[51] has to do with those who are subject to Church leadership and will come to believe because of the preaching of the apostles and those similar to them.[52] "The least" of v 40, he states, are

> " . . . the apostles and those similar to them who closely assist them, who voluntarily became poor and were subjected to various calamities in this world because of Christ . . . . In a more general and extensive manner, it can be correctly un-

derstood that any poor Christians whatsoever are meant, since through baptism and the grace of adoption they were made brothers of Christ."[53]

Christ calls his brothers by the adjective "least" to indicate either that Christians are considered humble, poor and abject by the world or that the object of his concern is the weakest among Christians.[54]

A considerable part of the commentary is taken up with a refutation of the opinions of the Reformers. The Matthean corporal works, to which, says Jansen, must be added the Tobian work of burying the dead,[55] are to be understood as including the seven spiritual works, and are used as the criteria for judgment to show that the faithful will be judged not according to their faith, but according to their works, especially their works of charity. "Against those who deny the merits of human works," he states, "it is to be observed that the just inherit the kingdom because of works, so that we might understand that eternal life is given to them as the reward of good works, and that the just merit it by their works, just as the wicked merit eternal punishment by their works."[56] He then continues the discussion emphasizing the causal nature of vv 35-36 and 41-42. Jansen is quick to add, however, that any good merits must be attributed to the divine mercy. They are not to be regarded as springing from ourselves, but rather seen as the result of "God's blessing and predestination" of the just in v 34. The saved are "blessed of the Father" in a twofold sense: by reason of their election from eternity, and by reason of their sharing in God's grace in time that enabled them to perform the necessary good works.[57]

In his commentary on v 41, by his emphasis on the observation that the eternal fire was not created for man but for the devil and his minions, Jansen stresses the point that God created no one for perdition.[58] This is surely in reaction to the predestinationist views of some of the Reformers.

The Douai-Rheims New Testament (AD 1582)

The New Testament of Jesus Christ,[59] commonly known as the Douai-Rheims New Testament, was translated from the Latin Vulgate. Begun at the English College at Douai and completed at Rheims in 1582, its publication is most closely associated with the names of Gregory Martin, Thomas Worthington, Richard Bristowe and William Allen. Its commentary on Matt 25:31-46 does not address the issue of the identity of "the least" at all but is more concerned with vv 35-36 and 42-43, stressing the expiatory value of good works and their necessity for salvation:

> Hereby we see how much almes-deeds and al Workes of mercy prevaile towards life everlasting and to blot out former sinnes . . . . He chargeth them not here that they beleeved not, but that they did not good workes. For such did beleeve, but they cared not for good workes, as though by dead faith they might have come to heaven.[60]

In the eyes of the commentators the subjects of the judgment will be good and evil Christians only and will not include the unbeliever, as the brief remark on v 32 seems to indicate: "Lo here is the separation for in the Church militant they lived both together. As for Heretikes, they went out of the church before, and separated themselves, and therefore are not to be separated here, as being judged already."[61]

Juan Maldonado (AD 1533 - 1583)

This Spanish Jesuit theologian and exegete, more commonly known as Maldonatus, does not even discuss the identity of "the least." In his commentary on Matt 25:31-46, found in his *Commentarii in quattuor evangelistas*,[62] vv 34-35 command his greatest attention as he attempts to counter the Calvinist views on predestination that used the phrase οἱ εὐλογημένοι τοῦ πατρός μου κληρονομήσατε in v 34 to prove that those saved are predestined to salvation and receive the kingdom, not because of labor or merit, but because of birth.[63] Maldonatus argues that the blessing in v 34 in no way refers to any past act of predestination, but to the future state of reward once the judgment is complete. He cites the absence of the Father's agency in the parallel v 41 and the fact that the punishment mentioned there was not prepared for men as proof that the subject of Christ's words in v 34 have to do with the glorification of the saved rather than their predestination.[64] He strongly insists on the point that salvation is a reward since it is often termed such in various passages of the Scriptures. To prove that salvation is given not only as a consequence of good deeds (*post laborem*) but as a reward for good works (*propter laborem*) as well, Maldonatus quotes vv 35 and 42, emphasizing the causal nature of the particle γάρ (*enim* in Latin) that is found in both verses:

> If there were no other passage but this, it would be clear that eternal life is given not only after works [post opera] but because of works [propter opera], and is therefore truly and properly a reward.... It is clear that [by the use of γάρ] not merely the consequence, as the above heretics say, but the true cause is shown.... For that it is properly a reward the heretics themselves are forced to confess, and given not only after labor but because of labor.[65]

A persistent thread running throughout Maldonatus' commentary is the idea that, in a metonymous sort of way, the scene described in Matt 25:31-46 is only one case that is meant to represent all other conceivable situations. Thus, he insists that at the judgment not only the corporal works of mercy will be the subject of discussion, but any and all works, in act or intention, that will be the cause of salvation or damnation:

> ... [some say that] in the judgment, as appears from the text, the question will be only of good and evil works. This I firmly deny, for the merits of each will be weighed, and these do not always consist of acts done, but sometimes in intention alone, or in grace alone ... it was not the intention of Christ to explain all the reasons of the salvation of some and the con-

demnation of others, but to give an example only of one kind from which the rest may be concluded.[66]

Maldonatus uses the same argument to prove the universality of πάντα τὰ ἔθνη in v 32. To those who argue that not all people will be gathered for judgment before the throne, since all are not capable of the acts mentioned in vv 35-36, he says that "Christ here puts one class for the whole race, as we often do . . . . Infants, therefore, and all men, believers or not, will be judged, and the reason of the salvation or condemnation of each will be given."[67]

Manoel De Sa (c. AD 1530 - 1596)

This Portuguese Jesuit, better known by the name Emmanuel Sa, has very little commentary on Matt 25:31-46 in his *Notationes in totam Scripturam Sacram*.[68] His only comment on v 32 has to do with συναχθήσονται rather than πάντα τὰ ἔθνη. The gathering, he says, will be accomplished by the ministry of the angels who accompany Christ.[69] His remarks on v 40 leave no doubt that his interpretation of "the least" is restrictive. The "brothers," he claims, are "the apostles and those similar to them," and "the least" are those who are "sick, lowly or abject among them."[70]

Protestant Authors

Ulrich Zwingli (AD 1484 - 1531)

This noted Swiss Reformer presented his interpretation of Matt 25:31-46 in his *Annotationes in Evangelium Matthaei*.[71] He is preoccupied in his commentary with stressing the point that the cause of the salvation of the just is not the Matthean works, but rather the faith in Jesus Christ that produced the works. In his commentary on v 31, Zwingli gives a brief introduction to the pericope and says that in the final judgment we will be examined to the point of exactitude [ad amussim] only in those matters which arise from faith in God. The condemned, he states, are those who were obliged to have faith, but did not, since faith is "our justice or injustice on account of which we are either saved or damned."[72] The six corporal works are only representative of all works, since "Christ, speaking according to Hebrew custom, names a certain few principal works from many and leaves the others to be understood by them."[73] Zwingli cites vv 34-35 against the "peddlers of justice and hypocrites" who go about selling a reward in exchange for works, reminding them that works are only signs of faith and merit nothing unless they spring from faith in Christ.[74]

His understanding of πάντα τὰ ἔθνη in v 32 is universal: "the judgment will be universal in which all deeds, words and thoughts of everyone [omnia omnium facta, dicta et cogitata] are to be made public and judged."[75] He must have understood "the least" to mean all the saved, since his only comment on v 40 is: "These words are spoken about those aforementioned who are situated at the right of the judge. What a great honor that the eternal Son of God and highest king calls us brothers."[76] In Zwingli's understanding only Christians could end up on the right of the judge, as his brief remarks on οἱ δίκαιοι in v 37 indicate: "Who are the just? Those who were justified by works? Not at all ... but those who, by the grace of God, were made just through faith."[77]

Martin Luther (AD 1483 - 1546)

The founder of the German Reformation and the most famous of all the Reformers commented only on the first twenty-four chapters of Matthew.[78] In his German translation of the scriptures, however, at the head of Chapter 25 he inserted his own short commentary on Matt 25:31-46 which revealed that his understanding of "the least" was restrictive:

> Those who ... use their gifts for themselves alone and do not share with others shall be the ones who will go into the curse and everlasting damnation, as the Lord Jesus himself makes

clear at the end of a parable such as this. He above all appeals to us in a friendly manner to help and advise one another as much as we can, and he says that what one does to the least Christians one has done to himself. He will praise and repay this on the last day.[79]

The same narrow interpretation of Matt 25:40 is likewise found in his only extant sermon on the Matthean judgment scene, which was delivered on November 26, 1537, the 26th Sunday after Trinity.[80] Luther very skillfully uses Matt 25:31-46 to muster financial support for the poor pastors, preachers, and schoolteachers of the evangelical Church who, once the break with Rome was complete, were forced to take on secular employment since they were no longer allowed the use of funds from established benefices. Granted, Luther included all who are Christ's "followers . . . and saints"[81] among the recipients of "the identity dialogue," but in a special way he regarded "the least" as the "poor pastors and preachers . . . who have suffered hunger, thirst, nakedness, persecution and the like, especially for [Christ] and his Word's sake" because they were deprived of their financial support by the goats, "the popes, cardinals, bishops, canons, priests and the whole diabolical rabble . . . at Rome . . . ."[82] "When ministers and pastors engage in worldly trades and pursuits," claims Luther, "they step outside of their proper calling. Therefore, they have to be supported, if they are to have anything to eat, from the begging that Christ is speaking about here . . . ."[83]

Luther's interpretation of πάντα τὰ ἔθνη is universal: Christ "will bring together by means of the resurrection all who have ever lived upon earth."[84] But the separation, according to Luther, will only take place between good and evil Christians and will be conducted in the sight of the accompanying angels and the unbelievers.[85] The unbeliever has no chance for salvation even though he perform the same works. In fact, the first reason Luther gives as to why Christ mentions only these six works (which he calls the works of the fifth commandment) and not any other works is because these are precisely the works practiced by the unbelievers, and by means of the "identity dialogue" Christ wishes to show that the Christian faith is necessary for works to be acceptable:

> ... the Turks do more works of this kind and boast more of them than we who are called Christians. . . . Certainly he does not mean to say that those also who are not Christians merit eternal life by reason of such works? Christ himself shows that he is speaking of the works of believing Christians . . . . There is no doubt that he who performs such works of mercy to Christians must himself be a Christian and a believer . . . .[86]

The second reason why only the works of the fifth commandment are mentioned here, says Luther, is to remind us that Christ was similarly merciful to us and redeemed us from the "wrath of God and the guilt of the fifth commandment." Hence, we are to act towards our neighbor in like manner, not because we are fearful of the judgment or wish to gain merit, but simply because we wish to follow the example of Christ.[87] Nowhere does Luther deny that the six Matthean works will be the criterion for judgment, but he constantly stresses the faith that produces such works. Because of this prerequisite faith, he states, the separation between the sheep and the goats is already going on in this life between those whose works are the result of their faith and those who have works but no faith.[88]

A thorough survey of Luther's extant works shows that he was rather consistent in his narrow interpretation of the "identity dialogue." Twelve out of the 18 quotations of Matt 25:40 found in his works are definitely used in the restrictive sense. In *First Psalm Lectures* 38. 5,[89] the Dedication of *Fourteen Consolations*,[90] the *17th Sermon on John 6* 6. 57,[91] *Selected Psalms* 110.1,[92] and *The Blessed Sacrament of Christ's Body* 6,[93] he encourages support for the individual Christian in need. In *Fourteen Consolations* 6[94] and *Treatise on Good Works* 3.16,[95] Luther is concerned with the needs of the entire church, while in four instances in *Lectures on Genesis* 18. 5[96] and 28. 20-22,[97] as well as in the *Third Sermon on John 4* 4.7,[98] he uses 25:40 to encourage Christians to support evangelical pastors, preachers, and schoolteachers, as well as their families.

John Calvin (AD 1509 - 1564)

This noted French reformer and theologian comments on Matt 25:31-46 in his *In Novum Testamentum commentarii*,[99] first published around 1555. Calvin does not interpret the pericope as a parable, but sees it as a clear explanation, "without figures,"[100] of the day of judgment. As one would expect of a proponent of Reformation theology, he devotes the major portion of his commentary to vv 34-35a.[101] He actually speaks of the kingdom as "the reward of good works [praemio bonorum operum],"[102] but quickly reminds his readers that the term εὐλογημένοι τοῦ πατρός μου in v 34 indicates that salvation proceeds, not from any work of man, but from the "undeserved favor of God;"[103] hence, it would be more correct to speak of the reward of grace.[104] This grace is given by the Father to "those who, under the guidance of the Spirit in this life aspire to righteousness, were predestined to life."[105] Calvin is aware of the exegesis of this verse by the opponents of predestination: " . . . that the reward was laid up with a view to their future merits,"[106] but he quickly dismisses it by emphasizing κληρονομήσατε τὴν ἡτοιμασμένην ὑμῖν βασιλείαν ἀπὸ καταβολῆς κόσμου, insisting that it indicates that the salvation of the righteous comes, not from any merits of theirs, but from the eternal gift of the Father.[107] He rejects outright the "Papists'" argument that γάρ in v 35a is a causal particle, stating that it is not to be taken causally but rather consequentially: "Their insistence on the causal particle is weak: we know that, when eternal life is promised to the righteous, *enim* does not always denote the cause, but rather the consequence."[108] He then seems to contradict himself, admitting, as it were, that there is a causal nature to γάρ, inasmuch as he argues that the kingdom, which depends on adoption, is the result of the Father's grace that enabled the righteous to perform good works.

As the righteous are predestined to salvation, so the wicked, says Calvin in his remarks on v 41, are predestined to eternal punishment by a secret judgment of God. As long as they have the possibility of eternal life, they cannot be considered "heirs of death or companions of Satan,"[109] he states, but their voluntary unbelief "uncovers and makes evident their perdition which had been formerly concealed."[110] He interprets the fire of v 41 metaphorically as a symbol for a "dreadful punishment that our senses cannot comprehend," so any inquiry into the material or form of the fire, he says, is foolish sophistry.[111]

Calvin sees the six Matthean works as mere examples of all the works of charity, corporal and spiritual, that a Christian must perform to indicate externally his internal faith and belief. Even a child, he says in his characteristically sarcastic fashion, seems to know what the "monks and other noisy talkers" have overlooked in their exegesis of vv 35-36: Christ does not mention more than six works because "he commends, by means of a synecdoche, all the duties of charity."[112] It cannot be argued from this pericope, insists Calvin, that the hallmark of righteousness is almsgiving, since the purpose of vv 35-36 is primarily to indicate that faith must give expression to works: " . . . Christ does not make the chief part of righteousness consist in almsgiving, but shows, by what may be called more evident signs, what it is to live a holy and righteous life: believers are not merely to profess their devotion to God, but to prove it with actual performances."[113]

In his remarks on v 32, Calvin does not mention, or even allude to, the ambiguity of πάντα τὰ ἔθνη. He states that one of the reasons for Christ's final coming would be to show that he intends his kingdom to be worldwide, "since he will be the judge of the entire world."[114] This is his only statement having universal import. He is not entirely clear as to whether non-Christians are included among the sheep and the goats, or whether the separation of the good and evil concerns only Christians. In his treatment of the separation in vv 32-33 one gets the distinct impression that the division is to be between those in the church, "those who now live together in the same flock of

God,"[115] while in his remarks on v 41, he calls the wicked "hypocrites who are now mixed with the righteous, as if they were closely allied to Christ."[116] This would also seem to indicate that in Calvin's understanding only Christians are included under the figures of sheep and goats. It is unfortunate that he is not clearer about his thinking in regards to non-Christians and their place, if any, at the judgment.

There is no such ambiguity, however, in Calvin's comments on v 40. He has a definite restrictive interpretation of "the least," but in no way does he restrict the charity of Christians to believers only:

> Believers only are expressly recommended to us; not that [Christ] bids us altogether to despise others, but because the more closely a man approaches God, the more highly he should be esteemed by us. Though there is a common tie that binds all the children of Adam, there is still a more sacred union among the children of God. Since those who belong to the houschold of the faith should be preferred to strangers, Christ makes special mention of them.[117]

Augustine Marloratus (AD 1506 - 1562)

This reformed theologian, in his *Novi Testamenti catholica expositio ecclesiastica*,[118] has very little of his own commentary to contribute. In his remarks on the Matthean judgment scene he slavishly copies Calvin's and Zwingli's commentaries with an insertion, every now and then, of his own thoughts.

Marloratus clarifies Calvin's ambiguity regarding πάντα τὰ ἔθνη by stating clearly that those to be gathered are "all the dead and those who will be found alive on that day . . . from every part of the earth."[119] The separation of vv 32-33, however, seems to be between Christians. Departing from Calvin's observations on the verse, he says that even though the work of final separation belongs properly to Christ on the last day, in the meantime it is the obligation of the church's ministers, by means of ecclesiastical discipline, to try to keep the sheep separate from the goats.[120]

By his additions to Calvin's comments on v 40, Marloratus shows himself to be just as restrictive as Calvin in his understanding of "the least," yet just as universal in his concept of Christian charity:

> Under the name brothers are meant all the faithful of Christ, the children of God. They are children of God, however, who believe in his name . . . and the children of God are the brothers of Christ . . . . Christ is to be recognized, therefore, in his faithful, who are called Christians. It is not allowed to reject anyone as not pertaining to Christ, when good is to be done, nor to set apart anyone from the flock of the faithful, for he says: What [you did] to one of these least. By these words he shows that no one is to be excluded, whoever he is . . . . Whoever is in need and seeks help because of Christ is to be considered a brother of Christ . . . . To Saul also he said: Saul, Saul, why do you persecute me? . . . when he was persecuting the Church.[121]

From the above quotation it seems that a necessary distinction must be made: Even though Marloratus had a restrictive understanding of "the least," he would nevertheless see all people as the proper object of Christian charity, as long as they made their request in the name of Christ.

The Seventeenth Century

Catholic Authors

Willem Hessels van Est (AD 1542 - 1613)

This Dutch exegete and professor at Douai, who more often went by Estius, his Latinized name, gives us his interpretation of Matt 25:31-46 in his *Annotationes in praecipua ac difficiliora sacrae scripturae loca*.[122]

In his commentary on v 32 he addresses the query, put by some, as to whether "all nations" necessarily means "all men," since, they argue, "all nations without exception" will be gathered before the throne, but that does not necessarily mean that every person without exception from every nation has to be represented. Estius responds that the judgment will be universal and that "no one at all will be excepted," not even infants and those incapable of reason [amentes].[123]

He holds a restrictive viewpoint with regard to "the least" of v 40, seeing them as all those Christians who are to be saved. He quotes Gal 6:10, however, to make his point that the verse cannot be used to put a limit on Christian charity. By specifically mentioning Christian recipients, Christ indicates, he says, that Christians are to be the primary concern of Christian charity, not necessarily the exclusive concern:

> When he says: *Of these, etc.*, the King or judge designates those who will be on his right, all of whom will be brothers of Christ. He singles out *the least*, however, those who will be weak among them, or rather, those who among Christians in this world will have been weak, that is, the most abject according to human judgment, as the poor, beggars, and afflicted are accustomed to be regarded. You say: Alms are to be given only to Christians, therefore, and to those who are good, since the wicked are not the brothers of Christ. Response: It does not follow. The meaning is that [alms] are to be given above all to such [i.e., Christians], as the Apostle warns: Let us do good to all, especially to those of the household of the faith.[124]

In his remarks on vv 34-35, Estius makes a point of rebutting the Reformers' position that works are not necessary for salvation. He states that "*enim* was added" in v 35a to show that the kingdom is given, not only because of sonship [jure filiationis], but also because of works of justice [propter opera justitiae].[125] He argues that it is charity that constitutes someone a son of God, and therefore in adulthood and old age good works are a necessity for salvation.[126] Christ speaks only of the corporal works of mercy, he says, because they can be detected by the five senses and can be performed by everyone. He does not mention the spiritual works of mercy since it would be impossible for Christ to say, "I wandered and you brought me back to the way of salvation; I sinned and you corrected me; I was ignorant and you taught me."[127] Likewise, he does not include the burial of the dead among the works, since it is rendered, not to a person, but merely to his dead body. The remaining six works of mercy have to do with persons.[128]

Sebastian Barradas (AD 1542 - 1615)

In his rather lengthy *Commentariorum in concordiam et historiam quatuor evangelistarum tomus* 9.16-17, 19,[129] first published in 1615, this Jesuit theologian treats Matt 25:31-46 as an accurate description of events that will occur on the last day. Hence he is concerned with every other scriptural passage that he feels has something to say about the final judgment and is overly taken up with smoothing over seeming inconsistencies. For example, he gives a considerable amount of attention to the separation mentioned in Matt 13:41 and whether it is the same separation mentioned in Matt 25:32 or not. It could be the same separation, he says, or there could be two: Matt 13:41 would be the first division on earth between the good and the bad, while Matt 25:32 would refer to the second separation brought about by the rapture of the just mentioned in 1 Thess 4:17. In that case, the right side would represent being up in the air with Christ, while the left side would mean remaining on the earth.[130]

Barradas differentiates between two judgments. In what he calls the "judgment of approbation or reprobation," everyone will be judged; while in the "judgment of discussion," described in Matt 25:31-46, only Christians, in full view of the remainder of humanity, will be judged as to their performance or non-performance of the Matthean works.[131] Nevertheless, πάντα τὰ ἔθνη in v 32 is to be interpreted in the widest sense: "There will be gathered before the supreme judge all peoples [omnes gentes], that is, all nations and all men [omnes nationes, omnesque homines]."[132] Even infants, baptized and unbaptized, will be included in the gathering, he says, but in an adult state.[133]

In his remarks on v 40, Barradas directly asks the question whether "the least" refers to all the poor or not, and decides that it does not. He sees "the least" as those Christians who stand at the right of the judge:

> I answer that Christ calls the blessed poor the least brothers, for he indicates with his hand those whom he calls brothers . . . . From these (he says) whom I point out. It does not seem feasible that at that time he will point out the reprobate and call them brothers; therefore, he will point out the holy ones. He calls the blessed poor, therefore, the least brothers.[134]

Barradas gives very little attention to the debate over the necessity of works for salavation, stating simply that v 40 is proof that "works are necessary for the attainment of eternal life, and that, because of works performed in grace and charity, man merits eternal happiness. Certain blind heretics cannot see this."[135] The six Matthean works are representative, he says, of all good endeavors, corporal and spiritual. Christ mentions only the six works of vv 35-36 to show that charity is a necessity for the Christian and is required by God before all else.[136]

Francis Luca of Bruges (ca. AD 1549 - 1619)

In his *Commentarius in sacrosancta quatuor Jesu Christi evangelia*,[137] Luca presents an extensive commentary on Matt 25:31-46.[138] His understanding of πάντα τὰ ἔθνη is universal, and in his remarks on v 32 he seems to indicate an awareness of the problem of the twofold meaning of ἔθνος: "nation" and "Gentile":

> *Nations*, that is, people [homines]; not only all nations, but each and every individual person of each nation, and therefore, in short, all people, of every time, every nation, every condition, every age, and of both sexes, from Adam and Eve . . . until the last human being, whether they shall have already

died or be found alive. No one whatsoever will be able to flee that judgment. He does not say people, however, but nations, so that you can more easily consider both the variety and the multitude of those to be judged and know that no nation is to be exempt, no matter how barbarous and far from the knowledge of God and Christ, and not think that only Israelites and Christians are to be judged.[139]

Against those who argue that everyone will be judged instantaneously wherever they happen to be on the earth, Luca argues from the term "will be gathered" that the judgment has to take place in a certain spot. That spot, for him, will be the valley between the Temple Mount and the Mount of Olives, as well as the environs to the north, west and south of the valley. Christ will be seated on a cloud to the east of the valley, directly over Mount Olivet.[140] As do so many other commentators, Luca refers to 1 Thess 4:17 in his exegesis of Matt 25:32-33. For him "the right" indicates "above the earth" where the just will be gathered, and "the left" symbolizes "on the earth" where the wicked will remain.[141]

His understanding of "the least" in v 40 is restrictive. In a lengthy commentary on the verse, he states that when Christ first uttered these words, he had in mind "the apostles whom he called brothers in Matt 12:49, but not only them, but all pious Christians . . . " since in 12:50 he says that anyone who does the will of the Father is his brother.[142] He then cites the restrictive Matt 10:42 and 18:5 to elucidate his point that in v 40 Christ is speaking of Christians:

> Christ stresses this word *brothers* and requires that our alms, if they are to receive the kingdom of heaven as a reward, be given to the poor as his brothers, that is, as children of God, the faithful of Christ, so that in them we might consider God and Christ in whom they believe and whom they serve.[143]

They are called "the least," not only because in their own humility they think that of themselves, but because they are considered that in the eyes of the world.[144]

Luca then asks the question whether non-Christians can be the object of Christian charity or not. He states that they can be, but that Christ is not concerned with them in Matt 25:40. There is a distinction, he says, between a natural work of mercy and a Christian work of mercy:

> To do good to a poor man simply because he is poor is a work of natural mercy, but to do good to a poor man because he is a poor brother of Jesus Christ, is a work of Christian mercy, which considers in the poor not only their poverty, but Christ himself .... Wherefore, Christ here commends by name only the faithful, not because he wishes all other poor to be despised, but because [he wishes to show] that a person should be dearer to us the closer he gets to God, and that the household members of the faith are to be preferred to outsiders ... [145]

Charity shown to non-Christians is not without fruit, says Luca, insofar as the infidel and the wicked have the potential to become Christians, and by such almsgiving might the more easily be led to Christ. It is obvious that he does not consider "the least" to be among those on the right since he asks whether these least brothers of Christ fall under the same sentence of approval in v 34 that those on the right fall under. Luca notes that "the least" seem to be "set apart from those who are judged." They are "indeed present for the judgment, but the sentence of the judge does not have to do with them." Will they be judged? he asks. They will, he says, but not according to the six Matthean works. Since under the one category of good works Christ intends all the others to be likewise included, "the least," claims Luca, will be judged by other works, such as patience, counsel and commiseration.[146]

In his remarks on vv 34-35, he attacks Calvin by name for his belief that *enim* is not causal, but consequential. Luca admits that the first, even though remote, cause of salvation is God's predestination, but he insists that the proximate cause is twofold: God's blessing and man's free will, which cooperates with God's grace and produces good works. The six corporal works are one species of good works that stand for every kind of good work and virtue. Christ mentions only these external works, he says, because they are discernible and visible to all, easy for everyone to do, and consequently more will be saved. In addition, charity is the "queen of the virtues," and therefore works of charity are the most appropriate external signs of love for God.[147]

Robert Bellarmine (AD 1542 - 1621)

Bellarmine did not leave a commentary on Matthew's Gospel, but in his sermons and theological works he often quoted Matt 25:31-46 so as to give some indication of his understanding of the pericope. In his extant sermons, which were published posthumously,[148] there are five quotations from the "identity dialogue." In four of the sermons, two preached on the Third Sunday of Advent,[149] one on Quinquagesima,[150] and one on the Assumption,[151] he remains neutral in his discussion of "the least," referring to them simply as "the poor." In a sermon on John 20:19, however, delivered on Low Sunday, 1603, with the intent to bring about greater cooperation and respect between religious superiors and subjects, Bellarmine interprets "the least" as Christians. He calls them "members of Christ" and cites the restrictive texts Acts 9:4 and 1 Cor 8:12 in conjunction with Matt 25:40 to emphasize the strict unity between the Christian and Christ.[152] The same narrow interpretation of "the least" is found in his *Explicatio psalmorum* 40.1: "Blessed also is he who has regard for the needy and poor Christ in his own members, of whom Matthew 25 will say: What you did to one of my least, you did to me."[153]

In a homily for the First Sunday of Advent, 1603, Bellarmine's brief comments on Matt 25:32 indicate that his understanding of πάντα τὰ ἔθνη was universal: "This power will be apparent first of all in the calling of everyone to judgment, Matt 25:32: *All peoples will be gathered before him.* And Matthew adds in the same place that just as a shepherd gathers his sheep, i.e., as a shepherd easily gathers a few sheep, so with greater ease will God gather all peoples."[154]

In his *Disputationes de controversiis Christianae fidei adversus hujus temporis haereticos* 2. 6, 5, Bellarmine gives us further insight into his understanding of Matt 25:31-46. Combatting those who would use the exclusive categories of right and left in Matthew 25 as an argument that unbaptized infants must go to hell, since they obviously cannot be included among the just, Bellarmine again indicates a universal understanding of πάντα τὰ ἔθνη, but he clearly states that the separation of vv 33-34, together with the ensuing "identity dialogue," applies only to Christians:

> I respond: The judgment will be universal and absolutely everyone will be present, the weak with the great, the faithful with the unfaithful, the just with sinners. But not all will be judged by the same format. Matthew 25 describes only the format by which those who are in the Church will be judged, and therefore this passage does not pertain to infants who are not in the Church . . . . The flock of the one shepherd corresponds to nothing other than the Church in which good and bad exist, but they are Christians. In the Scriptures the unbelievers are more customarily compared with wolves and dogs, rather than with goats.[155]

In *Disputationes de controversiis* 3,2. 5,3, Bellarmine uses Matt 25:34-35, together with Matt 25:21, 23 and Rev 7:14-15, as his third argument to show that the scriptures prove that the works of the just merit eternal life. The crux of his argument is that *enim* in Matt 25:35a, *quia* in Matt 25:21, 23, and *ideo* in Rev 7:15, are causal particles and cannot be interpreted in a consequential sense as Calvin and many of the reformers sought to do.[156] Not denying the notion of heredity in v 34, he states that the kingdom is given to the just for two reasons: heredity and merit, but God honors his children more by allowing them to gain eternity through their own meritorious works.[157]

James Tirinus (AD 1580 - 1636)

This Jesuit theologian has a relatively brief commentary on Matt 25:31-46 in his *Commentarius in Vetus et Novum Testa-*

mentum.[158] His understanding of πάντα τὰ ἔθνη is universal: "There will be gathered to the tribunal of the judge in the Valley of Josaphat all peoples [gentes], that is, all human beings, of whatever nation, secular condition, sex, or age they might be, either long or recently deceased."[159] Following Aquinas, he interprets the right side as "in the air" and the left side as "on the earth."[160]

He has no remarks as such on v 40, but his interpretation of "the least" is narrow, as evidenced by his interpolation of a restrictive comment into v 35a: "Vers. 35. *For I was hungry* in my members and my brothers, *and you gave me to eat.*"[161] Tirinus sees the Matthaen works as representative of all good works, claiming that "Christ wishes all categories of virtues to be understood under the one category of good works, namely of corporal mercy."[162]

Cornelis Cornelissen van den Steen (AD 1567 - 1637)

This Flemish Jesuit exegete, more commonly called by his Latinized name Cornelius a Lapide, has an extensive commentary on Matt 25:31-46 in his *Commentarii in quattuor evangelia*.[163] He plainly states that πάντα τὰ ἔθνη is to be taken in its widest sense as including "all men who are sprung from Adam, from the first to the last, of every family and nation, no matter how barbarous and fierce. Also little ones and infants, although the case and judgment of infants is not here properly treated, but only that of adults ...."[164] In his comments on v 32 he devotes considerable attention to the current theological problem of the fate of unbaptized infants, concluding that, although they will be present for the judgment, they will not be included among the sheep or the goats.[165]

In his comments on v 40, van den Steen adopts the position of Paschasius Radbertus and says that "the least" are primarily the apostles and religious who will sit with Christ as co-judges, but they are all poor Christians as well. Although he interprets "the least" in a restrictive manner, it seems he would not use the verse to argue that non-Christians should not be aided:

> The word *these* strictly denotes the apostles and religious and apostolic men like them who will sit as co-judges with Christ. In this world they were reckoned *the least* and the most abject.... In the second place, all poor Christians who, reborn in baptism, have by grace been made children of God and therefore brothers of Christ, are denoted by the word *these*. Notice that unbelievers and the reprobate, though they once may have been brothers of Christ, are not here counted worthy of the name. Yet he does not forbid giving them alms.[166]

His remarks on v 45 are just as restrictive: "Learn by these words how greatly to be esteemed are the lowly and the poor, especially the saints, religious, and apostolics, whom Christ here calls his own property, as it were."[167]

Aware that "there are many, such as paupers, children and religious, who can scarcely perform works of mercy,"[168] van den Steen argues that the Matthean corporal works, to which, he claims, must be added the seventh Tobian work, are merely representative of all good works, especially "the spiritual works of mercy which ... are as much superior to the corporal works as the soul is superior to the body."[169]

Cornelius Otto Jansen (AD 1585 - 1638)

Cornelius Jansen the Elder's more famous nephew, who was the Bishop of Ypres and gave his name to the rigoristic movement known as Jansenism, presents an exegesis of Matt 25:31-46 in his *Tetrateuchus, sive commentarius in sancta Jesu Christi evangelia*.[170] He understands the pericope, not as a parable, but as a graphic description of the events at the parousia,[171] during which, he argues, contrary to those who think only Christians are to be the subject of the Matthean judgment scene, "the peoples of all nations and ages" are to be gathered for judgment in the valley between the Mount of Calvary and the Mount of Olives, with the Valley of Gehenna, the symbol for hell, to the left of Christ, who will be seated facing them above Mount Olivet.[172]

Jansen's interpretation of "the least" in v 40 is narrow. Commenting on v 35a he says: "Therefore *I was hungry* in my members. For the entire Church, and Christ as its head, is one complete body, in which what happens to the head happens to the body, and vice-versa."[173] In his remarks on v 40, he says that, by means of this verse, Christ tacitly teaches that we are to consider "the afflicted, not only as a poor man, but as a Christian, a son of God, a brother and member of Christ;" and he cites the more restrictive Matt 18:5 and 10:42 as other examples of the unity between Christ and the Christian.[174]

Jansen states that the particle γάρ is causal but insists that it is to be taken with κληρονομήσατε in v 34 and not ἡτοιμασμένην. Thus, even though men are predestined to enter the kingdom, they cannot possess it without the response of meritorious works.[175]

John Bourgesius (d. AD 1653)

In his *Historia et harmonia evangelica*,[176] Bourgesius relies heavily on the commentary of the younger Jansen in his exegesis of Matt 25:31-46. His understanding of πάντα τὰ ἔθνη is universal: "all peoples of every age, from both hemispheres" will be gathered before Christ, who will be accompanied in judgment by the "Virgin Mother, the apostles and apostolic men."[177]

"The least" in his understanding are Christians. He makes the distinction between a work of natural mercy which is rendered to any poor man and a work of Christian mercy which is shown "because of Christ and God to a Christian, a brother, to Christ, since Christians are certainly the ones who have the capacity of being brothers of Christ."[178] Bourgesius cites the more restrictive Matt 10:42 to make his point that v 40 has to do with the poor man "not so much because he is poor, but because he is a Christian, a son of God, a brother and member of Christ."[179]

In his remarks on vv 34-35a, he opposes the Calvinist position regarding *enim* and states that "the most obvious truth" is that the particle is causal and that the kingdom can be regarded as a reward for good works. He makes the distinction between "election to grace," which is antecedent to good works, and "election to glory," which is subsequent to good works and, even though foreseen by God, is dependent on human perseverance in performing good works.[180]

Giovanni Stefano Menochio (AD 1575 - 1655)

This Italian Jesuit, in the brief exegesis of Matt 25:31-46 contained in his two-volume work *Commentarii totius sacrae scripturae*,[181] does not even discuss the problem of πάντα τὰ ἔθνη in v 32, but in his brief remarks on v 40 he clearly holds a narrow interpretation. He states that "my brothers" are "the apostles, disciples, [and] the faithful," while "the least" are "the lowest among them."[182]

Daniel van Breen (AD 1594 - 1664)

This Flemish theologian, commonly referred to by his Latinized name Brenius, presents an interpretation of the Matthean judgment scene in his *Opera theologica*.[183]

He states that πάντα τὰ ἔθνη of v 32 does not include the deceased, but only those living at the time of the parousia. Their gathering and separation, he says, is the same gathering and separation discussed in Matt 13:30,40,49. Furthermore, he states that πάντα τὰ ἔθνη refers to Christians only:

> *All peoples [gentes]* . . . is to be clearly understood as all peoples who profess the name of Christ, acknowledging him as their spouse, lord and only shepherd, at least as regards external profession . . . . There is the additional fact that an exact examination of works of mercy toward his chosen ones does not make sense except for those who profess the name of Christ and live intermingled with other Christians.[184]

From the above exegesis of v 32 it is clear that van Breen interprets the Matthean pericope as a judgment of Christians in regard to their works toward other Christians. This narrow interpretation of "the least" is more clearly delineated in his comments on v 40. He understands vv 35-36 to refer to the conditions that "the pious" will endure in a persecution against them shortly before the return of Christ, the same persecution mentioned in Dan 12:1, and he states that the Matthean works are to be exercised towards those "who will experience hunger and thirst . . . who for the sake of Christ will live as exiles, oppressed by nakedness and disease, some of whom will be held bound by prison and chains . . . ."[185]

Filippo Picinelli (fl. AD 1667)

The *Concetti della Sacra Bibbia*[186] of Don Filippo Picinelli is not meant as much to be a commentary on the Bible as it is an attempt to show parallels between the scriptures and the stories of Greek and Roman mythology. Consequently, in his treatment of the Matthean judgment scene,[187] he is not too apparent about his own understanding of Matt 25:31-46. He does indicate, however, that his concept of πάντα τὰ ἔθνη in v 32 is universal: "all the provinces of the earth . . . all creatures" will be gathered for the judgment.[188] He has no comment as such on v 40, but in his remarks on v 34 he cites the restrictive Matt 10:42 and compares it with the account of the Theban women who, as a reward, were allowed to enter the temple of Hercules after they had quenched the thirst of the god disguised as a poor man.[189] This citation of Matt 10:42 could be an indication that Picinelli held a restrictive interpretation of "the least," but this cannot be proven since he does not discuss v 40 and in his commentary gives no further clue of a narrow outlook.

Antoine Furetière (AD 1619 - 1688)

In the chapter "Parabole du jugement final" in his work *Les paraboles de l'évangile*,[190] a handbook of morality based on the Gospels, Furetiere treats Matt 25:31-46 as a parable. He says that it is an explanation of the previous Parable of the Talents, but does not elaborate further.[191] His understanding of πάντα τὰ ἔθνη is universal: "... Jesus Christ will come to judge all peoples."[192] In his treatment of the "identity dialogue" he does not address the problem of "the least" at all, but is more concerned with enunciating the moral principles that the omission of charitable works is grievous matter and that the six Matthean works are representative of all good works. There is nothing in his treatment of v 40 that would indicate a narrow interpretation; rather one gets the impression that his viewpoint is nonrestrictive.[193]

Charles Marie de Veil (d. AD 1690)

In his *Commentarius in sanctum Jesu Christi evangelium secundum Matthaeum et Marcum*,[194] de Veil is primarily concerned with the debate over the meritoriousness of good works. Hence, the majority of his comments have to do with vv 34-35a; he says nothing specifically about the identity of πάντα τὰ ἔθνη or "the least." He reiterates the Catholic position that γάρ in v 35a is a causal particle and that it gives the reason for the possession of the kingdom [κληρονομήσατε] rather than its preparation [ἡτοιμασμένην].[195] In a brief comment on v 42 he indicates that he understands the Matthean works to be representative of all works: "Definite works of mercy are given for the indefinite. Christ teaches that any work of mercy, whether corporal or spiritual, manifested to the neighbor will be rewarded at the judgment as if it had been done to himself."[196] There is nothing here to indicate a narrow perspective with regard to "the least."

An Anonymous Priest of The Oratory (fl. AD 1694)

In the anonymous work *Analyse de l'évangile selon l'ordre historique de la concorde*,[197] produced by a member of the French Oratory, there is a rather lengthy exegesis of Matt 25:31-46.[198] The interpretation of πάντα τὰ ἔθνη is universal: "

... he will reassemble all men after their resurrection . . . ,"[199] and the understanding of "the least" is decidedly narrow: " . . . as long as they have rendered them to the least of his brothers, that is, Christians, it is to Himself that they have rendered them."[200]

In a brief comment on vv 42-43, the author indicates his belief that the Matthean scenario has to do solely with the judgment of Christians: "This reproach will not be heard by the infidels, either those who have never heard of Christ or those who have known him only to persecute him or scorn him. Although they must appear before the judgment seat of Christ, this is not an indication of their judgment since they have already been judged by their unbelief."[201]

Jacques Bénigne Bossuet (AD 1627 - 1704)

This great French orator presents his views on the Matthean judgment scene in his *Méditations sur l'évangile* 91-97,[202] written sometime in the last decade of his life but not published until 1731, well after his death.[203] In *Méditations* 91 and 92 he clearly indicates his view that those to be gathered before the throne are all mankind,[204] including the infidels and enemies of the Church.[205] In *Méditation* 94, on vv 35-36, he holds a narrow interpretation of "the least." After comparing the restrictive Acts 9:4 to Matt 25:35-36, he states, " . . . it is because of the fellowship [la société], or rather the unity [l'unité], which exists between the head and his members; it is because he is the vine and we are the branches. It must be said here that, of all his members, the poor are those in which he is most [present]."[206]

Such a restrictive interpretation, however, is not found elsewhere in his works. In *Méditation* 95, also on vv 35-36, his comments show an openess to a more universal understanding of "the least." He calls the recipients of Christian charity "all those who have had to endure the same evils as Christ,"[207] and thus seems to identify Christ with any human being in need, although he never explicitly states that the unbaptized could be the objects of charity. This same openess to a universal view of "the least" is found in one of Bossuet's sermons, "Sur l'aumone,"[208] delivered on the text Matt 25:45. Throughout the sermon he describes those to be assisted as "all the destitute . . . all the captives . . . all the sick . . . all the afflicted . . . all the poor" and other such terms that give no indication of a narrow perspective."[209]

Pasquier Quesnel (AD 1634 - 1719)

This French Jansenist[210] presents his reflections on Matt 25:31-46 in *Le Nouveau Testament en françois avec des réflexions morales sur chaque verset*.[211] In his remarks on v 33 he betrays a universalist view of πάντα τὰ ἔθνη, stating that there will be a "separation of mankind for eternity."[212] His understanding of "the least" is narrow; commenting on v 39, he states: "Jesus Christ is continually humbled and suffers in his members until the end of the world. Happy are the poor who are religious and have eyes to see Christ residing and enduring poverty in themselves."[213] He uses the same designation, "members," to describe those identified with Christ in his remarks on vv 36, 38, and 42,[214] as well as in his commentary on v 45, where he says, "Everything is in common between the head and the members; but Jesus Christ is chiefly in the poor and the humble."[215]

Protestant Authors

David Pareus (AD 1548 - 1622)

In a twelve-page well-ordered, yet wryly sarcastic, exposition found in his *In Sancti Matthaei evangelium commentarius*,[216] Pareus gives his exegesis of Matt 25:31-46. He is a universalist with regard to v 32: "It will, therefore, be a universal judgment in which absolutely all tribes, peoples, nations, orders and positions of the entire earth will be judged: the great, the small, masters, servants, the rich, the poor. No one whatsoever - from Adam, the first person, until the last person - will be exempt."[217]

Pareus very clearly understands "the least" as Christians. He mentions that some think they are the apostles while others suppose them to be all Christians who are poor.[218] He does not seem to take a clear stand one way or the other except to make the point of distinguishing "the least" from those who ask the questions in vv 37-39:

> Some think the Apostles are meant, whom he calls his brothers in the gospel; they are said to be the least because they are despised in the world. Others [say] poor Christians: but then these will be with the sheep who say: When did we see you, etc. What is to be understood, therefore, is that, in the name of all, some who are closer to the judge will speak, and Christ, with his finger pointed at some other lesser people, will say: what you did to this particular least one in this crowd, etc., or else: whatever you greater ones did to the least, etc.[219]

In one of his answers as to why only works of charity are to be the criteria for judgment, Pareus, in a position similar to that of van Breen, says that Christ uttered the Matthean pericope in order to foretell the dangerous fate that would befall "the pious ones" in the future so as to encourage them and keep them from abandoning the faith: "For they [the pious] are the ones, before anyone else, who must go hungry, be thirsty, be exiled in nakedness and sickness, [and] struggle with persecutions in this world."[220] This same restrictive understanding of "the least" is found in six other places throughout the commentary where he speaks of the necessity of recognizing Christ "in his members."[221]

Pareus' main preoccupation with regard to Matt 25:31-46 is the debate over the meritoriousness of the works mentioned in vv 35-36 and the exact function of the particle γάρ.[222] He admits that γάρ is causal, but says that it indicates "the declarative cause of the just sentence given by the judge" and not "the meritorious cause of the kingdom."[223] He mentions the distinction made by the scholastics between a meritorious efficient cause (causa efficiens per modum meriti) and a mediate efficient cause (causa efficiens per modum viae et medii), but does not even allow good works to be called the mediate efficient cause of salvation. "Works of charity, therefore, can be the declarative cause of the piety of the sheep and of the sentence of the justice of the Judge; in no way can they be called the meritorious cause of the kingdom."[224] He spends a considerable amount of energy discussing the objection of the just in vv 37-39 and concludes that their ignorance of their works or their refusal to give any value to their works is "the most valid" argument against those who argue for the necessity of the works: "For indeed, if the just do not even recognize their works, how can they boast of them or consider them to be meritorious?"[225]

John Piscator (AD 1546 - 1625)

In his *Commentarii in omnes libros Veteris et Novi Testamentorum*,[226] this disciple of Calvin presents a rather complete exegesis of Matt 25:31-46.[227] He divides his commentary into three parts: a detailed "synopsis" of the pericope, a "scholion," in which he discusses textual variations and other matters of lower criticism, and "observations," wherein he gives his explanation of the meaning of the passage.

He understands πάντα τὰ ἔθνη in a universal manner. He describes the Matthean pericope as a "universal judgment of the entire human race,"[228] and says that *omnes gentes* signifies "all people whatsoever, as many as who have ever lived or will live up until the day of judgment."[229]

His understanding of "the least" is narrow. In the scholion on v 40 he states that *ex istis fratribus meis* is to be interpreted as "the devout poor and afflicted who were in need;"[230] while in his observations on vv 40 and 45 he makes his point even more clearly that "the least" are Christians:

> Since Christ here considers good works done to needy Christians as if they were done to himself . . . , we should be aroused from this passage to perform good deeds toward

needy Christians . . . . If Christ will punish those who omitted good works and charity toward needy Christians, then how much more will he gravely punish those who, in addition, cruelly persecute them?[231]

He then cites the more restrictive Acts 9:4 and 2 Thess 1:4 and states that Matt 25:40,45 is meant as a consolation for the faithful. This same thought is expressed in his opening reflections on the pericope, Observation 14: "The hope and expectation of that judge, therefore, serves as consolation for the devout when they are persecuted by the impious."[232]

The majority of Piscator's observations are taken up with the dispute over the efficacy of works. After a lengthy disputation of what he calls "the sophistry of Bellarmine," he concludes that "good works with respect to eternal life have to do with the efficient cause not as merits, . . . but as the path or the walkway by means of which one, through the ordination of God, arrives at eternal life."[233]

Huig de Groot (AD 1583 - 1645)

This Dutch jurist and theologian, more commonly known by his Latinized name Hugo Grotius, interpreted Matt 25:40 in a restrictive sense. In his brief remarks on the verse in his *Annotationes in Evangelium secundum Matthaeum*,[234] he says, "So great is the relationship of Christ and Christians . . . that Christ decrees that he is the receiver of benefits lavished on them and the vindicator of injuries inflicted [on them]. See above [Matt] 10:42."[235]

His commentary on v 32 is a bit more involved. De Groot states that πάντα τὰ ἔθνη could be understood to mean "all the living and deceased of the entire world," as indicated in Acts 10:42 and 17:31,[236] but then says that "the opinion of those who think . . . it has to do with those who, among all peoples, will profess the name of Christ"[237] is nevertheless probable. He cites the Parable of the Weeds (Matt 13:24-30), the Parable of the Net (Matt 13:47-50), and various quotations from Lactantius, Jerome, Theophylact, and Cyprian, as well as John 3:18, to press the point that only believers will be gathered before the throne for the final separation.[238]

Giovanni Diodati (AD 1576 - 1649)

In a brief comment on Matt 25:40, found in his *Pious Annotations upon the Holy Bible*,[239] Diodati very clearly espouses the narrow position with regard to "the least": " . . . for you have done it for my sake and in regard of me, Mt 10:40, 42, and that all believers are one and the same spiritual body with Christ their head."[240]

His only other comment on the pericope betrays the polemic of his day regarding the efficacy of good works for salvation. Commenting on v 35, he states: "*Not* that workes are indeed the cause of salvation--but because they are the true *fruit* of a lively faith in Christ, the only author of salvation . . . ."[241]

Joseph Hall (AD 1574 - 1656)

A Plaine and Familiar Explication of All the Hard Texts of the Whole Divine Scripture of the Old and New Testament,[242] the work of Joseph Hall, the Bishop of Exeter, contains very little commentary on Matt 25:31-46. From the brief remarks on v 35, however, it seems that he held a narrow interpretation of the identity of "the least": "For ye have manifested the truth of your faith (which can only give you just claim to heaven) by the fruits of your good and charitable workes: when I, in my poore members upon earth, was hungered, ye gave me meat, etc."[243]

Henry Hammond (AD 1605 - 1660)

This Anglican divine seems to have had a universal understanding of "the least." In his *Novum testamentum domini nostri Jesu Christi*,[244] commenting on v 40, he places this explanation on the lips of Christ: "To people of low estate, but sharers of the same nature which I deigned to assume."[245]

His understanding of πάντα τὰ ἔθνη in v 32 is likewise universal. He states that "the entire people of the Jews, believers, nonbelievers, and all people whatsoever who have ever led a mortal life on this earth"[246] will be gathered, by the ministry of angels, before the throne.

Matthew Poole (AD 1624 - 1679)

In his *Synopsis criticorum aliorumque sanctae scripturae interpretum*,[247] as the title suggests, Poole presents a medley of the opinions of other commentators on Matt 25:31-46; so it is very difficult to determine what his own thinking is.

In his remarks on v 32, he begins by stating that πάντα τὰ ἔθνη means "each and every person of all nations, times, ages . . . not only Israelites and Christians, but even barbaric peoples . . . ;"[248] but then he quotes the indecisiveness of de Groot on the matter and says that even though "it can be understood of all the living and the dead of the entire world . . . , probable is the opinion of those who think that here it has properly to do with those among all peoples who profess the name of Christ . . . ."[249] A bit further, commenting on v 33, he states that the separation of the sheep and goats means that "all peoples are to be divided into two classes."[250]

His understanding of the "the least" is less ambiguous. In fact, it is decidedly narrow. In response to the question as to why only works of charity are cited by Christ, he gives as his fourth answer: "So that he might console the Apostles who, he predicted, would be hungry, thirsty, etc. See 1 Cor 4:11. Christ teaches, therefore, both that he is hungry in them, and that he will never fail those who feed them when they are hungry, etc."[251] Commenting on v 37, he wonders how "the elect could have been unaware that they had fed Christ in Christians . . . ;"[252] and in his remarks on v 40 itself, before giving in full de Groot's narrow interpretation, Poole compares the situation to a marriage in which "an injury done to the wife is considered done to the husband."[253]

As is to be expected, he enters the polemic regarding the exact nature of the particle γάρ, even though he expressly states that he "does not wish to deal here with controversies."[254] His conclusion is that the works in v 35 cannot be seen as the efficient cause, or the meritorious cause, of salvation, but either the consequence of God's election in v 34 (as Calvin would hold) or the reason for the sentence openly proclaimed by the judge (as other Reformers believed).[255]

Richard Ward (ca. AD 1602 - 1684)

Ward gives a rather lengthy exegesis of Matt 25:31-46 in his *Theologicall Questions, Dogmaticall Observations, and Evangelicall Essays upon the Gospel of Jesus Christ according to Saint Matthew*.[256] His main concern in his remarks on v 32 is to dispute what he terms "the Papists' idea of Limbo," but in the midst of his own polemic, he betrays a universal understanding of πάντα τὰ ἔθνη: "All the world and all the men in the world" are to be gathered before Christ.[257]

Ward has no commentary on v 40 as such, but in his observations on vv 35-36, he very clearly espouses a restrictive interpretation of "the least":

> " . . . the estate of the godly is for the most part in this world full of calamity and misery . . . for it is the godly (for the most part) who are pinched and pained with hunger and thirst and persecution and the like . . . . This misery and affliction of theirs is his . . . hence Paul calls his sufferings Christ's sufferings (2 Cor 1), and this he learned from Christ himself who cried unto him when he was going to afflict the members of Christ . . . ."[258]

A good portion of Ward's discussion is concerned with the Catholic-Protestant polemic over the efficacy of good works for salvation and the role that vv 34-36 play in that debate. He admits that γάρ is a causal particle and that, as it is used in v 35a, it signifies a cause, "not the meritorious cause of the kingdom, but a declarative cause of the just sentence pronounced by the judge. By their works they showed they were Christ's sheep."259

Samuel Clarke (AD 1626 - 1701)

In his commentary on Matthew's Gospel contained in *A Survey of the Bible*,260 Clarke has very little to say about the Matthean judgment scene. He describes Matt 25:31-46 as a "scheme or draught and representation of the Last Judgment intermingled with many passages plainly parabolical."261 In a brief comment on v 32 he indicates a universal position, stating that πάντα τὰ ἔθνη means "all nations;"262 while in his remarks on v 40, he betrays a restrictive outlook, saying the verse has to do with "kindness shown to his [Christ's] members."263

NOTES TO CHAPTER IV

[1] *Sancti Bernardini Senensis opera omnia* (9 vols.; ed. P. M. Perantonus; Quaracchi-Firenze: College of St. Bonaventure, 1950-65) 1.119-131.

[2] Ibid., 3.197-229. Both of these sermons were delivered on the first Monday in Lent.

[3] Ibid., 1.126; 3. 213.

[4] Ibid., 1.125; 3. 212.

[5] Ibid., 3. 215-216.

[6] Ibid.

[7] Ibid., 3. 216; 1.127.

[8] Ibid., 3. 215; 1.128.

[9] Ibid., 3. 216.

[10] Ibid., 1.128.

[11] Ibid.

[12] (4 vols.; Cologne: Gymnicus & Hieratus, 1613). This work was first published in 1433.

[13] *Commentaria*, 4.197.

[14] Ibid., Question 393.
[15] Ibid., Question 392.
[16] Ibid., 4.197.
[17] Ibid., 4.198-199.
[18] Ibid., 4.199.
[19] Ibid.
[20] Ibid., 4. 200.
[21] *D. Dionysii Cartusiani opera omnia* (41 vols.; Montreuil: Cartusiae S. M. de Pratis, 1900) 11. 277-279.
[22] Ibid., 278.
[23] Ibid.
[24] Ibid.
[25] Ibid., 277.
[26] Ibid.
[27] Ibid., 279.
[28] Ibid.
[29] *Desiderii Erasmi Roterodami opera omnia* (10 vols.; Hildesheim: Olms, 1962) 6.131. See C. Augustijn, "Erasmus," *TRE* 10.1-18, esp. pp. 9-10.
[30] (Basel: Froben, 1524). A quarter of a century later the work was translated into English: *The First Tome or Volume of the Paraphrase of Erasmus upon the Newe Testamente* (London: Whitchurche, 1548).
[31] *Tomus primus paraphraseon*, 158; *The First Tome*, 98.
[32] Ibid.
[33] Ibid.
[34] Ibid.
[35] Ibid.
[36] *Tomus primus paraphraseon*, 158; *The First Tome*, 99.
[37] (Cologne: Quentell, 1539) 197-199.
[38] *Enarrationes*, 198.
[39] Ibid.
[40] Ibid., 199.
[41] (Paris: Julian, 1564) 211-212.
[42] *In sacrosanctum*, 212.
[43] Ibid., 211.
[44] Ibid., 212.

[45] Ibid., 211.
[46] Ibid.
[47] Ibid., 212.
[48] (Lyons: Plaignard, 1684) 850-854.
[49] *Commentarius*, 850.
[50] Ibid., 851.
[51] Ibid., 850.
[52] Ibid., 851.
[53] Ibid., 852.
[54] Ibid., 852-853.
[55] Ibid., 852.
[56] Ibid.
[57] Ibid.
[58] Ibid., 853.
[59] (Rheims: Fogny, 1582).
[60] *The New Testament*, 74.
[61] Ibid.
[62] (Pont-à-Mousson: Mercator, 1596) 576-583.
[63] *Commentarii in quattuor evangelistas*, 579. See also W. S. Kissinger, *The Parables of Jesus* (American Theological Library Association Bibliography 4; Metuchen, NJ: Scarecrow, 1979) 61-62.
[64] *Commentarii in quattuor evangelistas*, 580.
[65] Ibid., 579-580.
[66] Ibid., 578.
[67] Ibid.
[68] (Cologne: Kinchium, 1620). The work was first published in 1590.
[69] *Notationes*, 351.
[70] Ibid.
[71] *Opera Domini Huldrychi Zuinglii* (4 vols.; Zürich: Froschoverum, 1545) 4.139-140.
[72] *Annotationes*, 139.
[73] Ibid.
[74] Ibid.
[75] Ibid.
[76] Ibid., 140.
[77] Ibid.

[78] *Annotationes in aliquot capita Matthei* (WA 38. 447-667), first published in 1538, covers only the first seventeen chapters of Matthew. Luther's commentary on Matthew 18-24 can be found in his *Matthäus 18-24 in Predigten ausgelegt* (WA 47. 232-627) which was first published from 1537-40.

[79] *Biblia, das ist die gantze Heilige Schrift deudsch* (22d ed.; Wittenberg: Kraffts, 1581) 254. The work was first published in 1534.

[80] The sermon is found in two versions: a shorter one (WA 45. 324-329) and a lengthier one (WA 22:410-423).

[81] WA 22.411.

[82] Ibid., 22.417. Cf. WA 45. 328. See also W. Gähler, "Wer sind die geringsten Brüder?" *Die Christenlehre* 23 (1970) 3-16, esp. pp. 7-9.

[83] WA 22.421.

[84] WA 22.411. Cf. WA 45. 324.

[85] Ibid., 22.412.

[86] Ibid., 22.414. Cf. WA 45. 325.

[87] Ibid., 22.418. Cf. WA 45. 326.

[88] Ibid., 22.419. Cf. WA 45. 327.

[89] WA 3. 215.

[90] WA 6.105.

[91] WA 33. 233.

[92] WA 41.119-120.

[93] WA 2. 744.

[94] WA 6.132.

[95] WA 6. 242.

[96] WA 43. 2, 6, 8-9.

[97] WA 43. 609.

[98] WA 47. 222.

[99] (7 vols.; Berlin: Eichler, 1833). See W. Nijenhuis, "Johannes Calvin," *TRE* 7. 568-592, esp. pp. 579-580.

[100] *In Novum Testamentum commentarii*, 1. 293.

[101] See W. Gähler, *Die Christenlehre* 23 (1970) 9-10.

[102] Ibid., 294.

[103] Ibid., 295.

[104] Ibid., 296.

[105] Ibid., 295.

[106] Ibid.
[107] Ibid.
[108] Ibid.
[109] Ibid., 298.
[110] Ibid.
[111] Ibid.
[112] Ibid., 296.
[113] Ibid.
[114] Ibid., 294.
[115] Ibid.
[116] Ibid., 297.
[117] Ibid.
[118] (2d ed.; Geneva: Stephanus, 1564) 214-217.
[119] *Novi Testamenti expositio*, 215.
[120] Ibid.
[121] Ibid., 217.
[122] (Douai: Patté, 1629) 498-500.
[123] *Annotationes*, 499.
[124] Ibid., 500.
[125] Ibid., 499.
[126] Ibid.
[127] Ibid., 500.
[128] Ibid.
[129] (4 vols.; Augsburg/Graz: Veith, 1742).
[130] *Commentariorum*, 3. 689.
[131] Ibid., 3. 690.
[132] Ibid., 3. 689.
[133] Ibid.
[134] Ibid., 3. 697-698.
[135] Ibid., 3. 698.
[136] Ibid., 3. 697.
[137] (Antwerp: Moretum, 1606) 425-434.
[138] *Commentarius*, 425-434.
[139] Ibid., 425-426.
[140] Ibid., 425.

141 Ibid., 426.
142 Ibid., 430.
143 Ibid.
144 Ibid.
145 Ibid.
146 Ibid.
147 Ibid., 429.
148 *Sancti Roberti Bellarmini opera oratoria posthuma* (10 vols.; ed. S. Tromp; Rome: Gregorian University, 1942). See G. Galeota, "Roberto Bellarmini," *TRE* 5. 525-531, esp. pp. 527-528.
149 Ibid., 1.186; 5. 54. Both sermons, similar in content, are on John 1:26 and were preached in 1599 and 1603 respectively.
150 Ibid., 5.181. The sermon is on Luke 18:42 and was delivered in 1604.
151 Ibid., 8.167. Delivered in 1611, the homily is on the text Luke 10:38.
152 Ibid., 3.188-189. The exhortation was delivered before the Jesuit Provincial Council meeting at Rome.
153 *Roberti Bellarmini opera omnia* (6 vols.; Naples: Giuliano, 1856-62) 5.171.
154 *Bellarmini opera posthuma*, 5. 28. Bellarmine somewhat confuses the imagery of v 32. Matthew speaks of a shepherd separating, not gathering.
155 *Roberti Bellarmini opera omnia* (Editio nova juxta Venetam, 1721; 8 vols.; Naples: Lauriel, 1872) 4. 243.
156 Ibid., 4. 606.
157 Ibid., 4. 605.
158 (3 vols.; Antwerp: Nutium, 1632).
159 *Commentarius*, 3. 69.
160 Ibid.
161 Ibid.
162 Ibid.
163 (2 vols.; Lyons: Canier, Beaujolin, & Laurens, 1685).
164 *Commentarii*, 1. 455.
165 Ibid.
166 Ibid., 1.457.
167 Ibid., 1.459.

[168] Ibid., 1.456.
[169] Ibid., 1.457.
[170] (Brussels: T'Serstevens, 1639) 245-250.
[171] *Tetrateuchus*, 245.
[172] Ibid., 246.
[173] Ibid., 247.
[174] Ibid., 248.
[175] Ibid., 247.
[176] (Mons en Hainaut: Waudraei, 1644) 832-835.
[177] *Historia*, 833.
[178] Ibid., 835.
[179] Ibid.
[180] Ibid., 834.
[181] (2 vols.; Venice: Recurti, 1722).
[182] *Commentarii*, 2. 38.
[183] (Amsterdam: Cuperus, 1666) 39-40.
[184] *Opera theologica*, 40.
[185] Ibid.
[186] (Milan: Vigone, 1667).
[187] *Concetti*, 742-743.
[188] Ibid., 742.
[189] Ibid., 742-743.
[190] (Paris: Le Petit, 1672) 280-300, esp. pp. 286-293.
[191] *Les paraboles*, 286.
[192] Ibid.
[193] Ibid., 289.
[194] (Angers: Auril, 1674) 290-293.
[195] *Commentarius*, 292.
[196] Ibid.
[197] (4 vols.; Paris: Roulland & de Nully, 1694).
[198] *Analyse*, 3.191-199.
[199] Ibid., 3.192.
[200] Ibid., 3.195.
[201] Ibid., 3.197.

202 These meditations can be found in *Oeuvres complètes de Bossuet* (26 vols.; Paris: Gauthier, 1828) 5. 372-390. See also H. Wallon, *Les saints évangiles avec des réflexions de Bossuet* (2 vols.; Paris: LeClère, 1863) 1. 209-215.

203 See the article "Bossuet," *ODCC*, 191, as well as A. Largent, "Bossuet, Jacques-Bénigne," *DTC* 2/1.1049-1089.

204 *Oeuvres complètes*, 5.372-373.

205 Ibid., 5.374.

206 Ibid., 5.377.

207 Ibid., 5.380.

208 Ibid., 1.302-314.

209 Ibid., 1.303. See also pp. 311-313. The closest he comes to a restrictive meaning is on p. 312 when he refers to "the least" as "your brothers, my children." Nowhere in the sermon, however, does he give any indication that "brother" has to be interpreted "Christian."

210 See J. Carreyre, "Quesnel et le quesnellisme," *DTC* 13/2. 1460-1535, esp. cols. 1477-1481; as well as "Quesnel," *ODCC*, 1151.

211 (8 vols.; Paris: Prallard, 1696).

212 *Réflexions morales*, 1.344.

213 Ibid., 1.347-348. One cannot be sure, but the term "religious" in the quotation could have the meaning, as it does today, of a vowed person living in a monastic community.

214 Ibid., 1.346-347, 349.

215 Ibid., 1.350.

216 (Oxford: Lichfield, 1631) 644-656.

217 *Commentarius*, 646.

218 Ibid., 652.

219 Ibid.

220 Ibid., 650.

221 He speaks of "the least" as "members of Christ" once in his remarks on v 35 (p. 650), three times in his comments on v 37 (pp. 652-653), and twice in his reflections on v 42 (p. 655).

222 Five out of the twelve pages of his commentary are taken up with this issue (pp. 648-652).

223 *Commentarius*, 651.

224 Ibid., 652.

225Ibid., 653. He divides the just into three categories: the patriarchs and prophets of the OT who will object out of true ignorance because they never saw Christ or heard his words; the disciples of Christ during his 33 years on earth who will object from humility, refusing to boast of their ministrations to Christ; and all the church's faithful until the end of time who will truthfully object since they too never saw Christ or heard his words in person.

226(3 vols.; Herborn of Nassau: n. pub., 1638).

227*Commentarii*, 2.133-134.

228Observation 14. Ibid., 2.133.

229Ibid. These remarks are found in his synopsis of the pericope.

230Ibid.

231Observations 17 and 18. Ibid., 2.134.

232Ibid., 2.133.

233Observation 16. Ibid., 2.134.

234Found in his *Opera theologica* (4 vols.; Basel: Thurnisios, 1732) 2. 239-241, the work was originally published in 1642, three years before his death. See H. R. Guggisberg, "Hugo Grotius," *TRE* 14. 277-280, esp. pp. 278-279.

235"Annotationes," *Opera*, 2. 240.

236Ibid., 2. 239.

237Ibid.

238Ibid.

239(London: Fussell, 1643). See E. Ravarotto, "Italian Versions of the Bible," *NCE* 2.481-483, esp. p. 482.

240*Pious Annotations*, 31.

241Ibid.

242(London: Flesher, 1633).

243*A Plaine and Familiar Explication*, 50.

244(2 vols.; Frankfurt: Fritsch, 1714). The original work was published in 1653.

245*Novum testamentum*, 1.195.

246Ibid.

247(4 vols.; London: Flesher, 1674).

248*Synopsis*, 4. 603.

249Ibid.

250Ibid.

[251] Ibid., 4. 604-605.
[252] Ibid., 4. 605.
[253] Ibid.
[254] Ibid., 4. 604.
[255] Ibid.
[256] (London: Cole, 1640) 331-36.
[257] *Questions, Observations, and Essays*, 332.
[258] Ibid.
[259] Ibid., 334.
[260] (London: Robinson, 1693) 3-40.
[261] *Survey*, 35.
[262] Ibid.
[263] Ibid.

CHAPTER V

THE MODERN ERA

The Eighteenth Century

The majority of eighteenth-century exegetes interpret πάντα τὰ ἔθνη in Matt 25:32 in the universal sense. Among Protestant commentators who see all humanity as the subject of the final judgment are William Burkitt (AD 1650-1703),[1] Daniel Whitby (AD 1638-1726),[2] Matthew Henry (AD 1662-1714),[3] Joseph Priestley (AD 1733-1804),[4] P. Wright[5] and Thomas Scott (AD 1747-1821)[6] from the English School, as well as the Frenchman Jean Osterwald (AD 1663-1747)[7] and the Germans Johann Bengel (AD 1687-1752),[8] Immanuel Brastberger,[9] and Christoph Starke (AD 1684-1744).[10] Catholic authors who hold the universalist position include the Benedictine Augustin Calmet (AD 1672-1757),[11] the Capuchin Bernardin de Picquigny (AD 1633-1709),[12] and the Dominican Noël Alexander (d. AD 1724)[13] from the French School, as well as the Swiss Benedictine Germanus Cartier[14] and the Flemish author John C. Leerse.[15]

The only author from this period to understand πάντα τὰ ἔθνη as referring to non-Christians only is the English Protestant John Heylyn. In his *Theological Lectures at Westminster Abbey with an Interpretation of the New Testament*,[16] he translates τὰ ἔθνη as "the Heathen" and states that, since the judgment of Christians was the concern of the two previous parables, the Parable of the Virgins and the Parable of the Talents, Christians are not to be included in the judgment described in Matt 25:31-46.[17] He is unclear, however, as to the position of the Jews since he does not clarify whether "heathen" refers to all who are not Christian or to those who are not Christian or Jewish.

Three commentators from this period see πάντα τὰ ἔθνη as referring only to Christians. Commenting on v 32 in his *Verklaring van het Evangelium van Matthaeus*,[18] the Dutch Reformer Joannis van den Honert clearly states that only Christians will be gathered for judgment.[19] The same interpretation seems to be present in the commentaries of two French authors, the Protestant Isaac De Beausobre (AD 1659-1738)[20] and the Catholic Jean Baptiste DuHamel (AD 1624-1706).[21] They do not discuss πάντα τὰ ἔθνη as such, but state that the separation in v 32 is to be between Christians only, to whom will be addressed vv 35-36, 42-43.[22] The implication is that only Christians will be gathered before the throne.

The majority of eighteenth-century commentators interpret "the least" in the restrictive sense. Protestant authors who understand ἑνὶ τούτων τῶν ἀδελφῶν μου τῶν ἐλαχίστων in v 40 to mean all Christians include the English commentators William Burkitt,[23] Daniel Whitby,[24] Matthew Henry,[25] Thomas Scott,[26] John Heylyn,[27] P. Wright,[28] and John Wesley (AD 1703-1791),[29] the French authors Isaac De Beausobre[30] and Jean Osterwald,[31] as well as the Dutch commentator Joannis van den Honert,[32] and the German writers Christoph Starke,[33] Immanuel Brastberger,[34] and Johann Bengel.[35] The English commentator Joseph Priestley seems to have an even more restrictive interpretation of Matt 25:40. He refers to "the least" as "the apostles . . . and disciples,"[36] leaving his reader with the impression that he means only those who followed Christ before his death. Only two of the seven Catholic authors from this period hold the narrow interpretation of v 40: the French Capuchin Bernardin de Picquigny[37] and the Flemish theologian John Leerse.[38] Four Catholic authors, R. Witham, J.-B. DuHamel, A. Calmet, and G. Cartier, do not discuss v 40 at all.

In only two commentaries of this period is there an openess to the possibility that "the least" might be all people. The German Protestant Johann Christoph Wolfe (AD 1683-1739), commenting on Matt 25: 40 in his *Curae philologicae et criticae in quatuor sancta evangelia et actus apostolicos*,[39] simply states that "alms given to the poor are given to God;"[40] while the French Dominican Noël Alexander, in his original comments on v 40 in his *Expositio litteralis*, shows no sign of restrictiveness, stating that it is "Christ alone who begs in the entirety of all the poor."[41]

The strong emphasis on the nature of the particle γάρ in v 35a and the debate over the meritoriousness of the Matthean works that was so characteristic of the commentaries in the seventeenth and sixteenth centuries are noticeably on the wane in the works of the eighteenth century. Only eight of the twenty-three eighteenth-century commentators seem to be concerned with the issue and, as expected, the understanding of the efficacy of the six works divides along confessional lines. Among the Reformers, only five authors are concerned with the topic. Burkitt,[42] Scott,[43] Wolfe,[44] and Bengel[45] mention in passing that the works described in vv 35-36, 42-43 cannot be considered as the cause of inheriting the kingdom. Matthew Henry alone devotes a considerable portion of his commentary to a discussion of the works. He adopts Calvin's consequential understanding of the works and insists that they are "necessary to salvation," not as the cause of winning the kingdom, but rather as "proofs of our love."[46] Among Catholic theologians, de Picquigny[47] and Calmet[48] mention, likewise as an aside, that the Matthean works merit eternal life; only the Englishman Robert Witham (d. AD 1738), in his *Annotations on the New Testament of Jesus Christ*,[49] restricts his brief commentary to the issue of the efficacy of the works, stressing that the wicked, even though they possess faith, are condemned for their lack of works.[50]

Up to this time, all commentators viewed Matt 25:31-46 as a description, either realistic or parabolic, of an outward future universal judgment involving many people. The Swedish mystical thinker Emanuel Swedenborg (AD 1688-1772) departed drastically from this interpretation. In his *Commentary on the Gospel of Matthew*[51] he particularizes and interiorizes the Matthean judgment scene, stating that Matt 25:31-46 is a description of what will occur "with every man when he dies."[52] Consequently, the accompanying angels in v 31 are the Truths from heaven according to which man will be judged, while πάντα τὰ ἔθνη in v 32 are the individual moral strengths and weaknesses of each person that will be separated from each other and then judged.[53] The sheep, according to Swedenborg, represent "those who are in charity and thence in faith," while the goats are "those who are in the truths of faith without charity."[54] He totally spiritualizes the six Matthean works: the hungry are those who desire good; the thirsty, those who desire truth; the stranger is the one willing to be instructed; and the naked, sick and imprisoned are those who realize there is nothing of truth and goodness in themselves.[55] "The least" of v 40, for Swedenborg, do not have to be Christians; in that sense he can be said to have a universal interpretation. He does state, however, in his comments on v 40, that "they are called brethren who are in the good of charity and life."[56] Yet, according to his system of thought, those "in the good" are those who seek truth, desire good, and are willing to be instructed, presumably in the tenets of Swedenborg's spiritual fraternity called the New Church.[57] In that sense, his interpretation of "the least" could be considered narrow.

The Nineteenth Century

The Swedenborgian opinion from the previous century that Matt 25:31-46 was not concerned with a general judgment made some headway in the nineteenth century, but the overwhelming majority of commentators continued to regard the pericope as having to do with a final judgment in the manner of a great assize. Sixteen variously nuanced positions in regard to the meaning of "all nations" in v 32 and "the least" in v 40 surfaced during the nineteenth century. In this exposition I will attempt to group them into several major categories according to the following outline:

(I) Matt 25:31-46 is a Portrayal of the Final Judgment (98 witnesses)
    (A) "All Nations" are All Mankind (78 witnesses)
        (1) "The Least" are Everyone (33 witnesses)
        (2) "The Least" are All Christians (36 witnesses)
        (3) "The Least" are the Christian Missionaries (8 witnesses)
        (4) The Question of "The Least" is Left Open (1 witness)
    (B) "All Nations" are Christians (9 witnesses)
        (1) The Christianization of the World is Presupposed (7 witnesses)
            (a) "The Least" are Fellow Christians (5 witnesses)
            (b) "The Least" are the Christian Missionaries (2 witnesses)
        (2) The Christianization of the World is not Presupposed (2 witnesses)
            (a) "The Least" are Everyone (1 witness)
            (b) "The Least" are not Discussed (1 witness)
    (C) "All Nations" are All Non-Christians and Non-Jews (3 witnesses)
        (1) "The Least" are Everyone (1 witness)
        (2) "The Least" are All Christians (2 witness)
    (D) "All Nations" are All Non-Christians (8 witnesses)
        (1) "The Least" are Everyone (2 witnesses)
        (2) "The Least" are Christians (6 witness)

(II) Matt 25:31-46 is not a Portrayal of the Final Judgment (13 witnesses)
    (A) Matt 25:31-46 is a Premillennial Judgment (6 witnesses)
        (1) "The Least" are Jewish Missionaries (4 witnesses)

(2) "The Least" are Everyone or are not Discussed
   (2 witnesses)
(B) Matt 25:31-46 Refers to the Destruction of
   Jerusalem in AD 70 (3 witnesses)
(C) Matt 25:31-46 Refers to an Individual Judgment
   (4 witnesses)

(I) *Matt 25:31-46 is a Portrayal of the Final Judgment*

The vast majority of nineteenth-century commentators that were researched (ninety-eight out of a total of 111) understand the Matthean pericope as a description of, or a parable having to do with, the final judgment. Their commentaries reflect the following interpretations:

(A) *"All Nations" are All Mankind.* This is the widest possible interpretation of vv 32 and 40, 45 and is witnessed by thirty-three of the seventy-eight commentators who maintain, explicitly or implicitly, that πάντα τὰ ἔθνη is universal. Scholars who maintain this position argue in various ways that the outlook of Matthew's Gospel is universal and that all barriers between Jew and Gentile, believers and unbelievers are done away with. A popular argument is that the narrow Jewish concept of a judgment of Gentiles only is overturned in Matthew's Gospel by his use of the all-encompassing term πάντα τὰ ἔθνη to express a universal judgment. Proponents of this viewpoint will often argue that τὰ ἔθνη is used in a universal sense in Matt 24:9,14 and 28:18-19, as well as elsewhere in the NT (Acts 10:35; 17:26; Rev 5:9; 14:6, 8; 15:4).[58] Those who see "the least" as every human being likewise often argue from the univeralist tone of Matthew's gospel and the mention of the "Son of Man" in v 31. As the "Son of Man," they say, Jesus intends to identify himself with the entire human race.[59]

(1) *"The Least" are Everyone.* Among nineteenth-century commentaries that explicitly state that πάντα τὰ ἔθνη means all people without reservation and that "the least" refers to any human being whatsoever are the works of J. G. Rosenmüller,[60] Christian G. Kühnöl,[61] August Bisping,[62]

Wilhelm M. de Wette,[63] Charles Simeon,[64] John Stow,[65] Albert Barnes,[66] Richard Webster,[67] John M. Gibson,[68] C. M. Curci,[69] Lyman Abbott,[70] Philip Schaff,[71] and Joseph A. Exell.[72]

Fifteen commentators who state that πάντα τὰ ἔθνη is universal fail to be as explicit in their treatment of "the least;" their observations on vv 40, 45, however, contain no restrictive commentary and leave the reader with the impression that they are open to the universal interpretation. They include Franz Xaver Massl,[73] Johannes Gossner,[74] F. J. Knecht,[75] J. P. Migne,[76] A. Réville,[77] Constant Fouard,[78] Henri Lesetre,[79] Alfred Weber,[80] Beilby Porteus,[81] John C. Ryle,[82] David Thomas,[83] Clarke H. Irwin,[84] J. T. Beelen,[85] J. K. Zupanski,[86] and Johann Schwarz.[87]

Five authors do not allude at all to the problems involved in πάντα τὰ ἔθνη and "the least," but from their treatment of the passage leave the impression that they are open to the universal interpretation on both counts. These are the writers Mary Cornwallis,[88] A. Martini,[89] Joseph A. Alexander,[90] Henri Didon,[91] and J. O. Dykes.[92]

(2) *"The Least" are All Christians.* Proponents of this view will most often argue from passages such as Matt 10:40-42 and 18:6 to show that when Matthew uses the terms ἀδελφοί and οἱ μικροί, he has Christians in mind. According to this view, those who suffer the hardships of vv 35-36, 42-43 are, in the widest sense, members of the Christian community or, in the narrower sense, the apostles and missionaries sent to preach the gospel to all peoples. Some will argue from a passage such as Matt 19:28 that "the least" are not included among those to be judged but are co-judges with Christ of everyone else. Those who hold this opinion will often interpret Matt 25:31-46 as an account that is meant to give comforting assurance to the disciples for the time of suffering until the parousia.[93]

The largest number of commentators from the nineteenth century fall within this general category. Forty-four of the seventy-eight authors who maintain a universal interpretation of πάντα τὰ ἔθνη see "the least" in v 40 as a reference to

Christians. Those works which explicitly state that all Christians are Christ's concern in v 40 include the publications of Karl Friedrich Keil,[94] Theodor K. Innitzer,[95] Siegfried Goebel,[96] Joseph Knabenbauer,[97] E. LeCamus,[98] William Bree,[99] B. Bailey,[100] Adam Clarke,[101] George Holden,[102] William Trollope,[103] H. L. Mansel,[104] Francis J. Allnatt,[105] A. Carr,[106] Johannes H. van der Palm,[107] J. A. van Steenkiste,[108] István Végh,[109] J. MacEvilly,[110] Philip Doddridge,[111] S. T. Bloomfield,[112] John J. Owen,[113] Nathaniel M. Williams,[114] David Brown,[115] Petrus Lechner,[116] Howard Crosby,[117] John A. Broadus,[118] Edwin W. Rice,[119] and Anthony J. Maas.[120]

Six commentators in this general category accept a universal interpretation for v 32, but they never really discuss the exegetical options for v 40. Instead they leave the reader with the impression that their view of "the least" means all Christians. These include Frederic W. Farrar,[121] and Charles H. Spurgeon;[122] the anonymous author of the Bulgarian work *Kratko tulkovanic na Evangelie-to ot Matfeia s pytaniia i otgovory*;[123] as well as John Harriman Clark,[124] Ingram Cobbin,[125] and Henry Cowles.[126]

Three authors maintain a narrow perspective with regard to "the least," but in their commentaries fail to discuss πάντα τὰ ἔθνη. From their observations, however, it seems that they presuppose a universal gathering in v 32. Those in this category are B. Boothroyd,[127] Ezra M. Hunt,[128] and Francis W. Upham.[129]

(3) *"The Least" are the Christian Missionaries.* Among those who interpret v 32 in a universal sense and understand "the least" as Christians, there are eight commentators who hold the more narrow opinion that the recipients of the generosity mentioned in vv 35-36 are not Christians in general, but rather the apostles and missionaries who are sent to preach the gospel. They see "the least" in v 40 and the hardships described in vv 35-36, 42-43 as a reference to Matthew's concern with mission in 10:40-42; 24:14 and 28:19-20. Hence, the main concern of the pericope is not the doing of charitable works as such, but rather the acceptance in faith of the gospel. The

peoples of the earth will accordingly be judged as to their acceptance or rejection of Christ, represented by his missionary preachers.[130] Nineteenth-century authors who hold this opinion are Paul Schanz,[131] Willibald Beyschlag,[132] K. F. Nösgen,[133] Paul Wernle,[134] T. Kenrick,[135] D. D. Whedon,[136] George W. Clark,[137] and W. Sunderland Lewis and Henry M. Booth.[138]

(4) *The Question of "The Least" is Left Open.* One commentator from the nineteenth century, William A. Nast,[139] states explicitly that πάντα τὰ ἔθνη is universal, but leaves the question open with regard to the interpretation of "the least."

(B) *"All Nations" are Christians.* A variant of the universal understanding of πάντα τὰ ἔθνη, which will here be treated as a separate category, is the opinion that Matt 25:31-46 has to do with the judgment of Christians only with regard to their treatment of other Christians. The proponents of this interpretation argue from the fact that in vv 37 and 44 those who are judged address Christ as "Lord," indicating their belief in him. They also point out the improbability that the kingdom in v 34 would be given to non-Christians.[140] They often appeal to similar views held by Lactantius,[141] Jerome, and other patristic authors to buttress their case. Advocates of this view can be further divided into those who appeal to Matt 24:14 and 28:19-20 to argue that by the time of the parousia all will have become Christian, and those who will admit the existence of non-Christians by the time of the parousia, but do not include them among those judged in the Matthean pericope.

(1) *The Christianization of the World is Presupposed.*

(a) *"The Least" are Fellow Christians.* Five nineteenth-century works presuppose the christianization of the world by the time of the parousia and adopt the viewpoint that Matt 25:31-46 is a judgment of Christians with regard to their treatment of fellow Christians in general. They are the German commentaries of H. A. W. Meyer,[142] Friedrich W. Schütze,[143] and Johann Lange,[144] as well as the American publications of James G. Butler,[145] and James C. Gray.[146]

(b) *"The Least" are the Christian Missionaries.* August F. Vilmar[147] and Johann Peter Schegg[148] also presuppose the christianization of all peoples, but they see "the least" as the apostles or missionaries and interpret the Matthean pericope as a judgment of Christians vis-à-vis the treatment they give their leaders.

(2) *The Christianization of the World is not Presupposed.* Two works from the nineteenth century see Christians only as the subject of the judgment in Matt 25:31-46, but do not necessarily see an entirely christianized world at the parousia. They seem to admit to the existence of non-Christians, who are included in the universal πάντα τὰ ἔθνη, but place them outside the scope of the judgment. This viewpoint was attested as early as Origen, but more clearly formulated by Gregory the Great and Venerable Bede.

(a) *"The Least" are Everyone.* G. L. Haydock and F. C. Husenbeth[149] state that Matt 25:35-36 makes most sense if addressed to "Christians engaged in the cares of the world." In their treatment of v 40 they give no indication of a restrictive viewpoint but seem open to a universal understanding of "the least."[150]

(b) *"The Least" are not Discussed.* David T. Drummond sees Matt 25:31-46 in the same light as the two preceding parables of the Ten Virgins (Matt 25:1-13) and the Silver Pieces (Matt 25:14-30): "the day of reckoning with the servants of the house."[151] "The nations" of v 32, he claims, are those within the nations of the world at the time of Christ's second coming who will have become Christians. He does not at all discuss "the least" in v 40 and gives no indication whatsoever as to their identity.

(C) *"All Nations" are All Non-Christians and Non-Jews.* According to this viewpoint πάντα τὰ ἔθνη is equivalent to the OT term כָּל־הַגּוֹיִם and means all the Gentile nations, excluding both Christians and Jews. Proponents of this view would hold that following Matt 21:33-43 a mission to the Jewish people is no longer a part of the evangelist's vision. In Matthew's view, they claim, the Jews have already been condemned and will therefore not be among those assembled before the throne on the last day. Neither do Christians belong to "the nations." Matthew has already dealt with their judgment in the Parable of the Ten Virgins (25:1-13) and the Parable of the Silver Pieces (25:14-30). Some who hold this view will also argue from the element of surprise in the answers of the just and the unjust (vv 37-39, and 44) seeing it as a sure indication that those judged were not aware of Christ or his teaching.[152] Commentators in this category are further divided by their understanding of v 40. Those who understand "the least" as Christians see the heathens of v 32 being judged on their acceptance or rejection of Christ in the persons of his representatives, either missionary preachers or Christians in general. Those who understand "the least" in a universal sense see Matt 25:31-46 providing the answer as to how those who never heard of Christ will be judged. Since they cannot be judged by their faith in the Messiah, they will be judged by the criterion of charity, by their works. Only three commentators from the nineteenth century understand πάντα τὰ ἔθνη as those who are neither Christian nor Jewish.

(1) *"The Least" are Everyone.* Walter Lock adopts a universal understanding of "the least" and understands Matt 25:31-46 as a presentation of the ultimate standard of judgment for the Gentile nations who will have never heard of Christ. They will not be judged by faith, or lack of it, but rather by their deeds of kindness to all peoples.[153]

(2) *"The Least" are Christians.* Hans Heinrich Wendt[154] and Bernhard Weiss[155] interpret "the least" in a restrictive manner and see faith in Christ, or the lack thereof, as the criterion for the judgment of the heathen. They will be saved or condemned according to their acceptance or rejection of Christ as manifested by their treatment of Christians.

(D) *"All Nations" are All Non-Christians.* This viewpoint is similar to the preceding except that it includes the Jews among πάντα τὰ ἔθνη. Advocates of this position argue that just as the Israelites used the term כָּל־הַגּוֹיִם in contradistinction to Israel, the community of true believers, so Matthew uses the term πάντα τὰ ἔθνη in contradistinction to the true Israel, the Christian community.[156] As in all the foregoing categories, so in this classification authors can be further subdivided by whether they understand "the least" to be everyone, the apostles and Christian missionaries, or Christians in general.

(1) *"The Least" are Everyone.* Of the eight nineteenth-century commentators who fall into this category, only two have a universal interpretation of "the least." Henry Alford, seeing Matt 25:31-46 as a fulfillment of Gen 22:18, states that all non-Christians will be judged according to their conduct to "any of the great family of man."[157] Alexander B. Bruce sees "the least" as "the Christian poor and needy and suffering in the first place, but ultimately and inferentially any suffering people anywhere."[158]

(2) *"The Least" are Christians.* Six authors give v 40 a restrictive interpretation: one commentator understands "the least" in a special sense as the apostles or missionaries, while the remaining five see all Christians included in the term. Thomas Richey[159] sees "the least" primarily as the preachers of the gospel, while five writers, Otto Pfleiderer,[160] Karl August Gottlieb Keil,[161] H. Olshausen,[162] Heinrich J. Holtzmann,[163] and Franz von Holzendorff,[164] widen the term "the least" to include all Christians. They understand the criterion of judgment in Matt 25:31-46 to be primarily, not works, but faith or lack of faith in Christ as evidenced by their acceptance or rejection of all Christians, Christ's representatives.

(II) *Matt 25:31-46 is not a Portrayal of the Final Judgment*

A small minority of nineteenth-century authors (13 out of a total of 110) do not interpret the Matthean pericope in terms of the final judgment, but see it referring to one or another of God's intermediate judgments, whether general or individual, past or future, that will precede the final assize. The following interpretations in this category are attested in nineteenth-century works:

(A) *Matt 25:31-46 is a Premillennial Judgment.* According to the understanding of pre-millennialists, or dispensationalists as they are often called, there will be four distinct judgments:

(1) the judgment of Christians immediately following the rapture before the tribulation (see 1 Thess 4:16-17; 1 Cor 3:10-15; 2 Cor 5:9-11; Matt 25:1-30); (2) the regathering and judgment of the Jews when Christ returns to earth after the tribulation to begin his millennial reign (see Matt 24: 2-31; Deut 30:1-6; Ezek 20:33-38); (3) the judgment of individual Gentiles who are still alive after the tribulation when Christ reigns at Jerusalem at the beginning of the Millennium (Matt 25:31-46); and (4) the final judgment of all the unsaved dead after the thousand year reign (see Rev 20:11-15).[165]

(1) *"The Least" are Jewish Missionaries.* As can be seen from the above summary, according to dispensationalists Matt 25:31-46 is a description of the premillennial judgment which will come upon all living Gentiles who will manage to survive the seven-year period of tribulation that will be brought to an end by the battle of Armageddon. During the period of tribulation, according to the prophecies of Mic 5:2 and Isa 66:19, converted Jews, Jesus' own brothers according to the flesh (identified by the pre-millennialists with the 144,000 in Rev 7:1-8; 14:1) will take the place of the raptured Christians and will roam the earth preaching the Christian gospel. The Gentiles who survive the tribulation (there is no resurrection from the dead presupposed in this judgment scene from Matthew) will be judged according to their treatment of these Jewish messengers of Christ; those who accorded them hospitality will receive as their reward entrance into the millennial kingdom, the thousand-year peaceful reign of the Messiah on earth (Rev 20:1-6) that will precede the Great White Throne Judgment of Rev 20:11-15. Four nineteenth-century commentators interpret Matt 25:31-46 according to the classic pre-millenialist position: William Kelly,[166] John Nelson Darby,[167] William G. Carr,[168] and F. W. Grant.[169]

(2) *"The Least" are Everyone or are not Discussed.* This viewpoint is similar to the preceding, with the exception that the Jews are included together with the Gentiles in the term πάντα τά ἔθνη, and the concept of "the least" is not restricted to Jewish missionaries, but open to include all the poor and

needy. The two proponents of this nuanced pre-millennialist position are Edward B. Latch[170] and Albert B. Simpson.[171]

(B) *Matt 25:31-46 Refers to the Destruction of Jerusalem in AD 70.* Proponents of this view, which apparently had its origin among American Unitarians,[172] see the coming of the Son of Man in Matt 25:31 to be the same coming previously described in 16:27-28 and 24:29-35. Arguing from 16:28 and 24:34, which state that Jesus' generation will witness this coming, they conclude that the judgment described in Matt 25:31-46 was the historical event of God's visitation on the Jewish nation, evidenced by the Roman destruction of Jerusalem in AD 70. "The least" of v 40 are the disciples of Christ, while πάντα τὰ ἔθνη in v 32 has various interpretations, ranging from Jews only to a mixture of Jews and Gentiles. According to this interpretation the "kingdom" in v 34 is the Church, while Satan (v 41) is often seen as the personification of the Jewish hierarchy that persecuted nascent Christianity. The terms κόλασιν αἰώνιον and ζωὴν αἰώνιον in v 46, the most cogent stumbling blocks to this interpretation, are explained away in Origenian fashion as lengthy intervals of either disciplinary punishment or prosperity. The three nineteenth-century commentators who espouse this position are Lucius R. Paige,[173] Thomas Whittemore,[174] and Sylvanus Cobb.[175]

(C) *Matt 25:31-46 Refers to an Individual Judgment.* Four nineteenth-century authors stand apart in the sense that they interpret Matt 25:31-46 as having to do, not with a general judgment, but with the individual judgment of each human soul.

Two authors, John Clowes[176] and John Worcester,[177] are members of the New Church, founded by the Swedish mystic Emanuel Swedenborg. As to be expected, their interpretations of the Matthean judgment scene follow very closely those of Swedenborg, who understood Matt 25:31-46 to be primarily a description of the individual soul's judgment.[178] The "sheep and the goats" represent the moral strengths and weaknesses of each individual, while "the least" are, for the most part, understood in a restrictive sense.

Two other commentators, who give no indication of being followers of Swedenborg, likewise interpret Matt 25:31-46 as referring to the individual judgment. John H. Morison, arguing strongly against the idea that there is any presupposition of a general resurrection in v 32, states that the "individual manifestation, or coming, of Christ to each individual soul" at death is the same thing as "all the nations shall be gathered before him."[179] Sri Paránanda likewise understands πάντα τὰ ἔθνη in a universal, yet individual sense, as symbolic of the "righteous and unrighteous qualities of man that are naturally separated from each other when the spirit becomes freed from its fleshy rudiments. . . ."[180] He understands "the least" in a universal sense, insisting that "kindness to our fellow creatures is kindness done unto the Lord."[181]

The Twentieth Century

The eighty-six years of the twentieth century have so far produced more literature on Matt 25:31-46 than all the previous centuries combined. Thirty-two variously nuanced positions with regard to the meaning of πάντα τὰ ἔθνη and τῶν ἀδελφῶν μου find expression in the works of this century. I shall attempt to group them according to the following major categories:

(I) Matt 25:31-46 is a Portrayal of the Final Judgment (562 witnesses)
  (A) "All Nations" are All Mankind (440 witnesses)
    (1) "The Least" are Everyone (305 witnesses)
    (2) "The Least" are All Christians (86 witnesses)
    (3) "The Least" are Specific Christians (13 witnesses)
      (a) "The Least" are the Christian Missionaries (12 witnesses)
      (b) "The Least" are Jewish Christians (1 witness)
    (4) The Question of "The Least" is Left Open (3 witnesses)
    (5) The Question of "The Least" is not Discussed (33 witnesses)
  (B) "All Nations" are Christians (50 witnesses)

- (1) The Christianization of the World is Presupposed (17 witnesses)
  - (a) "The Least" are Fellow Christians (12 witnesses)
  - (b) "The Least" are the Christian Missionaries (1 witness)
  - (c) The Question of "The Least" is Left Open (1 witness)
  - (d) "The Least" are not Discussed (3 witnesses)
- (2) The Christianization of the World is not Presupposed (33 witnesses)
  - (a) "All Nations" are All Christians (31 witnesses)
    - (1) "The Least" are Everyone (15 witnesses)
    - (2) "The Least" are Fellow Christians (12 witnesses)
    - (3) "The Least" are not Discussed (4 witnesses)
  - (b) "All Nations" are the Christian Leaders (2 witnesses)
- (C) "All Nations" are All Non-Christians and Non-Jews (37 witnesses)
  - (1) "The Least" are Everyone (10 witnesses)
  - (2) "The Least" are All Christians (15 witnesses)
  - (3) "The Least" are the Christian Missionaries (7 witnesses)
  - (4) "The Least" are not Discussed (5 witnesses)
- (D) The Question of "All Nations" is Left Open (2 witnesses)
  - (1) "The Least" are All Christians (1 witness)
  - (2) The Question of "The Least" is Left Open (1 witness)
- (E) "All Nations" are All Non-Christians (21 witnesses)
  - (1) "The Least" are Everyone (5 witnesses)
  - (2) "The Least" are All Christians (11 witnesses)

                (3)   "The Least" are the Christian Missionaries (5 witnesses)
        (F)   "All Nations" are All Non-Jews (12 witnesses)
                (1)   "The Least" are Everyone (3 witnesses)
                (2)   "The Least" are All Christians (5 witnesses)
                (3)   "The Least" are Specific Christians (4 witnesses)
(II)   Matt 25:31-46 is not a portrayal of the Final Judgment (40 witnesses)
        (A)   Matt 25:31-46 is a Premillennial Judgment (35 witnesses)
                (1)   "The Least" are Jewish Missionaries (26 witnesses)
                (2)   "The Least" are Everyone (3 witnesses)
                (3)   "The Least" are Christians (4 witnesses)
                (4)   "The Least" are not Discussed (2 witnesses)
        (B)   Matt 25:31-46 Refers to the Destruction of Jerusalem in AD 70 (1 witness)
        (C)   Matt 25:31-46 Refers to an Individual Judgment (4 witnesses)

(I) *Matt 25:31-46 is a portrayal of the Final Judgment*

As was the case with nineteenth-century commentators, the overwhelming number of twentieth-century authors (562 out of a total of 602) understand the final judgment as the subject matter of Matt 25:31-46. Their commentaries reflect the following interpretations:

(A) *"All Nations" are All Mankind.*

(1) *"The Least" are Everyone.* Three hundred and five of the 440 commentators who regard πάντα τὰ ἔθνη in the universal sense fall into this category.[182] 136 authors state explicitly that πάντα τὰ ἔθνη of v 32 and "the least" of v 40 are to be understood in the widest possible sense. German language publications holding to this viewpoint include those of Johannes Weiss,[183] Werner G. Kümmel,[184] Moritz Meschler,[185]

Rudolf Bultmann,[186] Adolf Schlatter,[187] Franz M. William,[188] Hermann W. Beyer,[189] Friedrich Büchsel,[190] J. Theissing,[191] Heinrich Schlier,[192] Leonhard Ragaz,[193] Romano Guardini,[194] Karl Staab,[195] Josef Schmid,[196] Richard Gutzwiller,[197] Gustav Stählin,[198] Günther Bornkamm,[199] Martin Doerne,[200] Walter Grundmann,[201] Heinz Schürmann,[202] Ernst Barnikol,[203] Leonhard Goppelt,[204] David Bosch,[205] Rudolf Schnackenburg,[206] Wolfgang Trilling,[207] Gerhard Barth,[208] Georg Richter,[209] Ferdinand Hahn,[210] Heinz E. Tödt,[211] Gerhard Gross,[212] Paul Gaechter,[213] Alfred K. Läpple,[214] Siegfried Schulz,[215] Joachim Rohde,[216] Werner Pfendsack,[217] Herbert Braun,[218] Eduard Schweizer,[219] Otto Knoch,[220] Heinz Geist,[221] E. Rohner,[222] Armin Kretzer,[223] W. Hülsbusch,[224] H. P. Martensen,[225] J. Hamel,[226] Hubert Frankemölle,[227] Karl Hermann Schelkle,[228] Alexander Sand,[229] Paul Christian,[230] and Egon Brandenburger.[231] French language publications in this category include the works of Jules Lebreton,[232] François Mauriac,[233] Henri Daniel-Rops,[234] Theo Preiss,[235] André Feuillet,[236] Pierre Benoit,[237] Pierre R. Bernard,[238] J. Jomier,[239] Pierre Bonnard,[240] C. Dieterle,[241] Jacques Dupont,[242] Jean Radermakers,[243] Louis Evely,[244] Jean Zumstein,[245] Roger Parmentier,[246] Leopold Sabourin,[247] Charles Rochedieu,[248] Daniel Marguerat,[249] Victor K. Agbanou,[250] and André Chouraqui.[251] English language works representative of this view include the European publications of Alexander Maclaren,[252] Hubert H. Farmer,[253] Edward Hastings,[254] Alan H. M'Neile,[255] Ronald S. Wallace,[256] C. Leslie Mitton,[257] C. E. B. Cranfield,[258] G. Hebert,[259] Francis W. Beare,[260] H. E. W. Turner,[261] Sean Freyne,[262] R. S. McConnell,[263] David Hill,[264] and Nils Alstrup Dahl;[265] as well as the American publications of Francis N. Peloubet,[266] Andrew E. Breen,[267] A. L. Williams and W. J. Dean,[268] George H. Box and William F. Slater,[269] Hermann J. Cladder,[270] Halford E. Luccock,[271] J. Middleton Murry,[272] Patrick J. Carroll,[273] George A. Buttrick,[274] Herbert C. Alleman,[275] L. F. Miller,[276] Conrad

Noel,[277] Vincent McNabb,[278] Reuben S. Clymer,[279] Roswell C. Long,[280] Fritz Kunkel,[281] George S. Duncan,[282] Sherman E. Johnson,[283] Frank J. Sheed,[284] R. E. Nixon,[285] Alexander Jones,[286] Bruce Vawter,[287] C. C. Martindale,[288] Fulton J. Sheen,[289] William Barclay,[290] R. V. G. Tasker,[291] Suzanne de Dietrich,[292] Carroll Simcox,[293] Igino Giordani,[294] Herschel H. Hobbs,[295] Neil R. Lightfoot,[296] Béda Rigaux,[297] Howard C. Kee,[298] William A. Poovey,[299] T. C. Smith,[300] Charles E. Booth,[301] William E. McCumber,[302] Paul Nagano,[303] Herman C. Waetjen,[304] John P. Meier,[305] Ben Campbell Johnson,[306] Brian A. Nelson,[307] Wilfrid J. Harrington,[308] Pheme Perkins,[309] and George W. DeHoff.[310] Other witnesses of this universal viewpoint include the Dutch publications of F. W. Grossheide,[311] Jan T. Nielsen,[312] and W. J. C. Weren;[313] the Italian work of Angelo Lancellotti;[314] the Spanish commentaries of Francisco X. Peiró[315] and S. Del Paramo and J. Alonso;[316] the Norwegian author Terje Raddum,[317] and the Brazilian commentator Johan Konings.[318]

Fifty-two commentators in this general category expressly state that πάντα τὰ ἔθνη is universal, but are not as explicit in their treatment of "the least." Their commentary on v 40, however, contains nothing that would limit their interpretation; consequently, the reader is left with the definite impression that they are universalists. German language witnesses of this nuanced viewpoint include the works of Emil Dimmler,[319] Martin Porksen,[320] Alois Riedmann,[321] Josef Dillersberger,[322] Günther Schiwy,[323] Adrienne von Speyr,[324] A. Stöger,[325] L. Schottroff,[326] Georg Künzel,[327] and Martin Petzoldt.[328] French language publications include those of L. C. Fillion,[329] M.-J. Lagrange,[330] H. Lusseau,[331] Jean Deries,[332] and Violaine Monsarrat.[333] English language works in this category include the European publications of Archibald T. Robertson,[334] James A. Findley,[335] Hugh Martin,[336] P. J. Crean,[337] Floyd V. Filson,[338] Henry Wansbrough,[339] Philip H. Bligh,[340] and Robert G. Bratcher;[341] as well as the American works of Walter Elliott,[342] John Brown,[343] G. A.

McLaughlin,[344] B. C. Coffin,[345] Louis A. Banks,[346] Erik Thompson,[347] Isidore O'Brien,[348] Hall Caine,[349] Adam W. Miller,[350] F. D. Nichol,[351] Ray Summers,[352] David A. Redding,[353] David M. Stanley,[354] Ralph Earle,[355] John Killinger,[356] Daniel R. Seagren,[357] Myron S. Augsburger,[358] James M. Boice,[359] and LeRoy Lawson.[360] Other witnesses in this particular sub-category include the Dutch commentators W. S. van Leeuwen[361] and Herman Ridderbos;[362] the Italian publications of T. Garcia[363] and Domenico Squillaci;[364] the Spanish works of Andrés Fernández Truyols,[365] Xabier Pikaza,[366] José Alonso Diaz,[367] and Manuel de Tuya;[368] the Swedish author Christina Almgren,[369] and the Brazilian commentator Francisco de Araújo.[370]

Fifty-eight commentators hold an expressly universal interpretation of "the least," but fail to be as explicit regarding v 32. Either they treat πάντα τὰ ἔθνη in such a manner that one is left with the impression that a universal stance is presupposed, or they say nothing at all about v 32. Eight publications presuppose a universal understanding of v 32: the Italian work *La Sacra Bibbia*[371] and the American works of Elbert Russell,[372] J. Newton Davies,[373] Charles M. Good,[374] Eugene S. Wehrli,[375] Frank Earle,[376] William P. Barker,[377] and Malcolm O. Tolbert.[378] 50 works in this category, however, include no discussion of v 32: the German language works of W. Lütgart,[379] Heinz Dietrich Wendland,[380] Herbert Preisker,[381] Rudolf Otto,[382] Karl Barth,[383] E. Percy,[384] Oscar Cullmann,[385] Josef Ratzinger,[386] J. B. Soucek,[387] J. Gnilka,[388] Basilius Steidle,[389] Otto Betz,[390] P. Hoffmann,[391] Martin Hengel,[392] H. Rusche,[393] Adolf Holl,[394] and W. Lienemann;[395] the French language publications of Jacques Ellul,[396] S. de Dardel,[397] Jean Steinmann,[398] Francis Zorell,[399] J. M. Pelfrène,[400] and Pierre Géoltrain;[401] the English works of Hastings Rashdall,[402] Archibald Alexander,[403] Alfred E. Whitham,[404] H. W. Montefiore,[405] Geraint V. Jones,[406] A. L. Moore,[407] and Kenneth Slack;[408] as well as the American works of M. Dods,[409] John W. Russell,[410] J. Paterson Smyth,[411] James A. Richards,[412]

Frederick C. Grant,[413] Joseph Klausner,[414] Edward P. Blair,[415] Charles Miller,[416] David Granskou,[417] Stanley D. Walters,[418] Peter F. Ellis,[419] Charles A. Curran,[420] John T. Seamands,[421] Arthur Tonne,[422] Joseph A. Grassi,[423] and John F. Craghan.[424] The remaining witnesses in this category are the Italian publications of G. Castoldi[425] and D. Ruatti,[426] the Spanish article of Rudolf Obermüller,[427] and the work of the Brazilian commentator Walter Altmann.[428]

Fifty-nine commentators comprise the category of those who do not explicitly address the problems of vv 32 and 40 but by their comments indicate that their understanding of "the least" is open to the universal. These include the German language works of O. Karrer,[429] Wilhelm Hünermann,[430] Ernst Fuchs,[431] Karl Rahner,[432] Eugen Biser,[433] Josef Blinzler,[434] Hein Sprecklesen,[435] and Benedikt Schwank;[436] the French works of Daniel A. Mortier,[437] Theodore Salvagniac,[438] Paul De Surgy,[439] Raymond L. Bruckberger,[440] R. Swaeles,[441] Axel Lochen,[442] G. Dambricourt,[443] and Francis Martin;[444] the English works of George B. Stevens,[445] Joseph Dean,[446] Frederick W. Green,[447] and E. M. Blaiklock;[448] as well as the American publications of Francis G. Peabody,[449] William G. Ballantine,[450] Thomas C. Hall,[451] William L. Watkinson,[452] Herbert Moninger,[453] J. Watson,[454] Walter Rauschenbusch,[455] Charles R. Erdman,[456] Mary Gonzaga,[457] Henry T. Sell,[458] W. M. Wightman,[459] W. H. Russell,[460] Albert Kempin,[461] Jane M. Murray,[462] Frank Eakin,[463] Maisie Ward,[464] Edgar J. Goodspeed,[465] Bruce M. Metzger,[466] Menachem Israel,[467] Robert A. Spivey and D. Moody Smith,[468] D. B. J. Campbell,[469] Robert L. Cargill,[470] Richard Milham,[471] Donald P. Senior,[472] Robert E. Luccock,[473] Paul Hinnebusch,[474] Margaret Pamment,[475] James P. Martin,[476] Carolyn Osiek,[477] J. Barrie Shepherd,[478] John W. Miller,[479] Richard Edwards,[480] Eugene Kennedy,[481] and John Shea.[482] Other witnesses in this category are the Dutch commentator Anneus M. Brouwer,[483] the Italian authors Giovanni Papini[484] and Angelo Alberti,[485] the Hungarian writer Ottokar Proházska,[486] and the Russian author Dmitri Merezhkovskii.[487]

(2) *"The Least" are All Christians.* Eighty-six of the 440 commentators who understand πάντα τὰ ἔθνη in the universal sense regard "the least" as Christians in general.

Forty-eight authors explicitly state that v 32 is universal and that "the least" are all Christians.[488] These include the German publications of P. Dausch,[489] Hermann Cremers,[490] Erich Klostermann,[491] Willibald Lauck,[492] Georg Strecker,[493] Gerhard Sass,[494] Jindrich Mánek,[495] and the *Laien-Bibel*.[496] French language works in this category include *La Sainte Bible*[497] as well as the publications of Vincent Rose,[498] Ferdinand Prat,[499] Denis Buzy,[500] A. Durand,[501] François Amiot,[502] Xavier Léon-Dufour,[503] and Alphonse Maillot.[504] English language publications in this category include the European works of Arthur T. Cadoux,[505] Charles H. Dodd,[506] Basil F. Atkinson[507] A. W. Argyle,[508] A. E. Harvey,[509] and David R. Catchpole;[510] as well as the American publications of Arthur Ritchie,[511] J. W. McGarvey and P. Y. Pendleton,[512] James R. Miller,[513] J. A. MacDonald,[514] T. H. Robinson,[515] Richard C. H. Lenski,[516] Henry L. Boles,[517] John T. Mueller,[518] William Dallmann,[519] William P. Van Wyk,[520] Edward M. Zerr,[521] Walter E. Bundy,[522] Frank Stagg,[523] William H. Davis,[524] F. W. Dillemore,[525] Kevin O'Sullivan,[526] Herman C. Hanko,[527] Jack D. Kingsbury,[528] Albert Kirk and Robert Obach,[529] Simon Kistemaker,[530] Robert H. Gundry,[531] D. A. Carson,[532] Robert H. Mounce,[533] and John R. Donahue.[534] The Italian commentator Ortensio da Spinetoli[535] and the Belgian author François C. Ceulemans,[536] also fall within this category.

Thirty-one commentators in this general category explicitly argue that "the least" are Christians in general, but they are not as clear in their thinking with regard to πάντα τὰ ἔθνη. They either have nothing to say about v 32 or they leave the reader with the impression that a universal understanding is presupposed. These include the German language publications of Max Meinertz,[537] Oskar Holtzmann,[538] Albert Schweitzer,[539] Hans F. von Soden,[540] Heinrich Graffmann,[541] Wilhelm Michaelis,[542] E. Stauffer,[543] T. De Kruif,[544] Eduard Lohse,[545] and J. Beutler;[546] as well as the French language works of Emile Mersch,[547] Alphonse Tricot and Augustin Crampon,[548] and Raymond Thysman.[549] English language publications in this sub-category include the European works of Bo Reicke[550] and M. D. Goulder,[551] and the American works of Henry G. Weston,[552] Henry Cooke,[553] F. L. Rowe and John A. Klingman,[554] Charles J. Callan,[555] M. Kiddle,[556] Hugh Pope,[557] Ned B. Stonehouse,[558] William Hamilton,[559] Krister Stendahl,[560] W. Neil,[561] Angus J. Higgins,[562] H. L. Ellison,[563] J. Dheilly,[564] and John Drury.[565] The Italian author Marco Sales[566] and the Norwegian writer Sverre Aalen[567] are also to be included in this category.

Seven authors in this general category do not come right out and state that they understand "the least" to be Christians, but it is rather obvious from their commentaries that such is their thinking. These are L. Albrecht,[568] Ronald A. Knox,[569] J. R. Jones,[570] José M. Bover,[571] the anonymous author of the Bulgarian work *Bibliia*,[572] as well as the authors of the Russian publications *Bibliia*[573] and *Evangelie*.[574]

(3) *"The Least" are Specific Christians.*

(a) *"The Least" are the Christian Missionaries.* Thirteen commentators of the 440 who hold a universal interpretation of πάντα τὰ ἔθνη see "the least" as certain Christians. Nine works - the German publications of Otto Michel,[575] Johannes Wilckens,[576] and Samuel Prod'hom,[577] the French work of Antoine Duprez,[578] and the American publications of Apostolos Makrakis,[579] A. J. Mattill, Jr.,[580] Richard C. Oudersluys,[581] Carroll Stuhlmueller,[582] and Norman H. Young[583] - explicitly state that πάντα τὰ ἔθνη is all people and "the least" are the apostles and other Christian preachers of the gospel.[584] B. C. Butler[585] and Y. M. P. Jeng[586] do not discuss v 32, but they likewise insist that "the least" are Christian missionaries. Ernest J. Tinsley does not directly address himself to the identity of those in either v 32 or v 40, but his commentary is such that the meaning of Christian missionaries for "the least" is implied.[587]

(b) *"The Least" are Jewish Christians.* The German work of A. Szabo is unique in the sense that it understands "the least" as Jewish Christians.[588]

(4) *The Question of "The Least" is Left Open.* Three commentators in this general category leave the question of v 40 open to either a universal or restrictive interpretation. The American publication of Martin H. Franzmann[589] and the German work of Julius D. Schniewind[590] state that v 32 is universal, but they cannot decide whether "the least" are everyone, Christians in general, or only Christian missionaries; while the English writer J. A. T. Robinson[591] gives no information as to his opinion on v 32, but likewise leaves the identity of "the least" open.

(5) *The Question of "The Least" is Not Discussed.* Thirty-three twentieth-century authors in this general category do not discuss v 40 at all. Thirty-one of them explicitly state that πάντα τὰ ἔθνη is universal: the German language publications of Alfred Seeberg,[592] Adolf Jülicher,[593] Karl Ludwig Schmidt,[594] Karl Pieper,[595] Georg Bichlmair,[596] Innozenz Daumoser,[597] Ernst Lohmeyer,[598] Poul Nepper-Christensen,[599] Hans Grass,[600] Anton Vögtle,[601] Peter Stuhlmacher,[602] Hans Conzelmann,[603] W. Schenk,[604] Hans-Theo Wrege,[605] R. Pesch,[606] and Reinhart Hummel;[607] the French language works of Felix Klein,[608] D. Mollat,[609] and Hébert Roux;[610] the Italian publications of Giuseppe Ricciotti,[611] Carlo Baldi,[612] and M. Lago Toimil;[613] the Korean work of Song-gyom Pak;[614] as well as the American publications of Marvin R. Vincent,[615] William B. Riley,[616] Benjamin W. Bacon,[617] Thomas Albert,[618] Philippe Rolland,[619] B. J. Hubbard,[620] Thomas L. Kemp,[621] and Neil J. McEleney.[622] Two American authors, Norman Perrin[623] and Chuck Smith,[624] do not explicitly state that πάντα τὰ ἔθνη is universal, but that interpretation is implied in their commentaries.

(B) *"All Nations" are Christians.* There are fifty twentieth-century writers who understand πάντα τὰ ἔθνη to be Christians: seventeen of them presuppose the christianization of the entire world by the time of the parousia, while thirty-three do not necessarily presuppose this total conversion.[625]

(1) *The Christianization of the World is Presupposed.*

(a) *"The Least" are Fellow Christians.* The majority of those who presuppose the christianization of the world (twelve out of seventeen) understand "the least" in a universal sense, but since all are Christians by the time of the parousia, "the least" in their understanding are necessarily Christian. These include the German language publications of W. Brandt[626] and Günther Baumbach;[627] the work of the Belgian exegete Albert Descamps;[628] the English publications of A. Plummer,[629] William O. Oesterley,[630] and Arthur M. Ward;[631] the Spanish work of Isidro Goma Civit;[632] as well as the American publications of Robert F. Horton,[633] John R. Dummelow,[634] Ronald Cox,[635] A. Stock,[636] and Victor Furnish.[637]

(b) *"The Least" are the Christian Missionaries.* J. Ramsey Michaels[638] sees "the least" as the apostles and Christian missionaries.

(c) *The Question of "The Least" is Left Open.* Ulrich Wilckens[639] cannot decide whether "the least" are everyone (necessarily Christian) or only the apostles and missionaries.

(d) *"The Least" are not Discussed.* Three authors, Christian A. Bugge,[640] Leonhard Fendt,[641] and Lyder Brun,[642] presuppose the christianization of the world by the time of the judgment, but give no indication as to their views regarding the identity of "the least." One gets the sense that they are open to the universal (necessarily Christian) outlook.

(2) *The Christianization of the World is not Presupposed.* Thirty-three authors who fall into this general category do not presuppose that everyone is Christian by the time of the parousia, but see Christians only as the addressees of the Matthean judgment scene. 31 of these authors see those who are divided in v 32 as all Christians, while two commentators prefer to see Christian leaders as the object of the division.

(a) *"All Nations" are All Christians.*

(1) *"The Least" are Everyone.* Among those who do not presuppose the Christiani-zation of the world, yet understand Christians only to be the object of the division in v 32, 15 writers interpret "the least" in the widest sense to include everyone. Friedrich Spitta,[643] Ernst Käsemann,[644] R. Tuck,[645] A. J. Grieve,[646] Albert E. Barnett,[647] John B. Payne,[648] and Hendrikus Boers[649] state explicitly that "the least" are everyone, while Madame Cecelia,[650] B. T. D. Smith,[651] Harold A. Guy,[652] Charles W. F. Smith,[653] Bruce R. McConkie,[654] Manford G. Gutzke,[655] John L. McKenzie,[656] and Charles E. Carlston[657] do not directly address the question but leave the reader with the impression that their viewpoint is universal.

(2) *"The Least" are Fellow Christians.* Twelve authors in this category interpret "the least" in the narrow sense of fellow Christians. Eleven publications directly address the issue: those of Emanuel Hirsch,[658] Lucien Cerfaux,[659] Pierre Marcel,[660] Claude G. Montefiore,[661] the Catholic Biblical Association of America,[662] Paul Minear,[663] Harold Roper,[664] Emil G. Kraeling,[665] Mark Sheridan,[666] George Gay,[667] and Russell Pregeant.[668] One author, Julius Wellhausen,[669] does not explicitly identify "the least" as Christians, but leaves the impression that that is his understanding.

(3) *"The Least" are not Discussed.* Four authors in this general category *imply* that Christians only are the subject of the Matthean judgment scene and do not address the issue of the identity of "the least" at all. They are Charles F. Burney,[670] Benno Przybylski,[671] Stanley B. Marrow,[672] and James Breech.[673]

(b) *"All Nations" are the Christian Leaders.* Two commentators, Thomas L. Aborn[674] and Robert Maddox,[675] narrow the make-up of those who are divided in v 32 even more: they understand Matt 25:31-46 as a judgment of Christian leaders vis-à-vis their treatment of members of their flocks, especially children and weaker Christians.

(C) *"All Nations"* are All Non-Christians and Non-Jews. Thirty-seven witnesses from the twentieth century interpret πάντα τὰ ἔθνη to mean "heathens," that is, all who are not Christian or Jewish.[676]

(1) *"The Least" are Everyone.* Ten commentators in this category understand "the least" in a universal sense. Eight authors explicitly state this: Engelbert Neuhäusler,[677] E. H. Plumptre,[678] David Smith,[679] Philip A. Micklem,[680] John B. Lancelot,[681] William Strawson,[682] Charles J. Ellicott,[683] and Archibald M. Hunter;[684] while two commentators, Edward A. Armstrong[685] and Lloyd Gaston,[686] leave a definite impression that their conception of "the least" includes all.

(2) *"The Least" are All Christians.* Fifteen authors who maintain that "all the nations" are non-Christians and non-Jews restrictively interpret "the least" as all Christians: Joachim Jeremias,[687] Günter Haufe,[688] D. Gewalt,[689] Alfred Loisy,[690] Jean Rennes,[691] Max-Allain Chevallier,[692] Louis Monlobou,[693] William K. L. Clarke,[694] Frederick F. Bruce,[695] Schuyler Brown,[696] Francis B. Harris,[697] Ernest B. Gordon,[698] John Reumann,[699] Daniel Harrington,[700] and W. F. Pol Vonck.[701]

(3) *"The Least" are the Christian Missionaries.* Seven commentators, K. Bornhäuser,[702] F. Lau,[703] J. Lange,[704] W. D. Davies,[705] O. Lamar Cope,[706] Douglas R. A. Hare,[707] and Jan Lambrecht,[708] narrow the scope of v 40 even further and see "the least" as the apostles or Christian missionaries.

(4) *"The Least" are not Discussed.* Five exegetes in this general category identify πάντα τὰ ἔθνη as "the heathens," but never address the identity of "the least." They are N. Walter,[709] John Chapman,[710] Kenneth W. Clark,[711] August Van Ryn,[712] and Elwyn E. Tilden.[713]

(D) *The Question of "All Nations" is Left Open.* Two works leave the question open as to whether the term "all the nations" in v 32 refers to everyone or to all non-Christians and non-Jews.

(1) *The Question of "The Least" is Left Open.* The Catalán publication *La Biblia*[714] adopts this position and furthermore

remains undecided as to whether "the least" are everyone or only the apostles.

(2) *"The Least" are All Christians.* Ingo Broer,[715] however, while undecided about whether πάντα τὰ ἔθνη is universal or restrictive, is quite definite in his opinion that in Matthew's mind "the least" are Christians.

(E) *"All Nations" are All Non-Christians.* This viewpoint,[716] which understands the term τὰ ἔθνη in contradistinction to the Church, attests 21 witnesses from the present century.

(1) *"The Least" are Everyone.* Four publications in this category, those of James Hastings,[717] Alan Richardson,[718] R. Sterke and J. C. Hendrix,[719] and the Spanish work *La Biblia*,[720] explicitly identify "the least" as everyone, while W. F. Adeney[721] seems to have a universal interpretation of v 40, even though he does not directly address the question.

(2) *"The Least" are All Christians.* Eleven commentators who understand "all the nations" as referring to all non-Christians restrict the concept of "the least" to Christians in general. Ten works are definite in their restrictive interpretation of v 40: those of Wilhelm Pesch,[722] Johannes Friedrich,[723] Jean-Claude Ingelaere,[724] Francis Crawford Burkitt,[725] Thomas W. Manson,[726] Roger Mohrlang,[727] Paul P. Levertoff and H. L. Goudge,[728] George E. Ladd,[729] John C. Fenton,[730] and David L. Bartlett.[731] W. B. Godbey[732] does not directly address the issue of the identity of "the least" but implies that they are Christians.

(3) *"The Least" are the Christian Missionaries.* Five authors in this general category further restrict the understanding of "the least" to the apostles and Christian missionaries. Theodor von Zahn,[733] Winkelried Gähler,[734] William Manson[735] and Dan O. Via, Jr.[736] expressly identify "the least" in this very narrow perspective; while in the work of Fred W. Burnett[737] there is the strong implication that "the least" are the apostles and missionaries of the Christian church.

(F) *"All Nations" are All Non-Jews.* This interpretation of the Matthean judgment scene, maintained by twelve witnesses and not attested before the twentieth century, understands πάντα ἔθνη from the Jewish point of view as describing all those who do not belong to Israel. It is the sense of the term used by the prophets of the OT (Joel 4:2,11-12; Zeph 3:8; Obad 15-16; Zech 12:3; 14:2-3). Those who insist on this Jewish understanding of τὰ ἔθνη will often argue that Matthew was influenced by the prophets in his use of the term, since, in addition to its presence in 25:32, it is found elsewhere in his gospel (6:32; 10:5,18; 20:19; 28:19). Commentators who fall into this category will often argue that the judgment of the Jews in the Gospel of Matthew has already been pronounced (23:36-24:35)[738]

(1) *"The Least" are Everyone.* Three commentators who interpret πάντα τὰ ἔθνη as all non-Jews have a universal understanding of "the least." Rolf Walker[739] and William A. Curtis[740] state this universal stance explicitly, while in the work of Ray Greenhill[741] it is implied.

(2) *"The Least" are All Christians.* Five commentators in this general category interpret "the least," in a restrictive manner, as all Christians: Helge Hognestad,[742] H. B. Green,[743] William G. Thompson,[744] Duane Thebeau,[745] and Ethelbert W. Bullinger.[746]

(3) *"The Least are Specific Christians.* Four other commentators in this category restrict the meaning of v 40 even further, seeing "the least" as a segment of the Christian community: Henry B. Sharman,[747] Jacques Winandy,[748] and S. Légasse,[749] understand "the least" as the Christian apostles or missionaries, while W. C. Allen[750] maintains the unique theory that "the least" are Jewish Christians.

(II) *Matt 25:31-46 is not a Portrayal of the Final Judgment*

A rather small minority of twentieth-century authors (forty out of the total of 602) do not interpret the Matthean pericope in terms of the classic final judgment, but view it as an intermediate judgment of some sort that will precede the final event. The following interpretations in this category are attested in twentieth-century works:

(A) *Matt 25:31-46 is a Premillennial Judgment.* The vast majority of those who do not see Matt 25:31-46 as the final judgment (thirty-five out of the total of forty) interpret it along the lines of a premillennial judgment of non-Christians.

(1) *"The Least" are Jewish Missionaries.* Twenty-six commentators espouse the classic premillennialist view that πάντα τὰ ἔθνη are the living non-Christians and non-Jews who have survived the battle of Armageddon, while "the least" are the converted Jewish missionaries who have preached the Christian gospel during the tribulation.[751] These include George Williams,[752] William L. Pettingill,[753] Arno C. Gaebelein,[754] James M. Gray,[755] Leonard G. Broughton,[756] Keith L. Brooks,[757] Adolf E. Knoch,[758] Eugene S. English,[759] David L. Cooper,[760] Harry A. Ironside,[761] Howard F. Vos,[762] Homer A. Kent,[763] Merrill F. Unger,[764] Herman A. Hoyt,[765] John F. Walvoord,[766] Salem Kirban,[767] Walter K. Price,[768] Larry Richards,[769] R. L. Saucy,[770] Stanley D. Toussaint,[771] Lehman Strauss,[772] J. Dwight Pentecost,[773] Edward W. Hindson,[774] J. Vernon McGee,[775] Louis A. Barbieri, Jr.,[776] and W. H. Griffith Thomas.[777]

(2) *"The Least" are Everyone.* Seven authors differ from the standard pre-millen-nialist interpretation. Three commentators, Joseph Parker,[778] F. B. Meyer,[779] and William H. Ford[780] understand "the least" in a universal sense as anyone who happened to be alive during the period of tribulation.

(3) *"The Least" are Christians.* Four American publications, those of George C. Morgan,[781] Wallie A. Criswell,[782] Watchman Nee,[783] and John R. Rice,[784] interpret "the least" in a restrictive sense as all Christians who were not caught up in the rapture but remained on earth during the tribulation.

(4) *"The Least" are not Discussed.* Two authors, Ada R. Habershon[785] and Gerrit Verkuyl,[786] interpret πάντα τὰ ἔθνη along dispensationalist lines but give no indication of their views regarding the identity of "the least."

(B) *Matt 25:31-46 Refers to the Destruction of Jerusalem in AD 70.* This viewpoint is attested in only one work from the twentieth century. The French language publication of Georges Gander understands the Matthean judgment scene as a description of the Roman conquest of Jerusalem. The term πάντα τὰ ἔθνη includes the disciples of Christ and all the Jewish sects in existence in AD 70, while the "the least of my brothers" is given a universal interpretation to mean anyone.[787]

(C) *Matt 25:31-46 Refers to an Individual Judgment.* Four twentieth-century authors have a distinctive intepretation of Matt 25:31-46 in the sense that they do not regard the pericope as having anything to do with a public historical or transhistorical event, but view it rather as a description of a very private process within the individual soul at some time or other. John W. Doorly interprets the Matthean judgment scene in a highly psychological manner, somewhat after the fashion of the followers of Emanuel Swedenborg. The parable is concerned with all people, hence πάντα τὰ ἔθνη is viewed in a universal light. The sheep and the goats, however, represent good and evil or spiritual and material thinking within each individual. The blessed of v 34 are those who have the right consciousness of the Christ idea; they will inherit "the kingdom," that is, their true selfhood. "The least of my brothers" are likewise seen in a nonrestrictive manner, but the Matthean works are totally spiritualized. What Christ is demanding here, he argues, is that a sense of the Christ idea be given to those hungering and thirsting for it.[788]

Nigel Richmond sees Matt 25:31-46 in the same psychological light. For him also the sheep and the goats represent the forces of good and evil within every human being, while "the least" is interpreted to mean the repressed factors in human personality that need to be attended to, "fed, clothed, and brought home," in order to maintain a proper balance in the human psyche.[789]

Thomas F. Glasson argues forcefully that a close study of the original documents in no way supports the thesis that Jesus ever envisaged himself as the judge of the human race in some great assize at the end of time. Any division that Jesus was concerned with, he states, belonged to his present; in the ministry of Jesus there was a sifting of human souls. Glasson (without taking a position) discusses two possible interpretations of Matt 25:31-46, the first restrictive and the second universal: (1) either all people as individuals are continuously being judged by their acceptance or rejection of Christ in the persons of his disciples, or (2) in keeping with the thought of the OT prophets, the pericope is meant to be a pictorial representation of a judgment which runs through history, namely, that the survival of nations as a whole (not individuals) depends upon compassion and goodness for all the underprivileged.[790]

This theme of judgment in the ministry of Jesus, rather than a judgment at the end of time, is likewise emphasized in the discussion of Matt 25:31-46 in the commentary of William F. Albright and C. S. Mann.[791] There is no clear discussion of the identities of either πάντα τὰ ἔθνη or "the least," but the authors leave the reader with the strong impression that πάντα τὰ ἔθνη in the Matthean vocabulary means all non-Christians and "the least" are the apostles or missionaries. They are insistent that the parable be read in the same light as all the other Matthean parables. In the Matthean tradition, it is argued, the parables placed on the lips of Jesus are almost totally concerned with the account that Israel must give in the day of God's visitation, and this divine visitation is clearly identified by Jesus with his own ministry. The separation that is described, then, is that which inevitably occurs within everyone when confronted with the issue of Jesus' messiahship. The commentary insists on close links between the Matthean and Johannine traditions and sees the response made to the cross as the real acid test, for both Jew and Gentile.

NOTES TO CHAPTER V

[1]*Expository Notes with Practical Observations on the New Testament of Our Lord and Saviour Jesus Christ* (6th ed.; London: Wyat, 1716) 69-70, esp. p. 69.

2"The Gospel of St. Matthew," *A Critical Commentary and Paraphrase on the Old and New Testament* (4 vols.; ed. Simon Patrick et al.; Philadelphia: Carey & Hart, 1846-48) 4.33-205, esp. p. 170. The original work was *A Paraphrase and Commentary on the New Testament* (2 vols.; London: Bowyer, 1703).

3"An Exposition of the Gospel according to St. Matthew," *An Exposition of the First Four Books of the New Testament* (An Exposition of the Old and New Testament 5; Philadelphia: Barrington & Haswell, 1830) 11-351, esp. pp. 297-298. The original work was published in 1708-10. See "Matthew Henry," *ODCC*, 637.

4*Notes on the Harmony of the Four Evangelists* (Notes on All the Books of Scripture 3; Northumberland: Kennedy, 1804) 430. The work was first published in 1777. See "Joseph Priestley," *ODCC*, 1124.

5*The Complete British Family Bible* (London: Hogg, 1781). There is no pagination; Wright's commentary in found *ad loc.* at Matt 25:31-46.

6"The Gospel according to St. Matthew," *The New Testament of Our Lord and Saviour Jesus Christ* (Commentary on the Holy Bible 4; Philadelphia: Woodward, 1809) *ad loc.* Matt 25:32. The work was first issued in weekly numbers between 1788-92. See "Thomas Scott," *ODCC*, 1252.

7"The Gospel according to St. Matthew," *The Arguments of the Books and Chapters of the Old and New Testament* (6th ed.; 2 vols.; London: SPCK, 1799) 2. 271-329, esp. p. 321. See "French and Provençal Versions of the Bible," *EncJud* 4. 880-883, esp. p. 881.

8*Gnomon Novi Testamenti* (3d ed.; London: Nutt & Williams & Norgate, 1862) 136. The original edition was published at Tübingen by Schramm in 1742.

9"Predigt am 26. Sonntag nach Trinitatis: Evangelium Matt 25,31-46," *Evangelische Zeugnisse der Wahrheit* (Stuttgart: Mäntler, 1758) 839-856, esp. pp. 846-847.

10"Evangelium Matthaei," *Synopsis bibliothecae exegeticae in Novum Testamentum* (3 vols.; Kiel: Seilmann, 1746-48) 1. 29-702, esp. pp. 603-604.

11*Commentaire littéral sur tous les livres de l'ancien et du nouveau testament* (8 vols.; Paris: Emery, Saugrain, Martin, 1726) 7. 227.

12"Sancti Jesu Christi evangelii secundum Matthaeum triplex expositio," *Opera omnia Bernardini a Piconio* (5 vols.; Paris: Vivès, 1870-72) 1. 303-309, esp. p. 303. See H. Hurter, *NLTC*, 4. 815.

[13] *Expositio litteralis et moralis sancti evangelii Jesu Christi secundum Matthaeum* (2 vols.; Venice: Bettinelli, 1782) 1. 554-560, esp. p. 554. See Hurter, *NLTC*, 4.1179.

[14] *Biblia sacra vulgatae editionis* (2d ed.; 4 vols.; Constance: Bez, 1763) 4. 61. See Hurter, *NLTC*, 4.1425-26.

[15] *Spiritus dogmaticus et moralis evangelii* (2 vols.; Brussels: Leonard, 1776) 1. 634-636, esp. p. 634.

[16] (2 vols.; London: Tonson & Draper, 1749, 1761).

[17] *Theological Lectures*, 1. 219.

[18] (Amsterdam: Tirion & Loveringh, 1750).

[19] *Verklaring*, 543-548, esp. p. 543.

[20] *Le Nouveau Testament de notre seigneur Jésus-Christ* (2 vols.; Amsterdam: Humbert, 1718).

[21] *Biblia sacra vulgatae editionis* (Paris: DeLespine, 1705). See Hurter, *NLTC*, 4. 657.

[22] See De Beausobre, *Le Nouveau Testament*, 385, and Du Hamel, *Biblia sacra*, 256.

[23] *Expository Notes*, 70. "The least" are the "poorest and meanest members" of Christ.

[24] *Critical Commentary*, 4.170. He refers to the intimate union between Christ and his members and cites Matt 10:42 and Acts 9:4 in his exegesis of v 40.

[25] *Exposition*, 299-301. He calls "the least" Christ's "disciples and followers," "poor saints and poor ministers," and "poor Christians."

[26] *The New Testament, ad loc.* Matt 25:34-40. He sees "the least" as "poor, afflicted Christians" and insists that "none but believers are the brethren of Christ." He makes a point of arguing with those who would use Matt 25:40 as grounds for universal liberality and goes beyond the meaning of the text to insist that "love of Christ" must be the motive of the charity.

[27] *Theological Lectures*, 1. 219. "The least" are those Christians who were already judged in Matt 25:1-30; they will accompany Christ in his judgment of "the heathen" in vv 31-46.

[28] *Family Bible, ad loc.* Matt 25:40. He refers to "the least" as "his indigent members" and "the meanest of his people."

[29] *Explanatory Notes upon the New Testament* (4th American ed.; New York: Soule & Mason, 1818) 36. The original edition was published in 1754. Wesley cites v 40 as encouragement "to assist the household

of the faith," but also reminds his readers of their obligation "to do good to all men."

[30]*Le Nouveau Testament*, 1. 385. He states that "the least" are those on Christ's right hand. That he means Christians only is obvious from his remarks on v 32 where he says that the separation is between good and evil Christians.

[31]*Arguments*, 2. 321. "The least" are called "his members."

[32]*Verklaring*, 545-546. Van den Honert says "the least" are not only the Apostles but all who share the Christian faith. He cites the more restrictive Matt 10:42 and Acts 9:4 as further examples of the unity between Christ and the Christian.

[33]*Synopsis*, 1. 606. He refers to "the least" variously as "the believers," "the mystical body of Christ," and "the members" of Christ.

[34]*Evangelische Zeugnisse*, 852.

[35]*Gnomon*, 136-137. In a lengthy comment on v 40, Bengel states that "the least" are the disciples whom Christ, after his resurrection, called by the name "brothers." That his interpretation is broad enough to include all Christians, however, is evidenced by his remarks on v 35 where he refers to the recipients of the Matthean works as "the saints" and "the faithful."

[36]*Notes*, 431.

[37]"Triplex expositio," *Opera omnia*, 1. 305. He refers to "the least" as "sick, poor ... and destitute Christian brothers...."

[38]*Spiritus dogmaticus*, 1. 635. He refers to "the least" as "a disciple of Christ."

[39](3d ed.; 5 vols.; Hamburg: Herold, 1739).

[40]*Curae philologicae*, 4. 363.

[41]*Expositio litteralis*, 1. 557. This seeming universality in Alexander's own comments is offset by the fact that he also quotes at length the restrictive interpretations of Augustine and Cyprian. Nonetheless, the fact that in his own comments on v 40 there is no evidence of a restrictive interpretation could be an indication that Alexander sees "the least" as not only Christians, but all who are in need.

[42]*Expository Notes*, 70.

[43]*The New Testament, al loc.* Matt 25:34-40.

[44]*Curae philologicae*, 4. 361, 363.

[45]*Gnomon*, 136.

[46]*Exposition*, 299-300.

[47] "Triplex expositio," *Opera omnia*, 1. 305.

[48] *Commentaire littéral*, 7. 228.

[49] (2 vols.; London: n. pub., 1730). See S. Hartdegen, "Catholic English Versions of the Bible," *NCE* 2.465-470, esp. p. 465

[50] *Annotations*, 1.107.

[51] (Boston: New-Church Union, 1906).

[52] *Commentary*, 391.

[53] Ibid., 392.

[54] Ibid., 395.

[55] Ibid., 398-399.

[56] Ibid., 402.

[57] See the article "Emanuel Swedenborg" in *ODCC*, 1327-1328.

[58] For a good description of this viewpoint see E. W. Rice, *People's Commentary on the Gospel according to Matthew* (Philadelphia: The American Sundayschool Union, 1887) 257.

[59] A comprehensive discussion of the universalist stance with regard to v 40 is lacking in the works of the nineteenth century but is found in many works of the twentieth century. See G. E. Ladd, "The Parable of the Sheep and the Goats in Recent Interpretation," *New Dimensions in New Testament Study* (ed. R. Longenecker and M. Tenney; Grand Rapids: Zondervan, 1974) 191-199, esp. pp. 191-195; as well as J. A. Grassi, "I Was Hungry and You Gave Me to Eat," *BTB* 11(1981) 81-84, esp. p. 81.

[60] *Scholia in Novum Testamentum* (6th ed.; 5 vols.; Nuremberg: Officina Felseckeriana, 1815) 1. 502-508, esp. pp. 504, 506.

[61] *Commentarius in libros Novi Testamenti historicos* (4 vols.; Leipzig: Barth, 1823-27) 1. 670-683, esp. pp. 672, 674.

[62] *Erklärung des Evangeliums nach Matthäus* (2d ed.; Münster: Aschendorff, 1867) 494-496. The first edition was published in 1864.

[63] *Kurze Erklärung des Evangeliums Matthäi* (Kurzgefasstes exegetisches Handbuch zum Neuen Testament 1; Leipzig: Weidmann, 1845) 267-270, esp. pp. 267, 270. The work was first published in 1836.

[64] *Matthew* (Horae Homileticae 11; London: Holdsworth & Ball, 1832) 537-547, esp. pp. 538-539.

[65] *Thoughts on the Gospel of Jesus Christ the Son of God* (Greenwich: Richardson, 1846) 599-609, esp. pp. 600, 605-607.

[66] *Notes, Explanatory and Practical, on the New Testament* (London: Knight & Son, 1852) 121-122.

[67] *One Volume New Testament Commentary* (Grand Rapids: Baker, 1957) *ad loc.* The work was originally published as *The Methodist Commentary on the New Testament* (London: Kelley, 1893); the commentary by Richard Webster, however, was composed at some point before his death in 1856.

[68] *The Gospel of Saint Matthew* (The Expositor's Bible 29; London: Hodder & Stoughton, 1896) 366-375, esp. pp. 367, 374.

[69] *Il santo evangelo secondo Matteo* (Il Nuovo Testamento 1; Turin: Fratelli Bocca, 1879) 168-171, esp. pp. 168, 170.

[70] *A Popular Commentary on the Gospels according to Matthew and Mark* (New York: Barnes, 1876) 275-278, esp. pp. 275-276. In a popular work published a few years later (*A Life of Christ* [New York: Harper, 1882] 405), he holds the same universalist positions.

[71] *A Popular Commentary on the New Testament* (4 vols.; Edinburgh: Clark, 1879) 206-207.

[72] *The Biblical Illustrator* (8 vols.; New York: Randolf, 1880) 1. 590-600, esp. pp. 590, 594, 596.

[73] *Matthäus* (Erklärung der heiligen Schriften des Neuen Testamentes 2; Straubing: Schorner, 1841) 195-205, esp. pp. 196, 201.

[74] *Die heiligen Schriften des Neuen Testamentes* (8 vols.; Hamburg: Evangelische Buchhandlung der Niedersächsischen Gesellschaft, 1888-94) 1. 386-393, esp. pp. 387, 390.

[75] "The Last Judgment," *A Practical Commentary on Holy Scripture* (2 vols.; St. Louis: Herder, 1894) 2. 291-295, esp. pp. 292-293.

[76] *In Sanctum Matthaeum commentaria* (Scripturae sacrae cursus completus 21; Paris: Migne, 1841) 1065-1072, esp. pp. 1067, 1071.

[77] *Etudes critiques sur l'Evangile selon St. Matthieu* (Leiden: van Goor, 1862) 105.

[78] *La vie de notre Seigneur Jésus-Christ* (2 vols.; Paris: Lecoffre, 1880) 2. 262-263.

[79] *Notre seigneur Jésus-Christ dans son saint évangile* (2 vols.; Paris: Lethielleux, 1892) 2.148-151, esp. p. 149.

[80] *Le saint Evangile de notre seigneur Jésus-Christ* (Paris: Lefort, 1898) 377.

[81] *Lectures on the Gospel of St. Matthew* (London: Baynes, 1824) 285-288, esp. pp. 286, 288.

[82] *Expository Thoughts on the Gospels* (New York: Carter, 1860) 340-345, esp. pp. 341-342.

[83] *The Gospel of St. Matthew* (Grand Rapids: Baker, 1956) 483-487, esp. pp. 484, 486. This is a reprint of the original work, *The Genius of the Gospel* (London: Dickinson & Higham, 1873).

[84] "The Gospel according to St. Matthew," *The Universal Bible Commentary* (London: Religious Tract Society, 1928) 353-383, esp. p. 377. This work was first published in 1894.

[85] *Het Nieuwe Testament* (3 vols.; Bruges: Beyaert-Storie, 1891) 1.171-173.

[86] *Ewangelia Jezusa Chrystusa wedlug Swietego Mateusza* (Poznan: Nakladem Biblioteki Kórnickiej, 1892) 144-145.

[87] *Ein ewiges Evangelium* (Pittsburgh, PA: Man, 1835) 126-128.

[88] "The Gospel according to St. Matthew," *Observations, Critical, Explanatory, and Practical, on the Canonical Scriptures* (4 vols.; London: Baldwin, Cradock & Joy, 1820) 4.1-109, esp. pp. 79-80.

[89] *La Sacra Bibbia* (4 vols.; Naples: Marghieri, 1905) 4. 61. This work was first published in Florence: Pagni, 1829.

[90] *The Gospel according to Matthew* (New York: Scribner, 1861) 453-454.

[91] *Jesus Christ* (New York: Appleton, 1891) 233-235, esp. p. 234.

[92] As found in *A Homiletical Commentary on the Gospel according to St. Matthew* (The Preacher's Complete Homiletical Commentary 22; New York: Funk & Wagnalls, 1896) 583.

[93] For a more comprehensive treatment of this restrictive viewpoint it is again necessary to consult twentieth-century works. See G. E. Ladd, "Parable of the Sheep and the Goats," 197-199, as well as J. A. Grassi, *BTB* 11(1981) 81.

[94] *Commentar über das Evangelium des Matthäus* (Leipzig: Dörffling & Franke, 1877) 496-503, esp. pp. 498, 500. He argues that "my brothers" refers to Christians in general and that included among "the least," who are on the right of the judge, are the "poor, suffering, lowly and persecuted" mentioned in Matt 5:3-10.

[95] *Kurzgefasster Kommentar zu den vier heiligen Evangelien.* (4th ed.; 2 vols.; Graz: Styria, 1932) 1. 437. The work, originally published in 1880, was co-authored with F. X. Pölzl.

[96] *The Parables of Jesus* (Clark's Foreign Theological Library ns 15; Edinburgh: Clark, 1900) 418-419. The original is *Die Parabeln Jesu methodisch ausgelegt* (2 vols.; Gütersloh: Bertelsmann, 1879-80).

⁹⁷*Commentarius in Evangelium secundum S. Matthaeum* (2 vols.; Cursus Scripturae Sacrae 35-36; Paris: Lethielleux, 1892-93) 1. 376-386, esp. pp. 377, 383.

⁹⁸*La vie de notre seigneur Jésus-Christ* (3 vols.; Paris: Letouzey & Ané, 1887) 3.133-138, esp. pp. 133, 136.

⁹⁹"Notes on the Gospel according to St. Matthew," *The Plain Reader's Help in the Study of the Holy Scriptures* (2 vols.; Coventry: SPCK, 1822) 2.1-34, esp. pp. 28-29.

¹⁰⁰"The Sheep and the Goats," *An Exposition of the Parables of Our Lord* (London: Taylor, 1828) 477-493, esp. pp. 479, 486. He maintains that even the fallen angels will be among those gathered for judgment.

¹⁰¹"The Gospel according to St. Matthew," *The New Testament of Our Lord and Saviour Jesus Christ* (2 vols.; New York: Waugh & Mason, 1834) 1.23-266, esp. pp. 222-225.

¹⁰²"St. Matthew," *The Christian Expositor* (2 vols.; London: Rivington, 1834) 2. 2-126, esp. pp. 105-106.

¹⁰³*Analecta theologica* (2 vols.; London: Cadwell, 1842) 1. 305-308, esp. pp. 305, 308.

¹⁰⁴"The Gospel according to St. Matthew," *The Holy Bible with an Explanatory and Critical Commentary* (13 vols.; ed. F. Cook; London: Murray, 1878) 7.1-197, esp. pp. 152-153. He argues that "the least" are the Christians among those standing on the right side of the judge.

¹⁰⁵*The Witness of St. Matthew* (London: Paul, Trench, 1884) 246.

¹⁰⁶*The Gospel according to St. Matthew* (The Cambridge Bible for Schools and Colleges 33; Cambridge: University Press, 1898) 194-195. He is at first undecided whether πάντα τὰ ἔθνη refers to everyone or only to Gentiles but finally concludes it to be " . . . probable that Jews and Christians are not excluded from this picture of the judgment."

¹⁰⁷"Het Evangelium van Mattheüs," *Volledige Aanteekeningen tot de Vertaling des Bijbels* (3 vols.; Leiden: Du Mortier, 1835) 3.1-77, esp. pp. 64-66.

¹⁰⁸*Commentarius in evangelium secundum Matthaeum* (2 vols.; Bruges: Beyaert-Defoort, 1876) 1. 438-440. In a later work, *Sanctum Jesu Christi evangelium secundum Matthaeum* (4 vols.; Bruges: Desclée de Brouwer, 1880-81) 2. 878-883, esp. pp. 879, 882, the author espouses the same narrow view in regard to v 40 but with a slight difference. On page 882, in the body of the text, he states that "the least" are Christian poor. In a footnote, however, he states, " . . . needy

Christians . . . are directly indicated, but other men who are not Christians can in no way be excluded." The footnote may not be original but may be the observations of a later editor. If the footnote is original, the possibility exists that the universal element is a reflection of the author's views on the scope of Christian charity rather than the meaning of "the least." Because of such ambiguity and the narrow viewpoint of the earlier work, I prefer to place Steenkiste in the present category.

[109] *Világosító Jegyzemények Szent Máté Evangyeliomjára* (Pesten: Beimel József, 1840) 399-403, esp. pp. 400-401.

[110] *An Exposition of the Four Gospels* (4th ed.; Dublin: Gill, 1898) 481-489, esp. pp. 482, 485.

[111] *The Family Expositor: A Paraphrase and Version of the New Testament with Critical Notes* (Amherst, MA: Adams & Boltwood, 1837) 289-291. He admits the possibility that πάντα τὰ ἔθνη in v 32 could be "a direct intended opposition" to the notion among some Jews at Jesus' time that the Gentiles would have no part in the resurrection (289 n. 2).

[112] *The Greek Testament with English Notes* (2 vols.; Philadelphia: Clark & Hesser, 1854) 1.127-128.

[113] *A Commentary, Critical, Expository, and Practical, on the Gospels of Matthew and Mark* (New York: Leavitt & Allen, 1857) 339-347, esp. pp. 341, 343. He sees "the least" as included among the saved at the right of the judge.

[114] *The Gospel according to Matthew* (Boston: Gould & Lincoln, 1870) 275-280, esp. pp. 276-277. In a lengthy argument meant to portray the superiority of faith over works, he argues, contrary to the apparent meaning of the pericope, that the just were saved because they had the intention of doing good to Christ and therefore faith in him.

[115] "The Gospel according to St. Matthew," *A Commentary, Critical and Explanatory, on the Old and New Testaments* (2 vols.; ed. R. Jamieson, A. Fausset, and D. Brown; Hartford: Scranton, 1877) 2.3-64, esp. pp. 59-61.

[116] "Matthäus," *Die heilige Schrift des Neuen Testamentes* (Latrobe, PA: St. Vincent's Archabbey, 1881) 37-278, esp. pp. 240-241. He states that in the primary sense "the least" are the apostles and disciples in the time of Jesus, but in a wider sense they are all the believers.

[117] "The Gospel according to St. Matthew," *The New Testament* (Boston: Allen, 1884) 1-80, esp. p. 68.

[118] *Commentary on the Gospel of Matthew* (An American Commentary on the New Testament 1; Philadelphia: American Baptist Publication Society, 1886) 507-515, esp. pp. 508, 510, 515. He argues that "the least" are at the right of the judge among the sheep.

[119] *People's Commentary*, 256-260, esp. pp. 257, 259.

[120] *The Gospel according to Saint Matthew* (Saint Louis: Herder, 1898) *ad loc*. There is no pagination. In an earlier work, *The Life of Jesus Christ according to the Gospel History* (St. Louis: Herder, 1890) 436-439, he does not directly discuss the exegetical problem in v 40, but on p. 438 he leaves the reader with the sense that his interpretation could be open to the universal:" . . . we see clearly from this passage . . . that our neighbor represents to us Jesus himself."

[121] *The Life of Christ* (2 vols.; New York: Crowell, 1874) 2. 549. He simply refers to the recipients of v 40 as "His brethren." Technically, this gives us no more information than what is already contained in the verse; in the preceding pages, however, the author refers to Christians as Christ's brethren, so I interpret his comment on v 40 in the same restrictive sense.

[122] *Spurgeon's Popular Exposition of Matthew* (Grand Rapids: Zondervan, 1962) 228-230. This is a reprint of the original, *The Gospel of the Kingdom* (New York: Baker & Taylor, 1893). On page 229 he refers to "the least" as " . . . his tried and afflicted people."

[123] (Tsaringrad: Minaciiana & Cdrus, 1867) 520-524. This title, which is translated *A Short Commentary on the Gospel of Matthew in Question and Answer Form*, was most likely written by an Orthodox monk. His only observation on v 40 is to refer the reader to Matt 10:40-42; 18:5-6, and Mark 9:37, passages which refer to the disciples.

[124] "The Judgment of the World," *Our Lord's Prophecy* (Claremont, NH: Clark, 1874) 122-134, esp. pp. 123, 128. He states that Christ's reply in v 40 is based upon "the just grounds of Christian union."

[125] "The Gospel according to St. Matthew," *Commentary on the Bible* (2 vols.; New York: Hess, 1876) 2. 583-669, esp. pp. 655-656. On p. 656 he refers to "the least" as "those who love him," i.e. Christ.

[126] *Matthew and Mark* (New York: Appleton, 1881) 228-234, esp. pp. 229, 231. "The least" are referred to on p. 231 as "those who represent Jesus in this world."

[127] "The Gospel according to St. Matthew," *The Holy Bible* (London: Duncan, 1836) 1-41, esp. p. 34.

[128] "Notes on St. Matthew," *Bible Notes for Daily Readers* (2 vols.; New York: Scribner, 1870) 2.304-348, esp. p. 342.

[129] *St. Matthew's Witness* (New York: Hunt & Eaton, 1891) 373-375.

[130] For a more comprehensive treatment of this viewpoint it is again necessary to consult twentieth-century works. See J. Lambrecht, "The Last Judgment," *Once More Astonished* (New York: Crossroad, 1983) 196-235, esp. pp. 223-227.

[131] *Commentar über das Evangelium des heiligen Matthäus* (Freiburg: Herder, 1879) 497-501, esp. pp. 498, 500. "The least," he states, are primarily "the apostles who were in the company of Jesus." He would allow a widening of the concept to include "not all believers, but only the poor and unfortunate among them."

[132] *Neutestamentliche Theologie* (2 vols.; Halle: Strien, 1891-92) 1.215-216. He interprets Matt 25:31-46 as a development of 10:42 and sees "the least" as the "disciples in their mission to the world."

[133] *Die Evangelien nach Matthäus, Markus und Lukas* (Kurzgefasster Kommentar zu den heiligen Schriften des Alten und Neuen Testaments: NT 1; Munich: Beck, 1897) 172-180, esp. pp. 172-173, 178.

[134] *Die synoptische Frage* (Freiburg: Herder, 1899) 192.

[135] *An Exposition of the Historical Writings of the New Testament* (2d ed.; 3 vols.; Boston: Munroe & Francis, 1828). 1. 364-369, esp. pp. 364, 367. This is the earliest commentary on Matt 25:31-46 that I could find that was published in the United States

[136] *A Commentary on the Gospels of Matthew and Mark* (New York: Carlton & Porter, 1860) 297-301, esp. pp. 297, 299.

[137] *Notes on the Gospel of Matthew* (New York: Sheldon, 1870) 346-350, esp. pp. 346, 348.

[138] *A Homiletical Commentary on the Gospel according to St. Matthew* (The Preacher's Complete Homiletical Commentary 22; New York: Funk & Wagnalls, 1896) 578-580.

[139] *A Commentary on the Gospels of Matthew and Mark* (Cincinnati: Poe & Hitchcock, 1864) 554-559, esp. pp. 554, 557-558. He quotes from representatives of both the universalist and restrictive interpretations of v 40 without ever stating his own opinion.

[140] For the classic presentation of this viewpoint see H. A. W. Meyer, *Evangelium des Matthäus* (MeyerK 1; Göttingen: Vandenhoeck & Ruprecht, 1864) 525-527.

[141] A favorite reference is to Lactantius' *Divine Institutes* 7. 20 (CSEL 19. 647-650, esp. p. 649): "Nec tamen universi tunc a deo judicabuntur, sed ii tantum qui sunt in dei religione versati." It is obvious that Lac-

tantius is speaking of the final judgment in Chapter 7, but nowhere in the chapter does he cite Matt 25:31-46. Accordingly, one cannot use Lactantius as a witness to a particular interpretation of Matt 25:32.

[142] *Evangelium des Matthäus*, 525-530. In the English edition, *The Gospel of Matthew* (New York: Funk & Wagnalls, 1890) 443-447, esp. p. 444, he states that all the nations, who will be Christian by the time of the judgment, will be judged according to the "proportionable degree" in which they received Christ. This nuance seems to be missing from the original.

[143] *Das Evangelium des Matthäus* (Schullehrerbibel NT 1; Dresden/Leipzig: Arnold, 1846) 396-400, esp. pp. 396, 398. On p. 396 he says that "the pagans will have already been judged," but gives no further clarification.

[144] *Das Evangelium nach Matthäus* (Theologisch-homiletisches Bibelwerk, Die heilige Schrift, NT 1; Bielefeld: Velhagen & Klasing, 1861) 366-370. There is a slight ambiguity in his commentary. In the exegetical and critical section, he states (p. 367) that "the least" are "not the apostles alone, but Christians in general." In his homiletical and practical commentary, however, (p. 369) he says that men will be judged the way they treat "the suffering Christ in suffering humanity."

[145] *The Bible Readers' Commentary* (2 vols.; New York: Appleton, 1878) 1. 461-464.

[146] *Matthew and Mark* (The Biblical Encyclopedia and Museum 11; Cleveland: Barton, 1900) 194-197. Original, New York: Herrick, 1897. In seeming opposition to the obvious sense of the pericope, he insists that the intention to do good to Christ must be present. On p. 195 he states, "Those who do kindness to Christ's people, but not for Christ's sake, will lose the great reward."

[147] *Collegium biblicum--Praktische Erklärung der heiligen Schrift Alten und Neuen Testaments* (3 vols.; Gütersloh: Bertelsmann, 1879-83) 2. 338-339. With rather unveiled anti-Catholic rhetoric, he argues forcefully that the pericope is not a judgment of works, but of faith. It will occur at a time when "all the nations" will be equivalent to "the Church," and will be judged on the manner in which they received Christ who came to them in his messengers, the preachers of the gospel, the leaders of the community (p. 338).

[148] *Evangelium nach Matthäus* (3 vols.; München: Lentner, 1857) 3. 308-325, esp. pp. 309-311, 318. The apostles, he states, will not be among those judged, but "will quickly and gladly hurry to meet the Lord when

he does come for judgment and be immediately received as true servants."

[149] *The Holy Bible* (46 vols.; New York: Virtue, 1850) 37. 46. The authors give no indication as to the whereabouts or the fate of non-Christians.

[150] Ibid. ". . . the Son of God will accept all good offices done to the afflicted, as done to himself."

[151] "The Sheep and the Goats," *The Engravings of the New Testament* (Edinburgh: Kennedy, 1855) 537-539, esp. p. 537.

[152] For further treatment of this argument see J. Lambrecht, "The Last Judgment," 222-223. See also P. Bonnard, "Matthieu 25: 31-46: Questions de lecture et d'interprétation," *Foi et vie* 76 (1977) 81-87, esp. pp. 84-85.

[153] "The Sheep and the Goats," *Expositor* 5/10 (1899) 401-412, esp. pp. 402, 406, 409. On p. 408 he claims that the good that the heathen perform can be called "imperfect Christianity."

[154] *Die Lehre Jesu* (2d ed.; Göttingen: Vandenhoeck & Ruprecht, 1901) 186-188. The work was first published in 1886.

[155] In five major works, published over a span of 23 years, Bernhard Weiss gives varying, and often contradictory, interpretations of Matt 25:31-46. In *Die Vier Evangelien* (2d ed.; Leipzig: Hinrichs, 1905 [first published, 1899]) 149-150, and *Das Matthäus-Evangelium* (7th ed.; MeyerK 1; Göttingen: Vandenhoeck & Ruprecht, 1910 [first published, 1876]) 440-445, he states that, according to Matthew, the term πάντα τὰ ἔθνη indicates the heathen nations, while "the least" are Christians in general. In the original parable of Jesus, however, only Christians were gathered and judged according to their conduct toward their fellow Christians. This original meaning for the pericope is the only interpretation given in his *The Life of Christ* (3 vols.; Edinburgh: Clark, 1884) 3.137-138.

In his *Das Neue Testament* (2 vols.; Leipzig: Hinrichs, 1907 [first published, 1894]) 120-121, however, Weiss interprets πάντα τὰ ἔθνη as all mankind and understands "the least" as those standing on the right of the judge. There is no indication that Christians only are included in the term. This same universalistic stance is also found in his *Das Matthäusevangelium und seine Lucasparallelen* (Halle: Buchhandlung des Waisenhauses, 1876) 537-539. Because of this inconsistency it is difficult to categorize Weiss. I have included him in the present category of those who see Matt 25:31-46 as having to do with the judgment of the heathen with regard to their acceptance or rejection of Christians, because this interpretation surfaces most frequently in his works and is the interpretation used in his final commentary on the passage.

[156] See H. Olshausen, *Biblischer Commentar über sämmtliche Schriften des Neuen Testaments* (Köningsberg: Unzer, 1853) 924-932, esp. pp. 925-926.

[157] *The Greek Testament* (4 vols.; New York: Harper, 1859) 1. 235-238, esp. p. 237.

[158] ΚΑΤΑ ΜΑΤΘΑΙΟΝ ΕΥΑΓΓΗΛΙΟΝ, (2 vols.; The Expositor's Greek Testament; London: Hodder & Stoughton, 1897) 1. 61-340, esp. pp. 304-307. On p. 305 he thinks that, even though πάντα τὰ ἔθνη suggests the heathen peoples as distinct from the Jews, the Jews might very well be included in the term.

[159] "The Sheep and the Goats," *The Parables of the Lord Jesus according to St. Matthew* (New York: Young, 1888) 401-406, esp. pp. 402, 404, 406.

[160] *Das Urchristentum* (2d ed.; Berlin: Reimer, 1902) 596. The work was first published in 1887.

[161] *Analekten für das Studium der exegetischen und systematischen Theologie* (4 vols.; Leipzig: Barth, 1812-22) 1.177.

[162] *Biblischer Commentar*, 924-932, esp. p. 931.

[163] *Hand-Commentar zum Neuen Testament* (2 vols.; Freiburg: Mohr, 1892) 1. 270-271.

[164] "The Gospel according to Matthew," *A Short Protestant Commentary on the Books of the New Testament* (ed. P. W. Schmidt and F. vonHolzendorff; London: Williams & Norgate, 1882) 51-126, esp. p. 116. He understands the entire pericope to be an amplification of Matt 10: 40-42.

[165] See John R. Rice (ed.), "The Gospel according to Matthew," *The Rice Reference Bible* (Nashville: Nelson, 1981) 1001-1053, esp. p. 1045, and Salem Kirban, *The Beginning of Sorrows* (Huntingdon Valley, PA: Kirban, 1972) 138-141, for a more complete description of the dispensationalist viewpoint.

[166] *Lectures on the Gospel of Matthew* (6th ed.; New York: Loizeaux, 1950) 475-488, esp. pp. 479, 484-485.

[167] "Matthew," *Synopsis of the Books of the Bible* (5 vols.; New York: Loizeaux, 1942) 3. 29-209, esp. pp. 186-188. This work was written at some point during the nineteenth century as Darby, the founder of the Plymouth Brethren, lived from 1800-82.

[168] *The Gospel of the Kingdom by Matthew* (Rochester, NY: Genesee, 1896) 68-69. He insists that the judgment in Matt 25:31-46 is upon the Gentile nations, not upon individuals.

[169] "Matthew," *The Numerical Bible* (6 vols.; New York: Loizeaux, 1899) 4.39-272, esp. pp. 238-243.

[170] "The Gospel according to St. Matthew," *A Review of the Holy Bible* (Philadelphia: Lippincott, 1884) 379-418, esp. pp. 411-413.

[171] *Life of Christ* (Christ in the Bible 8; New York: Word, Work & World, 1888) 258. He never really discusses the issue of "the least" and, although he does prefer the interpretation of a premillenial judgment, he concedes that it could be postmillenial.

[172] See L. R. Paige, *A Commentary on the New Testament* (6 vols.; Boston: Mussey, 1844) 1. 285.

[173] Ibid., 285-290. He interprets πάντα τὰ ἔθνη as including Jews and Gentiles. The sheep are the God-fearing Gentiles who treated Christians kindly and, in fulfillment of Matt 21:43, are admitted to the church. The goats are the Jews, especially the religious leaders of Judaism, who persecuted the Christians.

[174] "Parable of the Sheep and the Goats," *Notes and Illustrations of the Parables of the New Testament* (Boston: Whittemore, 1832) 223-263, esp. pp. 224-229. He understands the pericope as the judgment of all non-Christians based on their acceptance or rejection of Christ's disciples.

[175] *The New Testament of Our Lord and Saviour Jesus Christ with Explanatory Notes and Practical Observations* (Boston: The Commentator, 1864) 77-81. "The least," he states, are the same disciples of Christ referred to in Matt 10:42 and 12:49-50, while "the nations" comprise all non-Christians, excluding infants and the heathen not visited by Christian missionaries.

[176] *The Gospel according to Matthew* (2d ed.; London: Hodson, 1819) 381-399, esp. pp. 383, 387. The major part of his commentary is excerpted from the various works of Swedenborg, so it is difficult to get an exact sense of Clowes' own understanding of the pericope. On p. 383 he manifests a universal understanding of πάντα τὰ ἔθνη when he states that "all nations" signifies "that the goods and evils of all shall be made manifest;" while on p. 399 he seems to exhibit a restrictive understanding of the recipients of the beneficence in vv 35-36. Commenting on ξένος in v 35c, Clowes makes the distinction between a "sojourner" (a seeker of Truth) and a "stranger" (someone adverse to

the Truth) and insists that the proper translation of ξένος is "sojourner," presumably one seeking the Truth of the New Church.

177 *Matthew's Gospel* (The Spiritual Interpretation of the Scriptures; Boston: Massachusetts New-Church Union, 1898) 128. He understands the Matthean pericope, in a more limited sense than Clowes, to refer to a separation within the Church itself. πάντα τὰ ἔθνη would thus symbolize all Christians: the sheep are those who cultivate charity along with knowledge, while the goats represent those who care for knowledge only. He never discusses the identity of "the least."

178 See above, pp. 255-256, for a more complete description of Swedenborg's viewpoint.

179 *Matthew* (3d ed.; Boston: American Unitarian Association, 1872) 434-438. He never discusses the identity of "the least."

180 *The Gospel of Jesus according to St. Matthew* (ed. R. L. Harrison; London: Paul, Trench, Trübner, 1898) 225-227, esp. p. 225. His understanding of the pericope is at times influenced by Hindu teaching. On p. 227, for example, commenting on v 46, he says that the κόλασιν αἰ- 'ώνιον is "the punishment of repeated incarnations for the period of an age or 'aeon.' "

181 Ibid., 226.

182 A description of this stance was given previously on pp. 257-258, and so will not be repeated here.

183 "Das Matthäus-Evangelium," *Die drei älteren Evangelien* (Die Schriften des Neuen Testaments 1; Göttingen: Vandenhoeck & Ruprecht, 1907) 229-406, esp. pp. 388-389.

184 In his *Einleitung in das Neue Testament* (17th ed.; Heidelberg: Quelle & Meyer, 1973) 116-117, he holds a universal interpretation of v 32 but does not discuss v 40. In his *Verheißung und Erfüllung* (2d ed.; ATANT 6; Zürich: Zwingli, 1953) 86-87, he expressly states a universalist preference for both vv 32 and 40.

185 *Das Leben unseres Herrn Jesu Christi des Sohnes Gottes* (2 vols.; Freiburg: Herder, 1912) 190-195, esp. pp. 190, 194.

186 *Geschichte der synoptischen Tradition* (Göttingen: Vandenhoeck & Ruprecht, 1957) 123-124. The work was originally published in 1921.

187 In *Der Evangelist Matthäus* (Stuttgart: Calwer, 1929) 723-731, esp. pp. 723, 725; and *Das Evangelium nach Matthäus* (Erlaüterungen zum Neuen Testament 1; Stutttgart: Calwer, 1947) 374-379, esp. pp. 375, 377, he maintains a universalist stance with regard to both verses.

188*The Life of Jesus Christ in the Land of Israel and among its People* (St. Louis: Herder, 1949) 370-372. This is a translation of *Das Leben Jesu in Lande und Volke Israel* (Freiburg: Herder, 1933).

189"ἐπισκέπτομαι," *TDNT* 2. 599-622, esp. p. 603, and "διακονέω," *TDNT* 2. 81-93, esp. p. 85.

190"κρίνω," *TDNT* 3. 921-941, esp. p. 936.

191*Die Lehre Jesu von der ewigen Seligkeit* (Breslau: Dissertation, 1940) 70.

192"Die Entscheidung für die Heidenmission in der Urchristenheit," *Die Zeit der Kirche* (2d ed.; Freiburg: Herder, 1958) 90-107, esp. p. 93. The work was first published in 1942.

193"Das Gericht," *Die Gleichnisse Jesu* (Der Stundenbücher 99; Hamburg: Furche, 1971)15-23, esp. pp. 16-18.

194*Der Herr* (2 vols.; Colmar: Alsatia, 1947) 2.43-44.

195*Das Evangelium nach Matthäus* (2 vols.; Die heilige Schrift in deutscher Übersetzung, Das Neue Testament 1-2; Würzburg: Echter, 1967)1.140-143. The work was first published in 1947.

196*Das Evangelium nach Matthäus* (RNT 1; Regensburg: Pustet, 1948) 242-246, esp. pp. 243, 245. The same views are reiterated in the revised edition of 1959, 350-356.

197*Jesus der Messias. Christus im Matthäusevangelium* (Einsiedeln: Benziger, 1949) 297. The same view is maintained in his later work, *Meditationen über Matthäus* (Einsiedeln: Benziger, 1959) 304-307.

198"ξένος," *TDNT* 5.1-36, esp. pp. 15-16.

199In his articles ("Matthäus als Interpret der Herrenworte," *TLZ* 79 [1954] 341-46, esp. pp. 343-344; "Vorletzter Sonntag im Kirchenjahr (Matt 25, 31-46)," *Göttinger Predigtmeditationen* 9 [1954-1955] 257-260, esp. p. 258) he expressly states that both verses are to be interpreted universally. In *Jesus von Nazareth* (Stuttgart: Kohlhammer, 1956) 131, he claims that "the least" are everyone. In a more recent article, however, ("Der Auferstandene und der Irdische: Matt 28, 16-20," *Überlieferung und Auslegung im Matthäusevangelium* [ed. G. Bornkamm, G. Barth, H. J. Held; WMANT 1; Neukirchen-Vluyn: Neukirchener Verlag, 1960] 289-310, esp. p. 309), he states that πάντα τὰ ἔθνη is universal.

200*Er kommt auch noch heute: Homiletische Auslegung der alten Evangelien* (4th ed.; Göttingen: Vandenhoeck & Ruprecht, 1956) 159, 161.

201 *Die Geschichte Jesu Christi* (Berlin: Evangelische Verlagsanstalt, 1957) 221. The same universal viewpoint is found in his later work, *Das Evangelium nach Matthäus* (THKNT 1; Berlin: Evangelische Verlagsanstalt, 1968) 524-529, esp. pp. 525, 527.

202 In *Jesu Abschiedsrede: Lk 22, 21-38* (NTAbh 20/5; Münster: Aschendorff, 1957) 111, he claims that "the least" are all; but in his later article, "Eschatologie und Liebesdienste in der Verkündigung Jesu" (*Kaufet die Zeit aus: Beiträge zur christlichen Eschatologie* [ed. H. Kirchhoff; Paderborn: Schöningh, 1959] 39-71, esp. pp. 50, 65), he holds for the universal interpretation of both verses.

203 *Das Leben Jesu* (Halle: Niemeyer, 1958) 474-475.

204 In "πεινάω (λίμος)," *TDNT* 6.12-22, esp. p. 20; and in "Die Herrschaft Christi und der Welt," *Christologie und Ethik: Aufsätze zum Neuen Testament* (Göttingen: Vandenhoeck & Ruprecht, 1968) 102-136, esp. pp. 106-107, he maintains a universalist stance with regard to both verses. In a later article, "Leben für die Barmherzigen. Mt 25, 31-46: Vorletzter Sonntag des Kirchenjahres," *Calwer Predigthilfen* 11 (1972) 221-228, esp. p. 224, he gives a universal interpretation to "the least."

205 *Die Heidenmission in der Zukunftsschau Jesu* (ATANT 36; Zürich: Zwingli, 1959) 142.

206 A universalist position for both verses is found in his *Gottes Herrschaft und Reich* (4th ed.; Freiburg: Herder, 1965) 117-118, and in his article "Mitmenschlichkeit im Horizont des Neuen Testaments," *Schriften zum Neuen Testament* (Exegese in Fortschritt und Wandel; Munich: Kösel, 1971) 435-458, esp. pp. 435-436, 451, and in his *The Moral Teaching of the New Testament* (Freiburg: Herder, 1965) 152. In his article "Der Heilaufstrag der Kirche in unserer Zeit," *Rechenschaft vom Glauben* (ed. E. Hesse and H. Erharter; Vienna: Herder, 1969) 97-116, esp. p. 115 n. 4, he likewise holds a universalist position with regard to v 40, but does not discuss v 32.

207 *The Gospel according to Saint Matthew* (2 vols.; New Testament for Spiritual Reading 2; New York: Herder & Herder, 1969) 2. 216-220. The work is a translation of *Das Evangelium nach Matthäus* (2 vols.; Geistliche Schriftlesung; Düsseldorf: Patmos, 1965). He is not consistent in his universal approach. In an earlier work, *Das wahre Israel. Studien zu einer Theologie des Matthäusevangeliums* (STANT 10; Munich: Kösel, 1964) 26-27, 155, he insists on a universal interpretation for πάντα τὰ ἔθνη but implies that "the least" are Christians. He is classified in this work according to his last published stance.

[208] "Das Gesetzesverständnis des Evangelisten Matthäus," *Überlieferung und Auslegung im Matthäusevangelium*, 54-154, esp. pp. 55-56, 89, 98.

[209] *Deutsches Wörterbuch zum Neuen Testament* (Regensburg: Pustet, 1962) 148, 963.

[210] *Christologische Hoheitstitel* (FRLANT 88; Göttingen: Vandenhoeck & Ruprecht, 1963) 187. See also his *Das Verständnis der Mission im Neuen Testament* (WMANT 13; Neukirchen-Vluyn: Neukirchener-Verlag, 1963) 30, 109-110.

[211] *The Son of Man in the Synoptic Tradition* (The New Testament Library; London: SCM, 1965) 73-77.

[212] "Die 'geringsten Brüder' Jesu im Mt 25:40 in Auseinandersetzung mit der neueren Exegese," *BibLeb* 5 (1964) 172-180, esp. p. 180.

[213] *Das Matthäus Evangelium* (Innsbruck: Tyrolia, 1964) 810-822, esp. pp. 813, 818, 820. In a later work, *Die literarische Kunst im Matthäusevangelium* (SBS 7; Stuttgart: KBW, 1965) 78-79, he remains open to the universal interpretation of both verses, but does not specifically address the issue.

[214] *Die Botschaft der Evangelien--heute* (Munich: Don Bosco, 1966) 324.

[215] *Die Stunde der Botschaft* (Hamburg: Furche, 1967) 233.

[216] *Rediscovering the Teaching of the Evangelists* (The New Testament Library; London: SCM, 1968) 50. This is a translation of *Die redaktionsgeschichtliche Methode. Einführung und Sichtung des Forschungsstandes* (Hamburg: Furche, 1968).

[217] *Die Kirche bleibt nicht im Dorf* (Basel: Reinhardt, 1968) 171-181, esp. pp. 172, 174-175.

[218] *Spätjüdisch-häretischer und frühchristlicher Radikalismus; Jesus von Nazareth und die essenische Qumransekte.* (2 vols.; BHT 24; Tübingen: Mohr, 1969) 2. 94 n. 2, 99, 123 n. 6. The same universalist stance is found in *Jesus. Der Mann aus Nazareth und seine Zeit* (Themen der Theologie 1; Stuttgart/Berlin: Kreuz, 1969) 127.

[219] This universal orientation is found in three later works: "Matthäus 21-25," *Orientierung an Jesus: zur Theologie der Synoptiker. Festschrift für W. Josef Schmid zum 80. Geburtstag* (ed. P. Hoffmann; Freiburg: Herder, 1973) 364-371, esp. p. 371; *The Good News according to Matthew* (Atlanta: Knox, 1975) 474-480; and *Matthäus und seine Gemeinde* (SBS 71; Stuttgart: KBW, 1974) 138-

170, esp. pp. 157-159. In two earlier articles, "The Matthean Church," *NTS* 20 (1973-74) 216, and "Observance of the Law and Charismatic Activity in Matthew," *NTS* 16 (1969-70) 213-230, esp. p. 229, he identifies "the least" as Christians.

[220]"Gott als Anwalt des Menschen," *BK* 24 (1969) 82-84.

[221]"Jesusverkündigung im Matthäusevangelium," *Jesus in den Evangelien* (SBS 45; Stuttgart: KBW, 1970) 105-126, esp. p. 120.

[222]*Die eschatologischen Reden der synoptischen Evangelien in der Verkündigung* (Münster: Dissertation, 1971) 132-135.

[223]*Die Herrschaft der Himmel und die Söhne des Reiches* (SBM 10; Würzburg: Echter; Stuttgart: KBW, 1971) 210-224, esp. pp. 211, 220.

[224]"Wenn der Menschensohn in seiner Herrlichkeit kommt," *BibLeb* 13 (1972) 207-214, esp. p. 209.

[225]"Predigthilfe für den Vorletzten Sonntag des Kirchenjahres," *Deutsches Pfarrerblatt* 73 (1973) 583.

[226]"Meditation: Vorletzter Sonntag nach Trinitatis. Matthäus 25, 31-46," *Göttinger Predigtmeditationen* 26 (1973) 474-481, esp. p. 476.

[227]"Amtskritik im Matthäusevangelium?" *Bib* 54 (1973) 247-262, esp. p. 252. See also his *Jahwebund und Kirche Christi. Studien zur Form - und Traditionsgeschichte des "Evangeliums" nach Matthäus* (NTAbh ns 10; Münster: Aschendorff, 1974) 122, 182, 280.

[228]*Theologie des Neuen Testaments* (Kommentare und Beiträge zum Alten und Neuen Testament; 4 vols.; Düsseldorf: Patmos, 1974) 4. 98-99.

[229]*Das Gesetz und die Propheten* (Biblische Untersuchungen 11; Regensburg: Pustet, 1974) 108, 166.

[230]*Jesus und seine geringsten Brüder* (Erfurter Theologische Schriften 12; Leipzig: St. -Benno, 1975) 36, 39, 56.

[231]*Das Recht des Weltenrichters* (SBS 99; Stuttgart: KBW, 1980) 119, 129, 131.

[232]*La vie et l'enseignement de Jésus-Christ notre seigneur* (16th ed.; 2 vols.; Paris: Beauchesne, 1947) 2. 216-228, esp. pp. 216-217, 221.

[233]*Vie de Jésus* (Paris: Flammarion, 1936) 198-199.

[234]*Jésus en son temps* (Paris: Fayard, 1945) 459-460. See also his later work, *The Life of Our Lord* (The Twentieth Century Encyclopedia of Catholicism 68; New York: Hawthorn, 1964) 143.

[235]"Le mystère du fils de l'homme," *Dieu Vivant* 8 (1947) 15-36, esp. pp. 26-28.

[236]"La synthèse eschatologique de saint Matthieu (XXIV-XXV)," *RB* 57 (1950) 62-91; 180-211, esp. pp. 182-185. He argues that just as the judgment against Jerusalem (Matt 24:1-44) brings an end to the epoch of the Jews, so Matt 25:31-46 brings an end to the epoch of the Gentiles. See also "Le caractère universel du jugement et la charité sans frontiers en Mt 25:31-46," *NRT* 102 (1980) 179-196, esp. pp. 186-187, 195-196.

[237]*L'Evangile selon saint Matthieu* (SBJ 31; Paris: Cerf, 1953) 147-148. See also P. Benoit et al. (eds.), *Nouveau Testament: Traduction oecuménique de la Bible* (Paris: Cerf, 1984) 112-113.

[238]*Le mystère de Jésus* (2 vols.; Paris: Amiot-Dumont, 1957) 312-317, esp. pp. 314-315.

[239]*La vie de Messie* (Paris: Cerf, 1963) 232-235.

[240]*L'Evangile selon saint Matthieu* (2d ed.; CNT 1; Paris: Delachaux & Niestlé, 1970) 364-367, esp. pp. 366-367.

[241]*Les petits et les enfants dans les évangiles synoptiques* (Lausanne: Dissertation, 1965) 65-70. See also his "A propos de la prédication synoptique sur les petits," *Le Semeur* 61 (1966) 55-72, esp. pp. 69-70.

[242]"L'Eglise et la pauvreté," *L'Eglise de Vatican II* (Paris: Cerf, 1966) 313-345, esp. pp. 341-342.

[243]*Au fil de l'évangile selon saint Matthieu* (2 vols.; Heverlée-Louvain: Institut d'études théologiques, 1972) 2. 315-317.

[244]"Le jugement dernier," *Méditations d'évangiles* (Paris: Editions universitaires, 1973) 112-116, esp. pp. 112-114.

[245]"L'Enjeu de l'éthique," *La condition du croyant dans l'Evangile selon Matthieu* (OBO 16; Göttingen: Vandenhoeck & Ruprecht, 1977) 327-350, esp. pp. 339-342.

[246]*L'Evangile autrement* (Paris: Le Centurion, 1977) 110-111.

[247]*The Gospel according to St. Matthew* (2 vols.; Bandra, Bombay: St. Paul Publications, 1982) 840-847, esp. pp. 844, 846.

[248]*Les trésors du Nouveau Testament* (St. Legier: Emmaüs, 1979) 57.

[249]"Le lieu de la fidelité chrétienne (Mt 25:31-46)," *Le jugement dans l'Evangile de Matthieu* (Le monde de la Bible; Geneva: Labor et Fides, 1981) 481-552, esp. pp. 494, 506, 510.

[250]"Mt 25, 31-46: L'annonce du jugement des nations," *Le discours eschatologique de Matthieu 24-25: Tradition et rédaction* (EBib ns 2; Paris: Gabalda, 1983) 172-207, esp. pp. 183-184, 191-192.

251"Matyah-Matthieu," *L'Univers de la Bible* (8 vols.; Paris: Lidis, 1985) 8.33-159, esp. pp. 139-140.

252*The Gospel according to St. Matthew* (3 vols.; London: Hodder & Stoughton, 1912) 3. 215-221, esp. pp. 215, 217, 219.

253"The Last Judgement," *The Healing Cross* (London: Nisbet, 1938) 160-168, esp. pp. 162-164.

254*The Gospel according to St. Matthew* (3 vols.; The Speaker's Bible 29-31; Aberdeen: The Speaker's Bible Office, 1938-40) 3.151-154.

255*The Gospel according to Saint Matthew* (London: Macmillan, 1952) 368-372. He argues that τῶν ἀδελφῶν μου is a gloss, added by someone who thought the ἐλάχιστοι were Christians.

256"The Sheep and the Goats," *Many Things in Parables* (Edinburgh: Oliver & Boyd. 1955) 185-192, esp. pp. 188-189.

257"Present Justification and Final Judgment: A Discussion of the Parable of the Sheep and the Goats," *ExpTim* 67 (1955-56) 46-50, esp. p. 48.

258"Diakonia," *London Quarterly and Holborn Review* 186 (1961) 275-281, esp. pp. 275-276. See also his *The Service of God* (London: Epworth, 1965) 24-25.

259"The Problem of the Gospel according to Matthew," *SJT* 14 (1961) 403-413, esp. p. 406.

260*The Earliest Records of Jesus* (Oxford: Blackwell, 1964) 218-219. See also his *The Gospel according to Matthew* (San Francisco: Harper & Row, 1981) 492-497, esp. pp. 493, 495.

261"The Parable of the Sheep and the Goats," *ExpTim* 77 (1965-66) 243-246, esp. p. 245. He argues that τούτων in v 40 is a redundant demonstrative and thus cannot be used to prove that "the brothers" are apart from those judged; in fact, he claims, they could be present among the condemned.

262This universal outlook is found in *Mark and Matthew* (Scripture Discussion Commentary 7; Chicago: Acta Foundation, 1971) 230, which he co-authored with Henry Wansbrough. In an earlier work, however, that he authored alone, (*The Twelve: Disciples and Apostles* [London: Sydney, Sheed & Ward, 1968] 178), he claims that "the least" are Christian missionaries.

263*Law and Prophecy in Matthew's Gospel* (Basel: Dissertation, 1969) 205.

264*The Gospel of Matthew* (NCB 1; London: Oliphants, 1972) 330-331.

[265]"Nations in the New Testament," *New Testament Christianity for Africa and the World. Essays in honour of Harry Sawyerr.* (ed. M. E. Glasswell and E. W. Fasholé-Luke; London: SPCK, 1974) 54-68.

[266]Peloubet, F. N., *The Teachers' Commentary on the Gospel according to Saint Matthew* (New York: Oxford University, 1901) 310-315, esp. pp. 310, 313.

[267]*A Harmonized Exposition of the Four Gospels* (4 vols.; Rochester, NY: Smith, 1908) 4. 77-90, esp. pp. 81, 84.

[268]*Matthew* (2 vols.; The Pulpit Commentary 33-34; New York: Funk & Wagnalls, 1910) 2. 481-485.

[269]*Saint Matthew* (NCB 22; New York: Frowde, 1922) 332-334.

[270]*In the Fullness of Time* (St. Louis: Herder, 1925) 323-329, esp. pp. 324-325.

[271]"The Last Judgment," Studies in the Parables of Jesus (Life and Service Series; New York: Methodist Book Concern, 1925) 123-131, esp. pp. 124-125.

[272]*Jesus, Man of Genius* (New York: Harper, 1926) 320.

[273]*The Man-God* (Chicago: Scott, Foresman, 1927) 263-264.

[274]*The Parables of Jesus* (Garden City, NY: Doubleday, 1928) 254-259.

[275]*New Testament Commentary* (Philadelphia: United Lutheran Church in America, 1936) 228.

[276]*The Gospel according to St. Matthew* (New York: Wagner, 1937) 302.

[277]*The Life of Jesus* (New York: Simon & Schuster, 1938) 478-479. He insists that the judgment will be of nations, not individuals.

[278]*A LIfe of Jesus Christ Our Lord* (New York: Sheed & Ward, 1938) 147-148.

[279]*The Interpretation of St. Matthew* (2 vols.; Quakertown, PA: Philosophical Publishing, 1945) 2. 232-235.

[280]"Serving the Saviour," *More Stewardship Parables of Jesus* (New York: Abingdon-Cokesbury, 1947) 90-104, esp. pp. 92, 94-95.

[281]*Creation Continues: A Psychological Interpretation of the First Gospel* (New York: Scribner, 1947) 249-250.

[282]*Jesus, Son of Man* (New York: Macmillan, 1948) 196-202, esp. pp. 198-199.

[283]"The Gospel according to Matthew, *IB* 7. 231-625, esp. pp. 562-566.

284In an early article, "The Last Judgment," *The Book of the Saviour* (ed. F. J. Sheed; New York: Sheed & Ward, 1952) 412-413, he is merely open to the universal interpretation of both verses. In a later work, however, *To Know Christ Jesus* (New York: Sheed & Ward, 1962) 320-321, his interpretation is explicitly universal.

285"Matthew," *The New Bible Commentary Revised* (ed. D. Guthrie and J. Motyer; Grand Rapids: Eerdmans, 1970) 813-850, esp. p. 846.

286"The Gospel of Jesus Christ according to Saint Matthew," *A Catholic Commentary on Holy Scripture* (ed. R. C. Fuller et al.; New York: Nelson, 1953) 851-904, esp. pp. 897-898. See also *The Jerusalem Bible* (ed. A. Jones; Garden City, NY: Doubleday, 1966) 57.

287*The Four Gospels* (2 vols.; Garden City, NY: Doubleday, 1967) 2.174-175. In an earlier work, however, (*A Popular Exposition of the Four Gospels* [2 vols.; Huntington, IN: Our Sunday Visitor, 1955] 2. 682-685) he identifies "the least" as Christians. He is classified in this dissertation according to his last published position on the matter.

288*The Gospel according to St. Matthew* (Stonyhurst Scripture Manuals; Westminster, MD: Newman, 1957) 189-191.

289*Life of Christ* (New York: McGraw-Hill, 1958) 171-173.

290*The Gospel of Matthew* (2d ed.; 2 vols.; The Daily Study Bible Series; Philadelphia: Westminster, 1958) 2. 358-361. See also his *Introduction to the First Three Gospels* (Philadelphia: Westminster, 1975) 166.

291*The Gospel according to Saint Matthew* (The Tyndale New Testament Commentaries 1; Grand Rapids: Eerdmans, 1961) 237-240.

292*The Gospel according to Matthew* (The Layman's Bible Commentary 16; Richmond: Knox, 1961) 131-132.

293"You Did it to Me," *The First Gospel* (Greenwich, CT: Seabury, 1963) 273-274.

294*Christ, Hope of the World* (Boston: St. Paul Editions, 1964) 378-381.

295*An Exposition of the Gospel of Matthew* (Grand Rapids: Baker, 1965) 352-357, esp. pp. 353-354.

296*Lessons from the Parables* (Grand Rapids: Baker, 1965) 179-183.

297*The Testimony of St. Matthew* (Chicago: Franciscan Herald, 1968) 91, 173.

298"The Gospel according to Matthew," *The Interpreter's One-volume Commentary on the Bible* (ed. C. M. Laymon; Nashville: Abingdon, 1971) 609-643, esp. pp. 639-640. See also "The Gospel according to

Matthew," *The Gospels* (Interpreter's Concise Commentary 6; ed. C. Laymon; Nashville: Abingdon, 1971) 1-96, esp. p. 87. In *Understanding the New Testament* (2d ed.; Englewood Cliffs, NJ: Prentice-Hall, 1965) 286, an earlier work which Kee co-authored with K. Froehlich and F. W. Young, there is no viewpoint expressed on πάντα τὰ ἔθνη and the identity of "the least" is not explicitly addressed, although the commentary remains open to the universal interpretation.

[299] *The Power of the Kingdom* (Minneapolis, MN: Augsburg, 1974) 124.

[300] "An Exegesis of Matthew 25:31-46," *Foundations* 19 (1976) 206-210, esp. pp. 207-208.

[301] "An Exegesis of Matthew 25:31-46," *Foundations* 19 (1976) 214-215.

[302] *Matthew* (Beacon Bible Expositions 1; Kansas City, MO: Beacon Hill, 1975) 192-194.

[303] "An Exegesis of Matthew 25:31-46," *Foundations* 19 (1976) 216-222, esp. p. 218.

[304] *The Origin and Destiny of Humanness* (Corte Madera, CA: Omega, 1976) 231-232.

[305] This universal outlook is found in his latest work, *Matthew* (New Testament Messsage 3; Wilmington, DE: Glazier, 1980) 302-304. In an earlier work, *The Vision of Matthew* (Theological Inquiries; New York: Paulist, 1979) 129, 177-178, Meier seems ambiguous about the identity of "the least." On p. 178, he claims that Christ identifies himself "with suffering mankind"; yet, on p. 129 he states that "the least" are "the humble members of the church." He is consistent, however, in his belief that πάντα τὰ ἔθνη is universal, arguing for that position not only in the two above-mentioned publications, but also in an earlier article, "Nations or Gentiles in Matthew 28:19?" *CBQ* 39 (1977) 94-102, esp. pp. 99-101.

[306] *Matthew and Mark* (Waco, TX: Word Books, 1978) 90-91.

[307] "How We're Going to be Separated," *Hustle Won't Bring the Kingdom of God* (St. Louis: Bethany, 1978) 81-85.

[308] "Christ the King," *The Saving Word* (3 vols.; ed. A. Flannery, T. Halton, W. Harrington; Wilmington, DE: Glazier, 1980) 1. 338-340.

[309] "The Sheep and the Goats," *Hearing the Parables of Jesus* (New York: Paulist, 1981) 158-165, esp. pp. 159-163. In an earlier work, however, (*Reading the New Testament* [New York: Paulist, 1978] 218) she holds that "all the nations" are non-Christians and "the least" are the Christians.

The Modern Era

310"The Gospel according to Saint Matthew," *Matthew--Acts* (DeHoff's Commentary 5; Murfreesboro, TN: DeHoff Publications, 1981) 27-129, esp. pp. 110-111.

311*Het heilig Evangelie volgens Mattheüs* (2d ed.; Commentaar op het Nieuwe Testament; Kampen: Kok, 1954) 283, 382.

312*Het Evangelie naar Mattheüs* (3 vols.; De Prediking van het Nieuwe Testament 1-3; Nijkerk: Callenbach, 1974) 3. 73-82, esp. pp. 74, 77.

313*De Broeders van de Mensenzoon* (Amsterdam: Bottenburg, 1979) 242.

314*Matteo* (Nuovissima versione della Bibbia dai testi originali 33; Roma: Edizioni paoline, 1975) 341-344.

315*El evangelio comentado* (2 vols.; Madrid: Editorial sapientia, 1954) 2. 555-565, esp. pp. 557, 562-563.

316*La Sagrada Escritura* (BAC, NT 1; 3d ed.; Madrid: Editorial católica, 1973) 264-267.

317*Mattheus Evangeliet* (Oslo: Universitets Forlaget, 1971) 244-245.

318"Quem e quem na 'parabola do ultimo juizo' (Mt 25:31-46)?" *Perspectiva teologica* 10 (1978) 367-402, esp. pp. 367, 393-394.

319*Das Evangelium nach Matthäus* (München/Gladbach: Volksvereins, 1911) 368-371.

320*Vom Herrn der Herrlichkeit: Tägliche Andachten aus dem Matthäus-Evangelium* (Schwerin: Bahn, 1937) 16-21.

321*Wie Jesus lebte, litt und starb* (Freiburg: Herder, 1953) 201-202.

322*Matthäus* (6 vols.; Salzburg: Müller, 1952-54) 5. 189-197.

323*Das Evangelium nach Matthäus, Markus und Lukas* (Weg ins Neue Testament 1; Würzburg: Echter, 1965) 168-171.

324"Das Weltgericht," *Gleichnisse des Herrn* (Einsiedeln: Johannes, 1966) 112-123, esp. pp. 114, 119-120.

325*Das Neue Testament* (Klosterneuburg: Österreichisches Katholisches Bibelwerk, 1975) 108.

326"Der Mensch Jesus im Spannungsfeld von politischer Theologie und Aufklärung," *Theologia Practica* 8 (1973) 243-257, esp. p. 253 n. 4.

327*Studien zum Gemeindeverständnis des Matthäus-Evangeliums* (Calwer theologische Monographien 10; Stuttgart: Calwer, 1978) 208-211. He argues forcefully against the idea that τῶν ἀδελφῶν μου of v 40 is an interpolation.

[328]"Vom Weltgericht," *Gleichnisse Jesu und christliche Dogmatik* (Göttingen: Vandenhoeck & Ruprecht, 1984) 72-77.

[329]*Vie de notre Seigneur Jésus-Christ* (3 vols.; Paris: Letouzey & Ané, 1922) 316-320.

[330]The universalist stance is characteristic of his *L'Evangile de Jésus-Christ* (4th ed.; Paris: Gabalda, 1929) 490-492. However, in an earlier work (*Evangile selon saint Matthieu* [3d ed.; Ebib; Paris: Gabalda, 1927] 484-489, esp. pp. 488-489) he implies very strongly that "the least" are Christians.

[331]*Les Evangiles* (Manuel d'Etudes Bibliques 4; Paris: Tequi, 1932) 744-745.

[332]*Les Evangiles* (3 vols.; Paris: Spes, 1944) 3. 60-64.

[333]"Matthieu 24-25," *Foi et vie* 76 (1977) 67-80, esp. pp. 71-72.

[334]This is his position in "The Gospel according to Matthew," *Word Pictures in the New Testament* (6 vols.; Nashville: Sunday School Board of the Southern Baptist Convention, 1930) 1.3-246, esp. pp. 200-201. In an earlier work, *The Gospel according to Matthew* (The Bible for Home and School 3; New York: Macmillan, 1911) 250-251, he does not discuss v 32 but is open to the universal interpretation of v 40.

[335]*Jesus in the First Gospel* (London: Hodder & Stoughton, 1925) 259-263. He argues that nations, not individuals, are to be judged.

[336]"The Sheep and the Goats," *The Parables of the Gospels* (London: SCM, 1937) 235-247, esp. p. 240.

[337]*Short Life of Our Lord* (Scripture Textbooks for Catholic Schools 1; London: Burns, Oates & Washbourne, 1945) 149-150.

[338]*A Commentary on the Gospel according to St. Matthew* (Black's New Testament Commentaries 1; London: Black, 1960) 266-268.

[339]"The Gospel according to Matthew," *The New Jerusalem Bible* (Garden City, NY: Doubleday, 1985) 1609-1659, esp. p. 1653. The same basic understanding of the pericope is found in *Mark and Matthew* (Scripture Discussion Commentary 7; Chicago: Acta Foundation, 1971) 230, a book he co-authored with Sean Freyne. In his "St. Matthew," *NCCHS*, 902-953, esp. p. 948, however, he holds that "the least" are Christians.

[340]"Eternal Fire, Eternal Punishment, Eternal Life," *ExpTim* 83 (1971-72) 9-11. He argues that the sheep are the Gentiles, while the goats are the Pharisees.

[341]*A Translator's Guide to the Gospel of Matthew* (Helps for Translators; London/New York: United Bible Societies, 1981) 322-325.

342*The Life of Jesus Christ* (New York: Catholic Book Exchange, 1902) 601-603.

343*The Students' Comprehensive Topical Bible Commentary* (Toledo, OH: Browning, 1909) 118.

344*Commentary on the Gospel according to Saint Matthew* (Chicago: Christian Witness, 1909) 342-346, esp. p. 344.

345As found in A. L. Williams and W. J. Deane, *Matthew* 2. 492-494.

346*Christ's Soul-searching Parables* (New York: Revell, 1925) 178-185, esp. p. 180.

347"The Universal and Final Judgment," *The Key to Revelation* (Grand Rapids: Zondervan, 1935) 105-116, esp. pp. 109, 112.

348*The Life of Christ* (Paterson, NJ: St. Anthony Guild, 1937) 423.

349*Life of Christ* (New York: Doubleday, Doran, 1938) 1090-1093.

350*The Gospel of Matthew* (Anderson, IN: Warner, 1944) 240-242.

351"The Gospel according to St. Matthew," *The Seventh-day Adventist Bible Commentary* (7 vols.; Washington, DC: Review & Herald, 1953-57) 5. 271-560, esp. pp. 511-512.

352*The Life Beyond* (Nashville: Broadman, 1959) 148-152. See also "Matthew 24-25: An Exposition," *RevExp* 59 (1962) 501-511, esp. p. 510.

353*The Parables He Told* (Westwood, NJ: Revell, 1962) 164-167.

354*The Gospel of St. Matthew* (2d ed.; New Testament Reading Guide 2; Collegeville: Liturgical Press, 1963) 105-106.

355"The Gospel according to St. Matthew," *Matthew--Acts* (The Wesleyan Bible Commentary 4; Grand Rapids: Eerdmans, 1964) 5-125, esp. p. 108. See also: "Matthew," *The New International Version Study Bible* (ed. K. Barker; Grand Rapids: Zondervan, 1985) 1439-1489, esp. p. 1483.

356*A Sense of His Presence* (Garden City, NY: Doubleday, 1977) 105. He claims that the goats are the scribes and Pharisees, while the sheep are to be equated with "the least" in v 40.

357"The Sheep and the Goats," *The Parables* (Wheaton, IL: Tyndale, 1978) 120-121.

358*Matthew* (The Communicator's Commentary 1; Waco, TX: Word Books, 1982) 282-284.

359"Unprofitable Servants and Unprofitable Goats," *The Parables of Jesus* (Chicago: Moody, 1983) 199-207, esp. pp. 202-203, 206.

360*The Lord of Parables* (Cincinnati: Standard Publishing, 1984) 82-83.

361"Het Evangelie naar Mattheus," *Commentaar op de Heilige Schrift* (ed. J. vor der Hake; Amsterdam: Paris, 1956) 850-899, esp. pp. 894-895.

362He is not totally consistent. The universal viewpoint is found in two of his works: *Matthew's Witness to Jesus Christ* (New York: Association, 1958) 81, and "Het Evangelie naar Mattheüs," *Beknopt Commentaar op de Bijbel in de Nieuwe Vertaling* (ed. W. Gispen, H. Ridderbos, R. Schippers; Kampen: Kok, 1963) 799-822, esp. p. 819. In his work *The Coming of the Kingdom* (Philadelphia: Presbyterian & Reformed Publishing, 1962) 349, 378, however, he strongly implies that πάντα τὰ ἔθνη are the heathen, while "the least" are Christians.

363*Praelectiones exegeticae de Novo Testamento* (2 vols.; Rome: Lateran University, 1956) 1. 331, 336.

364"Il discorso escatalogico," *Palestra del clero* 37 (1958) 72-77.

365*Vida de nuestro Señor Jesucristo* (Madrid: BAC 32, 1948) 620-621.

366He holds the universalist position in all five of his articles on Matt 25:31-46. See "Mateo 25,31-46 y la teología de la liberación," *CB* 31 (1974) 27-28; "Dios, hombre y Cristo en el mensaje de Jesús. Introducción al tema de la autenticidad jesuánica de Mt 25, 31-46," *Salmanticensis* 26 (1979) 5-50, esp. pp. 45, 50; "La bendición y maldición del hijo del hombre. Transfondo veterotestamentario del 'Benditos-Malditos' de Mt 25, 34. 41," *Salmanticensis* 26 (1979) 277-286, esp. p. 283; "Salvación y condeña del hijo del hombre. Transfondo Veterotestamentario y Judío de Mt 25, 34. 41. 46," *Salmanticensis* 27 (1980) 419-438, esp. p. 422; and "La estructura de Mt y su influencia en 25,31-46," *Salmanticensis* 30 (1983) 11-40, esp. pp. 19, 30-31, 37-40.

367"Sentido del 'judicio final' de Yahve en la apocalíptica y en Mt 25," *Studium Ovetense* 5 (1977) 77-98, esp. pp. 92-93. Cautioning against reading any element of a resurrection into v 32, he argues that all peoples will be judged, but not necessarily people who are not alive at the time of the parousia.

368"Evangelio de San Mateo," *Biblia comentada* (7 vols.; 3d ed.; BAC 239a; Madrid: Editorial católica, 1977) 5. 3-475, esp. pp. 408-410.

369*Vem var Jesus?* (Johanneshov: Solna, Seelig, 1968) 279-283, esp. p. 282.

370*Viver a palavra de Deus* (Petropolis, Brazil: Vozes, 1969) 27-28.

371*La Sacra Bibbia* (10 vols.; Florence: Salani, 1957) 8.115-116.

372"The Parables of the Judgment," *The Parables of Jesus* (Philadelphia: Winston, 1928) 152-168, esp. pp. 162-163. In an earlier work ("The King's Judgment," *The Parables of Jesus* [New York:

YWCA, 1909] 66-68) he does not discuss v 32 and remains open to a universal interpretation of v 40.

[373] "Matthew," *The Abingdon Bible Commentary* (ed. F. Eiselen, E. Lewis, and D. Downey; New York: Abingdon, 1929) 953-995, esp. p. 992.

[374] "The Parable of the Last Judgment," *The Parables of Jesus* (Boston: Christopher Publishing, 1961) 138-141.

[375] *Exploring the Parables* (Boston: United Church, 1963) 63-65.

[376] "The Gospel according to Matthew," *Matthew, Mark, Luke* (Beacon Bible Commentary 6; Kansas City, MO: Beacon Hill, 1964) 19-259, esp. pp. 228-229.

[377] *As Matthew Saw the Master* (Westwood, NJ: Revell, 1964) 127-129.

[378] *Good News from Matthew* (Nashville: Broadman, 1975) 213-215.

[379] *Die Liebe im Neuen Testament* (Leipzig: Deichert, 1905) 124.

[380] "Die dienende Kirche und das Diakonenamt," *Das diakonische Amt der Kirche* (2d ed.; ed. H. Krimm; Stuttgart: Evangelisches Verlagswerk, 1965) 519-554, esp. p. 520. He seems to have changed his mind with regard to the interpretation of v 40, for in an earlier work (*Die Eschatologie des Reiches Gottes bei Jesus* [Gütersloh: Bertelsmann, 1931] 246) he claims "the least" are Christians.

[381] *Das Ethos des Urchristentums* (Gütersloh: Bertelsmann, 1949) 155. The work was originally published by the same firm in 1933 under the title *Geist und Leben*.

[382] *Reich Gottes und Menschensohn* (3d ed.; Munich: Kösel, 1954) 159.

[383] *Kirchliche Dogmatik* (3 vols.; Zollikon: Verlag der evangelischen Buchhandlung, 1938, 1948, 1950) 1. 474; 3. 612.

[384] *Die Botschaft Jesu* (Lund: Gleerup, 1953) 165.

[385] *Die Christologie des Neuen Testaments* (3d ed.; Tübingen: Mohr, 1963) 161-162.

[386] *Die christliche Brüderlichkeit* (Munich: Kösel, 1960) 43. See also his article "Fraternité," in *Dictionnaire de spiritualité, ascétique, et mystique* (ed. M. Viller, F. Cavallera, and J. De Guibert; Paris: Beauchesne, 1932) 5. 1141-1167, esp. p. 1146.

[387] "Der Bruder und der Nächste," *Hören und Handeln* (ed. H. Gollwitzer and H. Traub; Munich: Kaiser, 1962) 362-371, esp. p. 367.

[388] "Die Kirche des Matthäus und die Gemeinde von Qumran," *BZ* 7 (1963) 43-63, esp. p. 52 n. 30. He argues that "the least" are the same people referred to in Matt 5:3-12.

389"Ich war krank und ihr habt mich besucht (Mt 25:36)," *Erbe und Auftrag* 40 (1964) 443-458, esp. p. 448.

390*Was wissen wir von Jesus?* (2d ed.; Stuttgart/Berlin: Kreuz, 1967) 50.

391"Selig sind die Armen . . . ," *BibLeb* 11 (1970) 89-104, esp. p. 103.

392*War Jesus Revolutionär?* (Calwer Hefte zür Forderung biblischen Glaubens und christlichen Lebens 110; Stuttgart: Calwer, 1970) 22.

393"Die erwählten Armen," *BibLeb* 11 (1970) 46-51, esp. pp. 49-50.

394*Jesus in schlechter Gesellschaft* (Stuttgart: Deutsche Verlagsanstalt, 1971) 113.

395"Solidarität mit den Schuldigen," *EvK* 6 (1973) 181.

396"Le pauvre," *Foi et vie* 49 (1951) 105-127, esp. p. 116.

397*L'Identification du Christ avec les pauvres.* (Lausanne: Dissertation, 1957) 104.

398*La Vie de Jésus* (Paris: Denoël, 1959) 216-217.

399*Lexicon Graecum Novi Testamenti* (Paris: Lethielleux, 1961) 23-24.

400"Tu aimera ton prochain comme toi-même," *AsSeign* (1st ser.) 66 (1966) 50-67, esp. pp. 66-67.

401"Notes sur Matthieu 24-25," *Foi et vie* 5 (1967) 26-35, esp. p. 35.

402*Principles and Precepts* (Oxford: Blackwell, 1927) 25.

403"The Church outside the Churches," *Feathers on the Moor* (London: Allenson, 1927) 169-172, esp. p. 170.

404"Creed and Conduct," *The Discipline and Culture of the Spiritual Life* (London: Hodder & Stoughton, 1938) 127-131, esp. p. 130.

405"God as Father in the Synoptic Gospels," *NTS* 3 (1956-57) 31-46, esp. p. 46.

406*The Art and Truth of the Parables* (London: SPCK, 1964) 105-106, 151-152.

407*The Parousia in the New Testament* (NovTSup 13; Leiden: Brill, 1966) 211 n. 3.

408*Matthew, Mark, Luke and Acts* (Mowbrays Mini-Commentaries 1; London: Mowbray, 1968) 34-35. See also *Matthew, Mark, Luke and Acts* (The Dimension Bible Guides 1; Denville, NJ: Dimension Books, 1970) 34-35.

409As found in A. L. Williams and W. J. Deane, *Matthew* 2. 501-502.

410*Nelson's Explanatory Testament* (New York: Nelson, 1912) 68-69.

411*The Gospel Story* (The Bible for School and Home 6; New York: Doran, 1923) 56-59.

412*Windows in Matthew* (Windows in the New Testament; New York: Long & Smith, 1932) 147-148.

413*The Gospel of Matthew* (2 vols.; Harper's Annotated Bible Series 10-11; New York: Harper, 1955) 2.46.

414*Jesus of Nazareth* (New York: Macmillan, 1959) 384.

415*Jesus in the Gospel of Matthew* (New York: Abingdon, 1960) 79, 108, 137.

416Miller, C., O. Miller and M. Roebert, "Stewards of Christ the King," *Announcing the Good News* (Staten Island, NY: Alba House, 1971) 193-196.

417"The Parable of the Last Judgment," *Preaching on the Parables* (The Preacher's Paperback Library; Philadelphia: Fortress, 1972) 124-127.

418"Mercy," *Baker's Dictionary of Christian Ethics* (ed. C. F. Henry; Grand Rapids: Baker, 1973) 418-419.

419*Matthew: His Mind and His Message* (Collegeville, MN: Liturgical Press, 1974) 88-94, esp. p. 93.

420"Feast of Christ the King," *The Word Becomes Flesh* (26 vols.; Apple River, IL: Counseling-Learning Institutes, 1975) 6. 81-84.

421*Power for the Day* (Nashville: Abingdon, 1976) 96.

422"Christ the King," *Five-Minute Homilies on the Gospels* (Hillsboro, KS: M. B. Publishing, 1977) 58.

423"I Was Hungry and You Gave Me to Eat," BTB 11 (1981) 81-84.

424"Christ the King," *Yesterday's Word Today* (Collegeville, MN: Liturgical Press, 1982) 158-160.

425*La Sacra Bibbia* (3d ed.; Florence: Libreria Editrice Fiorentina, 1934) 1338-1339.

426*Il judicio universale e le opere di misericordia (Mt 25,31-46)* (Rome: Gregorian University, 1959) 205.

427"¿Donde estuviste?" *RevistB* 35 (1973) 14-21, esp. p. 15 n. 2.

428"Libertação e justificação (Mt 25:31-46)," *Perspectiva teologica* 11 (1979) 5-15, esp. pp. 13-14.

429*Erklärung des Matthäusevangeliums* (Neues Testament 1; Munich: Ars sacra, 1959) 100-101.

430*Wir haben seine Herrlichkeit gesehen* (Innsbruck: Tyrolia, 1956) 345-347.

431*Zur Frage nach den historischen Jesus* (Gesammelte Aufsätze 2; Tübingen: Mohr, 1960) 313-314.

432"Gefangnisseelsorge," *Sendung und Gnade* (4th ed.; Innsbruck: Tyrolia, 1966) 447-463, esp. pp. 448-449. See also his "Über die Einheit von Nächsten- und Gottesliebe," *Schriften zur Theologie* (16 vols.; Einsiedeln: Benziger, 1954-84) 6. 277-298, esp. p. 280.

433"Das Gericht des Vollenders," *Die Gleichnisse Jesu* (Munich: Kösel, 1965) 145-151.

434*Die Brüder und Schwestern Jesu* (2d ed.; SBS 21; Stuttgart: KBW, 1967) 23.

435"Der Weltenrichter: Matthäus 25, 31-46," *Gleichnisse aus Altem und Neuem Testament* (Schriftauslegung für Predigt, Bibelarbeit, Unterricht 8; Stuttgart: Klotz, 1971) 310-316.

436"Der König der Juden," *Erbe und Auftrag* 55 (1979) 57-60.

437*L'Evangile* (Bruges: Desclée de Brouwer, 1925) 478-481.

438*Jésus de Nazareth, roi des juifs* (Paris: Lethielleux, 1935) 377.

439*The Mystery of Salvation* (Notre Dame: University of Notre Dame, 1966) 217.

440*L'Histoire de Jésus-Christ* (Paris: Grasset, 1965) 328-329.

441"Rassemblement et pèlerinage des dispersés," *AsSeign* (1st ser.) 78 (1965) 37-61, esp. p. 57.

442*L'Evangile raconté aux adultes* (Taizé: Les Presses de Taizé, 1970) 89-90.

443*Matthieu* (Toulouse: Privat, 1977) 151.

444"Le signe du fils de l'homme," *LumVie* 31 (1982) 61-77, esp. pp. 76-77.

445"The Parousia and the Judgment," *The Theology of the New Testament* (International Theological Library; New York: Scribner, 1920) 150-166, esp. pp. 163-165.

446*The Gospel according to Saint Matthew* (Westminster Version of the Sacred Scriptures, NT 1; London: Longmans, Green, 1928) 118-119.

447*The Gospel according to Saint Matthew* (The Clarendon Bible 7; Oxford: Clarendon, 1936) 238.

448*Commentary on the New Testament* (London: Hodder & Stoughton, 1977) 34.

449"The Teaching of Jesus concerning the Care of the Poor," *Jesus Christ and the Social Question* (New York: Macmillan, 1900) 226-266, esp. pp. 241, 266.

⁴⁵⁰*Inductive Studies in the Gospel of Matthew* (Inductive Bible Studies; New York: International Committee of the YMCA, 1900) 27.

⁴⁵¹*The Messages of Jesus according to the Synoptists* (The Messages of the Bible 9; New York: Scribner, 1901) 191-192.

⁴⁵²"The Surprises of the Judgment," *Studies in Christian Character, Work and Experience* (New York: Revell, 1903) 1-9.

⁴⁵³*Matthew's Gospel at the Point of Question* (2 vols.; Cincinnati: Standard Publishing, 1910) 2.142-143.

⁴⁵⁴"St. Matthew," *The Expositor's Dictionary of Texts* (2 vols.; ed. W. R. Nicoll and J. Stoddart; Grand Rapids: Baker, 1978) 1.769-987, esp. p. 954.

⁴⁵⁵*The Social Principles of Jesus* (College Voluntary Study Courses; New York: Association, 1916) 38.

⁴⁵⁶*The Gospel of Matthew* (Philadelphia: Westminster, 1966) 227-230.

⁴⁵⁷*Christ in the Old and the New Testament* (St. Louis: Herder, 1928) 596-597.

⁴⁵⁸"The Ten Virgins, The Talents, The Final Judgment," *Studies of the Parables* (Sell's Bible Study Text Books; New York: Revell, 1930) 75-81, esp. pp. 79-80.

⁴⁵⁹"The Gospel according to St. Matthew," *The Teacher's Commentary* (ed. H. Martin; New York: Harper, 1932) 280-296, esp. p. 295.

⁴⁶⁰*Christ the Leader* (Milwaukee: Bruce, 1937) 343-345.

⁴⁶¹"The Final Separation," *The King's Parables* (Anderson, IN: Gospel Trumpet, 1938) 112-119.

⁴⁶²*The Life of Our Lord* (The Christian Religion Series 1; Milwaukee: Bruce, 1942) 200-201.

⁴⁶³*Bible Study for Grownups* (New York: Macmillan, 1956) 327-328.

⁴⁶⁴*They Saw His Glory* (New York: Sheed & Ward, 1956) 84-85.

⁴⁶⁵*Matthew: Apostle and Evangelist* (Philadelphia: Winston, 1959) 96-97. He argues that Jesus' language in Matt 25:31-46 was colored by his familiarity with the apocryphal *Testament of the Twelve Patriarchs*.

⁴⁶⁶*The New Testament: Its Background, Growth and Content* (Nashville: Abingdon, 1965) 165.

⁴⁶⁷*The Record of Christ's Life and Doctrine* (New York: Exposition, 1968) 120-121.

⁴⁶⁸*Anatomy of the New Testament* (New York: Macmillan, 1969) 126-127.

[469] *The Synoptic Gospels* (New York: Seabury, 1969) 153.

[470] *All the Parables of Jesus* (Nashville: Broadman, 1970) 127.

[471] "A Look at the Goats," *Like it is Today* (Nashville: Broadman, 1970) 111-119; "A Look at the Sheep," ibid., 120-126.

[472] He is not consistent in his interpretation of Matt 25:31-46. He adopts the universalist position in *Matthew: A Gospel for the Church* (Herald Biblical Booklets; Chicago: Franciscan Herald, 1973) 78, in "The Gospel of Matthew and the Ministry of Social Justice," *Spirituality Today* 31 (1979) 14-25, esp. pp. 23-25, and in his latest publication, "The New Testament and the U. S. Economy," *TBT* 24 (1986) 357-362, esp. p. 361. In his *Gospel of Saint Matthew* (Read and Pray 1; Chicago: Franciscan Herald, 1974) 82, "the least" are Jesus' disciples, while πάντα τὰ ἔθνη are the Gentiles. In *Invitation to Matthew* (Doubleday New Testament Commentary Series; Garden City, NY: Doubleday, 1977) 243, he again understands "all the nations" as the Gentiles, while "the least" are seen as the Christian missionaries. In this work he is classified according to his last published position.

[473] *Preaching through Matthew* (Nashville: Abingdon, 1980) 202-205.

[474] *Saint Matthew's Earthquake* (Ann Arbor, MI: Servant Books, 1980) 55.

[475] "The Kingdom of Heaven according to the First Gospel," *NTS* 27 (1980-81) 211-232, esp. p. 216.

[476] "The Church in Matthew," *Interpreting the Gospels* (ed. J. L. Mays; Philadelphia: Fortress, 1981) 97-114, esp. p. 107.

[477] "The Ransom of Captives: Evolution of a Tradition," *HTR* 74 (1981) 365-386, esp. p. 368.

[478] "The Sheep and the Goats," *A Diary of Prayer* (Philadelphia: Westminster, 1981) 45-47.

[479] "The Last Judgment," *Step by Step through the Parables* (New York: Paulist, 1981) 80-84.

[480] *Matthew's Story of Jesus* (Philadelphia: Fortress, 1985) 83-84.

[481] *The Choice to be Human: Jesus Alive in the Gospel of Matthew* (Garden City, NY: Doubleday, 1985) 232-234.

[482] "Divine Judgment," *Chicago Studies* 24 (1985) 131-144, esp. p. 137.

[483] *De Gelijkenissen* (Leiden: Sijthoff, 1946) 178-179.

[484] *Storia di Cristo* (14th ed.; Florence: Vallechi, 1950) 382-384.

[485] *Il messagio degli evangeli* (Acqua viva 2; Milan: Massimo, 1956) 350-351.

486 *Meditations on the Gospels* (3 vols.; Westminster, MD: Newman, 1951) 3. 40-42.

487 *Jesus Manifest* (New York: Scribner, 1936) 372-373. This work is a translation of *Iisus Neizvjestnij* (Leningrad: Piroshkova, 1933).

488 Details of this viewpoint have already been discussed on p. 258.

489 *Die drei älteren Evangelien* (Die Heilige Schrift des Neuen Testaments 1; Bonn: P. Hanstein, 1923) 308-311.

490 *Biblisch-Theologisches Wörterbuch des neutestamentlichen Griechisch* (11th ed.; Stuttgart/Gotha: Perthes, 1923) 77, 384.

491 *Das Matthäusevangelium* (2d ed.; HNT 4; Tübingen: Mohr, 1927) 204-207.

492 *Das Evangelium des heiligen Matthäus und des heiligen Markus* (Herders Bibelkommentar 11; ed. E. Kalt and W. Lauck; Freiburg: Herder, 1936) 88-90.

493 *Der Weg der Gerechtigkeit* (FRLANT 82; Göttingen: Vandenhoeck & Ruprecht, 1962) 117-118, 145 n. 6, 149 n. 2, 191 n. 5, 218, 232, 236 n. 6, 240.

494 "Gericht nach den Wirken?" *Ungereimtes bei Matthäus* (Düsseldorf: Evangelische Kirche im Rheinland, 1968) 50-52.

495 "Mit wem identifiziert sich Jesus? Eine exegetische Rekonstruktion ad Matt 25:31-46," *Christ and Spirit in the New Testament. Essays in honour of C. F. D. Moule* (ed. B. Lindars and S. Smalley; London: Cambridge University, 1973) 15-25, esp. pp. 17-18, 22.

496 (Freiburg: Herder, 1938) 694-695.

497 L. C. Fillion (ed.), *La Sainte Bible* (3d ed.; 8 vols.; Paris: Letouzey & Ané, 1903) 7.166-167.

498 *Evangile selon Saint Matthieu* (La pensée chrétienne 1; Paris: Bloud, 1908) 196-198.

499 *Jesus Christ, His Life, Teaching and Work* (2 vols.; Milwaukee: Bruce, 1950) 2. 246-249.

500 *La Sainte Bible* (12 vols.; ed. L. Pirot and A. Clamer; Paris: Letouzey & Ané, 1946) 9. 337-339. See also his *Jésus comme il était* (Paris: Editions de l'Ecole, 1964) 306-307.

501 *Evangile selon saint Matthieu* (VS 1; Paris: Beauchesne, 1948) 461-464.

502 *Vie de notre seigneur Jésus-Christ* (Paris: Letouzey & Ané, 1958) 221-223.

[503] This is his position in the article which he co-authored with Armand Négrier: "Frère," *Vocabulaire de théologie biblique* (2d ed.; Paris: Cerf, 1970) 491-495, esp. p. 494. In an earlier work (*The Gospels and the Jesus of History* [New York: Desclée de Brouwer, 1968] 249) he holds for the universal interpretation of both v 32 and v 40.

[504] "Les brebis et les boucs," *Les paraboles de Jésus aujourd'hui* (Geneva: Labor et Fides, 1973) 83-90, esp. p. 84. He insists that it will be a judgment of nations, not individuals. With regard to v 40 he states that even though Matthew was thinking of the Christians of his era, it would be possible to extend the meaning of the verse today to all needy.

[505] "The Parable of the Sheep and the Goats," *ExpTim* 41 (1929-30) 559-562. See also *The Parables of Jesus* (London: Clarke, 1930) 237-241. Cadoux argues that τῶν ἀδελφῶν μου is a Matthean interpolation and that the original parable that he found in Q (which Luke omitted) had God as the judge and was universal in outlook. Matthew, he claims, limited "the least" to Christians.

[506] *New Testament Studies* (Manchester: Manchester University, 1953) 56-57, 62. See also his *The Parables of the Kingdom* (London: Nisbet, 1935) 85, 93 n. 1.

[507] "The Gospel according to Matthew," *The New Bible Commentary* (ed. F. Davidson et al; London: Inter-Varsity Fellowship, 1953) 771-805, esp. pp. 801-802.

[508] *The Gospel according to Matthew* (The Cambridge Bible Commentary, New English Bible; Cambridge: University Press, 1963) 193.

[509] *The New English Bible Companion to the New Testament* (Oxford: University Press, 1970) 99-100.

[510] "The Poor on Earth and the Son of Man in Heaven: A Re-appraisal of Matthew 25:31-46," *BJRL* 61 (1978-79) 355-397, esp. pp. 389, 393. He argues that τῶν ἀδελφῶν μου is a Matthean addition, restricting to Christians what was meant to be universal in the original parable of Jesus.

[511] *Spiritual Studies in St. Matthew's Gospel* (2 vols.; New York: Longmans, Green, 1902) 2. 289-305, esp. pp. 289, 295-296. "The least" are the saints who have previously died and now return with Christ in judgment.

[512] *The Fourfold Gospel* (2 vols.; Standard Bible Commentary 1-2; Cincinnati: The Standard Publishing, 1905-06) 2. 638-640.

[513] *The Gospel by Matthew* (Devotional Hours with the Bible 3; New York/London: Hodder & Stoughton, 1909) 267-273, esp. pp. 267, 270, 272.

[514] As found in A. L. Williams and W. J. Deane, *Matthew* 2. 506-507.

[515] *The Gospel of Matthew* (MNTC 1; New York: Harper, 1927) 208-209.

[516] *Interpretation of St. Matthew's Gospel* (Columbus, OH: Lutheran Book Concern, 1932) 964-980, esp. pp. 966, 973. He argues that "the least" are among those who are situated on the right side of the judge.

[517] *A Commentary on the Gospel according to Matthew* (Nashville: Gospel Advocate, 1936) 486-492, esp. pp. 487, 489-490.

[518] *The Concordia New Testament with Notes* (St. Louis: Concordia, 1942) 86-87.

[519] "The Sheep and the Goats," *Short Stories by Jesus* (St. Louis: Concordia, 1943) 215-219.

[520] "The Throne of Judgment," *My Sermon Notes on Parables and Metaphors* (Grand Rapids: Baker, 1947) 39-42.

[521] "Matthew," *Bible Commentary* (6 vols.; St. Louis: Mission Messenger, 1952) 5.1-111, esp. pp. 92-93.

[522] *Jesus and the First Three Gospels* (Cambridge, MA: Harvard University, 1955) 475-476.

[523] *New Testament Theology* (Nashville: Broadman, 1962) 193, 199, 332-333.

[524] *Davis' Notes on Matthew* (Nashville: Broadman, 1962) 95.

[525] "The Gospel according to Matthew," *Westminster Study Bible* (New York/Glasgow: Collins, 1965) 23-65, esp. p. 59.

[526] "Solemnity of Christ the King," *The Sunday Readings* (3 vols.; Paterson, NJ: St. Anthony Guild, 1970-72) 1. 389-395, esp. pp. 394-395.

[527] "The Final Judgment," *The Mysteries of the Kingdom* (Grand Rapids: Reformed Free Publishing, 1975) 295-306, esp. pp. 297-298, 302. He argues that individuals and nations will be judged.

[528] This is his general position in *Matthew as Story* (Philadelphia: Fortress, 1986) 14 n. 33, 98, 129 n. 20, and in *Matthew* (Proclamation Commentaries; Philadelphia: Fortress, 1977) 95, 101; although he can at times be seemingly contradictory. In *Matthew as Story*, 11, and in *Matthew*, 76, he leaves the reader with the impression that πάντα τὰ ἔθνη are all non-Jews. This is his position in *Matthew: Structure, Christology, Kingdom* (Philadelphia: Fortress, 1975) 119, 156. In *Jesus*

Christ in Matthew, Mark and Luke (Proclamation Commentaries; Philadelphia: Fortress, 1981) 73, he implies that πάντα τὰ ἔθνη is universal, and he describes "the least" as "the righteous." If this reflects a widening of his position with regard to "the least," it was short lived, for in his latest publication, *Matthew as Story*, 14 n. 33, 129 n. 20, he has a restrictive understanding of v 40.

[529] *A Commentary on the Gospel of Matthew* (New York: Paulist, 1978) 256-259.

[530] "Last Judgment," *The Parables of Jesus* (Grand Rapids: Baker, 1980) 146-157, esp. pp. 148, 151, 154.

[531] *Matthew* (Grand Rapids: Eerdmans, 1982) 511-516, esp. pp. 511, 514. He argues that "the least" are among those on the right of the judge.

[532] "Matthew," *The Expositor's Bible Commentary* (12 vols.; ed. F. E. Gaebelein and J. D. Douglas; Grand Rapids: Zondervan, 1984) 8. 3-599, esp. pp. 518-523.

[533] *Matthew* (Good News Commentary 1; San Francisco: Harper & Row, 1985) 242-244, esp. p. 244.

[534] "The 'Parable' of the Sheep and the Goats: A Challenge to Christian Ethics," *TS* 47 (1986) 3-31, esp. pp. 15-16, 25.

[535] *Matteo* (Assisi: Cittadella editrice, 1971) 566-574, esp. p. 569. See also his "L'Impostazione del problema escatologico in S. Matteo," *BeO* 8 (1966) 185-211, esp. p. 209.

[536] *Commentarius in Evangelium secundum Matthaeum* (3d ed.; Mechelen-lez-Deinze, Belgium: Dessain, 1928) 368-375, esp. pp. 369, 372.

[537] *Jesus und die Heidenmission* (NTAbh 1/1-2; Münster: Aschendorff, 1925) 157.

[538] *Das Neue Testament* (2 vols.; Giessen: Töpelmann, 1926) 1. 203. He states that the Jewish expectation that the Messiah would share in the sufferings of Israel led to Jesus' statement in v 40. The implication is that those who suffer are members of the Church, the new Israel.

[539] *Die Mystik des Apostels Paulus* (Tübingen: Mohr, 1930) 109.

[540] "ἀδελφός," *TDNT* 1. 144-146, esp. p. 145.

[541] "Das Gericht nach den Wirken im Matthäusevangelium," *Theologische Aufsätze. Festschrift für Karl Barth zum 50. Geburtstag* (ed. E. Wolf; Munich: Kaiser, 1936) 124-135, esp. pp. 125, 131.

[542] *Das Evangelium nach Matthäus* (2 vols.; Prophezei 1/1-2; Zürich: Zwingli, 1948) 2.111-112. See also his *Die Gleichnisse Jesu* (3d ed.; Hamburg: Furche, 1955) 170.

[543] "Das Evangelium vom barmherzigen Gott in Qumran und der Botschaft Jesu," *Deutsches Pfarrerblatt* 60 (1960) 73-150, esp. p. 126. He argues that in the original parable of Jesus the meaning of "the least of my brothers" was universal, but Matthew restricted it to Christians.

[544] *Der Sohn des lebendigen Gottes* (AnBib 16; Rome: Biblical Institute, 1962) 165-166.

[545] "Christus als der Weltenrichter," *Jesus Christus in Historie und Theologie. Neutestamentliche Festschrift für Hans Conzelmann zum 60. Geburtstag* (ed. G. Strecker; Tübingen: Mohr, 1975) 475-486, esp. p. 482.

[546] "ἀδελφός," *EWNT* 1. 67-71, esp. p. 70. In the original parable of Jesus, he argues, the meaning of v 40 was universal; Matthew restricted it.

[547] *Le Corps mystique du Christ* (2 vols.; Louvain: Museum Lessianum, 1933) 1. 60-61.

[548] *Le saint évangile de Jésus-Christ selon saint Matthieu* (Paris: Desclée de Brouwer, 1939) 118-119.

[549] *Communauté et directives éthiques: La catéchèse de Matthieu* (Récherches et synthèses, Section d'exégèse 1; Gembloux: Duculot, 1974) 28, 77, 88 n. 5.

[550] "The Conception of Reward," *Aux sources de la tradition chrétienne: mélanges offerts à Maurice Goguel à l'occasion de son 70. anniversaire.* (Paris: Delachaux & Niestlé, 1950) 195-206, esp. pp. 202-203.

[551] *Midrash and Lection in Matthew* (London: SPCK, 1974) 442-444. The ἐλάχιστοι, he argues, are a synonym for the μικροί of Matt 10:42 and 18:6, and are seated in judgment with Christ.

[552] *Matthew* (New York: Revell, 1900) 116-117.

[553] "The Gospel according to Saint Matthew," *The Self-Interpreting Bible* (4 vols.; St. Louis: Thompson, 1905) 4. 47-110, esp. p. 101.

[554] "Matthew," *The Bible in Questions and Answers* (Cincinnati: Rowe, 1916) 22.

[555] *The Four Gospels* (New York: Wagner, 1917) 163-164.

[556] "The Conflict between the Disciples, the Jews, and the Gentiles in St. Matthew's Gospel," *JTS* 36 (1935) 33-44, esp. p. 38 n. 3.

557 *The Layman's New Testament* (New York: Sheed & Ward, 1941) 94. His marginal notation, "The Mystical Body," alongside vv 37-40 certainly portrays a narrow interpretation.

558 *The Witness of Matthew and Mark to Christ* (Grand Rapids: Eerdmans, 1944) 175-176.

559 *The Modern Reader's Guide to Matthew and Luke* (New York: Association, 1959) 100.

560 "Matthew," *PCB*, 769-798, esp. p. 794. See also his *The School of Saint Matthew and its Use of the Old Testament*. (ASNU 20; Lund: Gleerup, 1968) 26 n. 5, where he states that because of v 40 Matt 25:31-46 should be regarded as a farewell address.

561 "The Gospel according to Saint Matthew," *Harper's Bible Commentary* (New York: Harper & Row, 1962) 333-348, esp. pp. 346-347. He argues that, even though Matthew had a narrow understanding of v 40, today's needs dictate a universal reading of the text.

562 *Jesus and the Son of Man* (Philadelphia: Fortress, 1964) 65, 114-117, esp. p. 116 n. 3. He agrees with those who see ἀδελφός as having had an originally universal meaning, but Christianized by Matthew.

563 "The Gospel according to Matthew," *A New Testament Commentary* (ed. G. C. Howley; Grand Rapids: Zondervan, 1969) 141-176, esp. p. 169. He understands Matt 12:49-50 as the key to the proper interpretation of 25:40.

564 "The Gospel according to Matthew," *The New Testament* (2 vols.; Boston: Daughters of St. Paul, 1975) 1.7-92, esp. p. 83.

565 *The Parables in the Gospels* (New York: Crossroad, 1985) 106-107.

566 "Vangelo di Gesù Cristo secondo San Matteo," *La Sacra Bibbia* (12 vols.; Turin: Berruti & Marietti, 1911) 11. 5-134, esp. pp. 113-114.

567 As indicated by his student Terje Raddum in his work *Mattheus Evangeliet* (Oslo: Universitets Forlaget, 1971) 245.

568 *Das Neue Testament* (Giessen/Basel: Brunnen, 1953) 93. At v 40 he has a cross reference to Matt 10:42.

569 *A Commentary on the Gospels* (New York: Sheed & Ward, 1952) 60.

570 J. R. Jones (ed.), *The New Testament of our Lord and Saviour Jesus Christ: A Comprehensive Commentary* (Philadelphia: n. pub., 1907) 29. Commenting on v 40, he states, "Everyone of us shall be judged ... by our treatment of Christ and His cause."

571 *Vida de nuestro señor Jesucristo* (Barcelona: Editorial Borgiana, 1956) 1148. He understands v 40 as the seed of Paul's later teaching on

the Mystical Body. In his earlier work, *El evangelio de san Mateo* (Biblioteca teologica de Balmesiana 3; Barcelona: Editorial Balmes, 1946) 432-433, he gives no clue as to his understanding of "the least."

[572]"Evangelie ot Mateia," *Bibliia* (Sofia: Izdava sv. Sinod na bulgarskata tsurkva, 1982) 1195-1232, esp. p. 1227. The only comment on v 40 is a cross-reference to Matt 10:42.

[573]"Ot Matfeia," *Bibli**ia* (Moscow: Evangelskich Christian-Baptistov, 1957) 1-37, esp. p. 31. The only comment on v 40 is a cross-reference to Matt 10:42.

[574]*Evangelie: Novyi Zavet i psaltir* (Washington, DC: The Russian Bible Society, 1958) 51. The only comment on v 40 is a cross-reference to Matt 10:42.

[575]"Diese Kleinen--eine Jüngerbezeichnung Jesu," *TSK* 108 (1937-38) 401-415, esp. p. 404. In "Freudenbotschaft und Völkerwelt," *Divus Thomas* 6 (1939) 45-68, esp. p. 63, he gives a universal interpretation of v 32, but does not discuss v 40. In "μικρός," *TDNT* 4. 648-659, esp. pp. 656-657, commenting on v 40, he gives both the universal and restrictive interpretations of "the least" but does not take a position.

[576]*Der König Israels* (Die urchristliche Botschaft 1; Berlin: Furche, 1937) 192-194.

[577]*Der verheissene König und sein Reich* (Zürich: Beröa, 1964) 304-310, esp. pp. 304, 307.

[578]"Le jugement dernier," *AsSeign* (2d ser.) 65 (1973) 17-28, esp. pp. 20-23, 25. He argues that in the original parable of Jesus the meaning was universal; Matthew changed it to mean the apostles and other followers of Jesus indicated in 19:28.

[579]"The Gospel according to Matthew," *The Four Gospels* (Interpretation of the Entire New Testament 1; Chicago: Orthodox Christian Educational Society, 1949) 23-472, esp. pp. 398-408. He understands "the least" as the apostles and other Christian preachers who co-judge with Christ according to Matt 19:28.

[580]In "Matthew 25:31-46 Relocated," *Restoration Quarterly* 17 (1974) 107-114, esp. pp. 109-110, he argues that πάντα τὰ ἔθνη is a Matthean interpolation in place of the original "house of Israel" and that the original parable was concerned with the treatment of Christian missionaries at the hands of the Jews, and was addressed to the Twelve at the conclusion of his charge to them, that is, "immediately after 10:42 and before 11:1." In an earlier article, ("What the World Owes the Church," *HPR* 71 [1971] 8-17, esp. pp. 11-13) he understands πάντα τὰ ἔθνη as inclusive of everyone, with the possible exception of

the Jews, and sees "the least" as not only the missionaries, but Christians in general.

[581] "The Parable of the Sheep and Goats," *Reformed Review* 26 (1973) 151-161, esp. 155-156.

[582] *Biblical Meditations for Ordinary Time* (3 vols.; New York: Paulist, 1984) 3.393-396, esp. p. 394.

[583] "The Sheep and the Goats," *Rebuke and Challenge* (Washington, DC: Review & Herald, 1985) 86-93, esp. pp. 89-90.

[584] Argumentation for this position was already given on p. 260 and so will not be repeated here.

[585] *The Originality of St. Matthew* (Cambridge: University Press, 1951) 97-98. See also his "M. Vaganay and the 'Community Discourse'," *NTS* 1 (1954-55) 283-290, esp. p. 287.

[586] *Die Adressaten der Heilsbotschaft Jesu. Die Worte über die Armen, Verlorenen, Unmündigen, Mühseligen-Beladenen und Kleinen-Kleinsten in der synoptischen Überlieferung* (Würzburg: Dissertation, 1970) 168, 178. He argues that in the original parable of Jesus "the least" were "the Twelve," while Matthew broadened the concept to include all Christian missionaries.

[587] *The Imitation of God in Christ* (The Library of History and Doctrine; Philadelphia: Westminster, 1960) 143 n. 6, 152. He sees a close connection between Matt 25:35-36, 42-43 and 2 Cor 11:23-28, the classic description of the sufferings of an apostle.

[588] "Anfänge einer jüdenchristlichen Theologie bei Matthäus," *Judaica* 16 (1960) 193-206, esp. p. 197.

[589] *Follow Me: Discipleship according to Saint Matthew* (St. Louis: Concordia, 1961) 183.

[590] *Das Evangelium nach Matthäus* (NTD; Göttingen: Vandenhoeck & Ruprecht, 1971) 250-254.

[591] "The 'Parable' of the Sheep and the Goats," *NTS* 2 (1955-56) 225-237, esp. p. 234-235. He sees a twofold development of an original parable about a shepherd: a pre-Matthean tradition could have used the parable as the basis for an allegory about the last judgment in which God is the judge, while Matthew further modified the parable to make Christ the judge. He sees τῶν ἀδελφῶν μου as an interpolation, but not necessarily an indication that Jesus would not have used ἀδελφός in a general sense. He does not seem to be able to come to a definitive conclusion regarding the identity of "the least," but at times borders close to the position that in the pre-Matthean account it was understood universally, while in the Matthean version it has a re-

strictive meaning. In his later work, *Jesus and His Coming* (Philadelphia: Westminster, 1957) 37, he gives no further elucidation as to his views on the interpretation of vv 32 and 40, but seems to understand Matt 25:31-46 as dealing originally with the judgment on every person brought about by "the crisis of the ministry of Jesus."

[592] *Der Katechismus der Urchristenheit* (Leipzig: Deichert, 1903) 84 n. 1.

[593] *Die Gleichnisreden Jesu* (Tübingen: Mohr, 1910) 429.

[594] "ἔθνος in the NT," *TDNT* 2. 369-372, esp. p. 369.

[595] *Heimat und Leben unsers Herrn Jesus Christus* (Münster: Aschendorff, 1947) 174.

[596] *Der Mann Jesus* (4th ed.; Vienna: Herder, 1948) 208.

[597] *Berufung und Erwählung bei den Synoptikern* (Stuttgart: KBW, 1954) 154.

[598] *Das Evangelium des Matthäus* (MeyerK Sonderband; 3d ed.; Göttingen: Vandenhoeck & Ruprecht, 1962) 418 n. 1.

[599] *Das Matthäusevangelium* (Acta theologica danica 1; Aarhus: Universitetsforlaget, 1958), esp. pp. 21 n. 57, 29 n. 101, 198.

[600] *Ostergeschehen und Osterberichte* (2d ed.; Göttingen: Vandenhoeck & Ruprecht, 1962) 31.

[601] "Das christologische und ekklesiologische Anliegen von Mt 28, 18-20," SE II. (TU 87. Berlin: Akademie, 1964) 266-294, esp. pp. 290-291.

[602] *Gerechtigkeit Gottes bei Paulus* (FRLANT 87; 2d ed.; Göttingen: Vandenhoeck & Ruprecht, 1966) 191.

[603] *Grundriss der Theologie des Neuen Testaments* (Munich: Kaiser, 1967) 167.

[604] *Der Segen im Neuen Testament* (Theologische Arbeiten 25; Berlin: Evangelische Verlagsanstalt, 1967) 165 n. 248.

[605] *Die Überlieferungsgeschichte der Bergpredigt* (WUNT 9; Tübingen: Mohr, 1968) 176 n. 1.

[606] "Heilszukunft und Zukunft des Heils," *Gestalt und Anspruch des Neuen Testamentes* (ed. J. Schreiner and G. Dautzenberg; Würzburg: Echter, 1969) 313-329, esp. p. 323. See also his "Eschatologie und Ethik," *BibLeb* 11 (1970) 223-238, esp. p. 235.

[607] *Das Auseinandersetzung zwischen Kirche und Judentum im Matthäusevangelium* (BEvT 33; Munich: Kaiser, 1966) 114, 140.

[608] *La vie humaine et divine de Jésus-Christ notre seigneur* (Paris: Bloud & Gay, 1933) 359.

[609]"Jugement dans le Nouveau Testament," *DBSup* 4. 1344-1394, esp. p. 1351.

[610]*L'Evangile du royaume: Commentaire sur l'évangile selon saint Matthieu* (2d ed.; Commentaires bibliques 2; Geneva: Labor et fides, 1956) 263.

[611]*Vita di Gesù Cristo* (Milan: Rizzoli, 1941) 554-555.

[612]*Il Messia del popolo* (Milan: Società Editrice "Vita e Pensiero," 1949) 340-342, esp. p. 341.

[613]"Allora il re dirà . . . ," *Palestra del clero* 47 (1968) 1318-1321, esp. p. 1318.

[614]*Matae pogum pyon* (Seoul: Korean Presbyterian Church, 1955) 272-273.

[615]*Word Studies in the New Testament* (4 vols.; New York: Scribner, 1905) 1. 135.

[616]*Matthew and the Synoptics* (The Bible of the Expositor and the Evangelist, NT 3; Cleveland: Union Gospel, 1926) 257-259.

[617]*Studies in Matthew* (New York: Holt, 1930) 75.

[618]*Manufacture of Christianity* (Philadelphia: Dorrance, 1946) 128. Although the judgment will be universal, he insists that it will occur on an individual basis. Therefore, there is no need, he claims, to take seriously the aspect of a universal gathering of all who have ever lived.

[619]"From the Genesis to the End of the World. The Plan of Matthew's Gospel," *BTB* 2 (1972) 155-176, esp. pp. 169-170.

[620]*The Matthean Redaction of a Primitive Apostolic Commissioning: An Exegesis of Matthew 28:16-20* (SBLDS 19; Missoula, MT: SBL & Scholar's Press, 1974) 84.

[621]"Christ the King," *Homilies on the Sunday Gospels* (Huntington, IN: Our Sunday Visitor, 1976) 112-114.

[622]*The Growth of the Gospels* (New York: Paulist, 1979) 58.

[623]*The New Testament: An Introduction* (New York: Harcourt Brace Jovanovich, 1974) 188. In an earlier work, *Rediscovering the Teaching of Jesus* (New York: Harper & Row, 1967) 113, he leaves the reader with the impression that the judgment has to do with Christians only.

[624]*The Gospel of Matthew for Growing Christians* (Old Tappan, NJ: Revell, 1973) 146. He insists that the judgment will take place on nations only, not individuals.

625Details of these two closely connected viewpoints have already been discussed on pp. 260-261.

626"Die geringsten Brüder: Aus dem Gespräch der Kirche mit Mt 25, 31-46," *Jahrbuch der theologisches Schule Bethel* 8 (1937) 1-28, esp. p. 25. See also his "Der Dienst Jesu," *Das diakonische Amt der Kirche* (2d ed.; ed. H. Krimm; Stuttgart: Evangelisches Verlagswerk, 1965) 15-60, esp. p. 39.

627"Die Mission im Matthäus-Evangelium," *TLZ* 92 (1967) 889-893, esp. p. 892.

628"Les chrétiens dans le cadre du jugement sur les oeuvres," *Les justes et la justice dans l'évangiles et le christianisme primitif* (Universitas catholica lovaniensis. Dissertationes ad gradum magistri in facultate theologica vel in facultate iuris canonici consequendum conscriptae 2/43; Louvain: Publications universitaires de Louvain, 1950) 250-269, esp. pp. 255-258.

629*An Exegetical Commentary on the Gospel according to St. Matthew* (London: Stock, 1909) 348-352, esp. pp. 350-351.

630"The Parable of the Sheep and the Goats," *The Gospel Parables in the Light of their Jewish Background* (London: SPCK, 1936) 150-156, esp. pp. 153, 156.

631*The Gospel according to St. Matthew* (Epworth Preacher's Commentaries, NT 1; London: Epworth, 1961) 144-145.

632*El evangelio según san Mateo* (2 vols.; Comentario al Nuevo Testamento 3; Colectanea san Paciano 22; Madrid: Marova, 1976) 2. 571-585, esp. pp. 572, 579.

633*A Devotional Commentary on the Gospel of St. Matthew* (New York: Revell, 1907) 225-228.

634"St. Matthew," *A Commentary on the Holy Bible* (New York: Macmillan, 1908) 617-721, esp. p. 707.

635*The Gospel Story* (New York: Sheed & Ward, 1944) 339-341.

636*Saint Matthew* (Saint Andrew Bible Commentary 28; Conception, MO: Conception Abbey, 1960) 99-100.

637*The Love Command in the New Testament* (Nashville: Abingdon, 1972) 82-83.

638"Apostolic Hardships and Righteous Gentiles," *JBL* 84 (1965) 27-37, esp. p. 28. In a later work which he co-authored with G. W. Barker and W. L. Lane (*The New Testament Speaks* [New York: Harper & Row, 1969] 271-272, 334 n. 11) πάντα τὰ ἔθνη are seen as all non-Christians and non-Jews, while it is implied that "the least" are Christian missionaries.

[639]"Gottes geringste Brüder--zu Mt 25:31-46," *Jesus und Paulus. Festschrift für W. G. Kümmel zum 70. Geburtstag* (ed. E. Ellis and E. Grasser; Göttingen: Vandenhoeck & Ruprecht, 1975) 363-383, esp. p. 382.

[640]*Die Hauptparabeln Jesu* (Giessen: Ricker, 1903) 381.

[641]*Die alten Perikopen für die theologische Praxis erläutert* (HNT 22; Tübingen: Mohr, 1931) 214 n. 1.

[642]*Segen und Fluch im Urchristentum* (Oslo: Dybwad, 1932) 19.

[643]*Jesus und die Heidenmission* (Giessen: Töpelmann, 1909) 10-12.

[644]"Kreuz und heilendes Handeln," *Ärztlicher Dienst weltweit* (ed. W. Erk and M. Scheel; Stuttgart: Steinkopf, 1974) 200-208, esp. p. 203.

[645]As found in A. L. Williams and W. J. Deane, *Matthew* 2. 512-513.

[646]"Matthew," *A Commentary on the Bible* (ed. A. S. Peake; New York: Nelson, 1920) 700-723, esp. p. 721.

[647]*Understanding the Parables of Our Lord* (Nashville: Cokesbury, 1940) 220-223.

[648]*The Imminent Appearing of Christ* (Grand Rapids: Eerdmans, 1962) 137-139.

[649]*Theology out of the Ghetto: A New Testament Exegetical Study concerning Religious Exclusiveness* (Leiden: Brill, 1971) 69.

[650]*The Gospel according to St. Matthew* (Catholic Scripture Manuals; London: Burns, Oates, & Washbourne, 1906) 188-189. She adopts the four categories of Gregory the Great regarding those present at the judgment. See p. 121 of this study.

[651]*The Gospel according to Saint Matthew* (The Cambridge Bible for Schools and Colleges 82; Cambridge: University Press, 1933) 149-150.

[652]*The Gospel of Matthew* (London: Macmillan, 1971) 135-136.

[653]"The Mixed State of the Church in Matthew's Gospel," *JBL* 82 (1963) 149-168, esp. pp. 158-160, 168. He sees the universal thrust of the Matthean passage as a deliberate attack on the exclusivist tendencies of the Essene community.

[654]*Doctrinal New Testament Commentary* (Salt Lake City, UT: Bookcraft, 1965) 691-692. In his opinion, those being judged in this pericope are members of the Church of Jesus Christ of Latter-day Saints.

655*Plain Talk on Matthew* (Grand Rapids: Zondervan, 1966) 211.

656"The Gospel according to Matthew," *JBC* 2. 62-114, esp. p. 107.

657"Interpreting the Gospel of Matthew," *Int* 29 (1975) 3-12, esp. p. 10.

658*Frühgeschichte des Evangeliums* (2 vols.; Tübingen: Mohr, 1941) 2. 322.

659"La charité fraternelle et le retour du Christ," *Recueil Lucien Cerfaux* (3 vols.; Gembloux: Duculot, 1954-62) 2. 27-40, esp. pp. 32-34.

660"Frères et soeurs du Christ (Matt 25:31-46)," *Revue Reformée* 16 (1965) 12-26, esp. pp. 13-14.

661*The Synoptic Gospels* (2d ed.; 2 vols.; Library of Biblical Studies; New York: Ktav, 1968) 2. 322-327, esp. p. 324. He does not consider the parable to be authentically from Jesus, but sees it as a product of the Christian church. In *Some Elements of the Religious Teaching of Jesus according to the Synoptic Gospels* (The Jewish People: History, Religion, Literature; New York: Arno, 1973) 156, he does not discuss v 32 at all but understands "the least" in a universal way. In his last work on the subject, *Rabbinic Literature and Gospel Teachings* (The Library of Biblical Studies; New York: Ktav, 1970) 332-340, esp. pp. 338-339, he again does not address the issue of πάντα τὰ ἔθνη but returns to his original position that "the least" are Christians.

662*A Commentary on the New Testament* (Washington, DC: CBA, 1942) 170-172.

663In his *The Kingdom and the Power* (Philadelphia: Westminster, 1950) 146, and *Images of the Church in the New Testament* (Philadelphia: Westminster, 1960) 147, 171, he implies that πάντα τὰ ἔθνη are Christians and that "the least" are likewise Christians. In another work, ("The Coming of the Son of Man," *TToday* 9 [1953] 489-493, esp. pp. 491-492) which was reprinted a year later in *Christian Hope and the Second Coming* (Philadelphia: Westminster, 1954) 101-105, he again implies that those to be judged are Christians, but in his treatment of "the least" he is open to a universal interpretation.

664*Jesus in His Own Words* (Westminster, MD: Newman, 1951) 245-246.

665*The Four Gospels* (The Clarified New Testament; New York: McGraw-Hill, 1962) 179.

666"Disciples and Discipleship in Matthew and Luke," *BTB* 3 (1973) 235-255, esp. pp. 249-251.

[667]"The Judgment of the Gentiles in Matthew's Theology," *Scripture, Tradition, and Interpretation* (ed. W. Gasque and W. LaSor; Grand Rapids: Eerdmans, 1978) 199-215, esp. pp. 208-213. He narrows the concept of those to be judged even further, stating that they are the Gentile Christians.

[668]*Christology beyond Dogma: Matthew's Christ in Process Hermeneutic* (SBL Semeia Supplements 7; Philadelphia: Fortress, 1978) 117-118, 122-123.

[669]*Das Evangelium Matthaei übersetzt und erklärt* (Berlin: Reimer, 1904) 133-135.

[670]"St. Matthew 25:31-46 as a Hebrew Poem," *JTS* 14 (1912-13) 414-424, esp. p. 415. In his attempt to render the pericope into what he thinks was its original Hebrew form, he translates πάντα τὰ ἔθνη by use of the Hebrew עם, used frequently in the MT for God's covenanted people, rather than the term גוי which is used primarily to denote those apart from Israel (see G. Bertram, "ἔθνος, ἐθνικός," *TDNT* 2. 364-369, esp. p. 365).

[671]*Righteousness in Matthew and his World of Thought* (SNTSMS 41; Cambridge: University Press, 1980) 103.

[672]*The Words of Jesus in our Gospels* (New York: Paulist, 1979) 104.

[673]*The Silence of Jesus* (Philadelphia: Fortress, 1983) 67.

[674]*The Lectures of St. Matthew* (Milwaukee: Morehouse, 1932) 508-515, esp. pp. 509, 512-513.

[675]"Who are the 'Sheep' and the 'Goats'?" *AusBR* 13 (1965) 19-28, esp. pp. 21, 25, 28. He argues that the masculine term αὐτούς in v 32 specifically refers to the leaders of the Christian community.

[676]The details of this particular viewpoint have already been discussed on p. 262.

[677]*Anspruch und Antwort Gottes* (Düsseldorf: Patmos, 1962) 210-211.

[678]*The Gospel according to St. Matthew* (Ellicott's Bible Commentary, New Testament 1; London: Cassell, 1902) 362-366.

[679]*The Gospel according to St. Matthew* (The Westminster New Testament 1; New York: Revell, 1915) 210-211. The same interpretation of vv 32 and 40 is found in his *The Disciple's Commentary on the Gospels* (3 vols., London: Hodder & Stoughton, 1928) 1. 400-403, which was republished in the United States as *Matthew* (Commentary on the Four Gospels 1; Garden City, NY: Doubleday, 1928) 426-429.

680*St. Matthew* (Westminster Commentaries 37; London: Methuen, 1917) 240-243.

681"The Sheep and the Goats," *Parables of Judgment* (London: The Church Book Room, 1936) 104-111, esp. pp. 105-107.

682*Jesus and the Future Life* (London: Epworth, 1959) 130-136, esp. pp. 131, 136.

683"Matthew," *Ellicott's Bible Commentary in One Volume* (ed. D. Bowdle; Grand Rapids: Zondervan, 1971) 681-757, esp. p. 743. C. J. Ellicott lived from 1819-1902, but an earlier edition of his commentary was unavailable to me.

684*Interpreting the Parables* (Philadelphia: Westminster, 1960) 88-91, esp. p. 90. See also his "The Last Judgment," *The Parables Then and Now* (Philadelphia: Westminster, 1971) 115-118, esp. pp. 116-117.

685"The Great Assize," *The Gospel Parables* (London: Hodder & Stoughton, 1967) 191-195, esp. p. 193. He suggests that in v 32 Matthew may have restricted what was an originally universal audience to the Gentiles.

686"The Messiah of Israel as Teacher of the Gentiles," *Interpreting the Gospels* (ed. J. L. Mays; Philadelphia: Fortress, 1981) 78-96, esp. p. 93.

687In seven different published works he has almost as many opinions. In *Die Gleichnisse Jesu* (8th ed.; Göttingen: Vandenhoeck & Ruprecht, 1970) 108 n. 2, 205-207, and in *Rediscovering the Parables* (New York: Scribner, 1966) 161-163, he understands πάντα τὰ ἔθνη as non-Christians and non-Jews and argues that "the least", even though limited by Matthew to the disciples, were in Jesus' original parable intended to refer to everyone. The same point of view is found in his last published work on the subject, *Neutestamentliche Theologie* (Gütersloh: Mohn, 1971) 113-115,167, 206. In *Jesus als Weltvollender* (BFCT 33/4; Gütersloh: Bertelsmann, 1930) 72 n. 4, πάντα τὰ ἔθνη are understood as all non-Christians. In *Jesu Verheißung für die Völker* (Stuttgart: Kohlhammer, 1956) 21, 40-41, he interprets "the least" as everyone and is ambivalent whether πάντα τὰ ἔθνη are everyone or only non-Jews. In his article "ποιμήν" (*TDNT* 6. 485-502, esp. p. 493) he sees "all the nations" as all non-Jews. In *Abba: Studien zür neutestamentlichen Theologie und Zeitsgeschichte* (Göttingen: Vandenhoeck & Ruprecht, 1966) 113, he does not discuss v 32, but is open to the universal interpretation of "the least."

688"Soviel ihr getan habt einem dieser meiner geringsten Brüder ... ," *Ruf und Antwort. Festgabe für Emil Fuchs zum 90. Geburtstag* (Leipzig: Koehler & Amelang, 1964) 484-493, esp. pp. 488-489.

689"Matthäus 25:31-46 im Erwartungshorizont heutiger Exegese," *LB* 3 (1973) 9-21, esp. pp. 13-15.

690*Les évangiles synoptiques* (2 vols.; Ceffonds: Chez l'auteur, 1907-08) 2. 483, 486.

691"A propos de Matthieu 25:31-46," *ETR* 44 (1969) 233-234.

692"Note à propos de l'exégèse de Mt 25:31-46," *RevScRel* 48 (1974) 398-400.

693*L'Evangile de Matthieu* (Mulhouse: Editions Salvator, 1977) 280-285, esp. pp. 282, 284.

694"The Gospel according to St. Matthew," *Concise Bible Commentary* (London: SPCK, 1952) 723-744, esp. pp. 742-743.

695*Matthew* (Understanding the New Testament; London: Scripture Union, 1978) 81-82. It was published in the United States as "St. Matthew," *Daily Bible Commentary* (4 vols.; Philadelphia: Holman, 1977) 3.10-103, esp. pp. 89-90. He argues that "the least" accompany the judge and are associated with him in judgment.

696"The Matthean Apocalypse," *JSNT* 4 (1979) 2-27, esp. pp. 18-19. He argues that Matthew's insertion of the element of a judgment of nations interferes with the judgment of individuals in the original parable, and that the universal sense of "the least" in the original was restricted by Matthew "to further community megalomania."

697"The Parable of the Sheep and the Goats," *The Kingdom of God* (Salem, OR: Harris, 1913) 97-103, esp. pp. 98-99, 101.

698*Notes from a Layman's Greek Testament* (Boston: Wilde, 1941) 40.

699*Jesus in the Church's Gospels* (Philadelphia: Fortress, 1968) 249-250. He argues that in the original parable those to be gathered were the followers of Christ, but Matthew, by the insertion of πάντα τὰ ἔθνη, changed the objects of the judgment to non-Christians and non-Jews.

700*The Gospel according to Matthew* (Collegeville Bible Commentary 1; Collegeville, MN: Liturgical Press, 1983) 100-101. The same interpretation of the pericope is found in an earlier article that he co-authored with Douglas R. A. Hare, "Make Disciples of all the Nations," *CBQ* 37 (1975) 359-369, esp. pp. 363-366.

701"The Last Judgment," *The Parables* (Spearhead 66; Eldoret, Kenya: Gaba, 1981) 50-52. He argues that Matthew changed the universal thrust of the original parable by the insertion of πάντα τὰ ἔθνη and by restricting his interpretation of "the least."

702"Zur Auslegung von Mt 25, 31-46," *Luthertum* 2 (1935) 77-82, esp. pp. 78-79. On p. 81, however, he gives the impression that "the least" are to include all Christians.

703*Das Matthäusevangelium* (Neutestamentliche Reihe 1; Berlin: de Gruyter, 1951) 157-158.

704*Das Erscheinen des Auferstandenen im Evangelium nach Matthäus* (FB 11; Würzburg: Echter, 1973) 296-299, 377-378.

705*The Setting of the Sermon on the Mount* (Cambridge: Cambridge University Press, 1964) 98.

706"Matt 25:31-46. The Sheep and the Goats Reinterpreted," *NovT* 11 (1969) 32-44, esp. pp. 37, 39, 41. The same interpretation of the pericope can be gleaned from his later work, *Matthew: A Scribe Trained for the Kingdom of Heaven* (CBQMS 5; Washington, DC: CBA, 1976) 42, 74, 116, 127, 130. He certainly does not exclude Christians in general from his interpretation of "the least," but his strong emphasis on the fact that they are primarily the missionaries is responsible for his classification in this work.

707This is the position of the article he co-authored with D. J. Harrington, "Make Disciples of all the Nations," *CBQ* 37 (1975) 359-369, esp. pp. 363-366. However, in an earlier work, (*The Theme of Jewish Persecution of Christians in the Gospel according to St. Matthew* [SNTSMS 6; Cambridge: University Press, 1967] 124) his interpretation of vv 32 and 40 is completely universal.

708"The Last Judgment," *Once More Astonished* (New York: Crossroad, 1983) 196-235, esp. pp. 220, 224-226. He argues that in the original parable of Jesus, those to be judged included everyone, while "the least" also had a universal interpretation. In an earlier work, "The Parousia Discourse: Composition and Content in *MT.*, XXIV-XXV," *L'Evangile selon saint Matthieu: Rédaction et théologie* (BETL 29; ed. M. Didier; Gembloux: Duculot, 1972) 309-342, esp. pp. 333-334, 338, he sees πάντα τὰ ἔθνη as all non-Christians and "the least" as poor Christians.

709"Ethnos," *EWNT* 1.928.

710*Matthew, Mark and Luke* (London: Longmans, Green, 1937) 256.

711"The Gentile Bias in Matthew," *JBL* 66 (1947) 165-172, esp. pp. 166-167.

712*Meditations in Matthew* (New York: Loizeaux, 1958) 101.

713"The Gospel of Matthew, "*The Oxford Annotated Bible with the Apocrypha* (eds. H. G. May and B. M. Metzger; New York: Oxford University, 1965) 1206.

714*La Biblia* (25 vols.; Montserrat: Monestir de Montserrat, 1963) 18. 298-300.

715"Das Gericht des Menschensohnes über die Völker," *BibLeb* 11 (1970) 273-295, esp. pp. 282, 284, 289, 291-294.

716The particulars of this interpretation were already discussed on p. 263.

717"Unto Me," *Saint Matthew* (Great Texts of the Bible 8; Edinburgh: Clark, 1914) 406-417, esp. pp. 407-410.

718*An Introduction to the Theology of the New Testament* (London: SCM, 1958) 89, 137, 244 n. 1, 251, 255, 324, 343,

719*Bij het Evangelie volgens Mattheüs* (In dienst van het woord 17; Haarlem: Gottmer, 1971) 90-91.

720R. Ricciardi and B. Hurault (eds.), *La Biblia* (Madrid: Ediciones Paulinas Verbo Divino, 1972) 55-56.

721As found in A. L. Williams and W. J. Deane, *Matthew* 2. 497-498.

722*Der Lohngedanke in der Lehre Jesu verglichen mit der religiösen Lohnlehre des Spätjudentums* (Münchener theologische Studien 7; Munich: Zink, 1955) 66. See also his *Matthäus der Seelsorger* (SBS 2; Stuttgart: KBW, 1966) 74.

723*Gott im Brüder? Eine methodenkritische Untersuchung von Redaktion, Überlieferung und Traditionen in Mt 25:31-46* (Stuttgart: Calwer, 1977) 238-239, 248-249, 253-254. He argues that in the original form, the meaning of vv 32 and 40 was universal; Matthew restricted those to be judged to non-Christians and likewise restricted "the least" to mean only Christians.

724"La 'parabole' du jugement dernier," *RHPR* 50 (1970) 23-60, esp. pp. 37, 52-53.

725*Jewish and Christian Apocalypses* (London: Milford, 1914) 25.

726*The Teaching of Jesus* (Cambridge: University Press, 1967) 265. In a later work, *The Sayings of Jesus* (London: SCM, 1971) 248-252, esp. pp. 249-251, he argues that the Christians, who are "the least," accompany Christ in judgment and together with Christ form a corporate Son of Man. This same idea of the corporate Son of Man is found in his article, "The Son of Man in Daniel, Enoch, and the Gospels," *BJRL* 32 (1949-50) 171-193, esp. p. 191.

727*Matthew and Paul* (SNTSMS 48; Cambridge: University Press, 1984) 56, 90, 106.

728"The Gospel according to St. Matthew," *A New Commentary on Holy Scripture* (3 vols.; ed. C. Gore, H. L. Goudge, and A. Guillaume; New York: Macmillan, 1928) 3. 124-205, esp. p. 196. This same interpretation of the pericope is found in a later work written by P. P. Levertoff alone: *St. Matthew* (Commentaries for Schools 1; London: Murby, 1940) 84-85.

729*A Theology of the New Testament* (Grand Rapids: Eerdmans, 1974) 118-119, 206, 545. In his article, "The Parable of the Sheep and the Goats in Recent Interpretation," *New Dimensions in New Testament Study* (ed. R. Longenecker and M. Tenney; Grand Rapids: Zondervan, 1974) 191-199, esp. pp. 197-199, he does not discuss πάντα τὰ ἔθνη but takes the view that "the least" are all Christians. This is a broadening of the interpretation found in his earlier works. In "Matthew," *The Biblical Expositor* (3 vols.; ed. C. F. Henry; Philadelphia: Holman, 1960) 3. 23-73, esp. pp. 65-66, and in *Jesus and the Kingdom* (New York: Harper & Row, 1964) 250, 272-273, 313, he interprets "the least" in a narrower sense as Christian missionaries, and seems to be more universal in his understanding of πάντα τὰ ἔθνη, seeing the term as inclusive of all.

730*The Gospel of Saint Matthew* (The Pelican Gospel Commentaries; Baltimore: Penguin, 1963) 400-402. His understanding is that in the original parable of Jesus "the least" probably referred to anyone in distress. He likewise holds for the Matthean insertion of πάντα τὰ ἔθνη and thus implies that here too Matthew might have reworked what was intended to be universal in the original.

731"An Exegesis of Matthew 25:31-46," *Foundations* 19 (1976) 211-213.

732*The Gospels Harmonized* (Commentary on the New Testament 7; Cincinnati, OH: Knapp, 1900) 362-365.

733*Das Evangelium des Matthäus* (4th ed.; Kommentar zum Neuen Testament 1; Leipzig: Deicher, 1922) 683-685.

734"Wer sind die geringsten Brüder?" *Die Christenlehre* 23 (1970) 3-16; 35-43, esp. pp. 38-39, 41-42.

735*Jesus the Messiah* (London: Hodder & Stoughton, 1943) 119. He argues that in the original parable of Jesus "the least" had a universal connotation.

736"The Church as the Body of Christ in the Gospel of Matthew," *SJT* 11 (1958) 271-286, esp. pp. 275-278. He argues that if the pericope originally stemmed from Jesus, then the term "the least of my brothers" would have had a universal significance. As the term stands in Matthew, however, it is most likely restricted to Christians, especially to the proclaimers of the gospel.

[737] *The Testament of Jesus-Sophia* (Lanham, MD: University Press of America, 1981) 288, 349, 390, 408 n. 3, 423-427.

[738] See J. Winandy, "La scène du jugement dernier," *ScEccl* 18 (1966) 169-186, esp. pp. 178-179.

[739] *Die Heilsgeschichte im ersten Evangelium* (FRLANT 91; Göttingen: Vandenhoeck & Ruprecht, 1967) 108-110.

[740] *Jesus Christ the Teacher* (3d ed.; London: Oxford University, 1945) 151.

[741] *The Gospel according to Matthew* (The Born-Again Bible 1; Atlanta, GA: Benjamin, 1978) 87.

[742] *Forkynnelse til oppbrudd: Studier i Matteusevangeliet og kirkens bruk av det.* (2 vols; Oslo: Universitetsforlaget, 1978) 127-128. He suspects that in the original saying those to be judged and "the least" included everyone, but Matthew reworked the story to have only the Gentiles judged according to their conduct towards Christians.

[743] *The Gospel according to Matthew* (The New Clarendon Bible, NT 1; Oxford: University Press, 1975) 206.

[744] "An Historical Perspective in the Gospel of Matthew," *JBL* 93 (1974) 243-262, esp. p. 258. In an earlier work, *Matthew's Advice to a Divided Community* (AnBib 44; Rome: Biblical Institute, 1970) 107, 121, 176 n. 1, he does not discuss v 32, but states that "the least" are Christians.

[745] "On Separating Sheep from Goats," *Christianity Today* 16 (1972) 1040-1041.

[746] *A Critical Lexicon and Concordance to the English and Greek New Testament* (Grand Rapids: Zondervan, 1975) 118, 516.

[747] *The Teaching of Jesus about the Future according to the Synoptic Gospels* (Chicago: University of Chicago, 1909) 235-245, esp. pp. 238, 242-243. In a later work, *Son of Man and Kingdom of God* (New York: Harper, 1943) 57-63, esp. pp. 61-62, he does not discuss v 32, but continues to insist that "the least" are Christian missioners.

[748] "La scène du jugement dernier," *ScEccl* 18 (1966) 169-186, esp. pp. 178-185.

⁷⁴⁹"La parabole du jugement dernier," *Jésus et l'enfant. "Enfants," "petits," et "simples" dans la tradition synoptique.* (EBib; Paris: Gabalda, 1969) 85-100, esp. pp. 94-98.

⁷⁵⁰*A Critical and Exegetical Commentary on the Gospel according to St. Matthew* (ICC 22; New York: Scribner, 1907) 265-266.

⁷⁵¹The particulars of this view have already been discussed on pp. 264-265.

⁷⁵²"Matthew," *The Student's Commentary on the Holy Scriptures* (Grand Rapids: Kregel, 1971) 696-731, esp. pp. 724-725.

⁷⁵³*Simple Studies in Matthew* (Harrisburg, PA: Kelker, 1910) 296-297.

⁷⁵⁴"The Gospel of Matthew," *The Gospels and the Book of Acts* (The Annotated Bible 4; New York: Our Hope, 1913) 53. It was republished a year later under the title *The Gospel of Matthew* (Bible Study Course 9; New York: Our Hope, 1914).

⁷⁵⁵"Matthew," *Christian Workers' Commentary on the Old and New Testaments* (New York: Revell, 1915) 293-313, esp. p. 310.

⁷⁵⁶*Blackboard Lectures on Matthew* (Nashville: Sunday School Board of the Southern Baptist Convention, 1919) 128.

⁷⁵⁷*Matthew's Gospel* (Los Angeles: Bible Institute of Los Angeles, 1923) 84.

⁷⁵⁸*Concordant Commentary on the New Testament* (3d ed.; Saugus, CA: Concordant, 1968) 49.

⁷⁵⁹*Studies in the Gospel according to Matthew* (New York: Revell, 1935) 188-189. In a later work, *A Companion to the New Scofield Reference Bible* (New York: Oxford University, 1972) 150, he broadens his interpretation of "the least" to include saved Gentiles who will survive the tribulation.

⁷⁶⁰"The Judgment of the Living Nations and the Establishment of the Kingdom of God," *Future Events Revealed* (Los Angeles: Cooper, 1935) 157-204, esp. pp. 161-162, 170, 205.

⁷⁶¹*Expository Notes on the Gospel of Matthew* (New York: Loizeaux, 1948) 337, 339.

⁷⁶²*Simple Survey of the New Testament for the Layman* (Grand Rapids: Zondervan, 1957) 26-27.

⁷⁶³"Matthew," *The New Testament and Wycliffe Bible Commentary* (ed. E. F. Harrison; New York: Iversen Associates, 1971) 93.

⁷⁶⁴*Study New Testament* (New York: Iversen-Norman Associates, 1979) 76.

[765] *The End Times* (Chicago: Moody, 1969) 142, 148, 220.

[766] "Christ's Olivet Discourse on the End of the Age," *BSac* 128 (1971) 109-116, esp. pp. 110, 113. His later works, "Christ's Olivet Discourse on the End of the Age: The Judgment of the Nations," *BSac* 129 (1972) 308-314, esp. pp. 310-311, 313; and *Matthew* (Chicago: Moody, 1974) 199-204, espouse the same pre-millenarian interpretation.

[767] *The Beginning of Sorrows* (Huntingdon Valley, PA: Kirban, 1972) 120.

[768] "The Future and the Gentile Nations," *Jesus' Prophetic Sermon* (Chicago: Moody, 1972) 140-146, esp. pp. 142-143. He insists that the judgment will be of nations, as opposed to individuals.

[769] *The Servant King* (Bible Alive Series; Elgin, IL: Cook, 1976) 165-167. He likewise argues that nations primarily will be judged according to v 32.

[770] "The Eschatology of the Bible," *The Expositor's Bible Commentary* (ed. F. Gaebelein; Grand Rapids: Zondervan, 1979) 1.103-126, esp. pp. 116-117. He too insists on the judgment of nations rather than individuals.

[771] *Behold the King* (Portland, OR: Multnomah, 1980) 288-292, esp. pp. 290-291. He argues that πάντα τὰ ἔθνη are primarily the Gentile nations, but also holds open the possibility that the term could refer "to the whole human race including Jews."

[772] *Prophetic Mysteries Revealed* (Neptune, NJ: Loizeaux, 1980) 116.

[773] *The Words and Works of Jesus Christ* (Grand Rapids: Zondervan, 1981) 409-411. In a later work, "The Sheep and the Goats," *The Parables of Jesus* (Grand Rapids: Zondervan, 1982) 157-160, esp. p. 158, he makes a distinction between the Jewish missionaries and the 144,000 mentioned in Rev 7: 4; 14:3, and says that the "best interpretation" of "the least" is that they are the 144,000.

[774] "The Gospel according to Matthew," *Liberty Bible Commentary* (2 vols.; ed. E. Hindson and W. Kroll; Lynchburg, VA: The Old-Time Gospel Hour, 1982) 2.1-98, esp. pp. 85-86.

[775] "The Gospel according to Matthew," *Matthew--Romans* (Thru the Bible with J. Vernon McGee 4; Nashville: Nelson, 1983) 1-155, esp. pp. 136-137.

[776] "Matthew," *The Bible Knowledge Commentary* (ed. J. Walvoord and R. Zuck; Wheaton, IL: Victor, 1983) 13-94, esp. pp. 80-81.

[777] *Outline Studies in Matthew* (Grand Rapids: Kregel, 1985) 363.

[778] *Matthew XI-XXVIII* (The People's Bible 19; London: Hazell, Watson, & Viney, 1900) 347-348.

[779] "The Gospel according to Matthew," *The Gospels* (Through the Bible Day by Day 5; Philadelphia: American Sunday-School Union, 1918) 62. On the primary level, he claims, "the least" are the Jewish missionaries of the tribulation period; on a wider level, however, the term can be interpreted to mean everyone.

[780] *Simple Sermons from the Gospel of Matthew* (Grand Rapids: Zondervan, 1963) 217-218.

[781] "Sheep and Goats," *The Parables and Metaphors of Our Lord* (New York: Revell, 1943) 157-163, esp. pp. 158, 161-162. In a much earlier work, *The Gospel according to Matthew* (The Analyzed Bible 10; New York: Revell, 1911) 271-272, he adheres to the strict pre-millenarian view and sees "the least" only as Jewish missionaries during the tribulation.

[782] *Expository Notes on the Gospel of Matthew* (Grand Rapids: Zondervan, 1961) 139-140.

[783] *The King and the Kingdom of Heaven* (New York: Christian Fellowship Publications, 1978) 376-386, esp. pp. 379-380, 382. In an earlier work, *Come, Lord Jesus* (New York: Christian Fellowship, 1976) 83, he retains a bit of the classic pre-millenarian stance, claiming that "the least" are the Jewish missionaries or Christians yet upon the earth.

[784] "The Gospel according to Matthew," *The Rice Reference Bible* (Nashville: Nelson, 1981) 1001-1053, esp. p. 1045.

[785] "His Coming Again," *The Study of the Parables* (Grand Rapids: Kregel, 1983) 77-97, esp. p. 93.

[786] "The Gospel according to Matthew," *The Holy Bible: The New Berkeley Version* (Grand Rapids: Zondervan, 1969) 1-35, esp. p. 30.

[787] *L'Evangile de l'église: commentaire de l'évangile selon Matthieu* (2 vols.; Etudes évangéliques 1-4; Geneva: Labor et Fides, 1967-70) 2. 469-476, esp. pp. 472-475.

[788] "Eighth Talk on Matthew," *Talks at Oxford Summer School-1948* (2 vols.; London: Foundational Book, 1948) 2.101-116, esp. pp. 105-106. See also "Fifth Talk on Matthew," *Talks at Oxford Summer School-1949* (2 vols.; London: Foundational Book, 1950) 1.121-140, esp. p. 128.

[789] *Christ's Drama* (London: Stuart, 1961) 176-177.

[790] *The Second Advent: The Origins of the New Testament Doctrine* (3d ed.; London: Epworth, 1963) 131-137. He argues that Matthew is

responsible for the framework of the passage, but clearly genuine words of Jesus lie behind the pericope.

[791]*Matthew* (AB 26; Garden City, NY: Doubleday, 1971) 306-310.

CHAPTER VI

CONCLUSIONS

Results of the Historical Study

The Second Century: Only in the writings of the later second century do we find authors who were certainly or possibly influenced by the Matthean pericope of final judgment. Justin Martyr is the first to give us an exact quotation from Matt 25:31-46, but he is so taken up with controversy regarding the Messiahship of Jesus that only those verses suitable for proving Christ's divinity are used by him. He is not concerned with the identity of "the least."

Neither is Irenaeus, even though he is the first church Father to quote from those verses having to do with the Christ/needy relationship. He is even more concerned than Justin with the false doctrines of heretics. Both times that he refers to the words of the needy Christ are in the larger context of combating certain tenets held by the Marcionites, so these two instances cannot safely be used to draw any firm conclusions as to whether his was a particularist or a universalist stance regarding the identity of the needy.

From the two anonymous writings discussed, *The Acts of Thomas* and *2 Clement*, if in fact they do allude to Matt 25:31-46, we are left with the impression that the later second century church might have regarded the "least of the brothers" as the apostles or elders. But this can only be conjecture. It is not until the third century that we begin to see concrete evidence favoring the particularist interpretation.

The Third Century: There seems to be a gradual shift in the use of Matt 25:31-46 that takes place in the third century. The writers of the late second century used the pericope, especially the verses having to do with Christ's glorification and his power to judge, primarily to combat heretical christological doctrines. While the same tendencies are present to a point in the authors of the third century, there is a definite growing moral and pastoral use of the passage. It begins with the Alexandrian Clement and reaches its clearest expression in the works of Cyprian.

Clement of Alexandria is the first of the eastern fathers to identify "the least" as Christians. This narrow interpretation that prevailed among writers of the third century, more so in the east than in the west, is most characteristic of Origen, the first to give us a commentary on Matthew and the first to attempt serious exegesis of the Matthean pericope. Like modern exegetes he at least recognized some of the difficulties that exist in the passage, but his interpretation of the pericope would make most moderns wince. He used the allegorical method (characteristic of the entire Alexandrian school) to reach what he called the "deeper sense" of the scriptures and thus interpreted the six Matthean acts of mercy in a highly spiritualized way.

In the west the North African Tertullian is the first to express a narrow interpretation of "the least."[1] In this he is followed by Cyprian, who seems less interested than Tertullian in using the work in an apologetic manner. It is with Cyprian that we have the first consistent use of the pericope to deal with pastoral and moral concerns. The more restrictive views of Tertullian and Cyprian, however, are not attested everywhere in the west. The authentic works of the Roman Hippolytus and the writings of Commodianus are representative of a more universal horizon. The fact that the two out of the eleven authors studied in the third century who have a more universal outlook (Hippolytus and Commodianus) happen to be representatives of the western church may be no mere coincidence. It could be reflective of a more universal mission in the west than in the east.

AD 325-431: A survey of what is sometimes called the great patristic century leads us to make six observations regarding the use of Matt 25:31-46 during this period: (1) for the first time the concern of the exact identity of "the least" is addressed; (2) there is a pervading restrictive viewpoint in the works of many authors; (3) at the same time, there are the beginnings of a true

Conclusions 333

universalism; (4) the apologetic use of the pericope has waned; (5) the tendency to spiritualize the Matthean acts of mercy, noticeable in the third century, continues in the fourth; and (6) a noticeable anti-Jewish sentiment is present in the observations of some writers.

Jerome, in his *Comm. in Matt.* 25. 33,[2] is the first to address the problem of the identity of "the least." Others before him commented on Matt 25:40, but Jerome is the first to give an indication that "the least of my brothers" presented a problem because it could be interpreted universally or restrictively. Jerome opted for the narrow interpretation. The mere fact, however, that he argues against the universal interpretation could be an indication that it was held by others in his own day. Paradoxically, even though Jerome opted for the restrictive interpretation of v 40, he can be regarded as somewhat of a universalist since he quotes from the "identity dialogue" on at least two occasions (*Apol. contra Ruf.* 3.17 and *Letter* 54.12),[3] where it seems his charitable concerns reach beyond the Christian community.

Of the thirty-five fourth-century authors researched, twelve (Basil of Ancyra, Cyril of Jerusalem, Asterius of Amasea, John the Dwarf, Palladius, Gaudentius of Brescia, Firmicus Maternus, Chromatius of Aquilea, Maximus of Turin, Pelagius, Paulus Orosius, and Sulpicius Severus) can be regarded as neutral (i.e., they simply refer to "the least" as poor and needy and give no indication whatsoever whether they mean only Christian poor or the poor in general); the remaining twenty-three writers can be considered in some sense to have a restrictive viewpoint (i.e., in at least one passage of their works they explicitly refer to "the least" as Christian needy and never offset that with an explicit universal reference). Among those authors expressing a restrictive viewpoint, however, John Chrysostom, the author of the "Clementines," and to some extent Jerome, can be regarded as universalists (i.e., at some point in their discussion of the identity dialogue they specifically refer to nonChristians as viable beneficiaries of the believers' charity). If the neutral authors are not included as part of the evidence, it is safe to say that the prevailing opinion of the fathers of the fourth century regarding the identity of "the least" was a restrictive one. I think it would be safe to say that, for the most part, they understood those with whom Christ identified himself in the Matthean judgment scene to be fellow Christians.

Yet, against this narrow background one can see the emergence of universalism. Chrysostom and the author of the "Clementines" in the east, and, to some extent, Jerome in the west, are the first to express a truly universal horizon in their interpretation of the dialogue of the needy Christ.[4]

For the most part, the authors of the fourth century use Matt 25:31-46 in the context of pastoral or moral concerns. With the exception of Aphraates, Pelagius and, to a lesser extent, Eusebius of Caesarea, the apologetic use of the pericope that was observed in the second and third centuries has all but disappeared in the fourth century.

The tendency to allegorize the six Matthean works is not overwhelming among the fathers of the fourth century, but it is there--surprisingly a bit more in the west (Ambrose, Chromatius, Aponius, and Jerome) than in the east (Eusebius of Caesarea and Macarius). This could perhaps be the effect of the lingering influence of Origen, especially in regard to Eusebius of Caesarea, Ambrose, and Jerome.

A noticeable anti-Jewish strand appears in the works of some fathers of the fourth century. I think it safe to say that the fourth-century authors would see only Christians among the saved; none would place the once "chosen people" among the sheep. But some (Aphraates, Athanasius, Asterius of Amasea, Jerome, and Augustine), in their comments on Matt 25:31-46, make a considerable point of including the Jews among the condemned goats, very often comparing the inability and the refusal of the goats to recognize the needs of "the least" to the inability and refusal of the Jews to recognize the Messiah.

AD 431-553: The century and some odd years between the Council of Ephesus (AD 431) and the Second Council of Constantinople (AD 553) produced thirty authors, eleven eastern and nineteen western, who referred to Matt 25:31-46. The most noticeable characteristic of these references during these years is the growth of a universal outlook with regard to the "identity dialogue." Of the thirty authors investigated, thirteen are technically neutral in that they give no indication one way or another as to the identity of "the least." Ten writers in all, four eastern (Basil of Seleucia, Theodoret of Cyrus, Ps-Eusebius, and John of Gaza) and six western (Peter Chrysologos, Patrick, Epiphanius Latinus, Prosper of Aquitane, Fulgentius of Ruspe, and Remigius of Rheims) can be considered representatives of the narrow outlook insofar as they explicitly postulate, in at least one passage of their works, a Christian identity to the beneficiaries without a universalistic corrective. Seven authors, however (Cyril of Alexandria in the east and six others [Valerian of Cemele, Leo the Great, Salvianus, Faustus of Riez, Caesarius of Arles, and Benedict] in the west), can be classified as universalists in their understanding of the Matthean pericope since they specifically mention the obligation of charity that Christians bear to all. Not surprisingly, the majority of those expressing this specifically universal viewpoint are western writers. Perhaps this can be attributed to the fact that during these years the west suffered more invasions than the east and consequently experienced, and had to learn to live with, a more pluralistic society. Among those expressing a universalist interpretation, Valerian of Cemele is the first, and the only one up to this point, to express a true universalism, i.e., he placed Christians and non-Christians on the same level of priority. Every other universalist author would, somehow or other, give preference to Christians.

In spite of the growth of the universal outlook, it cannot be denied that during these years there is still greater attestation of the narrow interpretation. Paradoxically, there is slightly more evidence of this narrow viewpoint among western authors. This can doubtlessly be attributed to the lingering influence of Augustine, especially in writers such as Prosper and Fulgentius. The popularity of reproducing Augustine's works is evidenced in Eugippius and, to a lesser extent, in Caesarius of Arles.

Perhaps one of the most noticeable differences between the second and third centuries and the century or more between AD 431 and 553 is the actual use of the "identity dialogue." The fifth and sixth centuries witnessed the rise of powerful preachers who, continuing the pattern begun in the fourth century, used Matt 25:31-46 for moral and pastoral, rather than dogmatic or apologetic, purposes. There is lingering evidence for the dogmatic use of the passage in the works of Cyril of Alexandria, Cassian, and Prosper of Aquitaine; but in the west especially, orators such as Laurentius of Novae, Peter Chrysologus, Valerian of Cemele, Leo the Great, Salvianus, Faustus of Riez, Fulgentius of Ruspe, and Caesarius of Arles referred to the "identity dialogue" out of the moral and pastoral concerns that the poor be taken care of. Seldom in these years, with the exception of Procopius of Gaza and Chrysostomus Latinus, is there evidence for the allegorical or spiritual interpretation of the six Matthean works. For the most part the passage is used in a strongly literal way.

The anti-Jewish element, observed in the fourth century, continues to be a factor in these years as well, although perhaps a bit abated. This tendency to single out the Jews for condemnation is mainly evident in the works of Cyril of Alexandria, Peter Chrysologus, and Quodvultdeus. To a lesser extent it might be attested to in the views of Prosper of Aquitaine and Caesarius of Arles that the Jews will not even be included in the final judgment since, due to their unbelief, they have already been judged. In the west, at least, such sentiment could be a further example of the preponderating influence of Augustine.

AD 554-750: In the two centuries that elapsed between the Second Council of Constantinople and the end of the patristic era, twenty-six authors - nine eastern and seventeen western - referred to the Matthean "identity dialogue." The majority of these writers were neutral in their use of Matt 25:35-40,42-45. Seven authors (Anastasius Apocrisarius, Cassiodorus, Leander of Seville, Donatus of Besançon, Valerius of Bancona, Fructuosus of Braga, and Venerable Bede) refer to the words of the needy Christ in a restrictive way with no universalizing corrective; while four writers (Antiochus the Monk, Gregory the Great, Isidore of Seville, and Audoenus of Rouen) manifest a distinct universalism in their outlook. During the last centuries of the patristic era there is a noticeable increase among western authors in the restrictive use of the "identity dialogue." This

Conclusions

could be due to the continuing influence of Augustine as well as the increasing popularity of monasticism in the west. Three of the six western restrictive uses of the "identity dialogue" (Leander of Seville, Donatus of Besançon, and Fructuosus of Braga) are found in monastic rules.

With the exception of Venerable Bede, there is no witness to the spiritual or allegorical interpretation of the six Matthean works that was popular in the third and fourth centuries. In the final two centuries of the patristic period Matt 25:31-46 is interpreted in a literal, realistic sense.

There is also no evidence for the dogmatic or apologetic use of the pericope in the final centuries of the patristic era. The moral and pastoral use of the "identity dialogue" that was so prevalent in the fifth and sixth centuries continues into the seventh and eighth.

The anti-Jewish rhetoric that was associated with commentary on Matt 25:31-46 in the earlier centuries is noticeably absent in this final period of the patristic era. The belief that the Jews would not be judged, found in Prosper of Aquitaine and Caesarius of Arles, is encountered again in the thought of Gregory the Great, Isidore of Seville, Julian of Toledo, and Bede. According to these last four authors, the Jews and everyone else outside the church will constitute that group at the judgment that will be punished without being judged, since they will have already been judged by their unbelief.

An overall perspective of the six and a half centuries that constitute the age of the Fathers shows that of the 504 references to the "identity dialogue" that were investigated, 312 (62 %) are used in a totally neutral way (i.e., they give no indication as to the identity of the needy). 166 references (33 %) are used in a narrow or restrictive sense (i. e., they refer to "the least" as Christian needy), and twenty-six passages (5%) are used in a truly universal sense (i.e., they explicitly or implicitly include non-Christians as beneficiaries of the Christians' charity).

If the neutral use of the "identity dialogue" is not taken into consideration, then it can be stated that a narrow interpretation of Matt 25:35-40,42-45 prevailed among the Fathers. In fact, the four Fathers (Origen, John Chrysostom, Hilary of Poitiers, and Bede)[5] who do specifically interpret the "identity dialogue" in their commentaries on Matthew understand "the least" as Christians. If, however, the neutral use is interpreted as an indication of nonrestrictiveness, then it is closer to the mark to state that a universal understanding of "the least" characterized the patristic era.

The restrictive interpretation of the "identity dialogue" was most prevalent in the third and fourth centuries, especially among eastern witnesses. It decreased in the centuries following the death of Augustine, but, most likely due to his influence, the majority of witnesses to the narrow usage (twenty-four out of thirty-eight) were from the west. The overwhelming majority of the universal usages (twelve out of fourteen) were likewise from the west in the centuries following Augustine's death. The following chart gives a much more detailed picture of the patristic era:

The Patristic Usage of Matt 25:35-40, 42-45

	Neutral use		Narrow use		Universal use	
	East	West	East	West	East	West
2nd cent. (4 uses)	0	2 (50%)	2 (50%)	0	0	0
3rd cent. (58 uses)	13	9 (38%)	23 (60%)	12	1 (2%)	0
AD 325-431 (265 uses)	106	57 (62%)	52 (34%)	39	5 (4%)	6

AD 431-553	18	59	9	10	1	8
(105 uses)	(73%)		(18%)		(9%)	

AD 553-750	13	35	5	14	1	4
(72 uses)	(66 2/3%)		(26 1/3%)		(7%)	

Total	150	162	91	75	8	18
(504)	(62%)		(33%)		(5%)	

Information regarding the Patristic interpretation of πάντα τὰ ἔθνη is much harder to come by. An overall view of the 114 Fathers investigated shows that the large majority (over 82%) did not discuss the issue. Five eastern witnesses (2 *Clement*, Origen, Cyril of Jerusalem, John Chrysostom, and Cyril of Alexandria) and nine western witnesses (Irenaeus, Ps-Hippolytus, Hilary of Poitiers, Rufinus of Aquilea, Jerome, Augustine, Leo, Epiphanius Latinus, and Audoenus of Rouen) give evidence of a universal interpretation of "all the nations." Six western Fathers (Prosper of Aquitane, Caesarius of Arles, Gregory the Great, Isidore of Seville, Julian of Toledo, and Venerable Bede) hold the opinion that the Matthean pericope has to do with the judgment of Christians only; they are not always clear though as to whether the rest of humanity will be gathered to witness the judgment or not.

The Medieval Period: The commentaries of the Middle Ages are characterized by a heavy dependence on the opinions of the Fathers; even the greatest authors of this period sometimes did no more than echo faithfully the past. In fact, it could be said that the most important contribution of medieval scholarship is that it preserved important material from earlier sources that might otherwise have been lost. In the east, the influence of John Chrysostom was predominant. His ideas on Matt 25:31-46 wielded influence in the west as well, but not so much as the ideas of Origen (most likely due to Rufinus' Latin translation), Jerome, Augustine, and Gregory the Great.

The overwhelming majority of medieval commentators interpret "the least" in a narrow way, especially in the west. Seventeen of the twenty-one medieval authors who comment on vv 40 and 45 see "the least" as Christians. Six of these (Paul the Deacon, Haymo, Paschasius, Rupert, Bonaventure and Ludolph) say that "the least" are the apostles and those who imitated the apostles in a complete divestiture of their possessions, namely, monks and religious. Paschasius Radbertus was the first to identify "the least" as those whom Gregory the Great, centuries earlier, had placed in the category of the elect who would not be judged but would judge. The only neutral or possibly universalist approach to the beneficiaries of vv 40, 45 is found, in the west, in the work of Albert and, in the east, in the commentaries of Theophylact, Theophane, and Dionysius. That there would be a far less restrictive viewpoint regarding "the least" among the eastern commentators is not surprising. They were unaffected by the interpretations of Jerome and Augustine, so influential in the west, and much more exposed to the less restrictive interpretation of John Chrysostom.

With regard to πάντα τὰ ἔθνη in v 32, the majority of the twenty-five medieval commentators are universalists. Eight authors (Theophane, Dionysius, Christian Druthmar, Haymo, Paschasius, Bruno, Bonaventure, and Ludolph) explicitly state this universalism; it can be implied in the works of five others (Rabanus, Remigius of Auxerre, Hugh of Saint Cher, Albert, and Nicholas of Lyra).

The four categories of Gregory the Great (according to which only Christians are subject to the judgment) are popular in the western commentaries from the Middle Ages. Of the seventeen western authors who address the question of who would be present at the judgment, six (Paul the Deacon, Anselm and Ralph of Laon, Rupert of Deutz, Zachary of Besançon, and Thomas

Aquinas) opt for the Gregorian tetrad. In the east, Euthymius, most likely unaware of Gregory's categories, is in agreement with Gregory that only Christians will be judged, but he says nothing about "the perfect" and the unbelievers. Three commentators (Paschasius, Bonaventure, and Albert) give evidence of a threefold division: "the perfect" who will co-judge with Christ, as well as "the sheep" and "the goats." They do not expressly indicate whether non-Christians are the subject of the judgment or not.

The Matthean works (vv 35-36) were the subject of much discussion in the Middle Ages. Thirteen of the nineteen authors expressing an opinion on vv 35-36 say that the works are to be interpreted spiritually as well as corporally. Not surprisingly, all of the eastern commentators, with the exception of Euthymius, give priority to the spiritual interpretation of the works. Euthymius, in the east, and Rupert, Peter Comestor, Albert the Great, and Nicholas of Lyra, among the western authors, speak of the works in a corporal vein only. Rupert of Deutz, Thomas Aquinas, and Nicholas of Lyra interpret the entire Matthean scene as a judgment only of those involved in the active life, as opposed to the contemplative or religious life. Peter Comestor was the first to introduce into the discussion the Tobian work of the burial of the dead; it took hold and every major commentator after him (Hugh of Saint Cher, Bonaventure, Albert, Thomas, Nicholas, and Ludolph) spoke of the "seven corporal works of mercy."

Almost every medieval witness approaches Matt 25:31-46 as if it were the actual description of the parousia. Only two commentators, Paschasius Radbertus and Nicholas of Lyra, refer to the pericope as a parable and, possibly influenced by Chrysostom,[6] see a linkage between Matt 25:31-46 and the two parables immediately preceding it.

Most likely as the result of the lingering influence of Augustine, the predestination of the just or the wicked is also a popular topic in western medieval commentaries, especially in the exegesis of vv 34 and 41. Ten authors are in agreement that v 34 can be used in one way or another to prove that the just are predestined. Only two commentators (Paul the Deacon and Bruno of

Asti) insist that the wicked are predestined in the same way. Rabanus Maurus and Anselm of Laon, however, are the only two to make the point that the wicked are not predestined to punishment.

The meaning of "the throne" in v 31 is also the subject of much medieval speculation. Of the nine authors who address the issue, seven (Paul the Deacon, Paschasius, Remigius, Anselm, Zachary, Hugh, and Ludolph) interpret it as the Church. Bonaventure sees it as the cross, and Thomas Aquinas, following the opinion of Origen,[7] says it will be the angels and the perfect who will accompany Christ.

With the caveat that we can seldom be certain that any given idea in the Middle Ages is new, it can be said that the heavy dependence of the medieval commentators on the Fathers did not prevent them from making their own unique contributions to the exegesis of Matt 25:31-46. Given the importance of the principle that a passage in a biblical work is best explained by another passage from the same work, rather than by a passage from elsewhere in Scripture, Paschasius Radbertus made an important breakthrough in his observation that "the least" of Matt 25:40,45 are "the perfect" in Matt 19:21,28. Origen had claimed that "the least" were not simply Christians, but "perfect" Christians. He quotes Ps 122:5 in their regard but does not directly connect them with "the perfect" in Matt 19:28.[8] Gregory the Great insisted that the so-called "perfect" of Matt 19:28 would come as co-judges with Christ,[9] but he never identified them as "the least" of Matt 25:40,45. It remained for Paschasius to combine the two ideas.

Perhaps the most significant advance in regard to Patristic commentary is to be seen in the well-organized scholastic commentaries of Albert the Great and Thomas Aquinas. In their insistence that the literal sense of scripture be taken seriously, they almost abandon the more spiritual approach to the Matthean works and attempt to use Aristotelian categories to emphasize their corporal nature. Their increased use of scripture to comment on scripture could be a further manifestation of their dissatisfaction with the allegorical approach of previous

Conclusions

commentators and their desire to give precedence to the literal interpretation.

The Renaissance and Reformation: The restrictive interpretation of "the least" that was so characteristic of the medieval authors is overwhelmingly attested to in the writings from the fifteenth to the seventeenth centuries. Twenty-nine of the thirty-six authors[10] who comment on vv 40 and 45 (eighteen Catholics[11] and eleven Reformers[12]) interpret "the least" as Christians, while only five witnesses (Alphonsus Tostatus, Denys van Leeuwen, John Wild, Augustine Marloratus, and Henry Hammond) definitely attest to a universal understanding. Two authors, Antoine Furetière and Charles Marie de Veil, can be said to be neutral in the sense that they give no indication of a restrictive understanding of v 40, but at the same time do not consciously embrace the universalist stance.

With regard to πάντα τὰ ἔθνη in v 32, the majority of the thirty-four authors from these centuries who discuss the issue[13] are universalists. Twenty-four commentators (seventeen Catholics[14] and seven Reformers[15]) understand those to be gathered for the judgment in the widest possible sense, while an additional nine witnesses (five Catholics[16] and four Reformers[17]) interpret πάντα τὰ ἔθνη to mean everyone, but see Christians only as the subjects for the judgment described in vv 34-45.

Daniel van Breen stands apart from the rest of the commentators of these three centuries: he alone sees πάντα τὰ ἔθνη as referring only to those Christians who will be alive at the time of Christ's coming. He is the first to state explicitly that the judgment described in Matt 25:31-46 does not entail or presuppose a resurrection from the dead.

As in the late second and early third centuries, so in the period of the Renaissance and Reformation, there is undeniable evidence that dogmatic controversies, rather than moral and pastoral considerations, lay behind a particular exegesis of Matt 25:31-46. Two theological controversies in particular, the role of works vis-à-vis faith and the existence of limbo, were at various times during this period intertwined with discussion of the Matthean judgment scene.

In the Middle Ages Rupert of Deutz had made the observation that there was a causal link between v 34 and vv 35-36. His insight went unnoticed and was not taken up in commentaries immediately subsequent to his; but the issue that he barely touched upon, the necessity of works for salvation, fueled by the debate over indulgences, was to flare up and become a *cause célèbre* during the Reformation. Twenty-one commentators from this period took an active part in the debate and, in their observations on Matt 25:31-46, devoted much of their energies to a discussion of the exact nature of the particle γάρ in v 35a. Catholic authors, insisting that works were necessary for salvation, tended to use the Matthean judgment scene as a proof text for their position. They regarded γάρ as causal in nature, resulting in the judge's invitation to salvation, the κληρονομήσατε of v 34.[18] In their response to the Catholic position, Protestants either stressed the faith that produced the works,[19] denied the causal nature of γάρ, or admitted its causality but refused to see it as a meritorious cause. Reformers who were influenced by Calvin's ideas of predestination argued that the particle was not causal but rather consequential in nature, and was to be linked with the word ἡτοιμασμένην rather than κληρονομήσατε. That is, because of God's grace, a certain elect are predestined to a kingdom that has been prepared for them from all time and, *as a consequence* of this divine grace of predestination, are able to carry out the works described in vv 35-36.[20] Some Reformers, however, did admit the causal nature of γάρ, but insisted that it indicated either the declarative cause of the judge's sentence (not the reward)[21] or else the *mediate* efficient cause of salvation, as opposed to the meritorious cause.[22]

As some Catholic exegetes overemphasized the role of γάρ in v 35a to prove their own theological positions, so some of the Reformers likewise misconstrued the separation in vv 32-33 and used it to further their own position. Calling attention to the exclusive categories of right and left in the Matthean judgment scene, the saved and the damned with no mention of a middle ground, they disputed the Catholic belief in the existence of limbo, a separate place for unbaptized infants, and argued that all the unbaptized were to be included among the damned.

The medieval tendency to allegorize the six Matthean works shows a remarkable decline in the centuries of the Renaissance and Reformation. Only twelve of the thirty-nine authors from this period interpret the works in an allegorical fashion. Most of them are Catholic writers;[23] only two Reformers understand the works described in vv 35-36 as representative of other works.[24]

As did the patristic and medieval commentators before them, the vast majority of the exegetes from the fifteenth to the seventeenth centuries treated Matt 25:31-46 as an accurate description of the parousia. Only Antoine Furetière calls the pericope a parable.

The Modern Era: The eighteenth through the twentieth centuries witnessed a veritable explosion of commentaries on Matt 25:31-46. The preceding seventeen centuries managed to yield to this investigatory study a total of 178 commentators on the Matthean pericope; already in the close to three centuries that comprise the modern period, 736 authors in over 800 works have had something to say about Matt 25:31-46.

1700-1799. The restrictive interpretation of the identity dialogue that is characteristic of the majority of commentaries from the Middle Ages and the Renaissance and Reformation continued throughout the eighteenth century. Sixteen of the twenty-three eighteenth-century commentators (about 70%), regarded "the least" as Christians; while fifteen of those commentators (over 65%) interpreted πάντα τὰ ἔθνη in the universal sense.[25] Not one eighteenth-century author expressed an explicitly universal understanding of the "identity dialogue," though two commentators (9%), J. C. Wolfe and N. Alexander, displayed an openess to that possibility.

There were two innovations in the eighteenth century that were to influence some future commentaries on Matt 25:31-46. In previous centuries the term πάντα τὰ ἔθνη was interpreted to mean everyone or only Christians; the publication of John Heylyn's commentary in 1749, however, witnessed for the first time the definite opinion that by "all the nations" Matthew had in mind "the Heathen."[26] The second innovation of the eighteenth century was that found in the writings of Swedenborg: there Matt 25:31-46 is not treated as a description of the final, universal judgment, but as the individual judgment of every human soul. Until this point in the history of the passage's interpretation, the judgment scene in Matthew had always been envisioned as a public event.

1800-1899. The most noticeable characteristic of the nineteenth century is the growth of the universalist position vis-à-vis the identity of "the least." Nineteen nineteenth-century writers (over 17%) hold an explicitly universal stance in this regard, while an additional twenty-one authors (almost 19%) can be termed "neutral" in the sense that they are open to the universal position; they do not expressly identify themselves as such, but there is nothing of a restrictive nature in their commentaries regarding the "identity dialogue." In spite of this universalist upsurge, however, the narrow stance with regard to v 40 continues to predominate; sixty-six of the 111 nineteenth-century exegetes (close to 60%) interpret "the least" as Christians or the pre-millennialist Jewish missionaries.

With regard to the interpretation of πάντα τὰ ἔθνη, the universalist position certainly dominates the nineteenth-century landscape: eighty-one authors (an overwhelming 73%) envision a gathering of all humanity. Yet the concept that "all the nations" refers only to those who are not Christian (attested for the first time in the previous century) sees a continual growth in two directions: slightly over 8% interpret πάντα τὰ ἔθνη as heathens, that is, non-Christians and non-Jews; while almost 10% understand the term to include the Jews and see it as coterminous with all non-Christians.

1900-1986. The nineteenth century attests for the first time in the interpretation of Matt 25:31-46 what has come to be known as the premillennialist or dispensationalist view, according to which πάντα τὰ ἔθνη are the *living* non-Christians and non-Jews at the time of the judgment and "the least" are Jewish missionaries who, in the absence of Christians, preach the gospel during the period of tribulation preceding the Battle of

Armageddon.[27] This interpretation makes its earliest appearance in the work of the English theologian, John Nelson Darby, the founder of the Plymouth Brethren;[28] but the seeds of this interpretation of the Matthean pericope could have been sown as early as the seventeenth century in Daniel van Breen's ideas that the judgment described in Matt 25:31-46 involves only those living at the time of Christ's return and that before his return there would be a period of persecution.[29]

A second innovation in the interpretation of Matt 25:31-46 that surfaces in the nineteenth century is the idea that the entire scene refers, not to the final judgment, but to the destruction of the Jewish Temple in AD 70.[30] This viewpoint had its strongest manifestation in this century (less than 3%) and is practically nonexistent (less than 1%) in the twentieth century.

The most noticeable characteristic of twentieth-century exegesis of Matt 25:31-46 is its universalism. The general interpretation of πάντα τὰ ἔθνη is certainly predominant in twentieth-century commentaries. 391 authors (nearly 65% of the total investigated) understand Matt 25:31-46 to be a judgment of all humanity, while fifty exegetes (a little over 8%) see it as a description of the judgment of only Christians. Of the latter fifty, seventeen writers presuppose the Christianization of the world by the time of the parousia and thus see all humanity as Christian, while thirty-one commentators imply a distinction between the two direct objects πάντα τὰ ἔθνη and αὐτούς in v 32 and envision Matt 25:31-46 as a judgment of Christians only against the backdrop of the rest of humanity gathered as a witness. Two authors espouse an interpretation of v 32 heretofore unattested: the αὐτούς of v 32, they claim, are the leaders of the Christian community, judged according to their treatment of Christians entrusted to them.

Another interpretation of πάντα τὰ ἔθνη that is unattested before the twentieth century is that that sees "all the nations" from the point of view of Israel and understands the gathering to comprise all non-Jews. This interpretation first surfaces in the first decade of the present century in the commentary of W. C. Allen[31] and is attested to by only 2% of the total number of twentieth-century authors. Seventy-two commentators (about

12%) interpet πάντα τὰ ἔθνη as all non-Christians and non-Jews, while twenty-two authors (close to 7%) would include the Jews in the term and see τὰ ἔθνη representing all non-Christians.

An analysis of the twentieth-century interpretation of Matt 25:31-46 brings to light a remarkable increase in the commentaries that espouse the universalist position with regard to "the least." 239 publications (almost 34% of the total) explicitly identify "the least" with everyone and an additional 135 works (a little over 19%) are neutral in the sense that they never directly address the question of the beneficiaries' identity, yet in their comments on "the least" there is nothing that betrays a narrow stance. If the neutral category can be interpreted as reflective of the universalist position, then it can be stated that the majority of twentieth-century authors (53%) are universalists and that for the first time in the interpretation of the pericope there is a major period in which proponents of the nonrestrictive stance outnumber those who opt for the narrow position. If, however, the neutral commentaries are not to be admitted as evidence of the universalist position, those who interpret "the least" in a restrictive manner have a slight edge, since 251 works (slightly more than 35%) understand "the least" in the narrow sense: 218 commentaries state that "the least" are Christians and thirty-three premillennialist works understand the term to mean Jewish missionaries during the tribulation.

What conclusions can be drawn from this lengthy study of Matt 25:31-46? An overall perspective of the four main periods in the history of the interpretation of πάντα τὰ ἔθνη reveals that 537 of the 914 interpreters (close to 59%) understand the Matthean pericope to be a judgment of all humanity. By far the greatest number of witnesses to this view are found in the modern period, yet in every period, where there is discussion of v 32, it is the majority opinion. The second largest category is that of "not discussed"; this is due principally to the fact that ninety-four of the 114 patristic authors investigated do not directly discuss v 32. The third-century exegete Origen was the first to ask the critical question as to the meaning of πάντα τὰ ἔθνη, but discussion of the issue was not pursued with any amount of frequency until the commentaries of the Middle Ages. The only other view to be attested in all four periods is a variant of the universal interpretation: Matt 25:31-46 is concerned only with the judgment of Christians. Proponents of this stance are divided into those who presuppose that all humanity will be Christian at the parousia and those who claim that only Christians will be judged before all the assembled non-Christian members of humanity. The remaining interpretations that πάντα τὰ ἔθνη refers to all non-Christians (with or without the inclusion of the Jews) or to all non-Jews did not surface until the modern era, and even then are not greatly attested. Origen first raised the question as to whether those gathered for the judgment would be all humanity or only those alive at the time of the parousia but, prior to the work of van Breen in the seventeenth century, there is no indication that anyone actually subscribed to the view that πάντα τὰ ἔθνη refers to only those living at the time of Christ's coming. The understanding of the first sixteen centuries is that Matt 25:32 presupposed a resurrection of the dead.

An overall perspective of the interpretation of v 40 fails to yield such clear-cut results. The issue is complicated by the strong showing of what is termed in this study the neutral, or nonrestrictive, position; that is, there is no statement that "the least" are everyone, and yet there is no indication of a narrow interpretation. If one accepts the neutral stance as indicative of universality, then it is clear that the majority of references (765 out of 1409 uses or close to 55%) understand "the least" to refer to anyone. The greatest number of witnesses to this universal/neutral position are found in the Patristic period (338 out of 504 uses or 67%) and in the nineteenth and twentieth centuries (414 out of 818 uses or 51%). In the intervening centuries this universalism is surprisingly almost nonexistent.

If one omits the neutral stance from the evidence, then it is clear that the narrow interpretation of "the least" is the predominant viewpoint throughout the centuries (545 out of 1409 uses or almost 39%). The restrictive stance regarding "the least" is most heavily attested in the Middle Ages (68%) and the Renaissance/Reformation (over 74%), but it maintains a very strong showing in every century, with the exception of the last three centuries of the patristic era. The explicitly universal interpretation of "the least," while attested in every historical period, is not attested to at all in the second and eighteenth centuries, and makes no significant impact on the charts until the twentieth century when it skyrockets to a surprising 34%, nearly equal to the percentage of the narrow use.

Why the sudden increase of the universal and neutral stances vis-à-vis "the least" in the twentieth century? A clue might be found in the careful analysis of the commentaries of each decade of this present century. Closer inspection of the twentieth-century interpretation of v 40 reveals that the century began with the narrow stance in the lead, but that there was an increase in the universal/neutral categories and a decrease in the restrictive categories (Christians/Tribulation Jews) in five ensuing decades: 1910-1929 and 1940-1969.[32] These were the decades most closely associated with the two World Wars and the phenomenon of the Second Vatican Council. Could the experiences of global human suffering that accompanied both World Wars, the "guilt" over the Jewish holocaust following World War II, and the atmosphere of ecumenism that surrounded the Second Vatican Council, have consciously or unconsciously influenced the growth of the universal interpretation of "the least of my brothers"? In the fourth decade of the century (1930-1939) there is a decrease in the universal/neutral stance and a significant rise in the restrictive interpretation. This same phenomenon is found near the end of the century in the 1970s and 1980s. Could these changes reflect the results of life for a number of years without a global conflict and the waning influence of the ecumenical atmosphere created by the Second Vatican Council? Could the significant increase of the premillennial interpretation since 1970 (which increases the restrictive ratio) be due to "end of millennium jitters"? The answers to these questions are not within the scope of this investigation. It could certainly never be proven (and it is not the intent of this study to do so), but it appears plausible to this writer that these three phenomena, World Wars I and II and the Second Vatican Council, could have had a part to play in the rapid rise in the twentieth century of the universalist stance with regard to the identity of "the least."

The French Sulpician André Feuillet, in his scholarly yet emotional article "Le caractère universel du jugement et la charité sans frontières en Mt 25,31-46,"[33] states with regard to the interpretation of "the least": "C'est, semble-t-il, la majorité des exégètes qui, parfois avec quelques différences, au surplus d'importance secondaire, opte pour l'explication résolument universaliste que nous venons d'esquisser."[34] This study shows that Feuillet's statement has to be qualified. If one takes into consideration the neutral evidence, then Feuillet's statement could be viewed as correct, provided he removes the adverb *résolument*. If the neutral evidence is not taken into consideration, however, then the above statement is false, even if he has only twentieth-century commentators in mind; for this study shows that, prescinding from the neutral evidence, throughout the centuries the combined restrictive interpretation of "the least" (38.68%) is nearly twice that of the universal interpretation (20.58%).

Observations

The primary purpose of this treatise was to present as complete a history as possible of the interpretation of Matt 25:31-46, with special emphasis on vv 32, 35-40, 42-45, in order to determine various currents of thought regarding the interpretation of πάντα τὰ ἔθνη and ἑνὶ τούτων τῶν ἀδελφῶν μου τῶν ἐλαχίστων. That has been accomplished. A secondary objective is to attempt to offer some broad critical assessment of the various interpretations. That attempt will now be made.

The two main exegetical pitfalls encountered in the commentaries of the preceding centuries, in my opinion, are (1) the failure to take into account the parabolic nature of Matt 25:31-46, and (2) the failure to realize that the Matthean judgment scene can be interpreted only in the context of the remainder of the gospel.

Much that had been written about Matt 25:31-46 during the past nineteen and a half centuries was influenced by each individual author's understanding of the passage's literary form. The overwhelming majority of commentators treat the Matthean judgment scene as a bona fide description of the parousia, in spite of the fact that it is immediately preceded by three parables: The Parable of the Watchful and Unwatchful Servants (24:43-51), The Parable of the Ten Virgins (25:1-13), and The Parable of the Silver Pieces (25:14-30). The number of commentators who do treat Matt 25:31-46 as a parable is minuscule in comparison. As was seen, the ninth-century author Paschasius Radbertus was the first to label the Matthean pericope a parable; yet almost five centuries were to elapse before Matt 25:31-46 was again described as a parable by the fourteenth-century theologian Nicholas of Lyra, followed three centuries later by Antoine Furetière. The possibility that the Matthean pericope might not be an actual description of parousiac events, but rather parabolic in nature, was slow in establishing a foothold, even in the modern era. E. Swedenborg is the sole eighteenth-century representative of this viewpoint, while only four[35] nineteenth-century commentators can be included in such a category. The twentieth-century, however, was to experience a drastic change: 105 of the 602 commentators of the present century either view Matt 25:31-46 as a parable or admit that it has strong parabolic elements.[36]

It is the view of the present writer that the failure to take into account seriously the parabolic nature of the Matthean judgment scene has led to many exegetical "derailments" in the history of its interpretation. Commentators insistent upon straddling the pericope with criteria demanded of factual reporting, rather than allowing the passage the flexibility and inconsistency inherent in a parable, often become stuck in the quagmire of interminable and unnecessary discussions about various aspects of its meaning. I will attempt to discuss these exegetical pitfalls in the order of verses.

Verse 32: The main point of the verse is the ease of recognition and the swiftness of separation. In other words, Matthew is comparing the Son of Man's ability to know the true nature of

Conclusions

those gathered before the throne with the facility of a shepherd to tell the difference between a sheep and a goat. While the symbolism of sheep and goats is, I believe, important to Matthew and imparts to the parable an ironic twist (to be discussed below), the countless commentators who exert so much of their literary energy in discussions of why the sheep represent the just and the goats the unjust miss the main thrust of the verse.

Another common error in the interpretation of v 32 is to make too much of the difference in gender between ἔθνη and αὐτούς and to conclude from this that those to be judged are not the same as those who are gathered, or that Matthew has taken a parable that was originally restrictive in nature and expanded it to include everyone. The obvious point of the parable is that those who are gathered are the ones who are separated and judged. To see a difference in the constituency of ἔθνη and αὐτούς because of the difference in gender imposes too strict a grammatical requirement on the parabolic literary form and fails to take into account the poetic license of the storyteller and the flexibility that can be inherent in a parable.[37]

Verses 35-36, 42-43: Those commentators who devote so much of their energies discussing why only six corporal works are mentioned, or whether the works can be taken in an allegorical sense, or who wonder about the fate of those who do not have the psychological or physical wherewithal to perform these corporal works, likewise fail to take into account the parabolic nature of the passage and the strong probability that the works are meant to be symbolic. The main point of the parable is the acceptance or the rejection of the Christian faith. The six corporal works are the parabolic stageprops, as it were, used to convey the primary meaning of the parable: it is not necessary to have personally encountered the preresurrection Jesus or the postresurrection Christ to come to believe in him; he is encountered in "the least," his representatives. In the opinion of this writer, the entire controversy during the Renaissance and Reformation over the issue of works versus faith could have been avoided if Protestant and Catholic writers had properly understood the symbolic nature of the corporal works.

Verses 37-39, 44: These verses are absolutely essential to the parable. The ignorance of the just and the unjust that Christ was present in "the least" is critical to the parable and must be taken at face value. In fact, without these verses vv 40 and 45 would lose much of their climactic impact. Consequently, commentators who use Matt 25:31-46 to prove that charitable works have value only if performed for love of Christ or with the intention of serving Christ miss the crucial point of the pericope: both the just and the unjust did not know they were encountering Christ in "the least." Likewise, those authors who, because of their own scandal over the fact that the saved would not have recognized Christ, try to play down the ignorance and the element of surprise in the response of the just do injustice to the parabolic literary form of Matt 25:31-46. The same is true of those writers who discuss at length why the response of the unjust (v 44) is shorter than that of the just (vv 37-39), or how the fact that both the just and the unjust call Christ "Lord" is to be taken as an indication that only Christians are judged. They likewise fail to take into consideration the fact that a parable, by its very nature, does not have to possess total inner consistency.

Verses 40, 45: The most common exegetical failing with regard to these verses, in my opinion, is the inability of many commentators to realize that "the least" form a distinct category and are not to be included among the sheep or the goats. This, I believe, is clearly indicated by the demonstrative τούτων. Another error made by some commentators is to understand "the least" of v 40 as being a different category than "the least" of v 45. There is no basis for such an understanding; the obvious sense of the pericope is that "the least" in both verses refers to the same category of people.

The second major exegetical pitfall often encountered is the failure on the part of commentators to take seriously the fact that Matt 25:31-46 is part of the unique synoptic tradition. Those guilty of this exegetical "sin" include those who distinguish the Matthean passage from a pre-Matthean pericope and those who interpret Matt 25:31-46 in the light of non-Matthean scriptural texts.

Conclusions

The Matthean judgment scene belongs to Matthew's *Sondergut*; consequently it cannot, in my opinion, be used to prove the existence or nonexistence of a previous account that Matthew might or might not have reworked. Those commentators who theorize whether the parable is authentically from Jesus, or whether it had the same meaning for Jesus as it did for Matthew, or whether Matthew combined two preexistent parables, fail to give serious consideration to the reality that when we deal with *unique* synoptic tradition, any hypothesis of a variant preexistent tradition is precisely that: an hypothesis. Since there are absolutely no external controls by which to judge redactional activity, in such a case it is the firm conviction of this writer that, when dealing with passages from the unique tradition, the presumption must always be in favor of composition by the author. The burden of proof lies with those who would argue otherwise. Commentators who claim that Matthew gives a restrictive interpretation to an account that was originally universal on the lips of Jesus may have clever arguments, but in the final analysis, since there are no external controls, their conclusions have to be placed in the category of conjecture.

Dispensationalist commentators and others who employ non-Matthean scriptural texts to interpret Matt 25:31-46 are likewise guilty of ignoring the fact that the Matthean judgment scene does not have parallels anywhere in the New Testament. If the exegetical principle that a scriptural text is best interpreted in the context of the work in which it is found is valid for synoptic passages in the double and triple tradition, then the need to abide by that principle is even more cogent when dealing with a passage such as Matt 25:31-46, found in the unique tradition. Commentators who refer to universal judgment scenes in the Pauline epistles to buttress their universal interpretation of πάντα τὰ ἔθνη or make use of apocalyptic passages in Revelation to elucidate their understanding of "the least" as Jewish missionaries during a pre-Armageddon period of tribulation, or compare the "identity dialogue" with the list of apostolic hardships in 2 Corinthians 11 to prove that "the least" are Christian missionaries, display a clever ability to argue their own interpretation of Matthean passages forcefully; unfortunately their exegesis sheds no light whatsoever on what Matthew might have had in mind.

In light of the foregoing critical observations, which interpretations of vv 32, 40, and 45 could be considered tenable? Obviously, any serious attempt at an exegesis of the three problem verses must be primarily concerned with the meaning of ἔθνος, ἐλάχιστος (μικρός), and ἀδελφός wherever else they are found in Matthew's Gospel.

Recent studies by D. R. A. Hare and D. J. Harrington[38] and J. P. Meier[39] have thoroughly investigated the fourteen Matthean uses of ἔθνος and have arrived at dissimilar conclusions. Hare and Harrington conclude that in no instance in Matthew's use of πάντα τὰ ἔθνη can it be proven that the phrase includes Israel. Rather, it "designates non-Jewish mankind in its entirety (with or without Gentile Christians)."[40] J. P. Meier, in a rebuttal to their conclusions, just as forcefully argues that in the Matthean vocabulary ἔθνος includes the Jews.[41] In light of the foregoing studies, it would seem then that, of the five various possibilities[42] for the meaning of πάντα τὰ ἔθνη, one could hold any of three positions: (1) τὰ ἔθνη are everyone, Christians and non-Christians, Jews and Gentiles; (2) τὰ ἔθνη include all non-Christians with the exception of the Jews; (3) τὰ ἔθνη include all non-Christians, including the Jews. The two opinions that see πάντα τὰ ἔθνη as Christians only would be exegetically untenable. There is no evidence that Matthew uses the term τὰ ἔθνη as a synonym for Christians, and it would seem inconceivable that he would use the term for Christian leaders. Those who argue from Matt 24:14 that at the parousia all will have been converted to Christianity are reading too much into the verse. It simply states that all will have heard the Gospel; it makes no claim whatsoever that all will have been converted. Those who argue that Christians only will be judged in the presence of all humanity make too much of the discrepancy between ἔθνη and αὐτούς, as I stated above, and fail to take into consideration that those gathered are the same as those judged. To see them as two distinct groups would do violence to the laws of literary logic. Matthew gives us no indication whatsoever that he has a distinct group in mind apart from those gathered. The switch from the neuter plural to the masculine plural would make sense if one took it as an indication of a shift in the author's thought pattern: he first envisions the gathering in a global sense, as units, and then thinks of the mass as individuals. The clinching argument to this writer that the shift from πάντα to αὐτούς in v 32 cannot be used as evidence that two different groups are meant or that Matthew redacted a pre-existent parable is the fact that an identical shift is found at Matt 28:19.

J. Winandy did a study of the Matthean uses of μικρός (Matt 10:42; 11:11; 18:6,10,14) and ἐλάχιστος (Matt 5:19) outside of the judgment scene and convincingly shows that whenever Jesus speaks of "little ones" or "the least," he refers to his disciples.[43] In a similar study of the majority of Matthean uses of ἀδελφός where the term is not used in the sense of a blood relationship (Matt 5:47; 12:49; 18:15; 23:8; 28:10), J.-C. Ingelaere comes to a similarly restrictive conclusion: "it appears that when Matthew uses the word 'brother,' he wishes to designate members of the community of disciples."[44] In view of the foregoing studies it would seem that "the least" of vv 40, 45 have to be Christians, disciples of Christ. Whether they are all Christians or only certain Christians is not readily clear, so that those commentators who maintain that "the least" are Christian missionaries, or Christians weak in faith, or Christians poor in material resources, or only Jewish Christians, might have exegetical support for their position. What is clear from the above studies is that there is hardly support for the view that "the least" are everyone. Likewise, to understand "the least" in the premillennialist sense as post-rapture Jewish missionaries has no support or precedent anywhere else in Matthew.

Regarding the time of the judgment in Matt 25:31-46, only two of the four interpretations[46] merit consideration: Matthew has in mind either the parousia or the destruction of Jerusalem. The concept that Matt 25:31-46 portrays an intermediate judgment after the battle of Armageddon, immediately before the inauguration of a millennial age, has no referent anywhere else in the gospel. Just as much in disharmony with the rest of Matthew is the idea that this judgment is a completely private or individual activity that will occur at each person's death.

It is not the intention of this study to present yet another detailed exegesis of Matt 25:31-46; in reality, another volume would be needed to do justice to such a task. Before bringing this treatise to an end, however, I would like to offer my own brief interpretations of the Matthean pericope as well as suggestions for further research.

It is my belief that Matt 25:31-46 portrays the classic judgment associated with the parousia. Although it could be argued that Matt 24-25 refers to the destruction of the Jewish temple,[47] I am more convinced by the arguments of those who state that in these two chapters Matthew distinguishes between the destruction of the temple and the parousia.[48]

It is also my conviction that "the least" are Christians in general and not any specific group of Christians. The demonstrative τούτων is important, I believe, but its purpose is to set "the least" apart from πάντα τὰ ἔθνη rather than to distinguish τῶν ἐλαχίστων from τῶν ἀδελφῶν.

Since "the least" are the Christians, they cannot be included in the term πάντα τὰ ἔθνη. Consequently, those to be gathered before the throne are non-Christians. I am persuaded by the arguments of those who would see the inclusion of the Jews, since I am convinced that for Matthew those Jews who did not accept the Messiah are considered as part of τὰ ἔθνη since the Church is now ὁ λάος τοῦ θεοῦ, the true Israel.

It is the conviction of this writer that what may be one of the keys to the meaning of Matt 25:31-46 has largely been ignored[49] in the history of its interpretation. I am speaking of the similarities[50] that exist between Matthew and *1 Enoch* and possibly other pre-Matthean Jewish apocalyptic literature.[51] If J.-C. Ingelaere is correct in his assessment that Matthew shared the view, found so often in Jewish intertestamental literature, that on the last day there would be two successive judgments, the first on Israel, and the second on the unbelievers,[52] then perhaps we are afforded another insight into the interpretation of Matt 25:31-46 that seems to have eluded most commentators. Does Matthew, in his magnificent judgment scene, exhibit one more instance of his reversal or replacement technique? I believe he does, but it would take another thesis to prove it. Throughout Matthew there continually surfaces the theme of the replacement of the Jews by the Gentiles. What is expected of or by the Jews is attributed to the Gentiles. Foreshadowings of this technique are found as early as the infancy narrative where the Jews (Herod and his court), whom one would expect to welcome the Messiah, actually reject him in contrast to the acceptance of the Gentile astrologers. It is also foreshadowed in 4:12-16, the account of the Jewish Messiah withdrawing to the more Gentile Galilee area to begin his mission to the Jews![53] The first text that corresponds to this reversal-replacement technique is 11:11 (the least Christian is greater than the best Israel has to offer), followed by 11:20-24 (Gentile cities are more receptive of God's word than Jewish cities),[54] 12:41-42 (the Gentiles at the judgment are cast in a more favorable light than the Jews); 19:30 (the first will be last and the last first); 20:1-16 (the latecomers get equal pay with the original workers);[55] 21:28-32 (the younger son exhibits more obedience than the elder son); 21:33-43 (the original tenants are ousted and new tenants brought in); and 22:1-10 (those by the wayside preempt those originally invited). Could we not continue this pattern one pericope further and see 25:31-46 in a similar light? Those who thought of themselves as the chosen sheep,[56] or believers (and thus expectant of inclusion in the first, or approving, judgment), find themselves classified as goats and unbelievers (included in the second, or condemnatory, judgment). Thus Matt 25:31-46 would be consistent with one of Matthew's main themes: the true sheep, the true Israel, are only those who accept the Messiah sent to Israel. This would mean that Matt 25:31-46, rather than having as its concern the performance of charitable works, would be more concerned with the acceptance of the Christian faith and would thus have an intimate connection with 28:16-20. If this is the case, then Matt 25:40 would be the elucidation of 28:20b.

NOTES TO CHAPTER VI

[1]*De Consumatione Mundi*, a work traditionally ascribed to Hippolytus, sees "the least" as Christians. If this work truly belonged to Hippolytus, it would be the first instance of the narrow interpretation of the "identity dialogue" in the west.

[2]CCL 77. 244.

[3]CCL 79. 89; PL 22. 556.

[4]It is uncertain whether the universalism in the "Clementines" is to be attributed to the anonymous author from the east or to Rufinus who was responsible for their translation and introduction to the west.

[5]Cyril of Alexandria and Philoxenus of Mabbug (ca. AD 440-523) also produced commentaries on the Gospel of Matthew. Cyril restricted his remarks to Matt 25:31 and Philoxenus commented only on vv 14-30 in Matthew 25. See *The 'Matthew-Luke Commentary' of Philoxenus* (SBLDS 43; ed. D. J. Fox; Ann Arbor, MI: Edwards, 1979).

[6]*Hom. in Matt.* 79. 2. PG 58. 718-719.

[7]*Comm. ser.* 70. GCS 38.166.

[8]*Comm. ser.* 73. GCS 38.174.

[9]*Hom. in evang.* 19. 5 (PL 76.1157); *Moralia* 26. 27, 50-51 (PL 76. 378-379).

[10]In all, thirty-nine witnesses from the period known as the Renaissance and Reformation were investigated, but three (the Douai-Rheims NT, Juan Maldonado, and Filippo Picinelli) give no indication whatsoever as to their views on the identity of "the least."

[11]Bernardine of Siena, Erasmus, Antonius Broickwy, Jansen the Elder, Manoel De Sa, Estius, Sebastian Barradas, Francis Luca, Bellarmine, Tirinus, Cornelius a Lapide, Jansen the Younger, John Bourgesius, Menochio, Brenius, the anonymous French Oratorian, Bossuet, and Quesnel. Of these eighteen only Manoel De Sa holds the most restrictive view that "the least" are the apostles and missionaries.

[12]Zwingli, Luther, Calvin, David Pareus, John Piscator, Grotius, Diodati, Joseph Hall, Matthew Poole, Richard Ward, and Samuel Clarke. Of these eleven only Matthew Poole espouses the stricter interpretation that "the least" are the apostles and the missionaries.

¹³Five authors, Manoel De Sa, Giovanni Menochio, Charles de Veil, Giovanni Diodati, and Joseph Hall, give no indication whatsoever as to their viewpoint regarding πάντα τὰ ἔθνη.

¹⁴Bernardine, Tostatus, Denis the Carthusian, Erasmus, Broickwy, Wild, Maldonado, Estius, Luca, Tirinus, Cornelius a Lapide, Jansen the Younger, Bourgesius, Picinelli, Furetiere, Bossuet, and Quesnel.

¹⁵Zwingli, Pareus, Piscator, Hammond, Poole, Ward, and Clarke.

¹⁶Jansen the Elder, the Douai-Rheims NT, Barradas, Bellarmine, and the anonymous French Oratorian.

¹⁷Luther, Calvin, Marloratus, and Grotius.

¹⁸Catholic authors involved in the debate included Wild, the elder Jansen, the authors of the Douai-Rheims NT, Maldonado, Estius, Barradas, Luca, Bellarmine, the younger Jansen, Bourgesius, and de Veil.

¹⁹Zwingli, Luther, Diodati, and Hall are in this category.

²⁰In addition to Calvin, Marloratus and Poole held this position.

²¹Pareus and Ward argued according to this line of thought.

²²John Piscator is the sole witness to this position.

²³Catholics who allegorize the Matthean works include Bernardine of Siena, Denis the Carthusian, the elder Jansen, Maldonado, Barradas, Luca, Tirinus, Cornelius a Lapide, Furetiere and de Veil.

²⁴The only two reformers in this category are the sixteenth-century authors Zwingli and Calvin; it is noticeable that not one of the seventeenth-century Reformers interpreted the works in a non-literal fashion.

²⁵If one includes in this category the works of Swedenborg, as well as those of van den Honert, De Beausobre, and DuHamel, who imply that everyone will be gathered to witness what will be a judgment of Christians only, then nineteen commentators (83%) can be said to hold for the universalist position with regard to πάντα τὰ ἔθνη.

²⁶*Theological Lectures*, 1. 219.

²⁷See the fuller description of this viewpoint on pp. 264-265.

²⁸See the articles "Darby, John Nelson" and "Plymouth Brethren" in *ODCC*, 376, 1104.

²⁹Breen's contemporary, David Pareus, also emphasized that before the return of Christ there would be a period of tribulation, and thus might have contributed as well to the rise of the pre-millenialist interpretation of Matt 25:31-46.

³⁰See p. 265 for a fuller description of this interpretation.

[31] *A Critical and Exegetical Commentary*, 265.

[32] In the decade 1960-69 there is an increase in the universal/neutral stances with no corresponding decrease in the restrictive viewpoint. The slight rise in the restrictive interpretation could be the result of two factors that might have been operative at the end of the decade: the distance in time from World War II and a greater use of the form critical method of exegesis and its insistence that a passage in Matthew can be properly interpreted by comparison only with other passages in Matthew.

[33] *NRT* 102 (1980)179-196.

[34] Ibid., 187.

[35] T. Whittemore, H. Olshausen, J. A. Alexander, and T. Richey.

[36] Those who understand Matt 25:31-46 as a parable or admit parabolic elements in it comprise a mere 17% of the entirety of twentieth-century commentators. They are too numerous to be listed individually.

[37] I agree wholeheartedly with the recent observation of J. Lambrecht (*Once More Astonished*, 213) that " . . . the shepherd-comparison and the King-metaphor do allow us to use the term 'parable' for this text, even if not in the strict sense." This represents a change from his earlier position ("The Parousia Discourse," 329-330) where he states: "One had better not talk of XXV, 31-46 as if it were a parable."

[38] *CBQ* 37 [1975] 359-369.

[39] *CBQ* 39 [1977] 94-102.

[40] *CBQ* 37 (1975) 366.

[41] *CBQ* 39 (1977) 101-102. His most cogent argument is found in his treatment of Matt 21:43 (pp. 97-98) where he convincingly proves that by ἔθνος Matthew means the Church, which in the Matthean Gospel is clearly comprised of Jews and Gentiles.

[42] These five possibilities are: (1) πάντα τὰ ἔθνη = everyone; (2) πάντα τὰ ἔθνη = non-Christians with the exclusion of the Jews; (3) πάντα τὰ ἔθνη = non-Christians with the inclusion of the Jews; (4) πάντα τὰ ἔθνη = all humanity that has been converted to Christianity; and (5) πάντα τὰ ἔθνη = Christian leaders. The view that only Christians will be judged before the gathering of all humanity is included in the first category.

[43] *ScEccl* 18 (1966) 181-183.

[44] *RHPR* 50 (1970) 51-52. His most convincing argument is the comparison of Matt 12:49 and its parallel Mark 3:34. Matthew deliberately inserts the phrase ἐπὶ τοὺς μαθητάς indicating his understanding that the brothers of Jesus are the disciples.

Conclusions 363

45Whether one interprets "the least" to mean all Christians or only certain Christians depends to a large extent on one's understanding of the role of the demonstrative τούτων and the nature of the genitive τῶν ἀδελφῶν μου. If one were to interpret τούτων as a superfluity (J. Jeremias, *Verheißung*, 21) and take τῶν ἀδελφῶν μου as an epexegetical gentive, i.e., in apposition to τῶν ἐλαχίστων, then it could easily be argued that Matthew has in mind all Christians, and is not speaking of a distinct group within the disciples.

46Those interpretations are: (1) Matt 25:31-46 deals with the parousia; (2) Matt 25:31-46 has to do with a pre-millenial judgment after the battle of Armageddon; (3) Matt 25:31-46 treats of the destruction of Jerusalem; and (4) Matt 25:31-46 deals with the particular judgment of each human being at death.

47The arguments for this interpretation usually take Matt 24:34 at face value and see the coming of Christ in Matt 25:31 as the very same coming described in 24:3, 27, 30.

48See J. Lambrecht, "The Parousia Discourse," 318-319. He argues that Matthew, in the rewriting of the Markan material, distinguishes better than his *Vorlage* between the destruction of the temple and the parousia. See also A. Feuillet, *RB* 57 (1950) 180. The theme of a public or general judgment is found frequently in Matthew (5:20, 21, 27; 7:2, 22; 11:22; 12:36; 13:24-30, 39, 49-50).

49The first commentator to consider seriously the connection with *1 Enoch* was C. H. Dodd (*Parables*, 92 n. 2); he said that the literary form of the Matthean judgment pericope is the same as that of the Son of Man passages in *1 Enoch* but was unwilling to admit further connections. J. A. T. Robinson (*NTS* 2 [1955-56] 230) and J. C. Ingelaere (*RHPR* 50 [1970] 28-29) are convinced of a Matthean-Enochian connection; while J. Winandy (*ScEccl* 18 [1966] 181-183) fails to see the need to resort to anything other than Pss 2 and 10 for the idea that the Messiah was constituted judge.

50There are strong thematic connections between Matt 25:31 and such passages as *1 Enoch* 45:3; 51:3; 55:4; 61:8; 62:2-3; and 69:27, 29. An even closer link can be detected between Matt 24:30 and *1 Enoch* 62:5 in the combination of motifs found in Zech 12:10b and Dan 7:13a. J. C. Ingelaere observes (*RHPR* 50 [1970] 29) that the focal point of Matthew's view of the Son of Man is his role as judge, an activity ascribed exclusively to God in Jewish and apocalyptic tradition, with the exception of *1 Enoch* where the Son of Man judges. He admits the possibility of Enochic influence on Matthew, not necessarily in a direct manner, but through the medium of an "archaic Palestinian tradition."

51It seems that the crux of the debate over Enochic influence on the New Testament centers on the dating of the Book of Parables (*1 Enoch* 37-71) where the references to the Son of Man as judge are found. J. T. Milik argues (*The Books of Enoch: Aramaic Fragments of Qumrân Cave 4* [Oxford: Clarendon, 1976] 74, 89-91) that since no manuscript evidence of the Book of Parables was found at Qumrân, it must be a later Christian work based on the New Testament, especially the Gospels, and interpolated by the Christians in place of the Book of Giants, which was found at Qumrân and was thus part of the original Enochic pentateuch. Not all, however, are quick to agree with Milik that the Book of Parables is a Christian composition. J. A. Fitzmyer ("Implications of the New Enoch Literature from Qumrân," *TS* 38 [1977] 332-345, esp. pp. 342-343), seeing the Enochic title Son of Man not as specifically Christian but having its roots in the Old Testament or Palestinian Jewish literature, asks whether the Book of Parables itself might not stem from pre-Christian Palestine. Others who are not so readily convinced by Milik's arguments include M. Black ("The 'Parables of Enoch' [1 En 37-71] and the 'Son of Man'," *ExpTim* 88 [1976-77] 5-8, esp. pp. 6-7) who argues for an Aramaic original behind 1 *Enoch* 65:10 and sees 1 *Enoch* 14 as the basis for the throne vision prophecy of 1 *Enoch* 71; T. F. Glasson ("The Son of Man Imagery: Enoch XIV and Daniel VII," *NTS* 23 [1976-77] 82-90) who claims that the author of Daniel 7 was inspired by 1 *Enoch* 14; J. C. Greenfield and M. E. Stone ("The Enochic Pentateuch and the Date of the Similitudes," *HTR* 70 [1977] 51-65, esp. pp. 60-61) who claim that the final composition of the Similitudes took place at some point during the first century C. E.; and M. A. Knibb ("The Date of the Parables of Enoch: A Critical Review," *NTS* 25 [1978-79] 345-359, esp. pp. 352, 358-359) who likewise argues for a late first-century date and entertains the idea that the composition of the Similitudes was prompted by the events of AD 66-73.

52*RHPR* 50 (1970) 40-41.

53Matthew also ends his Gospel in Galilee (28:16-20).

54Notice that Matt 11:23 contains a curse reminiscent of Isa 14:13-15 that was in the original applied to a pagan king. In Matthew it is directed against a Jewish town.

55Matt 20:1-16 ends with a reversal-replacement logion similar to that found at 19:30.

56The Enochic Book of Dreams (*1 Enoch* 89:10-90:42) shares with the Old Testament the same characteristic of portraying Israel as sheep.

BIBLIOGRAPHY

Abbott, L. *A Popular Commentary on the Gospels according to Matthew and Mark.* New York: Barnes, 1876.
──────. *A Life of Christ.* 2d ed. New York: Harper, 1882.
Aborn, T. L. *The Lectures of St. Matthew.* Milwaukee: Morehouse, 1932.
Achelis, H. *Hippolytstudien.* TU 16/4. Leipzig: Hinrichs, 1897.
Agbanou, V. K. *Le discours eschatologique de Matthieu 24-25: Tradition et rédaction.* EBib ns 2. Paris: Gabalda, 1983.
Albert, T. *Manufacture of Christianity.* Philadelphia: Dorrance, 1946.
Alberti, A. *Il messagio degli evangeli.* Acqua viva 2. Milan: Massimo, 1956.
Albrecht, L. *Das Neue Testament.* Giessen/Basel: Brunnen, 1953.
Albright, W. F., and C. S. Mann. *Matthew.* AB 26. Garden City, NY: Doubleday, 1971.
Alexander, A. *Feathers on the Moor.* London: Allenson, 1927.
Alexander, J. A. *The Gospel according to Matthew.* New York: Scribner, 1861.
Alexandro, N. *Expositio litteralis et moralis sancti Evangelii Jesu Christi secundum Matthaeum.* 2 vols. Venice: Bettinelli, 1782.
Alford, H. *The Greek Testament.* 4 vols. New York: Harper, 1859.
Alleman, H. C. *New Testament Commentary.* Philadelphia: United Lutheran Church in America, 1936.
Allen, W. C. *A Critical and Exegetical Commentary on the Gospel according to St. Matthew.* ICC 22. New York: Scribner, 1907.
Allen, W., R. Bristowe, G. Martin, and T. Worthington. *The New Testament of Jesus Christ.* Rheims: Fogny, 1582.

Allnatt, F. J. *The Witness of St. Matthew.* London: Paul, Trench, 1884.
Almgren, C. *Vem var Jesus?* Johanneshov: Solna, Seelig, 1968.
Altmann, W. "Libertação e justificação Mt 25:31-46." *Perspectiva teologica* 11 (1979) 5-15.
Altaner, B., and A. Stuiber. 9th ed. *Patrologie.* Freiburg: Herder, 1978.
Ambrose of Milan. *De fide.* PL 16.
――――――. *De mysteriis.* SC 25.
――――――. *De officiis ministrorum.* PL 16.
――――――. *De pentitentia.* SC 179.
――――――. *De viduis.* PL 16.
――――――. *Expositio evangelii secundam Lucam.* CCL 14.
――――――. *Letters.* PL 16.
Ambrosiaster. *Ad Corinthios Secunda.* CSEL 81/2.
――――――. *Ad Timotheum prima.* CSEL 81/3.
Amiot, F. *Vie de notre seigneur Jésus-Christ.* Paris: Letouzey & Ané, 1958.
Anastasius Apocrisiarius. *Epistula ad Theodosium.* PG 90.
Anastasius of Sinai. *Questions and Answers.* PG 89.
――――――. *In Hexaemeron.* PG 89.
Andrew of Crete. *Orationes.* PG 79.
Anonymous. *Analyse de l'Evangile selon l'ordre historique de la concorde.* 4 vols. Paris: Rouilland & de Nully, 1694.
――――――. *Ancient Hymn from the Fayûm.* PO 4.
――――――. *Bohairic Life of Pachomius.* CSCO 89; CS 45.
――――――. *De decem virginibus.* PLSup 1.
――――――. *De decem virginibus.* PL 88.
――――――. *Didascalia apostolorum.* CSCO 407.
――――――. *Ecclesiastical Canons of the Twelve Apostles.* TU 2.
――――――. *First Greek Life of Pachomius.* CS 45.
――――――. *Sahidic Life of Pachomius.* CSCO 99; CS 47.
――――――. *Scholia vetera in Matthaeum* 25. PG 106.
――――――. *Sermo de symbolo.* PLSup 4.
Anselm of Laon. *Enarrationes in Evangelium Matthaei.* PL 162.
Antiochus the Monk. *Pandecta scripturae sacrae.* PG 89.

Aphraates. "Demonstrations." *Patrologia Syriaca*. Ed. R. Graffin. 2 vols. Paris: Firmin-Didot, 1894,1907.
Aponius. *Explanatio in Canticum Canticorum*. PLSup 1.
de Araújo, F. *Viver a palavra de Deus*. Petropolis, Brazil: Vozes, 1969.
Argyle, A. W. *The Gospel according to Matthew*. The Cambridge Bible Commentary, New English Bible. Cambridge: University Press, 1963.
Armstrong, E. A. "The Great Assize." *The Gospel Parables*. London: Hodder & Stoughton, 1967. 191-195.
Arnobius the Younger. *Commentarium in Psalmos*. PL 53.
Assemani, J., and E. (eds.) *Sancti Ephraemi opera omnia, graece, syriace, latine*. 6 vols. Rome: Salvioni, 1732-1746.
Asterius of Amasea. *Homilies*. PG 40.
Athanasius of Alexandria. *Expositio in Psalmos*. PG 27.
_____. *Letters*. PG 26; LNPF 4.
_____. *Orationes quatuor contra Arianos*. PG 26.
Atkinson, B. F. "The Gospel according to Matthew." *The New Bible Commentary*. Ed. F. Davidson et al. London: Inter-Varsity Fellowship, 1953. 771-805.
Audoenus of Rouen. *Life of St. Eligius*. PL 87.
Augustijn, C. "Erasmus." *TRE* 10.1-18.
Augsburger, M. S. *Matthew*. The Communicator's Commentary 1. Waco, TX: Word Books, 1982.
Augustine of Hippo. *Contra Faustum*. CSEL 25.
_____. *Contra litteras Petiliani*. CSEL 52.
_____. *De agone christiano*. CSEL 41.
_____. *De baptismo contra Donatistas*. CSEL 51.
_____. *De catechezandis rudibus*. CCL 46.
_____. *De civitate dei*. CSEL 40.
_____. *De consensu evangelistarum*. CSEL 43.
_____. *De fide et operibus*. CSEL 41.
_____. *De fide et symbolo*. CSEL 41.
_____. *De gestis Pelagii*. CSEL 42.
_____. *De natura boni*. CSEL 25.
_____. *De nuptiis et concupiscentia*. CSEL 42.
_____. *De peccatorum meritis et remissione*. CSEL 60.
_____. *De perfectione justitiae hominis*. CSEL 42.

_____. *De sermone Domini in monte.* PL 34.
_____. *De spiritu et littera.* CSEL 60.
_____. *De symbolo ad catechumenos.* CCL 46.
_____. *De trinitate.* CCL 50, 50A.
_____. *Enchiridion.* PL 40.
_____. *Enarrationes in Psalmos.* CCL 38, 39, 40.
_____. *Sermo Lambot.* PLSup 2.
_____. *Sermo Mai.* PLSup 2.
_____. *Sermo Morin.* PLSup 2.
_____. *Sermo Morin Guelferbytanus.* PLSup 2.
_____. *Sermo Wilmart.* PLSup 2.
_____. *Sermons on NT Lessons.* PL 38; SC 116.
_____. *Speculum.* CSEL 12.
_____. *Tractates on John.* CCL 36.
_____. *Tractates on 1 John.* PL 35.
Avitus of Vienne. *Homily.* PLSup 3.
Bacon, B. W. *Studies in Matthew.* New York: Holt, 1930.
Bailey, B. *An Exposition of the Parables of Our Lord.* London: Taylor, 1828.
Baldi, C. *Il Messia del popolo.* Milan: Società Editrice "Vita e Pensiero," 1949.
Ballantine, W. G. *Inductive Studies in the Gospel of Matthew.* Inductive Bible Studies. New York: International Committee of the YMCA, 1900.
Banks, L. A. *Christ's Soul-searching Parables.* New York: Revell, 1925.
Barberiis, B. de. *Glossa in sacram scripturam secundum Bonaventuram.* 4 vols. Lyons: Anissonios, Posuel & Rigaud, 1685.
Barbieri, L. A. "Matthew." *The Bible Knowledge Commentary.* Ed. J. Walvoord and R. Zuck. Wheaton, IL: Victor, 1983. 13-94.
Barclay, W. *The Gospel of Matthew.* 2d ed. 2 vols. The Daily Study Bible Series. Philadelphia: Westminster, 1958.
_____. *Introduction to the First Three Gospels.* Philadelphia: Westminster, 1975.
Barker, G. W., W. L. Lane, and J. R. Michaels. *The New Testament Speaks.* New York: Harper & Row, 1969.

Barker, W. P. *As Matthew Saw the Master*. Westwood, NJ: Revell, 1964.
Barnes, A. *Notes, Explanatory and Practical, on the New Testament*. London: Knight, 1852.
Barnett, A. E. *Understanding the Parables of Our Lord*. Nashville: Cokesbury, 1940.
Barnikol, E. *Das Leben Jesu*. Halle: Niemeyer, 1958.
Barradas, S. *Commentariorum in concordiam et historiam quatuor evangelistarum tomus*. 4 vols. Augsburg/Graz: Veith, 1742.
Barth, G. "Das Gesetzesverständnis des Evangelisten Matthäus." *Überlieferung und Auslegung im Matthäusevangelium*. WMANT 1. Neukirchen-Vluyn: Neukirchner-Verlag, 1960. 54-154.
Barth, K. *Kirchliche Dogmatik*. 3 vols. Zollikon: Verlag der evangelischen Buchhandlung, 1938-1950.
Bartlett, D. L. "An Exegesis of Matthew 25:31-46." *Foundations* 19 (1976) 211-213.
Basil of Ancyra. *De virginitate*. PG 30.
Basil the Great. *Homilia in illud: Destruam*. PG 31.
_____. *Homilies on the Psalms*. PG 29.
_____. *Moralia*. PG 31.
_____. *Regulae brevius tractatae*. PG 31.
_____. *Regulae fusius tractatae*. PG 31.
Basil of Seleucia. *Orationes*. PG 85.
Baumbach, G. "Die Mission im Matthäus-Evangelium." *TLZ* 92 (1967) 889-893.
Baur, C. "Der Kanon des heiligen Johannes Chrysostomos." *TQ* 105 (1924) 258-271.
Beare, F. W. *The Earliest Records of Jesus*. Oxford: Blackwell, 1964.
_____. *The Gospel according to Matthew*. San Francisco: Harper & Row, 1981.
Beausobre, I. de and J. Lenfant. *Le Nouveau Testament de notre Seigneur Jésus-Christ*. 2 vols. Amsterdam: Humbert, 1718.
Bede the Venerable. *De muliere forti*. PL 91.
_____. *Explanatio Apocalypsis*. PL 93.
_____. *Expositio Actuum Apostolorum*. CCL 121.

_____. *Homilies*. CCL 122.
_____. *In Genesim*. CCL 118A.
_____. *In I Samuhelem*. CCL 119.
_____. *In Ezram et Neemiam*. CCL 119A.
_____. *In Psalmorum librum*. PL 93.
_____. *In Canticum Canticorum*. PL 91.
_____. *In Matthaeum*. PL 91.
_____. *In Marcum*. CCL 120.
_____. *In Lucam*. CCL 120.
_____. *In Joannem*. PL 92.
_____. *In Epistolam Jacobi*. CCL 121.
_____. *In Epistolam 1 Petri*. CCL 121.
_____. *In Epistolam 2 Petri*. CCL 121.
_____. *Retractatio in Actus Apostolorum*. CCL 121.
Beelen, J. T. *Het Nieuwe Testament*. 3 vols. Bruges: Beyaert-Storie, 1891.
Bellarmine, R. *Roberti Bellarmini opera omnia*. 6 vols. Naples: Giuliano, 1856-1862.
_____. *Roberti Bellarmini opera omnia: Editio nova iuxta Venetam anni 1721*. 8 vols. Naples: Lauriel, 1872.
Benedict of Nursia. *Regula*. SC 181,182.
Bengel, J. *Gnomon Novi Testamenti*. 3d ed. London: Nutt & Williams & Norgate, 1862.
Benoit, P. (ed.). *L'Evangile selon saint Matthieu*. SBJ 31. Paris: Cerf, 1953.
_____. *Nouveau Testament: Traduction oecuménique de la Bible*. Paris: Cerf, 1984.
Berardino, A. Di (ed.). *Patrology Vol. IV. The Golden Age of Latin Patristic Literature: From the Council of Nicea to the Council of Chalcedon*. Westminster, MD: Christian Classics, 1986.
Bernard, P. R. *Le mystère de Jésus*. 2 vols. Paris: Amiot-Dumont, 1957.
Bert, G. (ed.). "Die Unterweisung von der Unterstützung der Armen." TU 3 (1887) 89-113.
Betz, O. *Was wissen wir von Jesus*. 2d ed. Stuttgart/Berlin: Kreuz, 1967.
Beutler, J. "ἀδελφός." *EWNT* 1.70.

Beyer, H. W. "διακονέω." *TDNT* 2. 81-93.
──────. "ἐπισκέπτομαι." *TDNT* 2. 599-622.
Beyschlag, W. *Neutestamentliche Theologie*. 2 vols. Halle: Strien, 1891-1892.
Bibliia. Moscow: Evangelskich Christian-Baptistov, 1957.
Bibliia. Sofia: Izdava sv. Sinod na bulgarskata tsurkva, 1982.
Bibliorum sacrorum iuxta Vulgatam clementinam. Vatican: Typis polyglottis, 1951.
Bichlmair, G. *Der Mann Jesus*. 4th ed. Vienna: Herder, 1948.
Biser, E. "Das Gericht des Vollenders." *Die Gleichnisse Jesu*. Munich: Kösel, 1965. 145-151.
Bisping, A. *Erklärung des Evangeliums nach Matthäus*. 2d ed. Münster: Aschendorff, 1867.
Black, M. "The 'Parables of Enoch' (1 En 37-71) and the 'Son of Man'," *ExpTim* 88 (1976-77) 5-8.
Blaiklock, E. M. *Commentary on the New Testament*. London: Hodder & Stoughton, 1977.
Blair, E. *Jesus in the Gospel of Matthew*. New York: Abingdon, 1960.
Bligh, P. H. "Eternal Fire, Eternal Punishment, Eternal Life." *ExpTim* 83 (1971-72) 9-11.
Blinzler, J. *Die Brüder und Schwestern Jesu*. 2d ed. SBS 21. Stuttgart: KBW, 1967.
Bloomfield, S. T. *The Greek Testament with English Notes*. 2 vols. Philadelphia: Clark & Hesser, 1854.
Boers, H. *Theology out of the Ghetto. A New Testament Exegetical Study concerning Religious Exclusiveness*. Leiden: Brill, 1971.
Boice, J. M. "Unprofitable Servants and Unprofitable Goats." *The Parables of Jesus*. Chicago: Moody, 1983. 199-207.
Boles, H. L. *A Commentary on the Gospel according to Matthew*. Nashville: Gospel Advocate, 1936.
Bonnard, P. *L'Evangile selon saint Matthieu*. 2d ed. CNT 1. Paris: Delachaux & Niestlé, 1970.
──────. "Matt 25:31-46: Questions de lecture et d'interprétation." *Foi et vie* 76 (1977) 81-87.
Boon, A. *Pachomiana latina*. Louvain: Bureaux de la Revue, 1932.

Booth, C. E. "An Exegesis of Matthew 25:31-46." *Foundations* 19 (1976) 214-215.
Boothroyd, B. "The Gospel according to St. Matthew." *The Holy Bible*. London: Duncan, 1836. 1-41.
Borgnet, S. C. (ed.). *Alberti Magni opera omnia*. 38 vols. Paris: Vivès, 1890-1899.
Bornhäuser, K. "Zur Auslegung von Mt. 25,31-46." *Luthertum* 2 (1935) 77-82.
Bornkamm, G. "Der Auferstandene und der Irdische: Matt 28:16-20." *Überlieferung und Auslegung im Matthäusevangelium*. Ed. G. Bornkamm, G. Barth, and H. J. Held. WMANT 1. Neukirchen-Vluyn: Neukirchener Verlag, 1960. 289-310.
_____. *Jesus von Nazareth*. Stuttgart: Kohlhammer, 1956.
_____. "Matthäus als Interpret der Herrenworte," *TLZ* 79 (1954) 341-346.
_____. "Vorletzter Sonntag im Kirchenjahr Matt 25:31-46," *Göttinger Predigtmeditationen* 9 (1954-55) 257-260.
Bosch, D. *Die Heidenmission in der Zukunftsschau Jesu*. ATANT 36. Zürich: Zwingli, 1959.
Bossuet, J. B. *Oeuvres complètes de Bossuet*. 26 vols. Paris: Gauthier, 1828.
Bourgesius, J. *Historia et harmonia evangelica*. Mons en Hainaut: Waudraei, 1644.
Bover, J. M. *El evangelio de san Mateo*. Biblioteca teologica de Balmesiana 3. Barcelona: Balmes, 1946.
_____. *Vida de nuestro señor Jesucristo*. Barcelona: Borgiana, 1956.
Box, G. H., and W. F. Slater. *Saint Matthew*. NCB 22. New York: Frowde, 1922.
Brandenburger, E. *Das Recht des Weltenrichters*. SBS 99. Stuttgart: KBW, 1980.
Brändle, R. *Mt 25:31-46 im Werk des Johannes Chrysostomos*. BGBE 22. Tübingen: Mohr, 1979.
_____. "Zur Interpretation von Mt 25:31-46 im Matthäuskommentar des Origenes," *TZ* 36 (1980) 17-25.
_____. "Jean Chrysostome—L'importance de Matth. 25,31-46 pur son éthique." *VC* 31 (1977) 47-52.

Brandt, W. "Der Dienst Jesu." *Das diakonische Amt der Kirche.* Ed. H. Krimm. 2d ed. Stuttgart: Evangelisches Verlagswerk, 1965. 15-60.

_____. "Die geringsten Brüder. Aus dem Gespräch der Kirche mit Mt 25, 31-46." *Jahrbuch der theologischen Schule Bethel* 8 (1937) 1-28. Festschrift für F. von Bodelschwingh zum 60. Geburtstag.

Brastberger, I. G. "Predigt am 26. Sonntag nach Trinitatis. Evangelium Matt 25, 31-46." *Evangelische Zeugnisse der Wahrheit.* Stuttgart: Mäntler, 1758. 839-856.

Bratcher, R. G. *A Translator's Guide to the Gospel of Matthew.* Helps for Translators. London/New York: United Bible Societies, 1981.

Braun, H. *Jesus. Der Mann aus Nazareth und seine Zeit.* Themen der Theologie 1. Stuttgart/ Berlin: Kreuz, 1969.

_____. *Spätjüdisch-häretischer und frühchristlicher Radikalismus: Jesus von Nazareth und die essenische Qumransekte.* 2 vols. BHT 24. Tübingen: Mohr, 1969.

Bree, W. T. "Notes on the Gospel according to St. Matthew." *The Plain Reader's Help in the Study of the Holy Scriptures.* 2 vols. Coventry: SPCK, 1822. 2.1-34.

Breech, J. *The Silence of Jesus.* Philadelphia: Fortress, 1983.

Breen, A. E. *A Harmonized Exposition of the Four Gospels.* 4 vols. Rochester, NY: Smith, 1908.

Breen, D. van. *Opera theologica.* Amsterdam: Cuperus, 1666.

Broadus, J. A. *Commentary on the Gospel of Matthew.* An American Commentary on the New Testament 1. Philadelphia: American Baptist Publication Society, 1886.

Broer, I. "Das Gericht des Menschensohnes über die Völker." *BibLeb* 11 (1970) 273-295.

Broickwy, A. *Enarrationes in quatuor evangelia.* Cologne: Quentell, 1539.

Brooks, K. L. *Matthew's Gospel.* Los Angeles: Bible Institute of Los Angeles, 1923.

Broughton, L. G. *Blackboard Lectures on Matthew.* Nashville: Sunday School Board of the Southern Baptist Convention, 1919.

Brouwer, A. M. *De Gelijkenissen.* Leiden: Sijthoff, 1946.

Brown, D. "The Gospel according to St. Matthew." *A Commentary, Critical and Explanatory, on the Old and New Testaments*. 2 vols. Ed. R. Jamieson, A. Fausset, and D. Brown. Hartford: Scranton, 1877. 2.3-64.

Brown, J. *The Students' Comprehensive Topical Bible Commentary*. Toledo, OH: Browning, 1909.

Brown, S. "The Matthean Apocalypse." *JSNT* 4 (1979) 2-27.

Bruce, A. B. *KATA MATΘAION EYAΓΓHΛION*. The Expositor's Greek Testament. 2 vols. London: Hodder & Stoughton, 1897. 1. 61-340.

Bruce, F. F. *Matthew*. Understanding the New Testament. London: Scripture Union, 1978.

_____. "St. Matthew." *Daily Bible Commentary*. 4 vols. Philadelphia: Holman, 1977. 3.10-103.

Bruckberger, R. L. *L'Histoire de Jésus-Christ*. Paris: Grasset, 1965.

Brun, L. *Segen und Fluch im Urchristentum*. Oslo: Dybwad, 1932.

Bruno of Asti. *Commentaria in Matthaeum*. PL 165.

_____. *Homilies*. PL 165.

Büchsel, F. "κρίνω." *TDNT* 3. 921-941.

Bugge, C. A. *Die Hauptparabeln Jesu*. Giessen: Ricker, 1903.

Bullinger, E. W. *A Critical Lexicon and Concordance to the English and Greek New Testament*. Grand Rapids: Zondervan, 1975.

Bultmann, R. *Geschichte der synoptischen Tradition*. Göttingen: Vandenhoeck & Ruprecht, 1957.

Bundy, W. E. *Jesus and the First Three Gospels*. Cambridge, MA: Harvard University, 1955.

Burkitt, F. C. *Jewish and Christian Apocalypses*. London: Milford, 1914.

Burkitt, W. *Expository Notes with Practical Observations on the New Testament of Our Lord and Saviour Jesus Christ*. 6th ed. London: Wyat, 1716.

Burnett, F. W. *The Testament of Jesus-Sophia*. Lanham, MD: University Press of America, 1981.

Burney, C. F. "St. Matthew 25:31-46 as a Hebrew Poem." *JTS* 14 (1912-13) 414-424.

Busa, R. (ed.). *Sancti Thomae Aquinatis opera omnia*. 7 vols. Stuttgart/Bad Cannstatt: Frommann-Holzboog, 1980.
Butler, B. C. "M. Vaganay and the 'Community Discourse'." *NTS* 1 (1954-55) 283-290.
_____. *The Originality of St. Matthew*. Cambridge: University Press, 1951.
Butler, J. G. *The Bible Readers' Commentary*. 2 vols. New York: Appleton, 1878.
Buttrick, G. A. *The Parables of Jesus*. Garden City, NY: Doubleday, 1928.
Buytaert, E. M. (ed.). *Eusèbe d'Emèse: Discours conservés en latin*. 2 vols. Louvain: Bureaux de la Revue, 1953, 1957.
Buzy, D. *Jésus comme il était*. Paris: Editions de l'Ecole, 1964.
Cadoux, A. T. "The Parable of the Sheep and the Goats." *ExpTim* 41 (1929-30) 559-562.
_____. *The Parables of Jesus*. London: Clarke, 1930.
Caesarius of Arles. *Fragmenta*. PLSup 4.
_____. *Letters*. PL 67.
_____. *Sermons*. CCL 103, 104.
_____. *Testament*. PL 67.
Caine, H. *Life of Christ*. New York: Doubleday, Doran, 1938.
Callan, C. J. *The Four Gospels*. New York: Wagner, 1917.
Callinicus. *Vita sancti Hypatii*. SC 177.
Campbell, D. B. J. *The Synoptic Gospels*. New York: Seabury, 1969.
Calmet, A. *Commentaire littéral sur tous les livres de l'ancien et du nouveau testament*. 8 vols. Paris: Emery, Saugrain, & Martin, 1726.
Calvin, J. *In Novum Testamentum commentarii*. 7 vols. Berlin: Eichler, 1833.
Canévet, M. "Le 'De instituto christiano': est-il de Grégoire de Nysse? Problèmes de critique interne." *Revue des études grecques* 82 (1969) 404-423.
Cargill, R. L. *All the Parables of Jesus*. Nashville: Broadman, 1970.
Carlston, C. E. "Interpreting the Gospel of Matthew." *Int* 29 (1975) 3-12.

Carr, A. *The Gospel according to St. Matthew.* The Cambridge Bible for Schools and Colleges 33. Cambridge: University Press, 1898.

Carr, W. G. *The Gospel of the Kingdom by Matthew.* Rochester, NY: Genesee, 1896.

Carreyre, J. "Quesnel et le quesnellisme." *DTC* 13/2. 1460-1535.

Carrières, P. D. (ed.). *La Sainte Bible.* 6 vols. Paris: Gaume, 1856.

Carroll, P. J. *The Man-God.* Chicago: Scott, Foresman, 1927.

Carson, D. A. "Matthew." *The Expositor's Bible Commentary.* 12 vols. Ed. F. E. Gaebelein and J. D. Douglas. Grand Rapids: Zondervan, 1984. 8. 3-599.

Cartier, G. *Biblia sacra vulgatae editionis.* 2d ed. 4 vols. Constance: Bez, 1763.

Cassiodorus. *Expositio Psalmorum.* CCL 97, 98.

Castoldi, G. (ed.). *La Sacra Bibbia.* 3d ed. Florence: Libreria Editrice Fiorentina, 1934.

Catchpole, D. R. "The Poor on Earth and the Son of Man in Heaven. A Re-appraisal of Matthew 25:31-46." *BJRL* 61 (1978-79) 355-397.

Catholic Biblical Association, The. *A Commentary on the New Testament.* Washington, DC: CBA, 1942.

Cerfaux, L. "La charité fraternelle et le retour du Christ." *Recueil Lucien Cerfaux.* 3 vols. Gembloux: Duculot, 1954-62. 2. 27-40.

Ceulemans, F. C. *Commentarius in Evangelium secundum Matthaeum.* 3d ed. Mechelen-lez-Deinze: Dessain, 1928.

Chapman, J. *Matthew, Mark and Luke.* London: Longmans, Green, 1937.

Chevallier, M. "Note à propos de l'exégèse de Mt 25:31-46." *RevScRel* 48 (1974) 398-400.

Chitty, D. J. "Varsanuphius and John: Questions and Answers." *PO* 31 (1966) 449-616.

Chouraqui, A. (ed.). "Matyah-Matthieu." *L'Univers de la Bible.* 8 vols. Paris: Lidis, 1985. 8.33-159.

Christian Druthmar. *Expositio in Matthaeum.* PL 106.

Christian, P. *Jesus und seine geringsten Brüder.* Erfurter theologische Schriften 12. Leipzig: St. Benno, 1975.

Chromatius of Aquilea. *Tractatus*. CCL 9A.
Cladder, H. J. *In the Fulness of Time*. St. Louis: Herder, 1925.
Clark, G. W. *Notes on the Gospel of Matthew*. New York: Sheldon, 1870.
Clark, J. H. "The Judgment of the World." *Our Lord's Prophecy*. Claremont, NH: Clark, 1874. 122-134.
Clark, K. W. "The Gentile Bias in Matthew." *JBL* 66 (1947) 165-172.
Clarke, A. "The Gospel according to St. Matthew." *The New Testament of Our Lord and Saviour Jesus Christ*. 2 vols. New York: Waugh & Mason, 1834. 1. 23-266.
Clarke, S. "Matthew." *A Survey of the Bible*. London: Robinson, 1693. 3-40.
Clarke, W. K. "The Gospel according to St. Matthew." *Concise Bible Commentary*. London: SPCK, 1952. 723-744.
Clement of Alexandria. *Excerpta ex Theodoto*. GCS 17/2.
_____. *Protrepticus*. GCS 12.
_____. *Paedagogus*. GCS 12.
_____. *Quis Dives Salvetur?* GCS 17/2.
_____. *Stromata*. GCS 15, 17/2.
Clowes, J. *The Gospel according to Matthew*. London: Hodson, 1819.
Clymer, R. S. *The Interpretation of St. Matthew*. 2 vols. Quakertown, PA: Philosophical Publishing, 1945.
Cobb, S. *The New Testament of Our Lord and Saviour Jesus Christ with Explanatory Notes and Practical Observations*. Boston: The Commentator, 1864.
Cobbin, I. "The Gospel according to St. Matthew." *Commentary on the Bible*. 2 vols. New York: Hess, 1876. 583-669.
Committee of the Oxford Society of Historical Theology. *The New Testament in the Apostolic Fathers*. Oxford: Clarendon, 1905.
Commodianus. *Carmen de duobus populis*. CCL 128.
_____. *Instructiones*. CCL 128.
Conzelmann, H. *Grundriss der Theologie des Neuen Testaments*. Munich: Kaiser, 1967.

Cooke, H. "The Gospel according to Saint Matthew." *The Self-Interpreting Bible*. 4 vols. St. Louis: Thompson, 1905. 4. 47-110.
Cooper, D. L. "The Judgment of the Living Nations and the Establishment of the Kingdom of God." *Future Events Revealed*. Los Angeles: Cooper, 1935. 157-204.
Cope, L. "Matt 25:31-46. The Sheep and the Goats Reinterpreted." *NovT* 11 (1969) 32-44.
_____. *Matthew: A Scribe Trained for the Kingdom of Heaven*. CBQMS 5. Washington, DC: CBA, 1976.
Cornwallis, M. "The Gospel according to St. Matthew." *Observations, Critical, Explanatory, and Practical, on the Canonical Scriptures*. 4 vols. London: Baldwin, Cradock & Joy, 1820. 4.1-109.
Corwin, V. *Saint Ignatius and Christianity in Antioch*. New Haven: Yale University, 1960.
Council of Mâcon. *Canon 11*. CCL 148A.
Cowles, H. *Matthew and Mark*. New York: Appleton, 1881.
Cox, G. E. P. *The Gospel according to St. Matthew*. 2d ed. Torch Bible Commentaries. London: SCM, 1958.
Cox, R. *The Gospel Story*. New York: Sheed & Ward, 1944.
Craghan, J. F. "Christ the King." *Yesterday's Word Today*. Collegeville, MN: Liturgical Press, 1982. 158-160.
Cranenburgh, H. van. *La vie latine de Saint Pachome*. Subsidia hagiographica 46. Brussels: Société des Bollandistes, 1969.
Cranfield, C. E. B. "Diakonia." *London Quarterly and Holborn Review* 186 (1961) 275-281.
_____. *The Service of God*. London: Epworth, 1965.
Crean, P. J. *A Short Life of Our Lord*. Scripture Textbooks for Catholic Schools 1. London: Burns, Oates & Washbourne, 1945.
Cremers, H. *Biblisch-Theologisches Wörterbuch des neutestamentlichen Griechisch*. 11th ed. Stuttgart/Gotha: Perthes, 1923.
Criswell, W. *Expository Notes on the Gospel of Matthew*. Grand Rapids: Zondervan, 1961.
Crosby, H. "The Gospel according to St. Matthew." *The New Testament*. Boston: Allen, 1884. 1-80.

Cross, F. L., and E. A. Livingstone (eds.). *The Oxford Dictionary of the Christian Church*. 2d ed. London: Oxford University, 1974.
Cullmann, O. *Die Christologie des Neuen Testamnets*. 3d ed. Tübingen: Mohr, 1963.
Curci, C. M. *Il santo evangelo secondo Matteo*. Il Nuovo Testamento 1. Turin: Fratelli Bocca, 1879.
Curran, C. A. "Feast of Christ the King." *The Word Becomes Flesh*. 26 vols. Apple River, IL: Counseling-Learning Institutes, 1975. 6. 81-84.
Curtis, W. A. *Jesus Christ the Teacher*. London: Oxford University, 1945.
Cyprian of Carthage. *De dominica oratione*. CCL 3A.
―――――. *De lapsis*. CCL 3.
―――――. *De opere et eleemoysnis*. CCL 3A.
―――――. *De zelo et livore*. CCL 3A.
―――――. *Letter 60*. PL 4.
―――――. *Testimonia ad Quirinum*. CCL 3.
Cyril of Alexandria. *Commentary on Isaiah*. PG 70.
―――――. *Commentary on the Song of Songs*. PG 69.
―――――. *Contra Julianum*. PG 76.
―――――. *De adoratione*. PG 68.
―――――. *De recta fide ad Reginas*. PG 76.
―――――. *Explanatio in Psalmos*. PG 69.
―――――. *Glaphyrorum in Genesim*. PG 69.
―――――. *Homiliae diversae*. PG 77.
―――――. *Homiliae paschales*. PG 77.
―――――. *Letters*. PG 77.
―――――. *Quod Beata Virgo Maria sit Deipara*. PG 76.
―――――. *Quod unus sit Christus*. SC 97.
―――――. *Thesaurus*. PG 75.
Cyril of Jerusalem. *Catecheses*. PG 33.
Dahl, N. A. "Nations in the New Tetsament." *New Testament Christianity for Africa and the World. Essays in honour of Harry Sawyerr*. Ed. M. E. Glasswell and E. W. Fasholé-Luke. London: SPCK, 1974. 54-68.
Dallmann, W. "The Sheep and the Goats." *Short Stories by Jesus*. St. Louis: Concordia, 1943. 215-219.

Dambricourt, G. *Matthieu.* Toulouse: Privat, 1977.
Daniel-Rops, H. *Brève histoire du Christ-Jésus.* Paris: Fayard, 1964.
_____. *Jésus en son temps.* Paris: Fayard, 1945.
Darby, J. N. "Matthew." *Synopsis of the Books of the Bible.* 5 vols. New York: Loizeaux, 1942. 3. 29-209.
Dardel, S. de. *L'Identification du Christ avec les pauvres. Etude exégétique sur Mt 25, 31-46.* Dissertation. Lausanne, 1957.
Daumoser, I. *Berufung und Erwählung bei den Synoptikern.* Stuttgart: KBW, 1954.
Dausch, P. *Die drei älteren Evangelien.* Die Heilige Schrift des Neuen Testaments 1. Bonn: P. Hanstein, 1923.
Davies, J. N. "Matthew." *The Abingdon Bible Commentary.* Ed. F. Eiselen, E. Lewis, and D. Downey. New York: Abingdon, 1929. 953-995.
Davies, W. D. *The Setting of the Sermon on the Mount.* Cambridge: University Press, 1964.
Davis, W. H. *Davis' Notes on Matthew.* Nashville: Broadman, 1962.
Dean, J. *The Gospel according to Saint Matthew.* Westminster Version of the Sacred Scriptures, NT 1. London: Longmans, Green, 1928.
Deever, P. O. *Lending the Parables Our Ears.* Nashville: Tidings, 1975.
DeHoff, G. W. "The Gospel according to Saint Matthew." *Matthew—Acts.* DeHoff's Commentary 5. Murfreesboro, TN: DeHoff, 1981. 27-129.
Dekkers, E. *Clavis patrum latinorum.* Sacris erudiri 3. 2d ed. Steenbrugge: Abbatia S. Petri, 1961.
De Kruijf, T. *Der Sohn des lebendigen Gottes.* AnBib 16. Rome: Biblical Institute, 1962.
Del Paramo, S., and J. Alonso (eds.). *La Sagrada Escritura.* BAC, NT 1. 3rd ed. Madrid: Editorial católica, 1973.
Deries, J. *Les Evangiles.* 3 vols. Paris: Spes, 1944.
Descamps, A. "Les chrétiens dans le cadre du jugement sur les oeuvres." *Les justes et la justice dans l'évangiles et le christianisme primitif.* Universitas catholica lovaniensis.

Dissertationes ad gradum magistri in facultate theologica vel in facultate iuris canonici consequendum conscriptae 2/43; Louvain: Publications universitaires de Louvain, 1950. 250-269.

Dheilly, J. "The Gospel according to Matthew." *The New Testament*. 2 vols. Boston: Daughters of St. Paul, 1975. 1.7-92.

Diaz, J. A. "Sentido del 'judicio final' de Yahve en la apocalíptica y en Mt 25."*Studium Ovetense* 5 (1977) 77-98.

Didon, H. *Jesus Christ*. New York: Appleton, 1891.

Didymus the Blind. *In Zachariam*. SC 83, 84.

_____. *On the Trinity*. PG 39.

Dieterle, C. "A propos de la prédication synoptique sur les petits." *Le Semeur* 61 (1966) 55-72.

_____. *Les petits et les enfants dans les évangiles synoptiques*. Dissertation. Lausanne, 1965.

Dietrich, S. de. *The Gospel according to Matthew*. The Layman's Bible Commentary 16. Richmond: Knox, 1961.

Dillemore, F. W., et al. (eds.). "The Gospel according to Matthew." *Westminster Study Bible*. New York/Glasgow: Collins, 1965. 23-65.

Dillersberger, J. *Matthäus*. 6 vols. Salzburg: Müller, 1952-54.

Dimmler, E. *Das Evangelium nach Matthäus*. München/Gladbach: Volksvereins, 1911.

Diodati, G. *Pious Annotations upon the Holy Bible*. London: Fussell, 1643.

Dionysius Bar Salibi. *Comentarii in Evangelia*. CSCO 95.

Dodd., C. H. "Matthew and Paul." *ExpTim* 58 (1946-47) 293-298.

_____. *New Testament Studies*. Manchester: Manchester University, 1953.

_____. *The Parables of the Kingdom*. London: Nisbet, 1935.

Doddridge, P. *The Family Expositor: A Paraphrase and Version of the New Testament with Critical Notes*. Amherst, MA: Adams & Boltwood, 1837.

Doerne, M. *Er kommt auch noch heute: Homiletische Auslegung der alten Evangelien*. 4th ed. Göttingen: Vandenhoeck & Ruprecht, 1956.

Donahue, J. R. "The 'Parable' of the Sheep and the Goats: A Challenge to Christian Ethics." *TS* 47 (1986) 3-31.

Donatus of Besançon. *Regula ad virgines*. PL 87.

Doorly, J. W. "Eighth Talk on Matthew." *Talks at Oxford Summer School 1948*. 2 vols. London: Foundational Book, 1948. 2.101-116.

──────── . "Fifth Talk on Matthew." *Talks at Oxford Summer School 1949*. 2 vols. London: Foundational Book, 1950. 1.121-140.

Drummond, D. T. *The Engravings of the New Testament*. Edinburgh: Kennedy, 1855.

Drury, J. *The Parables in the Gospels*. New York: Crossroad, 1985.

DuHamel, J. B. *Biblia sacra vulgatae editionis*. Paris: DeLespine, 1705.

Dummelow, J. R. (ed.). "St. Matthew." *A Commentary on the Holy Bible*. New York: Macmillan, 1908. 617-721.

Duncan, G. S. *Jesus, Son of Man*. New York: Macmillan, 1948.

Dupont, J. "L'Eglise et la pauvrété." *L'Eglise de Vatican II*. Paris: Cerf, 1966, 313-345.

Duprez, A. "Le jugement dernier." *AsSeign* (2d ser.) 65 (1973) 17-28.

Durand, A. *Evangile selon saint Matthieu*. VS 1. Paris: Beauchesne, 1948.

Eakin, F. *Bible Study for Grownups*. New York: Macmillan, 1956.

Earle, F. *Matthew, Mark, Luke*. Beacon Bible Commentary 6. Kansas City, MO: Beacon Hill, 1964.

Earle, R. "The Gospel according to St. Matthew." *Matthew—Acts*. The Wesleyan Bible Commentary 4. Grand Rapids: Eerdmans, 1964. 5-125.

──────── . "Matthew." *The New International Version Study Bible*. Ed. K. Barker. Grand Rapids: Zondervan, 1985. 1439-1489.

Edwards, R. *Matthew's Story of Jesus*. Philadelphia: Fortress, 1985.

Eligius of Noyon. *Homilies*. PL 87.

Ellicott, C. J. "Matthew." *Ellicott's Bible Commentary in One Volume.* Ed. D. Bowdle. Grand Rapids: Zondervan, 1971. 681-757.

Elliott, W. *The Life of Jesus Christ.* New York: Catholic Book Exchange, 1902.

Ellis, P. F. *Matthew: His Mind and His Message.* Collegeville, MN: Liturgical Press, 1974.

Ellison, H. L. "The Gospel according to Matthew." *A New Testament Commentary.* Ed. G. C. Howley. Grand Rapids: Zondervan, 1969. 141-176.

Ellul, J. "Le pauvre." *Foi et Vie* 49 (1951) 105-127.

English, E. S. *A Companion to the New Scofield Reference Bible.* New York: Oxford University, 1972.

_____. *Studies in the Gospel according to Matthew.* New York: Revell, 1935.

Ephraem of Nisibis. *Commentary on the Gospel.* SC 121.

Epiphanius. *Panarion.* PG 41.

Epiphanius Latinus. *Interpretatio evangeliorum.* PLSup 3.

Erasmus, Desiderius. *Desiderii Erasmi Roterodami opera omnia.* 10 vols. Hildesheim: Olms, 1962.

_____. *Tomus primus paraphraseon D. Erasmi Roterodami in Novum Testamentum.* Basel: Froben, 1524.

Erdman, C. R. *The Gospel of Matthew.* Philadelphia: Westminster, 1966.

Erikson, A. *Sancti Epiphanii episcopi interpretatio evangeliorum.* Lund: Gleerup, 1939.

Est, W. H. van. *Annotationes in praecipua ac difficiliora sacrae scripturae loca.* Douai: Patté, 1629.

Eugippius. *Life of St. Severin.* PL 62.

_____. *Thesaurus Augustinianus.* CSEL 9.

Eusebius of Caesarea. *Commentary on the Psalms.* PG 23.

_____. *Commentary on Isaiah.* PG 24.

_____. *Commentary on Daniel.* PG 24.

_____. *De ecclesiastica theologia.* PG 24.

_____. *Demonstratio evangelica.* GCS 23.

Eusebius of Emesa. *De fide adversus Sabellium.* PG 24.

Euthymius Zigabenus. *Commentarium in Matthaeum.* PG 129.

Evangelie: Novyi Zavet i psaltir. Washington, DC: The Russian Bible Society, 1958.

Evely, L. "Le jugement dernier." *Méditations d'évangiles.* Paris: Editions universitaires, 1973.

Exell, J. S. *The Biblical Illustrator.* 8 vols. New York: Randolf, 1880.

Farmer, H. H. "The Last Judgment." *The Healing Cross.* London: Nisbet, 1938. 160-168.

Farrar, F. W. *The Life of Christ.* 2 vols. New York: Crowell, 1874.

_____. *Texts Explained.* New York: Dodd, Mead, 1899.

Faustus of Riez. *De revelatione corporis beati Stephani.* CCL 101B.

_____. *De spiritu sancto.* CSEL 21.

_____. *Epistles.* CSEL 21.

_____. *Homilies.* CCL 101A.

_____. *Sermons.* CSEL 21.

Fendt, L. *Die alten Perikopen für die theologische Praxis erläutert.* HNT 22. Tübingen: Mohr, 1931.

Fenton, J. C. *The Gospel of Saint Matthew.* The Pelican Gospel Commentaries. Baltimore: Penguin, 1963.

Fernández Truyols, A. *Vida de nuestro Señor Jesucristo.* BAC 32. Madrid: Editorial católica, 1948.

Feuillet, A. "Le caractère universel du jugement et la charité sans frontiers en Mt 25:31-46." *NRT* 102 (1980) 179-196.

_____. "La synthèse eschatologique de saint Matthieu XXIV-XXV." *RB* 56 (1949) 340-364; 57 (1950) 62-91; 180-211.

Fillion, L. C. (ed.) *La Sainte Bible.* 3d ed. 8 vols. Paris: Letouzey & Ané, 1903.

_____. *Vie de notre Seigneur Jésus-Christ.* 3 vols. Paris: Letouzey & Ané, 1922.

Filson, F. V. *A Commentary on the Gospel according to St. Matthew.* Black's New Testament Commentaries 1. London: Black, 1960.

Findley, J. A. *Jesus in the First Gospel.* London: Hodder & Stoughton, 1925.

Firmicus Maternus. *Consultationes.* PL 20.

Firmilian of Caesarea in Cappadocia. *Letter 75.* CSEL 3/2.

Fitzmyer, J. A. "Implications of the New Enoch Literature from Qumran." *TS* 38 (1977) 332-345.
Ford, W. H. *Simple Sermons from the Gospel of Matthew.* Grand Rapids: Zondervan, 1963.
Fouard, C. *La vie de notre Seigneur Jésus-Christ.* 2 vols. Paris: Lecoffre, 1880.
Fox, D. J. (ed.). *The Matthew-Luke Commentary of Philoxenus.* SBLDS 43. Ann Arbor: Edwards Brothers, 1979.
Frankemölle, H. *Jahwebund und Kirche Christi. Studien zur Form -und Traditionsgeschichte des "Evangeliums" nach Matthäus.* NTAbh ns 10. Münster: Aschendorff, 1974.
_____. "Amtskritik im Matthäusevangelium?" *Bib* 54 (1973) 247-262.
Franzmann, M. H. *Follow Me: Discipleship according to Saint Matthew.* St. Louis: Concordia, 1961.
Freyne, S. *The Twelve: Disciples and Apostles. A Study in the Theology of the first Three Gospels.* London: Sydney, Sheed & Ward, 1968.
_____, and H. Wansbrough. *Mark and Matthew.* Scripture Discussion Commentary 7. Chicago: Acta Foundation, 1971.
Friedrich, J. *Gott im Brüder? Eine methodenkritische Untersuchung von Redaktion,Uberlieferung und Traditionen in Mt 25:31-46.* Calwer theologische Monographien 7. Stuttgart: Calwer, 1977.
Froehlich, K., H. C. Kee, and F. W. Young. *Understanding the New Testament.* 2d ed. Englewood Cliffs: Prentice-Hall, 1965.
Fructuosus of Braga. *Regula monastica communis.* PL 87.
Fuchs, E. *Zur Frage nach den historischen Jesus.* Gesammelte Aufsätze 2. Tübingen: Mohr, 1960.
Fulgentius of Ruspe. *Ad Monimum.* CCL 91.
_____. *Ad Trasamundum.* CCL 91.
_____. *De fide.* CCL 91A.
_____. *De remissione peccatorum.* CCL 91A.
_____. *De veritate praedestinationis.* CCL 91A.
_____. *Epistulae.* CCL 91, 91A.
Funk, F. X. *Patres Apostolici.* 2 vols. Tübingen: Laupp, 1881.

Furnish, V. *The Love Command in the New Testament.* Nashville: Abingdon, 1972.

Furetière, A. "Parabole du jugement final." *Les paraboles de l'évangile.* Paris: Le Petit, 1672. 280-300.

Gaebelein, A. C. *The Gospel of Matthew.* Bible Study Course 9. New York: Our Hope, 1914.

_____. *The Gospels and the Book of Acts.* The Annotated Bible 4. New York: Our Hope, 1913.

Gaechter, P. *Die literarische Kunst im Matthäus-Evangelium.* SBS 7. Stuttgart: KBW, 1965.

_____. *Das Matthäus Evangelium.* Innsbruck: Tyrolia, 1964.

Gähler, W. "Wer sind die geringsten Brüder?" *Die Christenlehre* 23 (1970) 3-16; 35-43.

Galeota, G. "Roberto Bellarmini." *TRE* 5. 525-531.

Gander, G. *L'Evangile de l'église: commentaire de l'évangile selon Matthieu.* Etudes évangéliques 1-4. Geneva: Labor et Fides, 1967-70.

Garcia, T. *Praelectiones exegeticae de Novo Testamento.* 2 vols. Rome: Lateran University, 1956.

Gaston, L. "The Messiah of Israel as Teacher of the Gentiles." *Interpreting the Gospels.* Ed. J. L. Mays. Philadelphia: Fortress, 1981.

Gaudentius of Brescia. *Tractatus.* CSEL 68.

Gay, G. "The Judgment of the Gentiles in Matthew's Theology." *Scripture, Tradition, and Interpretation.* Ed. W. Gasque and W. LaSor. Grand Rapids: Eerdmans, 1978.

Geerard, M. *Clavis patrum graecorum.* 4 vols. Turnhout: Brépols, 1983.

Geist, H. "Jesusverkündigung im Matthäusevangelium." *Jesus in den Evangelien.* SBS 45. Stuttgart: KBW, 1970. 105-126.

Gennadius of Constantinople. *Commentary on Genesis.* PG 85.

Géoltrain, P. "Notes sur Matthieu 24-25." *Foi et vie* 5 (1967) 26-35.

Germanus of Constantinople. *In dominici corporis sepulturam.* PG 98.

_____. *Orationes.* PG 97.

_____. *Triodia majoris hebdomadis.* PG 97.

Gewalt, D. "Matthäus 25:31-46 im Erwartungshorizont heutiger Exegese." *LB* 3 (1973) 9-21.
Gibson, J. M. *The Gospel of St. Matthew.* The Expositor's Bible 29. London: Hodder & Stoughton, 1896.
Gignac, F. T. *A Grammar of the Greek Papyri of the Roman and Byzantine Periods.* 2 vols. Milan: Cisalpino, 1976, 1981.
Giordani, I. *Christ, Hope of the World.* Boston: St. Paul Editions, 1964.
Glasson, T. F. *The Second Advent: The Origins of the New Testament Doctrine.* 3d ed. London: Epworth, 1963.
_____. "The Son of Man Imagery: Enoch XIV and Daniel VII." *NTS* 23 (1976-77) 82-90.
Gnilka, J. "Die Kirche des Matthäus und die Gemeinde von Qumran." *BZ* ns 7 (1963) 43-63.
Godbey, W. B. *Commentary on the New Testament.* 7 vols. Cincinnati, OH: Knapp, 1896-1900.
Goebel, S. *Die Parabeln Jesu methodisch ausgelegt.* 2 vols. Gütersloh: Bertelsmann, 1879-80.
Goma Civit, I. *El evangelio según san Mateo.* 2 vols. Comentario al Nuevo Testamento 3. Colectanea san Paciano 22. Madrid: Marova, 1976.
Gonzaga, M. *Christ in the Old and the New Testament.* St. Louis: Herder, 1928.
Good, C. M. "The Parable of the Last Judgment." *The Parables of Jesus.* Boston: Christopher Publishing, 1961. 138-141.
Goodspeed, E. J. *Matthew: Apostle and Evangelist.* Philadelphia: Winston, 1959.
Goppelt, L. "Die Herrschaft Christi und die Welt." *Christologie und Ethik: Aufsätze zum Neuen Testament.* Göttingen: Vandenhoeck & Ruprecht, 1968. 102-136.
_____. "Leben für die Barmherzigen. Mt 25, 31-46: Vorletzter Sonntag des Kirchenjahres." *Calwer Predigthilfen* 11 (1972) 221-228.
_____. "πεινάω (λιμός)." *TDNT* 6.12-22.
Gordon, E. B. *Notes from a Layman's Greek Testament.* Boston: Wilde, 1941.

Gossner, J. *Die heiligen Schriften des Neuen Testamentes*. 8 vols. Hamburg: Evangelischen Buchhandlung der Niedersächsischen Gesellschaft, 1888-94.

Goudge, H. L. and P. P. Levertoff. "The Gospel according to St. Matthew." *A New Commentary on Holy Scripture*. 3 vols. Ed. C. Gore, H. L. Goudge, and A. Guillaume. New York: Macmillan, 1928. 3. 124-205.

Goulder, M. D. *Midrash and Lection in Matthew*. London: SPCK, 1974.

Graffmann, H. "Das Gericht nach den Wirken im Matthäusevangelium." *Theologische Aufsätze*. Ed. E. Wolf. Munich: Kaiser, 1936. 124-135.

Granskou, D. "The Parable of the Last Judgment." *Preaching on the Parables*. The Preacher's Paperback Library. Philadelphia: Fortress, 1972. 124-127.

Grant, F. C. *The Gospel of Matthew*. Harper's Annotated Bible Series 10-11. New York: Harper, 1955.

_____. "The Gospel according to Matthew." *The New Testament: The Gospels and the Acts of the Apostles*. Nelson's Bible Commentary 6. New York: Nelson, 1962. 24-136.

Grant, F. W. "Matthew." *The Numerical Bible*. 6 vols. New York: Loizeaux, 1899. 4.39-272.

Grant, R. *The Formation of the New Testament*. New York: Harper & Row, 1965.

Grass, H. *Ostergeschehen und Osterberichte*. 2d ed. Göttingen: Vandenhoeck & Ruprecht, 1962.

Grassi, J. A. "I Was Hungry and You Gave Me to Eat." *BTB* 11 (1981) 81-84.

Gray, J. C. *Matthew and Mark*. The Biblical Encyclopedia and Museum 11. Cleveland: Barton, 1900.

Gray, J. M. "Matthew." *Christian Workers' Commentary on the Old and New Testaments*. New York: Revell, 1915. 293-313.

Green, F. W. *The Gospel according to Saint Matthew*. The Clarendon Bible 7. Oxford: Clarendon, 1936.

Green, H. B. *The Gospel according to Matthew*. The New Clarendon Bible, NT 1. Oxford: University Press, 1975.

Greenfield, J. C. and M. E. Stone. "The Enochic Pentateuch and the Date of the Similitudes." *HTR* 70 (1977) 51-65.
Greenhill, R. *The Gospel according to Matthew*. The Born-Again Bible 1. Atlanta: Benjamin, 1978.
Gregory of Agrigentum. *Explanatio super Ecclesiasten*. PG 98.
Gregory the Great. *Book of the Morals*. CCL 143; SC 212, 221; PL 76.
_____. *Book of Pastoral Rule*. PL 77.
_____. *Dialogues*. PL 77.
_____. *Epistles*. CCL 140A.
_____. *In librum 1 Regum*. CCL 144.
_____. *Homilies on Ezekiel*. CCL 142.
_____. *Homilia in evangelia*. PL 76.
_____. *On the Seven Penitential Psalms*. PL 79.
Gregory Nazianzus. *Orationes*. SC 247, 270; PG 35, 36.
Gregory of Nyssa. *Commentary on the Song of Songs*. PG 44.
_____. *Contra Eunomium*. PG 45.
_____. *De beatitudinibus*. PG 44.
_____. *De instituto christiano*. PG 46.
_____. *De pauperibus amandis*. PG 46.
_____. *Oratio funebris de Flacilla*. PG 46.
Gregory Thaumaturgus. "Fragmenta in Jeremiam." *Analecta Sacra*. Ed. J. B. Pitra. 4 vols. Paris: Jouby & Roger, 1876-84.
Gregory of Tours. *History of the Franks*. PL 71.
_____. *Vita patrum*. PL 71.
Grenfell, B. P., and A. S. Hunt. *The Amherst Papyri*. 2 vols. London: Frowde, 1900.
Grieve, A. J. "Matthew." *A Commentary on the Bible*. Ed. A. Peck. New York: Nelson, 1920. 700-723.
Groot, H. de. *Opera theologica*. 4 vols. Basel: Thurnisios, 1732.
Gross, G. "Die 'geringsten Brüder' Jesu im Mt 25:40 in Auseinandersetzung mit der neueren Exegese," *BibLeb* 5 (1964) 172-180.
Grossheide, F. W. *Het heilig Evangelie volgens Matthaus*. Commentaar op het Nieuwe Testament. Kampen: Kok, 1954.
Grundmann, W. *Das Evangelium nach Matthäus*. THKNT 1. Berlin: Evangelische Verlagsanstalt, 1968.

_____. *Die Geschichte Jesu Christi.* Berlin: Evangelische Verlagsanstalt, 1957.
Guardini, R. *Der Herr.* 2 vols. Colmar: Alsatia, 1947.
Guggisberg, H. R. "Hugo Grotius." *TRE* 14. 277-280.
Gundry, R. H. *Matthew.* Grand Rapids: Eerdmans, 1982.
Gutzke, M. G. *Plain Talk on Matthew.* Grand Rapids: Zondervan, 1966.
Gutzwiller, R. *Jesus der Messias. Christus im Matthäusevangelium.* Einsiedeln: Benziger, 1949.
_____. *Meditationen über Matthäus.* Einsiedeln: Benziger, 1959.
Guy, H. A. *The Gospel of Matthew.* London: Macmillan, 1971.
Habershon, A. R. "His Coming Again." *The Study of the Parables.* Grand Rapids: Kregel, 1983. 77-97.
Hagner, D. A. *The Use of the Old and New Testaments in Clement of Rome.* NovTSup 34. Leiden: Brill, 1973.
Hahn, F. *Christologische Hoheitstitel.* FRLANT 88. Göttingen: Vandenhoeck & Ruprecht, 1963.
_____. *Das Verständnis der Mission im Neuen Testament.* WMANT 13. Neukirchen-Vluyn: Neukirchener-Verlag, 1963.
Hall, J. "The Gospel of St. Matthew." *A Plain and Familiar Explication of all the Hard Texts of the Whole Divine Scripture.* 2 vols. Oxford: Talboys, 1838, 2.124-188.
Hall, T. C. *The Messages of Jesus according to the Synoptists.* The Messages of the Bible 9. New York: Scribner, 1901.
Hamel, J. "Meditation: Vorletzter Sonntag nach Trinitatis. Matthäus 25,31-46." *Göttinger Predigtmeditationen* 26 (1973) 474-481.
Hamilton, W. *The Modern Reader's Guide to Matthew and Luke.* New York: Association, 1959.
Hammond, H. *Novum Testamentum Domini Nostri Jesu Christi.* 2d ed. 2 vols. Frankfurt: Fritsch, 1714.
Hanko, H. C. "The Final Judgment." *The Mysteries of the Kingdom.* Grand Rapids: Reformed Free Publishing, 1975. 295-306.

Hare, D. R. A. *The Theme of Jewish Persecution of Christians in the Gospel according to St Matthew.* SNTSMS 6. Cambridge: University Press, 1967.

_____, and D. J. Harrington. "Make Disciples of all the Nations." *CBQ* 37 (1975) 359-369.

Harnack, A. *Die Lehre der zwölf Apostel.* TU 2/1-2. Leipzig: Hinrichs, 1884.

Harrington, D. *The Gospel according to Matthew.* Collegeville Bible Commentary 1. Collegeville, MN: Liturgical Press, 1983.

Harrington, W. "Christ the King." *The Saving Word.* 3 vols. Ed. A. Flannery, T. Halton, and W. Harrington. Wilmington, DE: Glazier, 1980. 1. 338-340.

Harris, F. B. *The Kingdom of God.* Salem, OR: Harris, 1913.

Hartdegen, S. "Catholic English Versions of the Bible." *NCE* 2. 465-470.

Harvey, A. E. *The New English Bible Companion to the New Testament.* Oxford: University Press, 1970.

Hastings, E. *The Gospel according to St. Matthew.* 3 vols. The Speaker's Bible 29-31. Aberdeen: The Speaker's Bible Office, 1938-40.

Hastings, J. *Saint Matthew.* Great Texts of the Bible 8. Edinburgh: Clark, 1914.

Haufe, G. "Soviel ihr getan habt einem dieser meiner geringsten Brüder...." *Ruf und Antwort. Festgabe für Emil Fuchs zum 90. Geburtstag.* Leipzig: Koehler & Amelang, 1964. 484-493.

Haydock, G. L. and F. C. Husenbeth. *The Holy Bible.* 46 vols. New York: Virtue, 1850.

Haymo of Halberstadt. *Homiliae de tempore.* PL 118.

Hebert, G. "The Problem of the Gospel according to Matthew." *SJT* 14 (1961) 403-413.

Hengel, M. *War Jesus Revolutionär?* Calwer Hefte zür Forderung biblischen Glaubens und christlichen Lebens 110. Stuttgart: Calwer, 1970.

Henry, M. "An Exposition of the Gospel according to Saint Matthew." *An Exposition of the First Four Books of the New Testament.* An Exposition of the Old and New Testament 5. Philadelphia: Barrington & Haswell, 1830. 11-351.

_____., and T. Scott. "The Gospel according to Matthew." *The Family Commentary on the Holy Bible.* 2 vols. New York: Martin, 1853. 2.1-106.

Hesychius of Jerusalem. *Commentary on Leviticus.* PG 93.

_____. *In Psalmos.* PG 93.

Heylyn, J. *Theological Lectures at Westminster Abbey with an Interpretation of the New Testament.* 2 vols. London: Tonson & Draper, 1749, 1761.

Higgins, A. J. *Jesus and the Son of Man.* Philadelphia: Fortress, 1964.

Hilary of Poitiers. *Commentarium in Evangelium Matthaei.* SC 258.

_____. *De Trinitate.* PL 10.

Hill, D. *The Gospel of Matthew.* NCB 1. London: Oliphants, 1972.

Hindson, E. W. "The Gospel according to Matthew." *Liberty Bible Commentary.* 2 vols. Ed. E. Hindson and W. Kroll. Lynchburg, VA: The Old-Time Gospel Hour, 1982. 2.1-98.

Hinnebusch, P. *Saint Matthew's Earthquake.* Ann Arbor: Servant Books, 1980.

Hippolytus of Rome. *The Blessings of Moses.* PO 27.

_____. *Demonstratio de Christo et Anti-Christo.* GCS 1.

Hirsch, E. *Frühgeschichte des Evangeliums.* 2 vols. Tübingen: Mohr, 1941.

Hobbs, H. H. *An Exposition of the Gospel of Matthew.* Grand Rapids: Baker, 1965.

Hoffmann, P. "Selig sind die Armen...." *BibLeb* 11 (1970) 89-104.

Hognestad, H. *Forkynnelse til oppbrudd: Studier i Matteusevangeliet og kirkens bruk av det.* 2 vols. Oslo: Universitetsforlaget, 1978.

Holden, G. "St. Matthew." *The Christian Expositor.* 2 vols. London: Rivington, 1834. 2. 2-126.

Holl, A. *Jesus in schlechter Gesellschaft.* Stuttgart: Deutsche Verlagsanstalt, 1971.

Holtzmann, H. J. *Die Synoptiker.* Hand-Commentar zum Neuen Testament. 2 vols. Freiburg: Mohr, 1892.

Holtzmann, O. *Das Neue Testament.* 2 vols. Giessen: Töpelmann, 1926.

Holzendorff, F. von. "The Gospel according to Matthew." *A Short Protestant Commentary on the Books of the New Testament.* Ed. P. W. Schmidt and F. von Holzendorff. London: Williams & Norgate, 1882. 51-126.

Honert, J. van den. "Evangelium van Mattheus." *Verklaring van het Evangelium van Mattheus.* Amsterdam: Tirion & Loveringh, 1750. 1-627.

Horsiesi. *The Testament.* CS 47.

Horton, R. F. *A Devotional Commentary on the Gospel of St. Matthew.* New York: Revell, 1907.

Hoyt, H. A. *The End Times.* Chicago: Moody, 1969.

Hubbard, B. J. *The Matthean Redaction of a Primitive Apostolic Commissioning: An Exegesis of Matthew 28:16-20.* SBLDS 19. Missoula, MT: SBL & Scholar's Press, 1974.

Hugh of Saint Cher. *Hugonis de Sancto Charo opera omnia.* 8 vols. Lyons: Huguetan & Barbier, 1668-1669.

Hülsbusch, W. "Wenn der Menschensohn in seiner Herrlichkeit kommt." *BibLeb* 13 (1972) 207-214.

Hummel, R. *Das Auseinandersetzung zwischen Kirche und Judentum im Matthäusevangelium.* BEvT 33. Munich: Kaiser, 1966.

Hünermann, W. *Wir haben seine Herrlichkeit gesehen.* Innsbruck: Tyrolia, 1956.

Hunt, E. M. "Notes on St. Matthew." *Bible Notes for Daily Readers.* 2 vols. New York: Scribner, 1870. 2.304-348.

Hunter, A. *Interpreting the Parables.* Philadelphia: Westminster, 1960.

_____. *The Parables Then and Now.* Philadelphia: Westminster, 1971.

Ingelaere, J.-C. "La 'parabole' du jugement dernier." *RHPR* 50 (1970) 23-60.

Irenaeus of Lyons. *Adversus Haereses.* SC 100, 153, 211, 264, 294.

Ironside, H. A. *Expository Notes on the Gospel of Matthew.* New York: Loizeaux, 1948.

Irwin, C. H. "The Gospel according to St. Matthew." *The Universal Bible Commentary*. London: Religious Tract Society, 1928. 353-383.
Isho'dad of Merv. *The Commentaries of Isho'dad of Merv*. Ed. M. D. Gibson. 5 vols. Horae semiticae 5-6, 10-11. Cambridge: University Press, 1911-1916.
Isidore of Pelusium. *Epistles*. PG 78.
Isidore of Seville. *De ecclesiasticis officiis*. PL 83.
_____. *De ordine creaturarum*. PL 83.
_____. *Liber sententiarum*. PL 83.
_____. *Quaestiones in Vetus Testamentum*. PL 83.
Israel, M. *The Record of Christ's Life and Doctrine*. New York: Exposition, 1968.
Jaeger, W. *Two Rediscovered Works of Ancient Christian Literature: Gregory of Nyssa and Macarius*. Leiden: Brill, 1954.
Jansen (the Elder), C. *Commentarius in concordiam evangelicam*. Lyons: Plaignard, 1684.
Jansen (the Younger), C. O. *Tetrateuchus sive commentarius in sancta Jesu Christi evangelia*. Brussels: T'Serstevens, 1639.
Jeng, Y. M. P. *Die Adressaten der Heilsbotschaft Jesu. Die Worte über die Armen,Verlorenen, Unmündigen, Mühseligen-Beladenen und Kleinen-Kleinsten in der synoptischen Überlieferung*. Dissertation. Würzburg, 1970.
Jeremias, J. *Abba*. Göttingen: Vandenhoeck & Ruprecht, 1966.
_____. *Die Gleichnisse Jesu*. ATANT 11. Zürich: Zwingli, 1947.
_____. *Jesu Verheißung für die Völker*. Stuttgart: Kohlhammer, 1956.
_____. *Jesus als Weltvollender*. BFCT 33,4. Gütersloh: Bertelsmann, 1930.
_____. *Neutestamentliche Theologie*. Gütersloh: Mohn, 1971.
_____. "ποιμήν." *TDNT* 6. 485-502.
Jerome. *Apologia contra Rufinum*. CCL 79.
_____. *Commentary on Isaias*. CCL 73, 73A.
_____. *Commentary on Jeremiah*. CCL 74.
_____. *Commentary on Ezekiel*. CCL 75.
_____. *Commentary on Jonah*. CCL 76.

Bibliography

———. *Commentary on Matthew*. CCL 77.
———. *Contra Jovinianum*. PL 23.
———. *Epistula adversus Rufinum*. CCL 79.
———. *Letters*. PL 22.
———. *Tractatus de Ps 15*. CCL 78.
———. *Tractatus de Ps 50*. PLSup 2.
———. *Tractatus de Ps 90*. CCL 78.
Jobius. *De incarnatione*. PG 86, 2.
John Cassian. *De incarnatione domini*. PL 50.
———. *First Conference of Abba Isaac*. PL 49.
———. *First Conference of Abba Moses*. PL 49.
———. *Second Conference of Abba Moses*. PL 49.
John Chrysostom. *Ad Olympiadem*. SC 13.
———. *Adversus Judaeos*. PG 48.
———. *Commentary on the Psalms*. PG 55.
———. *Concerning the Statues*. PG 49.
———. *De compunctione: Ad Demetrium*. PG 47.
———. *De incomprehensibili Dei natura*. FC 72.
———. *De Lazaro*. PG 48.
———. *De petitione matris filiorum*. PG 48.
———. *De poenitentia*. PG 49.
———. *De virginitate*. SC 125.
———. *Homily 9 in Genesim*. PG 54.
———. *Homily 67 in Genesim*. PG 53, 54.
———. *Homilies on Matthew*. PG 57, 58.
———. *Homilies on John*. PG 59.
———. *Homilies on the Acts*. PG 60.
———. *Homilies On Romans*. PG 60.
———. *Homilies on 1 Corinthians*. PG 61.
———. *Homilies on 2 Corinthians*. PG 61.
———. *Homilies on Ephesians*. PG 62.
———. *Homilies on Philippians*. PG 62.
———. *Homilies on Colossians*. PG 62.
———. *Homilies on 1 Timothy*. PG 62.
———. *Homilies on 2 Timothy*. PG 62.
———. *Homilies on Hebrews*. PG 63.
———. *In Heliam et viduam*. PG 51.
———. *In illud: Habentes eundem spiritum*. PG 51.

———. *In illud: Salutate Priscillam*. PG 51.
———. *In illud: Vidua eligatur*. PG 51.
———. *In principium actorum*. PG 51.
———. *On the Power of Man to Resist the Devil*. PG 49.
———. *To the Fallen Theodore*. SC 117.
John Climacus. *Scala paradisi*. PG 88.
John Damascene. *De fide orthodoxa*. PG 94.
———. *De his qui in fide dormierunt*. PG 95.
———. *In epistolam primam ad Corinthios*. PG 95.
———. *Life of Barlaam and Joasaph*. LCL. London: Heinemann, 1914.
———. *Sacra parallela*. PG 95.
John the Dwarf. *Apophthegmata patrum*. PG 65.
John of Gaza. *Questions and Answers*. PO 31,3.
Johnson, B. C. *Matthew and Mark*. Waco, TX: Word Books, 1978.
Johnson, S. E. "The Gospel according to Matthew." *The Interpreter's Bible*. 12 vols. Ed. G. A. Buttrick. Nashville: Abingdon, 1951. 7. 231-625.
Jomier, J. *La vie de Messie*. Paris: Cerf, 1963.
Jones, A. "The Gospel of Jesus Christ according to Saint Matthew." *A Catholic Commentary on Holy Scripture*. Ed. R. C. Fuller et al. New York: Nelson, 1953. 851-904.
———. *The Gospel according to Saint Matthew*. New York: Sheed & Ward, 1965.
Jones, G. V. *The Art and Truth of the Parables*. London: SPCK, 1964.
Jones, J. R. *The New Testament of our Lord and Saviour Jesus Christ: A Comprehensive Commentary*. Philadelphia: n. pub., 1907.
Julian of Toledo. *Prognosticon futuri saeculi*. CCL 115.
Jülicher, A. *Die Gleichnisreden Jesu*. Tübingen: Mohr, 1910.
———., (ed.). *Itala: Das Neue Testament in altlateinischer Überlieferung*. 4 vols. Berlin: de Gruyter, 1938.
Justin Martyr. *Apologia*. PG 6.
———. *Dialogue with Tryphon*. PG 6.
Karrer, O. *Erklärung des Matthäus-evangeliums*. Neues Testament 1. Munich: Ars sacra, 1959.

Käsemann, E. "Kreuz und heilendes Handeln." *Ärztlicher Dienst weltweit*. Ed. W. Erk and M. Scheel. Stuttgart: Steinkopf, 1974. 200-208.

Kee, H. C. "The Gospel according to Matthew." *The Interpreter's One-volume Commentary on the Bible*. Ed. C. M. Laymon. Nashville: Abingdon, 1971. 609-643.

_____. *The Gospels*. Interpreter's Concise Commentary 6. Nashville: Abingdon, 1971.

Keil, K. A. G. *Analekten für das Studium der exegetischen und systematischen Theologie*. 4 vols. Leipzig: Barth, 1812-1822.

Keil, K. F. *Commentar über das Evangelium des Matthäus*. Leipzig: Dörffling & Franke, 1877.

Kelly, W. *Lectures on the Gospel of Matthew*. 6th ed. New York: Loizeaux, 1950.

Kemp, T. L. *Homilies on the Sunday Gospels*. Huntington, IN: Our Sunday Visitor, 1976.

Kempin, A. *The King's Parables*. Anderson, IN: Gospel Trumpet, 1938.

Kennedy, E. C. *The Choice to be Human: Jesus Alive in the Gospel of Matthew*. Garden City, NY: Doubleday, 1985.

Kenrick, T. *An Exposition of the Historical Writings of the New Testament*. 2d ed. 3 vols. Boston: Munroe & Francis, 1828.

Kent, H. A. "Matthew." *The New Testament and Wycliffe Bible Commentary*. Ed. E. F. Harrison. New York: Iversen Associates, 1971. 1-112.

Kiddle, M. "The Conflict between the Disciples, the Jews, and the Gentiles in St. Matthew's Gospel." *JTS* 36 (1935) 33-44.

Killinger, J. *A Sense of His Presence*. Garden City, NY: Doubleday, 1977.

Kingsbury, J. D. *Jesus Christ in Matthew, Mark and Luke*. Proclamation Commentaries. Philadelphia: Fortress, 1981.

_____. *Matthew*. Proclamation Commentaries. Philadelphia: Fortress, 1977.

_____. *Matthew as Story*. Philadelphia: Fortress, 1986.

_____. *Matthew: Structure, Christology, Kingdom*. Philadelphia: Fortress, 1975.

Kirban, S. *The Beginning of Sorrows*. Huntingdon Valley, PA: Kirban, 1972.

Kirk, A. and R. Obach. *A Commentary on the Gospel of Matthew*. New York: Paulist, 1978.

Kissinger, W. S. *The Parables of Jesus*. American Theological Library Association Bibliography 4. Metuchen, NJ: Scarecrow, 1979.

Kistemaker, S. *The Parables of Jesus*. Grand Rapids: Baker, 1980.

Kittel, G. (ed.). *Theologisches Wörterbuch zum Neuen Testament*. 10 vols. Stuttgart: Kohlhammer, 1933.

Klausner, J. *Jesus of Nazareth*. New York: Macmillan, 1959.

Klein, F. *La vie humaine et divine de Jésus-Christ notre seigneur*. Paris: Bloud & Gay, 1933.

Klostermann, E. *Das Matthäusevangelium*. 2d ed. HNT 4. Tübingen: Mohr, 1927.

Knabenbauer, J. *Commentarius in evangelium secundum S. Matthaeum*. 2 vols. Cursus Scripturae Sacrae 35-36. Paris: Lethielleux, 1892-93.

Knaake, J. C. F., et al. (eds.). *D. Martin Luthers Werke. Kritische Gesamtausgabe*. 79 vols. Weimar: Böhlau, 1883-1941.

Knecht, F. J. *A Practical Commentary on Holy Scripture*. 2 vols. St. Louis: Herder, 1894.

Knibb, M. A. *The Ethiopic Book of Enoch: A New Edition in the Light of the Aramaic Dead Sea Fragments*. 2 vols. Oxford: Clarendon, 1978.

_____. "The Date of the Parables of Enoch: A Critical Review." *NTS* 25 (1978-79) 345-359.

Knoch, A. E. *Concordant Commentary on the New Testament*. 3d ed. Saugus, CA: Concordant, 1968.

Knoch, O. "Gott als Anwalt des Menschen." *BK* 24 (1969) 82-84.

Knox, R. A. *A Commentary on the Gospels*. New York: Sheed & Ward, 1952.

Koester, H. *Synoptische Überlieferungen bei den apostolischen Vätern*. TU 65. Berlin: Akademie, 1957.

Konings, J. "Quem e quem na 'parabola do ultimo juizo' Mt 25:31-46?" *Perspectiva teologica* 10 (1978) 367-402.

Kornfeld, W. "Die Liebeswerke Mt 25:35-36, 42-43 in alttestamentlicher Überlieferung."*Theologia scientia eminens practica*. Ed. F. Zerbst. Vienna: Herder, 1979. 255-265.

Kraeling, E. G. *The Four Gospels*. The Clarified New Testament. New York: McGraw-Hill, 1962.
Kratko tulkovanic na Evangelie-to ot Matfeia s pytaniia i otgovory. Tsaringrad: A. Minaciiana & Cdrus, 1867.
Kretzer, A. *Die Herrschaft der Himmel und die Söhne des Reiches*. SBM 10. Würzburg: Echter; Stuttgart: KBW, 1971.
Kühnöl, C. G. *Commentarius in libros Novi Testamenti historicos*. 4 vols. Leipzig: Barth, 1823-27.
Kümmel, W. G. *Einleitung in das Neue Testament*. 17th ed. Heidelberg: Quelle & Meyer, 1973.
_____. *Verheißung und Erfüllung*. 3d ed. Zürich: Zwingli, 1956.
Kunkel, F. *Creation Continues: A Psychological Interpretation of the First Gospel*. New York: Scribner, 1947.
Künzel, G. *Studien zum Gemeindeverständnis des Matthäus-Evangeliums*. Calwer theologische Monographien 10. Stuttgart: Calwer, 1978.
La Biblia. 25 vols. Montserrat: Monestir de Montserrat, 1963.
Ladd, G. E. *Jesus and the Kingdom*. New York: Harper & Row, 1964.
_____. "Matthew." *The Biblical Expositor*. 3 vols. Philadelphia: Holman,1960. 3. 23-73.
_____. "The Parable of the Sheep and the Goats in Recent Interpretation." *New Dimensions in New Testament Study*. Ed. R. Longenecker and M. Tenney. Grand Rapids: Zondervan, 1974. 191-199.
_____. *A Theology of the New Testament*. Grand Rapids: Eerdmans, 1974.
Lagrange, M.-J. *L'Evangile selon saint Matthieu*. 3d ed. EBib. Paris: Gabalda, 1927.
_____. *L'Evangile de Jésus-Christ*. 4th ed. Paris: Gabalda, 1929.
Laien-Bibel. Freiburg: Herder, 1938.
Lambrecht, J. "The Last Judgment." *Once More Astonished*. New York: Crossroad, 1983. 196-235.
_____. "The Parousia Discourse: Composition and Content in *Mt*., XXIV-XXV." *L'Evangile selon saint Matthieu*:

Rédaction et théologie. BETL 29. Gembloux: Duculot, 1972. 309-342.
Lancellotti, A. *Matteo.* Nuovissima versione della Bibbia dai testi originali 33. Roma: Edizioni paoline, 1975.
Lancelot, J. B. *Parables of Judgment.* London: The Church Book Room, 1936.
Lange, J. *Das Erscheinen des Auferstandenen im Evangelium nach Matthäus.* FB 11. Würzburg: Echter, 1973.
Lange, J. P. *Das Evangelium nach Matthäus.* Theologisch-homiletisches Bibelwerk. Die heilige Schrift, NT 1. Bielefeld: Velhagen & Klasing, 1861.
Läpple, A. K. *Die Botschaft der Evangelien - heute.* Munich: Don Bosco, 1966.
Largent, A. "Bossuet, Jacques-Bénigne." *DTC* 2/1.1049-1089.
La Sacra Bibbia. 10 vols. Florence: Salani, 1957.
Latch, E. B. "The Gospel according to St. Matthew." *A Review of the Holy Bible.* Philadelphia: Lippincott, 1884. 379-418.
Lau, F. *Das Matthäusevangelium.* Neutestamentliche Reihe 1. Berlin: de Gruyter, 1951.
Lauck, W. *Das Evangelium des heiligen Matthäus und des heiligen Markus.* Herders Bibelkommentar 11. Freiburg: Herder, 1936.
Laurentius of Novae. *Homily 2.* PL 66.
Lawson, L. *The Lord of Parables.* Cincinnati: Standard Publishing, 1984.
Leander of Seville. *De institutione virginum et contemptu mundi.* Ed. A. C. Vega. Scriptores ecclesiastici hispano-latini veteris et medii aevi 16-17. Escorial: Monasterio Augustiniano, 1948.
Lebreton, J. *La vie et l'enseignement de Jésus-Christ notre seigneur.* 16th ed. 2 vols. Paris: Beauchesne, 1947.
LeCamus, E. *La vie de notre seigneur Jésus-Christ.* 3 vols. Paris: Letouzey & Ané, 1887.
Lechner, P. "Matthäus." *Die heilige Schrift des Neuen Testamentes.* Latrobe, PA: St. Vincent's Archabbey, 1881. 37-278.
Leclercq, J. "The Exposition and Exegesis of Scripture from Gregory the Great to St. Bernard." *The Cambridge History of*

the Bible. 3 vols. Ed. G. W. Lampe. Cambridge: University Press, 1969. 2.183-197.

Leerse, J. C. *Spiritus dogmaticus et moralis evangelii.* 2 vols. Brussels: Leonard, 1776.

Leeuwen, D. van. "Enarratio in Matthaeum." *D. Dionysii Cartusiani opera omnia.* 41 vols. Montreuil: Cartusiae S. M. de Pratis, 1896-1900.

Leeuwen, W. S. van. "Het Evangelie naar Mattheus." *Commentaar op de Heilige Schrift.* Ed. J. vor der Hake. Amsterdam: Paris, 1956. 850-899.

Légasse, S. "La parabole du jugement dernier." *Jésus et l'enfant. "Enfants," "petits," et "simples" dans la tradition synoptique.* EBib. Paris: Gabalda, 1969. 85-100.

Lenski, R. C. H. *Interpretation of St. Matthew's Gospel.* Columbus, OH: Lutheran Book Concern, 1932.

Leo the Great. *Sermons.* CCL 138,138A.

Léon-Dufour, X. *Les Evangiles et l'histoire de Jésus.* Paris: Editions du Seuil, 1963.

_____, and A. Négrier. "Frère." *Vocabulaire de théologie biblique.* 2d ed. Paris: Cerf, 1970. 491-495.

Lesetre, H. *Notre seigneur Jésus-Christ dans son saint évangile.* 2 vols. Paris: Lethielleux, 1892.

Levertoff, P. P. *St. Matthew.* Commentaries for Schools 1. London: Murby, 1940.

Lewis, W. S., and H. M. Booth. *A Homiletical Commentary on the Gospel according to St. Matthew.* The Preacher's Complete Homiletical Commentary 22. New York: Funk & Wagnalls, 1896.

Liddell, H. G., and R. Scott. *Greek-English Lexicon.* 2 vols. Revised, H. S. Jones and R. McKenzie. Oxford: Clarendon, 1951.

_____, and H. S. Jones. *A Greek-English Lexicon: A Supplement.* Ed. E. A. Barber et al. Oxford: Clarendon, 1968.

_____. *An Intermediate Greek-English Lexicon.* Oxford: Clarendon, 1975.

Lienemann, W. "Solidarität mit den Schuldigen." *EvK* 6 (1973) 181.

Lightfoot, J. B. *The Apostolic Fathers*. 2 vols. Hildesheim: Olms, 1973.

Lightfoot, N. R. *Lessons from the Parables*. Grand Rapids: Baker, 1965.

Lipsius, R. A., and M. Bonnet. *Acta Apostolorum Apocrypha*. 2 vols. Leipzig: Mendelssohn, 1891,1903.

Lochen, A. *L'Evangile raconté aux adultes*. Taizé: Les Presses de Taizé, 1970.

Lock, W. "The Sheep and the Goats." *Expositor* 5/10 (1899) 401-412.

Lohmeyer, E. *Das Evangelium des Matthäus*. MeyerK Sonderband. 3d ed. Göttingen: Vandenhoeck & Ruprecht, 1962.

Lohse, E. "Christus als der Weltenrichter." *Jesus Christus in Historie und Theologie. Neutestamentliche Festschrift für Hans Conzelmann zum 60. Geburtstag*. Ed. G. Strecker. Tübingen: Mohr, 1975. 475-486.

Loisy, A. *Les evangiles synoptiques*. 2 vols. Ceffonds: Chez l'auteur, 1907-08.

Long, R. C. *More Stewardship Parables of Jesus*. New York: Abingdon-Cokesbury, 1947.

Luca of Bruges, F. *Commentarius in sacrosancta quatuor Jesu Christi evangelia*. Antwerp: Moretum, 1606.

Luccock, H. E. *Studies in the Parables of Jesus*. Life and Service Series. New York: Methodist Book Concern, 1925.

Luccock, R. E. *Preaching through Matthew*. Nashville: Abingdon, 1980.

Ludolph of Saxony. *Vita domini nostri Jesu Christi e sacris quatuor evangeliis*. Lyons: Coffin & Plaignard, 1644.

Lusseau, H. *Les Evangiles*. Manuel d'Etudes Bibliques 4. Paris: Tequi, 1932.

Lütgart, W. *Die Liebe im Neuen Testament*. Leipzig: Deichert, 1905.

Luther, M. *Biblia, das ist die gantze Heilige Schrift deudsch*. 22d ed. Wittenberg: Kraffts, 1581.

Maas, A. J. *The Gospel according to Saint Matthew*. Saint Louis: Herder, 1898.

_____. *The Life of Jesus Christ according to the Gospel History*. 5th ed. St. Louis: Herder, 1909.

Macarius of Egypt. *De oratione.* PG 34.
———. *Fifty Spiritual Homilies.* Willits, CA: Eastern Orthodox Books, 1974.
MacEvilly, J. *An Exposition of the Four Gospels.* 4th ed. Dublin: Gill, 1898.
Maclaren, A. *The Gospel according to St. Matthew.* 3 vols. London: Hodder & Stoughton, 1912.
Madame Cecelia. *The Gospel according to St. Matthew.* Catholic Scripture Manuals. London: Burns, Oates, & Washbourne, 1906.
Maddox, R. "Who are the 'Sheep' and the 'Goats'?" *AusBR* 13 (1965) 19-28.
Maillot, A. "Les brebis et les boucs." *Les paraboles de Jésus aujourd'hui.* Geneva: Labor et Fides, 1973. 83-90.
Makrakis, A. "The Gospel according to Matthew." *The Four Gospels.* Interpretation of the Entire New Testament 1. Chicago: Orthodox Christian Educational Society, 1949.
Maldonado, J. *Commentarii in quattuor evangelistas.* Pont-à-Mousson: Mercator, 1596.
Mánek, J. "Mit wem identifiziert sich Jesus? Eine exegetische Rekonstruktion ad Matt 25:31-46." *Christ and Spirit in the New Testament. Essays in honour of C. F. D. Moule.* Ed. B. Lindars and S. Smalley. London: Cambridge University, 1973. 15-25.
Mansel, H. L. "The Gospel according to St. Matthew." *The Holy Bible with an Explanatory and Critical Commentary.* 13 vols. Ed. F. Cook. London: Murray, 1878. 7.1-197.
Manson, T. W. *The Sayings of Jesus.* London: SCM, 1971.
———. "The Son of Man in Daniel, Enoch, and the Gospels." *BJRL* 32 (1949-50) 171-93.
———. *The Teaching of Jesus.* Cambridge: University Press, 1967.
Manson, W. *Jesus the Messiah.* London: Hodder & Stoughton, 1943.
Marcel, P. "Frères et soeurs du Christ Matt 25:31-46," *Revue Reformée* 15 (1964) 18-30; 16 (1965) 12-26.

Marguerat, D. "Le lieu de la fidelité chrétienne Mt 25:31-46." *Le jugement dans l'Evangile de Matthieu.* Le monde de la Bible. Geneva: Labor et Fides, 1981. 481-520.

Marloratus, A. *Novi Testamenti catholica expositio ecclesiastica.* 2d ed. Geneva: Stephanus, 1564.

Marrow, S. B. *The Words of Jesus in our Gospels.* New York: Paulist, 1979.

Martensen, H. P. "Predigthilfe für den Vorletzten Sonntag des Kirchenjahres. 18. November, 1973. Matthäus 25,31-46." *Deutsches Pfarrerblatt* 73 (1973) 583.

Martin, F. "Le signe du fils de l'homme." *LumVie* 31 (1982) 61-77.

Martin, H. *The Parabales of the Gospels.* London: SCM, 1937.

Martin, J. P. "The Church in Matthew." *Interpreting the Gospels.* Ed. J. L. Mays. Philadelphia: Fortress, 1981. 97-114.

Martindale, C. C. *The Gospel according to St. Matthew.* Stonyhurst Scripture Manuals. Westminster, MD: Newman, 1957.

Martini, A. (ed.). *La Sacra Bibbia.* 4 vols. Naples: Marghieri, 1905.

Massaux, E. *Influence de l'Evangile de saint Matthieu sur la littérature chrétienne avant saint Irénée.* Leuven: Publications universitaires, 1950. Reprinted with *Supplement bibliographie 1950-1985* by B. Dehandschutter: BETL 75. Leuven: University Press, 1986.

Massl, F. X. *Matthäus.* Erklärung der heiligen Schriften des Neuen Testamentes 2. Straubing: Schorner, 1841.

Mattill, Jr., A. J. "Matthew 25:31-46 Relocated." *Restoration Quarterly* 17 (1974) 107-114.

_____. "What the World Owes the Church." *HPR* 71 (1971) 8-17.

Mauriac, F. *Vie de Jésus.* Paris: Flammarion, 1936.

Maximus the Confessor. *Capita de caritate.* PG 90.

_____. *Commentaries on the Works of Dionysius the Areopagite.* PG 4.

_____. *Epistles.* PG 91.

_____. *Expositio orationis dominicae.* PG 90.

_____. *Liber asceticus.* PG 90.

_____. *Mystagogia.* PG 91.
Maximus of Turin. *Sermons.* CCL 23.
McConkie, B. R. *Doctrinal New Testament Commentary.* Salt Lake City, UT: Bookcraft, 1965.
McConnell, R. S. *Law and Prophecy in Matthew's Gospel.* Dissertation. Basel, 1969.
McCumber, W. E. *Matthew.* Beacon Bible Expositions 1. Kansas City, MO: Beacon Hill, 1975.
McEleney, N. J. *The Growth of the Gospels.* New York: Paulist, 1979.
McGarvey, J. W., and P. Y. Pendleton. *The Fourfold Gospel.* Standard Bible Commentary 1-2. Cincinnati: Standard Publishing, 1905-1906.
McGee, J. V. "The Gospel according to Matthew." *Matthew—Romans.* Through the Bible with J. Vernon McGee 4. Nashville: Nelson, 1983. 1-155.
McKenzie, J. L. "The Gospel according to Matthew." *JBC* 2. 62-114.
McLaughlin, G. A. *Commentary on the Gospel according to Saint Matthew.* Chicago: Christian Witness, 1909.
McNabb, V. *A Life of Jesus Christ Our Lord.* New York: Sheed & Ward, 1938.
Meier, J. P. *Matthew.* New Testament Messsage 3. Wilmington, DE: Glazier, 1980.
_____. "Nations or Gentiles in Matthew 28:19?" *CBQ* 39 (1977) 94-102.
_____. *The Vision of Matthew.* Theological Inquiries. New York: Paulist, 1979.
Meinertz, M. *Jesus und die Heidenmission.* NTAbh 1/1-2. Münster: Aschendorff, 1925.
Menochio, G. S. *Commentarii totius sacrae scripturae.* 2 vols. Venice: Recurti, 1722.
Merezhkovskii, D. *Iisus Neizvjestnij.* Leningrad: Piroshkova, 1933.
Mersch, E. *Le Corps mystique du Christ.* 2 vols. Louvain: Museum Lessianum, 1933.
Meschler, M. *Das Leben unseres Herrn Jesu Christi des Sohnes Gottes.* 2 vols. Freiburg: Herder, 1912.

Methodius of Olympus. *De Lepra*. GCS 27.
_____. *De Vita*. GCS 27.
Metzger, B. M. *The New Testament: Its Background, Growth and Content*. Nashville: Abingdon, 1965.
_____. *A Textual Commentary on the Greek New Testament*. London/New York: United Bible Societies, 1971.
Meyer, F. B. "The Gospel according to Matthew." *The Gospels*. Through the Bible Day by Day 5. Philadelphia: American Sunday-School Union, 1918.
Meyer, H. A. W. *Evangelium des Matthäus*. MeyerK 1. Göttingen: Vandenhoeck & Ruprecht, 1864.
Michaels, J. R. "Apostolic Hardships and Righteous Gentiles." *JBL* 84 (1965) 27-37.
Michaelis, W. *Das Evangelium nach Matthäus*. Prophezei 1/1-2. Zürich: Zwingli, 1948.
_____. *Die Gleichnisse Jesu*. 3d ed. Hamburg: Furche, 1955.
Michel, O. "'Diese Kleinen' - eine Jüngerbezeichnung Jesu." *TSK* 108 (1937-38) 401-415.
_____. "Freudenbotschaft und Völkerwelt." *Divus Thomas* 6 (1939) 45-68.
_____. "μικρός." *TDNT* 4. 648-659.
Micklem, P. A. *St. Matthew*. Westminster Commentaries 37. London: Methuen, 1917.
Migne, J. P. *In Sanctum Matthaeum commentaria*. Scripturae Sacrae Cursus Completus 21. Paris: Migne, 1841.
Milham, R. *Like it is Today*. Nashville: Broadman, 1970.
Milik, J. T. and M. Black. *The Books of Enoch: Aramaic Fragments of Qumrân Cave 4*. Oxford: Clarendon, 1976.
Miller, A. W. *The Gospel of Matthew*. Anderson, IN: Warner, 1944.
Miller, C., O. Miller, and M. Roebert. *Announcing the Good News*. Staten Island, NY: Alba House, 1971.
Miller, J. R. *The Gospel by Matthew*. Devotional Hours with the Bible 3. New York/London: Hodder & Stoughton, 1909.
Miller, J. W. *Step by Step through the Parables*. New York: Paulist, 1981.

Miller, L. F. *The Gospel according to St. Matthew.* New York: Wagner, 1937.

Miller, S. M. *The Gospel by Matthew and Luke.* St. Paul, MN: Miller, 1925.

Minear, P. S. *Christian Hope and the Second Coming.* Philadelphia: Westminster, 1954.

_____. "The Coming of the Son of Man." *TToday* 9 (1953) 489-493.

_____. *Images of the Church in the New Testament.* Philadelphia: Westminster, 1960.

_____. *The Kingdom and the Power.* Philadelphia: Westminster, 1950.

Mitton, C. L. "Present Justification and Final Judgment: A Discussion of the Parable of the Sheep and the Goats." *ExpTim* 67 (1955-56) 46-50.

M'Neile, A. H. *The Gospel according to Saint Matthew.* London: Macmillan, 1952.

Mohrlang, R. *Matthew and Paul.* SNTSMS 48. Cambridge: University Press, 1984.

Mollat, D. "Jugement dans le Nouveau Testament." *DBSup* 4. 1344-1394.

Moninger, H. *Matthew's Gospel at the Point of Question.* 2 vols. Cincinnati: Standard Publishing, 1910.

Monlobou, L. *L'Evangile de Matthieu.* Mulhouse: Editions Salvator, 1977.

Monsarrat, V. "Matthieu 24-25." *Foi et vie* 76 (1977) 67-80.

Montefiore, C. G. *Rabbinic Literature and Gospel Teachings.* The Library of Biblical Studies. New York: Ktav, 1970.

_____. *Some Elements of the Religious Teaching of Jesus according to the Synoptic Gospels.* The Jewish People: History, Religion, Literature. New York: Arno, 1973.

_____. *The Synoptic Gospels.* 2d ed. 2 vols. Library of Biblical Studies. New York: Ktav, 1968.

Montefiore, H. W. "God as Father in the Synoptic Gospels." *NTS* 3 (1956-57) 31-46.

Moore, A. L. *The Parousia in the New Testament.* NovTSup 13. Leiden: Brill, 1966.

Morgan, G. C. *The Gospel according to Matthew.* The Analyzed Bible 10. New York: Revell, 1911.

_____. *The Parables and Metaphors of Our Lord.* New York: Revell, 1943.

Morison, J. H. *Matthew.* 3d ed. Boston: American Unitarian Association, 1872.

Mortier, D. A. *L'Evangile.* Bruges: Desclée de Brouwer, 1925.

Mounce, R. H. *Matthew.* Good News Commentary 1. San Francisco: Harper & Row, 1985.

Mueller, J. T. *The Concordia New Testament with Notes.* St. Louis: Concordia, 1942.

Murray, J. M. *The Life of Our Lord.* The Christian Religion Series 1. Milwaukee: Bruce, 1942.

Murry, J. M. *Jesus, Man of Genius.* New York: Harper, 1926.

Musurillo, H. (ed.). *Saint Methodius.* ACW 27. Westminster: Newman, 1958.

Nagano, P. M. "An Exegesis of Matthew 25:31-46." *Foundations* 19 (1976) 216-222.

Nast, W. *A Commentary on the Gospels of Matthew and Mark.* Cincinnati, OH: Poe & Hitchcock, 1864.

Nau, F. "Eusèbe d'Alexandrie." *DTC* 5/2. 1526-1527.

Nee, W. *Come Lord Jesus.* New York: Christian Fellowship Publications, 1976.

_____. *The King and the Kingdom of Heaven.* New York: Christian Fellowship Publications, 1978.

Neil, W. "The Gospel according to Saint Matthew." *Harper's Bible Commentary.* New York: Harper & Row, 1962. 333-348.

Nelson, B. A. *Hustle Won't Bring the Kingdom of God.* St. Louis: Bethany, 1978.

Nepper-Christensen, P. *Das Matthäusevangelium.* Acta theologica danica 1. Aarhus: Universitetsforlaget, 1958.

Nestle, E., E. Nestle, K. Aland, M. Black, C. Martini, B. Metzger, and A. Wikgren (eds.). *Novum Testamentum Graece.* 26th ed. Stuttgart: Deutsche Bibelstiftung, 1981.

Neuhäusler, E. *Anspruch und Antwort Gottes.* Düsseldorf: Patmos, 1962.

Nicephorus of Antioch. *Life of Simeon Stylites the Younger.* PG 86/2.

Nichol, F. D. "The Gospel according to St. Matthew." *The Seventh-day Adventist Bible Commentary*. 7 vols. Washington, DC: Review and Herald, 1953-57. 5. 271-560.
Nicholas of Lyra. *Postilla super totam Bibliam*. 4 vols. Strassburg: Mentelin, 1469.
Nielsen, J. T. *Het Evangelie naar Mattheüs*. 3 vols. De Prediking van het Nieuwe Testament 1-3. Nijkerk: Callenbach, 1974.
Nijenhuis, W. "Johannes Calvin." *TRE* 7.568-592.
Nilus of Ancyra. *De malignis cogitationibus*. PG 79.
_____. *Peristeria*. PG 79.
_____. *Tractatus ad Eulogium*. PG 79.
Nixon, R. E. "Matthew." *The New Bible Commentary Revised*. Ed. D. Guthrie and J. Motyer. Grand Rapids: Eerdmans, 1970. 813-850.
Noel, C. *The Life of Jesus*. New York: Simon & Schuster, 1938.
Nösgen, K. F. *Die Evangelien nach Matthäus, Markus und Lukas*. Kurzgefasster Kommentar zu den heiligen Schriften Alten und Neuen Testaments, NT 1. Munich: Beck, 1897.
Obermüller, R. "¿Donde estuviste?" *RevistB* 35 (1973) 14-21.
O'Brien, I. *The Life of Christ*. Paterson, NJ: St. Anthony Guild, 1937.
Oesterley, W. O. *The Gospel Parables in the Light of their Jewish Background*. London: SPCK, 1936.
Olshausen, H. *Biblischer Commentar über sämmtliche Schriften des Neuen Testaments*. Königsberg: Unzer, 1853.
Opitz, H. G. (ed.). *Athanasius Werke*. Berlin/Leipzig: de Gruyter, 1935.
Origen. *Commentary on the Song of Songs*. GCS 33.
_____. *Commentary on Matthew*. GCS 40.
_____. *Homily on Luke*. SC 87.
_____. *Commentary on John*. SC 120.
_____. *Commentary on Romans*. SC 226; PG 14.
_____. *Commentariorum series*. GCS 38.
_____. *Contra Celsum*. SC 150.
_____. *De oratione*. GCS 3.
_____. *De principiis*. SC 252, 268.
_____. *Fragment on Ps 36:22*. PG 17.

_____. *Fragment on Ps 68:24.* PG 12.
_____. *Fragment on Jer 22: 24-26.* GCS 6.
_____. *Homily on Genesis.* GCS 29.
_____. *Homily on Exodus.* GCS 29.
_____. *Homily on Numbers.* GCS 30.
_____. *Homily on Joshua.* SC 71.
_____. *Homily on Isaiah.* GCS 32.
_____. *Homily on Jeremiah.* SC 238.
_____. *Homily on Ezekiel.* GCS 33.
_____. *Homily on The Psalms.* PG 12.
_____. *Homily on The Song of Songs.* GCS 33.
_____. *Stromata.* PL 26.
Osiek, C."The Ransom of Captives: Evolution of a Tradition." HTR 74 (1981) 365-386.
Osterwald, J. F. "The Gospel according to St. Matthew." *The Arguments of the Books and Chapters of the Old and New Testament.* 6th ed. 2 vols. London: SPCK, 1799. 2. 271-329.
O'Sullivan, K. "Solemnity of Christ the King." *The Sunday Readings.* 3 vols. Paterson, NJ: St. Anthony Guild, 1970-1972. 1. 389-395.
Otto, R. *Reich Gottes und Menschensohn.* 3d ed. Munich: Kösel, 1954.
Oudersluys, R. C. "The Parable of the Sheep and Goats." *Reformed Review* 26 (1973) 151-161.
Owen, J. J. *A Commentary, Critical, Expository, and Practical, on the Gospels of Matthew and Mark.* New York: Leavitt & Allen, 1857.
Pachomius. *Instructions.* CSCO 159; CS 47.
_____. *Paralipomena.* CS 46.
_____. *Letter 3.* CS 47; CSCO 89.
Paige, L. R. *A Commentary on the New Testament.* 6 vols. Boston: Mussey,1844.
Pak, S. *Matae pogum pyon.* Seoul: Korean Presbyterian Church, 1955.
Palladius. *Dialogue of the Life of St. John Chrysostom.* PG 47.
Palm, J. H. van der. "Het Evangelium van Mattheüs." *Volledige Aanteekeningen tot de Vertaling des Bijbels.* 3 vols. Leiden: Du Mortier, 1835. 3.1-77.

Pamment, M. "The Kingdom of Heaven according to the First Gospel." *NTS* 27 (1980-81) 211-232.
Papini, G. *Storia di Cristo*. 14th ed. Florence: Vallechi, 1950.
Parānanda, S. *The Gospel of Jesus according to St. Matthew*. London: Paul, Trench, & Trübner, 1898.
Pareus, D. *In S. Matthaei evangelium commentarius*. Oxford: Lichfield, 1631.
Parker, J. *Matthew XI-XXVIII*. The People's Bible 19. London: Hazell, Watson, & Viney, 1900.
Parma, A. A.(ed.). *Sancti Bonaventurae opera omnia*. 10 vols. Quaracchi: College of St. Bonaventure, 1882-1901.
Parmentier, R. *L'Evangile autrement*. Paris: Le Centurion, 1977.
Paschasius Radbertus. *Expositio in Matthaeum*. CCM 56A, 56B.
Patrick of Ireland. *Confessions*. SC 249.
Paul the Deacon. *Homilies*. PL 95.
Paulinus of Nola. *Letters*. PL 61.
_____. *Poem*. PL 61.
Paulus Orosius. *Liber apologeticus contra Pelagium*. CSEL 5.
Payne, J. B. *The Imminent Appearing of Christ*. Grand Rapids: Eerdmans, 1962.
Peabody, F. G. *Jesus Christ and the Social Question*. New York: Macmillan, 1900.
Peiró, F. X. *El evangelio comentado*. 2 vols. Madrid: Editorial sapientia, 1954.
Pelagius. *Ad Demetriadem*. PL 33.
_____. *Epistola de malis doctoribus*. PLSup 1.
_____. *Fragmenta Vindobonensia*. PLSup 1.
_____. *In epistolam secundam ad Corinthios*. PLSup 1.
_____. *In epistolam ad Galatas*. PLSup 1.
Pelfrène, J. M. "Tu aimera ton prochain comme toi-même," *AsSeign* (1st ser.) 66 (1966) 50-67.
Peloubet, F. N. *Suggestive Illustrations on the Gospel according to Matthew*. New York: Herrick, 1897.
_____. *The Teachers' Commentary on the Gospel according to St. Matthew*. New York: Oxford University, 1901.
Pentecost, J. D. *The Parables of Jesus*. Grand Rapids: Zondervan, 1982.

_____. *The Words and Works of Jesus Christ.* Grand Rapids: Zondervan, 1981.
Perantonus, P. M. (ed.). *Sancti Bernardini senensis opera omnia.* 9 vols. Quaracchi: College of St. Bonaventure, 1950-1965.
Percy, E. *Die Botschaft Jesu.* Lund: Gleerup, 1953.
Perkins, P. *Hearing the Parables of Jesus.* New York: Paulist, 1981.
_____. *Reading the New Testament.* New York: Paulist, 1978.
Perrin, N. *The New Testament: An Introduction.* New York: Harcourt Brace Jovanovich, 1974.
_____. *Rediscovering the Teaching of Jesus.* New York: Harper & Row, 1967.
Pesch, R. "Eschatologie und Ethik." *BibLeb* 11 (1970) 223-238.
_____. "Heilszukunft und Zukunft des Heils." *Gestalt und Anspruch des Neuen Testamentes.* Ed. J. Schreiner and G. Dautzenberg. Würzburg: Echter, 1969. 313-329.
Pesch, W. *Der Lohngedanke in der Lehre Jesu verglichen mit der religiösen Lohnlehre des Spätjudentums.* Münchener theologische Studien 7. Munich: Zink, 1955.
_____. *Matthäus der Seelsorger.* SBS 2. Stuttgart: KBW, 1966.
Peter of Alexandria. "Homily 8." *Le Muséon* 45 (1932) 50, 69.
Peter Chrysologos. *Sermons.* CCL 24, 24A, 24B.
Peter Comestor. *In evangelia.* PL 198.
Pettingill, W. L. *Simple Studies in Matthew.* Harrisburg, PA: Kelker, 1910.
Petzoldt, M. *Gleichnisse Jesu und christliche Dogmatik.* Göttingen: Vandenhoeck & Ruprecht, 1984.
Pfendsack, W. *Die Kirche bleibt nicht im Dorf.* Basel: Reinhardt, 1968.
Pfleiderer, O. *Das Urchristentum.* 2d ed. Berlin: Reimer, 1902.
Picinelli, F. *Concetti della sacra Bibbia.* Milan: Vigone, 1667.
Picquigny, B. de. *Opera omnia Bernardini a Piconio.* 5 vols. Paris: Vivès, 1870-72.
Pieper, K. *Heimat und Leben unseres Herrn Jesus Christus.* Münster: Aschendorff, 1947.

Pikaza, X. "Dios, hombre y Cristo en el mensaje de Jesús. Introducción al tema de la autenticidad jesuánica de Mt 25, 31-46." *Salmanticensis* 26 (1979) 5-50.

_____. "La bendición y maldición del hijo del hombre. Transfondo veterotestamentario del 'Benditos-Malditos' de Mt 25, 34. 41." *Salmanticensis* 26 (1979) 277-286.

_____. "La estructura de Mt y su influencía en 25,31-46." *Salmanticensis* 30 (1983) 11-40.

_____. "Mateo 25,31-46 y la teología de la liberación." *CB* 31 (1974) 27-28.

_____. "Salvación y condena del hijo del hombre. Transfondo Veterotestamentario y Judío de Mt 25, 34. 41. 46." *Salmanticensis* 27 (1980) 419-438.

Pirot, L., and A. Clamer (eds.). *La Sainte Bible*. 12 vols. Paris: Letouzey & Ané, 1946.

Piscator, J. *Commentarii in omnes libros Veteris Testamenti et Novi Testamenti*. 3 vols. Herborn of Nassau: n. pub., 1638.

Pitra, J. B. (ed.). *Analecta sacra*. 4 vols. Paris: Jouby & Roger, 1876-84.

Plummer, A. *An Exegetical Commentary on the Gospel according to St. Matthew*. London: Stock, 1909.

Plumptre, E. H. *The Gospel according to St. Matthew*. Ellicott's Bible Commentary, New Testament 1. London: Cassell, 1902.

Podskalsky, G. "Euthymius Zigabenos." *TRE* 10. 557-558.

Pol Vonck, W. F. *The Parables*. Spearhead 66. Eldoret, Kenya: Gaba, 1981.

Pölzl, F. X., and T. K. Innitzer. *Kurzgefasster Kommentar zu den vier heiligen Evangelien*. 4th ed. 2 vols. Graz: Styria, 1932.

Pontianus of Rome. *Letter 2*. PG 10.

Poole, M. *Synopsis criticorum aliorumque sanctae scripturae interpretum*. 4 vols. London: Flesher, 1674.

Poovey, W. A. *The Power of the Kingdom*. Minneapolis, MN: Augsburg, 1974.

Pope, H. *The Layman's New Testament*. New York: Sheed & Ward, 1941.

Porksen, M. (ed.). *Vom Herrn der Herrlichkeit: Tägliche Andachten aus dem Matthäus-evangelium*. Schwerin: Bahn, 1937.

Porteus, B. *Lectures on the Gospel of St. Matthew.* London: Baynes, 1824.
Prat, F. *Jésus-Christ, sa vie, sa doctrine, son oeuvre.* 2 vols. Paris: Beauchesne, 1933.
Pregeant, R. *Christology beyond Dogma: Matthew's Christ in Process Hermeneutic.* SBL Semeia Supplements 7. Philadelphia: Fortress, 1978.
Preisker, H. *Das Ethos des Urchristentums.* Gütersloh: Bertelsmann,1949.
Preiss, T. "Le mystère du fils de l'homme." *Dieu Vivant* 8 (1947) 15-36.
Price, W. K. *Jesus' Prophetic Sermon.* Chicago: Moody, 1972.
Priestley, J. *Notes on the Harmony of the Four Evangelists.* Notes on All the Books of Scripture 3. Northumberland: Kennedy, 1804.
Procopius of Gaza. *Commentary on Isaiah.* PG 87/2.
_____. *Commentary on the Song of Songs.* PG 87/2.
Prod'hom, S. *Der verheissene König und sein Reich.* Zürich: Beröa, 1964.
Prohászka, O. *Meditations on the Gospels.* 3 vols. Westminster, MD: Newman, 1951.
Prosper of Aquitaine. *Answers to the Vincentian Articles.* PL 51.
_____. *De vocatione omnium gentium.* PL 51.
_____. *Expositio Psalmorum.* CCL 68A.
Przybylski, B. *Righteousness in Matthew and his World of Thought.* SNTSMS 41. Cambridge: University Press, 1980.
Pseudo-Athanasius. *In passionem et crucem domini.* PG 28.
_____. *Quaestiones ad Antiochum ducem.* PG 28.
Pseudo-Augustine. *Sermo Caillau-Saint-Yves.* PLSup 2.
_____. *Sermo Casinensis.* PLSup 2.
_____. *Sermo Mai.* PLSup 2.
_____. *Sermo Morin.* PLSup 2.
_____. *Testimonia adversus Pelagium.* PLSup 2.
Pseudo-Basil the Great. *Constitutiones asceticae.* PG 31.
_____. *Sermo de misericordia et judicio.* PG 31.
_____. *Sermo de renuntiatione saeculi.* PG 31.
_____. *Letter 8.* PG 32.
Pseudo-Chrysostom. *De caelo et Zacchaeo.* PG 59.

———. *De eleemosyna*. PG 60.
———. *De eleemosyna 2*. PG 64.
———. *De eleemosyna et hospitalitate*. PG 63.
———. *De futuro judicio*. PG 63.
———. *De jejunio*. PG 60.
———. *De jejunio et eleemosyna*. PG 48.
———. *De modo consequendi regnum caelorum*. PG 63.
———. *De poenitentia*. PG 60.
———. *Homilies*. PLSup 4.
———. *In catechumenos*. PG 60.
———. *In decem virgines*. PG 59.
———. *In illud: Attendite ne eleemosynam*. PG 59.
———. *In illud: Verumtamen*. PG 55.
———. *In mediam hebdomadam jejuniorum* PG 59.
———. *In paralyticum dimissum per tectum*. PG 51.
———. *In Psalmum 50*. PG 55.
———. *In secundum adventum*. PG 61.
———. *Opus imperfectum in Matthaeum*. PG 56.
———. *Sermons*. PLSup 4.
Pseudo-Clement. *Epistle of Clement to James*. GCS 42.
———. *Homilies*. GCS 42.
———. *Recognitions*. GCS 51.
Pseudo-Eusebius of Alexandria. *Sermons*. PG 86.
Pseudo-Eusebius of Emesa. *Homily 45*. CCL 101A.
———. *Sermon 1*. CCL 101B.
Pseudo-Hippolytus of Rome. *De Consummatione Mundi*. GCS 1.
Pseudo-Origen. *Homilies*. PLSup 4.
Pseudo-Pelagius. *Admonitio augiensis*. PLSup 1.
Pusey, P. E. (ed.). *Sancti Cyrilli archiepiscopi alexandrini opera*. 7 vols. Brussels: Culture et Civilization, 1965.
Puzicha, M. *Christus peregrinus*. Münster: Aschendorff, 1980.
Quasten, Johannes. *Patrology*. 3 vols. Westminster, MD: Newman, 1950-60.
Quecke, H. *Die Briefe Pachoms*. Textus patristici et liturgici 11. Regensburg: Pustet, 1975.
Quesnel, P. *Le Nouveau Testament en françois avec des reflexions morales sur chaque verset*. 8 vols. Paris: Prallard, 1696.
Quodvultdeus of Carthage. *De symbolo*. CCL 60.

———. *Dimidium temporis in signis Antichristi.* CCL 60.
———. *Liber promissionum.* CCL 60.
Rabanus Maurus. *Commentarium in Matthaeum.* PL 107.
———. *Sermons.* PL 110.
Raddum, T. *Mattheus Evangeliet.* Oslo: Universitets Forlaget, 1971.
Radermakers, J. *Au fil de l'évangile selon saint Matthieu.* 2 vols. Heverlée-Louvain: Institut d'études théologiques, 1972.
Ragaz, L. *Die Gleichnisse Jesu.* Der Stundenbücher 99. Hamburg: Furche, 1971.
Rahner, K. "Gefangnisseelsorge." *Sendung und Gnade.* 4th ed. Innsbruck: Tyrolia, 1966. 447-463.
———. "Über die Einheit von Nächsten- und Gottesliebe." *Schriften zur Theologie.* 16 vols. Einsiedeln: Benziger, 1954-1984. 6. 277-298.
Ralph of Laon. *Glossa ordinaria.* PL 114.
Rashdall, H. *Principles and Precepts.* Oxford: Blackwell, 1927.
Ratzinger, J. *Die christliche Brüderlichkeit.* Munich: Kösel, 1960.
———. "Fraternité." *Dictionnaire de spiritualité, ascétique et mystique.* 12 vols. Ed. M. Viller, F. Cavallera, and J. De Guibert. Paris: Beauchesne, 1937-84. 5.1141-1167.
Rauschenbusch, W. *The Social Principles of Jesus.* College Voluntary Study Courses. New York: Association, 1916.
Ravarotto, E. "Italian Versions of the Bible." *NCE* 2. 481-483.
Redding, D. A. *The Parabales He Told.* Westwood, NJ: Revell, 1962.
Reicke, B. "The Conception of Reward." *Aux sources de la tradition chrétienne: mélanges offerts à Maurice Goguel à l'occasion de son 70. anniversaire.* Paris: Delachaux & Niestlé, 1950. 195-206.
Remigius of Rheims. *Testament.* CCL 117.
Rennes, J. "A propos de Matthieu 25:31-46." *ETR* 44 (1969) 233-234.
Reumann, J. *Jesus in the Church's Gospels.* Philadelphia: Fortress, 1968.
Réville, A. *Etudes critiques sur l'Evangile selon St. Matthieu.* Leiden: van Goor, 1862.

Ricciardi, R. and B. Hurault (eds.). *La Biblia*. Madrid: Ediciones Paulinas Verbo Divino, 1972.
Ricciotti, G. *Vita di Gesù Cristo*. Milan: Rizzoli, 1941.
Rice, E. W. *People's Commentary on the Gospel according to Matthew*. Philadelphia: The American Sundayschool Union, 1887.
Rice, J. R. (ed.). "The Gospel according to Matthew." *The Rice Reference Bible*. Nashville: Nelson, 1981. 1001-1053.
Richards, J. A. *Windows in Matthew*. Windows in the New Testament. Ed. P. Hutchinson. New York: Long & Smith, 1932.
Richards, L. *The Servant King*. Bible Alive Series. Elgin, IL: Cook, 1976.
Richardson, A. *An Introduction to the Theology of the New Testament*. London: SCM, 1958.
Richey, T. *The Parables of the Lord Jesus according to St. Matthew*. New York: Young, 1888.
Richmond, N. *Christ's Drama*. London: Stuart, 1961.
Richter, G. *Deutsches Wörterbuch zum Neuen Testament*. Regensburg: Pustet, 1962.
Ridderbos, H. N. *The Coming of the Kingdom*. Philadelphia: Presbyterian & Reformed Publishing, 1962.
_____. "Het Evangelie naar Mattheüs." *Beknopt Commentaar op de Bijbel in de Nieuwe Vertaling*. Ed. W. Gispen, H. Ridderbos, and R. Schippers. Kampen: Kok, 1963. 799-822.
_____. *Matthew's Witness to Jesus Christ*. New York: Association, 1958.
Riedmann, A. *Wie Jesus lebte, litt und starb*. Freiburg: Herder, 1953.
Rienecker, F. *Das Evangelium des Matthäus*. Wuppertaler Studienbibel. 4th ed. Wuppertal: Brockhaus, 1966.
Rigaux, B. *The Testimony of St. Matthew*. Chicago: Franciscan Herald, 1968.
Riley, W. B. *Matthew and the Synoptics*. The Bible of the Expositor and the Evangelist, NT 3. Cleveland: Union Gospel, 1926.
Ritchie, A. *Spiritual Studies in St. Matthew's Gospel*. 2 vols. New York: Longmans, Green, 1902.

Roberts, A. and J. Donaldson (eds.). *The Ante-Nicene Fathers.* 11 vols. New York: Scribner, 1886-99. Reprinted, Grand Rapids: Eerdmans, 1979-82.

Robertson, A. T. *The Gospel according to Matthew.* The Bible for Home and School 3. New York: Macmillan, 1911.

_____. "The Gospel according to Matthew." *Word Pictures in the New Testament.* 6 vols. Nashville: Sunday School Board of the Southern Baptist Convention, 1930. 1.3-246.

Robinson, J. A. T. *Jesus and His Coming.* Philadelphia: Westminster, 1957.

_____. "The 'Parable' of the Sheep and the Goats." *NTS* 2 (1955-56) 225-237.

Robinson, T. H. *The Gospel of Matthew.* MNTC 1. New York: Harper, 1927.

Rochedieu, C. *Les trésors du Nouveau Testament.* St. Legier: Emmaüs, 1979.

Rohde, J. *Die redaktionsgeschichtliche Methode. Einführung und Sichtung des Forschungsstandes.* Hamburg: Furche, 1968.

Rohner, E. *Die eschatologischen Reden der synoptischen Evangelien in der Verkündigung.* Dissertation. Münster, 1971-1972.

Rolland, P. "From the Genesis to the End of the World. The Plan of Matthew's Gospel." *BTB* 2 (1972) 155-176.

Roper, H. *Jesus in His Own Words.* Westminster, MD: Newman, 1951.

Rose, V. *Evangile selon Saint Matthieu.* La pensée chrétienne 1. Paris: Bloud, 1908.

Rosenmüller, J. G. *Scholia in Novum Testamentum.* 6th ed. 5 vols. Nuremberg: Officina Felseckeriana, 1815.

Roux, H. *L'Evangile du Royaume: Commentaire sur l'évangile selon saint Matthieu.* Commentaires bibliques 2. Geneva: Labor et fides, 1956.

Rowe, F. L. and J. A. Klingman. *The Bible in Questions and Answers.* Cincinnati: Rowe, 1916.

Ruatti, D. *Il judicio universale et le opere di misericordia Mt 25,31-46.* Dissertation. Rome: Gregorian University, 1959.

Rufinus of Aquilea. *A Commentary on the Apostles' Creed.* CCL 20.

———. *Apologia ad Anastasium.* CCL 20.

———. *De benedictionibus patriarcharum.* CCL 20.

———. *Interpretatio novem orationum Gregorii.* CSEL 46.

———. *Praefationes in libros Periarchon.* CCL 20.

Rupert of Deutz. *Commentary on John.* CCM 9.

———. *De Trinitate et operibus eius.* CCM 21.

———. *In Canticum Canticorum.* CCM 26.

———. *Super Matthaeum.* CCM 29.

Rusche, H. "Die erwählten Armen." *BibLeb* 11 (1970) 46-51.

Russell, E. *The Parables of Jesus.* New York: YWCA, 1909.

———. *The Parables of Jesus.* Philadelphia: Winston, 1928.

Russell, J. W., et al. (eds.). *Nelson's Explanatory Testament.* New York: Nelson, 1912.

Russell, W. H. *Christ the Leader.* Milwaukee: Bruce, 1937.

Ryle, J. C. *Expository Thoughts on the Gospels.* New York: Carter, 1860.

Sa, M. de. *Notationes in totam scripturam sacram.* Cologne: Kinchium, 1620.

Sabourin, L. *The Gospel according to St. Matthew.* 2 vols. Bandra, Bombay: St. Paul Publications, 1982.

Sales, M. M. "Vangelo di Gesù Cristo secondo San Matteo." *La Sacra Bibbia.* 12 vols. Turin: Berruti & Marietti, 1911. 11. 5-134.

Salvagniac, T. *Jésus de Nazareth, roi des juifs.* Paris: Lethielleux, 1935.

Salvianus of Marseilles. *Adversus avaritiam.* CSEL 8.

Sand, A. *Das Gesetz und die Propheten.* Biblische Untersuchungen 11. Regensburg: Pustet, 1974.

Sass, G. *Ungereimtes bei Matthäus.* Düsseldorf: Evangelische Kirche im Rheinland, 1968.

Saucy, R. L. "The Eschatology of the Bible," *The Expositor's Bible Commentary.* 12 vols. Ed. F. E. Gaebelein and J. D. Douglas. Grand Rapids: Zondervan, 1979-84. 1.103-126.

Schaff, P. *A Popular Commentary on the New Testament*. 4 vols. Edinburgh: Clark, 1879.

_____, and H. Wace (eds.). *Select Library of Nicene and Post-Nicene Fathers*. 28 vols. New York: Scribner, 1886-1900. Reprinted, Grand Rapids: Eerdmans, 1978-83.

Schanz, P. *Commentar über das Evangelium des heiligen Matthäus*. Freiburg: Herder, 1879.

Schegg, J. P. *Evangelium nach Matthäus*. 3 vols. Münich: Lentner, 1857.

Schelkle, K. H. *Theologie des Neuen Testaments*. Kommentare und Beiträge zum Alten und Neuen Testament. 4 vols. Düsseldorf: Patmos, 1974.

Schenk, W. *Der Segen im Neuen Testament*. Theologische Arbeiten 25. Berlin: Evangelische Verlagsanstalt, 1967.

Schille, G. *Anfänge der Kirche*. BEvT 43. Munich: Kaiser, 1966.

Schiwy, G. *Weg ins Neue Testament*. 4 vols. Würzburg: Echter, 1965.

Schlatter, A. *Das Evangelium nach Matthäus*. Erläuterungen zum Neuen Testament 1. Stutttgart: Calwer, 1947.

_____. *Der Evangelist Matthäus*. Stuttgart: Calwer, 1929.

Schlier, H. *Die Zeit der Kirche*. 2d ed. Freiburg: Herder, 1958.

Schmid, J. *Das Evangelium nach Matthäus*. RNT 1. Regensburg: Pustet, 1959.

Schmidt, K. L. "ἔθνος in the NT." *TDNT* 2. 369-372.

Schnackenburg, R. *Die sittliche Botschaft des Neuen Testamentes*. Handbuch der Moraltheologie 6. Munich: Hueber, 1962.

_____. "Der Heilsauftrag der Kirche in unserer Zeit." *Rechenschaft vom Glauben*. Ed. E. Hesse and H. Erharter. Vienna: Herder, 1969. 97-116.

_____. *Gottes Herrschaft und Reich*. 4th ed. Freiburg: Herder, 1965.

_____. "Mitmenschlichkeit im Horizont des Neuen Testaments." *Schriften zum Neuen Testament*. Exegese in Fortschritt und Wandel. Munich: Kösel, 1971. 435-458.

Schniewind, J. D. *Das Evangelium nach Matthäus*. NTD 2. Göttingen: Vandenhoeck & Ruprecht, 1971.

Schoedel, W. R. *Ignatius of Antioch*. Hermeneia. Philadelphia: Fortress, 1985.
Schottroff, L. "Der Mensch Jesus im Spannungsfeld von politischer Theologie und Aufklärung." *Theologia Practica* 8 (1973) 243-257.
Schulz, S. *Die Stunde der Botschaft*. Hamburg: Furche, 1967.
Schürmann, H. *Jesu Abschiedsrede Lk 22, 21-38*. NTAbh 20/5. Münster: Aschendorff, 1957.
_____. *Kaufet die Zeit aus: Beiträge zur christlichen Eschatologie*. Ed. H. Kirchhoff. Paderborn: Schöningh, 1959.
Schütze, F. W. *Das Evangelium des Matthäus*. Schullehrerbibel NT 1. Dresden/Leipzig: Arnold, 1846.
Schwank, B. "Der König der Juden." *Erbe und Auftrag* 55 (1979) 57-60.
Schwarz, J. L. J. *Ein ewiges Evangelium*. Pittsburgh: Man, 1835.
Schweitzer, A. *Die Mystik des Apostels Paulus*. Tübingen: Mohr, 1930.
Schweizer, E. "Matthew's Church." *The Interpretation of Matthew*. Issues in Religion and Theology 3. Philadelphia: Fortress, 1983. 129-155.
_____. "Matthäus 21-25." *Orientierung an Jesus: zur Theologie der Synoptiker. Festschrift für W. Josef Schmid zum 80. Geburtstag*. Ed. P. Hoffmann. Freiburg: Herder, 1973. 364-371.
_____. "Observance of the Law and Charismatic Activity in Matthew." *NTS* 16 (1969-70) 213-230.
_____. *The Good News according to Matthew*. Atlanta: Knox, 1975.
_____. "The Matthean Church." *NTS* 20 (1973-74) 216.
Scott, T. *The New Testament of Our Lord and Saviour Jesus Christ*. Commentary on the Holy Bible 4. Philadelphia: Woodward, 1809.
Seagren, D. R. *The Parables*. Wheaton, IL: Tyndale, 1978.
Seamands, J. T. *Power for the Day*. Nashville: Abingdon, 1976.
Seeberg, A. *Der Katechismus der Urchristenheit*. Leipzig: Deichert, 1903.
Sell, H. T. *Studies of the Parables*. Sell's Bible Study Text Books. New York: Revell, 1930.

Senior, D. *Gospel of Saint Matthew*. Read and Pray 1. Chicago: Franciscan Herald, 1974.

_____. *Invitation to Matthew*. Doubleday New Testament Commentary Series. Garden City, NY: Doubleday, 1977.

_____. *Matthew: A Gospel for the Church*. Herald Biblical Booklets. Chicago: Franciscan Herald, 1973.

_____. "The Gospel of Matthew and the Ministry of Social Justice." *Spirituality Today* 31 (1979) 14-25.

_____. "The New Testament and the U. S. Economy." *TBT* 24 (1986) 357-362.

Sharman, H. B. *Son of Man and Kingdom of God*. New York: Harper, 1943.

_____. *The Teaching of Jesus about the Future according to the Synoptic Gospels*. Chicago: University of Chicago, 1909.

Shea, J. "Divine Judgment." *Chicago Studies* 24 (1985) 131-144.

Sheed, F. J. *The Book of the Saviour*. Ed. F. J. Sheed. New York: Sheed & Ward, 1952.

_____. *To Know Christ Jesus*. New York: Sheed & Ward, 1962.

Sheen, F. J. *Life of Christ*. New York: McGraw-Hill, 1958.

Shepherd, J. B. *A Diary of Prayer*. Philadelphia: Westminster, 1981.

Sheridan, M. "Disciples and Discipleship in Matthew and Luke." *BTB* 3 (1973) 235-255.

Sibinga, J. S. "The Structure of the Apocalyptic Discourse, Matthew 24 and 25." *ST* 22 (1975) 71-79.

Simcox, C. *The First Gospel*. Greenwich, CT: Seabury, 1963.

Simeon, C. *Matthew*. Horae Homileticae 11. London: Holdsworth & Ball, 1832.

Simon, P. "Albert der Große." *TRE* 2.177-184.

Simpson, A. B. *Life of Christ*. Christ in the Bible 8. New York: Word, Work & World, 1888.

Slack, K. *Matthew, Mark, Luke and Acts*. Mowbrays Mini-Commentaries 1. London: Mowbray, 1968.

Smalley, B. "The Bible in the Medieval Schools." *The Cambridge History of the Bible*. 3 vols. Ed. G. W. Lampe. Cambridge: University Press, 1969. 2.197-220.
Smith, B. T. D. (ed.). *The Gospel according to Saint Matthew*. The Cambridge Bible for Schools and Colleges 82. Cambridge: University Press, 1933.
Smith, C. W. F. "The Mixed State of the Church in Matthew's Gospel." *JBL* 82 (1963) 149-168.
Smith, C. *The Gospel of Matthew for Growing Christians*. Old Tappan, NJ: Revell, 1973.
Smith, D. *Matthew*. Commentary on the Four Gospels 1. Garden City, NY: Doubleday, 1928.
_____. *The Disciple's Commentary on the Gospels*. 3 vols., London: Hodder & Stoughton, 1928.
_____. *The Gospel according to St. Matthew*. The Westminster New Testament 1. New York: Revell, 1915.
Smith, T. C. "An Exegesis of Matthew 25:31-46." *Foundations* 19 (1976) 206-210.
Smith, W., and H. Wace. *A Dictionary of Christian Biography*. 4 vols. New York: AMS, 1967.
Smyth, J. P. *The Gospel Story*. The Bible for School and Home 6. New York: Doran, 1923.
Soden, H. von. "ἀδελφός." *TDNT* 1. 144-146.
Soucek, J. B. "Der Bruder und der Nächste." *Hören und Handeln*. Ed. H. Gollwitzer and H. Traub. Munich: Kaiser, 1962. 362-371.
Speyr, A. von. "Das Weltgericht." *Gleichnisse des Herrn*. Einsiedeln: Johannes, 1966. 112-123.
Spinetoli, O. da. "L'Impostazione del problema escatologico in S. Matteo." *BeO* 8 (1966) 185-211.
_____. *Matteo*. Assisi: Cittadella editrice, 1971.
Spitta, F. *Jesus und die Heidenmission*. Giessen: Töpelmann,1909.
Spivey, R. A., and D. M. Smith. *Anatomy of the New Testament*. New York: Macmillan, 1969.
Spreckelsen, H. "Der Weltenrichter: Matthäus 25, 31-46." *Gleichnisse aus Altem und Neuem Testament*.

Schriftauslegung für Predigt, Bibelarbeit, Unterricht 8. Stuttgart: Klotz, 1971. 310-316.

Spurgeon, C. H. *The Gospel of the Kingdom*. New York: Baker & Taylor, 1893.

Squillaci, D. "Il discorso escatologico." *Palestra del clero* 37 (1958) 72-77.

Squire, A. K. "Universal Compassion in Leo the Great." *Studia Patristica 13*. Ed. E. A. Livingstone. TU 116. Berlin: Akademie, 1975. 280-285.

Staab, K. *Das Evangelium nach Matthäus. Die heilige Schrift in deutscher Übersetzung, Das Neue Testament* 1-2. Würzburg: Echter, 1967.

Staats, R. *Makarios-Symeon: Epistola Magna. Eine messalianische Mönchsregel und ihre Umschrift in Gregors von Nyssa "De instituto christiano"*. Göttingen: AAW, 1984.

Stagg, F. *New Testament Theology*. Nashville: Broadman, 1962.

Stählin, G. "ξένος." *TDNT* 5. 1-36.

Stanley, D. M. *The Gospel of St. Matthew*. 2d ed. New Testament Reading Guide 4. Collegeville, MN: Liturgical Press, 1963.

Starke, C. "Evangelium Matthaei." *Synopsis bibliothecae exegeticae in Novum Testamentum*. 3 vols. Kiel: Seilmann, 1746-48. 1. 29-702.

Stauffer, E. "Das Evangelium vom barmherzigen Gott in Qumran und der Botschaft Jesu."*Deutsches Pfarrerblatt* 60 (1960) 73-150.

Steen, C. C. van den. *Commentarii in quattuor evangelia*. 2 vols. Lyons: Canier, Beaujolin, & Laurens, 1685.

Steenkiste, J. A. van. *Commentarius in evangelium secundum Matthaeum*. 2 vols. Bruges: Beyaert-Defoort, 1876.

_____. *Sanctum Jesu Christi evangelium secundum Matthaeum*. 4 vols. Bruges: Desclée de Brouwer, 1880-1881.

Steidle, B. "Ich war krank und ihr habt mich besucht Mt 25:36." *Erbe und Auftrag* 40 (1964) 443-458; 41 (1965) 36-46, 99-113, 189-206.

Steinmann, J. *La Vie de Jésus*. Paris: Denoël, 1959.

Stendahl, K. "Matthew." *PCB*. 769-798.

_____. *The School of Saint Matthew and its Use of the Old Testament*. ASNU 20. Lund: Gleerup, 1968.
Sterke, R., and J. C. Hendrix. *Bij het Evangelie volgens Mattheüs*. In dienst van het woord 17. Haarlem: Gottmer, 1971.
Stevens, G. B. *The Theology of the New Testament*. International Theological Library. New York: Scribner, 1920. 150-166.
Stock, A. *Saint Matthew*. Saint Andrew Bible Commentary 28. Conception, MO: Conception Abbey, 1960.
Stöger, A. *Das Neue Testament*. Klosterneuburg: Österreichisches Katholisches Bibelwerk, 1975.
Stonehouse, N. B. *The Witness of Matthew and Mark to Christ*. Grand Rapids: Eerdmans, 1944.
Stow, J. *Thoughts on the Gospel of Jesus Christ the Son of God*. Greenwich: Richardson, 1846.
Strauss, L. *Prophetic Mysteries Revealed*. Neptune, NJ: Loizeaux, 1980.
Strawson, W. *Jesus and the Future Life*. London: Epworth, 1959.
Strecker, G. *Das Judenchristentum in den Ps-Klementinen*. TU 70. Berlin: Akademie, 1958.
_____. *Der Weg der Gerechtigkeit*. FRLANT 82. Göttingen: Vandenhoeck & Ruprecht, 1962.
Stuhlmacher, P. *Gerechtigkeit Gottes bei Paulus*. FRLANT 87. 2d ed. Göttingen: Vandenhoeck & Ruprecht, 1966.
Stuhlmueller, C. *Biblical Meditations for Ordinary Time*. 3 vols. New York: Paulist, 1984.
Stuiber, A. "Ambrosiaster." *TRE* 2. 356-362.
Sulpicius Severus. *Letter 2*. PL 20.
_____. *A Life of St. Martin*. SC 133.
Summers, R. "Matthew 24-25: An Exposition." *RevExp* 59 (1962) 501-511.
_____. *The Life Beyond*. Nashville: Broadman, 1959.
Surgy, P. de. *Les grandes étapes du mystère du salut*. Paris: Les Editions Ouvrières, 1958.
Swaeles, R. "Rassemblement et pèlerinage des dispersés." *AsSeign* (1st ser.) 78 (1965) 37-61.

Swedenborg, E. *Commentary on the Gospel of Matthew.* Boston: New-Church Union, 1906.
Symeon the New Theologian. *Book of Ethics.* SC 129.
_____. *Catecheses.* SC 104, 113.
_____. *Gnostic and Practical Theological Chapters.* SC 51.
Szabo, A. "Anfänge einer jüdenchristlichen Theologie bei Matthäus." *Judaica* 16 (1960) 193-206.
Tasker, R. V. G. *The Gospel according to Saint Matthew.* The Tyndale New Testament Commentaries 1. Grand Rapids: Eerdmans, 1961.
Tertullian. *Ad Nationes.* CCL 1.
_____. *Adversus Hermogenum.* CCL 1.
_____. *Adversus Marcionem.* CCL 1.
_____. *De Carne Christi.* CCL 2.
_____. *De Oratione.* CCL 1.
_____. *De praescriptione haereticorum.* CCL 1.
_____. *De Resurrectione Mortuorum.* CCL 2.
_____. *Scorpiace.* CCL 2.
Thebeau, D. "On Separating Sheep from Goats." *Christianity Today* 16 (1972) 1040-1041.
Theissing, J. *Die Lehre Jesu von der ewigen Seligkeit.* Dissertation. Breslau, 1940.
Theodoret of Cyrus. *Dialogues.* PG 83.
_____. *Graecorum affectionum curatio.* SC 57.
_____. *In Canticum Canticorum.* PG 81.
_____. *Interpretatio in Psalmos.* PG 80.
_____. *Letters.* PG 83.
_____. *Quaestiones in Genesim.* PG 80.
_____. *Quaestiones in Leviticum.* PG 80.
Theophane Cerameus. *Homilies.* PG 132.
Theophylact of Bulgaria. *Enarratio in Evangelium Matthaei.* PG 123.
Thomas, D. *The Genius of the Gospel.* London: Dickinson & Higham, 1873.
Thomas, W. H. G. *Outline Studies in Matthew.* Grand Rapids: Kregel, 1985.

Thompson, E. *The Key to Revelation.* Grand Rapids: Zondervan, 1935.

Thompson, W. G. "An Historical Perspective in the Gospel of Matthew." *JBL* 93 (1974) 243-262.

_____. *Matthew's Advice to a Divided Community.* AnBib 44. Rome: Biblical Institute, 1970.

Thysman, R. *Communauté et directives éthiques: La catéchèse de Matthieu.* Récherches et synthèses, Section d'exégèse 1. Gembloux: Duculot, 1974.

Tilden, E. E. "The Gospel of Matthew." *The Oxford Annotated Bible with the Apocrypha.* Ed. H. G. May and B. M. Metzger. New York: Oxford University, 1965. 1171-1212.

Tinsley, E. J. *The Imitation of God in Christ.* The Library of History and Doctrine. Philadelphia: Westminster, 1960.

Tirinus, J. *Commentarius in Vetus Testamentum et Novum Testamentum.* 3 vols. Antwerp: Nutium, 1632.

Tischendorf, C. *Apocalypses apocryphae Mosis, Esdrae, Pauli, Johannis.* Leipzig: Mendelssohn, 1866.

Tödt, H. E. *Der Menschensohn in der synoptischen Überlieferung.* 2d ed. Gütersloh: Mohn, 1963.

Toimil, M. L. "Allora il re dirà...." *Palestra del clero* 47 (1968) 1318-1321.

Tolbert, M. O. *Good News from Matthew.* Nashville: Broadman, 1975.

Tonne, A. *Five-Minute Homilies on the Gospels.* Hillsboro, KS: M. B. Publishing, 1977.

Tostatus, A. *Commentaria in septem partes Matthaei.* 4 vols. Cologne: Gymnicus & Hieratus, 1613.

Toussaint, S. D. *Behold the King.* Portland, OR: Multnomah, 1980.

Tricot, A., and A. Crampon. *Le saint évangile de Jésus-Christ selon saint Matthieu.* Paris: Desclée de Brouwer, 1939.

Trilling, W. *Das wahre Israel: Studien zu einer Theologie des Matthäusevangeliums.* STANT 10. Munich: Kösel, 1964.

_____. *The Gospel according to Saint Matthew.* 2 vols. New Testament for Spiritual Reading 2. New York: Herder & Herder, 1969.

Trollope, W. *Analecta theologica.* 2 vols. London: Cadwell, 1842.
Tromp, S. (ed.). *Sancti Roberti Bellarmini opera oratoria postuma.* 10 vols. Rome: Gregorian University, 1942.
Turner, H. E. W. The Parable of the Sheep and the Goats." *ExpTim* 77 (1965-66) 243-246.
Tuya, M. de. "Evangelio de San Mateo." *Biblia comentada.* 7 vols. 3d ed. BAC 239a. Madrid: Editorial católica, 1977. 5. 3-475.
Unger, M. F. *Study New Testament.* New York: Iversen-Norman Associates, 1979.
Upham, F. W. *St. Matthew's Witness.* New York: Hunt & Eaton, 1891.
Valerian of Cemele. *Homilies.* PL 52.
Valerius of Bancona. *Opuscula.* PL 87.
Van Ryn, A. *Meditations in Matthew.* New York: Loizeaux, 1958.
Van Wyk, W. P. *My Sermon Notes on Parables and Metaphors.* Grand Rapids: Baker, 1947.
Vaux, R. de. (ed.). *La Bible de Jerusalem.* Paris: Cerf, 1961.
Vawter, B. *A Popular Exposition of the Four Gospels.* 2 vols. Huntington, IN: Our Sunday Visitor, 1955.
_____. *The Four Gospels.* 2 vols. Garden City, NY: Doubleday, 1967.
Vega, A. C. (ed.). *S. Leandri Hispalensis de institutione virginum et contemptu mundi.* Scriptores ecclesiastici hispanolatini veteris et medii aevi 16-17. Escorial: Monasterio Augustiniano, 1948.
Végh, I. *Világosító Jegyzemények Szent Máté Evangyeliomjára.* Pesten: Beimel József, 1840.
Veil, C. M. de. *Commentarius in sanctum Jesu Christi Evangelium secundum Matthaeum et Marcum.* Angers: Auril, 1674.
Veilleux, A. (ed.). *Pachomian Koinonia.* 3 vols. Cistercian Studies 45-47. Kalamazoo, MI: Cistercian Publications, 1980-82.
Verkuyl, G. (ed.). "The Gospel according to Matthew." *The Holy Bible: The New Berkeley Version.* Grand Rapids: Zondervan, 1969. 1-35.

Via, Jr., D. O. "The Church as the Body of Christ in the Gospel of Matthew." *SJT* 11 (1958) 271-286.

Vilmar, A. F. C. *Collegium biblicum—Praktische Erklärung der heiligen Schrift Alten und Neuen Testaments.* 3 vols. Gütersloh: Bertelsmann, 1879-1883.

Vincent, M. R. *Word Studies in the New Testament.* 4 vols. New York: Scribner, 1905.

Vögtle, A. "Das christologische und ekklesiologische Anliegen von Mt 28, 18-20." SE II. TU 87. Berlin: Akademie, 1964. 266-294.

Vos, H. F. *Simple Survey of the New Testament for the Layman.* Grand Rapids: Zondervan, 1957.

Waetjen, H. C. *The Origin and Destiny of Humanness.* Corte Madera, CA: Omega, 1976.

Waldebertus of Luxeuil. *Regula ad virgines.* PL 88.

Walker, R. *Die Heilsgeschichte im ersten Evangelium.* FRLANT 91. Göttingen: Vandenhoeck & Ruprecht, 1967.

Wallace, R. S. *Many Things in Parables.* Edinburgh: Oliver & Boyd. 1955.

Wallon, H. (ed.). *Les saints evangiles avec des reflexions de Bossuet.* 2 vols. Paris: Le Clère, 1863.

Walter, N."ἔθνος." *EWNT.* 1.928.

Walters, S. D. "Mercy." *Baker's Dictionary of Christian Ethics.* Ed. C. F. Henry. Grand Rapids: Baker, 1973. 418-419.

Walvoord, J. F. "Christ's Olivet Discourse on the End of the Age." *BSac* 128 (1971) 109-116; 129 (1972) 308-314.

_____. *Matthew.* Chicago: Moody, 1974.

Wansbrough, H. "St. Matthew," *A New Catholic Commentary on Holy Scripture.* Ed. R. C. Fuller. London: Nelson, 1969. 902-953.

_____ (ed.). "The Gospel according to Matthew." *The New Jerusalem Bible.* Garden City, NY: Doubleday, 1985. 1609-1659.

Ward, A. M. *The Gospel according to St. Matthew.* Epworth Preacher's Commentaries, NT 1. London: Epworth, 1961.

Ward, M. *They Saw His Glory.* New York: Sheed & Ward, 1956.

Ward, R. *Theologicall Questions, Dogmaticall Observations, and Evangelicall Essays upon the Gospel of Jesus Christ according to Saint Matthew.* London: Cole, 1640.
Watkinson, W. L. *Studies in Christian Character, Work and Experience.* New York: Revell, 1903.
Watson, J. "St. Matthew." *The Expositor's Dictionary of Texts.* 2 vols. Ed. W. R. Nicoll and J. Stoddart. Grand Rapids: Baker, 1978. 1/2. 769-987.
Weber, A. *Le saint Evangile de notre seigneur Jésus-Christ.* Paris: Lefort, 1898.
Weber, R. (ed.). *Biblia sacra iuxta vulgatam versionem.* 3d ed. 2 vols. Stuttgart: Deutsche Bibelgesellschaft, 1983.
Wehrli, E. S. *Exploring the Parables.* Boston: United Church, 1963.
Weiss, B. *Das Leben Jesu.* 2 vols. Berlin: Hertz, 1882.
_____. *Das Matthäus-Evangelium* 7th ed. MeyerK 1. Göttingen: Vandenhoeck & Ruprecht, 1910.
_____. *Das Matthäusevangelium und seine Lucasparallelen.* Halle: Buchhandlung des Waisenhauses, 1876.
_____. *Das Neue Testament.* 2 vols. Leipzig: Hinrichs, 1907.
_____. *Die Vier Evangelien.* 2d ed. Leipzig: Hinrichs, 1905.
Weiss, J., and W. Bousset. "Das Matthäus-Evangelium." *Die drei älteren Evangelien.* Die Schriften des Neuen Testaments 1. Göttingen: Vandenhoeck & Ruprecht, 1907. 229-406.
Wellhausen, J. *Das Evangelium Matthaei.* Berlin: Reimer, 1904.
Wendland, H. D. "Die dienende Kirche und das Diakonenamt." *Das diakonische Amt der Kirche.* Ed. Herbert Krimm. 2d ed. Stuttgart: Evangelisches Verlagswerk, 1965. 519-554.
_____. *Die Eschatologie des Reiches Gottes bei Jesus,* Gütersloh: Bertelsmann, 1931.
Wendt, H. H. *Die Lehre Jesu.* 2d ed. Göttingen: Vandenhoeck & Ruprecht, 1901.
Weren, W. J. C. *De Broeders van de Mensenzoon.* Amsterdam: Bottenburg, 1979.
Wernle, P. *Die synoptische Frage.* Freiburg: Herder, 1899.

Wesley, J. *Explanatory Notes upon the New Testament.* 4th American ed. New York: Soule & Mason, 1818.
_____, A. Clarke, M. Henry et al. *One Volume New Testament Commentary.* Grand Rapids: Baker, 1957.
Weston, H. G. *Matthew.* New York: Revell, 1900.
Wette, W. M. L. de. *Kurze Erklärung des Evangeliums Matthäi.* Kurzgefasstes exegetisches Handbuch zum Neuen Testament 1. Leipzig: Weidmann, 1845.
Whedon, D. D. *A Commentary on the Gospels of Matthew and Mark.* New York: Carlton & Porter, 1860.
Whitby, D. "The Gospel of St. Matthew." *A Critical Commentary and Paraphrase on the Old and New Testament.* 4 vols. Ed. Simon Patrick et al. Philadelphia: Carey & Hart, 1846-1848. 4. 33-205.
Whitham, A. E. *The Discipline and Culture of the Spiritual Life.* London: Hodder & Stoughton, 1938.
Whittemore, T. *Notes and Illustrations of the Parables of the New Testament.* Boston: Whittemore, 1832.
Wightman, W. M. "The Gospel according to St. Matthew." *The Teacher's Commentary.* Ed. H. Martin. New York: Harper, 1932. 280-296.
Wikenhauser, A. "Die Liebeswerke in dem Gerichtsgemälde Mt 25:31-46." *BZ* 20 (1932) 366-377.
Wilckens, J. *Der König Israels.* Die urchristliche Botschaft 1. Berlin: Furche, 1937.
Wilckens, U. "Gottes geringste Brüder-zu Mt 25:31-46." *Jesus und Paulus. Festschrift für W. G. Kümmel zum 70. Geburtstag.* Ed. E. Ellis and E. Grasser. Göttingen: Vandenhoeck & Ruprecht, 1975. 363-383.
Wild, J. *In sacrosanctum Jesu Christi domini nostri evangelium secundum Matthaeum commentariorum libri quatuor.* Paris: Julian, 1564.
William, F. M. *Das Leben Jesu in Lande und Volke Israel.* Freiburg: Herder, 1933.
Williams, A. L., and W. J. Deane. *Matthew.* 2 vols. The Pulpit Commentary 33-34. New York: Funk & Wagnalls, 1890-1919.
Williams, G. "Matthew." *The Student's Commentary on the Holy Scriptures.* Grand Rapids: Kregel, 1971. 696-731.

Williams, N. M. *The Gospel according to Matthew.* Boston: Gould & Lincoln, 1870.
Winandy, J. "La scène du jugement dernier." *ScEccl* 18 (1966) 169-186.
Witham, R. *Annotations on the New Testament of Jesus Christ.* 2 vols. Douai: n. pub., 1733.
Wolfe, J. C. *Curae philologicae et criticae in quatuor sancta evangelia et Actus Apostolicos.* 3d ed. 5 vols. Hamburg: Herold, 1739.
Worcester, J. *Matthew's Gospel. The Spiritual Interpretation of the Scriptures.* Boston: Massachusetts New-Church Union, 1898.
Wrege, H. T. *Die Überlieferungsgeschichte der Bergpredigt.* WUNT 9. Tübingen: Mohr, 1968.
Wright, P. *The Complete British Family Bible.* London: Hogg, 1781.
Wright, W. *Apocryphal Acts of the Apostles.* 2 vols. London: Williams & Norgate, 1871.
Wynne, R. *Annotations on the New Testament of Jesus Christ.* 2 vols. London: n. pub., 1730.
Young, N. H. *Rebuke and Challenge.* Washington, DC: Review & Herald, 1985.
Zachary of Besançon. *De concordia evangelistarum.* PL 186.
Zahn, T. von. *Das Evangelium des Matthäus.* 4th ed. Kommentar zum Neuen Testament 1. Leipzig: Deichert, 1922.
Zerr, E. M. "Matthew." *Bible Commentary.* 6 vols. St. Louis: Mission Messenger, 1952. 5.1-111.
Zorell, F. *Lexicon Graecum Novi Testamenti.* Paris: Lethielleux, 1961.
Zumstein, J. *La condition du croyant dans l'Evangile selon Matthieu.* OBO 16. Göttingen: Vandenhoeck & Ruprecht, 1977.
Zupanski, J. K. (ed.). *Ewangelia Jezusa Chrystusa wedlug Swietego Mateusza.* Poznan: Nakladem Biblioteki Kórnickiej, 1892.
Zwingli, U. *Opera Domini Huldrychi Zuinglii.* 4 vols. Zürich: Froschoverum, 1545.

AUTHOR INDEX

Aalen, S., 263.
Abbott, L., 247.
Aborn, T. L., 266.
Achelis, H., 130.
Acts of the Apostles, 14, 127.
Acts of Thomas, 14, 15, 127, 331.
Adeney, W. F., 268.
Agbanou, V. K., 258.
Aland, K., 10.
Albert the Great, 176-8, 179, 188, 192, 340, 341,342.
Albert, T., 264.
Alberti, A., 261.
Albrecht, L., 263.
Albright, W. F., 272.
Alexander, A., 260.
Alexander, J. A., 247, 362.
Alexander, N., 241, 243, 275, 345.
Alford, H., 252.
Alleman, H. C., 258.
Allen, W., 200.
Allen,W. C., 269, 347.
Allnatt, F. J., 248.
Almgren, C., 260.
Alonso, J., 259.
Altmann, W., 261.
Altaner, B., 126, 127, 131,141, 143.
Ambrose of Milan, 55, 57-9, 60, 72, 138, 334.
Ambrosiaster, 59-60, 138.
Amiot, F., 262.
Ammonius of Alexandria, 133, 170.
Analyse de l'évangile, 222-23, 360, 361.
Anastasius Apocrisiarius, 108, 336.
Anastasius of Sinai, 110-11.

Ancient Hymn from the Fayûm, 29, 30, 31.
Andrew of Crete, 112-13.
Anselm of Laon, 167-68, 170, 186, 340, 342.
Antiochus the Monk, 109-10, 336.
Aphraates, 33, 334.
Apocalypse of Peter (Greek), 14.
Aponius, 62, 334.
Apostolic Fathers, 11, 127.
de Araújo, F., 260.
Archelaus of Cascar, 23.
Argyle, A. W., 262.
Aristotle, 177, 179, 181, 183, 342.
Armstrong, E. A., 267.
Arnobius the Younger., 90-1.
Assemani, J., and E., 133.
Asterius of Amasea, 49, 333, 334.
Athanasius of Alexandria, 37-9, 132, 334.
Atkinson, B. F., 262.
Audoenus of Rouen, 122, 336, 339.
Augustijn, C., 232.
Augsburger, M. S., 260.
Augustine of Hippo, 6, 62, 63, 69-72, 95, 100, 101, 103, 145, 171, 178, 182, 183, 275, 334, 335, 336, 337, 338, 339, 340, 341.
Avitus of Vienne, 98-9.
Babion, G., 186.
Bacon, B. W., 7, 10, 264.
Bailey, B., 248.
Baldi, C., 264.
Ballantine, W. G., 261.
Banks, L. A., 260.
Barberiis, B. de, 174, 188.
Barbieri, L. A., 270.
Barclay, W., 259.
Barker, G. W., 317.
Barker, W. P., 260.
Barnes, A., 247.
Barnett, A. E., 266.
Barnikol, E., 258.

Barradas, S., 211-12, 360, 361.
Barth, G., 258.
Barth, K., 260.
Bartlett, D. L., 268.
Basil of Ancyra, 36-7, 333.
Basil the Great, 6, 42-4, 46,47, 111, 134, 146.
Basil of Seleucia, 79-80, 335.
Baumbach, G., 265.
Baur, C., 135.
Beare, F. W., 258.
Beausobre, I. de, 242, 361.
Bede the Venerable, 123-25, 147, 250, 336, 337, 338, 339.
Beelen, J. T., 247.
Bellarmine, R., 215-16, 227, 236, 360, 361.
Benedict of Nursia, 104-05, 335.
Bengel, J., 241, 242, 243.
Benoit, P., 258.
Berardino, A. Di, 371.
Bernard, P. R., 258.
Bernardine of Siena, 191-92, 231, 360, 361.
Bert, G., 131.
Betz, O., 260.
Beutler, J., 263.
Beyer, H. W., 258.
Beyschlag, W., 249.
Bibliia, 263.
Bibliorum sacrorum iuxta Vulgatam clementinam, 10.
Bichlmair, G., 264.
Biser, E., 261.
Bisping, A., 246.
Black, M., 10, 364.
Blaiklock, E. M., 261.
Blair, E., 261.
Bligh, P. H., 259.
Blinzler, J., 261.
Bloomfield, S. T., 248.
Boers, H., 266.
Bohairic Life of Pachomius, 34, 132.

Boice, J. M., 260.
Boles, H. L., 262.
Bonaventure, 174-76, 179, 188, 340, 341, 342.
Bonnard, P., 258.
Bonnet, M., 127.
Bonwetsch, G. N., 130.
Boon, A., 134.
Booth, C. E., 259.
Booth, H. M., 249.
Boothroyd, B., 248.
Borgnet, S. C., 188.
Bornhäuser, K., 267.
Bornkamm, G., 258.
Bosch, D., 258.
Bossuet, J. B., 223-24, 238, 360, 361.
Bourgesius, J., 219-20, 360, 361.
Bousset, W., 434.
Bover, J. M., 263.
Box, G. H., 258.
Brandenburger, E., 258.
Brändle, R., 9, 10, 50, 52, 135, 136.
Brandt, W., 265.
Brastberger, I. G., 241, 242.
Bratcher, R. G., 259.
Braun, H., 258.
Bree, W. T., 248.
Breech, J., 266.
Breen, A. E., 258.
Breen, D. van., 220-21, 225, 343, 347, 349, 360, 361.
Brenius, cf. D. van Breen.
Bristowe, R., 200.
Broadus, J. A., 248.
Broer, I., 268.
Broickwy, A., 196-97, 360, 361.
Brooks, K. L., 270.
Broughton, L. G., 270.
Brouwer, A. M., 261.
Brown, D., 248.

Brown, J., 259.
Brown, S., 267.
Bruce, A. B., 252.
Bruce, F. F., 267.
Bruckberger, R. L., 261.
Brun, L., 265.
Bruno of Asti, 168, 340, 341.
Büchsel, F., 257.
Bugge, C. A., 265.
Bullinger, E. W., 269.
Bultmann, R., 258.
Bundy, W. E., 262.
Burkitt, F. C., 268.
Burkitt, W., 241, 242, 243.
Burmester, O. H., 130.
Burnett, F. W., 268.
Burney, C. F., 266.
Busa, R., 186.
Butler, B. C., 263.
Butler, J. G., 249.
Buttrick, G. A., 258.
Buytaert, E. M., 132.
Buzy, D., 262.
Cadoux, A. T., 262, 308.
Caesarius of Arles, 101-04, 119, 145, 335, 336, 337, 339.
Caine, H., 260.
Callan, C. J., 263.
Callinicus, 78.
Campbell, D. B. J., 261.
Calmet, A., 241, 242, 243.
Calvin, J., 198, 200, 206-08, 209, 214, 216, 220, 226, 230, 234, 243, 344, 360, 361.
Canévet, M., 135.
Cargill, R. L., 261.
Carlston, C. E., 266.
Carpocrates, 16.
Carr, A., 248.
Carr, W. G., 253.

Carreyre, J., 238.
Carrières, P. D., 376.
Carroll, P. J., 258.
Carson, D. A., 262.
Cartier, G., 241, 242.
Cassiodorus, 114-15, 336.
Castoldi, G., 261.
Catchpole, D. R., 262.
Catholic Biblical Association, 266.
Cerfaux, L., 266.
Ceulemans, F. C., 262.
Chapman, J., 267.
Chevallier, M., 267.
Chitty, D. J., 143.
Chouraqui, A., 258.
Christian Druthmar, 160-61, 340.
Christian, P., 258.
Chromatius of Aquilea, 60, 333, 334.
Cladder, H. J., 258.
Clamer, A., 307.
Clark, G. W., 131, 249.
Clark, J. H., 248.
Clark, K. W., 267.
Clarke, A., 248.
Clarke, S., 231, 360, 361.
Clarke, W. K. L., 267.
Clement of Alexandria, 6, 16-7, 332.
Clement of Rome, 11, 73, 126, 131.
Clementines, 73-5, 141, 333, 334, 360.
Clowes, J., 254.
Clymer, R. S., 259.
Cobb, S., 254.
Cobbin, I., 248.
Coffin, B. C., 260.
Committee of the Oxford Society of Historical Theology, 14, 126, 127.
Commodianus, 29, 332.
Conzelmann, H., 264.

Cooke, H., 263.
Cooper, D. L., 270.
Cope, L., 7, 10, 267.
Cornelius a Lapide, 217-18, 360, 361.
Cornwallis, M., 247.
Corwin, V., 126.
Council of Mâcon, 115.
Cowles, H., 248.
Cox, R., 265.
Craghan, J. F., 261.
Crampon, A., 263.
Cranenburgh, H. van, 132.
Cranfield, C. E. B., 258.
Crean, P. J., 259.
Cremers, H., 262.
Criswell, W., 270.
Crosby, H., 248.
Cross, F. L., xx.
Cullmann, O., 260.
Curci, C. M., 247.
Curran, C. A., 261.
Curtis, W. A., 269.
Cyprian of Carthage, 6, 22, 27-8, 129, 227, 275, 332.
Cyril of Alexandria, 6, 75-7, 142, 147, 335, 336, 339, 360.
Cyril of Jerusalem, 45, 129, 333, 339.
Dahl, N. A., 258.
Dallmann, W., 262.
Dambricourt, G., 261.
Daniel-Rops, H., 258.
Darby, J. N., 253, 285, 347, 361.
Dardel, S. de, 260.
Daumoser, I., 264.
Dausch, P., 262.
Davies, J. N., 260.
Davies, W. D., 267.
Davis, W. H., 262.
Dean, J., 261.
Deane, W. J., 258.

De decem virginibus, 29, 30, 31, 125-26.
DeHoff, G. W., 259.
Dekkers, E., 145.
De Kruijf, T., 263.
Del Paramo, S., 259.
Denys van Leeuwen, cf. Dionysius (Denis) the Carthusian
Deries, J., 259.
Descamps, A., 265.
Dheilly, J., 263.
Diatessaron, 39, 133.
Diaz, J. A., 260.
Didascalia apostolorum, 29, 131.
Didon, H., 247.
Didymus the Blind, 6, 48.
Dieterle, C., 258.
Dietrich, S. de, 259.
Dillemore, F. W., 262.
Dillersberger, J., 259.
Dimmler, E., 259.
Diodati, G., 228, 360, 361.
Dionysius Bar Salibi, 155-56, 340.
Dionysius the Carthusian, 194-95, 232, 343, 361.
Dodd., C. H., 262, 363.
Doddridge, P., 248.
Dods, M., 260.
Doerne, M., 258.
Donahue, J. R., 262.
Donaldson, J., xvii.
Donatus of Besançon, 120, 336, 337.
Doorly, J. W., 271.
Douai-Rheims NT, 200, 360, 361.
Drummond, D. T., 250.
Drury, J., 263.
DuHamel, J. B., 242, 361.
Dummelow, J. R., 265.
Duncan, G. S., 259.
Dupont, J., 258.
Duprez, A., 263.

Durand, A., 262.
Dykes, J. O., 247.
Eakin, F., 261.
Earle, F., 260.
Earle, R., 260.
Ecclesiastical Canons of the Twelve Apostles, 29, 30.
Edwards, R., 261.
Eligius of Noyon, 121.
Ellicott, C. J., 267, 321.
Elliott, W., 259.
Ellis, P. F., 261.
Ellison, H. L., 263.
Ellul, J., 260.
English, E. S., 270.
Ephraem of Nisibis, 39-42, 130.
Epiphanius, 49-50, 127, 135.
Epiphanius Latinus, 94-5, 144, 335, 339.
Epistle of the Apostles, 14.
Erasmus, D., 138, 195-96, 232, 360, 361.
Erdman, C. R., 261.
Erikson, A., 144.
Est, W. H. van, 209-11, 360, 361.
Estius, cf. W. H. van Est
Eugippius, 100-01, 335.
"Eusebius of Alexandria," 82-3, 142.
Eusebius of Caesarea, 6, 31-3, 35, 127, 334.
Eusebius of Emesa, 35-6, 80, 132.
Euthymius Zigabenus, 153-54, 184, 341.
Evagrius Ponticus, 133, 137.
Evangelie: Novyi Zavet i psaltir, 263.
Evely, L., 258.
Exell, J. S., 247.
Farmer, H. H., 258.
Farrar, F. W., 248.
Faustus of Riez, 97-8, 145, 335, 336.
Fendt, L., 265.
Fenton, J. C., 268.
Fernández Truyols, A., 260.

Feuillet, A., 258, 351, 363.
Fillion, L. C., 259, 307.
Filson, F. V., 259.
Findley, J. A., 259.
Firmicus Maternus, 56, 333.
Firmilian of Caesarea in Cappadocia, 22.
First Greek Life of Pachomius, 34, 132.
Fitzmyer, J. A., 364.
Ford, W. H., 270.
Fouard, C., 247.
Fox, D. J., 386.
Frankemölle, H., 258.
Franzmann, M. H., 264.
Freyne, S., 258.
Friedrich, J., 268.
Froehlich, K., 296.
Fructuosus of Braga, 121, 336, 337.
Fuchs, E., 261.
Fulgentius of Ruspe, 99-100, 335.
Funk, F. X., 131.
Furnish, V., 265.
Furetière, A., 221-22, 343, 345, 352, 361.
Gaebelein, A. C., 270.
Gaechter, P., 258.
Gähler, W., 234, 268.
Galeota, G., 236.
Gander, G., 271.
Garcia, T., 260.
Gaston, L., 267.
Gaudentius of Brescia, 55-6, 333.
Gay, G., 266.
Geerard, M., 130, 132, 134, 137, 184.
Geist, H., 258.
Gennadius of Constantinople, 82.
Géoltrain, P., 260.
Germanus of Constantinople, 111-12.
Gewalt, D., 267.
Gibson, J. M., 247.

Gibson, M. D., 183.
Gignac, F. T., 142.
Giordani, I., 259.
Glasson, T. F., 271, 364.
Glossa ordinaria, 163, 170, 171, 172, 187.
Gnilka, J., 260.
Godbey, W. B., 268.
Goebel, S., 248.
Goma Civit, I., 265.
Gonzaga, M., Sr., 261.
Good, C. M., 260.
Goodspeed, E. J., 261.
Goppelt, L., 258.
Gordon, E. B., 267.
Gossner, J., 247.
Gottschalk, 162, 168.
Goudge, H. L., 268.
Goulder, M. D., 263
Graffin, R., 131.
Graffmann, H., 263.
Granskou, D., 261.
Grant, F. C., 261.
Grant, F. W., 253.
Grant, R., 126.
Grass, H., 264.
Grassi, J. A., 261, 276, 278.
Gray, J. C., 249.
Gray, J. M., 270.
Green, F. W., 261.
Green, H. B., 269.
Greenfield, J. C., 364.
Greenhill, R., 269.
Gregory of Agrigentum, 115.
Gregory the Great, 117-19, 122, 123, 158, 167, 169, 171, 178, 187, 250, 318, 336, 337, 339, 340, 341, 342.
Gregory Nazianzus, 46, 61, 138, 182, 183.
Gregory of Nyssa, 6, 47-8, 134, 135.
Gregory Thaumaturgus, 22-3.

Gregory of Tours, 116.
Grenfell, B. P., 131.
Grieve, A. J., 266.
Groot, H. de, 227-28, 229, 239, 360, 361.
Gross, G., 258.
Grossheide, F. W., 259.
Grotius, cf. H. de Groot.
Grundmann, W., 258.
Guardini, R., 258.
Guggisberg, H. R., 239.
Gundry, R. H., 262.
Gutzke, M. G., 266.
Gutzwiller, R., 258.
Guy, H. A., 266.
Habershon, A. R., 270.
Hagner, D. A., 126.
Hahn, F., 258.
Hall, J., 228, 360, 361.
Hall, T. C., 261.
Hamel, J., 258.
Hamilton, W., 263.
Hammond, H., 228-29, 343, 361.
Hanko, H. C., 262.
Hare, D. R. A., 267, 322, 356.
Harnack, A., 131.
Harrington, D. J., 267, 323, 356.
Harrington, W. J., 259.
Harris, F. B., 267.
Harvey, A. E., 262.
Hastings, E., 258.
Hastings, J., 268.
Haufe, G., 267.
Haydock, G. L., 250.
Haymo of Halberstadt, 161, 340.
Hebert, G., 258.
Hendrix, J. C., 268.
Hengel, M., 260.
Henry, M., 241, 242, 243.

Hesychius of Jerusalem, 78-9.
Heylyn, J., 241, 242, 345.
Higgins, A. J., 263.
Hilary of Poitiers, 6, 56-7, 147, 338, 339.
Hill, D., 258.
Hindson, E. W., 270.
Hinnebusch, P., 261.
Hippolytus of Rome, 6, 26-7, 127, 332, 360.
Hirsch, E., 266.
Hobbs, H. H., 259.
Hoffmann, P., 260.
Hognestad, H., 269.
Holden, G., 248.
Holl, A., 260.
Holtzmann, H. J., 252.
Holtzmann, O., 263.
Holzendorff, F. von, 252.
Honert, J. van den, 242, 361.
Horsiesi, 44-5, 134.
Horton, R. F., 265.
Hoyt, H. A., 270.
Hubbard, B. J., 264.
Hugh of Saint Cher, 172-74, 179, 182, 187, 340, 341, 342.
Hülsbusch, W., 258.
Hummel, R., 264.
Hünermann, W., 261.
Hunt, A. S., 131.
Hunt, E. M., 248.
Hunter, A., 267.
Hurault, B., 324.
Husenbeth, F. C., 250.
Ignatius of Antioch, 11, 126.
Ingelaere, J.-C., 268, 357, 358, 363.
Innitzer, T. K., 248.
Irenaeus of Lyons, 6, 12, 331, 339.
Ironside, H. A., 270.
Irwin, C. H., 247.
Isho'dad of Merv, 149, 155, 156, 183.

Isidore of Pelusium, 77-8, 142.
Isidore of Seville, 119-20, 122, 123, 336, 337, 339.
Israel, M., 261.
Jaeger, W., 135.
Jansen (the Elder), C., 198-99, 218, 360, 361.
Jansen (the Younger), C. O., 198, 218-19, 360, 361.
Jeng, Y. M. P., 263.
Jeremias, J., 267, 363.
Jerome, 27, 65-8, 70, 72, 75, 77, 126, 128, 134, 147, 157, 161, 162, 164, 165, 166, 167, 168, 170, 171, 173, 178, 182, 185, 194, 195, 227, 249, 333, 334, 339, 340.
Jobius, 85.
John Cassian, 86-7, 336.
John Chrysostom, 50-3, 54, 59, 68, 69, 70, 72, 75, 77, 78, 94, 97, 104, 111, 135, 136, 142, 146, 147, 157, 171, 173, 178, 182, 183, 333, 334, 338, 339, 340, 341.
John Climacus, 107.
John Damascene, 113, 146.
John the Dwarf, 53-4, 333.
John of Gaza, 84-5, 335.
Johnson, B. C., 259.
Johnson, S. E., 259.
Jomier, J., 258.
Jones, A., 259.
Jones, G. V., 260.
Jones, H. S., xx, 142.
Jones, J. R., 263, 312.
Julian of Toledo, 122-23, 337, 339.
Jülicher, A., 10, 264.
Justin Martyr, 6, 12, 131, 331.
Karrer, O., 261.
Käsemann, E., 266.
Kee, H. C., 259, 296.
Keil, K. A. G., 252.
Keil, K. F., 248.
Kelly, W., 253.
Kemp, T. L., 264.
Kempin, A., 261.

Kennedy, E. C., 261.
Kenrick, T., 249.
Kent, H. A., 270.
Kiddle, M., 263.
Killinger, J., 260.
Kingsbury, J. D., 262.
Kirban, S., 270, 285.
Kirk, A., 262.
Kissinger, W. S., 233.
Kistemaker, S., 262.
Kittel, G., 400.
Klausner, J., 261.
Klein, F., 264.
Klingman, J. A., 263.
Klostermann, E., 262.
Knabenbauer, J., 248.
Knaake, J. C. F., xxii.
Knecht, F. J., 247.
Knibb, M. A., 364.
Knoch, A. E., 270.
Knoch, O., 258.
Knox, R. A., 263.
Koester, H., 126.
Konings, J., 259.
Kraeling, E. G., 266.
Kratko tulkovanic na Evangelie-to ot Matfeia, 248.
Kretzer, A., 258.
Kühnöl, C. G., 246.
Kümmel, W. G., 257.
Kunkel, F., 259.
Künzel, G., 259.
La Biblia, 267, 268.
Lactantius, 2227, 249, 282.
Ladd, G. E., 2268, 276, 278.
Lagrange, M.-J., 259.
Laien-Bibel, 262.
Lambrecht, J., 7, 10, 267, 281, 362, 363.
Lampe, G. W., 187.

Lancellotti, A., 259.
Lancelot, J. B., 267.
Lane, W. L., 317.
Lange, J., 267.
Lange, J. P., 249.
Läpple, A. K., 258.
Largent, A., 238.
La Sacra Bibbia, 260.
La Sainte Bible, 262.
Latch, E. B., 254.
Lau, F., 267.
Lauck, W., 262.
Laurentius of Novae, 86, 336.
Lawson, L., 260.
Leander of Seville, 116, 146, 336, 337.
Lebreton, J., 258.
LeCamus, E., 248.
Lechner, P., 248.
Leclercq, J., 187.
Leerse, J. C., 241, 242.
Leeuwen, D. van, 194-95, 232, 343, 361.
Leeuwen, W. S. van, 260.
Légasse, S., 269.
Lenfant, J., 370.
Lenski, R. C. H., 262.
Leo the Great, 92-4, 95, 97, 144, 335, 336, 339.
Leo Patricius, 156.
Léon-Dufour, X., 262.
Lesetre, H., 247.
Letter of the Churches of Lyons andVienne, 14.
Levertoff, P. P., 268, 325.
Lewis, W. S., 249.
Liddell, H. G., xx, 142.
Lienemann, W., 260.
Lightfoot, J. B., 14, 126, 127.
Lightfoot, N. R., 259.
Lipsius, R. A., 127.
Livingstone, E. A., xv.

Lochen, A., 261.
Lock, W., 251.
Lohmeyer, E., 264.
Lohse, E., 263.
Loisy, A., 267.
Long, R. C., 259.
Luca of Bruges, F., 212-15, 360, 361.
Luccock, H. E., 258.
Luccock, R. E., 261.
Ludolph of Saxony, 167, 182-83, 186, 340, 341, 342.
Lusseau, H., 259.
Lütgart, W., 260.
Luther, M., 203-06, 234, 360, 361.
Maas, A. J., 248.
Macarius of Egypt, 46-7, 87, 134, 135, 334.
MacDonald, J. A., 262.
MacEvilly, J., 248.
Maclaren, A., 258.
Madame Cecelia, 266.
Maddox, R., 266.
Maillot, A., 262.
Makrakis, A., 263.
Maldonado, J., 200-02, 360, 361.
Mánek, J., 262.
Manes, 23.
Mann, C. S., 272.
Mansel, H. L., 248.
Manson, T. W., 268.
Manson, W., 268.
Marcel, P., 266.
Marcion, 13, 331.
Marguerat, D., 258.
Marloratus, A., 208-09, 343, 361.
Marrow, S. B., 266.
Martensen, H. P., 258.
Martin, F., 261.
Martin, G., 200.
Martin, H., 259.

Martin, J. P., 261.
Martindale, C. C., 259.
Martini, A., 247.
Martini, C., 10.
Martyrdom of Polycarp, 14.
Massaux, E., 126.
Massl, F. X., 247.
Mattill, Jr., A. J., 263.
Mauriac, F., 258.
Maximus the Confessor, 108-09.
Maximus of Turin, 60-1, 333.
McConkie, B. R., 266.
McConnell, R. S., 258.
McCumber, W. E., 259.
McEleney, N. J., 264.
McGarvey, J. W., 262.
McGee, J. V., 270.
McKenzie, J. L., 266.
McLaughlin, G. A., 260.
McNabb, V., 259.
Meier, J. P., 259, 356.
Meinertz, M., 263.
Menochio, G. S., 220, 360, 361.
Merezhkovskii, D., 262.
Mersch, E., 263.
Meschler, M., 257.
Methodius of Olympus, 23-24.
Metzger, B. M., 10, 261.
Meyer, F. B., 270.
Meyer, H. A. W., 249, 282.
Michaels, J. R., 15, 127, 131, 265.
Michaelis, W., 263.
Michel, O., 263.
Micklem, P. A., 267.
Migne, J. P., 137, 166, 185, 247.
Milham, R., 261.
Milik, J. T., 364.
Miller, A. W., 260.

Miller, C., 261, 303.
Miller, J. R., 262.
Miller, J. W., 261.
Miller, L. F., 258.
Miller, O., 303.
Miller, S. M., 409.
Minear, P. S., 266.
Mitton, C. L., 258.
M'Neile, A. H., 258.
Mohrlang, R., 268.
Mollat, D., 264.
Moninger, H., 261.
Monlobou, L., 267.
Monsarrat, V., 259.
Montefiore, C. G., 266.
Montefiore, H. W., 260.
Moore, A. L., 260.
Morgan, G. C., 270.
Morison, J. H., 255.
Mortier, D. A., 261.
Mounce, R. H., 262.
Mueller, J. T., 262.
Murray, J. M., 261.
Murry, J. M., 258.
Musurillo, H., 130.
Nagano, P. M., 259.
Nast, W., 249.
Nau, F., 142.
Nee, W., 270.
Négrier, A., 308.
Neil, W., 263.
Nelson, B. A., 259.
Nepper-Christensen, P., 264.
Nestle, E., 10.
Nestorius, 75.
Neuhäusler, E., 267.
Nicephorus of Antioch, 106-07.
Nichol, F. D., 260.

Nicholas of Lyra, 180-82, 183, 189, 192, 340, 341, 352.
Nielsen, J. T., 259.
Nijenhuis, W., 234.
Nilus of Ancyra, 54-5, 137.
Nixon, R. E., 259.
Noel, C., 259.
Nösgen, K. F., 249.
Obach, R., 262.
Obermüller, R., 261.
O'Brien, I., 260.
Oesterley, W. O., 265.
Olshausen, H., 252, 285, 362.
Opitz, H. G., 132.
Origen, 6, 17-22, 23, 24, 32, 57, 58, 66, 68, 72, 128, 129, 147, 161, 163, 164, 166, 167, 178, 179, 250, 254, 332, 334, 338, 339, 340, 342, 348, 349.
Orsisius, 44.
Osiek, C., 261.
Osterwald, J. F., 241, 242.
O'Sullivan, K., 262.
Otto, R., 260.
Oudersluys, R. C., 263.
Owen, J. J., 248.
Pachomius, 34-5, 44, 45, 87, 132.
Paige, L. R., 254, 286.
Pak, S., 264.
Palladius, 54, 333.
Palm, J. H. van der, 248.
Pamment, M., 261.
Papini, G., 261.
Parānanda, S., 255.
Pareus, D., 224-26, 360, 361.
Parker, J., 270.
Parma, A. A., 188.
Parmentier, R., 258.
Paschasius Radbertus, 163-66, 167, 185, 191, 217, 340, 341, 342, 352.
Patrick of Ireland, 91, 335.

Author Index

Paul the Deacon, 157-59, 162, 163, 167, 171, 340, 341, 342.
Paulinus of Nola, 66, 72-3.
Paulus Orosius, 62-3, 333.
Payne, J. B., 266.
Peabody, F. G., 261.
Peiró, F. X., 259.
Pelagius, 62, 63-5, 333, 334.
Pelfrène, J. M., 260.
Peloubet, F. N., 258.
Pendleton, P. Y., 262.
Pentecost, J. D., 270.
Perantonus, P. M., 231.
Percy, E., 260.
Perkins, P., 259.
Perrin, N., 264.
Pesch, R., 264.
Pesch, W., 268.
Peter of Alexandria, 24-5.
Peter Chrysologos, 87-9, 335, 336.
Peter Comestor, 171-72, 173, 341.
Petilianus, 6.
Pettingill, W. L., 270.
Petzoldt, M., 259.
Pfendsack, W., 258.
Pfleiderer, O., 252.
Philoxenus of Mabbug, 360.
Picinelli, F., 221, 360, 361.
Picquigny, B. de, 241, 242, 243.
Pieper, K., 264.
Pikaza, X., 260.
Pirot, L., 307.
Piscator, J., 226-27, 360, 361.
Pitra, J. B., 129.
Plummer, A., 265.
Plumptre, E. H., 267.
Podskalsky, G., 184.
Pol Vonck, W. F., 267.
Pölzl, F. X., 278.

Polycarp of Smyrna, 11, 126.
Pontianus of Rome, 27.
Poole, M., 229-30, 360, 361.
Poovey, W. A., 259.
Pope, H., 263.
Porksen, M., 259.
Porteus, B., 247.
Prat, F., 262.
Pregeant, R., 266.
Preisker, H., 260.
Preiss, T., 258.
Price, W. K., 270.
Priestley, J., 241, 242.
Procopius of Gaza, 83-4, 336.
Prod'hom, S., 263.
Prohászka, O., 262.
Prosper of Aquitaine, 95-6, 335, 336, 337, 339.
Przybylski, B., 266.
Pseudo-Athanasius, 38-9.
Pseudo-Augustine, 71-2, 417.
Pseudo-Basil the Great, 43-4.
Pseudo-Chrysostom, 52-3, 105-06, 336.
Pseudo-Clement of Alexandria, 6.
Pseudo-Clement of Rome, 14-5, 29-31, 73-5, 141, 333, 334, 360.
Pseudo-Ephraem, 41-2.
Pseudo-Eusebius of Alexandria, 82-3, 142.
Pseudo-Eusebius of Emesa, 36, 335.
Pseudo-Hippolytus of Rome, 26, 339, 360.
Pseudo-Macarius, 47.
Pseudo-Origen, 105-06.
Pseudo-Pelagius, 64-5.
Ptolemy, 13.
Pusey, P. E., 141.
Puzicha, M., 418.
Quasten, J., 127, 132, 133, 134, 135, 137, 141, 142.
Quecke, H., 132.
Quesnel, P., 224, 238, 360, 361.
Quodvultdeus of Carthage, 89-90, 336.

Rabanus Maurus, 162-63, 171, 178, 182, 340, 342.
Raddum, T., 259, 312.
Radermakers, J., 258.
Ragaz, L., 258.
Rahner, K., 261.
Ralph of Laon, 170, 340.
Rashdall, H., 260.
Ratzinger, J., 260.
Rauschenbusch, W., 261.
Ravarotto, E., 239.
Redding, D. A., 260.
Reicke, B., 263.
Remigius of Auxerre, 166-67, 178, 182, 186, 340, 342.
Remigius of Rheims, 100, 335.
Rennes, J., 267.
Reumann, J., 267.
Réville, A., 247.
Ricciardi, R., 324.
Ricciotti, G., 264.
Rice, E. W., 248, 276.
Rice, J. R., 270, 285.
Richards, J. A., 260.
Richards, L., 270.
Richardson, A., 268.
Richey, T., 252, 362.
Richmond, N., 271.
Richter, G., 258.
Ridderbos, H. N., 260.
Riedmann, A., 259.
Rigaux, B., 259.
Riley, W. B., 264.
Ritchie, A., 262.
Roberts, A., xvii.
Robertson, A. T., 259.
Robinson, J. A. T., 264, 363.
Robinson, T. H., 262.
Rochedieu, C., 258.
Roebert, M., 303.

Rohde, J., 258.
Rohner, E., 258.
Rolland, P., 264.
Roper, H., 266.
Rose, V., 262.
Rosenmüller, J. G., 246.
Roux, H., 264.
Rowe, F. L., 263.
Ruatti, D., 261.
Rufinus of Aquilea, 18, 19, 61-2, 134, 339, 340, 360.
Rupert of Deutz, 169-70, 187, 340, 341, 344.
Rusche, H., 260.
Russell, E., 260.
Russell, J. W., 260.
Russell, W. H., 261.
Ryle, J. C., 247.
Sa, M. de, 202, 360, 361.
Sabourin, L., 258.
Sales, M. M., 263.
Salvagniac, T., 261.
Salvianus of Marseilles, 96-7, 145, 335, 336.
Sand, A., 258.
Sass, G., 262.
Saucy, R. L., 270.
Schaff, P., 247.
Schanz, P., 249.
Schegg, J. P., 250.
Schelkle, K. H., 258.
Schenk, W., 264.
Schiwy, G., 259.
Schlatter, A., 258.
Schlier, H., 258.
Schmid, J., 257.
Schmidt, K. L., 264.
Schnackenburg, R., 258.
Schniewind, J. D., 264.
Schoedel, W. R., 127.
Scholia vetera in Matthaeum, 156-57.

Schottroff, L., 259.
Schulz, S., 258.
Schürmann, H., 258.
Schütze, F. W., 249.
Schwank, B., 261.
Schwarz, J. L. J., 247.
Schweitzer, A., 263.
Schweizer, E., 258.
Scott, R., xx, 142.
Scott, T., 241, 242, 243.
Seagren, D. R., 260.
Seamands, J. T., 261.
Second Clement, 14, 15, 331, 339.
Seeberg, A., 264.
Sell, H. T., 261.
Senior, D. P., 261.
Sentences of Sextus, 14.
Sermo de symbolo, 125.
Sharman, H. B., 269.
Shea, J., 261.
Sheed, F. J., 259.
Sheen, F. J., 259.
Shepherd, J. B., 261.
Sheridan, M., 266.
Sibinga, J. S., 10.
Sibylline Oracles, 14.
Simcox, C., 259.
Simeon, C., 247.
Simon, P., 188.
Simpson, A. B., 254.
Slack, K., 260.
Slater, W. F., 258.
Smalley, B., 187.
Smith, B. T. D., 266.
Smith, C., 264.
Smith, C. W. F., 266.
Smith, D., 267.
Smith, D. Moody, 261.

Smith, T. C., 259.
Smith, W., 144.
Smyth, J. P., 260.
Soden, H. von, 263.
Soucek, J. B., 260.
Speyr, A. von, 259.
Spinetoli, O. da, 262.
Spitta, F., 266.
Spivey, R. A., 261.
Spreckelsen, H., 261.
Spurgeon, C. H., 248.
Squillaci, D., 260.
Squire, A. K., 94, 144.
Staab, K., 258.
Staats, R., 134.
Stagg, F., 262.
Stählin, G., 258.
Stanley, D. M., 260.
Starke, C., 241, 242.
Stauffer, E., 263.
Steen, C. C. van den, 217-18, 360, 361.
Steenkiste, J. A. van, 248, 280.
Steidle, B., 260.
Steinmann, J., 260.
Stendahl, K., 263.
Stephen I, Pope, 22.
Sterke, R., 268.
Stevens, G. B., 261.
Stock, A., 265.
Stöger, A., 259.
Stone, M. E., 364.
Stonehouse, N. B., 263.
Stow, J., 247.
Strauss, L., 270.
Strawson, W., 267.
Strecker, G., 141, 262.
Stuhlmacher, P., 264.
Stuhlmueller, C., 263.

Stuiber, A., 126, 127, 131, 138, 141, 143.
Sulpicius Severus, 65, 73, 333.
Summers, R., 260.
Surgy, P. de, 261.
Swaeles, R., 261.
Swedenborg, E., 243-44, 254, 271, 346, 352, 361.
Symeon the New Theologian, 149-51, 152, 156.
Szabo, A., 264.
Tasker, R. V. G., 259.
Tatian, 39.
Tertullian, 6, 23, 25-6, 27, 332.
Thebeau, D., 269.
Theissing, J., 258.
Theodore of Mopsuestia, 149, 156.
Theodoret of Cyrus, 80-1, 335.
Theophane Cerameus, 154-55, 340.
Theophylact of Bulgaria, 152-53, 156, 227, 340.
Thomas Aquinas, 167, 178-80, 186, 189, 217, 340-41, 342.
Thomas, D., 247.
Thomas, W. H. G., 270.
Thompson, E., 260.
Thompson, W. G., 269.
Thysman, R., 263.
Tilden, E. E., 267.
Tinsley, E. J., 263.
Tirinus, J., 216-17, 360, 361.
Tödt, H. E., 258.
Toimil, M. L., 264.
Tolbert, M. O., 260.
Tonne, A., 261.
Tostatus, A., 192-94, 343, 361.
Toussaint, S. D., 270.
Tricot, A., 263.
Trilling, W., 258.
Trollope, W., 248.
Tromp, S., 236.
Tuck, R., 266.
Turner, H. E. W., 258.

Tuya, M. de, 260.
Unger, M. F., 270.
Upham, F. W., 248.
Valentinus, 13.
Valerian of Cemele, 91-2, 335, 336.
Valerius of Bancona, 120-21, 336.
Van Ryn, A., 267.
Van Wyk, W. P., 262.
Varsanuphius, 84, 143.
Vaux, R. de, 432.
Vawter, B., 259.
Vega, A. C., 146.
Végh, I., 248.
Veil, C. M. de, 222, 343, 361.
Veilleux, A., 132, 134.
Verkuyl, G., 270.
Via, Jr., D. O., 268.
Victor of Pettau, 31.
Vilmar, A. F. C., 250.
Vincent, M. R., 264.
Vögtle, A., 264.
Vos, H. F., 270.
Wace, H., 144.
Waetjen, H. C., 259.
Walafrid Strabo, 170.
Waldebertus of Luxeuil, 121.
Walker, R., 269.
Wallace, R. S., 258.
Wallon, H., 238.
Walter, N., 267.
Walters, S. D., 261.
Walvoord, J. F., 270.
Wansbrough, H., 259, 293.
Ward, A. M., 265.
Ward, M., 261.
Ward, R., 230-31, 360, 361.
Watkinson, W. L., 261.
Watson, J., 261.

Weber, A., 247.
Weber, R., 187.
Webster, R., 247, 277.
Wehrli, E. S., 260.
Weiss, B., 251, 284.
Weiss, J., 257.
Wellhausen, J., 266.
Wendland, H. D., 260.
Wendt, H. H., 251.
Weren, W. J. C., 259.
Wernle, P., 249.
Wesley, J., 242.
Wessely, C., 131.
Weston, H. G., 263.
Wette, W. M. L. de, 247.
Whedon, D. D., 249.
Whitby, D., 241, 242.
Whitham, A. E., 260.
Whittemore, T., 254, 362.
Wightman, W. M., 261.
Wikgren, A., 10.
Wilckens, J., 263.
Wilckens, U., 265.
Wild, J., 197-98, 343, 361.
William, F. M., 258.
Williams, A. L., 258, 299, 302, 309, 318, 324.
Williams, G., 270.
Williams, N. M., 248.
Winandy, J., 269, 326, 357, 363.
Witham, R., 242, 243.
Wolfe, J. C., 242, 243, 345.
Worcester, J., 254.
Worthington, T., 200.
Wrege, H. T., 264.
Wright, P., 241, 242.
Wright, W., 127.
Young, F. W., 296.
Young, N. H., 263.

Zachary of Besançon, 167, 170-71, 172, 186, 340, 342.
Zahn, T. von, 268.
Zerr, E. M., 262.
Zorell, F., 260.
Zumstein, J., 258.
Zupanski, J. K., 247.
Zwingli, U., 202-03, 208, 233, 360, 361.

www.ingramcontent.com/pod-product-compliance
Lightning Source LLC
Chambersburg PA
CBHW021350290426
44108CB00010B/174